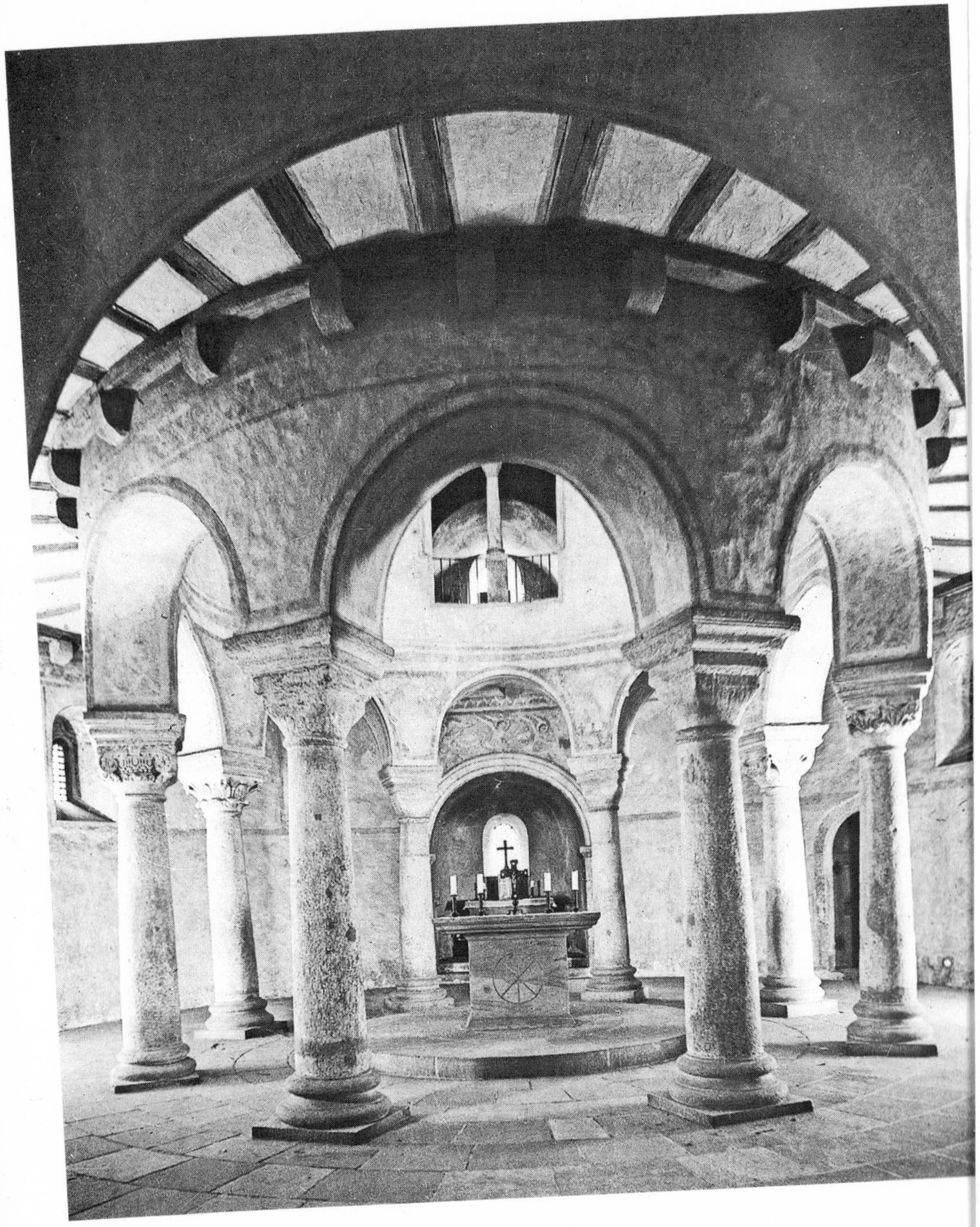

Saint Michael's Church, Fulda, Germany

THE EMPEROR AND THE SAINT

FOREWORD BY JOHN JULIUS NORWICH

THE EMPEROR AND THE SAINT

Frederick II of Hohenstaufen, Francis of Assisi, and Journeys to Medieval Places

RICHARD F. CASSADY

NORTHERN ILLINOIS UNIVERSITY PRESS / DEKALB

Published by the Northern Illinois University Press, DeKalb, Illinois 60115

Manufactured in the United States using postconsumer-recycled, acid-free paper.

Design by Julia Fauci

Library of Congress Cataloging-in-Publication Data

Cassady, Richard F., 1919–

The emperor and the saint: Frederick II of Hohenstaufen, Francis of Assisi, and journeys to medieval places / Richard F. Cassady; foreword by John Julius Norwich.

p. cm.

Includes bibliographical references and indexes.

ISBN 978-0-87580-439-2 (clothbound: acid-free paper)

1. Frederick II, Holy Roman Emperor, 1194-1250. 2. Frederick II, Holy Roman Emperor, 1194–1250—Influence. 3. Frederick II, Holy Roman Emperor, 1194–1250—Legends. 4. Holy Roman Empire—Kings and rulers—Biography. 5. Holy Roman Empire—History—843–1273. 6. Francis, of Assisi, Saint, 1182–1226. 7. Francis, of Assisi, Saint, 1182–1226—Legends. 8. Art, Medieval—History. 9. Architecture, Medieval—History. 10. Europe—History, Local. I. Title.

DG847.162.C37 2011

943'.025—dc22

[B] 2010051162

To ~

JOHN JULIUS NORWICH

who gave me my first encouragement

as a roaming recorder of the pageant of history,

its backstage gossip, its legends, and its settings.

Contents

Illustrations

FOREWORD

JOHN JULIUS NORWICH

The book that you hold in your hands is the biography of a giant: a giant who bestrode late medieval Europe and who is infinitely more deserving of the title Frederick the Great than that pipsqueak king of Prussia on whom it was so unaccountably conferred. That giant's fluency in six languages—including Arabic—was even rarer in the thirteenth century than it is now; he was a sensitive poet in whose court the sonnet was invented, a generous patron of the arts, a skilled general, a subtle statesman, and a superb naturalist. His book on falconry, *De arte venandi con avibus*, displays a knowledge and understanding of wildlife probably unparalleled in his time. It was to become a classic and is, I am told, still studied today. Frederick demonstrated his diplomatic skills when he recovered Jerusalem and the holy places for Christendom without shedding a drop of Christian—or Muslim—blood. (It was somehow characteristic of his relations with the papacy that he should have done so while under a papal sentence of excommunication.) A passionate intellectual curiosity—surely inherited from his Norman grandfather, King Roger II of Sicily—gave him more than a passing knowledge of philosophy and astronomy, geometry and algebra, medicine and the physical sciences. No wonder that he should have been given the sobriquet of *stupor mundi*; he was indeed, in his own highly individual way, a wonder of the world.

Not the least remarkable of Frederick's qualities was his talent for showmanship. His force of character alone, the sheer dazzle of his personality, would always have ensured that he impressed himself on everyone with whom he came in contact, but he deliberately built up his image still further: with his extraordinary menagerie, with his personal regiment of Saracens, even with his traveling harem. These last two attributes may have been regularly held against him by his enemies, but they too carried a clear message: the emperor was not as other men. He was a demigod, to whom the accepted rules of conduct simply failed to apply.

In a word, he had style. Now, style has always been, as it still is today, a speciality of the Italians; but Frederick—though he clearly thought himself Italian, loved southern Italy (especially Apulia) more than any other place, lived there for most of his life, and eventually died there—was not really Italian at all. His grandfather, King Roger, was a Norman whose own father had been one of that intrepid band of younger sons that had ridden down over the Alps into Italy during the eleventh century to seek their fortunes. In 1130 Roger had himself been crowned king of Sicily; Frederick's mother, Constance, Roger's posthumous daughter, had reluctantly married a German prince—Henry, the son and heir of the Holy Roman Emperor Frederick Barbarossa. It was the great tragedy of Norman Sicily that Roger's grandson, King William II, was childless. (He was married to Joanna, daughter of Henry II of England, which explains why there is a huge full-length mosaic portrait of St. Thomas Becket in Monreale Cathedral.) Thus, on the death of William II, the Sicilian throne ultimately passed through Constance to her husband, now the Emperor Henry VI, and the most astonishing kingdom of the Middle Ages—the only state in history to have been administered jointly and successfully by Latins, Greeks, and Muslims—came, after only sixty-four years, to its end.

Showmanship and style—many world rulers have possessed both qualities, but few have demonstrated them on the very day of their birth. When, on Christmas Day 1194, her husband Henry was crowned in Palermo Cathedral, Constance was not with him. Pregnant for the first time at the age of forty, she was determined on two things: first, that her child should be born safely; second, that it should be seen to be unquestionably hers. She did not cancel her journey to Sicily but traveled more slowly and in her own time; and she had got no farther than the little town of Jesi, some twenty miles west of Ancona, when she felt the pains of childbirth upon her. There, on the day after the coronation, in a tent erected in the main square to which free entry was allowed to any matron of the town who cared to witness the birth, she brought forth her only son—whom, a day or two later, she presented in that same square to the assembled inhabitants, proudly suckling the baby at her breast.

This story is, of course, told in greater detail in the pages that follow; it seemed worth a brief mention here, however, to illustrate the sheer glamour that Frederick so effortlessly—indeed, almost unconsciously—emanated literally every day of his life. He had, it must be admitted, a wonderful education—as far removed from that usually reserved for German princes as could possibly be imagined. Norman French, Latin, Greek, and Arabic had all been official languages of the Norman kingdom; German was the language of his father; brought up, as he was, in Sicily, Italian was never a problem. Ever since the days of his grandfather, Roger II, the court at Palermo had been the most cultivated in Europe, the meeting place of scholars and geographers, scientists and mathematicians, Christian, Jewish, and Muslim. Frederick could thus spend hours, not only in study but in long disputations on religion—Christianity or Islam—science, or philosophy. It was impossible to find a subject that did not interest him. Often, too, he would withdraw to one of the parks and palaces that, we are told, ringed the city like a necklace, watching the animals and birds that were his constant passion.

Thanks, then, to both his parentage and his extraordinary education, Frederick was probably one of the very first men—and in all of history there have been remarkably few—to have had a foot in both worlds, the Italian and the German, and to feel equally at home on either side of the Alps. But his heart remained in Italy, and rightly or wrongly, it is as an Italian that most of us—those of us outside of Germany, at any rate—tend to see him. Culturally, he gave that country much. Had the Provençal troubadours, fleeing from the horrors of the Albigensian Crusade, not found a warm welcome at the court of Palermo and fired the local poets with their ideals of courtly love, Italian literature might have taken a diametrically different course, and the *Divine Comedy* might never have been written.

In the field of architecture, too, he was an innovator. Alas, the immense fortified gateway to his frontier city of Capua, built to defend its bridge across the Vulturno river and designed by the emperor himself, no longer stands; but much of its sculpture is preserved in the local museum, from which it is clear that Frederick drew liberally on the decorative language of ancient Rome, anticipating the Renaissance well over a century before its time. Classical pediments and pilasters appear even more remarkably, in his magnificent hunting-box of Castel del Monte, a vast, turreted octagon in limestone crowning a remote Apulian hilltop. But perhaps we are wrong to be surprised. Frederick was after all a Roman emperor, and he was determined that we should not forget it.

Only politically was he a failure. His dream had been to forge Italy and Sicily into a united kingdom within the empire—the *regno*—with its capital at Rome; the overriding purpose of the Papacy, aided by the cities and towns of Lombardy, was to ensure that that dream should never be realized. It was unfortunate for Frederick that he should have had to contend with two such able and determined popes as Gregory IX and Innocent IV, but in the long run the struggle could have had no other outcome. Thanks—at least in part—to his long absences in the south, the empire had lost its strength and cohesion; no longer could the loyalty of the German princes, or even their deep concern, be relied upon. As for the Lombard cities of north and central Italy, never again would they be fooled by—let alone submit to—imperial bluster. Had Frederick only accepted this simple fact, the threat to the Papacy would have been removed and his beloved *regno* might well have been preserved. Alas, he rejected it, and in doing so he not only lost Italy, but he signed the death warrant of the imperial house of Hohenstaufen.

It should be clear from what I have said above that any would-be biographer of the Emperor Frederick must be a man—or woman—of considerable courage, with a fairly thorough mastery of the formidable complications of medieval European history. Ideally, he or she should, like Frederick himself, also have a foot in both camps, being equally at ease in the Italian world and in the German. It is on this rock, I believe, that several past essays have foundered—including the first of the recent important biographies, that of Ernst Kantorowicz. It was said of Kantorowicz that, had he not been a Jew, he would have been a Nazi; it was hardly surprising that he saw Frederick as a sort of spiritual führer, taking care to soft-pedal the Italian side of his character for all he was worth. Another biographer, Georgina Masson, lived permanently in Rome; for her, Frederick was an Italian through and through. Only one biography, by David Abulafia, seems to me to steer the perilous course between the German Scylla and the Italian Charybdis, avoiding shipwreck on either.

In this last regard my old friend Richard Cassady has kept an equally firm hand on the tiller; and his book can be recommended for another reason too. Being intended—as all really good books should be—not for scholars but for the average intelligent reader, it is, of all those that I have mentioned, the most easily accessible. Frederick II was always a lucky man; in his latest biographer he can count himself fortunate indeed.

Preface

This agglomeration which was called and which still calls itself the Holy Roman Empire is neither holy, nor Roman, nor an Empire.
Voltaire, *Essai sur les moeurs* (1756)

The humidity was awful, the kind that makes you feel that the earth itself is melting. The stores were open for business, but there were few southern Italians willing to brave the damp, not to mention the threatening storm lying just to the west over those vast Puglian plains known as "the Murge." Lightning, nearer with every flash, was close to the ground, and thunder not far behind chased the more resistant remaining pedestrians into cover. Then came the rain! Torrents of it—Noah's Deluge redux! I ducked into the bravely defiant stone building I was headed for in the interests of researching my first book, *The Norman Achievement*. On the cusp of the Italian boot, looking as though hanging on to keep from sliding down the Adriatic coast into the heel, Bari Castle was the scene of the introductory meeting of my life.

I was alone in a high-ceilinged room lit only now and then by searing flashes illuminating the single window. I was in an unfurnished, rectangular space of inappropriate smallness, considering that the castle was once an imperial abode and that this room was the venue of a most remarkable meeting—so remarkable that our knowledge of it is probably more legend than fact. According to a plaque on the wall it was here that Emperor Frederick II of Hohenstaufen, the predominant figure in all of Europe, met Francis Bernardone, a man born to be a saint if ever there was one. We are told that the two met to enjoy a profound discussion that must have been one of the most fascinating in history. And it was here that I experienced for the first time not only imperial brilliance but the figurative presence of my patron saint, assigned to my interests with the sprinkling of baptismal water and the recording of my middle name. My mind struggled to recreate a discussion that may never have taken place. But it did take place, I argued with myself. That plaque on the wall says it did! And in this very room!

Legend tells us that Frederick II of Hohenstaufen and Francis of Assisi met only once, and that was in Frederick's Norman-built castle at Bari. If they did meet, they must have had an enormous effect on one another. If they did not, it is safe to say they no doubt still influenced one another—from a distance. Each in his own way, Frederick and Francis can claim a curiously related, legitimate place in an even-to-them unsuspected historical relationship. The saint, through a personal, lyrical concept of a divinely created Nature under Brother Sun, was a calming spiritual balance in the world of Frederick's intrigue and violence in the name of God. On the other hand, Frederick's brilliance coupled with his uniquely self-centered intolerance gave poignant meaning to the pacifism of the shy saint's love of life and his dream of life after death. Frederick's volcanic personality rocked much of Europe, even the Holy Land, but did not allay Franciscan tranquility. The first half of the thirteenth century was as redolent of Francis's sweet perfume as of Frederick's bitter acid, though certainly the latter had the greater effect on the day-to-day struggles for survival in places that themselves sometimes did not survive. Francis died 24 years before Frederick, but he was Frederick's greatest contemporary. Frederick, utilizing an energetic, soaring intellect, stood in stark contrast to this intuitive man of God, this bearer of strange powers of understanding that the man of action may be excused for not appreciating. Together they round out their century.

I am an art historian and a romantic, not a political historian. I am comfortable with legends and have included them in my telling of the lives of both emperor and saint. Legends, whether grown out of love or propaganda, or both, rise up around the lives of certain historical figures and are handed down through the years until those reading about them at a distance cannot be sure which parts of them were true, if any. But the legends are a part of the story, and I have shared them here.

There is more to being a writer than fact and legend and the putting down of words. Myriad others ride herd on sentence structure, grammar and clarity of thought, on the writer's opinions and choice of subject matter, on his selection and placement of illustrations, cover designs, the number of copies to be printed, and selling price. For sympathetic understanding, patience, and never-flagging kindness I thank editor Amy Farranto with my entire being. Amy is the kind of unintrusive, inventive editor that every writer longs for but seldom finds. Her consideration for the author's feelings, interests, and occasional bursts of editorializing deserves more than commendation. It deserves a standing ovation.

Illustrations create complications that, thanks to the magical proficiency of my long-time friend John S. Scott, caused me no trouble. Not only did he enhance my photographs and prepare them to specifications ordered by NIUPress, Scotty generously allowed me to include his photograph—figure 30, Dome of the Rock, Jerusalem—in the text. Peaking those of prime importance is my best friend Alan Altshuld, computer wizard *extraordinaire*, eagle-eyed misspelling-spotter in the extreme, and patient re-reader beyond expectation. And I do not forget Massimo Ceresa, librarian in the Vatican Library in Rome, Italy, who guided me through the intricacies of the *Bibliotecca Scholastica Vaticana* to obtain my cover illustration. There are others—readers in this country and beyond, professionals in England, Sicily, Italy, France, Germany, Austria!—and especially John Julius Norwich in London, disadvantaged by a broken ankle and work on his own coming book on the papacy, yet cheering me on through the worst of it. To these and myriad others I am forever grateful. I hereby reiterate my thanks!

The English mottoes at the beginning of each chapter are translations of the *Dies Irae*, a sacred hymn used as part of the liturgy of the Roman Catholic Requiem Mass. The *Dies Irae* is attributed to Thomas of Celano, a Franciscan and a friend of Saint Francis of Assisi. This translation is used through the good graces of its owner, the Franciscan Archive, through whom it has been released to the public domain by its author. Items within round ( ) brackets are English words added to clarify the meaning of the denoted or connoted Latin signification. Items in square [ ] brackets are translations of terms in the Latin text from the new breviary. Items in braces { } represent translations of Latin terms that have simultaneous double meanings.

THE EMPEROR AND THE SAINT

Prologue

Day of wrath, day that
will dissolve the world into burning coals,
as David bore witness with the Sibyl.
***Dies Irae,* verse 1**

It was from an entirely unremarkable conical hill known as the Staufen, close to Esslingen in Swabia and a short distance east of Stuttgart, that the Hohenstaufen family derived its name. Frederick von Buren was the first of the dynasty, his name acquired through a Westphalian village that acknowledged him lord. He died in 1094, but not before producing a son, also called Frederick, a name used frequently in succeeding generations of the family. Young Frederick set the family on its upward trend by following in the train of the German king, who was also the Holy Roman emperor, Henry IV, and for his zealous loyalty was awarded the hand of the emperor's daughter, Agnes, whose dowry, by any standard, was lavish. Among the prizes was the duchy of Swabia, an area of southern Germany centering around Lake Constance. Young Frederick built a castle on the Staufen and coined the name Hohenstaufen—High Staufen. There is not much left of the castle today, though there are meager foundations, a few flights of steps, an occasional doorjamb or arch to make the strenuous climb worthwhile to the tourist who is interested in such things.

When Frederick died he left two sons, another Frederick, called "One Eye," who succeeded his father as duke of Swabia, and Conrad, who was appointed duke of Franconia by his uncle, Emperor Henry V. Though neither of the brothers was destined to wear the imperial diadem that he craved, they nonetheless never lacked for enemies—the dukes of Saxony and Bavaria, for example—and especially the Church, which, having created the first of the Holy Roman emperors in the person of Charlemagne, now three centuries later rightly viewed anything that smacked of imperial might as a threat to her own temporal ambitions. And in Germany the Church was backed by a powerful array of ecclesiastical princes, quarrelsome warrior-prelates who guarded their lands and wealth with tenacity, and who viewed German kingship as an elected office. So when Henry V died in 1125, with one-eyed Frederick inheriting his estates, the Hohenstaufens could expect only trouble.

Seeing himself as German king-designate first, and then, in keeping with the custom of the times and certainly more to his taste, as Holy Roman emperor, Frederick was thwarted in his ambitions, largely due to the machinations of the renowned and meddlesome Benedictine Abbot Suger, who came from France to lobby for papal interests. Lothair, duke of Saxony, was the pope's choice and as such was voted to the throne by the elector princes and crowned on September 13, 1125, at Aachen. Playing the spoilsport to the hilt, Frederick refused to surrender to the crown the estates that he had inherited from his late uncle. Lothair retaliated by pawning off his daughter Gertrude in marriage to Henry the Proud, son of the duke of Bavaria, thereby uniting two dedicated opponents of the Hohenstaufens. Some sources maintain that Henry the Proud was the great-grandson of an Italian, Azzo by name, a man interesting in his own right in that he is one of the earliest ancestors of Queen Victoria of England.[1] Henry the Proud's implied duty was to combat the duke of Swabia at every turn, a job he took seriously indeed, in one instance going so far as to lure Frederick into an abbey and then setting fire to it. His treachery failed. Creating consternation among the papists and royalists and confusion among later historians, Hohenstaufen sympathizers proceeded to elect Conrad king of Germany in opposition to the already crowned Lothair. As though two kings of Germany were not muddle enough, there were two popes vying with one another for the honor of occupying the unspacious throne of Saint Peter: Innocent II and Anacletus II, neither of whom could be persuaded to recognize Conrad as legitimate king. Both pontiffs saw him as dangerous to the future of the Church, even more so, apparently, than they thought themselves to be as they jostled and tugged first one way and then the other, each to secure his own position of power.

To bring to fruition his own imperial pretensions, Lothair recognized Innocent II's claims to the throne of Saint Peter. He was crowned emperor by Innocent's own hand in the Lateran, the Cathedral of Rome, which center of Christendom was already occupied by rival Pope Anacletus. Lothair immediately abandoned any pretense of loyalty to Innocent and returned to Germany in triumph, more determined than ever to bring the Hohenstaufen brothers to heel, while a resentful and embittered Innocent was himself forced by a rebellious populace to quit Rome two months later. Hohenstaufen submission was finally solemnized by oath in Bamberg in 1135. The brothers retained their estates, and Germany entered a period of respite from strife for the first time in fifty years. Adding to the general euphoria, Lothair was the one emperor from the middle of the eleventh century to the middle of the thirteenth who was not at one time or another placed under the papal ban, which gives some idea of the strenuousness of the struggles between the secular and spiritual heads of medieval Christendom. In the meantime, true to the Alsatian ditty about him—"he always had a castle tied to his tail"—Frederick Hohenstaufen was free to go on with his extensive castle-building programs, while brother Conrad denied his former claim to the German throne and joined the imperial forces, where he was awarded the position of standard-bearer.

With the death of Lothair in 1137, Conrad was again elected king of Germany, this time "legalized" by the presence of a papal legate. He was crowned Conrad III at Aachen, Henry the Proud being passed over by the electors as perhaps a little too proud for their tastes. War broke out between Conrad and Henry, continuing long after the death of the latter a couple of years later. His son, aptly known as Henry the Lion, carried on the struggle against the Hohenstaufens, even gaining a certain political prestige by marrying Matilda, daughter of King Henry II of England. Despite the political havoc caused by his quarrels with imperial ambition, his was a basically beneficial rule, marked by commercial expansion and the betterment of municipal life. Henry the Lion would make the headlines in 1983 for having commissioned an illuminated manuscript that brought the highest price paid up to that time for a work of art. Produced by a Benedictine monk on behalf of Henry the Lion, the missal fetched $11.8 million, according to Newsweek "a real bargain. . . . It is quite simply the most beautiful book in the world."

These endemic struggles between Saxony-Bavaria and Franconia-Swabia were laying the groundwork for the formation of a party system that ultimately determined the histories of Germany, Italy, and Europe in general, not to mention the twelfth- and thirteenth-century spin-offs in the Near East. Rivalry between the two German ducal families spilled over into Italy, where names for the factions were coined: Guelfi represented the German name Welf, borne by many men of rank, including Welf, Duke of Bavaria; Ghibellini referred to Waiblingen, a Hohenstaufen possession near the castle of the same name. Following the corruption of the designations into Italian and finally into English, the partisans of the popes, who leaned toward the Saxon-Bavarian house, came to be known as "Guelfs," while the followers of the Swabian emperors took the name "Ghibellines." The battle cries "Ho for the Guelfi!" and "Ho for the Waiblingen!" apparently originated during an action fought at Weinsberg in 1140 in which the defending garrison under the command of Henry the Proud's brother, Welf, was forced to surrender. Prevailed upon by the weeping women of the defeated community, victorious Hohenstaufen King Conrad agreed that they should be granted egress with as much of their property as they could carry, hardly expecting them to make their exit bearing husbands, fathers, grown sons, and babies. Conrad was good for his word, though, much to the disgust of brother Frederick. Conrad's chancellor is said to have complained that the women's act was a breach of the agreement, but Conrad would have none of it.

It is about a half-hour climb from the town of Weinsberg—charming, with pleasant shops, churches and public squares—to the Weibertreu ruins, that is, the castle looming over the settlement. It is an enjoyable ascent and worth the effort for the view, though one can drive up almost to the castle itself. A good portion of the old keep is still standing, round and forbidding, the more dour for its reddish stone. And there is an octagonal tower almost idyllically set amid lush, flowering trees. A pleasant caretaking couple might still be there, willing to explain certain aspects of the remains, and to show the visitor a dusty, but interesting, model of the burg as it once looked, and to sell cards and booklets.

King Conrad had troubles beyond those caused by the likes of Henry the Proud and his Saxon-Bavarian clan, difficulties that were finally ameliorated by Saint Bernard of Clairvaux's call to the second crusade. Conrad answered the summons, if somewhat reluctantly, and, accompanied by his nephew Frederick Barbarossa, marched eastward with a splendid banner-carrying army, only to have it decimated by disease and Turkish raids. He fulfilled his crusading vows, but really to no avail since he and his cohorts, despite a prolonged siege, were unable to take their main target, Damascus. Conrad himself was not faulted, though his generalship lacked imagination and inspiration. He displayed commendable valor, and one of his attacks is still known in German ballads as "the Swabian stroke." At the same time nephew Frederick gained for himself a notoriety for cruelty, augmented by his gratuitous firing of a monastery that had no bearing at all on his or his uncle's objectives in the East.

Conrad never seemed able to find the time to go to Rome to receive from the pope the imperial diadem, which he deserved as much as many lesser men who had enjoyed that exalted position. Basically a decent man, he was free of a certain taint of cruelty that seems to have persisted in every generation of the Hohenstaufens. He was intelligent, and wise enough to recognize that his own son was not emperor material. On his deathbed in 1152 he entrusted his insignia to his nephew Frederick "Red Beard," thereby indicating to the electors of Germany his choice of successor, a singular act of idealism, which effect on his seven-year-old son, Frederick of Rothenberg, is not recorded.

Ostensibly Conrad passed over his son on grounds of his youth. But the fact remains that he had become increasingly aware of the superior abilities of his nephew ever since the young man had accompanied him on crusade. Son of the one-eyed duke of Swabia, Frederick "Red Beard" was a genial man despite his reputation for ruthlessness and a tendency to tantrums and fits of anger that sent his lessers scurrying for cover. He was of medium height, well-knit, attractively blond-headed, and the fortunate possessor of a commanding Teutonic majesty and lordly mien. In envious admiration, the Italians nicknamed him "Barbarossa" in tribute to his dashing red beard, while contemporary commentators remarked on his eloquently expressive hands, a physical characteristic that shows up later in his even more comely grandson, Frederick II of Hohenstaufen.

Besides being a Hohenstaufen (and therefore Ghibelline), Barbarossa also had Guelf connections, his mother being Judith, sister of Henry the Proud, which made him a cousin to that very determined Guelf. With such a blood strain Otto of Freising, himself an uncle to Frederick, thought that Barbarossa might unite the two parties, which, indeed, he almost did. Germany was mighty under his stewardship, causing Chancellor Rainald of Dassel, archbishop of Cologne, to observe boastfully that Germany had an emperor while the rest of Europe had to be satisfied with petty kinglets. And certainly Barbarossa saw himself as the principal upholder of a God-created worldly order. The expression "Holy Empire" (and in his mind, at least, that included all of Italy, too) became commonplace in his time.

Frederick Barbarossa was purposeful and high-handed; his precrusading letter to the Muslim sultan, Saladin, giving him one year to quit Palestine, was a watermark of customary prideful arrogance. But he could debase himself too, as he did when Henry the Lion decided to desert the imperial cause. It is claimed that, in the agony of the moment, Frederick went so far as to fall on his knees before his Guelf cousin, but to no avail. He was capable of humanitarian acts and displays of justice as well. Thwarted in 1175 in his efforts to take the Lombard town of Alessandria della Paglia, defensively so ill-equipped as to be called

"Alessandria of Straw" and remaining today a town singularly devoid of historical interest, Barbarossa tried to bring about a surrender by threatening to blind anyone who attempted to provide the beleaguered town with supplies. Legend tells us that a young boy was captured and brought before him. Defiantly the lad claimed that he was not fighting emperor or empire; he was simply obeying his lord of the city and, even blind, he would continue to do so. Unable to stand against such devotion to duty, Barbarossa dismissed the youth unharmed. And he never took the town. It was in the aftermath of this "humiliation" that Henry the Lion supposedly deserted his cousin.

Like all German emperors, Barbarossa dreamed of uniting his German holdings with the Norman kingdom of Sicily, which included southern Italy. His politicking would lead to just such a takeover, but Frederick would not be around to enjoy the triumph. Ironically, his main difficulties stemmed from the hostility of the Lombards, a people whose origins centered in the region of the Elbe River at roughly the time of Christ, and then, after migrating southward, in Frederick's own Swabia. The Lombards entered Italy around 568, led by their King Alboin, who was killed shortly thereafter by his wife, Rosamunda, and her lover, the penalty for having forced her to drink from a cup made from her father's skull, which even in the most extravagantly permissive home must have been considered pretty kinky. "*Bevi, Rosamunda, nel teschio di tuo padre*"—"Drink, Rosamunda, from the skull of your father"—is a toast that the young of Italy jokingly use to this day. Alcohol has been the ruin of many men, but surely this is a new twist!

The Lombards set up a kingdom in Italy. Yet they remained essentially alien. After the usual succession of good and bad, weak and strong kings, they were subdued by the Franks under Pepin the Short, and then under his son Charlemagne, the two most responsible for establishing the Papal States, which would continue to exist, for better or for worse, until the nineteenth century. Since Charlemagne was the first of the Holy Roman emperors—crowned by Pope Leo III on Christmas Day in the year 800—it was through him that later emperors put claims on northern Italy in particular and all of Italy in general. While Charlemagne's successors proved unable to maintain the material unity of his empire, the idea of a Christian Roman empire persisted.

The most lasting effect of the rule of the Lombards in Italy was the residual establishment of a tradition of determined independence throughout their area of the peninsula. So, when the emperors of the Holy Roman Empire asserted their "rights" to make Lombardy subservient to imperial demands, they could expect only ferocious resistance.

And that most headstrong of emperors, Frederick Barbarossa, could expect an equally headstrong resistance when he moved against Milan, a city contentious in the extreme from the moment of her founding. Vexed by everlasting political and ecclesiastical difficulties, the people of Milan nurtured an anti-imperial spirit of independence and a resolute drive to look after themselves. Of the cities of northern Italy, Milan stood second only to Rome. Since the days of Saint Ambrose (in the fourth century), Milan's archbishops had exercised enormous influence over Italy's intricate affairs. One of these, the warlike Archbishop Heribert, invented the *carroccio,* an ox-drawn war chariot bearing the standard of the city. First employed in 1038 and quickly copied by other Italian cities, the heraldic wagon was the rallying point in battle, and its capture was a supreme humiliation.

Barbarossa would have none of Milan's treasonous insubordination. Was he not the successor of the magnificent Charlemagne? Were not he and his predecessors and successors entitled to loyalty, tax monies, and levies of warriors from this Italian city and the area that she seemed so intent on keeping in a state of seditious insurrection? Committed to depriving the Lombard cities of their consular self-government and to negating their proclaimed rights to make war on their own determination, Barbarossa descended upon Italy. In his mind Lombardy, through Milan, would be brought to her knees; then the rest of Italy would follow. The whole campaign would terminate in the glorious and final conquest of the Norman kingdom of Sicily.

But Frederick had not reckoned on the will of the Milanese, not a little inclined themselves to bullying their neighbors. On being advised of the stiff imperial terms for peace, they valiantly defended their city for over a year, not unaware that the eyes of their fellow Lombards were watching closely. In 1162, however, Milan was finally brought to the point of unconditionally accepting Barbarossa's demands, which included the destruction of all her defenses, the handing over of three hundred hostages, the acceptance of an imperially appointed podestà (mayor), not to mention extravagant fines, the construction of an imperial castle, and assurances of hospitality for Frederick and his troops whenever it was needed. To assuage the Hohenstaufen anger the city was almost completely destroyed—walls, churches, campaniles, even the cathedral. To this day the sightseer in Milan's Castello Sforzesco can see a figure of a crouching warrior with a dragon between his legs, thought to be a grotesque symbol of the emperor. It, along with reliefs showing the reentry of the Milanese into their city after Barbarossa's vengeance, was originally on the Porta Romana, constructed in 1171, and demolished finally in 1793. But the siege and destruction of this great city would be remembered by Italians forever.

It was because of Frederick's extravagant vengeance and in opposition to his ambitions that the Lombard League was formed, a political association with a Guelf point of view. The first steps were taken by Verona and Cremona in 1167, five years after Milan's destruction. Within a short time sixteen cities came together, swearing a solemn oath that they would join in their fight against common enemies (no one was fooled into thinking that the greatest common enemy was anyone but the German emperor), that they would never sue for separate peace, and that their primary objective was to restore Italy to the happier times she had known under certain previous emperors. The oaths taken by the consuls of the sixteen cities were solemn and unequivocal.

The Lombard League was given further incentive by Pope Alexander III, author and teacher, and anti-imperialist to the core, legitimately elected yet opposed by an antipope favored by the emperor. With Alexander III the emperor met his match. Yet Alexander was not to have an easy time of it. First one antipope (Victor IV), then another (Paschal III), and yet another (Calixtus III) was thrown in his way by antagonistic Frederick. Then, just before the formation of the Lombard League in 1167, Frederick headed for Rome. Pope Alexander fled for his life, decamping for the papal city of Benevento where he remained in exile from the Lateran for the next eleven years. But Frederick had no easier time of it. Having taken Rome, he was forced by an outbreak of malaria and dysentery among his troops to relinquish his hold almost immediately. He barely made it back to Germany alive, leaving some of his most loyal companions-in-arms behind in hastily dug graves, thus bearing out the words "Rome tames the proud necks of men . . . the fevers of Rome by a sure law are ever loyal to the Church," written a hundred years before by Peter Damian, an unattractive saint so puritanical he was scandalized by the sight of a bishop playing a game of chess. Bread and water, iron girdles, frequent flagellations, they all fit his concept of the best methods to salvation. Even in the heavenly abode where Dante places him, he remains faultfinding and complaining.

Thanks to the determination of the members of the Lombard League, when Frederick returned to Italy in 1174, he ran into a kind of opposition that a few years before he would have found unimaginable. Stopped cold at Legnano, near Milan, a defeat largely brought about by Henry the Lion's withdrawal of support, he was forced to conclude a six-year treaty with the Italian communes. As foreign lord and the most formidable power in Europe, Barbarossa was humiliated, even though the Italians claimed little beyond municipal authority and their cherished rights to declare their own wars against one another.

The imperial abasement was completed when Frederick agreed to meet Alexander III in Venice, a city well on its way to the heady glory for which it became so noted during the Renaissance and in modern times. Venice had reaped fantastic profit from those misguided crusades that had so far been undertaken; and there was more from the same source yet to come. Saint Mark's Cathedral, then serving as the doge's chapel, was already dominating her sparkling lagoon, a symbol of the wealthy commerce of Venice as well as her ability to remain somewhat aloof from the quarrels of her fractious neighbors. At Venice Barbarossa disavowed championing his antipopes and established a truce with the papacy. It was the only way of salvaging his power in Italy.

The sword having failed him, Frederick turned to diplomacy. His plans for southern Italy's Norman kingdom may have been destroyed—but only temporarily. He managed to negotiate an agreement to marry off his son, the future Henry VI, to Constance, the posthumous daughter of the great King Roger II. As aunt to reigning King William II, she was the only logical heir to the Sicilian throne should that monarch see fit to die without issue. Which is precisely what he did.

It was an astonishing and ill-advised policy, this willing away of the Norman kingdom, from the start being greeted by dire predictions. The dedicated and painstaking labors of several generations of Normans, who had stood firmly against imperial pretensions, went for naught with William's gifting of his Aunt Constance—to a German, of all people! Still, the ultimate heir, Barbarossa's energetic grandson, Frederick II, was one-quarter Norman. And that was to prove important. However, his father came first. With William's death in 1189, Henry Hohenstaufen, through his wife Constance, became the logical claimant to the Sicilian throne—not that logic always triumphed in these thorny situations. Apparently William II had foreseen the coming mischief of dissension in the ranks; he had persuaded his court to swear that the rights of his aunt would be upheld, thereby throwing open even wider the door through which the Germans could march into his lush southern kingdom, the richest, most refined, and certainly the most enlightened kingdom of the European Middle Ages. Normans were seldom as good as their word, and one wonders why William would have been lulled into complacency by mere sworn oaths.

Chapter One

How great a tremor is to be,
when the judge is to come
briskly shattering every (grave).
***Dies Irae,* verse 2**

Empress Constance had shown no inclination for an imperial role. Just the opposite. She had resisted with threats, tears, and finally with prophecies of damnation when "the shadow of the veil was ripped away" and "against her will and all propriety she was forced back to the world"[1] from the convent in which she had sought refuge from the rough-and-tumble life so relished by her family. But her nephew, King William II—"the Good"—had been adamant in the face of such impractical "propriety"; she would, he had insisted, recognize her heritage and duty as princess in Sicily's royal family.

The convent had been the one place in the world where Constance had found the quiet she had craved. As daughter of the most enlightened of the Norman Sicilian kings, Roger II, custom would relegate her to playing the part of political pawn, child bearer, and purveyor of wealth to an assuredly royal, or at least noble, husband. It must have been horrifying to Constance that her kingly nephew had bartered her off to the scion of the German imperial family, Henry VI—the speaker of a language whose guttural sounds must have sent chills up the back of every southern Italian, a man whose reputation for ruthlessness could not be gainsaid. On top of everything else, in contrast to the elegant silks from the royal workshop that she was accustomed to, his clothes were coarse and heavy, crude shields against the cold northern climate.

In truth the German nobility did not want Constance any more than she wanted them. They had always looked down on Italians and could never bring themselves to trust them. But even they had to admit that, should she produce for her husband a male heir, then Constance would achieve by motherhood what German emperors had been attempting for generations. They would be able to claim ownership of the most cultivated and sophisticated court of the western world. They would be undisputed proprietors of a multitude of warm-water, Mediterranean ports. Best of all, they would hem in the Papal States, that large block of land in central Italy dominated by princes of the Church, who would do better to look to the spiritual well-being of their flock than to their own temporal power.

According to contemporary gossip, Constance's mother, Beatrice, third wife of King Roger II, had been given to evil dreams and unnatural fears when on the verge of delivering his posthumous daughter. To avert predictions of dire ruin to be visited on her fatherland, Constance had been relegated to various nunneries. The story circulated that she was unwilling to marry at all. What possessed William II to drag Aunt Constance, complaining and protesting, from her convent retreat to be married to Barbarossa's eldest son is a historian's guess. From the start word was rife that she had been forced to deny her nun's vows, though we have no absolute proof that she ever took them. Certainly at this time it was customary for women to enter convents, to live out their lives in peace without committing themselves to the nuns' strict regimen. So be it! She had a role to fulfill outside the convent walls. She would see to it that even there her heart, her mind—her life—would remain forever virtuous.

1186

The wedding of Henry VI and Constance took place in Milan on January 27, 1186. In anticipation of the event, the Church of Sant'Ambrogio, used as a granary since Barbarossa's unparalleled destruction of the city twenty-three years before, was hastily scoured of the dirt of catastrophe. Milan had petitioned to be the scene of the glamorous and symbolically important union, even though the city was in no condition to entertain the multitudes that were expected to attend. Only partially rebuilt, with some streets still blocked and made inconvenient by the rubble of destruction, the cathedral barely in the initial stages of rebuilding, Milan still wanted to host the wedding of the century, a half-imaginary, half-realistic playing of its role in the new peace between the empire and the great Lombard League. Milan saw its very ruins as emblematic of its preeminence and courage, while much benefit would accrue by parading the evidence of its terrible war with Frederick in the name of Lombard freedom. As he progressed through the littered streets on his way to Sant'Ambrogio, Barbarossa, too, could draw comfort from the battered remains of his most dangerous adversary. With the circuitous reasoning of emperors, kings, popes, and presidents, he may even have derived satisfaction from the memory of his own defeat by the Milanese twelve years before with the thought that here was an enemy worthy of an emperor.

But the wedding had further symbolic importance that was not lost on old Pope Urban III, now only a year as pope and with only one more to go. The union of the Sicilian Hautevilles and the German Hohenstaufens should, if properly respected, mark the end of the long-standing antagonisms between the two houses, a peace not compatible with papal interests. Could a merging of the Sicilian kingdom with the northern empire be far behind? Was it in the cards for the papacy to find itself surrounded by a single redoubtable power, always on speaking terms with the Holy Father, but perpetually hostile and jealously defensive? The nightmare of generations of popes appeared on the verge of becoming a reality. And Frederick Barbarossa, for all his kissing of the late Alexander III's embroidered slipper in Venice, had brought it about not by the sword, but by diplomacy.

Romanesque arches weighed heavily on Sant'Ambrogio's dark interior, compressing into a stifling oneness the dense odors of incense, banks of flowers, and burning candles. Jewels and metallic-threaded silken fabrics worked to dispel the gloom of obscure corners and half-restored side chapels. As tall and fair as her Norman forebears, with the dignity of a princess born to the purple, Constance was escorted to the altar, pale, unsmiling, aware of the historic role she was playing on this cold January day. Historians have been mainly silent on her emotions, her longing for the convent on the one hand, and on the other her chagrin at being thrust into the heart of the most undisguisedly ambitious family on the continent, rough-talking and vulgar when compared to her own Oriental-leaning people. Surely she came to despise this calculating heir to the German throne she now faced in Milan's oldest church—if she did not do so already.

Following the elaborate marriage ritual, the newlyweds were crowned with the traditional iron crown of Lombardy by the patriarch of Aquileia, bringing down on his own head a papal interdict, which probably did not faze him a modicum as, worldly-wise and calculating, he saw a twenty-year-old future emperor's approbation as much more in harmony with his own ambitions than the skittish approval of a reactionary old pope. After Constance had been crowned queen of Germany (Barbarossa had seen to it that Henry had already been crowned king), the royal couple were hymned by the pealing bells of

Sant'Ambrogio and the few churches capable of mounting a resonant concert, announcing to the world that a new peace was in the land, that the gauntlet had been cast before the papal foot. Barbarossa led the procession through the spacious, magnificently proportioned atrium of the church to a specially erected pavilion to celebrate the wedding banquet. Even the half-ruined condition of the city could not mar the imperial celebration.

The expected papal fury was unbounded. A native archbishop of Milan, Urban III had been elected to the chair of Saint Peter because it was thought that he could be relied upon to maintain his natural hostility to the Hohenstaufens. The entire period of his two-year pontificate was spent in exile, first from Rome and then from Verona, where at the time of the royal wedding, he was in the process of drawing up an excommunication against the emperor for his part in arranging the union and, just as important, for being the power behind his son, who had recently invaded papal territories. The Veronese successfully petitioned Urban to delay his excommunication on the grounds that, as friends of the emperor, they had promised to defend him and to allow no harm to be aimed his way from their city. Urban never had the opportunity again. Expelled from Verona the next year (1187), he died on his way to Ferrara, eighteen days after receiving word that the city of Jerusalem had fallen to the supposedly infamous Saladin, which sent more shock waves through Christendom than even the death of the pope. The new pontiff (Gregory VIII) lasted barely eight weeks and was followed by Clement III, who managed in the short period of just over three years to do irreparable damage to the already shredded papal-imperial relationship. Having prevailed upon Barbarossa to make the crusading effort that would kill him, Clement then refused to condemn the pretender to the throne of Sicily, Tancred of Lecce, bastard grandson of Roger II. Tancred's claim was upheld by the Norman barons despite their pledge to honor the rights of Constance.

1190

Frederick Barbarossa lived just long enough to see his scheming begin to bear fruit. He died in 1190, well aware that there was no direct heir to the Sicilian throne but Constance. Confident as Caesar on his way to the senate, Frederick led a crusade off to Asia Minor where, swimming, or simply trying to cross the cold Calycadnus River, he drowned. He had been a good emperor basically, though in exercising his imperial claims to Italy, he had never been able to accept the

Italians as anything more than aliens in their own land. And there does seem to be something foolish in his persistent championing of three antipopes. Yet his own people genuinely mourned him. On hearing of his death, Walther von der Vogelweide, about twenty years old but already on his way to becoming the most celebrated of Germany's medieval poets, wrote: "My haughty crane's steps changed into dragging peacock's steps, I let my head hang down to my knees."[2] There had been something godlike about Frederick. If the picture of this crusty emperor that comes down to us is accurate, he was a man of no mean wit, an enjoyer of those scurrilous parodies of Rome so beloved of the goliards, itinerant scholar-student-poets, more notorious for their roistering and drinking than for scholarship, study, or poetry. "Caesar Frederick, prince of all earthly princes raised up by God above all other kings,"[3] wrote the Archpoet, a goliard under the patronage of Frederick's Grand Chancellor Rainald, archbishop of Cologne. Frederick Barbarossa would be long mourned.

So, with William II dying in 1189, Barbarossa in 1190, and Pope Clement III in 1191 while Henry VI was in the act of journeying to Rome for his imperial coronation, things in Italy were, at the very least, in a state of flux. However, Henry and Constance received their imperial crowns as one of the first acts of the new pope, Celestine III, a man with the show-stopping name of Hyacinth Bobo, whose family was shortly to adopt the name Orsini.

1190–1194

As for Henry VI's physical appearance, one is tempted to compare him to Shakespeare's Cassius, he of the "lean and hungry look," and indeed he has been so described. Scorning any kind of self-indulgence, he was rather frail of physique, pale, with a pleasant face. Highly educated, he could write love songs, was fluent in Latin, and versed in Roman and canon law. Megalomanic to his fingertips, he dreamed of ruling an empire including the Byzantine, and of calling the kings of Europe his vassals, with the pope little more than a worried, overawed ally bystander. Unlike his father, Henry was a cold, untrustworthy, heartless ruler, capable of unimaginable cruelties, traits that contradicted neither his masterful statesmanship nor his determination. Along with everything else he possessed an enormous energy. With the temporizing Pope Celestine recognizing neither Tancred nor the new emperor as a legitimate occupant of the Sicilian throne, Henry, in the name of his wife, determined to fight for that sun-drenched, Norman-enriched kingdom. Going along with him, and eager to cater to his apparent invincibility, the citizens of Salerno begged for the honor of housing the empress while her husband was off besieging the city of Naples, a preliminary step to taking over southern Italy, with its ultimate prize—the island of Sicily.

Both Salerno and Naples play distinctly checkered roles in the history of the Norman dominance of the south. In a land notorious for rebellions and counter-rebellions, seldom had either city been free of the taint of disloyalty. One would think that the citizens might have become tired unto death of rebuilding their castles and city walls, so often were they razed by order of one conqueror or another. In the wake of endemic sieges, the three medieval castles (two in Naples and one in Salerno), as well as Robert Guiscard's magnificent Salerno Cathedral, are miracles of survival.

At the time of Constance's stay in Salerno, the city was famous in Europe and over the entire Mediterranean for its medical school, the first in the western world. Legend has it that the school was founded by "four masters"—Latin, Greek, Jew, and Saracen—but this is probably just a way of illustrating the universal influences at work during its formative years. Famous throughout the Middle Ages for its research facilities and for the intercultural nature of its faculty—as well as, unhappily, for a lively trade in poisons and later for bogus degrees—the Salerno medical school treated some of the better-known personages of the period, including Bohemund (son of Robert Guiscard), Robert Curthose (brother to Henry I of England), and, not too long before Constance's visit, King Richard I, who, leading a crusade, was on his way to a Sicilian rendezvous with King Philip of France. Richard Lionheart stayed five days at Salerno where, it seems reasonable to assume, he would have consulted the learned doctors. Had Richard been in Salerno at the same time as Constance, and had they met, perhaps he might not have ended up just two years later as her husband's prisoner in Germany, patiently waiting for his mother, Eleanor of Aquitaine, to browbeat the English into coughing up the exorbitant ransom demanded by the emperor.

The school at Salerno went into decline with the opening of the University of Naples in 1224, but it managed to survive until 1812, when it was closed by Napoleon. Constance's great-uncle, Robert Guiscard, who took Salerno in 1077 and made it his capital, built the Cathedral of Saint Matthew on Lombard foundations, creating a forecourt of magnificent grace and majesty, with its two-tiered arcade of round arches in black-and-white stone, and with which even Milan's

Church of Sant'Ambrogio, with all its elegance, could not compete. A fountain in its center adds to the general graciousness of the ambience, and the medieval lions at both the atrium and church entrances seem—perhaps unintentionally—more welcoming than forbidding, more puppies than kings of beasts.

Henry VI was not at first successful in his attempt to take Naples and then Sicily. For once there was a sufficiently large contingent of southern barons agreeing to be a daunting force. The legitimate Hauteville male line may have become extinct with the death of William II, but illegitimate Tancred of Lecce managed to rally enough barons who believed that their land was not to be handed over to a German as though it were private property. Furthermore, having suffered through a couple of matriarchal regencies, the barons had an aversion to reigning queens. Constance's thoughts concerning her husband's assault on her homeland are not recorded, though one can assume that she was at least depressed. It is not beyond the limits of imagination to assume that she knew Tancred since he was an illegitimate grandson of her father. She must have seen him as a pretender to the throne, who was pushing aside her own legitimate claims and those of her unborn son. Tancred of Lecce had assumed the Sicilian rule, probably in an honest effort to preserve the Norman kingdom after William II's demise. One likes to think that it was not sheer self-interest that motivated him, for he was backed by a good-sized coalition of barons and courtiers, including powerful, but aging, Matthew of Aiello, who for the most part had been loyal all his life to three Norman kings and from the start had been the leader of the faction that stood against Constance's marriage to the German. But there is something pathetic about Tancred, a short man and appallingly ugly, when one considers his efforts to hold the kingdom together in the face of seditious internal destruction by certain barons, and the external threat of Henry VI and his tough, superbly trained imperial troops.

Emperor Henry was forced to cancel his initial attempt to take Naples because of sickness among his troops. As they had so often through history, southern Italian climate and epidemic disease combined to thwart the would-be northern invaders. The rumor even got about that Henry himself was dead of typhus, and this did nothing to bolster the morale of his troops or of his supporters at home. There was little to do but raise the siege of Naples and return to Germany. Here again the Salernitans proved only too willing to bend before the political winds. Having invited the empress—the only legitimate claimant of the Sicilian throne, remember—to await her husband in their city, the Salernitans now perceived

Henry as a defeated emperor. Unable to see beyond the present (countless precedents should have indicated to them that Henry would one day be hot for revenge), they turned on the hapless empress, taking her prisoner and sending her off to Messina to her husband's number-one enemy. With more vision than the Salernitans, Tancred knew that Henry's exit from Italy was only temporary, that he would be back, as sure as some of the barons would welcome him even against their own interests.

King Tancred squandered his trump card when he allowed Pope Celestine III to persuade him to turn Empress Constance over to papal custody until such a time as Henry and Tancred could work out a proper modus vivendi. While Constance was being escorted to Rome, her train was attacked by agents of the emperor, and she was whisked off to Germany. Thus was Tancred dealt out of the game. But Henry was not sitting in the winner's seat yet. Pope Celestine III was as much a weight around the imperial neck as Alexander III had been around Barbarossa's. It took no exceptional political savvy for Celestine to realize that German Henry intended Sicily to be a rich new part of his empire and that he, Celestine, must dedicate his whole mind to frustrating that ambition. He also knew that Henry had returned home to widespread dissatisfaction, bitterness at the failure of his southern campaign, and unrest between rival Guelfs and Ghibellines, and even, at times, Guelfs against Guelfs and Ghibellines against Ghibellines. It was the papal decision to do nothing to discourage this discord; indeed, Celestine could probably incite further discontent by giving the nod of approval to Tancred's claim to kingship, which is what he did in 1192. As for Henry, just when his ambition to sweep southern Italy into the imperial fold seemed most unfulfillable, he was, unexpectedly, dealt two winning hands. First, returning from crusade, Richard I of England—a king worth a king's ransom, brother-in-law to the formidable Guelf, Henry the Lion, friend and ally of Tancred—was captured and given into imperial custody. Then, in 1194, word was brought to Henry that Tancred had suddenly died, probably of sheer exhaustion from his struggles to save his kingdom from destruction. In the disarray that followed, the German emperor was able to take over the throne in his wife's name.

1194–1197

On Christmas Day 1194 Henry had himself crowned king of the unhappy island amid splendors that only royalty could command. On the following day he commenced his unspeakable reign of terror. The Sicilian aristocracy was decimated in cold blood. Tancred's Queen Sibylla, her son William (who would have been King William III), and her daughters were all sent north, the boy to vanish from the pages of history, some say murdered, others say castrated and relegated to a monastery to die an early death. Nobles and prelates alike endured fiendish cruelties. It was claimed that an unnamed ambitious man had a red-hot crown nailed to his head. Some had their eyes torn out, others were tortured, hanged, burned, even buried alive. Barbarous cruelties were visited on Tancred's old partisans. He and his sons were torn from their tombs and beheaded for the edification of the populace. The vengeful bloodletting went on and on. Later, in 1196, Germans bound for crusade passed through southern Italy, and Henry used their presence to tighten the screws. New taxes were levied. The walls of Naples and Capua were brought down. In the latter town Count Richard of Acerra, Queen Sibylla's brother, who had led Naples in successful resistance to Henry five years before, was captured, dragged through the streets at the tail of a horse, then hung by the legs from a scaffold. For two days he remained thus until a sympathetic samaritan tied a stone around his neck to end his agony.

On the very day that Henry initiated his satanic vengeance in Sicily, Constance gave birth to a son in Jesi (pronounced yay-zee), nineteen miles southwest of Ancona. It was an odd coincidence that the day after Christmas—Saint Stephen's Day 1194—marked both the start of the evil reign of Henry VI and the birth of his only child, appropriately named for nobler souls, his two brilliant grandfathers—Frederick Barbarossa and Roger II. With any luck Frederick Roger would be the answer to German prayers. He was, after all, a Hohenstaufen; but he was also part Norman. As Emperor Frederick II, he would in years to come do much to ameliorate the terrifying memories of his hideous father. The story goes that Empress Constance raised her infant son to the stares of the populace of Jesi and then suckled him in front of them, a forthright follow-up of her invitation to the women of the town to attend her during the birth ritual in the hastily erected tent in the city piazza that served as a delivery room. The effect of the empress's demonstration would have been enormous, especially so in that age when "divine" was an adjective frequently applied in connection with the person of the emperor. Considering her age, Frederick's birth—and her survival of it—was a small miracle. And the world needed to know that she, Empress of the Holy Roman Empire, daughter of King Roger II of Sicily, daughter-in-law to Frederick Barbarossa, had produced a male child directly in the line of succession to the imperial throne (though it was not a hereditary office), and more importantly, as far as she was concerned, to the royal throne of Sicily. Like every prominent man of his age, Frederick Hohenstaufen had his legends, and he was never one to let a good legend slip by unnoticed. Throughout his life he would sing the praises of his birthplace, calling Jesi his Bethlehem. He would imply that Constance was synonymous with the mother of Jesus—the further implications being obvious. Yet for all his hymning of Jesi, he would never spend much time there. In truth out-of-the-way Jesi seemed, and still seems, an entirely inappropriate setting to serve as birthplace for a future emperor, though it does command a majestic view of the Ancona Marches. There is a dearth of Frederick memorabilia, though the town still boasts its Piazza Federico II, the piazza in which Constance is said to have raised the tent wherein she birthed her son.

Some forbidding fourteenth-century stone walls with bulky, overhanging towers are beautifully preserved and solid enough to act as foundations for modern Jesi apartment buildings. In the twelfth century Jesi was a commune—that is, governed by a mayor and a municipal council. It was already an old community, possibly a settlement of the Umbri peoples, that was, as "Aesis," absorbed by the Romans in 247 BC. The upper city is the medieval quarter, with narrow, alternating sunny and shady streets, some of them stepped, and most of them echoing softly with Italian voices from behind heavy doors, solid and ponderously hinged. Occasionally the streets are arched by enclosed bridges connecting buildings from opposite sides, much used as vantage points for people-watching.

If later ages felt the need to equate the name of Frederick with divinity—and they did—then perhaps Jesi was by association a heaven-chosen spot. For barely thirty miles southeast in a direct line is the town of Loreto, considered by some to be the final resting place of the Santa Casa—the house of the Virgin Mary, carried there, it is said, by angels. It is not the only resting place commandeered for the holy house, as it was first brought from Nazareth to Rejika, near Trieste in Dalmatia, in 1291, and then three years later it was taken on its second lap across the Adriatic to Loreto, where it was set down in a laurel wood. The alleged transport of the house to Loreto was about forty-four years after Frederick's death, but it does, according to his apologists, indicate a divine regard for the area in which he was born. No one seems especially concerned that divinity has not touched the thousands upon thousands of souls who have been born in the vicinity of Loreto, many of them closer to the Virgin's house than Frederick ever was.

In the months following his birth, Constance placed Frederick in the care of the duchess of Spoleto. The duchess took him to Foligno, near Assisi, while his mother hastened south to join her husband at Bari, whence she moved on with him to the island of her origin. She must have gotten wind at once of what Henry was up to in Sicily, since he arrived at Bari with 160 horses burdened by the treasures that he had already confiscated, along with his royal prisoners who were later shunted off to Germany. According to some sources, Constance was so horrified by the barbarity of the new regime that she entered a conspiracy against her husband. On discovery of the plot, it was said, she was imprisoned for a time under the wardenship of Henry's trusted and selfishly ambitious Sicilian chancellor, Walter of Palear, bishop of Troia. Stories further circulated that the empress was forced to witness the gruesome dispatch of her co-conspirators. Yet, without the slightest catch in his voice, Henry could sanctimoniously brag to the German bishops of his pacification of the island kingdom, to the glory of the Christ who had embraced the cross for humanity's sins. Pacification or not, Henry's Germanization of the southern kingdom—and the rest of Italy with it—proceeded apace. His brother Philip was made duke of Tuscany while assorted comrades in horror were awarded important fiefs. Markward of Anweiler, a pushy, self-serving, treacherously unprincipled imperial interpreter served on occasion as Henry's deputy and would prove to be Frederick's childhood bogey. Nobody's fool, Pope Celestine III was ambivalent through all of this, especially in his reception of Henry's ambassadors, who brought straight-faced assurances of a new imperial crusade to the Holy Land. Celestine accurately saw them as mere excuses for summoning yet another army of unruly Germans into Italy. But as far as Henry was concerned, now that the conditions on which Barbarossa had gambled had been accomplished, it was time to head for Germany, there to browbeat his vassals and bribe them with the loot from Sicily until they agreed to elect infant Frederick as king of the Germans, the first step to his eventual occupancy of the imperial throne.

While the future emperor was being cared for at Foligno only a few miles away, Francesco Bernardone was running unchecked through the streets of his native Assisi. At thirteen Francis was showing promise of growing to only medium height. His face was inclined to be long, with prominent features and straight eyebrows. His hair was black. We are told that he had straight shoulders and delicate hands, that he was thin, with almost translucent skin. Though later he would develop the talents of a compelling speaker, and though his voice was strong, he would maintain through his life a sweet and lyrical speaking tone. A reputation for kindness and civility did not discourage him from embracing the dissolute life of the dark side of Assisi. Indeed, until his twenty-fifth year he squandered precious hours of his preordained brief life, indulging himself in every vice and vanity. "And thus overwhelmed by a host of evil companions, proud and high-minded, he walked about the streets of Babylon. . . ."[4] So the legends tell us.

Francis—in his love for his siblings in Nature, surely Christendom's sweetest saint—shared with Frederick the common experience of being spiritually cleansed in the same baptismal font, still in place in Assisi's Cathedral of San Rufino. A covered, stone cylinder imprisoned unattractively in a wrought-iron cage, it lends little to the romantic imagination. Historically, of course, it is interesting to note that it was Frederick's baptism that was special, attended as it was by fifteen prelates of the Church.

There may be a contrived aura of divinity surrounding the birth of Frederick promulgated by the man himself. But it is as nothing compared to the Franciscan legend of the detailed recreation of Bethlehem contrived by Francis's mother up to, but not including, the virgin birth,

Baptismal font, Cathedral, Assisi, Italy

which, even by Italian standards, was probably considered excessive. It is the spirit of Francis hovering over this Umbrian medieval city, even over streets full of the usual twenty-first-century tourist kitsch—the acres of cheap ceramics, the overtly sentimentalized "portraits" of the saint, the maudlin scenes from his life, quotes from *The Little Flowers of Saint Francis* and from his "Canticle to the Brother Sun" tastelessly memorialized on ashtrays, drink coasters, and coffee mugs. Yes, it is Francis who dominates Assisi, its stepped streets, stone-lined and edged by buildings of the same stone, festooned with vines and geraniums cascading from flower boxes, by the family laundry drying in the hot Umbrian sun. The secret corner nook still exudes an aura of gentle charm, simplicity, and calm. Sometimes Francis may be hard to find there, but Assisi does retain its pure, limpid air, its flocks of bird "sisters," its streets redolent of the Middle Ages, its daily siesta tranquility. It sings with the music of happiness, the joy of brotherhood. Where else on a clear moonlit night would one hear Schiller's "Ode to Joy" from Beethoven's Ninth Symphony being harmonized by young choristers enjoying a smoke during a respite from rehearsal? A city of the same clutter, filth, and corruption as any other, Assisi still retains an innocence lost to our century, a cleanliness that seems to have been just an hour ago washed by heavenly rains. No church fresco, no house, cave, or chapel can catch the smiling character of Assisi's lovable saint. We do not need to share his religious beliefs. And his practices sometimes seem a bit quirky. But we want to know him. Sometimes just a walk in the streets of Assisi causes one to come perhaps a little way toward that end.

The Cathedral of San Rufino was new when Francis and Frederick were baptized there, unfinished, its heavy Lombard-Romanesque facade dominating its small piazza. Unhesitatingly foursquare, its three round windows seem too small for the solid wall they penetrate; a miniature colonnade a third of the way up, while in detail delicately lacy in the clear sunlight, seems somehow ill advised, not exactly right, an architectural device to divide space and then not placed to greatest advantage. The Gate of Saint Peter, the best preserved of the eight openings in the city walls, was probably as familiar to Francis as the door of his childhood home, which, supposedly, is still there and dutifully pointed out to tourists, who just as dutifully photograph it. The Sant'Antimo Gate, originally Roman and the principal gate of the city, is square and arched, with restored marble columns on the exterior side. The inner side is part of the majestic original.

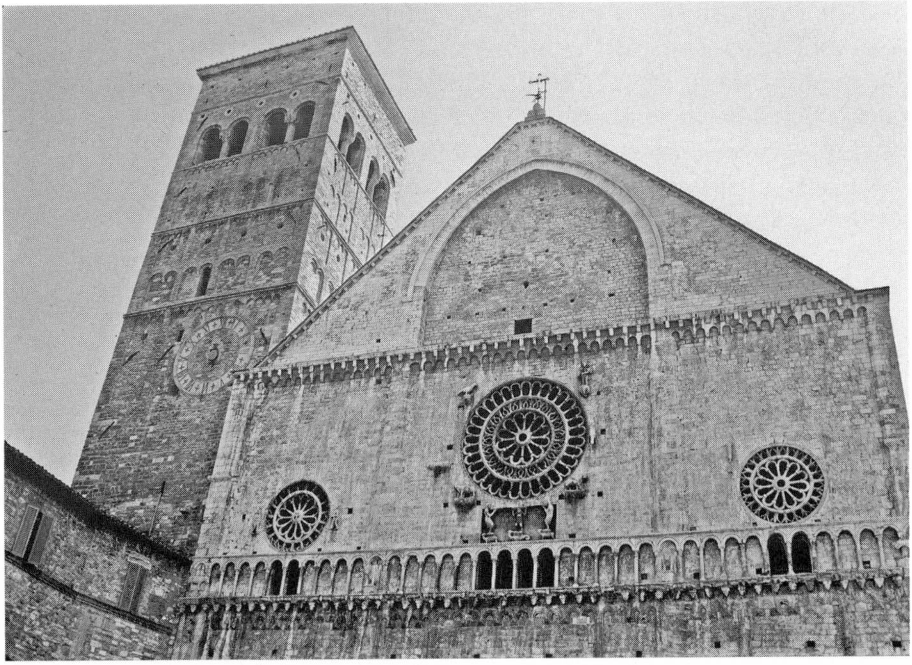

Cathedral San Rufino, Assisi, Italy

Toward the close of the twelfth century, Assisi belonged to the duchy of Spoleto and was rather casually ruled by Duke Conrad of that city—"Old Nit-Wit" is what they called him. Duke Conrad's favorite residence was the Rocca Maggiore, a giant castle lording over the city, which was destined to achieve its most lasting fame from the residence of a saint, rather than a maladroit nobleman. Conrad surrendered his landholdings to Rome during the anti-German reaction that followed the death of Henry VI in 1197. The citizens of Assisi celebrated Conrad's departure by pulling down his castle and reusing the stone for new city walls. The Rocca Maggiore, which we know today as a derelict ruin, was largely the work of the fourteenth-century Cardinal dell'Albornoz and so was known by neither Francis nor Frederick.

But the Church of San Damiano was familiar to both and proved to be a giant push in the legendary progression of Francis's march toward sainthood. As the story goes, Francis was praying one day before a crucifix in San Damiano. He "heard a voice" telling him to rebuild his church. Thinking the command to be a literal one, he immediately started a reconstruction program on the ill-repaired building. It was not until years later that he understood the heavenly admonition to be a command to rescue Mother Church from the degenerate ways into which it had been led by nonidealistic priests, prelates, and popes. And this is where his well-intentioned followers would collide with the politically ambitious, worldly Frederick Hohenstaufen.

Now was a time of trial, misery, and injustice. Political upheaval ravaged the cities. Famine reigned, and men were driven by unbearable hunger to eat wild grasses or to starve. Storms raged through the countryside uprooting trees, destroying what little fruits nature had managed to yield, and killing animals. Among the records of Assisi's cathedral was found an elegiac poem, a prayer to its patron, Saint Rufino, first bishop of Assisi and a man known to side invariably with the common man. It tells us more per line about the plight of medieval humanity than a whole volume of history:

> O Saint Rufinus, always protect your servants;
> Hear the prayer of your people, O Holy Saint.
> Protect us against devastating hail, devouring fire,
> Against hunger and pestilence, war and futile strifes.
> Grant that the harvests will be good,
> That the grapes will be safe.
> You who are pious and good, just, innocent, and kind. . . .[5]

CHAPTER TWO

A trumpet sounding an astonishing sound
through the tombs of the region
drives all (men) before the throne.
***Dies Irae*, verse 3**

1197–1201

For all the ambition that Henry entertained for his son, he probably saw him only once, at Foligno, when he was on his way northward to confront the German electors with demands that they recognize the infant Frederick as king. Henry was more interested in the succession of his line than in the personal development of his heir, about whom he had already heard disconcerting predictions from various doomsayers, including the respected Calabrian Cistercian abbot, Joachim of Flora, who foretold that a perverse and wicked Frederick would agitate the world and "wear out the saints of the Most Highest."[1] But Henry had no truck with the omens and little concern for Frederick, who remained in good hands in Foligno, a commercial center today, largely modern, though the town hall dates from the thirteenth to the seventeenth centuries, and one facade of the cathedral goes back to 1202. Having satisfied himself that the election to kingship of his son was certain, Henry hurried back to Sicily to quell rebellions with methods even more savage than anything the island kingdom had yet experienced. And all the time he continued to lay ambitious plans for his Euro-Mediterranean empire.

Then the unexpected—the kind of event that occurs with such frequency as to make one wonder why it is unexpected—happened. Henry died in September 1197 at Messina, apparently of a cold caught while hunting. A porphyry tomb in Palermo was his last resting place, in the cathedral, where the great Roger II himself was already resting—and where Frederick would eventually follow. The building has been so worked and reworked over the centuries as to bear little likeness to the probably-not-very-attractive, twelfth-century form envisioned by its builder, Walter of the Mill, the man who, as chief minister to King William II, was partly responsible for convincing his master to sign over his kingdom to the Germans. The building—"imposing in a messy sort of way," as John Julius Norwich puts it[2]—is as appropriate a place of entombment for Henry as for its founder. He was laid to ill-deserved rest swathed in silken textiles from Palermo's *tiraz* (workshop), overlaid by blond hanks of hair cut off by his widow as a demonstration of her grief, certainly unlamented by anyone but the Germans. In 1215 Frederick had the body of his father moved to a tomb that seemed more appropriately severe, while Constance, who lived only a year beyond her husband, was placed in Henry's former tomb.

Henry knew he was dying. In his death throes he was aware that he was leaving to his wife and child a troubled empire and an endemically violent kingdom, instead of a sweeping empire to rival that of the ancient Caesars. Seldom in history has the future of a land depended so completely on the guiding presence of a single man. Predictions of impending upheaval, mysterious, threatening visions, and alarming portents of disaster were rife. One report even had Theodoric the Ostrogoth, dead now six centuries, appearing on the banks of the Mosel River riding a black charger at the head of his hordes, a sure indication that anarchy was coming.

Before dying Henry did what he could to firm up the shaky situation and to set things right with other rulers. He absolved Richard I of England of his oath of vassalage, a debt established as a condition of that king's ransom. To disarm Pope Celestine's opposition to Frederick's eventual emperorship he made a will in which he commended his son to the care of the pope. He gave back certain papal territories that he had seized, encouraging the next pope, Innocent III, to claim yet more, thus establishing Church territory coast to coast across the Italian peninsula. Henry asked Celestine to recognize Frederick's succession and in exchange made the papacy the heir to the kingdom of Sicily should Frederick himself die without issue. It must have almost blown old Celestine III away. By an astonishing and totally unexpected transformation fifty years of papal concern about imperial aggression was suddenly eased. But the respite was only temporary. By the spring of the next year Pope Innocent III was firmly ensconced in Saint Peter's chair. Stubbornly defiant, he would have his own interests in mind, while ostensibly playing the guardian to the child heir to the empire. And civil wars were kindling in every inch of Germany and Italy.

Not the kind of woman to honor a will simply because its writer was emperor, king, and husband, the widowed Constance sent Henry's German confederates packing to their northern fatherland. Other notables and sympathizers she clapped into prison, including Chancellor Walter of Palear—a neat retribution for the similar insult she had endured at his hands, though it must be remembered that Constance's confinement had been on the orders of her husband. Devoid of concern for the empire, Constance hardly noticed when her brother-in-law, Philip of Swabia, Foligno-bound from the north to fetch Frederick and escort him to Germany for his coronation, suddenly reversed his direction on the news that Henry had died, thinking it wise to return home to protect family interests. Had Henry died only a few days later, Frederick would have been on his way to Germany where, as king, he would have been raised royally, with a totally different philosophy and set of political aims. By such a narrow margin of time was Frederick's future changed.

Constance may or may not have grieved, but for sure she inherited a passel of problems. Had Frederick been older she might have been content to return to her retreat in the convent of Saint Savior, close to him, but at the same time removed from the whirl of politics for which she had no aptitude, liking, or training. She did not view with favor a German coronation for her son. She was a southerner, and as far as she was concerned, so was he, a dedication she would instill so firmly in him that he would honor it until the day he died. Even in an age not noteworthy for beneficence, German savageries were appalling to her and her people. Germans were seen as barely out of their northern forests. They could well go back to their gloomy homeland and do what they wanted with their imperial throne! And they could take Markward of Anweiler, the dead emperor's interpreter and seneschal, with them, since he had, with stunning alacrity, proposed himself as vice-regent. As long as they all left Constance in peace to raise her son as heir to the Sicilian throne, that was sufficient. On the other hand, his mother's satisfaction with her son forfeiting his rights to the empire does not mean that Frederick, in his maturity, would feel the same way. Henry had seen to it that he had already been elected to the German throne; the imperial diadem was the next step. Born to the purple as he was, Frederick was not going to be done out of his rights through the denying attitude of his mother or the counterfeit arrogations of others, including his Uncle Philip, as it turned out.

After Henry's death Constance had Frederick brought to Palermo, preparatory to his being crowned king of Sicily. Desperately casting about for support, she turned to Pope Celestine, who was not so incapacitated by age as not to know a good bargaining ploy when he saw one. Constance's precarious position was obvious to him, an ideal situation for hard negotiating in favor of Church interests. To add weight to his argument before agreeing to sanction the coronation, Celestine even resurrected stories of Frederick's alleged issuance from the loins of a Jesi butcher, and Constance humiliatingly had to swear an oath that he was indeed her legitimate son. She was made to disavow certain special concessions that the Normans had won for Sicily, including the ecclesiastical rights of the crown in the selection and nomination of Sicilian bishops. Worse, an annual tribute of no little worth was agreed upon, payable to the pope, who was acknowledged suzerain of the island kingdom. Now Celestine would come to terms with the harried queen—for she was acting as queen of Sicily and not as empress. But there was a final discouragement: Celestine died before he could ratify the agreement.

Before long Constance reached an accord with the new Pope Innocent III, an even more dangerous man as far as the future of the kingdom was concerned. With his approval she arranged a joint coronation of herself and her three-and-one-half-year-old son on Whit Sunday 1198, which event took place with pomp and circumstance borrowed from the Byzantine court by her father and his Norman forebears. Clasping her baby in her arms, Constance showed herself to her subjects from the Cappella dell'Incoronata, the coronation balcony adjacent to Palermo's giant cathedral, and acknowledged the traditional acclaim "Christus vincit, Christus regnat, Christus imperat"—"Christ is victorious, Christ reigns, Christ rules over all"—a motto that, besides being visible on practically every southern Italian crucifix, was engraved on the seals of Frederick's early reign. Swathed in flowing linens and silks, Frederick was displayed—offered really—to his future subjects. An unattractive, in fact a rather ugly, veranda-like appendage to a sprawling cathedral served as stage for his entrance in a play beyond the merely ordinary, the story of a life, of events and legends strung link by link on a biographical chain as diverting and fascinating, sometimes beguiling, as any in history. By November 27 his mother was dead, and Frederick, in accord with her wishes, was the ward of the new pope. Constance's death may have been the most tragic loss of his life.

If nothing else, Pope Innocent III had good connections. His father, Trasimund, count of Segni (a town off the main road between Rome and Frosinone), was a proud man who traced his ancestry to the Lombard conquerors of old. He had married Clarissa of the noble Scotti family of Rome. Thus on both sides Innocent had position; but the connection to

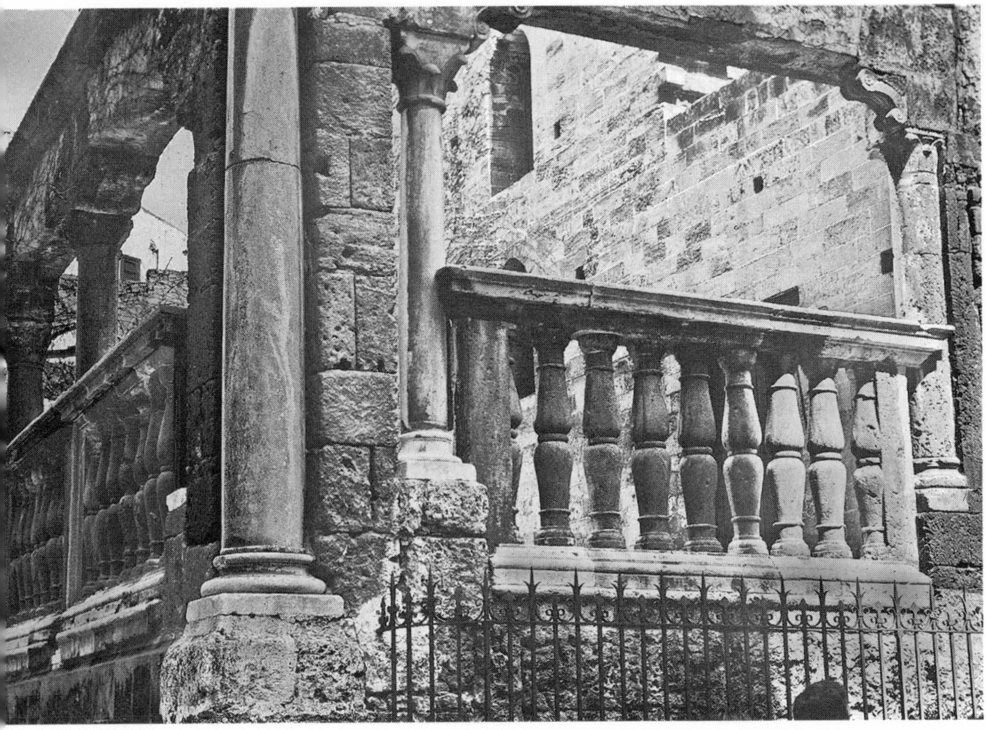

Cappella dell'Incoronata, Palermo, Sicily

Roman aristocracy stood him in better stead in his rise to the papacy. He was baptized Lothario, which should have said something right then as the name had an imperial ring. Innocent III is considered by many to be the greatest of all popes, the more strange that we know practically nothing of his childhood, other than that he had three brothers and that he studied in Rome, Paris, and Bologna, and that he traveled to England. Early on he was showing signs of becoming the pope of the century, a process enhanced when he was appointed cardinal by his nepotistic uncle, Pope Clement III.

Unfortunately Clement was succeeded by the late Celestine III. Lothario was only thirty-one years old and saw the election of that octogenarian as a step backward, a respite in the vital, assertive rule that the Church so obviously needed. Lothario's progressive intellect, his dominating will, his youth and energy were not looked upon with favor by the aged pontiff. Unable to do anything but bide his time, Lothario saw his career move into a seven-year eclipse. Celestine's pontificate may have been the respite needed to change the tenor of Church politics, for by the time he died in 1198, the College of Cardinals was decidedly in the mood to initiate basic changes toward reform. On the day that Celestine passed away, Lothario di Segni was chosen as Pope Innocent III by the cardinals, a conclave famous for the speed of its selections and for singling out the youngest member of the sacred college, a fact not lost on certain members of the lay community. Walther von der Vogelweide for one wailed to the Lord from beyond the Alps that the pope was too young and called on him to help his Christianity. But the doomsayers were misreading the man in question. Innocent was an extremely intelligent man, and his slight build and delicate features did not accurately reflect the vital energy stored within. Like Henry VI's role in the secular world, papal power was never so personified as it was in Innocent. His would be a period of the greatest papal power, a period when a pope-god ruled and manipulated not only the Church but most of the crowns of Europe. He had his work cut out for him, and from the start he took it seriously.

Innocent III followed a Spartan regimen, which he never hesitated to use as an example to his underlings, though he was not above moments of showy imperial ostentation. Pleasure and leisure were words not in his vocabulary. A small man, he had a youthful, good-looking face marked by penetrating eyes overscored by high, arching eyebrows. His mouth was small, but the voice that issued therefrom was rich and sonorous, more than able to give meaning to the shrewdly chosen words of Matthew 24:45 in his consecration ceremony: "Who then is a faithful and wise servant, whom his lord hath made ruler over his household. . . . ?" His speech set the tone for eighteen years of reign during which he steadfastly insisted that he, Innocent III, a man only too humanly weak, was chosen by God so that God's own power might be seen more clearly. Innocent saw himself as more than merely human, set in the middle between God and man, lower than God, but higher than Man. He admitted to the necessity of secular rulers in the scheme of things, even that their roles might be divinely ordained. But all rule culminated in his office—a secular as well as ecclesiastical lordship. Even from his former teachers, whom he respected with reverence, he would tolerate no opposition. Peter of Corbeil, raised by Innocent to the archbishopric of Sens, was himself the recipient of a thunderous letter when he acted against papal interest, The missive so took him aback that Innocent later apologized. To Innocent the theory of the supremacy of the Church over the State was a reality, a fact to be hammered home relentlessly. God was honored through the pope, he said, and when the pope was despised, God was despised. Perhaps his greatness lay in his single-mindedness. In any event the Church's time was nigh.

Innocent entertained awesome ambitions, not unreasonable ones in his eyes. Had not Henry VI envisioned himself leading a sweeping conquest of the Holy Land, and even of the last vestige of the Eastern Roman Empire, with its fabled city of Constantinople? Had he not died prior to finishing his building of a great armada to conquer the East, he might well have ended up as master of all Christendom. If Henry, why not Innocent?

Innocent could be just as attentive to the minutiae of governance. The growing menace of heresy did not rest lightly on his mind; nor did the plight of society's dishonored when he guaranteed that those who rescued a woman from a brothel would be forgiven their sins. For all his worldliness, Innocent maintained a high ideal for his clergy, and he vowed to correct breaches of pastoral impropriety. By the same token, as a result of his lofty view of the priest's role, the priest himself became greatly enhanced in dealings with the lay public. It was during Innocent's tenure that the priest began to perform the sacrifice of the Mass with his back to his congregation, facing the altar and the East. It was Innocent's Fourth Lateran Council (1215) that would raise the mystic miracle of Transubstantiation into dogma. He encouraged the clergy to lead celibate lives, to divorce themselves from society's sympathies, and to look to Rome as their source.

Innocent's most pressing problem concerned the inheritor of the German throne, with the precedent that such a king would reasonably claim the imperial throne as well. Surely it was out of the question that three-year-old Frederick Hohenstaufen even be considered a valid candidate, his reelection notwithstanding. Well, Innocent would get no argument from Constance on that score. But he and Constance were not the only ones who saw prospects of the succession of an infant to the German throne as distressing; the German electors did, too. Despite their having voted for Frederick under the whip of Henry VI, they seemed perfectly capable of reneging and taking sides with Henry's brother, Philip, or with the hulking Guelf teenager, Otto of Brunswick, both of whom desperately wanted the crown, indeed were already squabbling over it. Marches and counter-marches, a few battles, bribes of money and land, threats and letters to and from princes, kings, and pope, shifting loyalties, the best and worst of political honesty and hypocrisy, all became the order of the day as the two sides, Ghibelline and Guelf, squared off for a devastating civil war. The electors, in

March 1198, elected Philip of Swabia to the German throne. Thus was automatically revived the bogey of every medieval pope—the Papal States surrounded by Hohenstaufen might—especially since Philip let it be known even before his election that he planned to act as regent in his southern nephew's name. Then, after taking the crown at Magdeburg, he declared that he wore it only as a means of securing it for his house—a subtle difference. It would seem that Frederick's chances at the throne were lessening. Be that as it may, Philip wore the crown well.

Uncommonly handsome and genuinely pious, Philip was gracious of manner and generous of spirit. Perhaps too gentle and too mild for his day, he would never know peace in his reign. He had been trusted by his brother and appears to have been designated as Frederick's guardian, though Constance would have none of that. Henry VI had arranged for his brother's marriage to Irene, widowed daughter-in-law of King Tancred and daughter of Byzantine emperor Isaac Angelus. Having been shipped off to Germany with Tancred's widow, Queen Sibylla, her unhappy and frightened daughters, and her mutilated son, Irene must have been as astonished as anybody to find herself riding with husband Philip through the streets of Magdeburg during the 1198 Christmas festival, establishing herself as co-sovereign in Saxony, Otto of Brunswick's ancestral turf.

Opposition to Philip's election and coronation came almost at once, from his peers, from the pope, and from Otto of Brunswick, second son of Henry the Lion and Matilda, daughter of Henry II of England, hence nephew to Richard Lionheart. Otto had spent a good part of his youth at Richard's Angevin court, the result of his father's pointed lack of cooperation with Frederick Barbarossa. Seeing Otto as a worthy confederate in his everlasting quest to satisfy his continental ambitions, Richard made no bones about his affection for his nephew, even making him count of La Marche, and then count of Poitou. About five years younger than his opponent Philip, Otto was enormously tall and powerful of physique, with limbs and fists that allowed him to bear himself with aggressive arrogance. Guelf opposition to Philip, abetted by Archbishop Adolf of Cologne, secured the backing of the papal curia and caused the election of Otto as second king, whereupon Philip was excommunicated. It was clear that the pope's mind was made up. The bull issued as explanation of his reasons for disfavoring Philip as future emperor was, at best, a series of lame excuses: he was the son of a man who had stood against the Church; he had sworn fealty to Frederick and was therefore now perjured; the emperorship was not a hereditary office.

At the same time there were several reasons for the papal favor lavished on Otto. It was impossible for a pope—any pope—to approve of a Hohenstaufen—any Hohenstaufen—who could be counted on to try to unite the Sicilian and German realms. Otto was comparatively poor, especially after Richard I of England died in 1199, leaving the throne to his penurious brother, John Lackland. He was lacking in education and imagination. He would be putty in the hands of the strong pope that Innocent saw himself to be. Still, with that fighter's physique that Richard had so admired, Otto would be a worthy defender of Church interests. On top of everything else, he was stingy to the point of parsimony, a frugality scorned by poet and noble alike. Walther von der Vogelweide sputtered that, had Otto the generosity to match his physique, he would be a most virtuous man. Innocent's most spurious reasoning came when he pointed out that Otto may have received fewer votes than Philip, but when counting votes the influence of each elector was as important as his ballot.

Germany embarked on a ten-year period of dreadful civil war, not at all displeasing to the pope, who knew well that a weak empire meant a strong Church. Far from filling the role of peacemaker, the Church fanned the flames until the war went beyond a fight between two factions. Hired ruffians roamed the land, and partisans with endless quarrels fought their neighbors for the sake of mere plunder. The years were a prolonged horror show of the greed of men and the base self-interest of the Church.

One can justly wonder at the principles of a pope who had been appointed Frederick's guardian by the dying Constance but who seemed to do everything in his power to thwart the child's chances of ever taking over his elected place at the head of the German people. Innocent was a good judge of men and their abilities. He saw Frederick as a potential friend of the Church, but also as a potential stumbling block in his own bid for world power. His paranoia about being encircled by a German king-emperor and a king of Sicily in the same person was too powerful to let anything as trivial as loyalties stand in his way. Yet he foresaw danger in the policy he was pursuing himself, knowing that once Frederick reached maturity and realized that he had been robbed of his patrimony by the Roman Church, he would surely refuse her reverence and oppose her by every means he could. But Innocent could rationalize his way even out of that, holding that the Church had nothing to fear, for in reality it was Philip of Swabia who had robbed the child of his crown. It was not Innocent's most glorious moment of truth, any more than was a letter that he wrote to the ecclesiastical and lay princes of Germany. When the inevitable war between the rival claimants erupted, he wrote piously of the slaughter of men and the imperiling of their souls. He professed to be grieved and troubled. He then ordered them to look on the face of God and fear it. Pity the German people who, having just endured two years of flood and famine, were now faced with the prospect of a debilitating civil war. It was too much for minnesinger Walther von der Vogelweide, who sympathetically warned the German people. "Your honor is being destroyed," he cried. "Beware! These petty princes are a threat!"

On the surface of it Constance could not have made a better choice of guardian for her son, despite Innocent's trenchant warning that a country ruled by a child was destined to fail. By every measure of the day, Sicily was the garden spot of Europe, a bit of Eden flung down by the Almighty into the Mediterranean, just off the toe of the land to which it had once been attached. For centuries out of memory, the Germanic peoples had been on the move southward in quest of this warm promised land. Constance knew that her contemporaries were no different, that her son would have to draw on all the acquired wisdom and education that a conscientious guardian could impart to hold off the northern hordes. Frederick needed a guardian who had youth, industry, knowledge, and a keen awareness of political maneuvering. Innocent fulfilled those requirements. He had inherited social status. And with his righteous insistence on the superiority of the Church over all temporal institutions and the subjugation of empires, kingdoms, princedoms, and other political organizations, large or small, to that God-directed authority, he had clout. The one thing he lacked was a personal interest in Frederick. As far as he was concerned, the reign of Henry VI had come close enough to bringing about the dreaded union of the northern empire and the Sicilian kingdom to make papal hair stand on end. Now, with the Germans still eyeing Sicily, the Church, with Innocent as guide, was being given a second chance. It was therefore not surprising that the pope encouraged an outsider to meddle in the ever-volatile southern politics. Innocent supported Walter of Brienne, head of a noble house of Champagne, who had married Alberia, the late King Tancred's eldest daughter, and who was now trying to exercise a strangely convoluted claim in her name to the county of Lecce and the principality of Taranto. It seems that Henry VI, on taking Sicily, had granted these fiefs to Sibylla, mother of Alberia. He later rescinded the grant when he alleged Sibylla's involvement in that plot against his life and shipped her and her family off to Germany. Once free, Sibylla had gone to France where, being of noble blood, she had no difficulty marrying her daughter Alberia off to Walter. Innocent attempted to justify his support of Walter of Brienne by claiming that Walter had sworn to consider the child-king inviolate and to make absolutely no claims on Sicily. He explained to the young Frederick (that is, to his council) that he would prefer having Walter of Brienne as a friend rather than an enemy, all of which rings rather hollow, considering that the pope later encouraged Walter to take the island, a thing that Walter refused to do out of fear of jeopardizing his claims on Lecce and Taranto. Besides that, Walter foresaw a dim chance of gaining the crown in the event of Frederick's death, which, considering the situation, was extremely likely. In another effort to wrench Italy from German control, Innocent tried to arrange a marriage between Sancha, sister of King Pedro II of Aragon, and the baby Frederick, with Pedro furnishing substantial military assistance against the Germans—all of which fell through, though a similar plan was later realized.

None of this boded well for Frederick; it would seem that he was being swept further and further away from his thrones. To destabilize things even more, Innocent's championing of Walter of Brienne and his French friends immediately ruptured what little there was to bind Chancellor Walter of Palear to the pope. From Innocent's point of view the chancellor-bishop should have been the most trustworthy papal representative in the power struggle; had he, Innocent, not insisted to Constance that Walter of Palear occupy a prominent place in the Sicilian court even after she had banished him? More than anything Walter wanted to be archbishop of Palermo, to enjoy the vast resources and endless perquisites of that most-sought-after post. While not genuinely happily disposed toward Philip of Swabia, neither was he all that firmly in the papal camp. With Constance dead, his own interests were best served by feigning loyalty to Frederick, all the while enjoying his position of power as de facto regent by giving away whole sections of the royal domain as fiefs to various friends and relatives. Regent Palear wrote the end of his ecclesiastical dream, sinning in Innocent's eyes by sundering their relationship after papal recognition of the specious claims of Walter of Brienne. Henceforth Walter of Palear signed himself simply as chancellor of the kingdom of Sicily, omitting any reference to his sacerdotal standing.

Add to this witches' brew Markward of Anweiler—a brutal, unprincipled, ambitious man—whom Innocent despised with a passion reserved for him alone, seeing him as a supporter of Philip of Swabia and an unfaltering standard-bearer of Hohenstaufen power. In the anti-German hysteria following the death of Henry VI, Markward had been banished from southern Italy by Constance and deprived of his Henry-given duchy of Ravenna and the Marche of Ancona. On top of this, he was excommunicated by Innocent in a document that clearly spelled out the papal antipathy and that was to be reread on Sundays and on all feast days, the better to make it stick. "We excommunicate, anathematize, curse and damn him," he wrote, and then, calling on the Holy Trinity and the authority of Peter and Paul, he ordered that anyone who gave aid of any kind to Markward was damned.

Markward felt not the slightest tug of loyalty to Frederick—"the suppositious son" of Constance, he called him. As far as he was concerned the boy stood in the way of linking Sicily to the German imperium under Philip of Swabia, a union to which all of his energies were devoted. In addition, he was fighting for "rights" of his own against Walter of Palear's pretensions, claiming that Henry VI had willed the regency of the southern kingdom to him, which may have had a grain of truth in it. Did Markward want the kingdom for himself? Probably. But that guess could be contradicted by the fact that he maintained cordial relations with Philip of Swabia.

It is easy to see that each leading character on the stage of southern Italy—Innocent III, Walter of Palear, Walter of Brienne, Markward—was fighting for his own interests only. Add to this list an uncountable gang of hangers-on whose allegiances to one party or another were hardly durable and whose shifting loyalties depended solely on the direction and power of the political winds. Beyond these principals there were the Saracens on the island, denizens of earlier centuries and holdovers from the more enlightened rule, expecting little from a papal ward and taking advantage of the general anarchy to maraud the countryside. The Norman barons, notorious for restiveness, stirred the political stew, turning on one another when it was advantageous to do so—and it almost always was. A few northern Italian cities had trade interests in Sicily, mainly the maritime cities of Pisa and Genoa with their opposing political persuasions, the former usually loyal to the Germans and natural enemies of the latter. Nobles and churchmen, Frenchmen, Germans, and Italians were only too willing to contend with one another, to ravage the once-glorious kingdom of the brilliant Roger II, he who could, almost at will, assemble mighty fleets and dispatch them to Africa or to the very gates of Constantinople, who could summon an army to cow a pope or send an emperor scuttling back across the Alps. In truth, the Norman glory had tarnished, the vigorous mettle had been emasculated by easy living, lack of imagination, by self-serving stupidity and indolence. The old days of muscular determination were gone, a fact that caused the common folk to look back with nostalgia. Poor little Frederick!—lost in the shuffle and ignored, though each of the contending parties thought it imperative to be in possession of his royal person. And his "education" did not lack for frightening stories of his enemies, who, in his eyes at least, included just about everyone on the political stage.

We can sense the unease of six-year-old Frederick when he heard that his personal bogey, Markward of Anweiler, had returned from exile by way of Trapani on the extreme western tip of the island through the help of one Admiral Grasso (Admiral Fat, or maybe even Admiral Lewd), a Genoese seaman formerly in the employ of Henry VI. When word of Markward's return reached the pope, he responded by offering the same privileges and indulgences to any who would raise the sword against him as were offered to crusaders in Outremer. Markward was defeated in his first attempt to take Palermo (July 1200) by a rout at Monreale in the hills above the capital city, the town that grew up around King William II's last great testament of Norman magnificence, Monreale Cathedral. It was perhaps the first battle witnessed by Frederick, from a safe distance, of course. The rout was accomplished, at least in part, by papal troops, who deserted the cause immediately after their victory because of lack of pay, the intensity of the heat, and sickness. The papal cause was not served when always self-concerned Walter of Palear negotiated an alliance with Markward and signed away his own interests in the island except for the city of Palermo and the person of the young king, who was turned over to the custody of Walter's brother, Gentile. For his part, Walter of Palear was allowed free run on the Italian mainland, to which he repaired immediately.

The papal outlook brightened somewhat when the other Walter—Walter of Brienne—returned to Italy from France, where he had gone on a successful quest for monetary and military aid from King Philip Augustus. With the addition of papal troops, he scored a decisive triumph over Markward's still-belligerent adherents, who were partly under the generalship of Walter of Palear. So ended the alliance of Walter of Palear and Markward of Anweiler, and once again papal interests were being served on the mainland with Walter of Brienne firmly in the administrative saddle.

With the rupture of their tenuous relationship, Markward no longer felt it essential to honor his agreement with Walter of Palear that he would keep his hands off Palermo. It was incumbent upon him to gain possession of young King Frederick. He laid siege to Palermo at about the time that, according to some contemporary reports, a circular letter was sent to the courts of Christendom written on Frederick's behalf, pretentiously comparing him to Jesus with the statement that tormentors "draw lots for his garments," the type of comparison that would become more frequent and pointed in years to come. Seeing himself as the innocent boy-king he was, he begged the princes to relieve his plight. Writing of his parentless boyhood, and complaining of being hungry much of the time, he portrayed himself as a lamb among wolves, longing to regain his crown, and threatened the princes lest they, somehow, suffer the same fate.

No help was forthcoming.

Frederick had been trained to despise the name of Markward of Anweiler, to fear him above all enemies. Then, at ten in the morning on November 1, 1201, he was betrayed by a turncoat castellan, a certain "B of Accarino," who opened the Castellamare gates to Markward. It is easy to imagine the horror that six-year-old Frederick must have felt when, cornered in an inner room to which he had been whisked by his teacher, William Franciscus, he saw his archenemy burst through the door. Now here was his surly antagonist towering over him, backed by rough, guttural-speaking henchmen, the very people his mother had hated so much. There was no escape. Neither was there defense. Historic hearsay tells us that Frederick rose to heights expected of royalty. Already conscious of the sacredness of his position, he defied his enemies to lay hands on him, warding them off when they tried. Then, seeing his defense as hopeless, he proceeded to tear his clothes and flesh with his nails in his contempt for the defilers of his position. Through this story of the child, we get a glimpse of the man, the aggressiveness, the determination of one destined to hold the fate of Christendom in the palm of his hand. It was after his capture, apparently, that Frederick was allowed free rein in the city of Palermo, mainly because his captors were simply too busy with their own contentions to bother with him. It would seem now that Markward and his Germans had the kingdom for keeps.

Chroniclers tell sad and hair-raising tales of Frederick wandering the streets of Palermo unattended, literally *un ragazzo della strada*—a boy of the street. The accounts are persistent enough to compel belief, more so when one realizes that he was shunted from group to group, a valuable commodity for exploitation as it were, but revered by none. His loyal tutor, William Franciscus, did a remarkable job of educating Frederick under the circumstances, but rampant confusion, not to mention extended periods of actual want, is not conducive to easy learning. Ostensibly, Frederick lived in the fortress of Castellamare, but there were occasions when he was housed and fed by the Palermitan population, basically loyal to him since they saw him as a southerner and the grandson of Roger II, the rightful heir to the throne, and the living symbol of a more enlightened age. Try as *magister* William Franciscus might, Frederick would get the better education—a kind of street wisdom—from the alleys and marketplaces of Palermo.

Of all the cities of Europe, Palermo (from the Latin *Panormus*) could justly lay claim to being the most progressive, in many ways the most enlightened, and certainly the richest culturally and monetarily. It has changed in form radically since ancient days, and the shape of the modern city does little to suggest the original. When "Great Count" Roger I and Robert Guiscard conquered Palermo in 1091, the groundwork was laid for the magnificent flowering of East-West culture that the capital was to know under their successors. The Sicilian court became a vital center of Muslim-Christian culture and learning, where many of the great translations of Arabic and Greek scientific works were made and then disseminated throughout Europe. Muslims translated the Greek classics, while their colleague, the learned Idrissi, compiled his famous geography as a climax to fifteen years of investigative study. Court life was more Eastern than Western, more luxurious by far than anything found anywhere else in Europe, with the possible exception of the Arab holdings in Spain. Roger II, his son, and his grandson lived after the manner of Oriental potentates, enjoying their palaces and eunuch-guarded harems.

A crossroad of Eastern and Western cultures—Arab, Byzantine Greek, Norman, and native—Palermo thrived under the Normans. Add to this a sprinkling of Jews, mainland Italians, Spaniards, Germans, English, and French. Both the Latin and Greek Christian religions were allowed to flourish, as was Islam. Roger II himself would not permit Christian proselytizing of his Saracen troops, preferring them to remain loyal to their traditional beliefs. Arab workmen combined forces with Greek mosaicists to create Latin churches. Palermitan palaces were of a size and luxury to be equaled only by those of the Cordoban caliphs of Spain. Indeed, the gardens of Islam in al-Andalus (the Islamic Spanish territory) were models for the serene gardens, lake palaces described as pleasure domes on the hills around Palermo like the pearls of a necklace. The fertile plain in which Palermo lies—the Conca d'Oro (the Golden Conch Shell)—was rich with palm and orange groves, with myrtle and bay trees, with royal hunting parks and four luxurious palaces intended only for the pleasure of the semi-Orientalized Norman kings.

Despite the alleged undisciplined freedom of Frederick's early life, his freewheeling vagabondage in the streets of Palermo, surely he was not unfamiliar with more opulent pleasures, the aromatic scents, the perfume of citrus, the lightly blushing glories of the almond blossoms as they first reflected and then snowed into the lakes surrounding the pleasure palaces. Throughout his fifty-six years he cherished the beauties of Sicily, so much that he drew down the ire of more pious souls with a statement to the effect that God erred when he gave Palestine to his chosen people, a thing that "he never would have done had he ever seen my kingdom of Sicily."

Until the anarchy of Frederick's regency (if it can truly be called a regency), literature flourished along with the art of silk making and weaving. The sprawling Norman palace was there, built as an extension of a Saracen fortress, and today still housing the glorious jewel of Sicilian-Norman architecture, the mosaic-encrusted, glistening Cappella Palatina. The Arab-styled Norman churches of Martorana and San Cataldo stood in Frederick's day, as they do now, end to end in regal splendor on their plinth overlooking the piazza named for the composer Vincenzo Bellini. There were crowded synagogues and minaret-studded mosques.

The marketplace must have held special fascination for the seven- and eight-year-old Frederick, colorful, heavy with foreign odors, alive with divers tongues and exotic-looking products from throughout the Mediterranean: produce from the north coast of Africa, silk hangings from Greece, jewels and mosaics from Constantinople; there would be dark-skinned slaves from Egypt, books and manuscripts from the Holy Land, as well as leather bridles and weapons from Arab artisans. Streetwise as he was, Frederick could steal his share of the strange-tasting foods from the stands of strangely garbed vendors. He learned the speech of all these peoples and eventually mastered at least six languages, perhaps seven. But, though he may have had smatterings of education in the scriptures, a bit of mathematics here, some rhetoric there, he had nothing that could be even vaguely construed as a formal education to befit a king—not to mention an emperor.

With the alleys and marketplaces as his kingdom, with the noisy crowds as his subjects, Frederick still had his refuges: the Zisa, the Menani, the Cuba, and the Favara (the four park- and lake-surrounded pleasure palaces), the churches, and the quiet solitude of cloisters such as Saint John of the Hermits. At times he must have been overwhelmed by loneliness. Perhaps out of this sense of abandonment emerged his love for open space, for birds and animals—for nature—concerns which were, except in Francis Bernardone's world, out of kilter in a time of dangerous political intrigue and competitive infighting. Indeed, these considerations would not become vogue for another few centuries, during the later Renaissance. As an adult Frederick chose lonely, stark places for his lodges—"places of solace," he called them—to which he would repair with regularity when he had had his fill of imperial cares. They may have been lifesaving respites; and he may have developed a taste for them when, as a child, he wandered the rackety streets of his teeming capital city.

Chapter Three

Death will be stunned and (so) will Nature,
when arises (man) the creature
responding to the One judging.
***Dies Irae,* verse 4**

1202

On the verge of taking Messina, the one remaining city of Sicily that had not yet surrendered to him, Markward of Anweiler died in the autumn of 1202. He was at Patti, about thirty miles west of Messina, overlooking the azure blue water of the north coast of Sicily. Pope Innocent III was transported with joy, a little prematurely it turned out, since Markward's place was immediately filled by one William Capparone, about whom we know practically nothing other than that he was a German despite his name and that he had ridden in the train of Henry VI. On news of Markward's demise, Capparone sprang into presumptuous action. He seized both Frederick and the royal palace and took for himself the titles "Defender of the King" and "Grand Captain of Sicily" without so much as consulting either the pope or Philip of Swabia, who in fact appointed a confidant of his own to look after Frederick. That William Capparone managed to pull off his coup d'état gives some indication of how far government had deteriorated since the death of Henry VI. Complicating the power struggles, Walter of Palear, disenchanted by both his alliance with and betrayal by Markward, had returned to Sicily in his old position of chancellor. Even this did not intimidate Capparone who, with stunning brass, refused to give up his self-appointed custody of Frederick until 1206, at which time the twelve-year-old king was, according to Sicilian feudal law, approaching an age to succeed to his patrimony.

1204

As though these and assorted other interior despoilers were not enough to fragment the kingdom, outside forces were at work doing their destructive bits with impunity. A case in point: the turmoil during Frederick's formative years had allowed warlike Pisan merchants and sailors to occupy the city of Syracuse, driving out the bishop and much of the population, turning that ancient city into a center of piratical brigandage under the protection of Pisa. Now, in 1204, a Genoese fleet attacked Syracuse and, having put the Pisans to flight, set up a base on the lucrative trade route to the eastern Mediterranean. Again circumstance seemed to predict an impossible job for a boy within four years of his majority.

Along with street wisdom and emotional stability, Frederick's years of vagabondage also developed in him physical and mental propensities that would hold him in good stead for life. While he was not especially tall—nor would he ever be—he was firm of bone and sinewy, with a narrow waist. Archery and horsemanship had built broad shoulders and strong arms. Already he was showing signs of the expert huntsman he would become. And the steady directness of his gaze—he had blue-green eyes—was a clue to the stubborn, demanding, and inquisitive man of the future. Fencing was one of his favorite pastimes, one made more effective by hisexpressive, delicate hands. With Barbarossa's reddish hair, highlighted by a touch of gold, his quick and violent temper struck fear into the hearts of older companions. It was not unusual for him to go from activity to activity during the day, exercising at a ferocious clip and displaying his skill in the handling of all kinds of weapons, and then studying history far into the night. Settling into a regimen under tutor William Franciscus, and with a natural feel for languages, he read everything he could get his hands on. He was maturing so precociously that Innocent himself, normally not given to admiration, marveled that manhood was setting in before its time. To polish it all off, despite his demanding nature and temper he was disarmingly charming. When he took over his realm a few years later, admirers would see Frederick as the perfect man.

Intellectual pursuits aside, Frederick was not yet of the age to be automatically concerned with catastrophic events in the East, where events unparalleled in horror were unfolding. A new crusade, which had left Europe with the blessings of Innocent III, had, for a host of political reasons, been deflected to Constantinople. On the basis of one trumped-up excuse after another, the western Christians turned on their Byzantine brothers, raping, murdering, and sacking the city in one of the most tragic and barbarous lootings in history. It was a crime against mankind, a callous, preconceived, thoroughly planned display of wanton destruction, an everlasting stain on the motives of Western nobility and soldiery, who were supposedly on their way to worship at the shrines most sacred to Christendom. The richest city of the East for over nine centuries, filled with art treasures and examples of the most exquisite craftsmanship, some of it dating back to remotely ancient days, was almost totally despoiled of its wealth. If not destroyed outright the loot was hauled back to Europe, especially to Venice, the city that had, more than any other, instigated the calamity and the city that, more than any other, knew its value. It was precisely one of these shipments that brought to Venice the four bronze horses now prancing above the Piazza San Marco and seeming so much a part of the edifice they adorn. Byzantium's great Hagia Sophia, almost seven centuries old and one of the most stunning constructions known to man, was defiled and denuded of its priceless silk hangings, its silver iconostasis shredded, its precious books and icons scattered, and its sacred vessels desecrated by merrily imbibing drunken soldiers, who simultaneously enjoyed ribald songs sung by a prostitute from the patriarchal throne. Palaces, homes of the rich and poor, and churches crashed to rubble, while the dead and dying littered the streets. After three days of shameless pillaging and bloodshed, the once-proud city, so majestically situated on its Golden Horn, was reduced to a smoldering shambles. With unimaginable cynicism, the good Christian crusaders divvied up their plunder according to a prearranged agreement: three-eighths to the crusaders themselves; three-eighths to the Venetians; and the rest to the future Eastern emperor who was quickly selected and ceremoniously crowned in Hagia Sophia on May 16. He was Baldwin IX, count of Flanders and Hainault, who, it is pleasing to report, would never be comfortable on his stolen throne.

1205

One more contender for Frederick's realm was eliminated in 1205 when suicidally confident Walter of Brienne, overcome by bravado (he used to brag absurdly that armed Germans would not dare to attack even unarmed Frenchmen) became careless enough in battle to allow himself to be trapped and slain by Germans under a certain Diepold of Schweinspeunt, count of Acerra and a former trustee of

Henry VI. Walter left a son whom for many years Frederick regarded with unjust suspicion and jealousy, suspecting him as a possible pretender to his throne since the youngster was, after all, a grandson of the late King Tancred. Walter of Brienne might be missed by the pope, but certainly not by Frederick, nor by Walter of Palear, who was now free to tenuously reconcile himself to Innocent III, provided that his own personal gains were not compromised, of course. And Diepold of Schweinspeunt could go on his chosen path, following Markward's example of picking away at Frederick's holdings, firm in the belief that they were destined to be united to the fatherland. Sometimes a friend, sometimes a nuisance to Frederick, he could, on occasion, prove useful. For the moment, the best news for Frederick, more and more thinking it demeaning to be subjected to a regency and to be a ward of the pope, was that within the space of three years two contenders—Markward and Walter of Brienne—had been eliminated.

On the other hand, the situation in Germany was not one to instill confidence. Treachery was a way of life, violence widespread, and justice—well, simply nonexistent. While the civil war raged, King Otto IV of Brunswick had to own up that his support among the princes was dwindling. The most powerful of his adherents to desert so far was Archbishop Adolf of Cologne, a man who had lobbied extensively for his elevation. Duke Henry of Brabant followed suit, and even Otto's own brother Henry, count palatine of the Rhine, in a fit of pique because he had not been granted the rewards he thought he deserved, flopped over to the side of rival King Philip of Swabia.

Philip's policies were more than a little questionable. To gain the upper hand he mortgaged away some valuable Hohenstaufen lands and dispensed certain taxation and toll privileges as rewards for his supporters. His bribery paid off. Generosity put him in a better position than ever to firm up his claims to kingship, a fact not lost on the German princes. He had himself recrowned, but this time in Charlemagne's cathedral at Aachen by Archbishop Adolf on the Feast of Epiphany 1205. It may have been only a symbolic coronation but, as a direct repudiation of papal efforts to dominate the selection of German kings, it was important. Encouraged and echoed by the papacy, Otto's followers had always claimed that Philip's first coronation at Magdeburg lacked validity since it had not been performed in Aachen after the example of Charlemagne. Furthermore, tradition dictated that the crown be placed on the royal head by the archbishop of Cologne. Now both conditions had been realized.

Philip knew his politics. He saw the time was ripe to patch up his quarrels with the pope and to have the ban of excommunication lifted. Both men recognized that their disagreements had long passed the point of benefit for either of them. Philip had to persuade Innocent to sanction his claims to kingship and with any luck to eventual emperorship. He conceived the idea of suggesting that Frederick be married to Maria, daughter of his adherent, Henry of Brabant, knowing full well that the pontiff would see this only in the light of identifying Frederick with Germany. Again the specter of a Siculo-German empire rose in the papal vision. It was the perfect ploy to bring the pope around, for Philip knew that he still entertained the prospect of getting Frederick to the altar for a union with the House of Aragon, a shrewd concept since both Sicily and Aragon were nominally papal fiefs. In time Innocent and Philip would bargain their way out of their uncomfortable relationship with agreements beneficial to both. At least that was the optimistic way that Philip saw it. For now he could harass Otto, whose claims were being heard by a steadily evaporating group of princes.

Not to be left out of the adventures of his time, Francis Bernardone had, just the year before, set out for Apulia to join Walter of Brienne in his fight against the Germans. A man of action notorious for high living, Francis had already spent a year as a prisoner in Perugia after being captured during one of those absurd wars that were forever erupting between Italian cities, and even villages. While so many of these wars were hardly more than pageant-skirmishes, the antique hatred sputtering between Perugia and Assisi guaranteed savage battles and humiliating conditions visited on the ultimate victims. A crude rejoicing over the misery of the enemy by a Perugian of rather primitive letters tells the story of the fallen lords of Assisi, their limbs mangled and torn apart so they are unrecognizable.

As a result of the time on his hands during his imprisonment and the year of convalescence that followed, Francis was reaching a point of no return in his thinking. He was beginning a period of introspection and self-evaluation that would cause a personality change so great that it would lead him to sainthood. On the verge of experiencing the spiritual, emotional, and psychological transformation that would be the foundation of his life, Francis did not go far on his journey to Apulia, in fact no farther than Spoleto. Doubts assailed him; unsettling dreams brought about a change of heart, and he returned to Assisi where he did not endear himself to his father by selling off bolts of cloth from the family shop in order to raise money for his restoration of the crumbling Church of San Damiano.

1206

Signor Bernardone had had enough. Seeing his hard-earned money being squandered away to the sick, poor, and leprous of Assisi, he had no choice but to haul his willful son before Bishop Guido, a mistake as it turned out, but perhaps intentional. Francis remonstrated in a quasi-ritualistic ceremony of emancipation from paternal dominance performed by freedom-minded youths through the ages. But he went further. "Up until now I have called you father," he proclaimed before a growing crowd. "But from this day I can honestly say only 'Our Father who art in heaven.'" Doffing his clothes, he tossed them at the feet of his startled parent, spurring Bishop Guido into hastily draping him in his own embroidered cloak. It was the kind of renunciation to inspire generations of artists, most notably Giotto (born later this same century), who frescoed the scene in both the upper Church of Saint Francis at Assisi and in the Bardi Chapel of Santa Croce in Florence. Sassetta's fifteenth-century rendition of the story in the National Gallery of London is sweet and graceful and for that reason alone eludes the dramatic "moment of truth." The confrontation with his father behind him, free of material bonds, Francis marked his break with the bountiful life. He left Assisi to seek out quiet places of solace—as Frederick called his own retreats—where he could be alone, the better able to hear the secrets that God would reveal to him.

At the time that Francis and his father were reaching a parting of the ways, Diepold of Schweinspeunt, as disreputable and untrustworthy as any of the opportunistic, strutting nobles seeking to parlay their Hohenstaufen-given positions into total control of the kingdom, was working his way into the good graces of Innocent III. To prove himself, he convinced Frederick's self-appointed warden, William Capparone, to release both his captive and the royal palace at Palermo into the custody of the papal legate, a minor improvement over the last two years. In light of Frederick's restored status, Pope Innocent began bargaining with King Pedro II of Aragon for a wife for him, but this time dickering for another of the king's sisters—Constance, recently widowed by King Emeric of Hungary and ten years Frederick's senior. Even at the tender age of twelve Frederick could see the benefits that could accrue from the marriage: the proposed contract included a dower of five hundred Aragonese knights. It was King Pedro who voiced greatest misgivings about the proposed union on the grounds that Frederick was not properly royal, which causes one to wonder precisely what he had in mind: Frederick's paternal grandfather and father were both emperors and kings, his maternal grandfather and his uncle were kings, and his mother was both queen and empress. Pedro eventually came around, but only after being prodded by Innocent, who pointed out that Frederick was as much an offspring of emperors and kings as one had any right to expect, certainly higher ranking than Pedro himself, beyond his years in precociousness, and that his kingdom was very rich indeed. He advised Pedro to avoid no expense in sending his sister and troops to Sicily forthwith.

European men of consequence should have been looking east this year instead of grinding themselves down in their internecine squabbles and politically motivated marriages. On the banks of the River Onon, beyond the sweeping plains of the Asian steppes, the notables of Mongolia were gathering to hear one Temujin (Temuchin) declare himself ruler of an empire and to unanimously request that he take the title of Jenghis Khan—"Perfect Warrior." It was a momentous day, encouraging the Mongolian hordes to commence their march to the very gateway of western Europe, once and for all to bring about an end to European confident isolation. One can hardly blame the Europeans for being unaware of Jenghis Khan's existence. Mongolia was far away. But it would not always be thus: the Mongolians were about to start marching, and the earth would tremble beneath their feet and the hooves of their horses. All Europe would be transfixed and then despondent as the specter of death, pillage, and rape thundered to and then across its imaginary boundary. Though Frederick would never have to fight the waves of "Devil's horsemen," their presence on the eastern borders of his realm would later cause him no end of trouble with his German princes.

1208

By 1208 Frederick's year of coming of age, Philip of Swabia was riding high in Germany. Pope Innocent III had done several about-faces by withdrawing his support from Otto of Brunswick, recognizing Philip as king of Germany and lifting his ban of excommunication, adapting to himself the words of Proverbs 8:15, "By me kings reign, and princes decree justice." Philip had only to finish Otto off on the battlefield and make a pilgrimage to Rome. The empire would be his! The king-watchers of the day would see then whether or not Philip really intended to honor the claims of his nephew Frederick. Just when he was preparing to extinguish the last flicker of Otto's resistance, Philip was murdered at Bamberg in June by Otto of Wittelsbach, count palatine of Bavaria who, it seems, was more than a little disgruntled because he had been refused the hand of one of the royal daughters.

Established as Babenberg in the sixth century at a lovely spot where the Regnitz River flows astride an island about two miles above its junction with the Main River, Bamberg was elevated to a bishopric by Henry II, the last of the Saxon emperors, in 1007. In truth, the elevation may have been more a political than a religious move, as the city had been earmarked as a last-ditch defense against any invasion from the east. Bishops and abbots were appointed officers of the Crown and furnished Henry with copious supplies of knights. Henry further strengthened his favorite city by enlarging the castle, by establishing the cathedral (which burned down in 1185), and by building various monastic buildings on the surrounding hills. A peaceful man within the framework of his time despite the fact that he had a father with the evocative nickname of "the Quarrelsome," he was an enthusiastic believer in Church reform and was canonized by Pope Eugenius III in 1146. Henry II lies today in Bamberg Cathedral, in a tomb by the prolific north-German sculptor, Tilman Riemenschneider, which shows, lying in marvelous tranquility, both the emperor and his empress, Kunigunde. On guard over the imperial tomb, the life-size Bamberg Rider and his horse stand stonily against a column in regal dignity and chivalric pride, not at all mitigated by the absurdly inappropriate little French-style canopy over his head. Thought by some to be an idealized representation of Frederick II, and if not, surely an almost iconographic example of the political-imperial idea, he appears noble, youthful, imperturbable, eternal. He stares into space, not down at the tomb with its scenes from the life of the imperial couple, including the weighing of Henry's soul before Saint Lawrence and the dramatic ordeal by fire endured by Kunigunde on suspicion of adultery. (On the Untere Bruecke over the left branch of the Regnitz, there is a statue of Kunigunde, all gold-encrusted and simpering, not the kind of woman to walk on hot irons—or to commit adultery, for that matter.)

Besides the Cathedral there is the former episcopal and imperial palace in Bamberg, the Alte Hofhaltung (Old Residence), composed of half-timbered Gothic buildings with pitched roofs, beautifully ornate wooden balconies and rickety stairs, all surrounding a courtyard complete with fountain and spreading lime tree. For the sightseer of an eschatological turn of mind, there is the *Bamberg Apocalypse of Saint John*, a masterpiece of Ottonian illumination (c. 1020) from the scriptorium of the Benedictine Abbey at Reichenau and now in the Staatsbibliotek, on which the demons are represented as frogs. In addition there is the Old Town Hall, covered by trompe l'oeil frescoes and occupying the tiny island in the left branch of the Regnitz. The Altenburg, high over the city, is a well-preserved medieval castle.

With the murder of King Philip, Frederick was the last of the line of Hohenstaufen, for a few months yet the ward of an obstinate pope who long ago had set the same goals for him as had his mother—that he would not aspire beyond his island kingdom. But that was their conclusion, not Frederick's. As far as he was concerned, his northern inheritance was not to be frittered away in hands other than his own, despite the fact that his prospects sank to the nadir with the death of his Uncle Philip and the consequent sudden reticence of the elector princes to carry on the Hohenstaufen struggle. Apparently about as stable in their convictions as the pope, they reelected Otto of Brunswick king of Germany on November 11, 1208. The deed was done with full approbation of Innocent III, who wrote to Otto assuring him that he would spare nothing to see to it that no opposition could rise against him, though he admitted that factions of Germans already saw Frederick in the role of king-emperor. This papal mellowness was not proffered without the tit-for-tat gesture of Otto signing an agreement guaranteeing free episcopal elections in Germany, a development that emperors had fought for generations. Then there was the case of Sicily; Otto had to accept that Sicily was in fact a papal fief and as such was assuredly free of any threat of attack. Lands which had been greedily seized by the pope on the death of Henry VI were formally ceded to the Church, to act as an effective wedge between Sicily and the imperial northern holdings. At this point Innocent could realistically dream of an Italy united in the Church.

Otto IV was crowned king at Frankfurt by Conrad of Scharfenberg, bishop of Speyer and Metz. Who could doubt now that the emperorship was in his future? Making matters even worse, dead Philip's daughter, Beatrice, was betrothed to her father's enemy, a marriage encouraged by Innocent III and a host of German princes who were understandably fed up with the endless wars between the two houses. Once the marriage was performed, Otto would legally be able to claim the whole of Frederick's German patrimony. But Otto could afford to postpone the nuptials for a while.

Among those advising Otto, and who especially recommended his betrothal to Beatrice, was one of the interesting princes of the period, if also one of the more unreliable: Hermann, landgrave of Thuringia. He had already changed sides in this civil war in 1198, 1199, 1202, and 1204—and would once again in 1210. But Hermann had a more praiseworthy historical role to play. One did not change sides without profit. By his numerous vacillations he had amassed a sizeable fortune, which, to his credit, he used more creatively than most of his peers. On his invitation and reputation poets flocked to his magnificent Wartburg Castle in such numbers that, as Walther von der Vogelweide marveled, no sensitive person would be able to tolerate the din.

One of the best-preserved Romanesque castles on the continent, the Wartburg casts a dense shadow over Eisenach, a city formed in the twelfth century by the union of three separate communities. It was built, as most castles were built, high on a precipitous hill and under the auspices of another landgrave, Louis "the Springer" who died in 1123. But it was Hermann who turned the castle into a haven for artists, minstrels, writers, and thinkers. Martin Luther lived there for ten months in 1521–22, writing his translation of the New Testament—and throwing an inkwell at the devil, so they say. Johann Sebastian Bach was born in Eisenach. The crowds that frequented Hermann's ancestral home became legendary, partly thanks to such engaging recreations as a song contest held there, according to Richard Wagner's *Tannhäuser*, though some musicologists maintain that "it is practically certain . . . that in these contests music played no part; they were competitions not of musicians but of poets."[1] Walther von der Vogelweide (despite his report on the noise), Wolfram von Eschenbach, the greatest of medieval narrative poets, and Albert of Halberstadt were delighted to frequent Wartburg, seeing Hermann as the greatest art patron of his day. Besides that, the wine flowed abundantly.

Some of the finest poetry of the German Middle Ages came out of Hermann of Thuringia's Wartburg. Thanks to him this was a period of enormous, often politically critical, literary activity, as it had been since the days of Barbarossa when Heinrich der Glïchezäre wrote "Reineke Fuchs," a satire on the weaknesses and falsities of the Hohenstaufen empire. It was a period of not only the best works of the minnesingers (the German approximation of the troubadours) but of the best epics, which took their final form under the Hohenstaufens even though the works themselves often satirized the courtly world as one of lies and changing loyalties, which it was. The *Nibelungenlied* saw light of day at this time, as did Wolfram von Eschenbach's "Parzival" and "Willehalm" along with Gottfried von Strassburg's "Tristan und Isolde," an epic that shook the very foundations of long-established human institutions. "With apparent composure [Gottfried] explains that Tristan and Isolde have been anointed by their love. All other sacraments, the anointing of king and bishop, the consecration of the priest and the sacraments of marriage and communion, are superseded by this sacrament of love.

This new sacrament, the entire involvement of two lovers with each other at the deepest level of intimacy, struck a fatal blow at all hierarchies, secular, ecclesiastical and social."[2] More than this, Gottfried ventures into heretofore-forbidden fields by persuading readers to look sympathetically on the adulterous lovers. The notion of free speech and the toleration of conflicting ideals are not unique in our time. In truth, Germany was enjoying an awakening of the spirit of Imperial Rome, a southernization of the German spirit.

Let Hermann entertain his poets; let Otto of Brunswick and Pope Innocent III connive and haggle and change their minds over ways of doing Frederick out of his patrimony and at the same time practicing one-upmanship on the other. Pathetic little Queen Irene, two times a widow (of would-be king Roger III of Sicily and then of Philip of Swabia) found her own release. Her marriage to Philip may have been the one time in her life when she experienced anything remotely resembling affection, not to mention freedom from tension and sorrow. Her spirit broke under the treachery of her husband's murder. In seclusion at the castle at Staufen, perhaps in the agony of her untenable situation, she produced her fifth child, premature and stillborn. With that last futile attempt to perpetuate the family she died.

On his fourteenth birthday, December 26, Frederick reached his majority, and Innocent was obliged by Sicilian law to relinquish both his wardship and his regency. Trying to justify his years of serving Church interests at the expense of his ward, Innocent wrote a letter of congratulations in which he launched into an argument recounting the selfless work he had performed in Frederick's interest and out of loyalty to his mother, Constance. He assured Frederick of the endless sleepless nights he had endured, mulling over the youth's problems, not neglecting to mention the papal notaries who were so wearied writing letters on his behalf. He even insisted that he had postponed the business of the world in Frederick's interest and warned him to listen to his Church-directed counselors.

By this time Frederick had acquired an appropriately regal majesty, a dignified bearing without hauteur, and a graciousness of manner. His blue-green eyes were steady—like a serpent's, it was said. He had about him a serendipitous serenity, though how he managed that with his upbringing—or lack of it—is anyone's guess. The possessor of a ready wit, he was sometimes given to vulgarity and was intolerant of any kind of admonition, judging himself capable of correct decisions. He was, according to his contemporaries, wise beyond his years. It is not difficult to imagine what he thought of the pope's letter.

1209

With the zest and bravado of youth, Frederick lost no time in asserting himself to set his kingdom to rights. Though many of his early actions were in truth those of a fourteen-year-old, in others he showed a maturity that in anyone's eyes was impressive. He spurred himself to the task of leading an expedition to the northeast corner of the island, a military jaunt that served notice that he intended to regain those parts of his domain that had been whittled away by self- and family-ambitious officials during his minority. By August 1209 he had reestablished his domain in a triangular area marked by a line from Palermo to Catania, north to Messina, a generous third of the island. No small achievement for a fourteen-year-old!

Hardly had he won back the northeast zone of his island than Frederick was enticed back to Palermo by word that his bride, Princess Constance of Aragon, and her party had arrived. Though the marriage ceremony had already been performed by proxy at Saragossa Cathedral, a second of impoverished splendor was held almost immediately, a kind of tattered pageantry that tried to appeal to the barons who were in attendance. Side by side, Frederick and Constance put the best face on it, stepping out on the Cappella dell'Incoronata to receive the plaudits of the crowds who, dazzled by royalty and putting their trust in the energetic, good-looking young man whom they had observed wandering their streets for years, did not see the bleak prospects before the couple. They knew only that accompanying the attractive Constance were her brother, Count Alfonso of Provence, and the five hundred Aragonese knights who had been promised as part of the wedding contract and who were intended to help Frederick win back his patrimony and incidentally to help the pope settle himself more securely on the mainland. They were the trump card in the marriage contract game played in Frederick's name by Innocent III and Pedro II. Like most marriages between noble houses, romance had nothing to do with it. Power and politics were the only considerations. But the subject people could think only that perhaps now their time of trial was over.

Chroniclers do not enlighten us as to their reactions to one another, but twenty-four-year-old Constance was no doubt the most sophisticated woman yet encountered by Frederick. Raised in a land as rich in Arab culture as was Sicily, she had already been married to King Emeric of Hungary by whom she had produced a son who died tragically when she had fled with him to Austria to avoid persecution by her brother-in-law on her husband's death. Her blood brother, Alfonso of Provence, stood for chivalry, cultural acuteness, and understanding, for poetry and troubadours. Her other brother, King Pedro II, rather indolent and given to wallowing in Eastern-style luxury, was not out of step with Frederick's opulent heritage. Constance's knights, ladies, troubadours, and hangers-on must have opened Frederick's eyes to a world that was his to fight for. From this inauspicious, unromantic tie the relationship between Frederick and Constance developed into a meaningful one, rounded out by a feeling of genuine respect, if not affection. A new profundity was awakened in Frederick; for the first time in his life there was someone at his side who shared his interests and whose advice and encouragement could not be put down as first of all for personal gain. Frederick's queen became a source of inspiration and support when he needed it most. Living as a princess in Aragon, as a queen in Hungary, and then again in Aragon as a widowed queen, Constance knew her way through the horrors and pleasures of court life. Love of culture, of the songs of Aquitaine and Provence were not foreign to her; but neither was the cold bargaining, nor the dog-eat-dog conspiratorial self-interest of every court worthy of the name.

The role of helpmate was not entirely one sided. Within two months of her arrival in Sicily, Frederick was comforting Constance for the loss of her younger brother and the major part of the contingent of five hundred knights who had accompanied her, all killed off by plague. So often in the past these epidemics had fought the battles for the Italians and Sicilians, driving off would-be conquerors from the north, who, for all their trouble, had no alternative but to lead decimated armies back over the Alps in humiliating defeat. But this time nature turned against the Sicilians. Watched by an array of discontented barons headed by the likes of Diepold of Schweinspeunt, Frederick grappled with the meaning of the knights' deaths in terms of setting his kingdom in order. Outwardly playing the part of the king hunting in the woods and wild marshes of Lentini, south of Catania, where he and his bride had gone to escape the plague, he was considering means of pursuing his policies by another tack. He needed foreign allies; historically loyal Genoa would be the most obvious. For starters he named to his council a Genoese, Count Alaman da Costa, whose dedicated friendship would be a great boon in the next few years when Frederick's need would be most dire.

As though he did not have problems enough, the year marked Frederick's first direct brush with the forbidding power of the papacy. With the archbishopric of Palermo falling vacant, the cathedral chapter obtained permission from the king to elect a new prelate, just as they had in the happier days of the Hauteville kings. Certain members of the chapter, however, averred with reason that Frederick's mother had signed away that royal privilege in her agreements with popes Celestine and Innocent. In a rage Frederick banished them from the realm. They appealed to the pope, bringing down on the novice king's head a letter which, if not thundering, was at least rumbling—a warning of the coming storm that would be the normal chaos of Frederick's dealings with popes for the rest of his days. Innocent expressed amazement that Frederick's advisors would counsel him into such a move. Imperiously he warned the king to be content with the temporal power that he, the pope, had given him, thereby setting forth the papal attitude for the future. As he saw it, Frederick's crown had been a papal gift and he, Frederick, should never forget it. He should be grateful. Frederick would do well not to usurp the papal office by dealing in things spiritual. He was reminded of the fates of Uzzah, who was struck dead for presuming to lay a hand on the Ark of God, and of Uzziah, who was afflicted with leprosy for transgressing the duties of the priests of the Lord. Frederick was in the wrong. He may have had spine and ability to match his ancestors, but it was going to take more to bring events into line with his destiny. He was not yet ready to take on a pope. He had no choice but to comply with papal wishes and recall the canons.

At precisely the time that Frederick was establishing himself in his world of intrigue and violence, Francis Bernardone was setting up his own lifestyle, totally at odds with the Hohenstaufen world. In 1208, with a friend and first follower, one Bernardo of Quintavalle, a nobleman who owned a mansion and who had already renounced his worldly wealth to follow him, Francis attended Mass. He begged the priest to set him in a philosophical direction. According to the oft-told story the priest opened a Bible three times, producing three precepts from Matthew, which became the basis for the establishment of a new order of religious brothers. Francis interpreted the readings as mandates directing him to start his lifetime of itinerant preaching, poverty, and charity. His journey to sainthood had begun. Also set in motion was a movement that, while in the short run of far less importance than the immediate business of the empire, was in the long run of significant consequence for the world.

Caught up in his initial enthusiasm, Francis reached the conclusion that the observance of poverty and the return to the austerity of Christ that he and his few friends practiced should receive the sanction of the Church. He determined to approach the pope in person. But first he had to convince his recalcitrant brothers: Brother Giles, the energetic traveler and speaker of "golden sayings"; Brother Leo, "Pecorello di Dio"—"Little Lamb of God"—who, with brothers Rufino and Angelo, would later set their memories of Francis into writing; shy, stammering Brother Rufino who, on Francis's command, gave a sermon half-naked in a church of Assisi; Brother Pacifico, a jongleur, designated "King of Verses" by Frederick II; Brother Masseo, he who when levitated by Francis felt "sweet sensations in his soul," not to mention consolations from the Holy Spirit beyond anything he had known. And who can forget "the plaything of God," the simple, childlike Brother Juniper, one of Francis's favorites? Francis told them of a recent dream in which, walking along a road, he came upon a tree, enormously tall, in full leaf and mighty of girth. He found himself growing taller until at length he was the same height as the tree, which he took to hand, bending it down to touch the ground. The tree, he interpreted, was the mighty Innocent III, who would eventually bend to their request.

Francis and his ragtag followers set out for Rome early in the summer. The sun was warm on their faces, the Umbrian air limpid, and travel on foot pleasant. The group's optimism was obvious to everyone they encountered, and they had little trouble finding barns to sleep in and food, which was given to them by charitable people along the way. On arriving in Rome they were surprised to meet Bishop Guido of Assisi, the same bishop who had draped Francis in temporary raiment before his stunned father three years ago. Despite Guido's inclination for violence and quick temper, he was sympathetic to soft-spoken Francis and his friends. With genuine concern he tried to talk them out of their determination to follow a rigorously impoverished lifestyle, feeling that their doctrines could easily slip into the heretical practices of the Albigenses, a religious sect thriving in southern France and holding that all riches were instruments of the devil and that anyone who owned any goods was not a true follower of Christ. Guido's efforts to reason with members of Francis's budding order were more the act of a kindly father playing the role of *advocatus diaboli* to sons who already know the positive side of the way of life they propose to adopt. Fearing that Innocent would be inclined to ridicule the tattered band of brothers, Guido introduced them to Cardinal John of Saint Paul, a member of the prominent Colonna family, a pious man sharing many of Francis's biblically inspired ideals. His response to Francis's stated principle was the same as Guido's. Perhaps it would be better if the brothers simply entered an existing order that had already obtained Church recognition. In time, however, being somewhat of a kindred spirit, the cardinal arranged a meeting with Innocent.

It was a strange confrontation there in the Lateran palace—one of the humblest men of God in an age of humble men of God face-to-face with the boldest pope in an age of bold popes. Francis, preaching poverty, simplicity, and penance, kneeling before a man of Spartan mold but an advocate of worldwide theocracy, still managed to impress the enthroned pontiff with his seriousness of purpose. Innocent sized Francis up, seeing him as a possible leader in his fight against heresy, which was an avowed goal almost beyond that of a politically triumphant papacy. By example this simple man could fight the Church's battle against heresy and establish more firmly the kingdom of Christ here on earth. Dominic Guzman, future founder of the Dominicans, was rallying spiritual forces to fight the Albigenses in southern France. What Dominic was doing by argument Francis could do by example. After voicing a string of delaying objections, Innocent finally suggested that the group meet with him again to know the divine will after prayers, contemplation, and a good night's sleep.

As was the way with so many medieval happenings, according to popular legends Innocent III experienced a dream that night which played an important part in his decision. In his vision he saw the Church of Saint John Lateran crumbling, the center of Christendom buckling and trembling in the throes of some invisible destructive force. Then his eyes fell on the figure of a man dressed in the garb of a monk, putting his shoulder to the edifice to prevent its collapse, a papal counterpart, it would seem, of the voice which had instructed Francis to rebuild the Church. At once Innocent identified the self-effacing, ingratiating leader of the little group of penitents from Assisi who had stood in his presence the day before.

The papal Curia met to debate the case of the petitioners from Assisi. Objections were raised, especially that their aspirations were too difficult for attainment and that they could soon lapse into heresy. Look what had happened to the Albigenses, who had started out espousing poverty and then, before long, ended up accusing the pope and his bishops of being in league with the devil and calling the Church the "whore of Babylon"! Finally Cardinal John arose, reminding the others that Francis and his followers were asking only that they be allowed to live according to the precepts of the Gospels. If the Curia denied these holy men that right, they were, in effect, denying the teachings of Jesus. End of discussion. Innocent gave the holy men permission to preach, though they could not establish doctrine. Between Dominic Guzman's aggressive preaching and Francis's pious example and soft-toned persuasion, Innocent figured he had given the Church two fresh teams of fighters.

Taking leave of the pope and happy with their triumph over Church bureaucracy, the brothers headed north, stopping briefly at Orte, a town of little interest today but for its dramatic situation on an abrupt outcropping of rock, where they affirmed their love for "Lady Poverty." Then, at Francis's behest, and all of them believing that "from a hovel one ascends more quickly to heaven than from a palace,"[3] they settled temporarily in an abandoned cowshed at Rivo Torto where the smallness of the place would not frustrate contemplation. But not for long.

King Otto IV was on the move, marching "on pilgrimage" to Rome to receive the imperial diadem from the papal hand, escorted and protected by all manner of boisterous followers who were anxious to see for themselves the official crowning. The pandemonium—it must have seemed like a resurgence of the barbarian hordes of old to the people of quiet Umbria—was too much for Francis Bernardone and his men, who were trying to achieve a contemplative life in their cowshed. Staring down from his magnificent height, Otto was unimpressed when accosted by what seemed a fanatic who had been sent out to lecture him on the evanescence of worldly fame and material possessions. He laughed in his vulgar way and moved on to his meeting with the pope.

What with further intrusions into their space, Francis and his friends packed their meager possessions and left Rivo Torto, finally coming to rest at the tiny Chapel of the Porziuncola—"the Little Portion," because of its size—in the valley below Assisi. Here the brothers built their huts of boughs around their new headquarters, the first real home of the Franciscan order, though they could not claim ownership since it was merely on loan to them by the Benedictine Abbot of the monastery above Assisi on Mount Subasio in exchange for an offering of lake fish every year on the feast of Saint Benedict. In return, Francis was given a jar of oil.

Despite the sixteenth- and seventeenth-century excesses of Galeazzo Alessi's mighty baroque Church of Santa Maria degli Angeli, which encapsulates and completely dwarfs the precious little Porziuncola, the assertive structure—a monument to bad taste—cannot silence the sweet Franciscan hymn or eradicate the gentle spirit of Francis Bernardone that seems to permeate every crack and crevice of every abode that he frequented—tourist clamor and the sometimes uncharacteristic crossness of the Franciscan fathers who watch over these lovely places aside. Tiny is the Porziuncola, and blackened by centuries of candle smoke. It is desecrated with frescoes that do not help it a whit, though Ilario da Viterbo's fourteenth-century *Annunciation*, echoing an earlier work of Simone Martini, does possess a

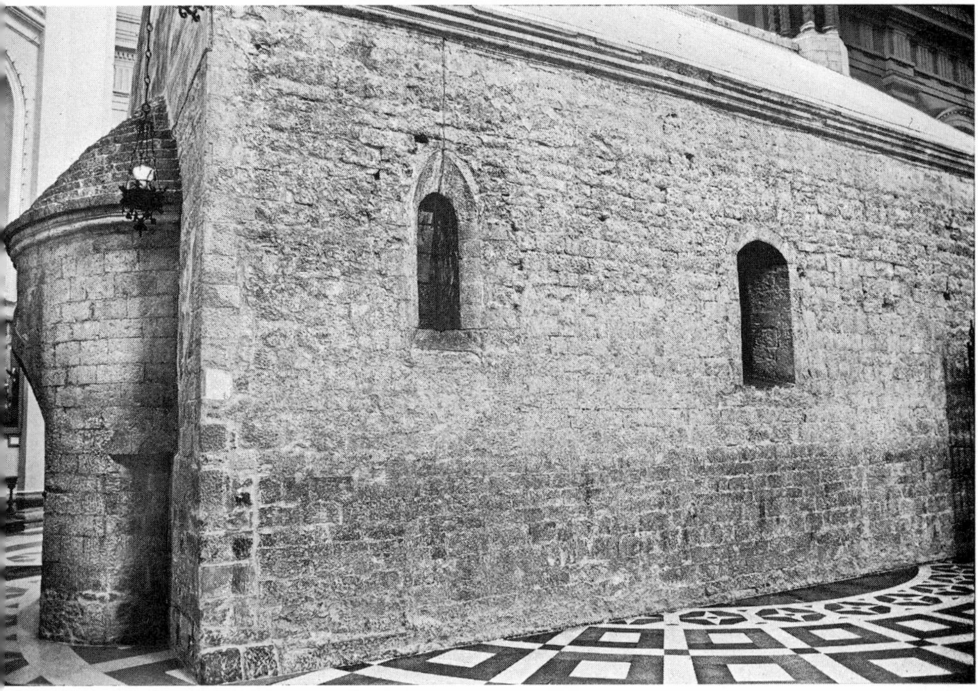

Porziuncola, Assisi, Italy

graceful charm. With its wee slit windows and a tiny apse, this entirely inauspicious structure seems an unlikely place for the fledgling Franciscan order to get its start. But the fabled *Little Flowers of Saint Francis* assures us that this was the joyful, idyllic period of Francis's new order. Gathering companion followers from every corner, the numbers were not yet so large to be a problem.

With the crowning of Emperor Otto IV of Brunswick in October 1209, Pope Innocent was satisfied that the threat of isolation of the Church by a union of Sicily and the empire had been avoided. But his peace of mind was not to last. Hardly had he been crowned when Emperor Otto repudiated the agreements of the year before, even laughing outright in the face of the disgruntled pope when he was reminded of them. Especially anguishing was Otto's scorning of the agreements regarding German episcopal elections, papal territories, and the "fact" that Sicily was a papal fief and therefore beyond imperial interests. His promises were invalid, Otto proclaimed, because they had not received the approval of the German princes. It became clear at once that Otto, in papal eyes an unimaginative, unintellectual boor, was not going to be anyone's lackey. Innocent remonstrated with him, reminding him that those agreements had been the stepping-stones to the imperium. But perjured Otto replied with characteristic rudeness that must have shaken the recipient's whole being, going so far as to use similar arguments that Innocent himself had recently used with Frederick. "Be content with your spiritual functions," he warned, and then he went on that men of the cloth are not fit to wield the secular sword.

To add to the bad news for both Frederick and Innocent, Otto had already welcomed into his presence, at Pisa, the treacherous Diepold of Schweinspeunt. A marcher in the footsteps of Markward of Anweiler, Diepold was stubbornly convinced that Sicily was correctly an appendage of the German empire and that Frederick was no more than a temporary block in the path of such a union. As a leader of the Apulian barons Diepold played into Otto's hands, making it clear that he wanted to rule the southern kingdom. Otto kept Diepold on his team by making him duke of the papal duchy of Spoleto, an act of open hostility to Innocent in that he, Otto, thereby negated all papal hopes of a strong Church buffer between southern Italy and the German north. Then Otto set about preparing for a Sicilian campaign, knowing full well that Innocent claimed suzerainty over that region.

1210

The pope flew into a pontifical rage. Again there was looming that dreadful specter of the Papal States standing hostage to a Siculo-German empire. But, like Frederick, Innocent was not one to let events guide him. It was not in his personality to go along with the times. A maker of history, a creator of events, a manipulator, Innocent set to the task at once, writing encyclicals to the German bishops and divisive letters to the secular princes, including an astonishing one to King Philip Augustus of France, always a hater of Otto, if for no other reason than that he was a nephew of the king of England. In his letter Innocent was forced to acknowledge the error of his judgment, admitting that Philip had warned him against granting the imperial crown to Otto. But Innocent had sneered at such negative opinion, stating categorically that he was in a better position to judge such weighty matters. The German bishops set to work conspiring with the princes, a dissatisfied lot and never wholly convinced of the benefits of having Otto as emperor. When Otto moved into Frederick's Apulia in late 1210, he was automatically excommunicated by a pope who knew full well that he was touching off another civil war in Germany, but who was no longer in the mood for the negotiating table. He was determined that Otto should be deposed; such was the extent of his hatred. Suddenly Frederick was very vulnerable.

In the two years since his majority, displaying an almost awesome energy and an adult manner that amazed his disconcerted nobles, Frederick had systematically put down a revolt touched off by the deaths of his brother-in-law, Alfonso of Provence, and his Spanish knights. Then his nobles stood thunderstruck as he won back more and more of his realm that had been nibbled away during his minority. He issued an edict demanding that all landowners submit to the royal curia their deeds of ownership for arbitration. This legally justified minute examination of conditions in his realm was the kind of thing that was going to puzzle his enemies throughout his career. He knew what he was doing and had obviously anticipated his actions earlier, when he had watched his barons whittling away his demesne and had stood by helplessly while Walter of Palear had given great chunks of it to his own favorites. One of the leaders of the barons, Anfuso de Rota, count of Tropea, was indignant and insulted Frederick to his face, only to find himself cooling his heels in prison. Frederick then wrote a circular letter to the barons and the prelates of the realms, calling by name the members of his baronage who had robbed him and plotted against him, especially Anfuso. By this time even Walter of Palear had been relegated to a see at Catania, retaining the title of chancellor, albeit by now an empty one. The message was clear to all: Frederick might be the last of the Hohenstaufens and impoverished to boot, but he was a Hohenstaufen worthy of the name and, as much as the most determined of his ancestors, a force to be reckoned with.

1211

"It repenteth me," cried Innocent III, quoting I Samuel 15:11, "that I have set up Saul to be king: for he is turned back from following me, and hath not performed my commandments." By March 1211 it had become clear to the pope, to the German princes, and to Philip Augustus of France that nothing could stop Emperor Otto, short of insurrection at home. So it was that on March 31 Otto's excommunication was given elaborate publicity, including the word that his followers were tarred by the same brush, that his subjects were absolved from any oaths of fidelity they might have sworn, and that all places that allowed Otto shelter were laid under interdict, a formidable weapon unique to papal practice and used to bring the most recalcitrant prince and brazen warrior into line. In its strictest application the citizens of a city or area under the ban were forbidden to maintain their allegiance to their prince. They were denied the benefit of the sacraments, even the right to worship. Church bells were silenced, the dead remained unburied, the citizens uncomforted by their religion. Used judiciously the interdict was a fearsome papal revenge, a condition calculated to strike fear into the hearts and, as in the case of Germany at this time, revolt into the minds of intimidated subjects. Revolt was the idea that Innocent had in mind, and revolt was precisely what he got.

Though Innocent's actions in company with the German princes, all of them egged on by Philip Augustus, would eventually bring Otto down, for the moment the least-envied character on the political stage was Frederick Hohenstaufen. Poor as he was, there was no way he could withstand the coming onslaught of German might. He may recently have overcome his Apulian barons, but he clearly was not yet master of his own house. With the exception of his wife Constance there was, apparently, no one in the kingdom to be trusted since the nobility, trying to feather their own nests, had already swung over to the German emperor. Even the Saracens who still resided in the Sicilian highlands had communicated to Otto their promises of obedience. On the advice of his wife, Frederick finally had to depose Bishop Walter of Palear from his figurative chancellorship because he was on intimate terms with Diepold of Schweinspeunt. In a trumpeting fury Innocent fired off a letter to Frederick, telling him that he was past childhood and should ignore recommendations for such action, that he should restore the deposed chancellor in gratitude for all the work he had done for him during his minority, an assertion which must have brought a wry smile to Frederick's lips. Despite the fatherly tone of parts of the letter, Innocent had already proven his own lack of friendship by exacting from financially strapped Frederick a pledge of reimbursement for the expenses of the regency. He was quite capable of talking out of both sides of his mouth, a fact noticed with undisguised bitterness by Walther von der Vogelweide:

> For God makes kings of whom he will . . .
> This word fills simple men with hope—
> But then again priests say it is the Pope.
> Tell us in sooth,
> Which is the truth?
> Two voices in one mouth—it likes me ill.[4]

In one respect at least Innocent was right; Frederick was past childhood. But he was also in a better position than the pope to judge the merits of keeping unreliable Walter of Palear in the royal service. He did not obey the papal injunction, though whether or not he helped himself by the refusal is a moot point. On the positive side, however, he did learn that he could stand against a bullying pope: and the pope learned a new respect for the young king, a man as headstrong as he—and as difficult to intimidate.

Politically speaking there seemed to be no way out for Frederick, with voracious Otto taking his mainland holdings from him in bite-size chunks. He attempted to negotiate with Otto, going so far as to offer to cede to him all of his Swabian heritage. But he was no more successful in his dealings with the high-riding Guelf than had been Innocent III. The emperor was in possession of all of the mainland part of his realm and was waiting now in Calabria for the arrival of a confederate Pisan fleet before making the leap across the Straits of Messina. Frederick had no choice but to ready a galley in the harbor of Palermo, a getaway hatch to Africa when the inevitable invasion occurred. It must have seemed strange to king-watchers that he chose this low point of his life to embellish his coat of arms with the sun and the moon, both symbols of world dominion. It was a hint of the king's zestful optimism that was to become typical.

With the tensions in Europe, the intrigues and endless one-upmanship, the battles and the lustings after naked power, no one cared that Jenghis Khan had this year penetrated the Great Wall of China and was directing his ravening armies to overrun the Chinese empire. Typical nomads, his subjects yearned for new lands to conquer, for booty, slaves, and riches. The world had never known an army such as this: cavalry, lancers, archers, men, and beasts alike accustomed to hard living, long treks across open deserts, and frequent periods of little sustenance. It would take Jenghis Khan another few years to finish China off, but in the end he would gain tributes of five hundred youths and maidens, including two princesses of the imperial house, and three thousand horses. City by city, province by province, he was building an empire which, before mid-century, would cause Europe to think there was no stopping the avalanche. For the moment, however, Europe was caught up in its own frustrations; and a despondent, defenseless Frederick waited in Palermo for the German onslaught, hoping against rational expectation for a miraculous intervention. Then came the miracle.

Chapter Four

The written book will be brought forth,
in which the whole (record of evidence) is contained
whence the world is to be judged.
***Dies Irae*, verse 5**

1211

If proud Otto was unimpressed by his excommunication, the same cannot be said for a good number of his princes, who were already leery of his growing power and alarmed lest he should—emulating his grandfather, Henry II of England—supplant German feudal tradition with new, modern bureaucracy. Pope Innocent, gambling on the complexities of Germany's political games, added further itch to the rash of disloyalty by reminding the electors that with Otto's excommunication came an exemption from their oaths of allegiance. It was a good time for Innocent to stir the political stew, for he knew that both Guelf and Ghibelline factions were tired unto death of the endemic upheavals. Egged on by Ghibelline sympathizer Philip Augustus of France, the Guelf princes held a September assembly in Nuremberg, the city of the Meistersingers, to declare the excommunicated Otto IV to be ex-king and ex-emperor. By the end of the month, they had drafted their proclamation declaring Frederick their new choice for king and emperor, voicing, after the usual religious formalities, their determination to exercise their rights of selection. Their statement indicated their conviction that despite Frederick's youth he was mature in character and blessed with the virtues of the legitimate Caesars of Germany. The Ghibelline princes were ecstatic. While Guelf messengers were dispatched to Otto's camp in Calabria with the sorry news, Ghibelline ambassadors were sent first to Rome for papal approval, and then to Palermo to ascertain whether or not Frederick was in a position to accept the royal honors.

Having orchestrated Otto's dethronement and the elevation of Frederick Hohenstaufen, Innocent's mind was made up long before the Ghibelline legates reached him, though he did entertain misgivings about the German princes choosing their king without expressed papal approval. But other considerations outweighed that objection. In Innocent's mind Frederick was beholden to him in too many ways to be anything but an obedient son of the Church and an enthusiastic protector of the Papal States. It seems an incredible contradiction that Innocent, so defensive of Church interests, so adamant in his opposition to even the vaguest suggestion of a union of southern Italy and Germany, could walk into such a trap. To allow his abhorrence of Otto to cause him to embrace Frederick's cause in Germany was surely the greatest blunder of his career. The marriage of Frederick's father and mother had been nothing compared to this disservice to papal interests. Innocent could not have been so naive as not to realize that, with the election of the king of Sicily to the German throne, the imperial diadem was almost certain to adorn the same head that wore the two crowns.

Arrogant and boorish as ever, Otto reacted instantly to the German messengers, breaking camp and heading for home with an urgency that he had not so far exhibited. He may have been overly alarmed (it was told that he was influenced by a dream in which a bear invaded his bed, growing ever larger until it pushed him out) for it seems clear that had he followed his original plan, moved into Sicily, taken the person of the young king and then headed north, he probably would have been able to save his position. His abrupt change of plans ultimately doomed his imperium. With a last stab of grandeur in a brilliant court at Lodi, Otto moved across the snowbanked Alps in midwinter, taking Diepold of Schweinspeunt, count of Acerra and new duke of Spoleto, with him. By March 1212 he was in Frankfurt.

1212

Unlike Otto, Frederick hesitated. Just recently Constance had presented her seventeen-year-old husband with his first son, Henry. Shortly thereafter his first illegitimate child, Enzo, was born, the initial evidence of a sensual nature so overt as to become, in time, the gossip of a Europe accustomed to overlooking royal infidelities. Frederick was for heading north at once. One can understand the eagerness of a teenage king of an all-but-derelict realm, suddenly thrust into the limelight by being offered the most influential ruling position on the continent. He would have to fight for it, yes; but with the rich German Ghibellines on his side, he could realistically envision success. Conservative members of his court advised against his acceptance, feeling that the quixotic German princes might turn against him even before he managed to cross the Alps. In fact, word had reached Palermo that a few of those who had elected to invite Frederick to Germany had already deserted and returned to Otto's side. Others of the southern court did not trust the pope, fearing that, should the wind suddenly blow from another direction, he, with the political expediency that he seemed so adept at displaying, would do an about-face in his present hostile-to-Otto course, personal bonds having little to do with the decision.

More than anyone it was Queen Constance who gave Frederick pause. She knew who her enemies were. Genuinely fond of her younger husband, her concern was more conjugal, even maternal, than political. She was worldly-wise beyond many men of her time. She saw that, once Frederick took a predominant position in the affairs of Europe, she would lose him to the kingdom, the empire, and the bloody battling and treacherous politicking so much a norm of the day. She could see herself once again a widow, perhaps more tragic than the widow she had been as queen of Hungary. Her personal loss would be severe, but as she saw it not so severe as that of her infant son. Constance argued that Frederick should remain in his shaky kingdom, shoring it up against the insidious forces that would destroy it from within, thus making it more secure for his heir's eventual takeover. Henry's future was at stake, especially if Frederick ventured off in pursuit of his rightful patrimony.

On the other hand, Frederick saw himself as the legitimate scion of the imperial family. His mother's wishes and Innocent's original determination that he live out his life in Sicily administering the kingdom of his Norman ancestors and carrying on their traditions of enlightened culture stood for nothing now. He saw the German princes' invitation as a miracle, a manifestation of God's favor and will that he take over the Empire as a heaven-inspired son of the Church. In his own eyes he was an instrument of divine providence, God's regent. According to him even the pope acted under a blessed compulsion to preserve the ultimate power of the house of Hohenstaufen. There was not much argument against that kind of reasoning. Others, friends and enemies, might in affection or derision speak of the "boy of Apulia," but as far as Frederick was concerned he was a man now with an unrelenting confidence in his own God-given ability to fight the most daunting powers for his just inheritance of the two thrones of his father. His determination was boisterous, self-serving, youthful. Flying in the face of the most considered advice, Frederick set out for Germany in March but not before bowing to the demands of Pope Innocent, who still thought to head off the centering of power in one man. He had his son, Henry, crowned king of Sicily and named his wife regent of the realm.

Frederick must have cut a curious figure indeed as he left his beloved Sicily, not to return for another eight years. In worn-out, ragged clothes—more beggar boy than king—he boarded ship at Messina with a company of retainers that was skimpy for an emperor-elect and probably not much better outfitted. The most favored of his few confederates was Berard of Castacca, bishop of Bari and future archbishop of Palermo, a man whose loyalty was unswerving and one of the few friends for whom Frederick would always feel genuine affection. Newly appointed as papal legate, Berard was destined to be a lifelong intimate of his king and emperor, clinging faithfully to his master through excommunication and vilification, and finally administering to him the last sacraments. When Frederick needed Berard he was there. In Berard's perpetual presence lay his greatness.

Guelf-sympathizing Pisa had galleys on the prowl to intercept the king-elect, a threat serious enough to force Frederick's ship to cover at Gaeta on the coast between Naples and Rome. Delayed there a month, inhabiting a castle that today is largely nonexistent, so marked is it by the additions of later generations, Frederick was champing the bit to get his venture going. He probably had only impatient eyes for the Cathedral of Saint Elmo, patron saint of sailors, with its handsome twelfth-century Romano-Moorish campanile, which still stands, more Moorish in style than Christian, square, and with an eight-sided pinnacle. Its heaviness is artfully lessened by two lighted windows and by friezes of judiciously placed blind arches. Not in the mood for sightseeing, Frederick could afford to bypass the impressive Montagna Spaccata, the vertical fissure in a mountain said to have split at the moment of Christ's death; likewise the tomb of Lucius Munatius Plancus (called "Orlando's Tower") perched on the summit of a promontory, the final resting place of the friend of Julius Caesar who was later successively attached to Brutus, Antony, and Octavian. Horace addressed his ode 7, book 1 to Plancus, ending with words that Frederick could have taken to heart and that, well-read as he was, he may have known:

> . . . now drink with me, brave men.
> Banish with wine your sorrow;
> We'll sail again the wide sea tomorrow!

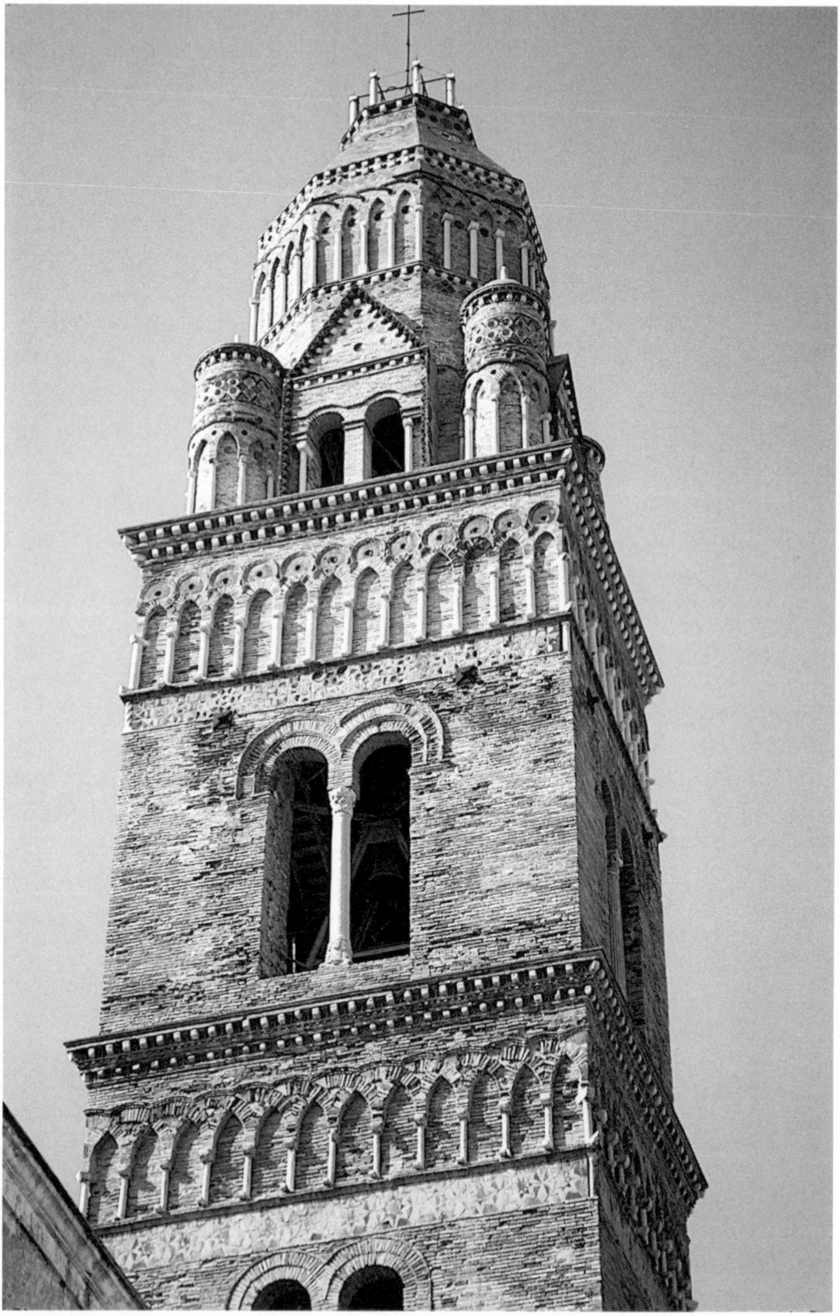

Cathedral campanile, Gaeta, Italy

Frederick moved on by land to Rome for the one face-to-face meeting of his life with Innocent III. Here he was at the heart of the ancient empire that he was consciously setting out to re-create, in the city of the Caesars, the long-dead men from whom he took his title Kaiser. He could not have been anything but impressed by the republican and imperial glories, the tombs, the ruined villas, temples, and lesser reminders of former brilliance, not to mention the monuments of early Christianity—the churches, many of which had been built from the rubble of the decaying empire, and even the pagan arena and circuses which served as graphic testimony of antireligious depravity.

The meeting of Frederick and Innocent III was a coming together of ascendant and descendant powers, all the more strange in that practically nothing was recorded of the event other than that Frederick was warmly received on Easter Sunday after he had performed his act of homage on his knees, his hands in those of the pope, his head bowed. Looking down on the beardless youth with the sparkling blue-green eyes and red-gold hair, Innocent saw none of the residual anger, the budding seeds of resentment and outright contempt that his own self-serving guardianship had planted in Frederick's heart. He should have looked more deeply into the eyes of his former ward. He would have detected that edge of resentment and ruthless determination that only a long period of hate, want, and fear could have provoked. Accomplished politician that he was, Innocent should have recognized another in the making when he saw Frederick at his feet. But in the vanity of his present accomplishments, Innocent had eyes only for growing temporal power. For all his experience in acting the judge, this worldly pope—perhaps the most worldly of them all—failed to estimate the rancor, the pride even greater than his own, the awful determination of an eighteen-year-old who had been all but done out of his heritage. Innocent saw only the immaturity, the handsomely sensual mouth, and the studied humility of the pose. But it was of no matter. In four years Innocent would be dead.

Frederick knew well enough that the chaos in his kingdom was due to both papal negligence and manipulation. And when Innocent did the worst of all things he could possibly have done under the circumstances—making Frederick swear fealty to Sicily, the single remnant of his patrimony that had always, even in the bleakest hours, been his—Frederick knew that he would never hold to it, oath or not. Why should any veneration be owed to this oval-faced, ascetic-looking, steady-eyed prelate staring down at him, he who was just then beginning to realize his magnificent destiny? He saw the papal welcome, the encouragement to seek his destiny not in the light of a just pursuit of his patrimony, but for the fact that he was an enemy of a papal enemy. Frederick awakened then to his place in the scheme of things other than as lackey and defender of Church worldliness.

Innocent had already asked himself the unanswerable questions. He knew the risk he was taking. Once Frederick occupied the throne of Germany would he not automatically entertain the aspirations of his ancestors, the union of Germany, including northern Italy, with Sicily? Frederick was young. Would later popes be able to hold their own against his energy? Anticipatory questions or not, Innocent had no way of knowing that this agreeable young man would develop into "Stupor Mundi"—"Wonder of the World"—a man of such fixed ideology and belief in expediency as to cause the next four popes anxieties unparalleled in the history of their office. But for the moment there was such accord that Innocent could afford to foot the bill for Frederick's visit, as well he might, seeing that his former ward, pauperism aside, was theoretically the most promising papal protector in sight. It was no matter that a few Romans were amused by Frederick's short stature and openly dubious of his abilities to cut heroically built Otto down to size. It was the warm display of loyalty and the thrilling send-off on the part of the notoriously fickle Romans who saw in him a resurgence of their own lost dreams and glory that caused Frederick to experience emperorship for the first time. But it was a brief moment of glory.

Once he was out of the Eternal City, papal expenditure on Frederick's behalf ceased. It was the small northern city of Pavia that guaranteed his expenses on the next leg of his journey. There was no proud ritual procession northward. Because Emperor Otto's garrisons made land travel too dangerous for him, Frederick had to sail from Civitavecchia on a Genoese galley, landing in Genoa on May 1. The "Son of the Church" (the pope's phrase), the "Priestling-Emperor" (to quote Fredrick's adversaries) expected, and received, a ceremonious and joyful reception at this staunchly Ghibelline city. But even here Otto's power was a ruling factor; imperial might still made the roads unsafe, necessitating a delay of about three months.

Rivaling Venice and Pisa as predominant Italian maritime power, Genoa was enjoying a building boom from profits reaped for her part in the crusades, though these benefits were being steadily drained by persistent wars with two competitors. Strategically located at the top of the Ligurian Sea, Genoa is one of the old cities of Italy, having been occupied by Greeks as early as the fourth century BC, though the only proof of that is the existence there of a Greek cemetery. The settlement was destroyed by Carthaginians, then later became the Roman Genua. A flourishing seaport town, it was later reduced to fishing village status by Ostrogoth and Lombard raids. It had revived sufficiently by the tenth century to drive the Saracens from Corsica and Sardinia and then—in one of the unique times in the city's history when it allied with Pisa—out of Italian waters altogether. The crusades gave Genoa the necessary financial boost and rapid expansion followed, echoed today in soaring gateways, the Porta dei Vacca and the Porta Soprana, as well as in twelfth-century walls that extended the confines of the city to the sea, important to survival, as the thirteenth-century bank (now known as the Palazzo San Giorgio) at portside indicates. In Frederick's time Genoa served as a trading depot rather than an industrial center. In this sense Genoa was similar to other great medieval cities such as London, Bruges, and Lübeck on the Baltic Sea north of Hamburg. Genoa had established herself in Sicily as a commercial affront to a Pisa loyal in principle not only to the Germans, but to the Guelfs. This fact

Cathedral tympanum, Genoa, Italy

alone would foster Genoa as a natural ally to Frederick Hohenstaufen, his doorway to the empire—Genua—Janua—door, gate. The history of Genoa during the Middle Ages is not much different from that of the other Italian communes—strife, intercity rivalry, and the steady acceleration of commerce and banking. But it is interesting to note that there would be "no blue jeans but for the city of Genoa, *Gênes,* where the blue cotton cloth was first produced, and no Genoa jibs."[1]

When Frederick sat out his time there, much of Genoa resembled what its old section looks like today. There are solemn basilicas with bicolored walls and high polygonal domes reminiscent of Burgundy. The Cathedral of San Lorzo, consecrated almost a century before Frederick but still in the process of construction when he saw it, reflects Gothic features that appeared early in Liguria and that eventually gave Genoa a flamboyantly Gothic air. Even then San Lorenzo retains its Romanesque character due at least in part to its dichromatic ornamentation. A stern, majestic Christ surrounded by abstract symbols of the evangelists dominates the facade. And there below is Saint Lawrence himself being grilled before Emperor Decius, who signals to his men to pump the bellows more energetically. It is all very ornate, but tasteful, with an especially interesting south side porch. The nave, even though transitional between Romanesque and Gothic, is handsome. The treasury displays a glass *sacro catino,* supposedly given to Solomon by the Queen of Sheba, and from which Christ, surprisingly, is alleged to have drunk during the Last Supper. The whole idea is so palpably false as to be embarrassing! There is also a metal box there that is said to have belonged to Frederick Barbarossa. San Lorenzo's crowning dome was built after designs by Galeazzo Alessi (he of the Church of Santa Maria degli Angeli near Assisi), who played a fundamental sixteenth-century role in the city's planning.

And then the streets!—what streets they are! The Via Garibaldi is gorgeous and opulent of days past, as rich and heady as the Street of the Goldsmiths is dark, hidden, and tawdry, the former broad, sweeping, and breathtaking, the latter painfully narrow, secretive—and fascinating. But the author's favorite spot in all of Genoa is the picturesque Piazza San Matteo, where aristocratic black-and-white-striped buildings and the church of the saint form a small, quiet square of arresting dignity. Tucked away in one corner—kitty-corner from the church—is number 17, given by a grateful city of Genoa to condottiere and admiral Andrea Doria (1466–1560). The joys of Genoa are sumptuous, notwithstanding a populace that strikes one as being a little dour and un-Italian in their lack of ebullience.

For his three-month layover in Genoa, Frederick stayed at the home of Niccolo Doria, the head of a family that would remain loyally Ghibelline even when the city became a papal stronghold. It was probably at this time that Frederick met poet Percival Doria, who attached himself to the Sicilian court and helped make it the most brilliant of the thirteenth century. He also met Manfred Lancia in Genoa, a young man about his own age, whose sister or niece (we do not know which) would later be his mistress, perhaps even his wife, and the mother of his favorite son.

Despite its treasury being slowly depleted by endemic wars with maritime rivals, Genoa still managed to cough up enough money to cover Frederick's expenses while he bided his time there but, with typical business savvy, only in exchange for a packet of promissory notes with the curious postscripts "valid for the day when I become emperor." At length, to Frederick's and probably Genoa's relief, it was time to get on with the trek over the Alps before the summer ran out, plans having been laid with allied cities to see him through the imperially infested regions of northern Italy. A ploy was devised wherein Frederick headed westward toward Asti, then northeast to Pavia, where he arrived on July 28 to the cheers of the populace and the ringing of church bells, including those of San Michele, the Romanesque portals of which are lovingly carved into lavish fantasies of natural and geometric decoration. How lovingly are the stone plants nurtured! How expertly are they trained to weave their way through figures and abstract trellises provided by the sculptors, frustrated gardeners all! Surely believing churchgoers through the ages have felt a rise in spirit, a stirring in the soul on passing through these heavenly portals!

No church is more rewarding to study than San Michele. It is redolent of Frederick's age—bold, solid, with large areas of smooth sandstone emphasized and balanced by horizontal bands of Lombard Romanesque sculptural reliefs. How arresting is that small cross piercing the facade high up and between two circular windows! This is not to ignore the masterfully conceived stepped colonnade under the front eaves and the wonderfully complex sculptures on the three portals. Leaves, flowers, and vine patterns; cats of all kinds and griffins; birds, fish, and snakes; saints and sinners, freakish composite figures whose legs become reptilian; palm fronds, shells, and abstract, nonobjective patterns; Saint Michael himself, wings at rest and orb in hand. They are all there in such a wealth of form and detail as to make total comprehension impossible. The mind must work mightily to fathom the rich subject matter in this twelfth-century flowering of a style influenced

Center door decoration, San Michele, Pavia, Italy

by the great Anselmo Campione and his followers, about whom we will hear more later. No sculpture has been more lovingly caressed into being, no saints more sweetly conceived, no imps imbued with more evil. Even allowing for the fakery of San Michele's facade—a device typical of the day, which makes buildings appear from the street a good deal larger than they are—the church stands as one of the most satisfying structures of the twelfth century. And the elaborately carved capitals in the interior echo what we have seen without, adding to the orchestration of the octagonal dome at the crossing, the raised choir, and the galleries. The twelfth-century crucifix of silver repoussé in a side chapel and an eloquently simple Annunciation relief on the south transept exterior are the final exclamation points. If Frederick saw all of this—and one hopes he did—he must have been thrilled. With his mental makeup he would never have forgotten it.

Young Frederick could feel at home in Pavia, which preserved in his day, as it does in ours, the rectilinear street pattern of its Roman development. After Rome it served as the Lombard capital, a rich and sensuous city of palaces, baths, and colonnades. Surely more important to Frederick, Pavia was the scene of the Lombard undoing by the first of the Holy Roman emperors, Charlemagne. The Lombard king, Liutprand (711–744), is buried there, in San Pietro in Cielo d'Oro (a church similar to San Michele and of the same period). An enlightened man, Liutprand decreed in 731 that the marriage of boys younger than thirteen was forthwith prohibited, which goes only half way in the eternal battle for gender equality. Saint Augustine of Hippo lies in state above the high altar of San Pietro, above even the remains of the revered Boethius, who is a comparative newcomer, having lain in the church only since 1923. Beyond that, Pavia was the birthplace of the brilliant Lanfranc, archbishop of Canterbury and devoted friend of William the Conqueror. Lanfranc probably founded the law school at Pavia, which later grew into the university.

Frederick stayed the night in this former Lombard capital. So far, so good. Now the trick was to get him through hostile Guelf territory belonging to Milan and Piacenza and into friendly Cremona. The Pavians schemed with the Cremonese for a dawn rendezvous on the banks of the Lambro River just south of Lodi, at which time they would deliver the king-elect over to them for a continuation of his journey north. To the accompaniment of vesper bells, Frederick and his escort of armed townsmen-guides set out at dusk on July 29. All went well as long as it was dark. At dawn the following morning they were surprised by a band of Milanesi who had gotten wind of the presence of their quarry. Cremonese troops showed up at the same time. Frederick leaped upon a saddleless horse and plunged into the river to meet them as they approached, leaving his Pavian guides to the mercies of the frustrated Milanese. With Milanese taunts of "Frederick wet his britches in the Lambro!" ringing in his ears, the future king of Germany was welcomed into Cremona.

As for some heavenly visitor, the church bells of Cremona pealed their joyous welcome. Frederick's triumphal procession headed for the sweeping Cathedral Piazza, defined even today by some of the finest buildings to be found in Lombardy, an area synonymous with fine architecture. The cathedral—massively foursquare but for the porch jutting out over the main portal, the two horizontal arcades one above the other, and the rose window added later in the century—was comparatively new, having been consecrated in 1190 after a rebuilding necessitated by an earthquake. High on the porch Saint Homobonus, patron saint of the city, cloth workers, and tailors, looks down benevolently on the sprawling piazza

Cathedral, Cremona, Italy

below. He was a native merchant and, as his name implies, a man of outstanding goodness and charity to the poor. He died in Frederick's time. The interior of the cathedral is nice, perhaps a little disappointing after the splendid exterior, due to being so drastically modified in later years. Even the transepts were subsequent additions, transforming the original basilica rectangular plan to a Latin cross. But the cathedral is rich in frescoes by Cremonese masters of the sixteenth century, augmented by fifteenth-century inlaid wooden stalls and seventeenth-century tapestries. Far and away the most winning attraction here are the lions standing guard at the central door, supporting the columns of the porch and looking for all the world like guilty dogs caught in some naughty act and soliciting our forgiveness.

The approximately 365-foot high cathedral bell tower was not begun until 1250, the year of Frederick's death. It was topped finally in 1284 and proclaimed the highest campanile in Italy. Together with the cathedral it forms a moment of arresting architectural balance, harmony, and proportion, especially as seen from the apsidal end of the church. The solid, octagonal Romanesque baptistry has a high arcade echoing the

Lion sculpture, Cathedral, Cremona, Italy

facade of the cathedral and running around its eight sides. The Palazzo del Comune, with its public speaking rostrum, was in the throes of being built at the time of Frederick's triumphal visit, but it would not be finished until 1246. To the left of the palace is the Soldiers' Loggia of the thirteenth century.

Cremona is a most beguiling city to explore, emanating a warm, reddish color from its buildings of brick and terra cotta as well as from its tile roofs. There are colorful markets and crowds. Always crowds in Italy! But it is to the Piazza del Duomo, a center of enormous civic pride, that one always returns. It bears a kinship to other Italian town centers, and yet it is unique in its flavor, its spaciousness, its soft color. "Looking down the long avenue of time," H. V. Morton observes, "one can discern a moment in the early Middle Ages when these towns vied with each other in the size and beauty of their cathedrals, the height of their towers, the dignity of their town halls, and, though they used the same formula, each city created something different. Such conformity, yet such lovely variety, in cities separated rarely by more than thirty miles, is as though a number of musicians had all composed variations on the same theme."[2] This is a singularly apt metaphor if we recall that Antonio Stradivari lived there, as did the violin-making families Amati and Guarneri.

Looked upon and patronized as the manifestation of a miraculous presence, Frederick enjoyed the festivities in Cremona until August 20, when he headed for one friendly city (Verona) by way of another (Mantua). Then we lose track of him. We can be certain that he set out for Trento but winter, so far holding off but nonetheless in the making, convinced him that veering west and then north was the route to take, thereby allowing him also the benefit of avoiding the hostile territories of Otto's adherents, the dukes of Merano and Bavaria. It was by daring and luck that he negotiated his way through the bleakest mountain tracts imaginable in late summer rather than winter. Early in September he surfaced in Swabia, his land by rights of inheritance, at Chur, a romantically situated town on the Vorder Rhine, in clear sight of the snowcapped Alps and in the shadows of the towering Mittenburg and Pizokel. Having presented himself at the palace of Archbishop Arnold, one of the more powerful German spiritual princes, Frederick was made aware that the severity of his plight would be diminished from now on, mainly because the pope had finally come through with an admonition to Germany's churchmen to lend their support.

There are three Saint Luciuses to choose from when trying to decide which is the patron of the cathedral at Chur. Pope Lucius I, who died in

254 after reigning for only eight months, would seem to be the logical designate, though logic does not always have a great deal to do with these matters. There is another Saint Lucius who may not even have lived, a legendary English king of the second century, mentioned by the Venerable Bede in his *Ecclesiastical History*. He is the one most often nominated as patron, the reason for the choice being an interesting idea for a doctoral dissertation. There is yet another, a fourth-century bishop of Adrianople in Turkey who was caught up in the Arian controversy. One of these may have been the "Luz" interred in the monastery of that name and in Frederick's time peopled by Premonstratensians, an austere offshoot of the Augustinians founded thirty years earlier by Saint Norbert, archbishop of Magdeburg.

Though probably in use, the weighty, primitive Cathedral of Saint Lucius was in the process of construction when Frederick came to Chur, its setting demanding a strenuous climb up steep streets and through the Marsöltor Gate. Colorfully inlaid ribs arch the main entrance, which lets into a three-aisled, dark, Romanesque interior, with what little light there is coming mainly though high windows on the south side. The forbidding atmosphere is in harmony with an almost surreal misalignment of the nave and chancel. (Was this done on purpose?) The crypt is a remarkable semicircular, barrel-vaulted passage beneath the apse dating from Carolingian times. Surely Frederick attended Mass in the cathedral, if for no other reason than he was the guest of Archbishop Arnold. He was depending on the Archbishop as an escort in the land that he was there to claim. Any act that smacked of subservience would be interpreted as meaning to show Frederick as a soldier of the faith, a warrior willing to take to the field in the Church's interest. And being young added shine to his image.

It is lovely to spend a quiet Sunday morning in Chur just as the town awakens: no traffic or confusion; church bells echoing against the surrounding hills and mountains; coffee or brandy (depending on how early it is) at sparsely patronized sidewalk cafes in piazzas animated by churchgoers and occasional bicyclists. And how diverting to hear Italian spoken in this peculiar, lightly German-sounding way!

Otto IV had not been idle. His popularity had experienced a rebound by the simple fact that he had come back to Germany. Eighty princes had attended him at his first court in Frankfurt in mid-March, not a few of whom had previously signed the proclamation declaring for Frederick. Then there were those who were undecided, who vacillated until Otto was there to whip them into line. Experiencing a resurgence of optimism, and using the Frankfurt gathering as his springboard, Otto soared into action, finally achieving a secure enough position by midsummer that it seemed even to the most antagonistic that he would soon surmount papal enmity and hold the empire in a tighter grip than ever.

Well might Otto exude confidence! It seemed that Frederick, if he stood a chance at all, would be faced with years of struggle to breach the wall that Otto was building against him. But, true to Otto's personality, with confidence came contempt. While he was besieging Weissensee, near Erfurt—a part of his revenge against Hermann of Thuringia for taking part in the rebellion against him—Otto received word that Frederick was on his way north to claim his patrimony, indeed that he had already reached Genoa. He greeted the message with scorn, but he was not as unperturbed as he made out. Groping for a means of avoiding a showdown with Frederick, it occurred to him that he had not yet married Beatrice Hohenstaufen, Philip of Swabia's daughter, to whom he had been betrothed since 1209. What better way to rally Swabian support than to marry her at once and sweep the duchy of Swabia into the Guelf camp? All very well until Beatrice died mysteriously three weeks after the wedding, shattering Otto's expectation of an heir, of the duchy as a part of his wife's dowry, and of his hopes of pulling any wavering Hohenstaufen partisans into his camp.

By the time of Otto's marriage, Frederick had reached Cremona. As word got around that he was approaching, both Swabia and Bavaria declared for him. Otto became alarmed. He abandoned his siege of Weissensee, which he should not have been wasting his time on anyway, and hastened south to head off Frederick. Otto worried over the growing popular conviction that his adversary was living under divine sponsorship, maybe under a particularly favorable star or with foreign allies. Otto may even have believed such himself. As for Frederick, with his increasing success to buoy him, he believed that his mission in life was being fulfilled, wherein he would do providential work and ultimately bring about a divinely conceived world order. And it did seem that miraculous guidance got him to and through Germany, first here, then there, always gathering adherents and every day becoming stronger. In Frederick's favor was the fact that Otto had been excommunicated and so was simply reaping his just reward, a veritable creed that did not hurt Frederick's case in the least. Still, conscious that time was of the essence, Frederick did not linger long at Chur. Following the Rhine River north under the guidance of Archbishop Arnold, Abbot Ulrich of Saint Gall, and Henry of Sax, he set out for the monastery of Saint Gall. Through informers he learned that Otto was moving south from Weissensee and would in all probability head for the city of Constance. But for the moment, in the transalpine custom, Frederick and his approximately three hundred men were welcomed at the Abbey of Saint Gall, a Benedictine settlement so large and well endowed that it resembled more a town than a monastery.

Aside from his Irish birth we know little of the early life of Saint Gallus, who came to Switzerland sometime in the seventh century as a companion to Saint Columbanus. Gallus was a man of somewhat the same reputation as Francis of Assisi for his power over and kinship with animals. It was said that squirrels nestled in the folds of his cowl, that he once tamed a bear and her cub and, on another occasion, a wolf. Gallus was an intelligent man and a clever linguist. Most of the stories about him are legendary, but one concerning him and a bear has become an appropriate modern symbol worth a retelling. While searching out a place for a hermitage in the desolate valley of the Steinbach River, Gallus tripped and fell. Believing that Providence had in this way indicated the spot, he erected a wooden cross to mark it. That night, while he was praying before his rough shrine, a bear wandered into the circle of light cast by his fire. Interrupting his prayer, Gallus directed the bear to put another log on the blaze, which act was accomplished. After being fed some bread and being warned to cause no more bother, the bear shuffled off to become the emblem of the modern city and the Swiss canton of Saint Gallen—a bear holding a log. But the legend goes on. Gallus and a guide set to work the next morning to construct his first primitive hermitage, the origin of the great Abbey of Saint Gall, which within a century of the saint's death had acquired a reputation for being a nucleus of learning, especially in literature, music, and manuscript illumination, indeed the only eastern Frankish scriptorium to create manuscripts important in the development of book illumination.

By the time Frederick made his stopover Saint Gall was an important medieval center of knowledge, not only in the sense of collecting learning through an extensive library, but also in disseminating original literature and music that would play important roles in the cultural development of following centuries. Notker Balbulus had already lived and died there, busying himself writing anecdotes of the life of Charlemagne and originating "sequences," a sacred poetry to be incorporated into the Mass as a chant of praise at the conclusion of the "Alleluia" and immediately preceding the gospel. At first free verse, the sequence metamorphosed into a metrical form and so had a telling influence on later secular poetry. Though impossible to prove definitively, some musicologists hold that one of loveliest of hymns in Latin sacred poetry—the "Golden Sequence," "*Veni, Sancte Spiritus*"—was written by Pope Innocent III himself. Others hold out for King Robert II of France, son of Hugh Capet, and still others for Stephen Langton, archbishop of Canterbury. Notker composed more church music, compiled a martyrology, and did numerous translations. In the tenth century Ekkehard I was a monk at Saint Gall, writing his "Waltharius," a swashbuckling romance of the Middle Ages.

It was not until about 820 that the colony of simple hermit cells begun two centuries before by Saint Gall was replaced by the well-planned, now nonexistent Benedictine monastery that in time developed into the enormous institution it was in the thirteenth century. Thought of as a nearly utopian architectural design to set the pace for Benedictine monastery planning for centuries, it took the form of a grid, a veritable town of separate buildings organized into a rectangular plan divided by narrow streets, all placed in such a way as to aid the efficient running of the establishment. As was proper in a monastery, the church and cloister were pinpointed as the center of activity. Those buildings appropriate to daily living were clustered around the monks' cloister, which was located along the south side of the great abbey church, thereby taking advantage of the southern sun, valuable in a land where any warmth was appreciated. It is curious that in a monastery as famous for manuscript production as Saint Gall the scriptorium was located on the north side of the chancel, basking in a perpetually chilly shadow that denied the prerequisite warm hands for the painfully delicate work. Near the cloister were located the refectory and kitchen, the cellar for storage, the calefactory—the only room artificially heated and so used as a social room—with a dormitory upstairs. The cloister arcades provided shelter for intercourse between many of the most-used buildings.

Off the eastern apse of the church were the master's room, the infirmary, the novices' house, a refectory for the novices, along with their dormitory and school. Also to the east and south were gardens, orchards, a cemetery, and an herb garden. Various buildings devoted to hospitality were in evidence: special accommodations for paupers and poor travelers, and more elaborate quarters for hobnobbing with emperors and kings, archbishops and well-heeled nobles and their elaborate entourages. Add to these the working buildings: stables, a factory for artisans, kilns, mills, threshing floors, barns, sheepfolds, goat sheds, a buttery, a brew house, laundry, bake house, baths, accommodations for servants and lay workers, hen and duck houses, gardeners' and poultry keepers' rooms, and equipment storage sheds. These functional buildings were dispersed throughout the community to guarantee minimum interference with one another. The important visitor and his pompous and ritualistic activities—such as can be envisioned even in the case of pfennig-pinching Frederick—were accommodated in the northwest sector, not allowed to interrupt the study, worship, and manual labor of the 110 monks within the cloister and the 160 workers doing their tasks throughout the community and in the fields. The complex was fully self-sufficient. The monks came to the monastery to stay, consciously desiring to shut out the evil world with its intrigue, its unending violence, its plagues and hopeless poverty. In about 954 the entire community was walled against marauders. And so originated the city of Saint Gallen. Allowing for modifications to accommodate individual sites, conditions, and preferences, most Benedictine monasteries followed these basic ideas. Saint Gall, however, was one of the largest; some idea of the size can be gained by realizing that the abbey church contained seventeen altars.

Alas, the mostly wooden monastery familiar to Frederick is gone now. But we are fortunate to have at Saint Gall a ninth-century parchment plan of the building layout that he could have known, an architectural manifestation of the time of Charlemagne that stands as an early example of Western community planning. There is also a reasonably authentic model of the ninth-century abbey in the local Historisches Museum. The old abbey church has been supplanted by an ornate rococo building of the eighteenth century, the inside all angels and arabesques, gilded plaster rays of light, puffy plaster clouds, and flowers arrested in perpetual eighteenth-century bloom, undulating curves and surfaces, marble inlays, and a gaudy, soaring rotunda, the work of many German architects, painters, and sculptors. To the viewer who finds rococo excessive—and the author confesses to this persuasion—Saint Gall is a bit more bearable than some, but only a bit. Seeing the overdone interior one does get the feeling, on occasion, of having swallowed a fur. And yet the curlicues and mighty bulk of the edifice can do wonderful things to the intricate and baroque ornament of a Bach cantata, say the 140th—"Awake! cries to us the voice"—with its measured cadences and elaborate musical decorations. For the viewer interested in a more intimate art, the Stiftsbibliotek, a remarkable library constructed of inlaid and carved wood, houses a superlative collection of Irish, Carolingian, and Romanesque manuscripts, ivory book covers, and assorted medieval art, all of which must be viewed while skating over precious, shining wood floors in special shoe covers that polish as well as preserve.

With Otto bearing down from the north, this was hardly the time for Frederick to tarry at Saint Gall. The city of Constance (Konstanz), situated in a shimmer of light on the south shore of the lake of the same name where it narrows back into the Rhine, was singled out as Frederick's gateway to the future. But he had to get there before Otto, who was known to be already at Überlingen, on the opposite shore of the lake. Frederick raced for Constance and, with his luck still holding, beat the emperor by a scant three hours. At the city gate Frederick's way was barred by order of the archbishop, who was indecisively trying to balance his loyalties to pope and to emperor. Standing like Lazarus at the home of the rich man, with winter approaching, the Alps rising menacingly behind him, and the prospect of his enemy looming in his immediate future, Frederick must have thought that his power bid had reached dead end. With Otto's advance party already within the city preparing a sumptuous feast for their excommunicated master, Frederick's predicament was daunting. Not for the first or for the last time his loyal adherent, papal nuncio Berard of Castacca stepped forward, saving the day, to remind the archbishop that Otto was living under the papal ban and that, if the vacillating man wished to be counted as a loyal churchman, he had best obey Innocent's bidding and side with Frederick. The gates were thrown open forthwith, and Frederick's party entered a city already lavishly decked out for Otto's anticipated triumphal arrival. Guards were posted and the great gates were barred. That evening Frederick and his men dined on a repast prepared for his understandably frustrated enemy. The chroniclers do not record Otto's understandable, if profitless, expletives.

One of the delights of exploring history is the opportunity to imagine what individuals might have said to one another. What kind of dreams did they have? Were they dapper dressers, or just plain slobs? How many of them were insomniacs; and if one or another was, what kind of night thoughts did he endure? One of the more pleasant fantasies is imagining what someone (in this case an emperor-to-be) ate.

It is entertaining to imagine Frederick and his troop of supporters and well-wishers enjoying a celebration party originally planned for Otto IV. How would parsley soup be for a starter? "Take parsley and fry it in butter," advises a medieval cookbook, "then pour boiling water on to it and boil it and add salt and serve your sops."[3] One especially tantalizing dish could have been fowl and veal cooked in water and wine with bacon, and then sprinkled with coriander seeds, pomegranate seeds, and fried almonds. Medieval herbalists held that coriander seeds were "'good to do away with the fevers that come the third day' and when 'drunken with honey' will slay worms."[4] In light of an ancient Roman maxim that no two men can eat from the same bowl and remain enemies, it is amusing to imagine Frederick and his followers enjoying a comradely cheese fondue, a dish invented by the Alpine Swiss as a rich, filling, and hot use of their native Emmenthaler and Gruyère cheeses. Cheese as we know it did not exist in Frederick's day; but generic cheese did, being an ancient food, as is indicated in I and II Samuel, and Job himself threatens to complain to God: "Hast thou not poured me out like milk, and curdled me like cheese?" Would history have followed the same course had Frederick and Otto been able to dip chunks of crusty bread into a common fondue pot, each warning the other that he who loses the first piece buys the next drink? Would they have been able to resist conversation? And then friendship?

The three-hour jump that Frederick had on Otto marked the beginning of the end of the latter's dream of undisputed imperial power. By the same token, had Frederick been the late arrival he could have kissed his kingdom and empire goodbye. When Otto found the roads blocked and the bridge across the Rhine from Überlingen guarded, he took the only course of action that he could. He turned back, aware, perhaps, that bragging self-confidence, kinship with the English crown, high-handedness, and awesome physique were not enough to maintain his hold on the empire of Charlemagne.

Otto's first stop was at the town of Breisach on the east bank of the Rhine, a city with its own stormy history. In ancient days the site of a Roman camp guarding the Rhine against German barbarians, Breisach became an imperial holding, "the cushion and key" of the empire during the Middle Ages. Eighteenth-century devastations followed by those of World War II almost destroyed the city, sparing only two hefty medieval gates and the cathedral, situated somberly on its hill throne, from which it dominates miles of wide, sluggishly moving Rhine River. The Romanesque cathedral nave is made more solid and noble by contrast with the Gothic choir that was added about 1300, and the whole building is the richer for the wooden, astonishingly complex, superbly excessive high altarpiece (1523–1526) by Master H. L. (Hans Loi?).

Despite his haste, Otto must have had a difficult time getting to Breisach. The northern extremity of the Jura Mountains and the Black Forest, for all our impressions of Hänsel and Gretel and cuckoo clocks, are even today something to negotiate, what with sharp turns, steep grades, and some of the most breathtaking scenery to be found in Central Europe. In any event Otto did not last long in Breisach, as he was soon driven out by the citizens who refused to tolerate the general licentiousness of his troops. In contrast to Frederick's joyously accelerating triumph, Otto found himself more and more bereft of followers, frequently denied entry into cities, and increasingly hard-pressed for funds. Unwilling to back a lost cause, his penurious uncle, King John of England, found it ever more difficult to finance his quest for power. Besides, John had problems of his own with his restive barons moving steadily closer to a writing of the Magna Carta. And all the while King Philip of France smirked happily. The pope, of course, was jubilant.

Loathe to allow Otto one moment of peace, Frederick prepared to leave Constance, a city which, by virtue of the number of Late Gothic and Renaissance houses, fortifications, gates and towers, and the old market hall at the harbor, still maintains an aura of another age. We do not know the archbishop's reaction to the departure, but a good guess is that he heaved a sigh of relief, even though protocol demanded that he accompany Frederick at least for a while. As a prince of the Holy Roman Empire, the archbishop ruled the city and its surrounding territory like an autocrat, and his successors would continue to do so until the Reformation. His cathedral was built in the eleventh century on the ruins of an ancient Roman encampment, to him a fitting symbol of the Church's temporal power. The original Romanesque nave columns still stand, but the structure was largely rebuilt in the more frivolous Gothic style. The interesting crypt houses tombs of diocese patrons Saint Pelagius and Bishop-Saint Conrad, a man so cool it is said that while celebrating Mass, and out of respect for the Eucharist, he once swallowed down a spider that had dropped into the chalice, though all spiders were thought to be poisonous. Today Conrad maintains his cool detachment as, standing in stone by the River Rhine, he turns his back on it and on the Rheintorturm, a medieval gate that was a key structure in the city's defense system. Constance could not have been big enough for both the archbishop and the boisterous soldiers of the aspiring king-emperor, though the city was not unfamiliar with an imperial presence. In 1183 Frederick's grandfather had signed the Treaty of Constance there, it is said, in the Gasthaus zum Barbarossa, establishing a peace of sorts with the Lombards. A painted scene on a *Rathaus* wall commemorates the event, along with a representation of Frederick himself entering the city that year, crowned and with long hair and a beard, looking middle aged instead of his actual eighteen years and riding a rigidly posed, fiery steed. The quiet courtyard of the *Rathaus*, even on a rainy day, is a soothing antidote to the modern hubbub, a nook of silence in an enchanting city, and is the setting for a lovely sixteenth-century house.

Serving as a focal point of intrigue, Constance continued to play a dominant part in the conflicts and upheavals of the later centuries. In July 1415 a tumultuous Church council there condemned and burned John Huss, Bohemian reformer, spiritual leader, and preacher against clerical abuses. As he died in the waves of smoke and flames he was heard singing the Kyrie Eleison. In the following year Jerome of Prague, student at Oxford, Paris, Cologne, and Heidelberg, a friend of Huss and like him a condemner of clerical evils—especially the selling of indulgences—was executed there in like manner, giving impetus to the kind of thought that would be so monumentally manifest in the next century by Martin Luther.

It is pleasant to think that, while Frederick moved on to Basel, he might have stopped off at the island of Reichenau, which is only about four-and-a-half miles from Constance and now connected to the mainland by a poplar-lined causeway. In the tenth and eleventh centuries Reichenau Island was a center of learning, ivory carving, and a most outstanding, productive, and influential school of manuscript illumination that in the twelfth century went astray when at least one of the good monks indulged in a black market of forged documents. The first point of interest is Oberzell and its Church of Saint George housing a fresco cycle depicting the miracles of Christ. Against naively simple, flat, geometric backgrounds biblical characters gesture and pose, properly angular in the manner of the eleventh century, stiff, and dressed in clothes that are crisply lineal, more rhythmical than descriptive. It is astonishing that artists painting in the forced, geometric mode of their time could achieve such telling effects, even to the suggestion of fluttering bits of drapery. Magnificent in their storytelling clarity, the frescoes are the triumphs of Saint George's church. The *Miracle of the Curing of the Woman with the Issue of Blood* is especially moving in the almost balletic grace with which Jesus turns to the afflicted woman, inclining his head sympathetically toward her to say, "Daughter, be of good comfort; thy faith hath made thee whole." The frescoes were damaged by inept nineteenth-century restorations, but they are among the best of the few remaining Ottonian examples. When last visited by the author they were in the process of being expertly and meticulously restored to a better approximation of their original state.

Farther into the island of Reichenau one comes on the stout Klosterkirche at Mittelzell, Ottonian and superbly constructed in Romanesque red-and-white stone striping. The brawny heaviness of the west tower is relieved by sensitively spaced friezes of Lombard arches and circular and arched openings. While the wooden-beamed church

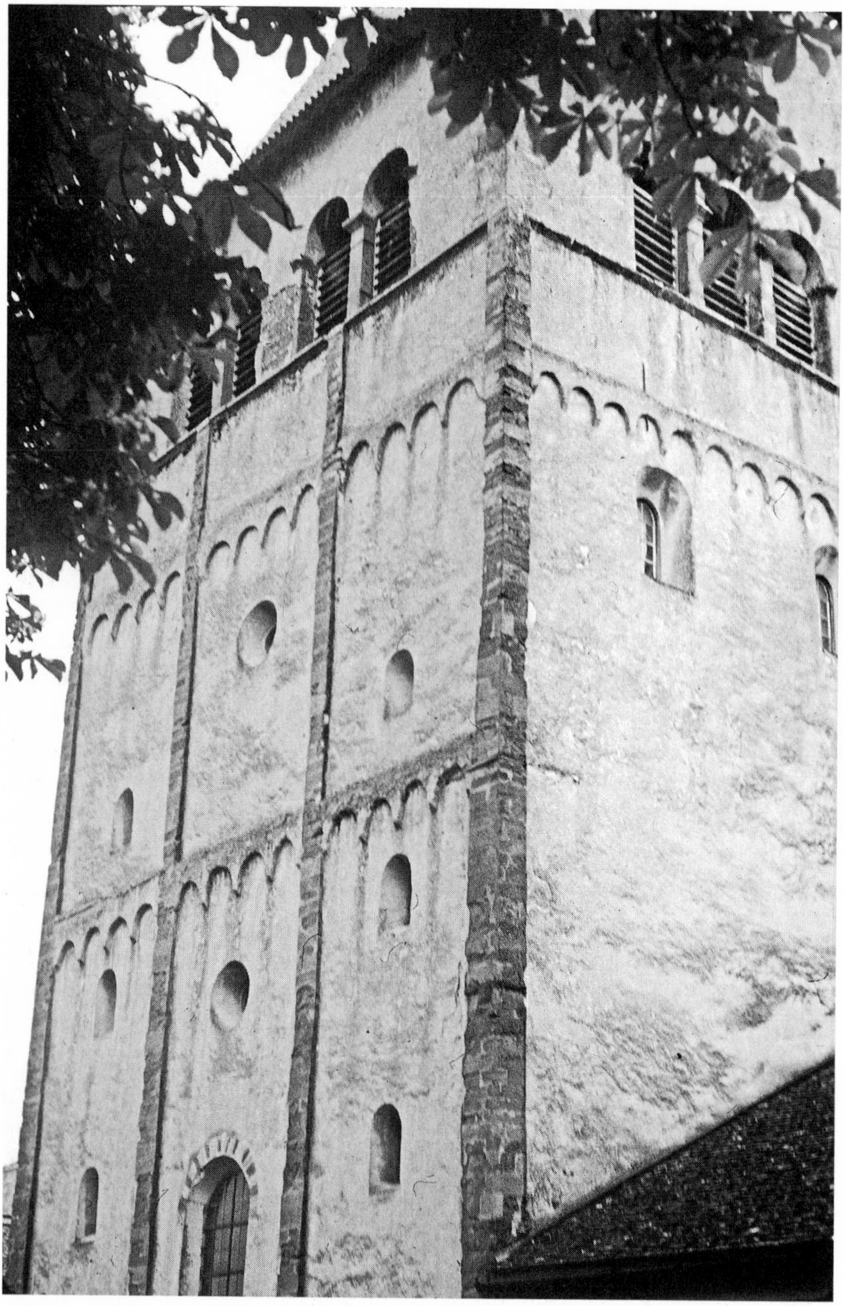

Klosterkirche, Mittelzell (Reichenau), Germany

interior has been expertly reconstructed to give an accurate idea of how it looked in Frederick's day when the institution stood as a renowned seat of learning, it is the tower that stands as exemplary eleventh-century architecture, a step up from the modest monastic structures of the ninth. It has about it an obvious muscularity, a "come on!" attitude that would give pause to any would-be reformer of Romanish doctrine or instigator of Satanic heresies.

Frederick's appearance in Germany, if not the equal of a second coming, continued to be greeted as a miraculous happening. News of the providentially assisted arrival of the youthful, good-looking, red-haired Hohenstaufen was spreading like fire throughout the land. Castles and villages were festooned with decorations and thrown open to him. Nobles vied with one another to court his favor. The princes and intellectuals of the Upper Rhine and beyond flocked to his banner: "Wherefore have I for many a day and many a dark night suffered heat and cold, that I might depart from town and country to follow a noble and worthy count,"[5] wrote Peirol, a troubadour from Auvergne, and hordes of common folk emulated his example. Peirol, who was born about 1160, may himself have been a petty knight, possibly holding a castle or small town in fief. Since he was French he owed no allegiance to Frederick, though, as he claims in one song, it is possible that he was present at Frederick's coronation.

In addition to the new magnates marching to his drum, the archbishop of Strasbourg provided Frederick with five hundred men to augment his still meager, but ever-growing armed forces. Frederick seemed agreeable to making expedient sweeping promises of monetary rewards for services payable, according to the IOUs, in the vague but foreseeable future when he would be better able to soothe palms. His prodigal generosity with money and lands, perhaps wise in terms of the moment, boded ill for the future when the princes became more independent and powerful, leading eventually to the dissolution of Germany into a conglomeration of semi-independent princedoms. But that was beyond Frederick's time. For now, his generosity served his purpose, and he was praised the length and breadth of the land for his liberality. Minnesingers rejoiced in singing that no characteristic so became a good king, comparing Frederick to Alexander the Great, another young conqueror noted for generosity. As for Frederick himself, he held that prestige could only gain by the lavish giving of gifts, whether to individuals or communities. In the face of Frederick's success, half-bought and half-sincere, Emperor Otto had no choice but to abandon the Upper Rhine to his younger adversary. But Frederick still had his work cut out for him: Otto needed to be eliminated; Guelf dissidents would need to be wooed into his camp, and the appalling dislocations of the years since his father's death would have to be rectified. By taking Constance first and then Basel, Frederick would climb merely the first step on the long ascent to the imperial throne. But it was there for all to see that the "boy of Apulia" had grown up. He was a conqueror now.

In every sense it was a triumphant royal retinue that marched into Basel, made up in part by the archbishops of Chur and Constance, counts Ulrich of the well-fortified stronghold city of Kyburg, Rudolph of Hapsburg, and the abbots of Saint Gall and Reichenau. But for the curving presence of the Rhine River, the Basel of our day bears little resemblance to that of Frederick's, even the bridges connecting Gross Basel on the south bank with Klein Basel on the north being built at later dates, though the first of them was constructed in his time (1225). Basel's big moment in history came when it hosted the last of three fifteenth-century reforming Church councils (Pisa and Constance being the other two hosts), whose unrealized aim was to destroy the absolute supremacy of the pope, but which succeeded only in causing a ten-year schism and an affirmation of the monarchical character of Church governance.

Were Frederick reincarnated today there is one building he would surely recognize in Basel—the fine cathedral, part of which was built on a Carolingian three-apse foundation. Dramatically high on its "Cathedral Hill," it dates from 1200, with parts of an older structure still visible in its west facade, most of which is a Gothic product of the thirteenth century and beyond. Of basic Romanesque plan, the church rises in a glory of red sandstone, rich in sculptural ornamentation, especially on the capitals in the crypt and in the galleries. It was more opulent in Frederick's day for the presence of a gold altar presented to the cathedral, presumably on its dedication by Emperor Henry II and his Empress Kunigunde, a masterpiece now, alas, in the Musée de Cluny in Paris. Magnificent it is, shimmering in its golden splendor, exhibiting on its front in five arches Saints Benedict and Michael, Gabriel and Raphael, all facing toward the center and doing homage to the slightly taller Christ. The five are augmented by rich patterns of arabesques and are further enhanced by the plain, sheet-gold backgrounds against which they stand. Precious jewels are used solely in the haloes of the figures, which further sets them off from their intricately ornamental surroundings. The altar stands as one of the supreme creations of eleventh-century Germanic art; in its day it was the fitting focal point of interest in Basel Cathedral.

Apse exterior, Cathedral, Basel, Switzerland

The cathedral transept terminates in the Saint Gallus portal, the most elaborate Romanesque doorway of figurative sculpture in all Switzerland. Arranged in high relief are apostles, all with outsize hands and solemn expressions, and stories from the life of Saint Lawrence by the Campionesi, Lombard sculptors so called after their place of origin (Campione di Lugano) who in the twelfth and thirteenth centuries extended their activities northward beyond the Alps. Their reliefs on the Saint Gallus portal seem almost early Christian in their clear Romanesque simplicity.

From the point of view of pure form, though, it is the exterior of the apse that is altogether arresting, with a dramatic ground-level blind arcade of round arches and a fan of buttresses pierced with bluntly pointed openings through which one can stroll while looking down on a panoramic curve of the Rhine. A kind of theatrical arrangement of solids and voids conjures thoughts and emotions of a distant past, of an age not unlike our own. The stone forms move upward out of the earth, as organic in concept as a modern building of glass and steel. The young couple moving arm-in-arm slowly through the arches without giving the weather-smoothed medieval stone a glance; the rotund little Swiss lady—she must be someone's aunt—laden with the day's shopping and having difficulty balancing the bottle of wine on the top of the heap; the tired old man sitting on a bench among the trees between the apse and the edge of the steep escarpment, hands resting on a cane almost as old as he, and staring solemnly at the magnificent pile of red sandstone; the quarrelsome children shouting and kicking a soccer ball over the gravel esplanade—none of them disturbs the age-old tranquility. They bring the twentieth century to the walls. But only to the walls. Not beyond. The Münster, the chapter house, the courtyard are still silent, silent as a shadow, making soft footfalls sound like thunderclaps, maintaining a heroic dignity in an age of poison-spitting internal-combustion engines, riverboat whistles, and overhead jets. Even Saint George on the western facade, acting the hero, the aggressive Christian rescuer, even Saint George maintains an anachronistic calm. The tree-planted cathedral square with its Gothic and baroque houses is a cocoon of protective quiet in a world where one no longer has rights to quiet.

Basel boasts a sixteenth-century *Rathaus*, all red and bright blue and gold, aptly located in a central marketplace animated by a steady stream of trams, open-air produce stalls, young peoples' demonstrations—and maybe still the charming sidewalk-cafe waitress who speaks unaccented English after having spent a mere three months in England! Several museums create worlds of culture of their own in Basel, especially the Kunstmuseum with its important showings of Gothic and Renaissance German and Swiss art, plus a fine collection of modern masters. And there are those incredible Holbeins—all three of them—particularly Hans "the Younger," who lived in Basel for about fifteen years and had as one of his first patrons the great humanist Erasmus of Rotterdam, who also resided there and posed for a portrait shown in the Kunstmuseum.

On leaving Basel, Frederick marched his impressively enlarged court down the Rhine to Hagenau in Alsace, a lovely town, now mostly modern, with flower-planted squares and a church with the oldest bells in France—but, alas, nothing of Frederick remaining. This was Hohenstaufen country. Here more than any place outside of Sicily, Frederick discovered his roots. At every step along the Rhine, he found evidence of the castle-building propensities of his forebears. Son of Sicily that he was, Frederick never liked living north of the Alps. But if he had to be there, then Hagenau castle, built by Frederick Barbarossa on the site of a hunting lodge enjoyed by the dukes of Swabia, was his favorite. It touched a nerve in him, for years later he would speak of Alsace, and Hagenau in particular, as places "most dear to my heart."

From Frederick's point of view, Hagenau offered two great advantages: extensive forests for hunting, and one of the finest libraries in the realm. The palace, we are told, was enormous, with elaborate rooms of state and floors of red marble. But it went beyond that. Besides serving as an imperial residence, it was also a seat of power, for Barbarossa had incorporated into its design a chapel in which were stored the elaborately jeweled imperial crown, scepter, orb, and the sword of Charlemagne. It would be some time before Frederick would see these valuable symbols of imperial dignity since Otto—no fool—had taken them on the road in a practical application of the northern European equivalent of "a bird in the hand is worth two in the bush." Divested of its crown jewels, the chapel served as a reminder to the determined king-elect of the battles he had yet to fight and of the determined stubbornness of his adversary.

Unable to rally his forces to stop Frederick's progress, Otto finally came to rest at Cologne, where he was always welcome because of his English connections and that city's commercial contacts with the island kingdom. While collecting himself, Otto summoned his magnates to meet him at Aachen, Charlemagne's city, where he intended to block the formal enthronement of Frederick, as well as halt his further infiltration into the empire. On both counts he would be disappointed and made to face the realization that the day was approaching when France and England would be dragged into the struggle, a measure of the dreadful state of things in the empire.

Neither of the German factions had the wherewithal to fight an all-out war. Outsiders were needed to define the situation. A favorable point for Frederick lay in the fact that, though he was gaining followers but had not yet had time to muster a sizeable fighting force, Otto was fast losing his. Both sides needed cash persuaders to coax the German princes into declaring for one or the other. King John of England had overcome his natural parsimoniousness and was presently pouring funds into his nephew Otto's coffers. John and his realm were already under papal interdict, and just this year he had been "deposed" by the pope for his recalcitrance in accepting the already consecrated Stephen Langton as new archbishop of Canterbury. That Pope Innocent III was on the side of the Hohenstaufen, as was Philip Augustus, a handsome, well-built man who liked his wine and women and who was eager to cut down anyone with English royal family connections, were facts enough to loosen John's purse strings. To John, always at loggerheads with his barons and suspecting that under papal prodding King Philip was hatching ambitious plans to invade his island, any friend—especially a relation on the German throne—was worth every pence needed to keep him there. Conversely, to Philip Augustus, who in truth entertained no great affection for Frederick, a Hohenstaufen king-emperor was far and away better than a nephew of the English crown. A meeting was arranged between Philip and Frederick near Vaucouleurs on the Meuse River, a land to be rich in memories of Joan of Arc, who in two hundred years would be born in nearby Domremy. Tales, true or false, are told of the hazards to which Frederick was exposed during his journey to meet Philip Augustus, the most provocative being a bedroom assassination plot to be paid for by Otto. The plot was discovered, and an ill-fated servant was substituted in the bed of the king-elect.

The meeting came off well for both Frederick and Philip. Among the agreements Frederick pledged that only with Philip's blessings would he make peace with either King John or Otto—or even with Otto's supporters. In return Philip, who could be generous when he tried, promised an enormous endowment, which was promptly dissipated in the fulfillment of Frederick's pledges to his German loyalists. Myriad voices joined to chorus the wisdom of Frederick's generosity and, both implicitly and explicitly, the stupidity of his avaricious rival. So it was that Frederick, thanks to the self-interested efforts of Pope Innocent III, to the wealth of King Philip of France, and to his own generosity and determination, became master of southern Germany and was being hailed as hereditary sovereign. Suggestive tales that he was the bastard son of a butcher of Jesi, or even of a papal official, did nothing to dim his glory. Everyone loves a giver. Especially a giver on the rise.

On December 5, in Frankfurt am Main, amid a horde of celebrants including French envoys, Frederick was confirmed in his office as king of the Germans. He was crowned four days later at Mainz, though the ceremonial luster was tarnished a trifle in that the ritual did not take place at Aachen as was traditional, and that the regalia was a tacky imitation since Otto was still in possession of the original articles. For all its lack of traditional legitimacy, the occasion was a joyous one, with Frederick, still a few weeks short of his eighteenth birthday, the hero of a success story that pales fiction. He was a miracle incarnate, the regent of God, under divine protection since the days of the Sicilian anarchy. In the common eye he was a young savior, a David fighting a Goliath, the public defender taking on forces beyond the rude imagination, an attractive, well-spoken, extremely intelligent leader who had risen from the murk of European intrigue to gain the backing of one of the most autocratic popes in history, as well as of the firmly established monarch of the nation next-door. To the troubadours, the minnesingers, and the goliards he was a romantic sensation.

Mainz's ponderous red sandstone cathedral rang with song and acclamation. The cavernous nave and eastern end were already about seventy-five years old, while the western end was in the process of being rebuilt. Two previous cathedrals on the same site had been destroyed by fire; the first, established by one Archbishop Willigis in 975, had burned down even before its consecration. Of the two chancels, the simpler one is the more interesting, with its traditionally curved apse acting as a raised extension of the nave. The choir screens of Frederick's day (there are some fragments in the diocesan museum) are among the best works of the "Naumburg master," who is generally thought of as the most accomplished of thirteenth-century German sculptors. From without the enormous architectural mass is a wondrous crescendo of arcades, arches, steeples, gables, and domes, some of which were added in the eighteenth century. Viewed from the Leichhofplatz, the complicated pattern of ridge roofs, the soaring lantern tower and apsidal curves and arcades seem somehow related to the baroquely decorated marzipan that one sees in the windows of the absolutely sinfully tempting confectioneries of the neighborhood.

It was a deal from the underside of the deck that pitted Frederick Hohenstaufen and Otto of Brunswick against one another for supremacy in the empire. In a sense both of them were foreigners to the land they claimed. True, Otto's family had originally been Swabian, as had Frederick's. But it must be remembered that Otto had spent a large part of his early life in the English court of Richard I, after his father's estrangement from Barbarossa. As much a stranger to the land and the people as Otto, Frederick was perceived as the more likable of the two, more appealing to the popular imagination, more able to cry "foul!" before the court of world opinion. He was rhapsodized as young, fair, good, brave, knowing, and generous. As soon as he was able, Frederick made good his promises to the cities that had been so loyal and without whose help he would never have made it across the Alps and to his triumphal progress through Bavaria, Swabia, and Alsace. In every instance he rewarded where he thought it due. There can be no other way of explaining why Diepold of Schweinspeunt was welcomed, or maybe just tolerated, as one of Frederick's loyalists. But not for long. Obviously preferring the rough-and-tumble of Italian chaos, Diepold deserted his new benefactor and returned to his old intrigues as duke of Spoleto—not the kind of thing that Frederick took calmly, especially since that office of duke had been bestowed by Otto.

Unlike his Hohenstaufen rival, Otto squandered whatever favor he might questionably have had with the princes and the people. He was severe, unsmiling, arrogant, selfish, and petty in his justice. He favored English foreigners and Saxons. He annoyed everyone with his vulgar lack of courtesy and his total misunderstanding of the word "royalty," not to mention "imperial." Hated in Italy, he was looked down upon even by his own. It has been pointed out that Otto simply was not intellectual enough to manage the rule of the empire. With the growing fund of knowledge that is one of the characteristics of the thirteenth century, clear-sightedness—definitely not one of Otto's strong points—was the order of the day. He was, indeed, the embodiment of the old adage that, however mighty their dukes, the Guelfs will be forever vassals, the Ghibellines forever emperors.

Chapter Five

Therefore when the Judge shall sit,
whatever lay hidden will appear;
nothing unavenged will remain.
***Dies Irae*, verse 6**

1212

Chiara Favarone came from a well-to-do Umbrian family. Her father, Favorino Scifi, a man of standing in Assisi, was the lord of several small castles and a townhouse on the cathedral Piazza San Rufino. The head of a family of high livers, he was robust and overbearing, as were all the males who made up Chiara's kin. Her mother, Ortolana, was of the same ilk, perhaps more delicate in manner but nonetheless headstrong. Unwilling to accept the fact of her barrenness—a shameful indication of providential disfavor—Ortolana had visited Monte Sant'Angelo on the Gargano peninsula to beg the intercession of Saint Michael, in addition to making the rounds of the miracle-working shrines of Rome. Then, probably in 1192, accompanied only by a young cousin, Pacifica di Guelfuccio (the name itself saying plenty about her family's political leanings), she had made the most hazardous pilgrimage of all—to Jerusalem, to visit there the places sacred to the memory of Jesus Christ, especially the Holy Sepulcher. As Ortolana had predicted when convincing her husband to fund the pilgrimage, she was soon blessed with child, though the father's noisy joy was somewhat mitigated by the fact that it turned out to be a girl rather than the promised son. But Signor Favarone was a doting parent, and he brought his daughter up to the finer and richer things of life, seeing to it that she was properly trained in the feminine arts and the reading and speaking of Latin. She grew into a refined, well-mannered young lady, beautiful, tall, with a kind of regal dignity, and crowned by glorious blond hair. Though youthful, she was mature in spirit, wise, and humble.

Chiara matured into adolescence hearing of the eccentricities of the kind and loving Francis Bernardone. For one thing she was extremely fond of her cousin, Rufino Offreduccio, one of Francis's first followers. Rufino was a shy young man with a tendency to stammer. He was not zealous enough for such an outspoken man as Francis, who put him through the ultimate humiliation for a stammerer. Francis once commanded Brother Rufino to strip to his underclothes and take himself to a church of Assisi to deliver a sermon. Much abashed, Rufino did as he was ordered, to the delight and mocking laughter of the congregation, while Francis himself came out on the short end of the experiment. Suffering pangs of guilt for having subjected a follower and a member of a noble family to such blushing mortification, he convinced himself that, in the name of God, he should suffer what he demanded of others. The churchgoers of Assisi were more delighted than ever when Francis, similarly unclad, approached his stammering, embarrassed brother and climbed into the pulpit to preach so movingly on the contempt of the world, on poverty and the sacraments, on the humiliation of Jesus as he hung dying and naked on the cross, that his audience was moved to tears. For all the ridiculousness of the tale, Brother Rufino was one of the most virtuous men to become a member of Francis's community and, Francis maintained, was canonized in heaven while he was still alive on earth. And this, he said, had been revealed to him in a vision.

Little did Francis suspect early this year that it was going to be through Brother Rufino that he would be brought into contact with the most unrelenting sweetness of his life: Chiara Favarone. By this time she was much aware of the gentle presence of "il poverello d'Assisi." How could she not be? He was the talk of the town, either mocked or adored, regarded with derision or with encompassing affection. One local theory held that Francis and his followers had gone insane. Another cherished their presence and revered their leader with a passion not spent on ordained priests and prelates. Living on the cathedral piazza—the Piazza del Duomo—as she did, Clare must have heard plenty of gossip about his "crazy" sermon, not to mention an ample number of derogative discussions in her father's house. Unlike the rest of her prominent family, she was not offended by the story, or by the other gossip concerning the self-effacing "Brothers Minor," so named by Francis that they would not presume to go beyond their lowly station as followers of Christ.

As the story was told, during the Lenten season of 1211, Chiara Favarone had heard a sermon by Francis, one of his addresses so intimately sincere that each listener came away feeling that had been spoken to alone. About seventeen years old at the time, Clare arranged a meeting through Rufino. Throughout the rest of the year, she and Francis had frequent long talks during which he counseled her, lecturing her on the idea so dear to the Middle Ages: the mystic union with Jesus Christ. They were, Francis and Clare, in every sense spiritual lovers, though Francis abhorred the thought of bodily contact between the sexes and even turned his eyes away when addressing a woman, advising his followers to do likewise. Their meetings were secrets shared only by Clare's sister, Caterina, and Pacifica Guelfuccio; better to keep the secret since pressure was building that Clare should start thinking in terms of a husband. Was she not, her family argued, the most desirable of the marriageable girls of Assisi? A good match could be arranged with no trouble. Her family had to be negated; and Clare always found herself talking around their arguments. Francis's influence on her was profound and would become total. He had revealed to her a new meaning of life, the joy of submission to a higher power. He had taught her the pleasures of sacred love, in every way superior to profane love. Steps for her liberation from the world had to be taken.

On the evening of Palm Sunday 1212, Clare let herself out through a little-used back door of her father's house, a door usually unlocked only in emergencies. She met Pacifica in the Via del Parlascio, and from there the two left Assisi through the Moiano Gate and descended the hill to the plain where, according to plan, a procession of the Brothers Minor met them with torches to light their way to the humble Porziuncola. Clare approached the tiny altar and, smiling faintly, one by one laid her jewels and her girdle of precious stones on the sacred table. Then she received from Francis's own hand the drab garb of the Friar Minor. Pacifica performed the same ritual. Kneeling at Francis's feet then, Clare loosed her hair, which fell to the floor under the scissors that Francis wielded. Pacifica followed the example. The two girls had put the frivolous life behind them; in those few moments they had become sisters of poverty.

Francis escorted the two new members of his order to the Benedictine convent commonly called Saint Paul of the Abbesses, where they remained for five days, until Good Friday. Accosting her there and seeing her rough coiffure, Clare's parents remonstrated so vehemently over the shame she had brought down on the family that it was decided the convent would exercise its right to refuse entry. Francis arranged to put the girls up at the convent of Sant'Angelo di Panzo on Mount Subasio where Clare's sister, Caterina, joined them. Now the future order of "Poor Clares" boasted three members. With the additional desertion the Favarone family indulged in paroxysms of fury, so out of control that they tried to storm the convent and carry the girls off by force. They did manage to lay hands on Caterina but were finally reduced to frustrated inaction by Clare's soothing defensive arguments. It was then that Francis conceived the idea of housing them in poverty at San Damiano, the reconstruction of which had started him on his way to sainthood. There followed a veritable procession of women to the door of San Damiano—including, eventually, Clare's own mother, Ortolana—until it seemed that some of the finest houses of Umbria were being emptied of their womenfolk. In a disregard of protocol, Francis—he was not a priest—appointed Clare the abbess of San Damiano. Under her supervision that tiny church, hardly more than a wayside oratory, was enlarged to house a sizeable number of nuns. Clare also organized there a small charity hospital. The sisters were called the Poor Ladies of San Damiano, then later the Second Order of Saint Francis. But so overwhelming was the influence of the gentle Clare that the sisters called themselves after her name: in Italy the "Clarisse," in France the "Clarisses," in England the "Poor Clares." As Thomas of Celano put it, she, "the most precious and the firmest stone of the whole structure, was the foundation."[1]

Sometime this year Francis met another woman, according to Thomas of Celano the only woman besides Clare and her little group whom he knew by name: Lady Jacopa dei Settesoli, called by Francis "Brother Jacopa" because in his eyes she was the Franciscan par excellence. Lady Jacopa may have heard him preaching in Rome, where she lived in the rundown Palazzo Septizonium. Descended from the Normans who had conquered Sicily, she had married into the Frangipani family, believed to be descendants of Flavius Anicius, who generously distributed bread to the starving Romans during the famine of 717 AD, earning the name Frangens Panem—breaking bread. (Flavius's ancestors added further glory to the name by claiming to trace their ancestry back to the Trojan hero, Aeneas, the founder of the Roman race.) Brother Jacopa had been recently widowed. So impressed was she by Francis that she probably would have joined the Poor Clares had she not property to manage and two young sons to raise. For the present she could be Francis's friend, attending to his housing when he was in Rome, making for him a special sweet pastry with almonds, which he seemed to dote on, probably made from a family recipe and to this day called frangipani by the Romans. (This is all open for debate, of course. Some writers on Francis claim that the sweet made by Jacopa was what the Romans call *mostaccioli.* On the other hand, Ada Boni, in

Italian Regional Cooking, claims this biscuit to be of Arab origin and to contain chocolate. As with most "facts" concerning Francis, the reader may decide for himself what is to be believed and disbelieved.) Occasionally Lady Jacopa supplied Francis with a new or repaired wardrobe. She would be a source of never-ending strength to him, even, by some miracle of unspoken, unwritten summons, rushing to comfort him in his final hours.

For all the unselfish love of Francis and Clare and their followers, one wonders at the group reaction to an event that must have been considered a disaster without parallel, even in their day when commonplace tragedy was remembered with legendary exaggeration: the children's crusade, a movement with stories so persistent that they defy disbelief. Legend may contradict fact, but neither relieves the pathos of the picture of thousands of children being stirred to such a pitch of religious heat that they undertook to win from the Muslims the far-off places sacred to the memory of Jesus. Coming from the small town of Cloyes in the Orléannais, a young boy by the name of Stephen approached French King Philip at Saint Denis where he was holding court. Displaying the fanatical confidence of a person with a mission, Stephen showed the king a letter, which he claimed was given to him by Christ and which was supposed to validate his intent to preach a crusade. King Philip offhandedly advised the lad to return home to his job of shepherding, which, as to be expected with young people, only made him more determined.

Stephen set out across France, gathering thousands of children—boys and girls, peasant and noble—whom he assured he would lead to Outremer, but only after the sea miraculously parted for them as it had for Moses. "Awed contemporaries spoke of thirty thousand, not one over twelve years of age. There were certainly several thousand."[2] When the sea refused to separate at Marseilles, a bit of the spirit went out of the movement. Some of the children returned home, though apparently the greater number stuck loyally with their young leader. Rumor had it that a couple of merchants with the astonishingly appropriates names of Hugh de Fer (of Iron) and William Porcus (Pig) put seven vessels at the children's disposal, on which they sailed triumphantly out of Marseilles harbor, not to be heard of again for eighteen years. A priest who claimed to have been a part of the misguided venture asserted that five boatloads of the children had been betrayed and sold into slavery in Africa and Egypt. The remaining two boats were lost off the coast of Sardinia with all hands. As for the merchants, their paths would cross Frederick's, and their sins would be punished—at least according to thirteenth-century propaganda.

Shrine of the Magi, Cologne, Germany

But this is not the end of the dreadful tale. A German youngster by the name of Nicholas, perhaps wanting to share Stephen's notoriety, began preaching a similar message at the Shrine of the Magi in a side chapel of Cologne Cathedral. He chose a wonderful stage for his exhortations. Medieval tradition held that the three kings of the Christmas story had died true Christians, having been baptized by Saint Thomas when he was proselytizing in India. Magian relics had been brought from Milan by Frederick Barbarossa in 1164, to be deposited in the cathedral at Cologne where they still reside in a gold, enameled, and jeweled shrine, one of the major works of itinerant goldsmith Nicholas of Verdun, "the last truly great enamel artist."[3] Altered over the years, the shrine is still magnificent, with fourteen figures on each of the long sides, seven above and seven below. The enamel pairs of columns between the figures and delineating the niches in which they sit are exquisite. The prophet figures in the lower register are powerful almost to the point of movement, their turned heads expressive as they gaze into the unknown. The reliquary is no longer in the Chapel of the Magi—or even in the same cathedral—as the old cathedral was destroyed by fire in 1248; it is now behind the high altar, viewable, but, alas, inaccessible.

The second children's expedition set out with young Nicholas leading a large contingent of young people across the Alps to Genoa, with only about a third of the volunteers getting there. When the sea was as adamant in its refusal to divide as it had been for the French group, Nicholas and his children moved on to Pisa, leaving a small number behind to become citizens of Genoa. Determined to forge on, Nicholas and his followers marched to Rome, where they held audience with Pope Innocent III, who was impressed by their innocence and piety but appalled by their lack of wisdom. He told them to return home to wait patiently for the day when they could fight the infidels as adults. Part of the group went on as far as Brindisi, where some of them managed to sail for the East. Of the larger number who tried to make it back to their homes not many succeeded. Nicholas himself probably never returned home; and his father was hanged for allegedly having encouraged his son as a self-publicizing gimmick.

Francis must have been profoundly moved by the horrid spectacle. Innocent III saw that the taking of the Holy Land was not a job for children. But pragmatic to the core, he could use the misguided adventure to advantage. The children put adults to shame, he wrote, by their willingness to risk their lives to conquer the land of the living Christ. Only eight years before Innocent had launched the crusade that had aborted in the shocking orgy at Constantinople, though he cannot justly be blamed for that debacle. Ever a believer in a new crusade—popes apparently have just as hard a time learning from experience as anyone else—and using the children as examples, his call to arms would become increasingly strident.

1213

The time was ripe for Francis Bernardone's most famous sermon. Nothing stands in more stunning contrast to the hideous children's crusade and its political, material-oriented age than the story of St. Francis's sermon to the birds. On a preaching mission Francis and two of his companions, Brother Angelo and Brother Masseo, approached the town of Bevagna, more specifically a nearby plain known today as the Pian dell'Arca, where a great number of birds had congregated. It was a sunny day, bathed in that light that Umbrians so eloquently speak of as *limpida,* the kind of day to make Francis even more aware than usual of his place in the God-created universal scheme. By nature feeling an affinity for all living things, sensing through a common Creator a kinship with animals, and birds, water, fire, stars—the universe—Francis determined to speak his message of divine love to the twittering birds. Leaving his brothers behind, he approached, whereupon the birds became silent, many of them gliding to the ground to gather attentively around him. When they were settled, he began one of his loveliest and best-loved sermons.

> Little birds: You owe much to your Creator, my sisters, and you should praise Him forever in every way you can. He has given you a change of feathers for every season and wings to fly with greatest freedom. He preserved your seed in Noah's ark so your generations would not perish from the earth and now supplies you with food to eat and fresh water to drink. He gives you air to breathe, mountains and valleys to enjoy and safety in high trees. You neither sow nor reap for God gives clothes to you and your children. In these ways he proves his love. Beware, little sisters, that you are never guilty of the sin of ingratitude and that you praise God always and forever.

Francis made the sign of the cross over the flock, dismissing them. Singing, they rose into the air in the form of a cross, and then flew off to the four cardinal points, indicating that the preaching of Francis and his brothers was to be carried throughout the world.

Unknown to Francis in Italy and Frederick in Germany, a quiet revolution was taking place. A new force was being born. Frederick, who knew no world but one of political power, was going to meet his match. The Hohenstaufen stand against religious hegemony loomed ever in the foreground of popular vision, but Franciscan spiritual strength still lurked in the minds of men. "The inference was clear—a renewal of Christ must necessarily beget the Anti-Christ."[4]

The first of Frederick's eight years in Germany was being spent as much to his advantage as to Otto's disadvantage. It was a learning from the past to control the future: due to the unkept promises of Otto concerning church lands, the elections of German prelates, and various other points of imperial-Church business that emperors had agonized over for generations, Frederick was prompted to acquiesce to the demands of Pope Innocent III and to issue the Golden Bull of Eger. The pope had had enough of the broken promises of emperors. The Bull of Eger, once signed by Frederick, became a binding law of the kingdom and eventually of the empire, recognizing therein the central Italian territorial demands of the papacy.

The city of the formulation and signing of the Bull of Eger was strategically important, lying on the western edges of Bohemia, a kingdom that had only the year before gained political privileges, while yet remaining a fief of the empire. It may have been pragmatically wise for Frederick to sign the Bull of Eger, but with it he surrendered what control he had over the elections of German prince-bishops with the promise that no toll centers or mints would be erected on territory belonging to those princes of the Church and, furthermore, that no new cities would be built on their lands. The ecclesiastics were given the rights of sovereigns, with the pope in Rome as their suzerain, not the German king. Thus the German Church was freed of imperial control, and the eventual breakup of the empire was guaranteed. But for the moment everything was rosy.

Unlike his rival, whose energetic labor bolstered his position, and in spite of receiving in January a generous grant from his uncle, King John of England, Otto was frittering his time and money away in futile harassments of various princely enemies, in vengeance for their desertions to the Ghibelline camp. His actions were, in the main, instinctive knee-jerk responses to political stimuli. Had he from the start organized his efforts and used his finances and human resources systematically, he could have stopped Frederick cold. And, as always, it was the peasants, excluded from these political shenanigans, who were the ultimate sufferers. They saw their cities razed, their houses torn down around them, their wives and daughters raped, their fields burned and crops devoured, their animals stolen by marauding armies. By October Frederick's troops were estimated to be sixty thousand, vastly more than those claimed by his enemy, and certainly enough for him to keep up the pressure. Yet in some ways Otto still had the advantage; he was the defender who could fall back to established points of defense, scorching the earth as he retreated. Otto had so devastated the countryside that Frederick's pursuing forces found foraging difficult. And it might seem to the observer that Otto had yet another possible advantage: a perceptible shift in Pope Innocent's loyalties vis-à-vis John Lackland.

King John had come to the belated realization that peace with the pope was a less unpleasant pill to swallow than the bitter accusations and vituperations that had been the norm for years. He knew that Innocent was actively pressuring Philip of France to sail against the "deposed" king of England on the theory that any humiliation of the English ruler would undercut his nephew in Germany, thus benefiting Frederick. Could John be sure that his barons would rise to his defense if Philip invaded? John was mean and petty, a vicious, irreligious man of absolutely no charm. "Even his sins had no boldness or splendour about them."[5] By the same token he was, like most of his ilk, intensely superstitious. When it came to his attention that a certain monk, Peter of Wakefield, was openly predicting that by Ascension Day John would no longer be king, the scales were tipped. With the undependable loyalty of his subjects of this world coupled with almost certain condemnation in the next hovering in his vision, John suddenly and unexpectedly made his total submission to the pope. In addition to paying a large tribute, he offered the most abject demonstration of all by handing over as papal fiefs his kingdoms of England and Ireland. To John, accustomed to the political entanglements of the day, that may have been a reasonable act. But surely he could not expect anyone, looking through the binoculars of history, to see it as anything but a shameless expediency. Archbishop Steven Langton, over whom much of the argument with Rome had started in the first place, was allowed to take his place in Canterbury, the interdict was lifted from the kingdom, John was absolved from his excommunication, and Philip, to his consternation, was commanded to stop his preparations for invading England, a scheme that had been heartily instigated by Innocent himself. The knowledge that John was now a vassal of the pope—who could have imagined it a few months before?—threw Philip into tantrums of fury. But Innocent himself was caught in a bind. Unable to ignore John's acts of submission and vassalage, he found himself in the uncomfortable position of indirectly aiding his enemy, Otto, to the disadvantage of his former ward, Frederick. In the smallness of royal pique, King Philip lashed out punitively at the count of Flanders, who had refused a part in the projected, but now cancelled, invasion of England. The upshot was that Philip's fleet was surprised by the English in the navigable channel called the Zwyn, the port of the now decayed city of Damme, which connected that city with Bruges, four-and-one-half miles to the southwest. The English, commanded by John's half brother, William Longsword, third earl of Salisbury, so damaged the French fleet that Philip was forced to destroy the remainder to prevent it from falling into enemy hands.

The machinations of the kings of England and France and the pope were of utmost importance to both Frederick and Otto, though the reverse did not necessarily hold true, the plights of the emperor and would-be emperor being merely asides to kingly conniving. Should

John, Philip, or Innocent fail in this game, it would be disastrous for one or the other of the German contenders. As things stood Otto already was the predictable loser. There was a steady stream of desertions from his ranks. While a confident Frederick enjoyed Christmas festivities at Speyer, Otto was being distracted by affairs that, in his predicament, should never have entered his range of vision. He was plotting with his English uncle a simultaneous attack on France, thinking to take advantage of Philip's weakness after the loss of his fleet. But uncle and nephew misread Philip's precariousness.

1214

In the spring of 1214, John landed at La Rochelle, while Otto invaded France from the northeast. Intending to come to the aid of his French mentor, Frederick mustered his troops; but his help was not called for. The French heir apparent, the future Louis VIII, won a smashing victory over John in the south at La-Roche-aux-Moins. At the same time Philip finished off Otto and his assorted Flemish allies in the memorable battle of Bouvines between Tournai and Lille, a rundown little town, when last seen by the author, in a lush green setting. Even its main Church of Saint Pierre, which gives Lille what passes for a skyline, displayed a number of broken windows. There are red poppies scattered through the surrounding green to liven up untidy French gardens, and any map shows nearby towns that ring out in memory of another war, greater in its tragedy of lost young lives—Cambrai, Douai, Armentières, Arras.

It was a steamy Sunday afternoon on July 27 when Philip decided the fates of three countries by winning what some consider to be the most meaningful battle of the Middle Ages. Philip may have had as many as twenty-five thousand men with him, of whom five hundred knights constituted one of the best fighting machines in the world. The French carried their oriflamme of Saint Denis overhead, crimson silk, with two or three points; the Germans bore a great dragon surmounted by a golden eagle on a kind of *carroccio*. When his rearguard was attacked, Philip coolly arranged his troops across the marshy plain of Bouvines with the sun at their backs. This would be the forty-nine-year-old Philip's great moment. His position at the center of his troops was marked by his banner, scarlet with gold fleur-de-lis. Confronting his troops on this fateful afternoon, Philip delivered an address worthy of Shakespeare, later remembered by William the Breton, who stood behind him:

> In God is all our hope, all our trust. King Otto and his army have been excommunicated by the Pope, for they are enemies and persecutors of Holy Church. The payroll for his soldiers comes from the tears of the poor, from the pillage of lands belonging to God and to the clergy. As for us, we are Christians, in peace and communion with Holy Church. Sinners though we are, we are in accord with the servants of God. . . . Thus we may count on divine mercy. The Lord will give us means of triumphing over our enemies, who are ours![6]

An interesting speech for a man who had just recently managed to wriggle out of an excommunication!

During the clashing melee Philip was unhorsed by the hooks and pikes of German foot soldiers. His armor was so well made that no opening could be found through which to stab him, and he was finally rescued, thanks to the combined efforts of a knight who shielded him, to his standard-bearer who signaled for help, and finally to Guillaume des Barres, one of his commanders, who helped him to remount. There followed a terrible slaughter of the German infantry. Determined as befit a man of his size and station, Otto was in the thick of difficulty. His horse had been seized and then stabbed in the eye, a blow intended for Otto. The mortally wounded animal reared, shied away from battle, and then collapsed under Otto, who was saved by one of his barons, who hoisted him aboard his own mount. But Otto had to fight off Guillaume des Barres who, pressing his steed against the emperor's, had grabbed him by the soft neck armor and was choking him. Guillaume was finally unhorsed, and in the confusion that followed Otto escaped. With that the Germans started a broad retreat. A number of Otto's loyal dukes and barons were captured, but Otto reached safety in Valenciennes.

Bouvines was Philip's last battle. Hereafter he left fighting to younger men. He enjoyed the certainty that his victorious country was free of fear of an English invasion for an indeterminate future. More important, he saw his nation moving inexorably toward increased central control, another step in the rising power of his monarchy to which history offers few parallels. As for John, who had set out with flamboyant fanfare and spectacle for his invasion of France, he returned to his island kingdom completely humbled. His barons saw him as more contemptible now than ever, his defeat giving them exactly the opportunity they needed to rise in revolt against his excesses. By June 15, 1215, they had him on the field at Runnymede where they wrung from him the great Magna Carta.

The French victory at Bouvines was a windfall for Frederick. Except for Cologne, Aachen, and the imperial palace at Düsseldorf, he was in possession of practically the entire Rhineland. It would not be long before he would own those few remaining Guelf strongholds. Otto was finished and, holed up in Cologne with a new bride, was living off the merchants of the city, who supported him only because Uncle John had granted them lucrative trading privileges as long as they did so. Encumbered by his wife's passionate predilection for gambling, he continued to fight on doggedly without the direct financial help of his uncle. But the time was approaching when the few German princes still loyal to his banner would realize the futility of fighting and spending for a cause without future, and he knew it. Already the duke of Brabant had submitted to Frederick's charisma, despite his dice-loving daughter's being current empress. Yet Frederick took the proper precaution against being hoodwinked. Since the duke was not known for his steadfastness (Otto had married his daughter only to assure his loyalty), Frederick wisely demanded his son as hostage-collateral against future shilly-shallying. In September he added the duke of Limburg and the counts of Jülich and Kleve to his widening circle. Add to that his taking the castle of Trifels from the Guelfs.

Eight miles west of Landau in the Bavarian Palatinate, high (1,600 feet) on the Sonnenberg overlooking the Queich River and the oak, beech, and fir forests of the Hardt Mountains, Berg Trifels must have been of special interest to Frederick. It had been one of his father's strongholds in the area and was the almost-out-of-reach fortress that had served as one of the prisons for Otto's uncle, Richard Lionheart, after he had been captured on his way home from crusade. Frowning down on charming little Anweiler, a town of modest industry, Trifels even in its ruins looks impenetrable when one makes the climb on foot and enters its precinct through the soaring, heavy-arched gate. It seems the perfect place to imprison an active, rambunctious hero such as Richard. (The lesson was not lost on Adolph Hitler, who planned, it is said, to imprison both Winston Churchill and Franklin D. Roosevelt in the same lockup—the ultimate irony of that devious mind.) Constructed of magnificent ashlar, it is typical Hohenstaufen military architecture, with its defense walls and ring of watchtowers. Berg Trifels would figure later in Frederick's stormy relations with his son Henry.

Despite the happy outcome of the battle of Bouvines as far as Frederick was concerned, Germany's internal disintegration was obvious to the world, especially to those two outside powers who had in a sense decided between them the next occupant of the imperial throne.

Though not even there to fight for his own future, Frederick received from Philip the battered symbolic golden eagle that Otto had carried into battle. Frederick did not burnish the sagging German reputation when, in December, while holding court at Metz, he recognized without argument the claims of Danish King Waldemar II to imperial lands north of the Elde and Elbe rivers (Schleswig-Holstein).

The Christmas court at Metz was impressive. What better place for a future emperor to celebrate Christmas, the anniversary of Charlemagne's crowning, than this ancient city at the juncture of the Mosel and Seille rivers? Caesar himself described Metz as one of the oldest and most important cities of Gaul. An important station on a network of military roads that included Toul, Langres, Lyons, Strasbourg, Verdun, Rheims, and Trier, it was fortified by the Romans, who built a supplying aqueduct, a few arches of which are still standing. There remain also the *tepidarium* of the Roman bath and some walls of a large amphitheater. Over the centuries Metz has been mauled and mutilated, passed back and forth among warring nations. Attila sacked the city in 451. In 1871 the French ceded it to Germany, and then after World War I it was re-ceded to France. And this is not to mention World War II.

Christianity came early to Metz—in the third century—and it was not long before it was a religious center and a bishopric. In the ninth century Holy Roman Emperor Lothair I, grandson of Charlemagne, made Metz the capital of his portion of the divided Carolingian empire. It was during the reigns of Lothair I and his father, Louis the Pious, that Metz developed into an active art center, mainly due to the encouragement of Bishop Drogo, another son of Charlemagne, but this one illegitimate.

A man of enormously high intellectual disciplines, Drogo patronized the arts, especially painting and ivory carving, raising the quality of the Metz artists to such standards as to carry into Frederick's day and beyond. This was especially true in the illustrators' use of letters adorned with significant ornamental figures as a basic part of the decorative element of manuscripts. Now in the Bibliothèque Nationale in Paris, the Drogo Sacramentary, the masterpiece of the Metz school made for Drogo sometime after 844, has no full-page illustrations, but only those marvelous historiated letters containing tiny figures important to the text. A truly intimate art form (a manuscript is intended to be held in the hand and viewed by one or two people at a time), manuscripts such as Drogo's are rewarding of themselves to anyone willing to give them the contemplative time they deserve. Text aside, each exquisite letter, so elaborately stated, so fascinatingly intricate, can become as absorbing as the most complicated and extensive fresco, mosaic, or sculptured frieze. As interesting as the decorated letters of Drogo's Sacramentary are the covers, both front and back, which exhibit openwork relief carvings in ivory—small, lifelike figures shown in animated detail and illustrating scenes from the life of Christ, as well as liturgical motifs.

Adopting Christianity so early, Metz would be expected to preserve remains of that nascent religion. The Church of Saint-Pierre-de-la-Citadelle has incorporated within its seventh-century walls courses of bricks that are datable to the fourth century, making it perhaps the oldest church in France, though it was not vaulted until the fifteenth century. There are other churches in Metz to indicate an active building boom between the eleventh and sixteenth centuries, though none of them stood in their present form at the time of Frederick's Christmas court. The Cathedral of Saint-Etienne itself was not begun until six years later and was worked on well into the next century, with certain parts of the work being carried on even to our own time. Up-to-date in the extreme, it boasts among other wonders some windows by Jacques Villon (died 1963), breathtaking floods of organized color depicting the Last Supper, the crucifixion, the marriage at Cana, and Moses striking the rock in Horeb. In addition there are several windows by Marc Chagall, telling in shimmering yellows and glowing blues, red, and greens the stories of Genesis, of Moses and David, the sacrifice of Abraham, and two events in the life of Jacob. The cathedral treasury houses a tenth-century embroidered cloak known as "Charlemagne's coat," an obvious misadjustment of historical chronology.

1215

The new year ushered in a period of personal triumph for Frederick. It started with his January move to Gelnhausen, built on an island in the Kinzig River by Frederick Barbarossa and finished by Henry VI. Barbarossa's case against Otto's father, Henry the Lion, was argued here, and it may have been in this castle that Barbarossa went down on his knees to his recalcitrant vassal. Even in its present state the castle is important because of the quality of its decoration, and it stands as the most important example of Swabian architecture in Germany. There are some specimens of interlocking arches, as well as a surrounding wall, a handsome two-nave porch, some well-preserved towers, a columned hall, and parts of the residential quarters, all of them indicating the efficient construction methods of twelfth- and thirteenth-century Germany. Furthermore, keeping abreast of similar tendencies in

Norman England, Germany was experiencing a growing concern for creature comfort (speaking, of course, of royal and imperial comfort) and appearances. There was a new awareness of luxury and the enjoyment of day-to-day living, of warmth and light and privacy. We find an increased use of decoration to please, of larger windows to allow fresh air and sunshine to penetrate dank interiors, of fireplaces with innovative flues. The Europeans had not yet reached the point long ago accomplished by the Byzantines—the use of rugs and sumptuous wall hangings on a scale so luxurious as to appear effeminate, if not sybaritic, to more rugged western visitors. Certainly Frederick Barbarossa had an eye out for comfort, as is reflected in his Gelnhausen palace, a characteristic that rubbed off on his grandson.

The four-towered Marienkirche (the tower over the transept is unaccountably crooked) was undergoing a rebuilding program when Frederick was there. Sculptors trained in France were not above introducing on a capital a rendition of a witch riding a broom, one of the oldest to be found. A magnificent twelfth-century stone rood loft stands before the choir, graphic in its agonizing depictions of the Last Judgment. The dead arise, adore the Judge, are encircled by stout chains, and are then dragged off screaming to a fiend-infested hell, complete with horned Satan and fire-breathing monsters—enough to frighten any good Christian of the Middle Ages into toeing the line!

Frederick's meandering through Germany this year was leading him inexorably to Aachen, the seat of German imperial power, still in the hands of the Guelfs. One of the most astonishing things to the person who pursues the study of medieval history (and ancient history, too, for that matter) is the ability of those people to get around—hundreds, thousands of miles seeming to be all in a day's work. The idea is breathtaking when one remembers that most of these vagabonding troops were moving on foot, with only the nobles and knights on horseback. Yet we read that between January of this year, when Frederick was in Naumburg, and July, when he was at the gates of Aachen, he had visited Altenburg in Thuringia, Augsburg in Swabia, and then gone to Speyer in Franconia. He spent Easter at his favorite Hagenau in Upper Lorraine, and later moved on to Andernach in the duchy of Lower Lorraine (now Alsace). Originally an ancient Roman encampment on the Rhine, later a walled city, Andernach is now a thriving center with a fine twelfth-century Romanesque church. It was while relaxing there that Frederick summoned a meeting of his princes for May 1, to discuss a new Rhine campaign with the objective of taking the cities of Aachen and Cologne. He hardly needed to have bothered.

In July, just when the imperial forces were about to march, Frederick received word that the Aachenians were tired of riding in the trail of Otto's fast-extinguishing comet. Their city gates were open to him if he cared to march through them. Perhaps the citizens were edgy over rumors that Frederick was breaking bivouac and would be heading their way. Whatever their reasons, they had driven out their governor and now wanted to come to terms with Frederick as their rightful lord. In the mind's eye it is pleasant to see Frederick parading his troops through the clumsily hulking gate, the Marschiertor, and down the gentle incline to the town center and Charlemagne's church. He entered the city as a conqueror, albeit without swinging a sword, but with pomp befitting a Roman emperor. Accompanied by his princes and members of the ranking families of Germany, by papal legates—even one from the king of France—to the cheers of the citizens and the ringing of church bells, king-elect Frederick II laid claim to the city of Aachen. It was a triumphal procession strutting through the decorated streets jammed with citizens cheering their new deliverer.

Frederick would approve of Aachen as it is now, with its life-size bronze statues scattered about the sidewalks, doing things that people do—reading books, waiting for buses, bouncing balls, gathering around a fountain—and especially the intriguing *Puppenbrunnen,* a fountain composed of moveable marionette-like figures that can be turned and twisted any which way by children and the young at heart. Charlemagne, who may have been born there, had established Aachen as his capital, building his grand, gray-stone palace, with its enormous state hall and columns of porphyry and green marble reminiscent of Ravenna, its frescoes depicting scenes of battle, all gone now and replaced by a fourteenth-century town hall. One of Charlemagne's scholars, the poet Modoin, indicated clearly that his master saw Aachen as being transformed into a second home, a "golden city."

The day after Frederick's triumphal entry was fraught with significance. The heavy, delicately decorated bronze doors—dating from the ninth century and each, despite its size, cast in a single piece but for the two attached lions' heads, which at one time held giant rings—swung ponderously open to receive Frederick into Charlemagne's palatine church. Frederick knew that the first Holy Roman emperor had established this mosaic-shimmering court chapel, which had been designed by Odo of Metz. It is our finest Carolingian structure, indeed, the first truly monumental building in German art history. It is generally conceded that the cathedral at Aachen owes much to San Vitale in Ravenna, though the relationship is spiritual rather than formal. In Charlemagne's day Ravenna was the glamour capital of Europe, the last capital of the western Roman emperors. And because San Vitale was considered the imperial palace chapel, Charlemagne wanted to confirm his authority by symbol and chose it as a model for his chapel at Aachen. That is also why he chose Aachen as his last resting place. But Charlemagne's church was not imposing in scale, hardly larger than a chapel. Visitors, even in his time, began speaking of the capital as Aix, the chapel.

Almost everything that Frederick's eyes lit upon suggested to him his noble heritage: the heavy, inelegantly conceived slab-marble throne of Charlemagne, held together with crude, unconcealed iron clamps, the seat hewn too small to accommodate Charlemagne's oversize hips; the golden altar, which had been a gift of Otto III (died 1001) or Henry II (died 1024); the gold cross of Lothair with its inset cameo of Augustus; the massive pulpit of Henry II, made of gold-plated copper and embedded with precious and semi-precious stones, with reliefs and six ivory sculptures; and, more meaningful than anything else to Frederick, the huge gilded-copper chandelier hung there by his grandfather, Barbarossa, ringed by the arched upper gallery, and domed by

Cathedral chandelier, Aachen, Germany

shimmering mosaics of Christ in a mandorla surrounded by symbols of his evangelists and John's "four and twenty elders" holding their crowns of gold. Designed by one Master Wibert, the forty-eight-candled chandelier is in the form of a circular city with protecting towers. It is the city of light, the inscription tells us, the heavenly Jerusalem. The vast ring of candles and copper imaging Revelation 21:24 of Saint John deserved study by Frederick: "And the nations of them which are saved shall walk in the light of it: and the kings of the earth do bring their glory and honor into it. And the gates of it shall not be shut at all by day: for there shall be no night there."

Few royal coronations of the thirty that have been held in Aachen Cathedral have been so charged with emotion as the colorful pageant honoring the young, golden-haired "boy from Apulia." How few years had passed since he had been the child haunted and hunted in the streets of Palermo! How many of his fawning magnates now gathered in Charles the Great's imperial chapel understood, or even remembered, the pathos of the royal urchin wandering the teeming alleys and byways of the noisy Sicilian capital, more familiar with the crush of the common folk, the Arabic-sounding Italian of the hawkers, and the self-interested, but nonetheless kind, charity of the natives who fed the boy because he was out of Queen-Empress Constance? What a short time it had been, and how many things had happened, since power-hungry Markward of Anweiler had broken into Frederick's hiding place in the palace. Did anyone present at the coronation allow his thoughts to envelop once again the letter that had made the rounds of the European courts in his name, claiming he was no king and was forced to beg favors of others, rather than granting them himself. Now, at the height of his glory, did Frederick himself recall that it was barely four years ago that, worried for his safety and that of his wife and new child, he had prepared a ship to flee his Sicily should the dreaded Otto cross the narrow straits from Italy?

Here at Aachen, in the seat of the empire, a center of Western politics, learning, and culture and the symbolic nucleus of a sprawling power structure—with barely an offensive blow struck, almost as if events, once moving, continued on their own—here was the anointed king of Germany, dazzling in the light of Barbarossa's chandelier, enthroned, crowned-and-sceptered, surrounded by a centuries-old cathedral and mystic pageantry. Even special gloves and slippers were made to adorn the royal person on his great day and which today may be the ones exhibited in the Kunsthistorische Museum in Vienna. In his youthful energy he was ready, and able by tradition, to lay formal claim on the empire itself. This would take some doing yet. But it is true that in his later days Frederick calculated his imperium as starting with his royal coronation at Aachen.

If the onlookers thought they had seen the ultimate in the drama of Frederick's rise and takeover of power, they were in for further surprise. Immediately after hearing a rousing sermon preached in the name of Innocent III, wherein an appeal was voiced to the nobles to mount a new crusade against the Muslims in the Holy Land, Frederick made a typical flamboyant gesture, one that would haunt him for the rest of his days. It is difficult to see what prompted Frederick to his dramatic demonstration. There was nothing new in the pope's message; he had been fanning the flames of crusade for years now. Enthusiastic response had been less than encouraging in the aftermath of the fiasco of the children's crusade. Frederick might have been overcome by the magnificence of his own coronation. Or, undergoing the historic ritual and enthroned in the seat of the empire, he might have been awed by romantic thought of the great Charles (called "the destroyer of heathens," even though he had never marched against the East; indeed, he enjoyed decent relations with the Muslims) or of his paternal grandfather, Barbarossa, who died on crusade. He may even have seen his action in a divine light, a quid pro quo for myriad blessings heaped on his young shoulders. The question is further muddled by the facts that he had lived the large part of his life in half-Muslim Sicily, that he had always been friendly and sympathetic with the Muslims, never sharing Europe's negative sentiments for the infidel. Certainly Innocent III had not as yet pressured him directly to go to the East, though he envisioned such a plan for the future. But first the pope wanted to see the Church secure and in a dominant position vis-à-vis the empire, a condition he was convinced Frederick would bring to fruition.

Whatever the cause, the story goes that Frederick suddenly leaped to his feet in the church at Aachen, declaring that he would undertake a crusade to free the Holy Land and its sacred shrines from the heathen grasp. Putting the best face on it, many of his princes followed suit. Thus Frederick inadvertently opened a Pandora's box of troubles: endless hounding by a string of popes; perpetual expenditures of money, the sums which, at present, he could not imagine; concomitant recruiting and disbanding of armies; the assembling of fleets; excommunications. Frederick's oath was a heroic gesture in a lifetime of heroic gestures, and one of several that he lived to regret. He may have gotten the message of future trouble when the pope sedulously ignored his vow.

In Innocent's eyes Frederick's drama was a brilliant move to place himself at the head of militant Christendom. However, Innocent had ideas of his own. He envisioned a fifth crusade as a manifestation of Church militancy, accomplished at the behest, guidance, and approval of the pope and the Curia. Even though Frederick made the initial move to accomplish what the pope had long been exhorting, it did not fit in with the papal concept of protocol. Frederick was, in fact, stealing Innocent's thunder, after he had gone so far as to toy with ideas of leading the people's army into Outremer himself. A man as headstrong and as self-aggrandizing as Innocent found it next to impossible to take a back seat to anyone, much less a twenty-year-old whom he had protected, in his own eyes at least, through his difficult childhood years and then propelled to his present position. For a time all this could wait while Innocent prepared to assemble the greatest of Church conclaves—the Fourth Lateran Council.

There was yet another theatrical performance to stage before Frederick considered his several days of celebration complete. After Mass on July 27, he witnessed the placing of the remains of Charlemagne in a handsome new reliquary of silver, gold, and enamel, still to be seen on the high altar of the cathedral of Aachen. Frederick's own effigy, along with those of his predecessors and scenes from the life of the king it honors, are a part of the embossed images, the whole so rich in three-dimensional ornamentation as to be almost baroque in effect. There is an especially animated relief of the razing of the walls of Pamplona in Navarre, destruction ordained by Charlemagne in 778 as part of his retreat from Spain and the terrible defeat of his rearguard at Roncesvalles, as we read in the *Chanson de Roland*. While Charlemagne had been venerated by his successors through history, none of them paid him the tribute that Frederick did when he doffed his kingly apparel to assist the workmen in fastening down the lid of the reliquary. Frederick's view of himself as the latest of the long line of emperors was unmistakably romantic, and his absorption in the history of the empire is evident, as is his lofty intention to restore the might, magnificence, and justice of the ancient Roman Empire. If his grandfather could have Charlemagne canonized (he is not listed on the official roster of saints because the ritual was not performed by a legitimate pope), then Frederick could make a gesture—albeit an almost adolescent gesture—of closeness to his forebear. And the gesture was not lost on his attendant followers. But now it was time to move on.

The capitulation of Aachen and the subsequent coronation opened the floodgates of submission. There was no reason to resist the Hohenstaufen further. Frederick's mediators persuaded even Cologne to join the stampede. The citizens of that largest city in Germany offered Otto and his gambling wife enough money to see them to Brunswick, Otto's family seat. Anything to be rid of them! Without raising a hand Frederick entered this Guelf stronghold by one gate, while Otto and his wife, disguised as pilgrims, left by another.

Originally a town of the Ubii, Cologne had been established as Colonia in the year 50 by the Roman emperor Claudius to satisfy a whim of his murderous wife, Agrippina, who had been born there, and whose monumental evil has been memorialized on the page—in an endless stream of works by playwrights, historians, novelists—and even melodically, by George Frederick Handel. The town was renamed Colonia Agrippina, for whose satisfaction it should be obvious. Preserved under the present city hall are remains of the Roman governor's residence and, near the cathedral, parts of another Roman house and some mosaics. Cologne was established as a bishop's see in the fourth century, and from that time onward its history was largely caught up in struggles between churchmen and prosperous city merchants, many of whom were involved in weaving and other crafts for which the city was famous. It was not until after Frederick's time that Cologne was granted a charter of self-government, but even then quarrels between the archbishops and the elector-princes were not resolved until as late as 1671.

But for a host of churches, since the catastrophic air raids of World War II there is not much left of the Cologne that Frederick knew. Of the thirteen original chapter and monastic churches that form a kind of protective semicircle around the cathedral, Saint Gereon is the oldest. Gereon and 318 of his Theban Legion—a third-century military body—refused to persecute their fellow Christians and were themselves exterminated in Cologne during the reign of Emperor Maximian. The citizens lost no time building a church to their memory, starting it about 370, but revamping and adding to it over the centuries. In Frederick's time it was still being praised, notably by a monk named Helinand, for its oval plan with a tower-like central structure enlivened by eight niches, some galleries, corridors, and a ribbed dome, for its columns, its ornamentation, and its glittering gold decoration. Richly colored, but quite ordinary, stained glass cannot dim the magnificence of its architectural form. Some important Romanesque pavements representing scenes from the lives of David and Solomon are in the crypt, where reside the remains of Gereon and some of his fellow martyrs.

It is the massive bulk of the exterior, viewed from the east, that arrests the attention, with two square towers reaching for heaven, flanking an extremely handsome apse composed of two tiers of blind arches,

Apsidal end, Saint Gereon, Cologne, Germany

so majestic as to appear indestructible. The two rows of small open arches, one atop the apse, the other aesthetically connecting the towers, are marvels of lightening emptiness, sensitively placed and impeccably sized for best effect. The deep-throated bells of Saint Gereon's towers add exactly the timbre to keep sight and sound of a piece. Few Romanesque buildings can hold the interest and conjure the emotions of this little-visited church in Cologne.

Saint Maria im Kapitol was built, significantly, on the ruins of a Roman temple, with a triapsal choir—the first in the Rhineland—of which only the south one remains. It still preserves its unique, vigorously carved wooden doors of the mid-eleventh century (though no longer hanging) and a plague crucifix dated 1304. The massive Church of Saint Pantaleone was part of an outstanding Benedictine monastery that probably housed a school of book illuminators and ivory carvers. The patron saint was a fourth-century martyr whose veins were said to have spouted milk when he was beheaded, but whose blood, notwithstanding, is claimed to be preserved in Constantinople, Madrid, and Ravello, where, in the latter case, it is supposed to liquefy yearly on his feast day of July 27. With Frederick's winning of the cities of the Lower Rhine it would seem that peace had finally come to Germany; and Frederick was her savior.

Yet on the international side both Frederick and Philip of France were being upstaged.

More than ever seeing himself and the Church as a sun casting light throughout the world, with the secular courts as barely more than lunar reflections, Pope Innocent III could see no better way of demonstrating the amazing power of the papacy that had been reached under his aegis than by calling the Fourth Lateran Council, the most dazzling in the history of Christendom. There were 2,283 official delegates present, including ambassadors from most of the Western countries, from the Latin emperor of Constantinople, and from both Otto and Frederick. It is interesting that, of the 405 bishops and archbishops present, 105 of them were from Sicily, a count disproportionate with the size of the island, and one that should have given Frederick pause. At one gathering the crowd was so great that the archbishop of Amalfi was crushed to death. Francis was there from Assisi, and it may have been on this visit to Rome that he met Dominic Guzman, founder of the Dominicans. There was also a man present whom Frederick had not as yet met but who would become for the next twenty years a highly respected and favorite emissary between him and the papacy, not to mention a loyal personal friend: Hermann von Salza.

The council was a display of papal muscle if ever there was one, from the start geared to establishing the superiority of ecclesiastics over laity, with Innocent militantly at their head. It was here that the theory of transubstantiation was declared dogma, a canon that, along with the ordaining that all Christians beyond the age of reason must confess at least once a year and receive the Holy Eucharist at Easter, gave the medieval priesthood the kind of exaggerated power that Frederick would combat in a far less reverent spirit than later Protestant reformers. During the council's three sessions seventy resolutions were passed, among them the suppression of heresy, the prohibiting of trial by ordeal and judicial duels, the strengthening of the episcopal inquisition, divers laws concerning marriage, convents, ecclesiastical courts, problems having to do with Christian intercourse with Jews and Saracens, and finally, as though Frederick's taking of the crusader's cross had gone unnoticed, one calling for a new crusade with a departure date specified as July 1, 1217, with Egypt the designated target.

Probably the most politically important of the questions discussed at this Fourth Lateran Council was that of Frederick's claim to empire. His case was argued during the second session, November 20, by the persuasive and loyal Archbishop Berard. A rebuttal in the name of Otto was offered by a Milanese lawyer, who was so conclusively talked down that the meeting degenerated into a near brawl, necessitating Innocent's hasty departure. Frederick's election to the throne of the empire was upheld at the last session of the council, a triumph for Frederick and for Innocent's policy. But this deposition of a Roman emperor by a Church council was an ominous precedent, and the medieval papacy had best prepare itself to face the most formidable political adversary it had ever known. Frederick's position was secured, and there was no reason to expect him to do anything but rise still higher. With his Church-verified position he could afford greater liberality than ever, which he practiced with enormous prodigality. Cities were granted privileges of trading, freedom from taxes, freedom from certain civil services. It may have been about this time that Frederick granted a small fief in Franconia to lyric poet Walther von der Vogelweide, making him forever his eulogist and causing him to rejoice in his good fortune.

All in all, it had been a momentous year, remarkable for three events even greater than Walther's fiefdom: the crowning of Frederick, the gathering of the Fourth Lateran Council, and the signing of the Magna Carta, the three of them—at Aachen, Rome, and Runnymede—combining to ruffle the pages of history for seven and a half centuries.

Chapter Six

What am I the wretch then to say?
what patron I to beseech?
when scarcely the just (man) be secure.
***Dies Irae*, verse 7**

1216

Europe had cause to remember Innocent III's prophetic intoning of the words of Christ in Luke 22:15 when he had opened his Fourth Lateran Council last year: "With desire I have desired to eat this passover with you before I suffer." On July 16, 1216, barely a half year after his remarkable triumph in Rome, Innocent died in the city of Perugia, the first of four popes who within the next eighty-nine years would die in that city. Determined to the end to arouse Christendom against the infidels in Palestine, he had set out for Pisa and Genoa in April, hoping to bring peace to those two eternal enemies so that, their eyes turned from one another, they could more readily heed his call for crusade. His first stop was Viterbo, in the heart of papal territory known as "the Patrimony of Saint Peter," extensive lands in central Italy supposed to have been willed to the Church by Emperor Constantine the Great.

With a history that goes back to Roman days and beyond, Viterbo preserves even today the darkly dramatic medieval San Pellegrino Quarter, all towers and balconies and outside staircases rising from shadowed, narrow streets that look more theatrical than real. Self-contained, secretive but for the natural gregariousness of the inhabitants, the Quartiere San Pellegrino leads one to days more basic to the human condition. Corner shrines, small gardens hidden behind protective high walls, shots of joyful color from window planters that enliven the general drabness, a decorated arch here, a modest entablature there, a highly polished brass doorknob—all these everyday items seem personal, not just the products of the anonymous makers' hands

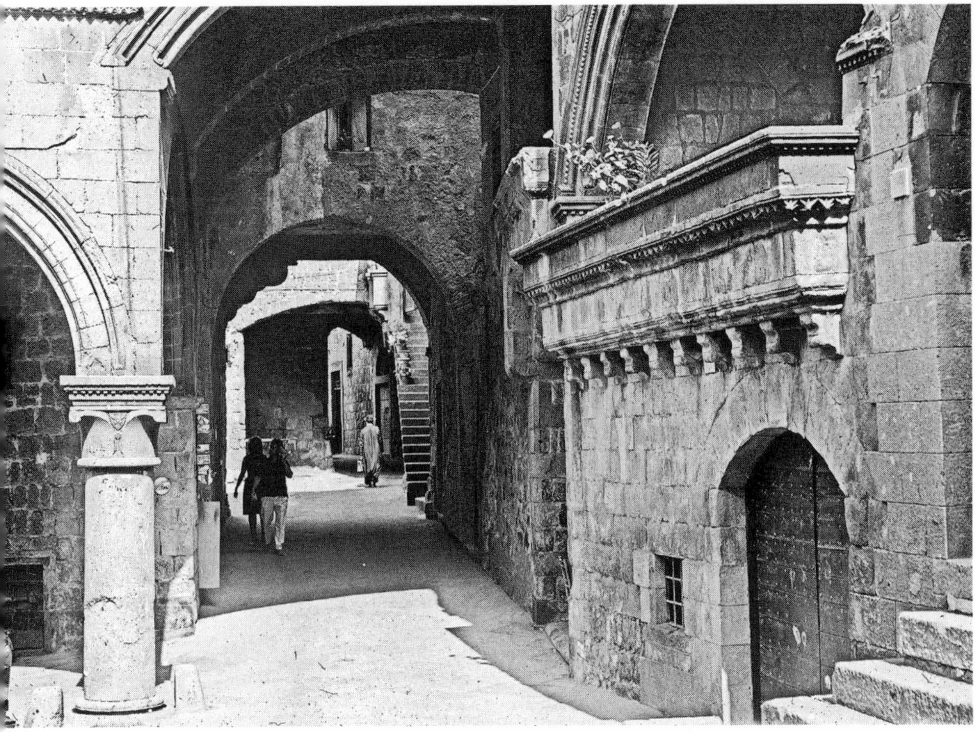

Quartiere San Pellegrino, Viterbo, Italy

but of their very being, their own quiet escapes from the typical raucousness of the Italian city. It is a quarter for secret dealings and covert acts, for opera and theater, for vendettas and feuds. There is a peculiar intimacy about certain nooks in the world: Fulda's Church of Saint Michael; the cloister of San Giovanni degli Eremiti in Palermo; Rome's Piazza Mattei, with its gracefully beguiling Fountain of Turtles, and Borromini's Sant' Ivo, near the Pantheon in the same city. Such places are designed for private contemplation, for lonely enjoyment. So is the Quartiere San Pellegrino, where even the surfaces of the cobbled streets soothe aching soles.

The small Piazza San Pellegrino may be one of the finest thirteenth-century piazzas in Italy. But there is also the Piazza San Lorenzo, occupying the site of an ancient Etruscan acropolis and ringed with old houses, some built on Etruscan foundations. Besides setting off an excellent Goth campanile, it glories in the basilica cathedral of the twelfth century with its handsome columns and fantastic capitals that are so much a part of the Romanesque and which was, in Innocent's time, flat roofed. Whether or not Innocent III had eyes for the sights of Viterbo, he had to move on to Perugia.

One wonders whether Innocent put time aside to contemplate the city of Assisi from the heights of his papal palace in Perugia, one of the most violence-addicted cities of the continent. There in the distant hills was the humble abode of the same man who had so impressed him by preaching a return to fundamentals, a way unlike that which any pope of the age enjoyed—even Innocent, as spartan as he was. Innocent had come to a redoubtable city so much into mayhem that her citizens actually played at it. A unique game enjoyed by the Perugini was to divide themselves into teams, pad themselves with deer-hair-stuffed clothing and, wearing eagle- or hawk-shaped helmets, stone one another in the streets until the city was littered with the dead and wounded. Apparently the belief was that such savage pastimes better prepared the citizenry for the defense of their community.

Among its excesses Perugia can lay claim to the dubious fame of having launched the medieval armies of flagellants who whipped and groaned their way across the face of Europe. Flagellation was meant to be the perfect imitation of Christ. Not unique to Christianity by any means, and its obvious psychosexual overtones aside, this flamboyant manner of expiating sin became widespread as a manifestation of a period of spiritual revival. In 1260, with Perugia as its point of origin, groups of wailing, bleeding penitents began parading the streets with lash and stick, reaching their most hysterical zenith in northern Italy and the low countries by the end of the next century, by which time the practice had been declared heretical. At first extolled by the Church, it was later found difficult to comprehend how "the perfectly orthodox belief in the efficacy of the scourge as a means and an outward sign of repentance could degenerate into a depraved and animal delight in self-torture, combined with a mystic and wholly unlawful belief that flagellation was not only a sacrament but the only lawful sacrament."[1] The custom was appealing to practitioners as an independent route to heaven, in a sense freeing them of a need for Holy Mother Church, a peculiar kind of anarchy in the name of eternal salvation. If Christians generally took to whipping and torturing themselves into states of purity, obviously there would be no need for the confessional. The Church felt called upon to curtail the practice, indeed within a century to anathematize it and to declare its devotees heretics.

Cloaked in time-darkened walls, Perugia is divided and interspersed by split levels, sloping walks—the dark and narrow Via dei Priori is especially rewarding on a hot summer afternoon—massive palazzi, exuberant fountains, sober, shadowed arches, all peopled by a determinedly independent citizenry as far back as the sixth century BC, when it was one of the most important of the twelve federated cities of Etruria. More than most Italian cities Perugia maintains its medieval appearance. Should Pope Innocent III, by some quirk of the natural process, suddenly find himself in modern Perugia, there are a number of buildings that he would have no trouble recognizing. The round Early Christian Church of Sant'Angelo, with its circular ambulatory and sixteen ancient columns supporting the central drum, is a case in point. Then there is the tenth-century Church of San Prospero, much remodeled, but with an eighth-century ciborium over the high altar. The eleventh-century San Pietro, with every available inch of space covered by frescoes, still maintains its original basilica form and, on top of everything else, a lovely Pietà by favorite citizen Pietro Perugino.

One feels that the Cathedral of San Lorenzo, from the outside at any rate, expresses the nature of medieval and Renaissance Perugia. It is at the same time majestic and rustic, handsome and ugly. Standing artlessly in its piazza, it gives the impression of never having been completed—and such is indeed the case—since its masonry walls remain uncovered by finer facing. There is, however, a five-arched loggia and a noble flight of stairs leading to a porch on which sits Pope Julius III in green-patinaed bronze finery. There is also an outside pulpit from which many a fire-and-brimstone preacher harangued in more strident ages. The Renaissance portal is by Galeazzo Alessi, whose path we have already crossed. Inside, for tourist edification, are some fine wooden stalls, the Virgin's wedding ring, sculptures, and paintings.

Throughout Perugia there are excellent examples of secular art from the age of Innocent. The twelfth-century Sciri House and its adjacent tower are interesting. Facing the cathedral the Gothic Palazzo Comunale, begun in the thirteenth century and sometimes called the Palazzo dei Priori, has a majestic fan staircase, a recurring visual theme in Italy. Over the stairs the griffin of Perugia and the Guelf lion, both in bronze, pose on stone brackets. Between them dangle chains and rods, which some claim are relics from a fourteenth-century assault against Siena or Assisi; but the truth of the matter is that those relics were carried off in 1799, and what we have now are only the chains from which they hung.

The most pleasant of Perugia's secular monuments, the Fontana Maggiore, splashes happily in the piazza between the cathedral and the Palazzo dei Priori. Designed and carved by father and son, Nicola and Giovanni Pisano, it is a pleasing arrangement of two concentric basins

Palazzo Communale, Perugia, Italy

one above the other and is topped by a bronze bowl with three nymphs supporting a wreath. Jets of water from the summit stream from basin to basin, adding a soft animation to the piazza and lightening the gloom of the heavy, brown-colored buildings that surround and tower over it. Better known for his pulpits at Siena and Pisa, Nicola, the father, is held by some to have been originally inspired in the arts by the "Renaissance" of the reign of Frederick II, especially as we see it in Apulia, from where Nicola may have originated. Be that as it may, his fountain at Perugia is a splendid example of his work and a fine coming-together of the talents of father and son. Even Giovanni's exuberant and temperamental use of the chisel cannot dim his father's milder, more considered manner. And Nicola's precise outlines and concentration of volumes on two panels of the lower basin—one of a cavalier and a companion piece of a horsewoman with a falcon on her wrist—are clearly of a very high expressive quality, despite the erosion of time and weather.

Pope Innocent arrived in Perugia in May. He was exhausted by his travels, as well as by the labors of his monumental Fourth Lateran Council just past. At first when he caught a tertian fever it seemed as though he would have the strength to shake it off. But a relapse followed, a paralysis complicated things, and by July 16 he was dead. With events moving at an uncommonly brisk pace, and with his crusade scheduled for the following year, it was imperative to elect a new pope as quickly as possible. Innocent's body was laid in state, but no vigils were kept by members of the papal court, who were off politicking for the next occupant of Saint Peter's chair. Alas, with no guards standing watch, Innocent's jewels and fine vestments proved too tempting. Ethics were no match against greed, and the oppportunity to moralize was not missed by Cardinal Jacques de Vitry, canon of Namur, soon to be named Bishop of Acre in the Holy Land, who arrived in Perugia on the very day that Innocent breathed his last. "During the night some robbers had stripped him of his valuable clothes and left his body, which was lying in the middle of the church, almost naked and giving off a nauseating odor. I went there and saw with my own eyes how brief, vain, and ephemeral is the glory of this world."[2]

The medieval papacy had reached its secular apogee under Innocent III, for none would come after him who would be such a judge—even if self-appointed—of the destinies of Europe. It is no matter that too often his plans misfired, that his intrigues ended in disaster, that his idealism turned evil. The heresy "crusade" in southern France and the sack of Constantinople are well-cited cases to illustrate the latter point. Though it may be a measure of questionable merit, it remains for all to see that, by the time he died, the Papal States were more than doubled in size, occupying a solid block of land midway in the Italian peninsula that served to buffer the imperial domains from the kingdom of Sicily. He was not a builder, but he did leave us the truncated Conti Tower in Rome, now only a stump of the original, which was damaged by an earthquake in 1348. Innocent built the tower as a policing device for protecting papal processions on the route to the Lateran. Almost on the corner of the Via Cavour and the Via dei Fori Imperiali, it stands as one of Rome's more somber monuments, now looking indestructible and serving as a modern tenement, with clothes hanging out of windows to dry.

No, Innocent's talents were clearly administrative. The whole government of the Church had been streamlined as Innocent, with little respect for tradition, had brushed aside the cobwebs of inefficiency and the institutionalized superfluities so beloved of large organizations. In such a spirit, and with an acuteness deemed at the time supernatural, he recognized that enthusiastic men might be utilized in the service of the Church instead of being diverted to the ranks of her enemies. For undeniably the distinctive religious feature of his pontificate was the founding of the mendicant orders, which kept papal power on an even keel for the next two centuries at least. Both Dominic Guzman and Francis Bernardone had been coldly received at first. But eventually Innocent had come around. The fact is he understood and respected greatness, especially when it approached or surpassed his own. Under his guidance and protection the two most notable men of the immediate future had been given their chances: Francis of Assisi and Frederick II. By this alone he achieved lasting merit.

Passionately ambitious to establish the supremacy of the papacy and a rigid believer in an imperial priesthood through Proverbs 8:15, "by me kings reign, and princes decree justice," Innocent's interference in the affairs of Europe and Constantinople had been persistent and consequential, too much so from the lay point of view. He always sought a legal basis for his claims, but certainly his view that all worldly power be dispensed from the papal chair was nonsense. Despite denials by his apologists, the thin line between religion and politics often became blurred, as when he offered a new form of redemption to crusaders: full remission of their sins regardless of the heinousness of their crimes and the circumstances under which they were committed.

Innocent could flatter with the best of them, especially the monarchs with whom he had to deal—his many "best beloveds." But he could pound his crosier on political daises enough to bring royalty to their knees, as he did with John Lackland, and Philip Augustus too, when he forced him to give up his mistress and return to his queen's bed. In an incident-crammed life one wonders how Innocent managed to devote time to the minutiae of his position. Only shortly before his demise he had granted to Francis's Clare and her Poor Ladies the *privilegium paupertatis*, authorizing them to live without possessions or endowments, in poverty similar to that advocated by Francis. And he wrote the document with his own hand. In the end, in a providential truism as contradictory as the vilification of his corpse, the idea of a material, power-craving papal monarchy went the way of all unsound ideas.

Frederick's reaction to the death of Innocent III can only be imagined, but it must have been multifaceted. Only a few weeks before, Frederick had sent his former mentor assurances that his command to bring his baby son, Henry, to Germany should not cause anxiety. Frederick knew full well that word of his summons would cause the pope's hair to stand on end. Though Innocent never received the message, the fact that Frederick sent it indicated his belief that a papal-royal dialogue had to be maintained. Now, on the death of Innocent, if Frederick thought his loyalties to the papacy and his anticipated troubles with that office were of the past, he could not have been more wrong. Popes who followed in Innocent's wake—and what a wave that must have been to ride!—were perfectly capable of causing him no end of frustration and outrage. Even dead the Pope, claimed Walther von der Vogelweide, led the clergy "by the devil's rein." Frederick, on the other hand, proclaimed indebtedness to Innocent, though that had to be window trimming. Still, casting aside political conditions and personal ideas of expediency, they must have felt a natural attraction one to the other. There is no reason to doubt that Frederick saw Innocent as the vicar of Christ, the proper successor to Saint Peter, and that Innocent saw his former ward as the sword arm of a politically victorious Church. For all of Innocent's aggressive reforms, within two days of his passing, the Church moved right back into its old groove: the cardinals at Perugia elected an able administrator, a remarkable financier, the conciliatory traditionalist, conservative, sixty-six-year old vice-chancellor of the Holy See, Censius Savelli, who took the name of Honorius III. A man not inclined to the machinations and deceptions indigenous to politics, he was, on top of everything else, unwell. He would be no match for the virile young Frederick Hohenstaufen.

At about the time that Innocent lay dying in Perugia, Queen Constance and the five-year-old Henry were leaving Sicily, perhaps in the company of Hermann von Salza, recently returned from seven years in Outremer. About to step onto the stage of imperial politics, Hermann von Salza was set to initiate his new role as close friend and confidant of Frederick II. He was a good man to guide the queen and her son across Sicily. The island had fallen on hard times with the prolonged absence of the king. Walter of Palear was left in charge of a realm virtually without government. He had his work cut out for him as whole provinces of the kingdom, whose untrustworthy barons had declared for Otto in the past and were not yet used to the idea that his was a lost cause, remained stubbornly in a state of insurrection. Risky as the journey was for the royal family, it was made safely, and the party arrived at Frederick's court in Nuremberg in December for a jubilant reunion after five years. Now, for the first time, Frederick the king and Hermann von Salza, the grand master of the Teutonic Knights, got to know one another. And both were impressed.

The Order of the Teutonic Knights was German and the newest of the military-religious orders that had come into existence during the Holy Land crusades. The Templars, another, but mainly French order, had fought in that blood-stained region, as had the largely Italian Order of the Hospital Knights of Saint John of Jerusalem (more frequently known as the Hospitallers), sometimes even one against the other, though it was expressly forbidden in the Templar Rule to kill or injure another Christian. At the behest of Pope Innocent III, the Teutonic Knights had adopted the Rule of the Templars. Henry VI had seen the value of the German organization, but only so far as it could help him achieve his Eastern pretensions. When he died so did interest in the order, to an extent retarded by its own insistence that it was open only to knights of German birth. So the Teutonic Knights never aspired to the benefaction and wealth that the other two groups enjoyed, but neither did it sink into such corruption.

As with the other two, it was from the ashes of violence and plague that the Teutonic Order arose. In the winter of 1190–91 a two-year siege of the city of Acre had ground to a halt. The defenders had fought adamantly enough to draw grudging admiration even from the Christian camp. Starvation and sickness were the orders of the day. Out of this chaos some merchants from Bremen and Lübeck established a hospital in a boat, which they had beached near the city. Within a short time the hospital was attached to the Church of Saint Mary in Jerusalem, to be, in March 1198, raised to the rank of an order of knights by the remnants of Henry VI's abortive precrusade. From then on, it emulated the other two organizations, finally developing into an elite military club, exercising its own rights of sovereignty over lands given to it by Frederick. With his journey to the Holy Land in mind, Frederick anticipated that he would have need of crusade-thinking German knights. Under his encouragement the order became courtly, with two brethren in permanent attendance on his person and the grand master himself forming a part of the royal household. The revitalized growth of the Teutonic Order was due to the combined efforts of Frederick and Hermann von Salza, who did more to advance the cause of this brotherhood in his twenty-nine years of leadership than any other of its masters. Their friendship would persist for over twenty years, with Hermann serving as Frederick's most trusted and valued intimate by reason of his indispensability.

Hermann von Salza was born in Thuringia near Lagensalza, about twenty miles northwest of Erfurt. He had all the worthwhile qualities to recommend him for his post as grand master of the Teutonic Knights: he was wise, brave, eloquent, and honorable. Above almost all other men of consequence, his word was believed. Von Salza was the thirteenth-century model of prestige and manly virtue. Over the Christmas season he and Frederick cultivated their budding relationship in the castle (the Kaiserschloss) of Nuremberg. One likes to imagine them cementing their friendship over steins of good beer and a plateful of marvelous Nuremberger bratwurst, even if neither had been invented yet, at least as we know them. Not much is known of either the castle or Nuremberg before about 1050, and it would seem that the building of the fortress brought the city itself into existence. During the twelfth century Nuremberg suffered the usual sieges, demolitions, and rebuilding that were normal to the age, which did not prevent it from becoming an extremely wealthy center, situated as it is on the Pegnitz River and the trade route between northern Europe on the one hand and Italy and the East on the other. By 1219 Frederick would grant it rights of a free imperial city with the accompanying perquisites.

Nuremberg's finest triumphs have come through its artists, all of them from the centuries after Frederick. Aside from Albrecht Dürer, Nuremberg's most famous son is unquestionably the poet, dramatist, and cobbler Hans Sachs, immortalized for modern audiences in Richard Wagner's *Die Meistersinger von Nuremberg*. But Nuremberg's greatest notoriety was yet to come, when Adolph Hitler chose it as the city for staging his massive Reichs Party Convention demonstrations, and when the victorious allies chose it for the scene of history's most magnificent justice: the Nuremberg trials.

Badly wrecked during World War II, most of Nuremberg has been rebuilt, some of it in the historical styles. The streets are narrow and twisting, the houses red-tiled and in the manner of the sixteenth century. There are lovely things to see in Nuremberg (the Schöne Brunnen—Beautiful Fountain—in the main market square is splendid) but little from Frederick's day except for parts of the castle and the imperial chapel therein, which dates from the twelfth century. A sprawling structure measuring over seven hundred feet in overall length, the castle came into Hohenstaufen proprietorship in 1138. The complex is mostly of stone, but with much wood, with weathered balconies and outside staircases, a deep, housed well, defiant towers, women's quarters, and a knights' hall with thirty oak beams held up by an enormous timber running the full length, which is in turn supported by oak columns. The textures and patterns of the woodwork, contrasting with rough-hewn stone, the angles and somber shadows, the cloudy glass windows and creaking floors—all of these speak of imperial Germany, though not all of it as long ago as Frederick.

The most arresting point of interest in the castle is the simple, quietly melancholy imperial chapel, two-tiered, one directly above the other, the upper exclusively for the use of the emperor and his court, the lower allocated from this year for the use of the Teutonic Knights. The two chapels are united aesthetically and liturgically by the clever use of a central bay that rises to the ceiling height of the upper gallery. The lower chapel—the handsomer of the two from the point of view of the author—is more rigorously Romanesque, squat, somber, shadowed. This is not to imply that the two levels are of different periods. They were constructed, as a matter of fact, in a single operation. Because of its texture, sandstone does not lend itself to elaborately detailed carving. Yet the capitals and the bands of decoration are fine beyond reasonable expectation. In the upper, gracefully columned chapel, the head of Christ, so tragically brutalized yet empty of a trace of rancor, is a memorable moment in the development of sculpture during the Hohenstaufen era.

Of interest to any student of medieval lore is the German National Museum of Nuremberg, though it does not specialize in that period alone. The eleventh-century manuscript, the Codex Aureus of Echternach, with its colorful, highly animated scenes from the life of Christ, is there. The figure of the risen Christ shrinking from Mary Magdalene's adoring touch is a masterpiece of graceful, but not unloving denial. And what about the especially noteworthy Christ in Majesty surrounded by four prophets and the symbols of the four evangelists? The central figure, unbearded, and with robes delineated by rigid lines in the Romanesque manner, is dignified beyond measure, aloof, judgmental, of another world, and yet welcoming and friendly. The medieval Gods and Christs can, indeed, invite worship because they are of another plane, beyond reality, removed from vulgar humankind. The Gloria of the Codex Aureus is the sort of thing to compel belief, to cause wonder, to thrill with an anticipation of a higher existence. The enameled armband of Frederick Barbarossa in the same museum is another thing entirely: here is a world-wearied, crucified Christ, mourned on either

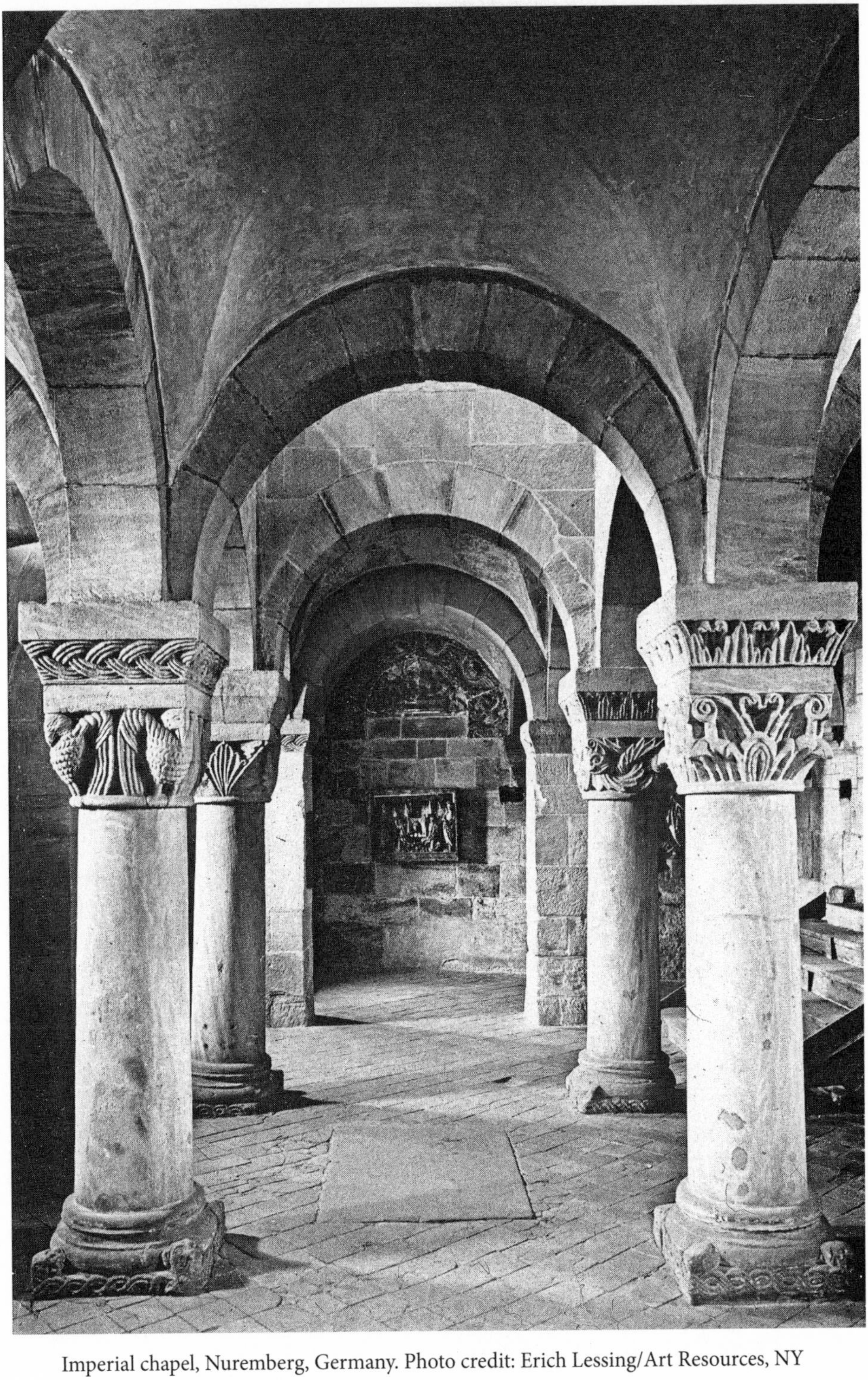

Imperial chapel, Nuremberg, Germany. Photo credit: Erich Lessing/Art Resources, NY

hand by Mary and John, being pierced in the side by the nonbeliever Longinus and being given water and vinegar by an unsympathetic lackey while soldiers divide the seamless robe at his feet and angels comfort him from heaven. Colorful and graphic it is, entirely on our plane.

If one gets tired of museums, castles, and churches in Nuremberg, there are always the enchanting courtyards to explore and oriels to admire—and the Nuremberger *Lebkuchen* made of sugar, nuts, spices, and ginger, the *Eierzucker* (egg sugar), marzipan and other sweets, not to mention the *Weinstuben* with the gentle, light, Nuremberg ale.

1217

One of the first things that Frederick did on the arrival of his wife and son from Sicily was to have young Henry, already the acknowledged king of Sicily, installed as duke of Swabia, a first step to getting him the German crown while Frederick donned the imperial regalia. Pope Honorius was not now, and never would be, an Innocent III. One can imagine the invective that would have been heaped on Frederick's head had Innocent still been alive to hear of the investiture; one even wonders if Frederick would have dared make such a move. But Innocent was dead, and Honorius, by his silence, indicated to the astute Frederick a not-altogether-accurate picture of the nature of the years to come.

The question naturally arises, why did Frederick not go to Rome and cinch his emperorship? Emperor Otto IV had, after all, been uncrowned by the Fourth Lateran Council two years ago, a declaration that was almost in the nature of a coup de grâce since it caused so many waverers to swing over to the increasingly popular young Hohenstaufen. There was nothing standing in Frederick's way. It would seem to be an especially propitious time for him to demand his own coronation, what with the comparatively compliant Honorius III in Saint Peter's chair. But everything in good time. There were several reasons for his extended stay in Germany, not the least important being Otto himself.

Since his humiliating flight from Cologne with his high-living wife, torn between vanity and despair, Otto had continued to act the part of emperor from his family lair in Braunschweig. There he could work hand in glove with his brother Henry, as well as with a powerful, but dwindling, group of nobles on Germany's northeast frontier, disgruntled to a man since Frederick had ceded away, three years ago, to King Waldemar II of Denmark, that land north of the rivers Elbe and Elde in which so many of them held vital interests. With Otto's encouragement Guelf forces tried futilely to take back these lands in a war that dragged on interminably with no gain for Otto's side. In fact, it was just the opposite. The protracted effort wore down the Guelf forces to a point of weakness that they could ill afford. And the brutal devastations of the countryside guaranteed a scarcity of supplies, so obvious a shortfall that no foreign power could be persuaded to waste its energy or money on so hopeless a cause.

All in all, Otto was no longer a threat to Frederick. But his was a disruptive presence because he tempted others to waver in their loyalties. The most unstable of the lot of them, Hermann, landgrave of Thuringia, was contemplating yet another switch in loyalties, conveniently forgetting that he was part of the intrigue that had brought Frederick to Germany in the first place. His death in April could not have grieved Frederick, or Otto either for that matter. Totally unstable in his loyalties, it was too bad that he had not devoted himself to those cultural pursuits at which he excelled and left politics to the more adept. On the other hand, since Hermann had accumulated much of his wealth through accepting bribes, he might very well have found himself impoverished had he led a decent life. His son, Louis, who inherited the estates, was more steadfast, a characteristic that was encouraged by his wife, the extremely long-suffering and austere Elizabeth—later a saint, no less—whom he had married when she was thirteen. Hermann's widowed wife was apparently not a whole lot better than Hermann, jealously doing everything in her power to guarantee her daughter-in-law's sainthood by making her life a living hell.

1218

Historians may accuse Otto of all kinds of perfidies, of swimming through life in a torrent of lies, broken promises, and cruel revenges that served no purpose other than to salve a wounded ego. Even alive he was spoken of as a boor, ignorant, bad mannered, in fact as a man without saving grace but for that magnificent physique. Yet it must be said that, regardless of his reasons—his fears for his own neck, his desire to pump up a totally deflated self-esteem, a misguided family pride—he fought doggedly and with unflagging courage to the bitter end. Total humiliation was spared him when, at Harzburg Castle, at the northern extreme of the Harz Mountains, fighting to regain a nonexistent empire, with nothing in his hand of that empire but the regalia which he continued to lug around with him, he fell sick of dysentery. His condition was worsened by an overdose of purgative. He was not a man without remorse—the familiar deathbed penance of despicable rulers. A circle of priests surrounded his bed, chanting and scourging him with whips while Otto sobbed out the words of the *Miserere*, and between phrases admonished them to lay on more severely. Even the household scullions had their turns with the lash. So Otto passed away at forty-three years of age, miserable to his last agonizing breath on May 19, just seven years after he had been crowned emperor by Innocent III and had threatened the island kingdom of the ascendant Frederick, who was even now moving in triumphant progress through his realm. Earlier that month a future emperor was born to the house of Habsburg. It is said that Frederick pleased his vassals by acting as godfather, little knowing that the babe, Rudolph, would found one of the great houses of Europe from which the rulers of Spain and Austria would claim descent. To his dying moment Otto insisted on his right to the imperial title, going so far as to leave instructions that he be buried in the accoutrements of the office and that his brother Henry retain the imperial cross, lance, crown, and orb for twenty weeks following his demise.

It was probably not a heartbroken cortege that escorted the body of Otto IV to Braunschweig for burial in a clumsy, rectangular tomb at the head of the north aisle of the cathedral of Saint Blaise, an edifice erected by Otto's ambitious father, Henry the Lion, who was already interred there with his consort, Matilda of England. As one of the Fourteen Holy Helpers, a group of saints honored more for their abilities to do certain acts than for their piety, Saint Blaise is much revered in France and Germany. He was said to have possessed healing powers, a gift that extended to animals as well as to humans. He is the patron saint of animals, wool combers, and people who suffer afflictions of the throat, the relevancy of this last being that he once saved a boy who almost suffocated when a fishbone lodged therein. His cathedral at Braunschweig is twelfth-century Romanesque, the first completely vaulted building in northern Germany. It has a chancel decorated with important twelfth-century frescoes and a north aisle with columns twisting in alternating directions, which do tend to give one a squeamish turn. Hardly the least interesting of the cathedral treasures is an enormous twelfth-century, seven-branched candelabrum, elegant and gracefully curved; and the large triumphal cross, the Christ of Imerward, is worth a long, studied look.

Braunschweig would never have reached the point of flowering had it not been for the Guelf dukes, particularly Henry the Lion, a man, like most men of power, both hated and feared. He was a prince of princes, rapacious, greedy, high-handed, and a master of men. A word from him could change the history of the duchy of Saxony. In addition to his cathedral, Henry built the much-restored, extremely handsome

Guelf lion, Braunschweig, Germany

Dankwarderode Castle, housing a collection of brilliant Guelf gold work, not to mention the "cope of Otto IV," which may be of English origin, a not unreasonable assumption considering the length of time Otto spent in the court of Richard Lionheart. On a brilliant red ground, agile, pop-eyed lions cavort among a scattering of stars and moons, all edged by a border of angels and Fatamid palmettes. Eastern influences are obvious in the general layout but not so in the lions, which are at the same time heraldic and playful—and a little bit whimsical in their joyous gamboling.

Dankwarderode Castle, a clear-cut attempt to eclipse similar imperial structures, is fronted by a bronze Guelf lion facing eastward, Henry's major danger zone, the lands to the north as far as the Baltic shores already being under his iron-handed control at the time of the castle's construction. A noble beast it is too, standing on its lofty plinth in the Burg-Platz like a champion dog posing in the judging ring, head high, tail low, and with a handsome mane composed of overlapping, triangular-shaped tufts. Had the Guelfs displayed half the brazen nobility of their adopted symbol history might have read differently.

The medieval aspect of Braunschweig is preserved in the monumental relationship of the cathedral, the Gewandhaus (Cloth Merchants' Hall), the gorgeous Altstadtrathaus (one of the first city halls in Germany), and the Church of Saint Peter. Old houses with carved facades and steep gables abound in Braunschweig, and three parish churches, despite their later renovations, maintain a stylistic kinship with the cathedral. For all its architecture, its science and art collections, its book and weaving trades, Braunschweig is probably most famous to gustatory-minded moderns for its native Braunschweiger liver sausage. Pity those who have never tried the local Kartoffelpuffer (potato pancakes) or the Altbierbowle (strawberries in beer), which the natives down with obvious relish!

Finally rid of his principle antagonist, Frederick held court at Fulda. He could feel at home in Fulda, with its many Carolingian associations. It had for centuries been acknowledged as a center of theological learning, counting among its teachers the great humanist and pedagogue, Hrabanus Maurus, himself a student of the noted Alcuin, friend and teacher of Charlemagne. That is not forgetting Walafrid Strabo, a prolific writer of theological, historical, and geographic subject matter along with his famous lyrical poem, *The Book on the Art of Gardening*, an accurate description of herbs that he grew in his garden and of their medicinal uses. And what of Servatus Lupus, the first German humorist? The Benedictine abbey that housed these men was established in 744 by a disciple of that prolific founder of abbeys, Saint Boniface, who had been born near Exeter in England. A most tactless missionary, Boniface was notorious for his impatient turning-over of idols and for chopping down the sacred oak of Donar in full view of its heathen worshippers, showing himself a man of little tolerance, albeit one of personal bravery. For his oak-destroying venture Boniface is credited in Germany with inventing the idea of the Christmas tree, a myth a little more extended than most. But still one wonders at his methods.

Intellectual argument and superstition aside, medieval monasteries like Boniface's contributed much to secular-religious activities. Once the labors of the year were accomplished with the completion of the harvest, the change of pace brought about presentations of plays and sporting events for the amusement of the field workers, even the monks themselves. Franciscans were especially active in these endeavors, probably as a means of popularizing their own preaching and the messages of the Testaments. They amused themselves and the local people by applying popular airs to hymns, always in the vernacular rather than the churchy Latin. Francis would have been proud of them! They were fostering the creation of the organum, which led to the grassroots development of the motet and the *conductus*, both of which could be either religious or secular. Music knows no national, racial, or even religious boundaries, and these new forms spread throughout the medieval world.

Boniface had no way of knowing that Fulda, the best known of the foundations in his name, would become a center of medieval learning with two schools, one for goldsmithing and the other for manuscript illumination. The latter produced the Sacramentary of Fulda, famous for its flat, but nonetheless graceful, ornamentations. It is now in the University Library at Göttingen, while still others are found in Bamberg and in the Vatican. The double-apsed abbey church at Fulda, now the cathedral, was enlarged to the west to accommodate a growing pilgrimage business to the tomb of Saint Boniface, which is in the crypt of the present eighteenth-century baroque building, and which is remarkable for its almost humorous representation of a recumbent Boniface impatiently pushing his grave slab aside and crawling out from under with ill-disguised lack of dignity. The church finally ended up with a transept large enough to rival the public basilicas of ancient Rome. More easily encompassed, and certainly more rewarding to visit, is the small, round Michaelkirche, erected in 822 in imitation of the Church of the Holy Sepulcher in Jerusalem.

There are places in the world that create in the visitor the notion that one has come back to the beginning, that one has returned to origins, to roots. Saint Michael's Church in Fulda is that kind of place. Small enough to be easily taken in without supreme effort, sufficiently simple and undecorated to neither tease nor distract from the contemplation of the whole, one feels that in its very directness it sweeps one into its embrace, not relying on particular creed or special prejudice. One needs only to sit quietly in the dim light of this beautifully proportioned rotunda church to experience genuine inner aloneness—awareness. The columns are so stalwart, the capitals such wonderful spots of pattern, the arches at once earthbound and upward-reaching that one is tempted to feel the presence of divinity. Every age breeds its opposites; only an age erroneously dubbed "dark" could produce a temple so exquisitely eloquent of intense belief. The cruelties of the age belie the dramatic beauty. And the crypt, with its squat, muscular columns and its central single column supporting a principle vaulting so low

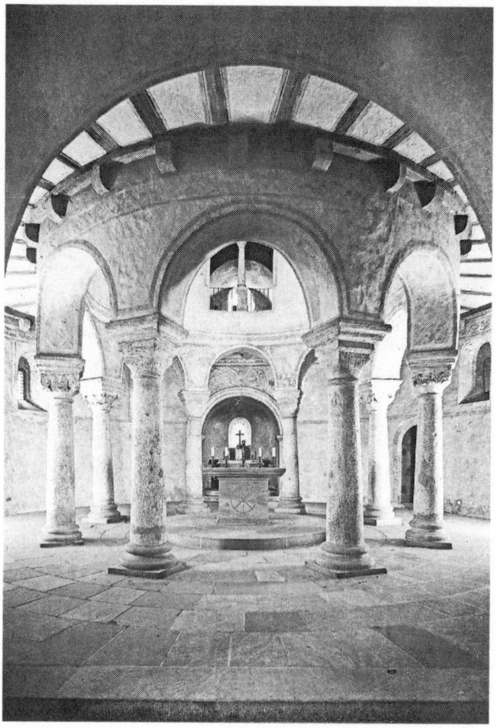

Saint Michael's Church, Fulda, Germany

that one must stoop to navigate the tiny space—all this only adds to the general aura of faith. The exterior is more than a little forbidding with two witches' cap towers looming over the cathedral square from a massive retaining wall base.

Imperial objectives progressed at Fulda when Otto's partisans, at last realizing the hopelessness of further resistance, did fealty to their emperor-to-be. It was not until the following July, however, at Goslar, that Frederick smoothed things over with the more reticent brother of Otto, Henry of Saxony, who finally surrendered the imperial regalia to his lord, even then only after a papal thunder of possible excommunication and an interdict on Braunschweig should he persist in hanging on to the cherished emblems. So was brought to an end the Guelf-Hohenstaufen struggle that had begun early in the twelfth century with the rivalry of Henry the Proud and the first of the Hohenstaufen kings, Conrad. Guelf family estates were passed on to Otto IV's nephew (another Otto) who, coming into the confidence of the young king, was given the dukedom of Braunschweig-Lüneburg. For his humiliating submission, Henry of Saxony was appointed vicar-general of the empire.

It had been a relaxing Christmas season, and Frederick now saw his way clear to march on Rome to claim the imperium. Pope Honorius III envisioned him as finally fulfilling his crusading vows. Welcome news, indeed—ambiguous, perhaps, and in any case maybe too late. In truth the fifth crusade, a papal enterprise from its start in the summer and autumn of 1217, had been a manifest failure, coming to a grinding halt at the foot of the walls of Damietta, Egypt, where it waited now for supply ships, promised time after time but never forthcoming. Following the example of Innocent III, Honorius had studiously ignored Frederick's coronation crusading pledge. Like his predecessor, he had seen this newest attempt to wrest the Holy Land from the infidel foe as the triumph of a Christendom united under papal leadership.

The choice of Damietta as the target of this fifth crusade had been Innocent III's, following the opinion of Richard Lionheart that if Egypt were brought to her knees then the Holy Land would fall too, caught in a pincers movement between Acre in the north and Egypt in the south. Damietta was located two miles inland from the Mediterranean, on the eastern branch of the Nile between the east bank and Lake Manzaleh. (The modern city is about four miles farther south, built there when the old Damietta was razed around 1260 as a defense against attacks from the sea.) Not until the whole misguided crusading endeavor had shifted from the Holy Land, and then stalemated at Damietta, did sixty-eight-year-old Honorius belatedly come to the conclusion that only a youthful imperial presence could salvage it. And he was probably correct in this. Frederick, however, had other inclinations, though he had, the previous December at Fulda, made arrangements for meeting his princes at Magdeburg the following March to focus on details of a crusade, all of which may have been merely a gesture to assuage papal anxieties.

With the pacification of Germany brought about by Henry of Saxony's appointment as vicar-general, Frederick could feel confident of continued governance in his absence. This was reassuring to Pope Honorius. What was not so reassuring was news that Frederick's son, Henry, designated duke of Swabia, was now to be made regent of the kingdom of Burgundy. It was enough to make a pope's flesh crawl. Could the kingship of Germany be far behind? Frederick replied to the pope's suspicious questioning by claiming that he had no intention of uniting the Sicilian realm to the empire. His main intent, he soothed, was to guarantee young Henry's place should anything happen to him, Frederick, while he was off fighting for Jesus Christ. But Honorius was not fooled. He could rightly see Henry as king of Germany, and Frederick as king of Sicily and German emperor, thereby uniting the two offices in one person, the very bugaboo that popes had feared for centuries. Frederick was required to renew assurances he had made to Innocent III, that he recognized the Church's feudal rights over Sicily, that he would give the kingdom of Sicily to his son on his coming of age, keeping the empire for himself. For the present, however, both men viewed the coming imperial coronation with eagerness, Frederick as a step to naked power, Honorius as a prelude to the launching of a rescue mission to the mismanaged, ill-advised, foundering fifth crusade. And then there was that Eastern presence!

Rather than thinking in terms of the Outremer infidels, Honorius and Frederick would have done better to recognize the greater potential threat: Jenghis Khan was on the move and headed for central Europe. But neither had thoughts for that, having been encouraged by reports that a Christian monarch from Asia was preparing to march against the heathen. In 1217 Jacques de Vitry, bishop of Acre, had written to Honorius that Asian Christians were massing under the banner of the legendary Prestor John, whipping up a storm of enthusiasm for the crusade, especially in Austria and Hungary. But that was about the extent of it. Forged letters lent credence to the bishop's assertion. One of them induced the Jewish population of Europe to contribute vastly to the cause of the Eastern Christians who were allegedly on the march. But the gold never got beyond the Caucasus, where it fell into the hands of Georgian bandits and probably into the coffers of Jenghis Khan. What Jacques de Vitry never realized was that there was indeed an army of Christians in the East—but they were Nestorian Christian heretics riding with Jenghis Khan. And they were moving on Khwarizm, east of the Caspian Sea.

1219

By now it was clear to Pope Honorius that Frederick was playing games with him. Frederick had established June 24 as the departure date for his crusading expedition. Then, for one reason or another, the Magdeburg meeting at which the princes were to discuss the venture did not take place. Frederick asked Honorius for a postponement of the sailing date, to which the pope agreed. That does not mean that Honorius stopped barking at the heels of the ambitious Frederick. His frequent letters chided him to get on with preparing his ships and recruiting his men in obedience to Divine Will and in the manner of his grandfather, Barbarossa. Frederick is a young man, Honorius writes, God expects more from him than from another: "Forgo sleep! Hurry!"

Frederick, distracted by dickering with his princes over the coronation of his son as king of the Germans, had no time for papal messages. If the truth were out, Henry's future was his reason for requesting another delay of the journey to Outremer. Pope Honorius agreed to one more postponement, to March 21, 1220, with the warning that a further putting-off would bring down an excommunication.

In his own eyes at least Honorius had reason to resort to the by-now threadbare practice of excommunication. If something was not done pretty soon, his fifth crusade was going to peter out in the bleached sands of the Nile delta at the foot of the walls of Damietta. Now the crusaders were wrangling among themselves. Just the year before they had been joined by a fleet of cohorts that Honorius had managed to rustle up and finance, and at whose head he had put one Cardinal Pelagius, a Spaniard of remarkable industry, but lacking in judgment. The good cardinal was not about to take a backseat to any secular prince, and on landing he let it be known that, since he was papal legate, he was in command and he would remain supreme commander until the promised arrival of Frederick Hohenstaufen and his imperial army.

Present commander, John of Brienne, regent king of Jerusalem by virtue of having married the late Queen Maria of Montferrat, would have none of that. Admittedly impoverished and a bit long in the tooth, John was nonetheless able and courageous, cut from the same cloth as his brother, Walter of Brienne. Despite his sixty-plus years he had earned and held the respect of his men. Tall in stature and robust, he was so expert in the art of war that his men spoke of him as another Charlemagne. The Saracens fled at the sight of him, seeing him as the devil or a lion ready to devour them. Having lost his wife after one year of marriage, John was left with a kingdom, an infant daughter, Yolanda, and the zeal to increase his own power by routing the Muslims from the Holy Land.

The crusading troops biding their time in the shadow of Damietta's walls, like four previous armies, found themselves being led by incessantly wrangling commanders, who cared for nothing but their own positions in the military hierarchy and who did not know the meaning of the word *compromise*. By August things were so bad that the soldiers took matters into their own hands, attacking the Muslims in a disorderly rabble devoid of leaders or strategy and ending in tumultuous pandemonium for the Christians, six thousand of whom were killed or captured. Those who were rescued could thank John of Brienne and his knights for a skillful turnabout of a tragic situation. They could also indirectly thank the most unlikely of personages to be in Egypt at this time, Francis of Assisi.

By now Francis's growing army of Friars Minor was radiating from its hub at the Porziuncola to distant lands and far corners, taking its message of love and humility to any people who would listen. To France, Germany, and Spain went the soldiers of the Church, to Asia Minor, the Greek islands, and the Near East. Brother Egidio and Brother Eletto sailed off to Tunisia; Brother Benedetto of Arezzo went to Greece; six brothers, about whom we know little but their names, happily set off for Morocco, five of them making it. They may have been as humble as Francis wanted them to be, and naive, but they were also abrasive. Having been ordered to leave Morocco by Emperor Miramolin Abu-Yâqub, who was understandably irate at their preaching against the Mohammedan religion, they managed to worm their way back. Caught again in the act of preaching, they were subjected to frightful tortures and finally beheaded, it was reported, at the hands of Abu-Yâqub himself.

We do not know from which port Francis sailed for Egypt, shrouded in legend as he is. We hear only that he left Italy in June with twelve companions, five of whose names are recorded, the one especially appealing in that he had taken a name that is a veritable reflection of the light found by his Brothers in Poverty: Brother Illuminato. Francis left eleven of his brothers with Brother Elias in Syria and then hurried off to Egypt with only Illuminato as his traveling mate. He was dismayed at what he found.

The man of peace had never seen such a fortified city: soaring double walls protected it on the river side, with triple walls landward; barbicans and bastions, over a hundred towers, and twenty-two gates. A chain stretched across the river just north of the city had been hacked into pieces to allow the Europeans to arrive at the foot of the great walls. Epidemic alone had depleted the crusading army by one-sixth. Women of the camp—army wives, daughters, and just followers—were in force, capable of great deeds, like women in war through history. But their very presence and all that it implied must have been appalling to a man who, so it was said, could barely bring himself to look a woman in the eyes. Francis watched assault after assault on the ancient city. He who dreamed of the brotherhood and love of all mankind watched the instruments of the death of his Christ flaunted as banners of war. He watched as captive Muslim spies were tortured and mutilated by means that only demons in the souls of the European Christians could have conjured. Having an eye cut out or a finger lopped off were kindnesses. As bad as anything was the dissension he witnessed among the Christians. When Francis saw events leading up to the spontaneous and misguided attack of August 29, he protested. But he was talked down.

Like so many men before and since his time, Francis had gone to a foreign land in good faith, thinking to bring peace. What he found there was too much for him. Such hatred, cruelty, and senseless antagonism he had never imagined. Finally, perhaps in desperation, he allowed that there was yet one untried way to achieve peace. If he could convert the defending sultan, al-Kamil, nephew of the brilliant Saladin, then further battle would be unnecessary. Like most of the simple soldiers who were fighting this war, he naively saw it as a religious war—the error of deluded victims through history. The crusades had long since become political exercises meant to garner material rewards of land and wealth for the lords who commanded the troops. Certain popes may have seen them as holy wars, but even that is reasonably suspect and certainly a contradiction in terms. Never doubting that they could convert Sultan al-Kamil to Christianity, Francis and Illuminato begged permission from Cardinal Pelagius to cross enemy lines under a flag of truce. At first the cardinal rejected their proposal. "'If you go, you will never come back,' he said. 'If we go,' they replied, 'there will be no fault imputable to you; for you wouldn't be sending us; you would merely refrain from putting obstacles in our way.' The cardinal finally relented, disclaiming all responsibility, washing his hands in the ancient metaphorical way, and no doubt feeling relief at getting the pair of fanatics out of his way."[3]

The Muslim guards were reticent and suspicious but eventually decided that Francis and Illuminato were so innocent and gentle that they were mad. Francis did not succeed in converting al-Kamil, who listened patiently to their Christian arguments. Nor would the Muslim agree to a demonstration of faith through an ordeal by fire. Disappointed, Francis and Illuminato were given gifts and then, after a several-day layover as guests of al-Kamil, were escorted back through the no-man's-land surrounding Damietta. Kind and civilized as al-Kamil was, Francis saw that it was not he who was prolonging the war but the Europeans who, for their own less-than-uplifting reasons, wanted to score an unconditional surrender; any taking of Damietta was going to be a hollow victory.

Like so many of his forebears, particularly like his uncle, Saladin, al-Kamil was an honorable man, brilliantly civilized, considerate, and an admirer of Westerners, their literature, and their languages. Basically he was a man of peace whose major problems, like those of the other Ayyubite rulers, were with his own people. He had none of the barbarous hatreds and cruel streaks of vindictiveness so characteristic of the Europeans who opposed him. By October he realized that Damietta could no longer be defended. The population had been decimated by disease, and there were not enough of them left to man the walls.

He made a final offer to the Christians: if they would but leave Egypt, he would return to them the True Cross, Jerusalem, Bethlehem, and Nazareth. Again the command voices wrangled, with Cardinal Pelagius winning out. He believed it wrong to come to terms with an infidel, and furthermore, he believed the Muslim forces in general were on the verge of collapse.

On November 5 Damietta fell before an awesome rush of Christians, who were delighted with the treasures they found, the supplies and equipment. These were divided among the commanders, with the rank and file enjoying the inevitable looting that is the follow-up of every conquest. Of a population of about eighty thousand Muslims, only about three thousand were still living, too sick to look after themselves or even to bury their dead. Three hundred of them were immediately selected as hostages, young children were given over for instruction in the Christian religion, and the rest were sold into slavery. Al-Kamil, in the meantime, had simply moved upstream to Mansourah.

1220

Throughout the new year the crusading forces were stalemated at Damietta. King John of Jerusalem, whose rapport with Cardinal Pelagius was, by this time, so bad that there was no point for him to remain in Egypt, left for Armenia, to which he intended to lay claim in the name of his second wife, Stephanie of Armenia, and their infant son. That kingdom had been up for grabs since the summer of 1219 when its king, Leo II, died. John had not even reached Armenia when Stephanie died, a result, it was noised about, of a severe beating which he had administered for her unsuccessful attempt to poison her stepdaughter Yolanda, no doubt in the interest of her own son. Then a few weeks later the son died, ending any claim that John might entertain on Armenia. He did not return to Egypt but went instead to Jerusalem, where he remained, looking after the rights of Yolanda, hereditary queen through his first wife, Maria of Montferrat.

During the Damiettan impasse some small rebuilding began and a few walls were repaired. The chief mosque was blessed and rededicated as a cathedral in the name of the Virgin. But mostly the crusaders waited. Pope Honorius kept sending assurances that Frederick would be on his way, but even that did not ring true since it was known that Frederick had just requested one more delay of his departure. He cited conditions in Germany as his excuse, but Honorius was not gullible enough for that. He had known Frederick as a child in Sicily. He had deeper insights into the king's motivations and pragmatic actions than the adult Frederick cared to admit. Honorius sent him a rather surly letter in response to his request for delay, equating him with a common criminal and giving him a date, the first of May, to set forth as was God's Will, for all Christendom was at stake. Had he known, Honorius might have pointed out to his advantage that *il poverello* and Brother Illuminato had set the example, and in a sense stolen Frederick's thunder, by getting to the Holy Land ahead of him, and then by visiting Jerusalem and the most holy Sepulcher of Christ. But things were not going well for Francis either. He had heard that, despite his outward-looking proselytizing, his new order was fragmenting. His carefully laid-out rules were being set aside, brothers were leaving the order, and fervent sons of poverty were being isolated by changes instigated sometimes from without. It was reported to Francis that even Brother Giovanni della Capella had apostatized and was forming a new order. There Francis had his Judas. All things considered, it was time to return home.

There is no denying that Francis made light of intellectual exercise. He was not anti-intellectual; he simply did not consider learning to be useful to his friars. To him learning was a stumbling block to poverty and humility. There is a story about Francis at this time that does neither his sanctity nor his love a good turn. On returning from Outremer, he stopped off at Bologna, where he heard that Brother Peter Staccia, knowledgeable in law, had taken over the Franciscan rest house and turned it into a place for study and the teaching of canon law. This was in direct defiance of Francis's principles. He stormed into the house, driving out all the occupants—even the sick—and closing the place down. By this time his temper was thoroughly unleashed. He accused the intimidated Peter Staccia of trying to destroy the order and shouted his desire that the brothers pray rather than read. He brought down on the legal-minded friar a curse so terrible that the victim fell on his knees, begging the future saint to retract it. Francis ranted that it was impossible since Christ Himself had already confirmed it in heaven. It was irrevocable. Thoroughly inconsolable, the professor took to bed where he was destroyed by sulphur from heaven perforating both him and the bed. The poor man exuded a frightful smell as he was being delivered into the hands of the devil. If there is even a grain of truth in the story, Francis does not shine in an amiable light.

The order had grown too large to be managed on a person-to-person basis. And despite his heavenly inspiration, Francis was no administrator. He saw that Cardinal-Bishop Ugolino of Ostia, a man sincerely interested in him and the movement he had started, would make an effective guardian angel. Around this time Francis appealed to Pope Honorius III to appoint Ugolino the authoritative protector and "corrector" of the brotherhood. As a new patron Ugolino played a minor role, but as time went on he became increasingly active, more and more relieving Francis of his duties, reassuring and sometimes discomfiting and hurting. An admirer of Francis and his ideals, Ugolino was also a prince of the Church. As Pope Gregory IX and with the order backing him, Ugolino would try to reform the Church by increasing Franciscan authority while negating Frederick's. Francis, too, set out to reform the Church, but not in the manner of Ugolino. Frederick would reform the world and men's ways of looking at it. In this, he and Francis clasp hands. But not in the same spirit.

Frederick had reached a point past denial that he was angling for his son's royal coronation—and that he intended to keep his beloved Sicily for himself. Frederick had carefully formulated his plans. He would go on crusade, but more in his father's empire-building spirit than through any compunction to piety, and only when he had accomplished all the things at home that needed doing. The pope could not have been surprised when he received a letter from Frederick: "We hope to obtain from your beatitude the favourable issue to our demand that we keep to ourselves the Realm of Sicily for our life."[4] Frederick had always insisted that he meant to keep his sworn vow that he would turn the island kingdom over to his son when he reached his majority. Had he not had Henry crowned king of Sicily when he was still an infant? But now Frederick had come right out with it. And there was a new shade of meaning to his words. Now he felt strong enough to use the word "demand." Even "intention" would have been more tactful. And at just the time that Honorius, in Viterbo, was receiving Frederick's letter, the German princes contrived a meeting in Frankfurt to stage a "surprise" election of Frederick's son as Henry VII, king of the Romans, a bit of playacting that ensued when Frederick was "absent," thereby lending a phony aura to his claim that it came to him as much a surprise as he thought it would be to the pope He could honestly point out that he had not been present to stop the election. Why it should have come as a surprise to Honorius defies reason, for surely he had been advised by wiser members of the Curia that this is what Frederick had been contemplating all along. Perhaps only the brazenness of the move could be termed surprising. But, contradicting even that, Walther von der Vogelweide—admittedly beholden to Frederick for his fief—had already publicly chided the princes for resisting Frederick's plans, masking the argument under a thin veil of humor:

> . . . Just let him have his way and go,
> Perhaps he thus will never vex you more!
> If he dies there [on crusade]—which Heaven forfend—you score;
> If he return to us, his friends, the more
> We praise the fate that doth our lord restore.[5]

Before Frederick convened his diet in Frankfurt he had already done the groundwork, greasing palms, rewarding, buying loyalty, restoring order. The election of young Henry probably took place in the cathedral (not the present one), which had been built by King Louis "the German" (804–876) and which was later dedicated to Saint Bartholomew. It was difficult for Pope Honorius to complain about the election since the ecclesiastical princes, now the dominant elements, bore the brunt of responsibility. It became obvious that Frederick had been working on the bishops, and probably working for months, when three days after the election he signed the *Privilegium in favorem principum ecclesiasticorum*, which was, in a sense, a document that solidified the already-signed Bull of Eger of 1213 and was obviously a quid pro quo gesture to the bishops. From now on the ecclesiastical princes were absolute lords over their own Church lands within the boundaries of Germany, from which all imperial authority was excluded. The privilege made up a body of laws that in almost every way dealt with the relationship of the Church to the sovereign, sometimes even reducing him to a status beneath that of the ecclesiastical princes, as when it established that should a man be excommunicated by a bishop and not absolved within six weeks, then he was automatically subject to the ban of the empire. It would seem that Frederick was dangerously curtailing his own power; and to some extent he was. But that was the price he had to pay if he wanted Henry established on the throne of Germany while he, Frederick, returned to Sicily as emperor. The document that Frederick signed isolated Germany from the progressive movement of national unity being nurtured by Philip Augustus of neighboring France, with effects that were long lasting. It can reasonably be claimed that the later fragmentation of Germany into principalities originated on April 26, 1220, when Frederick took pen in hand. In the end the Church benefited from the privilege, which did not make the crowning of Henry less annoying to Honorius. And if the Curia had not already learned the lesson, surely by this time it was driven home that Frederick's promises to both Innocent III and Honorius had been simply words without meaning, the letters and oaths he had signed mere refuse.

Frederick had learned his methods well, mainly from the popes themselves, as Innocent III had predicted years before. This is not to excuse his broken pledges and his use of expediency in the cause of self-interest. He was playing the game according to the rules and practices of his time, if indeed there were rules. And when one examines the case closely, the thought occurs that, for all his dissembling, he was merely exploiting a flaw in the various written oaths he had sworn. He had, often enough, renounced personal union of the crowns of Italy and Germany; no mention had ever been made of Henry. In his eyes there was no breach of any treaty here. The treaties had been made in Frederick's name. Certainly Frederick owed no great debt of gratitude to the papacy. Innocent III had exploited him and used him as a pawn in the most obvious way, as he had his mother, Constance. Frederick may be cited for his callous conduct, but it must be remembered that within the context of his time he was doing nothing out of the ordinary. Ethical considerations aside, he had set the stage for his coronation march on Rome and, the pope could hope, for his crusade.

There is not much left of the thirteenth century in Frankfurt except for the Saalhof Chapel, actually a wee part of the imperial palace that has been reconstructed and made a part of the History Museum. The twelfth-century city walls and moat are gone now, what is left of them marked only by streets with names ending in *graben*—ditch. Saint Leonard's Church on the right bank was only one year into building at the time of Frederick's court. Too bad that he missed his personally commissioned relief sculptures by Master Englebertus, which were about to be placed over the two main entrances but due to later reconstruction are now inside. Minus sunlight, alas, they lose their intensity, their emotional impact, and to a point their reason for being. But they still speak to us. Especially rewarding is the Jesus receiving the adoration of John the Evangelist, Mary, Peter, and Saint George, the first and last on their knees as they are in corner recesses. With what ceremonial dignity the five face us as we enter Saint Leonard's! Mary makes a gesture of peace. Peter holds the key to heaven, John his book, and George his accoutrements of battle. George wears the faintest trace of a friendly smile, as though he sees something vaguely humorous or embarrassing about his soldierly presence in that august company. The simple, flat background all the better rivets our attention to the gorgeous Romanesque carving. Again, this is genuine hieratic sculpture attempting to plumb an imaginary other-world, a cleaner world than ours, in a sense the womb-beginning of us all. Man strives for perfection; but, being imperfect, how can man imagine perfection? In a sense Master Englebertus did it for us. And on his second doorway, Saint James the Great maintains the same unruffled dignity; existing on a plane beyond mere mundane reality, he holds the cockleshell emblem of the multitudes who were currently making pilgrimages to his shrine in Spain.

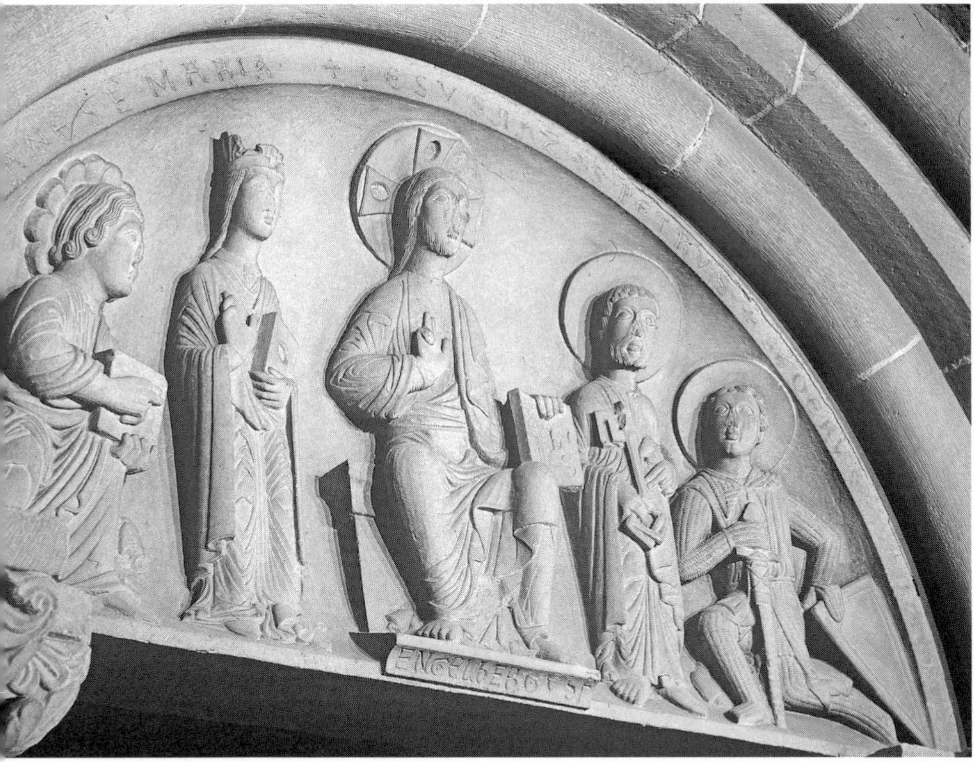

St. Leonard's Church, Frankfurt, Germany

By now enough of the cold and dark of northern Europe for Frederick! Having swept all blocks aside, he prepared to move to a southland that had been crying for eight years for his return. By now the cry had become shrill. He thankfully gave over the cares of ruling Germany in the name of his eight-year-old son to a subordinate government entrusted to Englebert, archbishop of Cologne, a man devoted to protecting the common good against the greedy interests of the princes and lesser lords. He would serve both the empire and his ward with distinction. Frederick convened his final German court in Augsburg in Bavaria, the jumping-off place for Italy since ancient days when it was founded by Emperor Augustus. Gathering an enormous host—the best of German manhood—at Augsburg, with Queen Constance in attendance, and perhaps remembering his own lonely childhood, Frederick enjoyed a last few days with little Henry. It would be twelve years before father and son would meet again, and then not under the best of circumstances; Constance would never see her child again.

Chapter Seven

King of tremendous Majesty,
who saves those-to-be-saved free,
save me, Fount of piety.
***Dies Irae*, verse 8**

1220

To his lessers there seemed to be something God-given about this twenty-six-year-old king and would-be emperor. He had circumvented the expressed wishes of one of the cleverest popes of the Middle Ages, and now he had forced his successor and the Curia to accept the fact that he would crusade in his good time—even then only when and if he received the imperial crown. Frederick had seen the end of his enemies in Germany, or at least he had immobilized them. It behooved him now to put an end to his enemies in Italy as well. To avoid hostility from Spoleto on his triumphant march to Rome, he ordered the arrest of its duke, Diepold of Schweinspeunt, who was taken into custody by his own son-in-law, James of Severino. Frederick's empire would suffer as a result of some of the questionable wheeling and dealing by which he coaxed the princes into his orbit. While the privileges granted to the ecclesiastical princes stood as good examples, as did his giving away of German land, on occasion he alienated with his untoward generosity the very princes on whom he needed to rely. For the moment, though, things were going swimmingly, and Frederick knew it. His last diet in Germany—the one at Augsburg—would be a joyous pageant of high living with only one thing lacking: he was the acknowledged emperor, but not *in fact* emperor until he received the sacred emblems of office from the reigning pontiff. Galling to Honorius and the Roman Curia as it might be, it was inevitable. Lionization was the order of the day!

Augsburg's day was pending. It became one of the most important cities in Germany during the Renaissance, at which time it hosted the Luther-inspired "confession" of Protestant belief as well as fostering the arts, especially of the important Holbein family of painters. Both Leopold Mozart, father of Amadeus, and Bertolt Brecht were born there. Still Augsburg could claim a certain notoriety in the thirteenth century. It was jammed with traffic moving to and from the Brenner Pass into Italy. Had Frederick, on his entrance into Germany eight years ago, been traveling more conventionally, he no doubt would have passed through Augsburg. By contrast, now in the flush of success and secure that all was well in his world, he intended to set out from Augsburg and to follow the most-used route over the Alps to what all his life he would consider his homeland. Augsburg had a cathedral worthy of the active center of commerce that it was, with patina-encrusted bronze doors considered to be among the most important by German craftsmen of the Middle Ages. Cast in thirty-two separate panels attached to a wooden ground, they display graceful figures against flat backgrounds, with no attempt to create any feeling of natural surroundings. Grinning lions hold circular doorpulls in their mouths. There are centaurs and rampant lions, representations of the seasons, figures leaping and cavorting as though some kind of strange current were sweeping through them. Warriors threaten, assuming eloquent, balletic poses that contrast with customary representations of militancy.

While a medieval Eve is being tempted by the serpent, Adam gives in to temptation, striking a bacchantic pose while merely plucking a cluster of grapes. Better, he could serve as a Debussy balletic faun in an afternoon indulgence or, at the very least, a Shakespearean Puck, so casual is his enjoyment, so without hesitation or self-consciousness his appropriation of nature's gift. Samson, as told in Judges 14:6, is attacked by a lion and portrayed at the moment when "the Spirit of the Lord came mightily upon him, and he rent him as he would have rent a kid, and he had nothing in his hand: but he told not his father or his mother what he had done." Striving for spiritual expression, these figures show the influence of Byzantine art, and not a little of ancient Rome, putting them outside the Ottonian style, which ended in the eleventh century with the death of Emperor Henry II. Despite the building's five stained glass windows—the oldest significant German examples to be found—the Romanesque cathedral itself, alas, has been hidden beneath a layering of Gothic additions.

Italy was enjoying an uncharacteristic moment of peace, thanks in part to the political machinations of the cardinal-bishop of Ostia, Ugolino dei Conti, Francis Bernardone's protector, and Frederick's future evil genius. As headstrong as his uncle Innocent III, and like him destined to be a political pope, Ugolino was an ideal prelate to

Adam, south door, Augsburg Cathedral, Germany

institute the Inquisition several years later. But all that was coming. For now, even the knowledge that he was walking into a land where discord and personal hostility lay barely beneath the surface could not dim Frederick's ardor. Skirting Innsbruck, he headed for the Brenner Pass. When he descended on the south side of the Alps he followed the River Isarco to Vipiteno. From this charming mountain village—a chic resort today with a laughter-filled main street terminating at a severe fifteenth-century gate—Frederick led his party to the Tirolean town of Bressanone at the confluence of the rivers Isarco and Rienza, secure behind her two-hundred-year-old walls, and still proudly showing the twentieth-century early Romanesque and later Gothic-style frescoes in the Church of San Giovanni Battista. Bressanone lies in a plain in sight of mountains so gentle in their rise that they seem to beckon, to envelope the travel-weary, characteristics that must have been lost on Frederick, so anxious was he to move south. Continuing to follow the Isarco, the royal party reached Bolzano, with its three nearby castles. A fourth, the Castel Roncolo, an aerie balanced precariously on a huge rock outcropping and, interestingly, preserving Gothic frescoes of the Tristan and Isolde legend, was probably in the planning stage about the time of Frederick's visit. Five centuries later Goethe would gush over the Adige River where "the foothills [of the Alps] are covered with vineyards. The vines are trained on long, low trellises and the purple grapes hang gracefully from the roof and ripen in the warmth of the soil so close beneath them."[1] Trento, with embattled walls seemingly intended to dam the valley of the Adige, was inhabited by a prehistoric people known as the Riatians, then by the Romans, Ostrogoths, Lombards, Franks, militant German bishops, by Austria, and finally by Napoleon's forces. It was not until the sixteenth century that Trent came of age with the Council of Trent, which did so much to reunify the Church after the onslaught of the Protestant Reformation. The cathedral, dating from the eleventh century, has been rebuilt, altered, and restored over the centuries until 1889, even to the present as the unfinished tower attests. The castle at Trento is really three structures, only one of which is medieval, and even it—the Castelvecchio—was enlarged in the fifteenth century with a Venetian Gothic loggia. The mingling of the Venetian and Alpine styles creates a curious architectural ambience in Trento, the overhanging roofs adding a strange feature to the more elegant and familiar Venetian.

It was in an entirely different spirit that Frederick visited the region now than when, eight years before and going in the opposite direction, he had turned aside to sneak into a kingdom that was rightfully his. This time, with banners flying high, the young king rode in tumultuous triumph, though his subjects, apparently expecting a more heroic figure, were a little put out that he looked so much a boy. Exaggerated to the extreme, his exploits in Germany had been noised about in northern Italy—and southern, too—and a more regally imperial figure than Frederick now cut had been anticipated—no, yearned for.

Frederick made it a point not to enter the cities on the way to Rome but instead camped outside the walls, giving none of them an inkling as to his sympathies now or for the future. Moving on another fifty-six miles, he arrived at the outskirts of Verona, where he pitched his camp in sunny splendor. Germans escaping from under their darker skies and shrinking from their colder winters have always relished this part of Italy. After enduring his years north of the Alps, Frederick was no exception. He luxuriated with his train of followers in a tent city awash in Italian sunshine outside of Verona, within earshot of the city where literature's great lovers, Romeo and Juliet, would live, love, and die before the century was out. It casts additional light on their tragic story to remember that their brawling families were on opposite sides of the political stage, the Montagues being Guelfs, the Capulets Ghibellines.

It may have been from Verona that Frederick sent to Pope Honorius a notification of his anticipated arrival in Rome, for the first time entrusting Hermann von Salza as his ambassador. Frederick received representatives from most of the communes of northern Italy, whose missions were to confirm privileges of self-interest vis-à-vis the kingdom of Sicily as well as the empire. Remembering papal suspicions, Frederick scrupulously avoided any deals with them as king of Sicily, only confirming their rights concerning the empire. It was a disappointment and a shock to envoys from cities that had been loyal to him when he was so desperately in need of their help eight years before. Genoa's ruffled feelings were hardly soothed by Frederick's granting them control of the Ligurian coast, especially when it was learned that Caesarean largesse extended even to their old enemy, Pisa. In fact, they were so unsoothed that the Genoese ambassadors stormed out of the royal presence in a huff and refused to send representatives to his coronation, preferring to chalk that ceremony off with a few gifts. In lieu of Frederick's promises eight years ago to grant them the same privileges that had been bestowed by his forerunners, they had the right, they felt, to expect a statement of their benefits concerning the kingdom of Sicily. Frederick refused to make any commitment, informing them that these things would be studied in good time when he was back in his kingdom. He was determined to move on Rome in a peaceful Italy, with none of the endemic jealousies and perennial warring that was the norm among the cities, and he was going to be recognized as emperor by the recalcitrant communes of northern Italy. Both of these feats, with certain minor aberrations, he managed. His problems were beyond inter-city haggling. He was playing two roles. The problem of getting the northern cities to settle down in peace, by implication abandoning their independence, was gigantic enough. But with the pope adamantly against his establishing the kingship of Sicily in the same person as the emperorship and capable of fomenting much trouble by his opposition, Frederick had limited options. No slightest gesture could be made at this point to indicate that papal wishes were going to be abridged, that he did indeed have it in mind to unite the two offices in his own being and later in that of his son Henry.

The one low moment for Frederick—and it was only a moment—came when Milan petulantly refused to grant him the iron crown of Lombardy in spite of the fact that he was recognized as uncrowned emperor. It was a harbinger of things to come, though in his flush of success Frederick could hardly be expected to see it as a hint of a reconstituted Lombard League, which had proven such a thorn in the side of his grandfather, Barbarossa. On the other hand, and balancing the rejection by Milan, the Venetians were eager to maintain an aura of neutrality. Doge Pietro Ziani, whose wife was a daughter of erstwhile King Tancred of Sicily, sent an embassy to sign a treaty with the future emperor by which, among other considerations, the Venetians won a privilege of freedom from custom duties within the empire, the doge promising in return an annual tribute of cash, pepper, and a fine robe. Near Mantua Frederick had his first meeting with precocious, fifteen-year-old Azzo VII, marquis of Este, in whose favor he settled a dispute with Padua. Azzo's family had always been an on-again off-again threat to the imperial cause. Azzo VII would prove just as wavering in his support. Loyal now, but give him another few years.

The only exception Frederick made to his rule of not entering and spending time in the cities of his imperium north of Rome was Bologna. Curious and given to learning, he was intrigued by the city that hosted the first true university in Europe famous for its studies on canon and civil law and now, in the thirteenth century, on medicine and the liberal arts. It is said that eventually the school would attract as many as ten thousand students. In Frederick's time it was a loosely organized entity, if it was organized at all. Such a thing as a campus did not exist, but rather the university was scattered throughout the city wherever it was convenient for the professors to lecture, be it in homes, in rented rooms, or simply out-of-doors. The lecturers were hired by students (often older than teachers) who arranged contractually the amount of pay and the conditions of instruction. It was only in later centuries that the master-apprentice relationship was established. Finally, in the sixteenth century the professors were given quarters, and the university itself was housed in the single new palazzo that serves now as a municipal library. It is somewhat surprising to learn that during the Middle Ages certain women professors were given places of distinction at the university. One of them—Novella Calderini—was allegedly so beautiful that she lectured from behind a screen, or hidden by a thick veil, to keep lusting students' minds in the upper spheres of education where they belonged.

Frederick wallowed in the hospitality lavished on him by the good-natured Bolognesi, a fun-loving people, and handsome too, though they do seem prone to markedly prominent noses. Their cordiality can be measured by noting that a short time after Frederick's visit Bologna's most celebrated jurist, Roffredo of Benevento, joined his court, indicating the direction of imperial thinking: legal justice for all, a concept that would attract to him a large intellectual elite. The Church might for a long time hold sway over the masses, but Frederick, thanks to his policies, would attract an ever-enlarging cultural and intellectual aristocracy. For a young man Frederick had his options in order. But the gesture of taking Bologna's prime jurist into his court was, in the long run, politically futile since this city in years to come invariably sympathized with the opposing Guelfs.

Another personage, slightly older than Frederick, of humble origin, but a master of that florid style of writing so much admired in the Middle Ages, joined Frederick's train. Pier delle Vigne, instead of studying for the priesthood—the most commonly accepted way for a man of scant means to set up a successful career for himself—had managed to study at the University of Bologna. More important than his higher training was the fact that he had come from Capua, which was renowned for its school of *ars dictandi,* the formal Latin prose writing that he would eventually make his prime strength. Knowing that Frederick had per-

Pier delle Vigne, Museo Provinciale Campano, Capua, Italy

petual need for a master of courtly correspondence, Archbishop Berard of Palermo introduced Pier delle Vigne into the court, where he worked first on minor official business and in later years became the leading civil servant in Frederick's Sicilian prototype of the modern lay state. In 1230 Pier would be tapped for a comparatively lightweight diplomatic mission, launching him into another field in which he excelled. Judging from the battered portrait in the Museo Provinciale Campano in Capua, Pier was a man of quiet, retiring nature and not without a sense of humor. There is about his portrait a vague hauteur—or perhaps pride, for which he would be justified—but never vanity or arrogance. He looks to have been a friendly and sociable person, a little overfed, and very intelligent. Pier would prove an invaluable member of the imperial court and Frederick's much-loved friend, until years later when his terrible and tragic end seemed to indicate otherwise.

Such vivacity among the Bolognese! They stroll their arcaded walkways rain or shine, socializing in sidewalk cafes, dry and shaded, and shouting above the noise of the traffic. Among other reasons for thanks, Bologna gave to America her favorite sandwich meat as well as her synonym for foolish or exaggerated talk. Bologna as the gastronomic capital of Italy is a fact attested to by any fair-thinking Italian—even a Frenchman. The teeming city is one of the most exciting of northern Italy, with every *alimentare* (delicatessen) tempting the hungry eye. And the restaurants! To enjoy ravioli cooked in a sealed balloon of flaky puff pastry filled with creamy cheese sauce—is an experience made in heaven. And, of course, there is always the classic sauce bolognese! Only the Italian language, gestures, and facial expressions can approximate adequate appreciation.

Culinary delights and friendly citizens notwithstanding, an endless array of historical associations and visual treats makes Bologna one of the most intriguing of European cities. Located at the foot of a spur of the Apennines called Monte della Guardia (in days past sentries were posted there to keep an eye on hostile Modena) and between two rivers, the Reno and the Savena, Bologna was inhabited as early as the Bronze Age, with subsequent settlements during the Iron Age, and then the Etruscan period when the city was known as Felsina. Only rare traces remain of the Celtic Boii, who settled at Bononia (hence the Roman-derived name Bologna) and who were driven out by the Romans and went on to settle in Bohemia (also a name for which they are derivative). Bologna was held successively by the Lombards and the papacy, thanks to a donation by Pippin III, father of Charlemagne, and then was finally sacked in 902 by the Hungarians.

The Roman city can be traced by the right-angled streets that are oriented to the cardinal points. The Romans encircled the town with walls that were refortified in the tenth century and extended on the southern and eastern sides. The Via Emilia ran through Bologna; a part of it was later unearthed in the construction of the modern subterranean mall beneath the city's central piazza. Finally recognized as a city of worth by virtue of the founding of the university, it was granted its first charter by Frederick Barbarossa. Bologna rose to special magnificence in Frederick's day and in the following century. Dante and Petrarch studied at the university, and in 1506 Bologna was brought under the protection of the papacy by Pope Julius II, patron-nemesis of Michelangelo, and remained so shielded until 1860, when it became part of the kingdom of Italy.

As in most Italian cities, the Renaissance left its mark on Bologna; but the overwhelming impression is of the Middle Ages. The most spectacular medieval evidence is surely the two leaning towers, citified versions of the European castle keep. Both are square brick towers: the Asinelli is 320 feet high and four feet out of perpendicular; the Garisenda, which remains unfinished, is 163 feet high and ten feet out of perpendicular. (The more famous, and admittedly more handsome, leaning tower at Pisa is sixteen feet out of perpendicular.) There are remains of other towers in Bologna, but none so spectacular or preposterous as these. At one time similar towers rose all over the city, sprouting like cactus as every man of means persisted in looking down on his neighbors. They were defensive in nature but, all things considered, were born first of all of monied madness! Other towns have family towers. Siena, Florence, and most spectacularly by sheer numbers San Gimignano, but nowhere are there two so close together and both leaning, creating a picture of a topsy-turvy world. Climbing them is a little like experiencing a "dizzy room" in an amusement park.

Medieval architecture in Bologna is usually two stories (not counting the ground level) with two- and three-lighted mullioned windows on the upper floors. The Piazza Maggiore is ringed by such pleasing buildings, some of them of Frederick's time. King Enzo's palace is the most interesting of several on the piazza, a brick building of the thirteenth century topped by the winged, or forked, battlements of the Ghibellines—ironically, since this is the palace in which Enzo, Frederick's natural son, who will enter our story later, was imprisoned for the long last years of his life. Enzo was never able to look down, alas, on the commanding presence of the god Neptune presiding over a host of nymphs, putti, and dolphins—all adorning a sixteenth century bronze fountain by Giambologna (a Frenchman, despite his name).

The Piazza della Mercanzia is elegant with its Loggia dei Mercanti, a brick building with enormous pointed arches on the ground floor and delicately traceried windows above. From between two windows protrudes the Gothic balcony from which court decisions and bankruptcies were announced. Canopied and ornate, the entire ensemble is crowned by a rigid row of winged Ghibelline battlements. In the same piazza are the thirteenth-century Torre Alberici and a shop dated 1273.

The staggering list of churches and works of art in Bologna includes the Church of Saint Dominic, more interesting historically than aesthetically. Dominic spent the last years of his life journeying between Toulouse and Bologna. In fact he was here this year presiding over the first chapter of his order, during which its final constitutions were established. The constitutions were seen as "one of the most remarkable legislative achievements of western Christendom" to which "must be attributed the continuing vigor and unity of the Dominican Order."[2] The Church of Saint Dominic was started in 1221, the year of his death in Bologna, and houses his tomb-altar, attributed to Nicola Pisano, with two angels thought to be by Michelangelo. There is also in the church a stylistically thrilling crucifix by another native Pisan, Giunta Pisano, important for introducing a new concept—a dead Christ, sagging pathetically, limp-armed, eyes closed, in contrast to the stiffer, posed, rigidly erect and unreal figures then in vogue. The Renaissance was approaching. The visual world, as opposed to the realm of the spirit, was becoming ever more important to artists and learned men. Frederick himself has been labeled "the first of Renaissance princes two hundred years before his time."[3]

The largest church in Bologna is dedicated to San Petronio, fifth-century patron and bishop of the city. Size has nothing to do with its main glory, the central doorway by Jacopo della Quercia, only a part of which is from his hand, though the original contract called for him to design the entire ensemble. In a series of stridently sensual bas-reliefs of the Old and New Testaments, Jacopo created a whole new concept, peaks of tension as figures strain against one another, nullifying any feeling for negative space. In a kind of stone poetry Adam and Eve work out their penalty for committing the first sin while infants Cain and Abel play at their feet. Familiar biblical stories are told in a new language, the realistic, almost naturalistic, terms of the coming age. History is the study of change, of progress, not a conservative study of the status quo. Artists, scientists, philosophers, all types of thinking men and women have encouraged our forward movement. And here at San Petronio's church Jacopo della Quercia opens one small door to the future. A small door—a great achievement.

Frederick's journey south to Rome by the Via Flaminia took him across the Apennines, passing, but not visiting, meaningful places of his origin—Jesi, Assisi, Foligno, Spoleto. At last he reached the outskirts of the Eternal City and raised his imperial encampment on Monte Mario (then called Monte Malo), a height used by almost every conqueror, would-be looter, and friend through history. Frederick's father and grandfather had viewed Rome from this vantage point, as had his Norman great-uncle, Robert Guiscard, before his appalling rape of the city in the name of Pope Gregory VII. But Frederick had come in peace. He had already received papal emissaries to whom he reiterated his intentions of crusade and gave absolute assurances that he had every intent of keeping Sicily separate from the Holy Roman Empire—a hollow promise if ever there was one. He had even put it into writing in a letter to the uneasy Honorius III: "Who could be more obedient to the Church than he who was nursed at her breast and had rested in her lap? Who more loyal? Who could be so mindful of benefits already received, or so prepared to acknowledge his obligations according to the will and pleasure of his benefactors?"[4] But Frederick had few qualms over his lie; if the pope needed words as a deposit on the imperial crown, then words were what the pope would get.

The pope may have been doddering, but he was not stupid. He had not frequented the corridors of power all these years for nothing. He could see as plainly as anyone that prelates and magnates were arriving from Sicily in unprecedented numbers, invited to the coronation by the recipient of the crown himself who, it went without saying, further demanded of them new oaths of fealty. It was enough to arouse the least suspicious mind in the world. But Frederick assured the pope that he viewed his claim to Sicily not through inheritance from his father, but rather through his mother's line, and everyone knew that she had held Sicily as a fief of the Church. He further promised to keep separate the administrations of the empire and the kingdom, a promise that he kept, formally associating his son's name with his own on all official documents until Henry's death.

Other than his coronation and a few related activities, we have no record of how Frederick used his time during his short period in Rome. We assume that he had little opportunity for a serious study of the city's highlights, most of which he probably had missed the first time around. If anything, it would have been the ancient aspects of Rome that held him. We speculate that his Capuan gate of the future, his Apulian castles, and in his own image on his later coinage all verify it. And that is not to mention his persistent reverence for the Caesars as models for emulation. Classical remains were just then beginning to be appreciated in the historical sense, a fundamental activity of the coming Renaissance. From Monte Mario Frederick could pick out the major points of interest: the Colosseum still echoing in the universal subconscious with the screams of the tortured; the imperial forums; the Pantheon with its spectacular concrete dome; the palaces of the Caesars on their wooded hilltop; the stadium of Domitian—the scene of the martyrdom of Saint Agnes, today the Piazza Navona with three fountains and rich with odors wafting from thriving restaurants. More of the ancient city was standing in Frederick's day than in ours: the Renaissance popes used it as a convenient stone quarry for church building. But pragmatic as he was, Frederick could forgo the pleasure of on-the-spot delving into Rome's past, knowing in his own mind that he would be back again another day in a role more securely locked into that of the ancients—a pleasure, as it turned out, not in the cards for him. This visit to Rome, the very symbol of his expectations and pretensions, was his second and last.

On November 22, Frederick and Queen Constance set out from the royal encampment in splendor, descending to the city along the Via Triumphalis. They crossed the Tiber, moving eastward to the ancient Porta Collina, which was discovered in 1873 a few blocks short of the Porta Pia, at the junction of the Via Goito and the Via Venti Settembre. At the Castra Praetoria they were close approaching that source of the empire's power that Frederick wished to recreate, and he might have dwelt a little on the role played by that crack body of imperial guards. In the military sense the word *praetorium* means the headquarters of a commander-in-chief or of the emperor himself. A well-known paranoid, Emperor Tiberius (42 BC–AD 37) had insisted on strict discipline for his Praetorian guards, removed from the temptations and corruptions of his capital city. He housed them in luxurious barracks, the Castra Praetoria, outside the walls of the city, now in the vicinity of Mussolini's magnificent railroad terminal. The Praetorian Guard grew into the most formidable power in the Roman state, leading to that most melancholy scene in Roman history, when they shut themselves within their camp after the murder of aging Emperor Pertinax and put the throne up for auction. So was the fate of the empire decided when Julian bought his way into power while the Praetorian guards remained barricaded in their sumptuous barracks. Julian got his, though, ruling only sixty-six days before he, too, was murdered, to be succeeded by Septimius Severus (193 AD).

Having progressed as far as the Porta Collina, Frederick was met by a crucifix- and censer-bearing clergyman who escorted him toward Saint Peter's Basilica, chanting from Exodus 23:20, "Behold, I send an Angel before thee, to keep thee in the way, and to bring thee into the place which I have prepared." In a gesture reminiscent of ancient bread and circuses, gifts were scattered to the cheering mobs as the procession moved through the autumn sunlight. There would be none of the riotous bloodletting that marked the coronations of his grandfather and his father if Frederick had anything to say about it! Some questionable sources maintain that the holiday mood did not prevail throughout the several scheduled days of celebration. It seems that a certain cardinal promised the present of a dog to the ambassador from Florence. Forgetting that he had committed the animal to the Florentine, the cardinal gave it to the Pisan envoy, causing a riot in the streets when the two met. "The Devil took the shape of a dog . . . as we see by the mischief that followed."[5] Resentments were carried so far that a war flared up between these leading cities of Tuscany. For the most part, however, everyone put his best foot forward, German and Italian, Ghibelline and Guelf, churchman and layman, the Roman population itself, so notoriously skittery and disloyal. For once almost everyone was in agreement. It was a festive and proud day for Rome.

In the piazza before the venerable Saint Peter's (it still had another three hundred years to go before being torn down to make room for the present structure), the Roman senator[6] and certain counselors stepped forward to hold the emperor's horse. Pope Honorius III emerged in solemn procession from the church and waited at the head of the stairs. As he approached with the surety of youth, Frederick observed the bank of cardinals on the pope's right and on his left the cardinal-deacons. He himself was surrounded by attendants, men in long robes, and powerful, armor-clad knights, with legs and arms encased in chain mail, lugging long, narrow swords, and crested by close-fitting flat helmets. Without hesitation, with real or implied reverence, Frederick mounted the stairs, knelt to kiss the papal slipper, and then made his expected, and no doubt avidly anticipated, tribute of gold. With that, he was helped to his feet and embraced by a grateful Honorius. Did Honorius look back fourteen years to remember the gauche, street-running ragamuffin whom he had known in Palermo, whose domains now rivaled those of the ancient Caesars and were washed by the waters of the North Sea, the Baltic, and the Mediterranean? Side by side, with Frederick on the right, the two moved to a side chapel where Frederick reiterated his promise to protect the Church, its pontiff, and its property. He was then received as a canon of Saint Peter's.

It was not until then that Frederick was clad in the imperial vestments and the cloak of his grandfather, King Roger II of Sicily, deep red, with a golden embroidery of lions attacking camels, and embellished with Kufic characters and Byzantine-like arabesques, a product of the Palermitan Tiraz—the palace workshop. Now resplendently clad, Frederick was allowed to enter the basilica through the silver gate. Greeted and blessed by cardinals, he was escorted to the tomb of Saint Peter, where he paused for contemplation and prayer. He was anointed then at the tomb of Saint Maurice, the third-century Roman officer who perished with his friend, Gereon, and his Theban Legion, a company that, as we have seen, is said to be entombed in the Church of Saint Gereon in Cologne. With preliminaries out of the way, Frederick advanced to the candle-lit altar, where he confessed to the pope and received the kiss of peace.

After prayers came the ultimate triumph! Frederick was crowned first with the miter, then with the opulently bejeweled imperial crown, probably made for Emperor Otto I in the second half of the tenth century. Along with the robe of Roger II and additional items made for Frederick this year, and perhaps used in this ceremony (jeweled gloves and slippers, for example), the crown is a high point of the Imperial Treasury in the Hofburg in Vienna. Thought to be a product of the Benedictine Abbey at Reichenau, it was conceived as a hinged octagon, the believed ground plan of the heavenly Jerusalem. With twelve great stones set on the front, symbolizing the twelve apostles as well as, by an interesting juxtaposition, the twelve tribes of Israel, it is connected front to back by a jeweled arch reminiscent of Roman imperial helmets. Four enamel panels, including representations of Isaiah and Kings Solomon and David, enliven the sides and are augmented by additional panels heavily encrusted with jewels. It is a complicated statement, symbolizing the commonality of peoples and held together by interlacings creating the very form of the crown itself, different from any other known in the Western world. It remains a stunning climax to a fabulous collection!

Once crowned, Frederick was handed the imperial sword with which he made threatening and showy gestures as the protector of the Church. To complete the ceremony he was given the scepter and the imperial orb, which had first been used in the coronation ceremony of his father, while the choir intoned a hymn to his glory. Then Frederick stepped aside to watch while his queen was crowned empress.

For the Mass, which he celebrated as subdeacon assistant to the pope, the new emperor doffed his imperial emblems to dress in priestly robes and a heavily embroidered blue-and-gold dalmatic showing, among other things, the symbols of universal power—the sun and the moon.

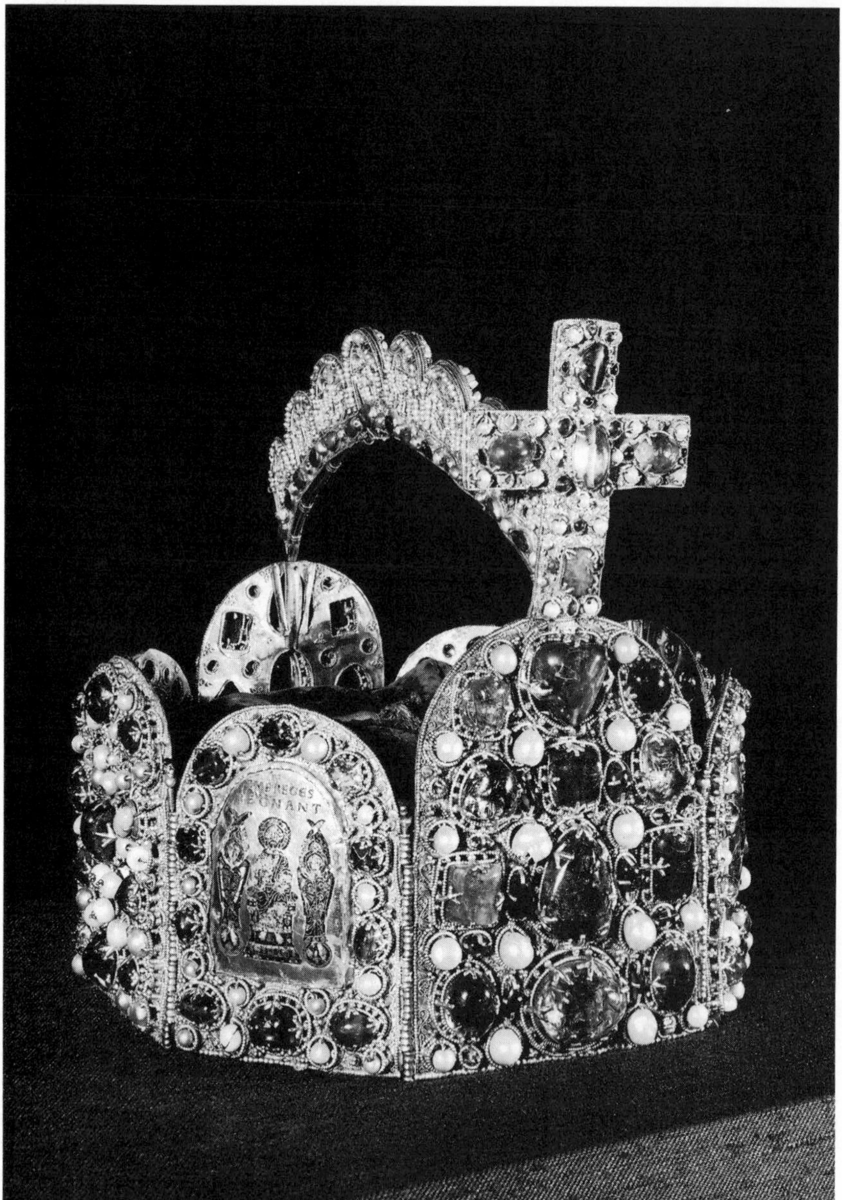

Imperial crown, Kunsthistorische Museum, Vienna, Austria. Photo credit: Erich Lessing/
Art Resources, NY

Both emperor and empress received the Eucharist from the hand of Honorius. The candles were extinguished, and a proclamation was read excommunicating all heretics. The secular and ecclesiastical powers were going hand in hand in matters of heresy, and by implication in matters of rebellion within the empire, a neat tit-for-tat agreement for Frederick. Both considerations would be conveniently called up in the future. There then followed a ceremony that was to haunt Frederick for years. Upon being handed the crusaders' cross by Cardinal Ugolino dei Conti, Frederick, blatantly catering to the Church, swore his promise to set out the following August on his long-heralded crusade. He appointed the cardinal, already papal legate, as his own legate in Italy along with Conrad of Metz. How was Frederick to know that Ugolino was destined to be the next pope and his most formidable adversary? At the moment all was tranquil. But it was only a moment of calm, an oasis as it were between the treacherously shifting sands of the reigns of Innocent III and Ugolino dei Conti as Pope Gregory IX.

Outside Saint Peter's Frederick held the papal stirrup while Honorius, who was about seventy now, climbed aboard his mount. Thus Frederick fulfilled a symbolic gesture of menial servitude, a stumbling block in relations between emperors and popes in the past, most recently between Frederick's grandfather, Barbarossa, and the only English pope, Adrian IV. But Frederick was not going to carp over symbols. He was the crowned emperor, and he had kept his kingdom of Sicily to boot. With Honorius leading and Frederick and Constance preceded by his imperial sword bearer, the splendidly caparisoned procession set off through the narrow streets toward the Tiber. At the Church of Santa Maria in Traspontina, these two most important men of their time parted with an embrace. Frederick and Constance returned to Monte Mario, while Honorius, probably in deeper thought than the emperor, adjourned to his palace. The Church of Santa Maria brings to mind another meeting of the secular and the Church: the Lateran Treaty of 1929 meeting between Mussolini and Pope Pius XI.

Frederick tidied up a few loose ends in and around Rome. Securely enthroned, he could afford to be magnanimous. It was probably at this time that he granted the release of Diepold of Schweinspeunt, who was still being held in custody by his son-in-law, James of Severino. But there were strings attached. Diepold's brother, Siegfried, was forced to surrender two important castles in the Volturno River valley that could have hindered Frederick's progress into his southern realm. Diepold was escorted over the Alps and deposited in Germany, his belligerent nature to be allowed further outlet through his associations with the Teutonic Knights.

Eager to get back to Sicily, Frederick struck camp three days after his coronation, leading his court and small army south on the Via Labican, thence to its juncture with the Via Latina. The imperial progress took them past the villa of Julia Agrippina, she who devised the murder of her husband, Claudius, to pass his estate and the Roman imperial title on to her son, Nero. Along the way there were the ruins of ancient Tusculum, traditionally founded by the son of Ulysses and Circe but destroyed by the Romans only three years before Frederick was born. Cicero had a villa at Tusculum, and it was here that he wrote his Tusculan Disputations. Not the least of its important citizens, Cato the Elder was born there.

At Fregellae (about one-half mile east of modern Ceprano) Frederick crossed the Liris River and was finally, after eight years, in his native territory. His self-imposed exile in Germany was over. He came in peace, unlike Hannibal, who in 212 BC came all the way from Carthage only to be stopped cold when the Fregellaeans destroyed their bridges. Frederick urged his party on to Capua where he called his first diet on home soil. His thoughts were for the south, for Palermo and the shade of Mount Pelegrino, for the noisy streets and markets, for the cool of his father's gardens and pleasure palaces so conducive to relaxation and study and Norman ceremony. It must have been difficult for a man, emperor or not, suffering the impatient agitation of youth, to wait out the seven months it would take him to get there.

Chapter Eight

Remember, faithful Jesus,
because I am the cause of your journey:
do not lose me on that day.
***Dies Irae*, verse 9**

1220

Hardly had Frederick received his imperial crown and turned his face southward than discord broke out in northern Italy. There was no way, at least as long as he was absent, of maintaining even a semblance of peace for any appreciable time. With the major cities forever at one another's throats, countryside spoliation was the order of the day, the expected norm. In truth, the communes preferred their autonomy to peace. Better to make war of one's own volition than to have peace dictated from above. Eventually the philosophy of autonomy would come into head-on collision with Frederick's notion that liberty not be allowed to jeopardize the calm of the empire.

Only occasionally lifting a sword, Frederick systematically won back great chunks of his realm that had been filched away since his father died. He started his repossession while still in Germany by laying claim against lands of the traitorous Count Rainer of Manente, a foe from the time of his infancy. Rainer, a Tuscan and a man of an effrontery that beggars description, had been introduced into Sicily by Frederick's mother, whereupon at the first opportunity he linked up with Markward of Anweiler and William Capparone. While Frederick was still running the streets of Palermo, Rainer was increasingly in clover, coolly prospering at the expense of the demesne. As soon as Frederick's wife left Sicily to join him in Germany, Rainer leaped to rebellion, short-lived as it turned out, for with Emperor Otto's death he knew he had no choice but submission. The young king was not easily mollified. When Rainer came to Germany without invitation or safe conduct to effect a reconciliation, Frederick clapped him into prison, releasing him only on condition that he cough up his ill-gotten Sicilian estates. But Rainer was still a man to watch. Even in custody he displayed a determined propensity for troublemaking, illustrated when he incited his Tuscan relatives to further mischief in Sicily until Frederick resolved the issue by closing the island to shipments of arms and reinforcements from this troublesome family.

Even before returning to his southern realm, and mainly to guarantee his own safe passage through it, Frederick had forced certain other notables to disgorge properties, the kinds of holdings that could be used against him. The abbot of Monte Cassino relinquished Rocca d'Evandro, an imposing castle silently defensive on a steep needle of a mountain. Under reconstruction when last visited by the author, it is still a pleasant site to visit despite a strenuous climb through narrow streets and sun-drenched little piazzas. Atina was also surrendered by the abbot, a town of little interest but for its fifteenth-century ducal palace. Sora, straddling the Liri River, with its castle called Sorella (once the property of Pope Innocent III, but given over to his brother Richard), was put at Frederick's disposal. Count Roger of Aquila gave up Mondragone, a dreary little town with broken castle remains atop a promontory; Teano, with its ruins of Roman city walls, a theater, an amphitheater, and baths; and Sessa Aurunca.

Sessa Aurunca is one of those towns, gratifying the way only a Campanian town can be, with flowering window boxes, drying laundry strung across narrow streets, Moorish-looking yellow-and-green majolica tile domes and campanile roofs, stepped streets and secretive cul-de-sacs. An ancient town of a people known to the Romans as the Aurunci, Sessa hangs to the southwest slope of the extinct volcano called Rocca Monfina. Replete with ruins, including a twenty-arched Roman bridge and bits of a gymnasium or a theater, there are medieval city walls, a small early Christian church, and the castle with its square tower that Frederick also wrenched from recalcitrant Roger of Aquila. The cathedral, begun in 1103, was made mostly from salvaged Roman materials, some of which can be easily identified, including some sculpture over the three main portals. At the central door is a lioness nursing her cub, a strangely tender and charming sculpture to find in that particular place.

The basilican interior of nave and two aisles was remodeled—abused may be the better word—with baroque surfacing, which, as usual, works to the disadvantage of the original structure. Some of the earlier furnishings remain, however, including the parapet of the organ loft, the altar, the barber pole-like Paschal candlestick, and the pulpit with a desk supported by a pathetic male figure whose head is caught firmly in an eagle's talons while his arm is being bitten by a serpent, a graphic symbol of the wages of sin! All of these are marble with mosaic incrustations, showing Moorish influences. The old nave columns are still standing, and there is a handsome geometric floor in the Cosmatiesque manner, so beautiful as to forbid foot contact. The crypt, except for the steps down, is original.

The spirit of Sessa Aurunca is outside and meant to be enjoyed: the hurrying, book-packing students, the shrilly shouting children, the mouth-watering aromas that you can almost taste of pasta and pizza, the poor but proud people who are not afraid to work hard and who look as though they do. Perhaps that lioness and her cub say more about Sessa and its people than at first one suspects.

Regardless of what his retainers thought of his land-grabbing techniques, Frederick's plan was clear to all. In Germany he had been forced by circumstance to cater to the established, though not definitive, bureaucracy, to make donations, give gifts, pander. His kingdom of Sicily was of a different color. Thirty years of chaos there had bred anarchy and self-interest and had shaken to their foundations those institutions of government that still existed. Frederick was not prepared to yield ground as he had in Germany. He played the Sicilian barons off one against the other, employing weaker barons to help him fight the stronger, in this way dissipating energies for mischief and whittling the mighty down to size. Using barons as allies, he set out to fight barons. Something vaguely Machiavellian echoes in Frederick's political reasoning and use of the barons in this way, though that Italian political philosopher would not be born for another 248 years to give his name to the philosophy "that a prince ought never to make common cause with one more powerful than himself to injure another."[1] When the chips were down, Frederick was not averse to using force. He was a principal mover in a violent age, though the concept that it was an age devoted to irresponsible and arbitrary mayhem and force is a mistaken impression. More often than not, men tried to make laws work; when the laws were not strong enough, they would resort to war.

In no way was Frederick playing by ear; his plans had been formulated in Germany and were now being systematically realized. Throughout his lifetime he would exhibit an uncanny ability for organization, which, tempered by common sense, would put him in the vanguard of creating the framework for one of the first modern European states. Frederick's Norman forebears had already cemented together the best organized, most enlightened, opulent, and wealthy state of medieval Europe. Now their scion, following the example, was about to do it again, but this time a little more generously, creating order out of chaos, reinstituting governing bureaucracies, encouraging and building traditions in all the arts, and more important to his subjects, bringing some welcome peace to their battered homeland. His ways were not always exemplary. Once in a while he turned despotic. But he was enlightened and, at least for historical moments, brought tranquility and quiet in his wake.

Frederick lost no time getting his plan moving. Now he was not appealing to a group of resisting German princes. In his Sicilian kingdom he ruled by fiat, his laws emanating straight from the throne. "Our will and pleasure" became the law. At Capua in December he issued ordinances especially hard on his nobles. Frederick's ancestors, both Norman and German, had established order by brute force. In this, Frederick was different. He was determined to create his new order based on law. To support and advise him he had the most brilliant juror of the day, Roffredo of Benevento, at his elbow. First off, Frederick attacked the sources of possible insurrection: the castles and military strongholds of the ambitious, insurrection-minded, questionably loyal barons, who knew as well as he that castles built without royal permission (and there were many created since the days of Henry VI) were illegal. Frederick ordered that they all be turned over to the royal will or, if that were too grim a prospect for the owners, that they be torn down. Royal consent was necessary if the nobles desired to exit their castles accompanied by more than four unarmed men. In almost every way the legal and political status quo at the time of the last legitimate Norman king, William II, was to be reestablished. Taxes were reinstituted as they had been at the death of Frederick's mother, eventually establishing the most efficient system of taxation known to western Europe since the ancient Roman Empire. The common folk applauded Frederick's dictum that not everyone should be allowed to bear arms but only those who had been granted permission in the reign of King William II. For the commoners better yet was coming their way. And if the barons were disheartened by the imperial dictates—well, worse was coming theirs.

The *de resignandis privilegiis*—the resignation of privileges—required that all privileges granted since the reign of William II be submitted to the Royal Chancery by Easter 1221 on the mainland, and by Whit Sunday (seventh Sunday after Easter) in Sicily, for confirmation or denial. When Pope Honorius admonished him for reclaiming any special rights that had been assumed without papal approval, as well as for retaking scrounged strongholds of the realm, Frederick responded rather curtly: "The Emperor, our father, gave away much of the Kingdom which he ought to have retained, in the expectation of reclaiming it, and, after the death of the Empress many privileges were illegally granted under his seal, as a result of which the greater part of our domain was taken. Therefore we demand that all privileges be surrendered into our hands."[2] So it was that at Capua, in a single legal and brilliantly manipulated diet, Frederick contrived through systematic planning to impose order after years of destructive anarchy. He went even further by regulating that holders of fiefs could not marry or will their property to heirs without direct imperial consent, thus seeing to it that the fiefs reverted to the Crown, to be kept or parceled out at will, an effective way of forcing disgruntled nobles and their sons to toe the line.

In addition vassals were encouraged to emulate their emperor by reasserting rights that had been usurped during the years of upheaval, a measure designed not wholly in the interests of the fief-holder. The Crown could benefit as well in cases of reversion by avoiding the subdivision of the fief. So even this gesture, ostensibly in the interest of the vassals, became an effective concentration of power within a pattern, carefully designed and yet basically simple, admirable material for constructing the new edifice of government. It followed naturally that out of these Capuan assizes there developed an early national "department of defense," enabling Frederick to put two squadrons of ships to sea by the end of the year and to change castles from residences of noble families to strongholds inhabited by fighting men only. The imperial fortress of Lucera—to be dealt with presently—for all the world like a Roman *castrum* (garrisoned town), was one of the type that started springing up after 1221.

The palace in which Frederick held his Capuan diet is still standing, at least in part, and displays a magnificent rectangular, crenellated tower. Heavy with regularly cut blocks, it is all straight lines and vertical heights. Much of the medieval building material was quarried from nearby Santa Maria Capua Vetere (the ancient Roman Capua), which was sacked by Saracens in 840. Indeed, Capua itself was founded by fugitives from that ill-starred city, an ancient bawdy town, if ever there was one. The Cathedral of Santo Stefano, which dates from 856 and was destroyed during World War II and rebuilt, displays a Paschal candlestick of the thirteenth century, a porch of antique columns, and a soaring ninth-century Lombard campanile.

One likes to think that Frederick could have taken a bit of time off from tiresome meetings to journey about three miles east to the small church that had been reconstructed and decorated by Abbot Desiderius of Monte Cassino, who was also a prince of Benevento. Desiderius later became Pope Victor III and ruled for a single tragic year (1086–87) at the height of the eleventh-century papal-imperial struggles for supremacy. There, at Sant'Angelo in Formis, Frederick would have found a church glowing in colorful frescoes of the New and Old Testaments, a narrative cycle of incomparable beauty, done under the careful hands and eyes of Byzantine artists imported to this lonely spot from Sicily and Constantinople. The scenes depicted are rich examples of some of the finest storytelling painting of the Middle Ages, stylized, yes, and iconographic at times, but clear in their adherence to earthly detail and the human side of some very human stories. Sant'Angelo in Formis is yet another example of the changing aesthetic interest: the otherworldly existence of the spirit is giving way slowly to the more mundane here-and-now, the coming Renaissance.

1221

Following his assizes at Capua, Frederick toured his realm, visiting Naples, Sessa Aurunca again, Foggia, Troia, Salerno, Brindisi, and Trani, all cities with proud Norman heritages, and Trani with possibly the most spectacularly sited cathedral of all, on a quay jutting into the Adriatic. Only Foggia today lacks good evidence of this Norman background. Castles and cathedrals abound—the cathedral at Troia being something special, though not large, and that of Salerno, built by Robert Guiscard himself, with its forecourt of incomparable proportions and beauty. After eight years in Germany, such strongholds reinstilled in Frederick a pride in the Norman branch of his family, a new insight into the brave, if sometimes ruthlessly despotic determination of his Hauteville ancestors to establish their enlightened, culturally superior kingdom in the face of daunting odds, not the least being the papacy. And, like his forebears, neither religious nor lay opposition caused him to anticipate the future with fear.

Thomas, duke of Molise, an enemy from the time of Henry VI's death and a stubborn supporter of Emperor Otto IV, learned by Rainer of Manente's example, but too late as it turned out. After an unsuccessful bid for imperial clemency for enough misdeeds to turn a more magnanimous lord than Frederick against him, the duke dug in his heels at the prospect of losing what he thought were his two impregnable Molise strongholds, Boiano and Roccamandolfi. It would have been better had he remained loyal and been satisfied with Boiano's stupendous views of both the Matese and Sannio mountains. Today only meager remains of that castle crown a daunting height about eight miles southwest of Campobasso. Boiano was taken by force, while Thomas's wife herself opened the gates of Roccamondolfi, its very position a flouting, implied dare to attack. Near Boiano, it is dramatically and perhaps dangerously perched on a precipitous outcropping of diagonally stratified rock. Cavalry horses must have been hard pressed to negotiate the climb, not to mention the burden of carting the clumsy machines of medieval siege warfare. Think of the challenge to a footsore army! Thomas finally holed up in his Abruzzi castle at Ovindoli, now a popular resort town with sumptuous hotels, pools, tennis courts, saunas, and other requisite joys of twenty-first-century lotus-eaters. Settlement was finally achieved when the count's possessions were vested in his wife, his sons given over as hostages to Hermann von Salza, and the glum duke of Molise shipped off on the first boat to the Holy Land, no doubt to his wife's vast relief.

Frederick's treaty with Thomas did not, however, save that traitor's town of Celano, whose origin went back to ancient, more precisely, Lombard days. Mercifully allowed to cart off their possessions, the citizens were driven out and the town destroyed but for the single Church of San Giovanni, which for some unexplained reason stands unmolested with its colorful, well-preserved frescoes intact. Within a few years Celano's luckless inhabitants would be imported to Sicily to work the soil vacated by Muslims, who had been exported in Frederick's Christianization of the island. In 1227 Frederick did a limited reconstruction on the castle at Celano. It was restored again in 1392 but was demolished by an earthquake in 1915. Since then it has been rebuilt—stunningly, too—with inner court, arcades, defensive towers, all overlooking drained Lake Fucino, the agriculturally rich Conca del Fucino, which gives nearby Avezzano its reason for being. The castle is now used as a museum. Eventually Frederick confiscated all of Thomas's lands, which was probably what he had in mind in the first place, granting them in 1227 to his special friend, Conrad of Hohenlohe.

Frederick finally crossed the narrow Straits of Messina into Sicily in May 1221. At Messina he set to work on a new diet by which he regulated the affairs of those citizens who were not directly affected by the assizes of Capua and feudal practices generally. He meant to bring the kingdom totally under his jurisdiction and to instill in his subjects an abject fear of his displeasure. The imperial will was the activator of the realm. No impulse or activity would stem from any another source. Some of the laws were curiously backward looking, surprising in a man so conscious of his own enlightenment and of the changes he wished to bring about. Jews, for example, were singled out to wear identifying costumes—blue tunics with yellow swatches sewn thereon. They were compelled to let their beards grow, perhaps as a sop to the Roman Curia, for his law observes that without these marks the practitioners of both faiths might be confused, in itself a confusing idea. Other of his edicts strike us as being narrowly prudish and petty: since "one sick sheep infects the herd," prostitutes were prohibited from living in town and could not use public baths with the more virtuous of their sex; players and minstrels were not to "disturb the Emperor's peace with ribald songs," and, in a master statement of bigotry, since the former were given to blasphemy, they were not to associate with churchmen because the latter were to "uphold the standard of right living in conduct and in speech."[3]

Even more uncharacteristic is Frederick's law that vengeance taken against malicious jesters was not deemed an offense against the peace and was not subject to punishment. We can detect the finger of the pope in this sticky law, as he tried to halt the popular, insulting, and insubordinate refrains that were directed at the clergy. The emperor may have felt the need to cater to papal desires since, with all the work to be done in the realm, he was already planning to excuse his way out of going on crusade. For him to depart this year would have been to throw the land into chaos, with every newly tamed baron reverting to the old lawlessness. Nor would the state finances bear the burden. Neither of these valid excuses could be expected to mollify the pope nor to mitigate criticism from certain lower quarters. Troubadour Peirol of Auvergne even questions God's judgment in allowing Frederick to be emperor, despite Peirol's own conviction that the crusades were no longer products of religious conviction, but rather now governed almost solely by material and political considerations:

> Fair Lord God, if thou didst act according to my mind, thou wouldst take good care whom thou didst create emperors and make kings and to whom thou gavest castles and strongholds; for the richer men are, the more they hold thee to scorn. For I saw the Emperor take many an oath last year which he now seeks to evade.[4]

To strengthen his case with the pope, while he was at Messina Frederick sent two small fleets to succor the Christian troops still barricaded behind the walls of Damietta, the first commanded by Duke Louis of Bavaria and the bishop of Passau, the second by Anselm of Justingen who, it will be remembered, was the German ambassador who had brought the news to Frederick that he had been elected king and emperor. Raising these fleets had not been easy. Frederick had set to work building his fleets, both merchant and naval, but shipbuilding takes time. In the interim he commandeered boats putting into Sicilian ports from Italian coastal towns. These, in conjunction with the new boats that were being constructed, constituted the nucleus of an imperial navy and merchant marine that, though nominally of the kingdom of Sicily, flew the Hohenstaufen imperial eagle from the start. Supply ships were sent to Damietta with some soldier reinforcements and three commanders explicitly admonished not to take part in any adventure against the Muslims until a segment of the reviving royal navy under Henry of Malta and Chancellor Walter of Palear, now bishop of Catania, arrived in July.

Still holed up behind the barricaded gates of Damietta, papal legate and self-appointed crusade commander Cardinal Pelagius rejoiced at the news of the approaching fleets. By this time John of Brienne, regent of Jerusalem in the name of his twelve-year-old motherless daughter, Yolanda, had returned to the fray, not out of any real concern for the foundering project, but because he did not want to be branded a coward. On the surface, at least, his presence gave renewed strength to the crusading pilgrims, as they called themselves. When al-Kamil offered honorable peace terms again, and even though Pope Honorius had clearly ordered that any such offer not be turned down without first consulting Rome, Pelagius flatly rejected the suggestion. This was when Louis of Bavaria and his two fellow commanders arrived. Louis was eager to engage the infidel and, despite the orders of no contact from Frederick, he fell in with Pelagius's irresponsible exhortations to attack Cairo. The Christian forces were decimated by overconfidence, by al-Kamil's defense, a rising Nile, and infidel-opened sluices along the right bank of the river. Pelagius was not the kind of man to face the music with his mud-mired, drowning army. He was carried to safety, and as he had with him the medical supplies and much of the provisions, his escape was a calamity. On top of the slaughter of thousands of his screaming, cursing crusaders, many Christian ships were lost or captured.

Even knowing that Damietta was adequately supplied and that further Sicilian rescue ships were on the way, al-Kamil was still aware that he had the crusading army at his mercy. It was finally agreed that the Christians would abandon Damietta and that there would be an eight-year-truce. Basically a fair-minded man, al-Kamil agreed, further, to give back the most sacred of Christian relics, the remnant of the True

Cross. Pelagius, King John of Jerusalem, the duke of Bavaria, the masters of the orders, and an assortment of counts and bishops were to be handed over as hostages until Damietta was surrendered. Count Henry of Malta and Walter of Palear arrived during the negotiations and did what they could to salvage the situation. But the Christians knew perfectly well that al-Kamil held the winning hand. The sultan entertained King John at a sumptuous banquet. He revictualized the crusading army for their retreat. The hostages were released. And on September 8, the crusaders embarked for home, and the sultan returned to Damietta. So the fifth crusade ended, having come within a hair of success. As a final dollop of shame, adding to the bitterness, misery, and despair of nonaccomplishment, when the time came to hand the relic of the True Cross over to the Europeans, it could not be found. It was a bitter Peirol who looked back on the receding Egyptian shores.

The crusade had been wrecked by ego and one-upmanship. Pelagius had been abrasive. John of Jerusalem had lacked the wherewithal to command an international force. Francis of Bernardone had done what he could, and his was certainly the most selfless effort. But his situation had been impossible. The only person who could have saved the day—Frederick II of Hohenstaufen—had not shown up. The troubadour Peirol, who witnessed the final catastrophic days, called Frederick to account: "Emperor, Damietta awaits you and night and day the White Tower weeps for your eagle . . . which a vulture has cast down therefrom; cowardly is the eagle that is captured by a vulture! Shame is thereby yours and honour accrues to the Sultan."[5]

Among those who sailed homeward with Peirol none was more miserable than Chancellor Walter of Palear. For all his cynical self-interest during Frederick's regency, Walter had been entrusted with an active part in the mission to Damietta, or perhaps it was merely Frederick's way of getting him out of the kingdom. In any event, he could not bear the anticipation of a face-to-face meeting with his master. Rather than enduring the ordeal as official bearer of the disastrous tidings, he fled to Venice where, it is said, he died in abject poverty. As a maker of history Walter was no more or less self-interested than most others playing the power politics of his day. But his end seems a sad commentary on a man who had been chancellor of the realm, bishop of Troia, and bishop of Catania. Had he been of a different ilk he might have fared better. Frederick never appointed another to fill Walter's vacated ex-chancellorship. He had had his troubles with Walter and had, several times, relegated him to his see of Catania, unable to replace him since the position, once granted, was legally nontransferable. Once Walter was dead Frederick left the office vacant. He was not the type to appoint to a position any man who could defy the imperial right to fire him.

While dispensing niggling laws intended to separate groups of malcontents who were already separated, Frederick lashed out at foreign powers with vested interests in the kingdom. If the Genovesi had been irked by Frederick's refusal to grant them commercial privileges when they had approached him in Modena, they were in for a jolt now that he was back in home territory. In Frederick's absence they had benefited mightily by usurping a major part of the lucrative shipping interests, especially in grain, that had in better days been Sicilian. They, and the Venetians and Pisans too, had held rights since the days of the regency. After aiding Frederick on his secret march to Germany, the Genovesi understandably expected preferential treatment, even though their motives had been mainly to frustrate the Otto-sympathizing Pisans. Frederick was not ungrateful; he even had a special place in his heart for Genoa. But Sicily and his power came first. Favors could be granted pertaining to the empire; but the rights of his kingdom Frederick guarded jealously. Quite unceremoniously the Genovesi, along with the Pisans and Venetians, were ousted from the realm. Ingratitude was the only word the Genovesi could find to describe the king's behavior. Relations between the two deteriorated, eventually developing into open hostility. But Frederick would not be sidetracked. Sicily came first.

William Porcus, alleged abductor of crusading children, fled the country seething with resentment as though he had cause for it. The story goes, he had linked up with his old accomplice and alleged child seller, Hugh de Fer; but he was out of his league when he chose to bear a grudge against imperial determination by acting the pirate in Sicilian waters, and by doing everything in his power to frustrate Frederick's budding war with the island Muslims. Popular rumor has it that by the following summer both William and Hugh were dangling from the gallows.

Laws passed "at our will and pleasure" at both Capua and Messina should have indicated the tenor of Frederick's laws yet to come, for they were the foundation of his legislation. In time it became more and more obvious that he was out to curb corruption, private and governmental, to regulate the actions and fees of public servants, to insist that officials denounce infractions of the laws and disobedience to the imperial will, to punish the issuance of counterfeit coinage, and to establish fair wages for laborers, tailors, cobblers, and carpenters. In these interests he remained consistent throughout his career.

There was no denying it; Frederick was back where he belonged. The German part of his empire would continue to swim against the mainstream, perpetuating its petty princedoms and elector-controlled territories almost until modern times. So Germany would always be secondary to him, and his preference for Sicily says much about the man. The summery skies, the more polished manners, the gleaming cities edging the blue Mediterranean, the arts, poetry, and history—all of these, plus the romance of the south, were more congenial to Frederick's lifestyle than the chilly north. As he saw it, the uncouth barbarism, the ruder pomp and feudal backwardness of his German liegemen were difficult to take, though they did influence him and his way of thinking. But then he absorbed influences from every source. It was claimed by his detractors that he had become more foreign, especially more Mohammedan, than was becoming a Christian prince. He spoke Italian, French, German, Greek, Latin, and Arabic fluently, was interested in exotic philosophies and caused several of them to be translated into Latin. He was accused of allowing Saracen women the run of his court, where they were free to corrupt Christian morals. Historically more important than any of this, by instigating a vernacular court poetry he caused the birth of modern Italian literature years ahead of Dante.

1222

On the Italian mainland in April 1222, Frederick met Pope Honorius in the small mountain town of Veroli, a few miles northeast of Frosinone, a settlement with a fortress-like gate—the Porta di Santa Croce—and some remains of ancient walls. On a high summit was the castle where, no doubt, the meeting occurred. The basically homely cathedral of Sant'Andrea cherishes a breviary of Saint Louis of Toulouse, over 1,200 ninth-century manuscripts, and a gilded silver, marvelously primitive, thirteenth-century bust of Saint Andrew. Considering that one seldom hears the name of Veroli, it is interesting to note that the Victoria and Albert Museum in London owns the tenth-century Veroli casket, of ivory carved to represent pneumatic little putti belaboring a variety of equally graceless animals, serpents, and birds.

The steep streets of Veroli (the Vicolo Terribile, for example) are fascinating to explore, with steps up the center of some, and bordered by crusty old houses, including a medieval one on the Via Cavour. Veroli is a grand town for gate-peeping into secret courtyards, with arches and outside staircases banked with potted plants, and quiet, shaded gardens that defy intrusion but tempt with an opulence of ripe lemons and oranges. Old men play cards in sidewalk cafes, children play soccer in the streets, and women—well, they work. Several sites smack of

Frederick's time and before: the Church of San Leucio in a high part of the town, hard to reach even by car, but worth the effort for its rugged, blocky Romanesque simplicity and seasoned wooden roof and beams; the basilica of Sant'Erasmo, where a legate of Barbarossa once met with Pope Alexander II to try to establish a modus vivendi; the Church of Santa Salomè with its small but beautifully frescoed crypt, built where her bones were found in 1209.

A bit stouter now than he had been two years ago in Rome, and showing a premature baldness, Frederick impressed upon the aged Honorius the need for further delay in his expedition against the Muslims of Outremer. He was, he explained quite rightly, in the process of organizing an assault against the Muslims but closer to home, indeed, on the island of Sicily itself where, he was sure the Holy Father would agree, they were more of a threat to Christianity than they were in the far-off Holy Land.

Saracens had been inhabiting Sicily for four centuries, at times as masters and then again as a second-class society, but always in contact with their point of origin, the north coast of Africa. Native Sicilians, the Byzantine Greeks, the Lombards, all had been at odds with the Saracens, and with one another for that matter. It had taken Frederick's Norman predecessors to bring order out of the endemic conflicts, to weld the four distinctly separate peoples into a tolerant live-and-let-live society that had lasted until the end of the Norman hegemony. Now three decades after the last of the Norman kings, settlements of defiantly hostile Muslim warriors and their families lived in nearly impregnable mountain aeries such as Iato, about twenty-five miles south of Monreale—too close to Palermo! They had settled in Iato after taking the cathedral, some surrounding villages, farms, and castles, capturing the archbishop and driving out most of the inhabitants. Agrigento, on the south coast, had also been taken. An imperial campaign against these increasingly pugnacious Muslims was called for, and was not long in coming.

Having succeeded in convincing Pope Honorius that the crusade could wait until the Muslim problem in Sicily was wrapped up, Frederick rode on another six miles to the Cistercian abbey at Casamari, where a new church had been consecrated by Honorius only five years before. Frederick may have been putting on a good show for the pontiff in this venture, for he knew that Honorius was a dedicated patron of the abbey and held it in esteem. As a matter of fact, the construction of the church itself was a result of Honorius's generosity, and he was currently in the area to consecrate a new altar there. On the other hand, with a need to feed a growing population, Frederick may have been motivated by a genuine interest in the farming science of the Cistercians, since they were the most forward-thinking medieval pioneers in scientific agriculture and animal husbandry. Certainly it would have been true to his character to show an interest in their farming methods. Beyond that, the Casamari foundation had been protected by his own father and mother. Frederick and his parents may be commemorated in the cloister that was in construction about this time, as three capitals show the heads of two men, both crowned, one clean-shaven, as was Frederick, and one bearded, as was his father, and the veiled head of a woman, perhaps Frederick's mother, Constance.

Marking the plebeian birthplace of Gaius Marius (Casamari—"home of Marius"), the Roman general and consul who married the aunt of Julius Caesar, the abbey is an excellent example of Burgundian early-Gothic style and is sometimes compared to its near contemporary, Fossanova. A massive gateway greets the visitor, two-arched, one for pedestrians, and one for vehicles. A spacious courtyard lends grandeur to the facing abbey church with its rose window, transept tower, and noble portal. The inside is cruciform in plan, with enormous columns

Frederick (?), Casamari Abbey, Italy

supporting soaring, pointed arches. The twin-columned cloister is rewarding—in addition to giving us a look at what may have been the Sicilian royal family—for being a quiet retreat in a country where noise pollution too frequently reaches the hundredth percentile. A fine chapter house is supported by massive bundle-columns. True to Cistercian custom a number of lay brothers were employed to work the fields and care for the animals. Their outside corridor to the church, where they were relegated to the western end, is still preserved between the cloister and their humble rooms.

In July Frederick received the disheartening news that his wife, queen, and empress, Constance, had died of malaria in Catania at age forty-three. Despite the bitter hardship of her early life in Hungary, she was said to be youthfully beautiful to the end, with the long, fair hair that was her glory and a continuing zest and enthusiasm for imperial living. She had been a good wife to Frederick, though once his life had taken a more sybaritic turn after the birth of son Henry, she had probably not administered to him in a conjugal way. Wrapped in a robe of deep crimson embroidered with gold and pearls, she was buried in Palermo Cathedral in the same side chapel where lay Frederick's mother and father and his grandfather, Roger II. At her side was placed a casket containing a Byzantine diadem encrusted with jewels, dolphins, and Kufic characters, and with jeweled chains hanging from the sides. Frederick would miss his empress. She was far and away the most important woman in his life, admittedly a life not known for the roles women played. And in the long run she would prove to be his most successful wife. Over a distance of seven hundred years, it is apparent that he never treated another woman with the tender respect with which he favored Constance.

As though to mitigate the bad news, Frederick was encouraged by messages from Germany. His regent there and the guardian of his son Henry, Archbishop Engelbert of Cologne, had done much to suppress the scattered revolts that were the way of life in the northern reaches of the empire. If this were not gratifying news enough, Frederick also learned that his son was, this year, anointed king by Archbishop Engelbert in Charlemagne's church at Aachen, the same historic site that served for Frederick's reception of similar honor. With his son in his wake, and with such a devoted and experienced regent as Engelbert in charge, Frederick's plans for his line were assured. It was even noised about that King Henry III of England was proffering the hand of his sister Isabella to the adolescent king. In the meantime Frederick moved on to Cosenza.

Straggling outward on either side of its steep main street that rises from between the Crati and the Busento rivers, Cosenza looks every bit the product of frequent earthquakes. About halfway up, facing on a small theatrical-looking piazza, the cathedral is glowering and majestic, gothically dark and wearing memories of better days with angry longing. Many of the tenements in the area were formerly palaces, identifiable by handsome Renaissance doorways, today humbly, if colorfully, festooned with billowing swags of drying laundry. Completed in 1222, the church was consecrated that same year, as though on cue for Frederick. The legate of Rome, Bishop Nicholas of Tusculum of the great Sicilian house of Chiaramonte, was the dignitary in charge and was there on invitation of Archbishop Luke who, by the way, had been secretary to that cranky seer who had predicted such a dire future for Frederick at his birth: Abbot Joachim of Flora. There was a growing interest in French architectural forms in southern Italy at this time, and Cosenza's cathedral adapted the Cistercian Gothic style to its own needs, though the pseudo-Gothic facade was added in 1831. The three portals and the restored rose window are parts of the original church. It is properly moody inside, with three apses and great semicircular arches marching up the nave and serving to divide it from its two side aisles. A noble building it is, and different enough in its hint of French delicacy to be arresting. Carrying out the idea is the tomb of Isabella of Aragon, the wife of Philip III of France, who died at Cosenza after falling from her horse there.

In honor of the dedication, Frederick presented a gift to the cathedral—a gold filigree, Byzantine reliquary cross, still to be seen in the palace of the archbishop. Exquisitely beautiful, the crucifix is reversible, with the sagging Christ on one side, flanked by the apostle John in a medallion on his left hand, and Mary opposite on his right. The archangel Michael is in a medallion at the head of the cross—a figure that to Frederick, with his Norman blood, should have been especially meaningful—holding symbols of divine justice. At Christ's feet the representation of an altar with the chalice of wine and the bread, along with a dove, symbolize the soul, which is nurtured by the miraculous food. On the reverse side Christ in Glory occupies the central medallion, while at the extremities of the cross are the four evangelists. These figures and those on the obverse side are rendered in enamel, stylized by the very nature of enamel in combinations of bright and dull, intense and subtle colors. Below the Christ under a crystal protective cover is what is said to be a tiny remnant of the True Cross. The whole ensemble is edged with gold beads, and the reverse side is further embellished with jewels mounted in tiny cups of gold.

Cosenza is the legendary burial place of Alaric, fifth-century Gothic despoiler of Rome, for whose grave the Busento River was diverted from its bed, to be returned only after the mourned chieftain had been deposited in his rock-lined tomb with a treasure horde of stolen loot and the spot made secret by the savage massacre of the prisoners who had been employed to execute the work. Even further back in legendary time Cosenza is also the final resting place of Alexander I, king of Epirus, brother of the witch-mother of Alexander the Great. Reader and linguist that he was, Frederick must have been familiar with the spurious romance of Alexander the Great, which had been translated into Latin as early as the third century AD and was currently making the rounds among the intelligentsia. It is pleasant to think of Frederick in his Norman castle at Cosenza (probably in the process of being remodeled then, as it always seems to be today), arguing with his confidants the merits of both of these Alexanders. High above the medieval and modern zones of the city and surrounded by a seedy neighborhood, the castle enjoys a sweeping view of the glorious peaks of the Sila Massif ("Italy's Little Switzerland") to the east, near enough to be enjoyed, but distant enough not to seem oppressive. Surely Archbishop Luke was a regular at the castle, and from him Frederick must have heard lively stories of Joachim, how the renowned old grump had forced mother Constance to her knees when she confessed and, on the other hand, how he had given all his clothes to the poor of Calabria during the disastrous winter of 1202, the year of his death. But, according to legend, this year Frederick made the acquaintance of one greater, and certainly more revered, than Joachim.

Stories tell of an unlikely meeting at Bari, a meeting of the two most imaginative men of their time: Frederick Hohenstaufen, *stupor mundi,* and Francis Bernardone, *il poverello.* With no factual basis in the chronicles of the time, the coming together of these diametrically opposed personalities has teased the imaginations and stimulated the creative genies of artists and storytellers through the ages—and still does. Legends have always helped shape certain figures of history into full-fledged characters who breathe and cry, who make music, laugh, and sing, who sleep, make love, and perhaps work miracles. If not provable, legends are at least a part of history. *The Little Flowers of Saint Francis* tells a tale of Francis on his return from Outremer, though some authorities maintain that he returned via Venice. In the more popular instance, according to his apologists, Francis was in the vicinity of Bari, in Apulia, preaching salvation through penance and a return of the Church to its proper ecclesiastical purpose. Frederick had heard of this sainted man and invited him to lodge at his great castle. One can imagine how Frederick's harem, courtiers, guards, and imperial menagerie went over with his antipathetic guest!

Francis was assigned a tower room while Frederick elected to play the part of tempter. With the skepticism of a man more and more inclined to libertinism, and always the despiser of poseurs, charlatans, and false piety, and certainly contrary to his personality as we have come to think of it, he arranged to watch through a peephole as an alluring courtesan was introduced into Francis's room. But Francis was not to be brought down by anyone so earthy as a seductress—or a voyeur emperor either, for that matter. He put her to flight with fire—some legends say with a fiery shield, others claim he lay close beside a red-hot, coal-filled brazier and invited her to join him there. Unable to endure the scorching heat, the woman was thunderstruck, so it is said, repented of her sins, and converted to Christianity on the spot. Frederick was so impressed by the virtuous "groom of Lady Poverty" that he stayed up the rest of the night in heated conversation with Francis.

Though it had existed many years before the coming of the Normans in the eleventh century, a good part of Bari Castle, a solid, coastal structure, moody, with dramatic arches and sweeping staircases, had been built by those redoubtable fortress builders. During a 1950 restoration of the castle, a stone plaque was uncovered from beneath coats of plaster. It bears the date of 1635 and states in Latin: "Dressed in an ash-grey robe, Francis here subdued with fire a wanton temptress like unto a ferocious Hydra." The plaque proves nothing, set in place as it had been four centuries after the fact. It does indicate, however, that the tradition of the event was honored and commemorated even at that late date. What is sorely missed in every instance is the conversation allegedly enjoyed by these two leaders, a conversation that would have been a gem to record! Whether the tale is true or not begs the point of the greatest men of their day, the one who was already notorious for his sensual tastes, and the other who had abandoned the world and was beloved of Lady Poverty, sitting down together for a friendly chat. Frederick would have found it difficult—if not impossible—to resist the sincere and persuasive arguments of Francis when he spoke as a man on fire with divine love. And Frederick would have found it equally difficult, if not inconceivable, to accept the message concerning his "sister birds" if Francis had the opportunity to deliver it at this, their only meeting, as he had asserted he would like to do:

> If I were to speak to the Emperor, I would, supplicating and persuading him, tell him for the love of God and me to make a special law that no man should take or kill Sister Larks, nor do them any harm. Likewise, that all the Podestas of the towns, and the Lords of castles and villages, should be bound every year on Christmas day to compel men to throw wheat and other grains outside the cities and castles, that our Sister Larks may have something to eat, and also the other birds, on a day of such solemnity. And that for the reverence of the Son of God, Who rested on that night with the most blessed Virgin Mary between an Ox and an Ass in the manger, whoever shall have an Ox and an Ass shall be bound to provide for them on that night the best of good fodder. Likewise on that day, all poor men should be satisfied by the rich with good food.[6]

How would Frederick, one of the most sophisticated men of his time, an expert falconer and crack hunter, and the most ambitious ruler of Europe, have responded to such a message? Interested as he must have been in Francis's philosophy of living and concept of salvation, this little speech, so naive in concept and manner, would have taxed Frederick's credulity to the limit. In later years, when he was embroiled in a hate-filled struggle with the Church demeaning to both sides, Frederick castigated the "pious rich," the luxury-loving religious hierarchy, and the hypocrisy of pontiffs for their opulent living and worldly power. If the night with Francis was not mere legend, Frederick would have cause to remember it when, in the future, the Franciscans themselves tried to rally the Church faithful against an emperor under the ban.

In the same year that Francis is supposed to have met and conversed with Frederick, he preached in Bologna, according to one of only two firsthand accounts we have of his sermons. The impressions on hearing this devout, determinedly poor man were graphically recorded by Thomas of Spalato:

> I was studying in that city when I had an opportunity of hearing Francis preach on the square of the Public Palace, where almost the whole population had assembled. He preached of angels, men, and demons with such eloquence and precision that the most learned were amazed that an untutored man could express himself so well. His discourse had nothing of the tone or mannerisms of the preacher. Rather it was like a conversation whose sole object was to extinguish hatred and restore peace. The orator was wretchedly garbed, his appearance frail, his face

> without beauty; but this did not hinder his words from reconciling the Bolognese nobles who had been slaughtering one another for generations. And so great was the enthusiasm that men and women rushed up to him to tear his garments to shreds and make off with the pieces.[7]

So would be cherished generation after generation purloined relics of this sainted man.

1222–1226

Practically speaking, the Saracens controlled a fair part of Sicily, handily maintaining contact with their North African supply centers from their main base at Agrigento. Working on the theory that they were merely taking back lands that had, under the Normans, been filched from them, lands that had been theirs for over two centuries, they had moved north and west from Agrigento through the island's mountainous interior until they were trespassing on Monreale property and threatening Palermo itself. Frederick could ill afford to let the situation continue. He had to lash out against the Saracen menace before daring to leave his kingdom again.

The mountain fastness of Iato was Frederick's first objective. After two months of siege, Iato's emir, Ibn Abbad, realizing the long-run hopelessness of his situation, had no stomach for further resistance. He and his two sons went personally before the emperor to sue for peace. When they flung themselves at his feet, they were treated to an object lesson on just how mercilessly angry this emperor could be: he ripped the emir's side open with his spur. Without granting him a comforting amenity Frederick had Ibn Abbad and his sons hanged as rebels. Iato fell to Frederick's forces, but before the winter was out the imperial forces were betrayed and massacred. Admiral Henry of Malta, in charge of the town and powerless in the face of the Muslim rally, was divested of his holding of Malta.

By summer 1223 Frederick had decided that the only way to bring the Arabs into line was through all-out warfare, and then the only way to neutralize them permanently was through revolutionary Draconian measures. He started by attacking them on several fronts, slowly dividing them into smaller units, and then mopping up bit by bit. The Muslims fought desperately, believing the only alternative was death. But Frederick had a display of surprising magnanimity in store for them. There were at least 25,000 Muslims, a number formidable enough to make imperial progress at the very least painfully slow. Frederick distracted them by sending a fleet against the island of Djerba off the coast of Tunisia, a main supply depot. He took the island, captured its inhabitants, and brought them home to undergo the same fate he had in store for his Sicilian prisoners, a most original and cleverly conceived remedy for this Muslim threat.

Frederick initiated a master plan by which he not only solved the problems of the Muslims on his island but also created in them a willing loyalty to the imperial banner and to him personally. Between 1223 and 1226, when his war with the Muslims ended, Frederick transported 16,000 of them from Sicily and from Djerba—whether they had been belligerents or not—to Lucera, west and slightly north of Foggia on the Italian mainland. Here he set them up in their own community, free of molestation and able to pursue their own religious and social customs. They were even allowed a degree of autonomy under their emirs and sheiks, who taught them skills of farming, horse breeding, and various crafts at which they excelled. In time they became, instead of a drain on the kingdom's treasury and manpower, an asset and a pillar of military support, fanatically loyal to Frederick and obedient to his every command and whim. He was a hero in their eyes, and they were willing to serve him in every way they could—as farmers making productive the barren hillsides of northern Apulia; as metalworkers shaping weapons and domestic utensils; as servants, keepers of the menagerie, trusted palace guards, warriors and light cavalry. His slightest expression was a signal for them to leap to action. Arab women played their roles, too: as domestic servants, weavers, and of course as inmates of the notorious imperial harem that so scandalized the age. But for his grandfather, Roger II, no other European ruler of the island kingdom could even begin to approach the approbation that Frederick enjoyed from these hard-to-manage former enemies become dedicated allies. Best of all, they owed no allegiance to the pope and so could afford to be utterly unheeding of his bans. When the pope objected to Frederick's use of Saracen guards and soldiers, the emperor, tongue in cheek, excused himself on grounds that surely his was the better way of waging war, for were not Saracen souls more expendable than Christian? And the pope had to be satisfied with that. Frederick, his eyes always on the lookout for ready cash, still managed to levy taxes on his Saracens: the *jizyah* in exchange for their religious autonomy; the *terragium* for their use of the soil. Both of these devices for picking up quick money he had learned from the Saracens themselves.

The city of Lucera had been of some importance under the Romans, when it was prominent enough to be known as "the key of Apulia." Its temple of Minerva was said to house the Trojan Palladium, the sacred statue of Pallas Athena on which the safety of ancient Troy had depended, and which had been carried off by Diomedes—the muscular Greek warrior, second only to Achilles—in company with Odysseus. Lucera was destroyed by Eastern Roman Emperor Constans II in 663 as part of the last effort to reestablish Rome as the center of a reunited empire. Though it was taken over by the Normans it never amounted to much under them, and it was only when Frederick determined to establish his Muslims there that general prosperity revived. The cathedral was turned into a mosque, minarets and all, losing points for Frederick in the Lateran Palace. It must have been appalling to Christian ears to hear the muezzins' five daily calls to prayer. (Lucera's present cathedral dates from after 1300 and is considered one of the best-preserved Angevin churches in southern Italy.)

The castle that Frederick built at a later date, now largely in ruins, earned for him the nickname "Sultan of Lucera." Here, in a massive stone structure surrounding a spacious, fountain-enlivened courtyard, he housed his Saracen bodyguards, his harem and treasury, along with his own apartments embellished with every luxury. (The impressive pentagonally planned half-mile wall with its evenly spaced towers that one sees encircling the castle ruins was built around 1300 by Charles II of Anjou.) Like his forebears Frederick had embraced the Oriental concept of luxury, granting to himself a style of living that was the talk and scandal of the century. He was not totally alone in this as many of his barons, as well as knights of Spain and elsewhere, were only too willing to embrace the softer manner of the East. But Frederick was certainly the most theatrical about it. With his harem, with bears, monkeys, and Arabian mares—even a giraffe—his camel and dromedary gifts from al-Kamil carrying the imperial treasury, with his Saracen guards, his hounds trotting beside him eagerly panting for the hunt—it was all a pointed display put on by a quasi-Oriental ruler heading the richest, most liberal and civilized of Occidental courts.

Imperial passages through Italy may have been showy, even vulgar, but Frederick's setting up of Lucera as a Muslim city in Christian surroundings was a stroke of genius and enlightenment far ahead of his time. Even after his death, when he had been succeeded by his ill-starred son Manfred, the ambassador from Egypt and Syria could only marvel at Frederick's vision: "The inhabitants [of Lucera] were Muslims, originally of Sicily. There were celebrated the Friday prayers, and the rites of Islam were openly observed. I noted that the principal officers of the Emperor Manfred were Muslims and that in his camp was observed the call to prayers."[8]

Frederick was not quite thirty when he set into motion his plans for the pacification of the Muslims. One is not surprised to learn that his Muslim community was a stumbling block to any kind of dealings with the Church. Papal protests indicated the gulf between Frederick and an institution governed by narrow-thinking men who were meddling in areas that were a far cry from the spiritual vocations that they claimed to espouse. Comparatively peaceful their relationship might be; but to anyone as perceptive as Frederick, the coming split must already have appeared inevitable.

1223

For all his confidence Frederick was not prepared for the proposition that was thrown his way by his trusted associate, Hermann von Salza. Hermann had been to Rome to negotiate a meeting between pope and emperor. On returning to the imperial court (it was in session at Cassino, called then San Germano) Hermann put out feelers to Frederick: what would be the imperial response to suggestions of a marriage to Yolanda, the twelve-year-old queen of Jerusalem? Frederick knew that Yolanda's father, John of Brienne, had been in Rome coincidentally with Hermann. He knew also that such a marriage would establish a bond between himself and the Holy Land by making him titular king of Jerusalem, thus putting him in line with papal insistence on an immediate crusade. As king of Jerusalem how could he reasonably procrastinate further? And everyone knew that the kingdom of Jerusalem's name had been reduced to just that—a name—and that its queen was as impoverished as her father, unable to bring into the marriage a dower other than her vacant title. In short, Frederick was unenthusiastic.

Hermann must have played on Hohenstaufen genes in this game of political marriage. Now an intimate of the emperor for over seven years, he knew how to go about doing that. He knew as well as his employer that father Henry VI had entertained visions of an enormous empire extending from Germany to the Holy Land, in a sense a duplication of the ancient Roman Empire. The only thing preventing him from attempting such a bravura effort had been his own death. These themes may well have been played by Hermann von Salza in his arguments with Frederick. Whatever he did, it was remarkable that he could persuade Frederick to agree to marry an impoverished and dowerless queen.

The projected meeting between pope and emperor took place in Ferentino, a hilltop city with stepped streets, whose ancient Roman walls still survive, strengthened by gates and towers restored during the Middle Ages. The episcopal palace where the meeting probably occurred is on a jutting eastern corner of the city heights and may have been built on remains of an ancient temple foundation. Also on the acropolis, the small Romanesque cathedral was over a hundred years old at the time of the meeting, its beamed ceiling sheltering a lovely Cosmati floor, while the altar under the heavy, domed ciborium (signed by Drudo di Trivio, thirteenth century) is decorated with two large rondelles of porphyry.

Cathedral door, cat relief, Ferentino, Italy

The left side-aisle portal shows delightful cats' heads on the arches, at the same time malevolent and comical, witty, but with more than a hint of the villain. The right entrance displays equally amusing goats with no trace of malice, it being impossible to conceive of an evil-looking bovid. Always interested in the real world, the medieval artist could not resist inventing his own real world, abstract, simplified in form by geometric statements rightfully his own but nonetheless engaging. So is this strange menagerie decorating, of all things, a "house of God." A weighty, yet soaring, campanile with twin- and triple-lighted openings could well be the favorite of one given to choose such things. The Church of Santa Maria Maggiore in the lower city relieves the Romanesque heaviness with its graceful Gothic exterior. Witnessing the meeting of Honorius and Frederick were Hermann von Salza, John of Brienne, and the patriarch of Jerusalem. The cards were clearly stacked against any last-minute effort by Frederick to wriggle out of an agreement to marry the queen of Jerusalem, or to avoid a crusade. Before the array of prominent witnesses, Frederick agreed to the marriage and vowed that he would depart on June 24—the Feast of the Nativity of Saint John the Baptist—1225. Recruiters for the crusade were dispatched in all directions, with Hermann von Salza going to Germany, and even crusty old John of Brienne—he was over seventy now—doing his bit by proselytizing in France, England, and Spain. For the present Frederick had only two years' grace to mop up the Muslims in his realm, which, as we have seen, he did with panache.

Chapter Nine

Thou has sat down as one wearied seeking me,
Thou has redeemed (me) having suffered the Cross:
so much labor let it not be lost.
***Dies Irae*, verse 10**

1223

Lady Jacopa dei Settesoli lived in the Septizonium, which had been acquired from the Camaldolesi monks in 1145 by her husband's family, the Frangipani. An ancient edifice, it had been a magnificent palazzo in its day, though no one really knows its purpose; some hold that it was built by emperor-builder Septimius Severus (146–211) to impress Roman sightseers by screening a confused jumble of unsightly buildings behind it. Lady Jacopa was about thirty-three years old now; she hospitably housed Francis Bernardone in her Septizonium while he was in Rome to present his laboriously worked, definitive Rule to Pope Honorius III. Francis must have been grateful for the shelter, for it was November, and the Roman damp was not salutary to his steadily declining health. His hostess was happy in the presence of her idol, always enjoying the continuation of their holy friendship and grateful for company beyond that of her two teenage children. As always, she made for him the almond-and-sugar spice cakes that he so doted on—*mostaccioli.* No one—but *no one*—could make those cakes like "Brother Jacopa" who used exactly the right amount of sugar—making it not too sweet—to give Francis one of his few culinary pleasures.

Francis had been invited to stay with Cardinal Ugolino in his residence next to the Church of San Marcellino, which still stands on the corner of the Via Labicana and the Via Merulana. But the hubbub of Church business tended to frustrate Francis's yearning for contemplative quiet, and he refused the offer of his mentor. Turning down another offer to bed at the house of Cardinal Leone Brancaleone, Francis opted for the more tranquil, if partially ruined palazzo of the Septizonium.

Here among the decaying statuary and derelict gardens he could at least maintain his peace of mind. He would need it.

Francis's group of "penitents from Assisi," as they called themselves now, were finally organized according to ideals known as the Rule. The order had grown

> as more souls began to follow him
> in poverty—whose wonder-working life
> were better sung among the seraphim.[1]

From now on the Franciscans were a full-fledged order like any other. Francis was aware that one of the differences between his doctrine and the teachings of some of the heretical sects—Humiliati, Waldensians, Albigensians—was dependence on Church approbation. Even he, poor organizer that he was, understood the need for papal approval to prevent his ideas of poverty, freedom in nature, and the direct communion of the soul with God without the mediation of priests from being mired in heresy and the eventual wake of persecution. And there was the rub. In time, the brothers would more and more be drawn into squabbles and political intrigues of popes, bishops, even parish priests—and emperors. On more than a few occasions, Frederick Hohenstaufen would feel called upon to squelch Franciscan influence as the brothers fanned out to act as papal propagandists. Already there were *fratres minores* in England, France, Germany, Bohemia, Spain, North Africa, Hungary, and the Holy Land. Like most such organizations, the brothers would find themselves involved even in philosophical and administrative struggles within the order.

The Rule had difficulty earning the approval of Honorius III. Francis himself was not happy with the wording and never would be after he saw that Cardinal Ugolino had reworded parts of it, altering or striking out the all-important rule of poverty. He was depressed when he saw what a far cry the finished document was compared to that which he had envisioned. Still Ugolino, whether Francis liked the new version or not, made *il poverello's* doctrines official by introducing the Franciscan spirit into the Roman Church.

In his dejection Francis took leave of Lady Jacopa and hid himself in a cave near the Umbrian town of Greccio. Alone in his retreat for several winter months, he communed with himself, with nature, and with his times. The tall woods, the rocks, and the numerous cascades set an ideal stage for the kind of introspection he favored. And here took place one of the most memorable stories in the life of this gentle man.

As Christmas approached Francis determined to experience in his unassuming way the hardships of the infant Christ. He had straw and hay brought into a small cave where he proposed to preach a sermon during the Christmas Mass. He approached a friend, John of Vellita, who had prepared his rock cell for him, to procure an ox and an ass that would duplicate the Nativity of Christ in the manger for members of the religious community, local peasants, shepherds, and their families who flocked to the cave for the Mass. As usual with Francis, his sermon was remembered for ardor and beatific joy more than for content. Miracles were ascribed to the touching, eating, or possession of the hay from the manger. Exaggerated? Perhaps. But nonetheless it is a lovely story and is often singled out as the origin of the widespread use of the Christmas crèche.

It is difficult to reconcile this display of love and tender devotion with the persistent reports of Francis's failing health and depression. He was slowly weakening, and it is thought today that he may have been suffering a form of cancer. His sight was becoming increasingly bad. Furthermore, he was worried. His order was not being fulfilled the way he had anticipated. It was sufficient to drive this haunted man of God into fits of depression—not that it held him back from preaching and traveling around Italy, though he did depend now on being carried on the back of a donkey.

For the present, residing in his Greccio hideout, Francis was oblivious to some earthshaking realities. Pope Honorius III was enthusiastically sniffing the sweet smell of crusade. Small matter that it would be a blatant war of conquest for purposes of expanding Frederick's empire, already so large that it brought shudders to the aging pontiff's frame. More important, perhaps Honorius's name would be cleared of the shame of the dismally disastrous fifth crusade. And Frederick would be the one to clean the record. Let him try to worm his way out of this one as he had in the past. Too many witnesses at Ferentino had heard him vow to sail within two years.

1224

By now it was obvious to all, even to old Honorius III, that mustering a new crusade was going to be a matter of more than mere persuasion, or even cajolery. John of Brienne found no takers in France. King Philip Augustus had died in July 1223, and with King Louis VIII on the throne, French participation was out of the question. John of Brienne stayed on in France long enough to attend both Philip's funeral and the coronation of Louis VIII. Then he moved on to Spain. He made a pilgrimage to Santiago de Compostela and then hung around Castile for some months, during which time (at the age of seventy-five) he married King Ferdinand III's sister, Berengaria, and returned to Italy sometime the following year. With seventeen-year-old Henry III on the throne—King John Lackland had died eight years ago—England could be counted on to offer no help, especially since Henry's defenders were preoccupied with asserting the prerogatives of the minor king against ambitious barons and foreign mercenaries. In Germany persuader par excellence Hermann von Salza got only hesitant support from the princes. For a moment he claimed a minor success when Danish King Waldemar III agreed to sustain the effort—and then backed out. It looked as though Frederick would end up bearing the brunt of the long-promised sixth crusade, if it ever came to pass. And he knew, as did Hermann von Salza and John of Brienne, that only a carefully planned and heavily financed effort would prevail against the Muslims.

Pope Honorius had to make the grudging admittance that Frederick, for one, had been doing his share of the preparation. When he wrote to Honorius in March, the emperor could claim one hundred galleys ready and seaworthy, plus fifty additional transports in the construction stage, capable of carrying two thousand knights and ten thousand men-at-arms. In a sense the prototype of twentieth-century military landing craft, they were built in such a manner, asserted Frederick, that the knights could disembark armed and mounted, a trick he may have learned from the records of William the Conqueror. Disappointed at the singular lack of success of the smooth-talking men dispatched to encourage the crusade, Honorius was himself energized to appeal to the Western leaders—with as little luck.

Nagged by the pope and by the pressures of the physical preparations for the crusade, Frederick still found time for one of his most ambitious new schemes. Of all the innovations of the tireless young ruler probably the most enduring was in the field of education, an effort that would do more than any other to raise the intellectual level of his subjects. Unlike so many rulers both ancient and modern, Frederick anticipated a literate, intellectually astute body of subjects. For a couple of hundred years now the school of medicine at Salerno had been the only institution of higher education in southern Italy. Students who desired to better themselves outside the field of medicine had to go to northern Italy, to Paris, perhaps to England, and especially to Spain. The teeming city of Naples, with its noisy streets, sparkling bay, and rumbling volcano, was singled out as the site for Frederick's new Studium Universale. In his charter Frederick stated his aims:

> We propose to rear many clever and clearsighted men, by the draught of knowledge and the seed of learning; men made eloquent by study and by the observation of just law, who will serve the God of all and will please us by the cult of Justice. . . . We invite learned men to our service, men full of zeal for the study of *Jus* and *Justitia,* to whom we can entrust our administration without fear.[2]

Frederick beckoned, and scholars flocked to his new university on the cobalt-blue, Vesuvius-sentineled bay, raucous, alive and teeming, sometimes gray under a leaden sky, but mustering one gorgeous daily blush in the light of morning's rosy dawn. Capri and Ischia smiled from their offshore anchorages, close enough to entice to frivolity on days of rest, but not enough to distract from the more important business of this foundation of the modern University of Naples. Remembering his own harrowing struggle for survival in the alleys of Palermo, his hunger, and the handouts from sympathetic strangers, Frederick remained ever mindful of the needs of the poor students, the hardships of self-betterment, and the agonies of creative endeavor. He wanted no blocks other than personal capacity to obstruct a student's progress. Scholarships were set up for the needy, who, by arrangement, could be lodged and fed at reduced rates.

Frederick had it in mind—and it was no secret since it was explicitly stated in his charter—to train minds for imperial service. His first concern was the realm, of course. "Sicily is the mother of tyrants," he wrote atop one of his later edicts, borrowing the phrase from Paulus Orosius, the historian and theologian who flourished about 415. There was defiance, perhaps impertinence, in his statement, since "tyrant" to a Christian mind had come to smack of Satan himself. But Frederick wanted no mistake to be made: he was in control, and there he intended to stay. His next concern was law, law in the abstract and as an ideal. For this reason the legal scholar and imperial judge, Roffredo of Benevento, was assigned a professorial position along with other leading jurists. It was clear even at the time that Frederick was working toward an "age of law," a term that has been used to describe the last hundred years of the Middle Ages. His plan was to train professional jurists and judges, along with notaries (basically recorders and certifiers of transactions) with legal training. Lofty as were his designs for the good of mankind, his application of legal thinking to the secular state was not totally original. But his insistence on legal justice was original. And if his appointed authorities could combine secular law with canon law, why, so much the better. He did not want to turn his back on the Church, but he would assert above all the supremacy of the State. All of this did not preclude the teaching of other subjects (the arts, Aristotle's natural philosophy, grammar), and the natural sciences were eventually lorded over by the great Peter of Ireland, teacher of Thomas Aquinas.

The emperor and his jurists had watched attentively the rising generation of functionaries, and now with the foundation of the University of Naples they had more opportunity than ever to control young careers. His methods of achieving his goals have sometimes been justly criticized by latter-day pundits, who recognize that they bear no little resemblance to the ways of modern totalitarian states. To educate the youth of his realm in his own spirit, to retain them within the state, Frederick would allow no foreign distractions. No scholar from within the kingdom could go outside for education, and those who had started their educational processes beyond its borders were forced to return. They had no options. His dream was of a rigidly organized society where everyone had his place, or, as in cases of wandering singers, knights, and itinerant scholars, no place at all. He was determined to rule men's thinking. And he was only thirty.

In a way, Frederick's university was in opposition to the law school of Bologna. It was not that he felt any animosity to that revered school; he simply did not want his young people going outside the kingdom to learn the ways of the freethinking, rebellious communes to the north, with whom he understandably had little sympathy. He was determined to hang on to the new generation of intellectuals. There remained only one unified force to stand up to him, to give him pause: the Church, with its claims of a holiness that set it above all secular bodies. And the Church was going to get one more example of its projected sanctity in the person of its holiest brother, Francis Bernardone.

Mount La Verna, about twenty-seven miles north of Arezzo, to which Francis Bernardone had taken himself, had been given to him and his friars as a place for penance and contemplation by one Count Roland, lord of nearby Chiusi di Casentino. Long after both Francis and Roland were dead, a deed was signed by Roland's sons, stating that the gift of the mount had been made on May 8, 1213. By 1216 Francis had established a monastery there, almost four thousand feet in the azure blue of the Tuscan sky, overlooking gleaming chalk cliffs and nestled in the solitary quiet of a grove of pine and beech trees. There are limitless picnic spots there, of which Francis would certainly approve. But thousands of tourists, masses of automobiles, snarling motorcycles, screaming, ball-playing children, and angry parents crowd up to the sacred spot, which cries out to be experienced, not merely seen. Despite signs begging for silence, the clatter is omnipresent. And it is not only tourists sundering the quiet; visiting nuns and resident Franciscans contribute their share.

The dank Sassa Spicca is a natural ravine where it is claimed that Francis liked to come to pray. The so-called bed of Saint Francis (a metal grill all of about four feet long) is entirely spurious, though the cave in which it is located is a reasonable retreat for a saint. It is clear that Francis, his later hymn to the Brother Sun notwithstanding, was as much a part of the dark and damp side of the world as he was of the open, sun-drenched mountains, of the leafy and piney forests. Now vacationers drown out the songs of his sisters, the birds, and the whirring breath of brother wind through the pines. Away from the center of the raucous activity, you may hear his voice—a whisper—over a quiet picnic.

A short distance from the friary Francis had constructed for himself a rough cell as an ideal place for meditation. The air was clean, the sun strong. The natural crevices were fresh with springs and dripping outlets. It was a good spot for him to be. He was tired and worried. His eyesight was steadily deteriorating, which continued to depress him, though he bore the infirmity with his usual patience. He still had two years to live but seemed to be weakening daily. It was here at his cell on Mount La Verna, on the eve of the Feast of the Exaltation of the Cross—a popular feast day that commemorated the defeat of Persian King Chosroës by Byzantine Emperor Heraclius, and the consequent repossession of the relic of the True Cross (c. 629)—that the greatest miracle of Francis's legend-filled life would take place. Absorbed in contemplation of the crucified Christ, Francis beheld the vision of an angel that advised him to prepare himself to receive a sacred gift. Francis affirmed that he was ready.

The next day he was meditating again on the passion of Christ. It was several hours before sunrise, according to the most gripping parable in the biography of this wondrous man. Extenuated by fasting, Francis "was filled unto overflowing, and as never before, with the sweetness of heavenly contemplation."[3] He turned his face eastward to pray:

> [T]wo graces do I pray Thee to grant unto me ere I die: the first, that while I live I may feel in my body and in my soul, so far as is possible, that sorrow, sweet Lord, that Thou didst suffer in the hour of Thy bitterest Passion; the second is, that I may feel in my heart, so far as may be possible, that exceeding love wherewith . . . Thou wast enkindled to endure willingly for us sinners.[4]

Francis remained a long time dwelling on the passion. At last he saw above him a seraph, crucified, and possessing six glowing wings: two for flying, two over its head, and two wrapped about its body. Puzzled by the meaning of the apparition and filled with wonder, Francis was pleased by the graciousness with which the seraph regarded him. Suddenly Mount La Verna appeared in flames bright enough to create what seemed to be an early day. Frightened shepherds swore that the light lasted for over an hour. Muleteers saddled their animals and headed for work as the light faded and the real sun arose. And Francis heard the words: "Knowest thou what I have done to thee? I have given thee the stigmas that are the marks of my Passion, in order that thou be My Standard-bearer."[5] It was a perplexing vision. Moments later Francis became aware of marks appearing on his hands and feet as he had seen in the seraphic vision. At the same time a lance wound appeared in his right side. The wounds were festering and bleeding and would continue to bleed many times in the future.

At first Francis tried to conceal the evidence of his stigmata. Retiring by nature, he wanted to hide the divine manifestation, to attract as little attention as possible. But as time passed it became increasingly obvious that he had to inform his friars of the miracle that had been inflicted on him. He was close to Brother Illuminato, who provided the answer, telling him that it was not for him alone that God performed this miracle but for the profit of others as well. It was only then that Francis made known to the brothers the nature of the miracle and some of the words that had been spoken to him.

Finally Francis made ready to depart for the Porziuncola. In a fond farewell he once more allowed the friars to see his wounds, to touch and to kiss them. With that he left them and went down from the sacred mountain.[6]

1225

No one can know the inner feelings of little Yolanda of Jerusalem as she contemplated the prospect of marrying the most powerful ruler of Europe, worse, a man with a reputation approaching the fabulous. She was recorded by chroniclers as weeping uncontrollably as she took leave of her aunt, Queen Alice of Cyprus, after a brief call at that island before sailing for Italy. As the day of her meeting with Frederick neared, she must have felt at least awed; a man of Frederick's sybaritic propensities and reputation would have given pause to anyone walking into such a union, more so to a fourteen-year-old. Yet Yolanda's feeling may have been mixed, especially at first, when the celebrations in Jerusalem commenced with the arrival of Henry of Malta and a fleet of fourteen imperial galleys sent with proper fanfare to fetch this wisp of a girl who, while not quite a beggar, was unable to bring much beyond her almost meaningless title into a marriage that would make her an empress. There was a round of glittering parties preceding and following her proxy marriage to Frederick in the Church of the Holy Cross at Acre, with Frederick's representative slipping the ring on her finger. There was further rejoicing when Yolanda was crowned queen of Jerusalem at Tyre. Though she would not be of age officially until she was sixteen, the barons of the realms proffered their homage, a display that had to be delightful to a child born to the purple.

That Yolanda was not a second Constance is self-evident. Twice a queen and then empress, Constance was older than Frederick, a widow, a woman of worldly experience, familiar with tragedy. She had brought as her dowry the strength of the House of Aragon and, though they proved useless through no one's fault, a contingent of valiant Spanish knights. She had been Frederick's most reliable guide when he needed advice. On top of everything else, she was the mother of his son, thus far his only legitimate child, who would himself be married this year.

By the time of this second marriage, Frederick had already fathered a covey of illegitimate children. We do not know for sure the actual birthdates of these offspring—nor do we know how many he eventually sired, though among the eleven we do know there are sons and daughters worthy of note: Enzo (born shortly after Henry); Frederick of Antioch (by legend said to be the child of a Syrian girl conceived at the time of Frederick's crusade in 1228, though his status as a lord by 1240 would seem to indicate an earlier birth); Richard of Teate; and, most famous of all, ill-crossed Manfredi. Then there were three girls: Selvaggio, Violante, and Margaret. In addition to the very legitimate Henry, his first-born, there would be two more legitimate sons of the emperor: Henry—one would think that one Henry would have been sufficient—and Conrad IV. Promiscuity is the word that best characterizes Frederick's sexual activities, not necessarily considered a vice in his day. With the high infant mortality rate he must have had other unrecorded children. As time went on and the luxuries and size of his harem were increasingly noised about, his sex life came to be regarded as an open scandal by the Guelf faction, and probably the Ghibelline, too.

For her trip to Italy, Yolanda was accompanied by the requisite parade of nobles, bishops, and ladies-in-waiting, including one slightly older cousin, the daughter of the late Walter of Brienne. Historical gossip has it that Frederick nurtured a passion for the young lady and tradition carries the story further, saying that one of the four extant poems thought to be from Frederick's hand was dedicated to her. If that is true, his passion was indeed profound. It is one of the most charming of love poems, with many an overtone that rings clearly in the twenty-first-century ear. Frederick's misery toward the end of the poem at thoughts of his separation from the object of his desires is a genuine cry from a lover's heart.

> O my God, how crazy I was
> when I left the place
> Where I had been in such grace!
> And dearly do I pay for it,
> and melt down like snow,
> thinking that someone else may have all that in his power now!
> And it seems to me that a thousand years must go by
> before I can return to you, my lady;
> this awful thought presses upon me so heavily
> that it does not let me laugh or play.[7]

If the poem is by Frederick, and it may well be, and if he is indeed writing to Yolanda's lady-in-waiting, then it lends credence to some of the sordid speculation concerning his wedding night and its aftermath.

When Yolanda landed at Brindisi, she found her father and Frederick with a significant part of the imperial court waiting on her. John of Brienne had been close to Frederick's side for a couple of months now, and the two, in anticipation of their new relationship, had become close friends. But friendships can be tenuous things. Yolanda was faced by a husband more than twice her age, still handsome and well built, but giving way to corpulence despite his general abstemiousness and innate love of physical exercise. His red Hohenstaufen hair was beginning to recede at the forehead. But his bride must have been struck by his arresting eyes: they were green, cold, steady, penetrating, and devoid of any expression of kindness. Yolanda's impression must have been of a man of steely strength, yet generous, and considerate to those who were loyal and honorable. She must have been impressed that her husband could speak to her in six languages and that he was a composer of love poetry in the Provençal form but in his native Italian—even if his verses were not directed her way.

The marriage of Frederick and Yolanda was ratified in a face-to-face ceremony on November 9 in the cathedral at Brindisi, not a particularly handsome building, though it is spacious. Its present problem is that so much of it has been rebuilt following an earthquake in 1743, the only twelfth-century parts left being the apse and some mosaic flooring. The Piazza del Duomo is quite another thing, with its ruined Portico of the Knights Templar, a striking three-arched remnant calling vividly to mind the fourteenth century when those knights were conspicuously active in Brindisi. While Frederick could not have been familiar with the portico, he surely would have known Brindisi's round church, San Giovanni al Sepolcro, built by the Templars, and the monastery of San Benedetto, which is Norman. The lintel at the south entrance of San Benedetto, showing in low relief men hunting and fighting various animals, is lively and filled with vigorous action. San Giovanni al Sepolcro is exactly the opposite, all quiet repose with its Romanesque porch guarded by two weathered, very sedate lions. The inside—a miracle of golden light—still preserves its ring of old columns and some traces of fourteenth-century frescoes. It fronts on its own tiny piazza, animated beyond its size by a couple of friendly bars where locals respond to inconsequential and innocent questions with instant, almost intimate, friendship.

The chief jumping-off port for Corfu, Greece, Crete, and Rhodes, Brindisi has suffered much over the centuries. There were the Romans and Goths, Lombards, Byzantines and Normans, Angevins, the Aragonese, soldiers of World War II, and the hordes of rowdy crusaders who embarked there for the Holy Land—unruly mobs who did more for its prosperity, outside of Frederick himself, than anyone until the modern tourist and the Montedison Petrochemical complex. The city was plundered by Saracens in 836, sacked at least twice later, almost eradicated by pestilence in 1348, and as though all of that were not enough, devastated by frequent earthquakes. Frederick's hand is felt in Brindisi, especially in the castle looming like some clumsy monster from the Adriatic. A sturdy building it is, its naked walls constructed of golden, exactingly cut stone. Frederick did not start its construction until two years after his marriage to Yolanda, when he laid out its rectangular plan. In 1481 the castle was enlarged and strengthened by the addition of a barbican and four round towers. Later, in 1551, it was further extended by Emperor Charles V. Since it is the principal medieval secular architecture in Brindisi, it is a pity that it cannot be enjoyed by tourists; it remains today the headquarters for the Comando Militare Marittimo.

In no way could Frederick's second marriage be called ideal. First, he had a raging disagreement with his new father-in-law when he, Frederick, assumed the title of king of Jerusalem, henceforth using it immediately following his title of emperor and preceding that of king of Sicily. Somehow John of Brienne had been led to believe that he would retain that title, though he had no legal right to it, until Yolanda reached her majority in two years. Ever aspiring to the Caesarean might of the ancients, Frederick would have none of it, to the point that John stomped off to Rome, where he found a host of sympathetic bishops and barons who had been similarly slighted by being deprived of their sees or holdings. In cahoots with the pope, the lot of them formed a tornado of contention to encourage disagreements that were soon to break out between Honorius and Frederick. Honorius instinctively sided with John of Brienne. But Frederick refused to budge and went jubilantly on his way as king of Jerusalem.

According to legends lurid in the extreme, none of them probably accurate, there were other causes for Frederick's quarrel with John of Brienne. They start with Frederick's beating Yolanda. We know that he could be self-interested and sly, but it is doubtful that he was given to child-wife beating! Seducing her attractive older cousin—the one who caused him to "melt down like snow"—without even appearing in the nuptial chamber is perhaps another thing entirely. Knowing Frederick's lusty appetite, there is nothing surprising in the story of his faithlessness to so young a bride. Surely any man in his position would have preferred to bed down with a nubile twenty-year-old lady-in-waiting rather than with a girl in her early teens.

The most believable of the wedding aftermath stories is that Frederick abruptly left Brindisi the next morning and when John of Brienne, in a fury over nuptial rumors, finally caught up with him, the father-in-law was dealt the jolting story of the groom's assumption of the title of king of Jerusalem. We can understand the bitterness of the pill as John watched his former liegemen doing homage to a new master. Why Frederick acted so unexpectedly remains a question for speculators to toy with for another several centuries. We do know that Frederick was entertaining fits of resentment against John of Brienne, who refused to cough up fifty thousand silver marks that the late King Philip had bequeathed to the kingdom of Jerusalem. Frederick could have used that money, preoccupied as he was with his coming crusade. And he had more on his mind. His son, King Henry of Germany, was about to be married to Margaret, daughter of Leopold VI of Austria, in a union that had been carefully arranged by faithful regent Archbishop

Engelbert and that was scheduled to take place in twenty days. Tragically, the good Engelbert had just been assassinated by his own cousin, principally for having so effectively put down the restless lawlessness that prevailed in Germany. His murderer was hauled before the proper authority within a year, confessed his guilt, and died on the rack, while the aging Walther von der Vogelweide called down on him an awesome curse. Earlier this year—in July—Frederick had met with Pope Honorius at San Germano, the modern Cassino at the foot of the mountain bearing Saint Benedict's abbey known by the same name. Frederick came out not a little humiliated for a man who aspired to better the ancient Caesars.

At San Germano Honorius made it clear to Frederick that something had to be done to get a crusade rolling. In his own mind Frederick had reason enough for putting it off again. He argued, quite rightly, that he was doing his share of Saracen bashing by defeating and relocating those of Sicily. But his better argument was the recalcitrance of the rest of Europe. It gained for him an extension of another two years. At the time of the meeting, John of Brienne was still Frederick's friend. And Hermann von Salza was on his side, and always would be. Even the patriarch of Jerusalem agreed with Frederick's argument that an ill-planned venture to Outremer would be doomed to failure. Experience had convinced most secular leaders of Europe that they had had enough of papal predilections for organizing crusades, as well as for the inexperienced leadership of papal- and self-appointed bishops and cardinals.

Ten years after having been crowned in Charlemagne's chapel at Aachen, Frederick stood before the high altar in the cathedral at San Germano with his hand on the bible. With two cardinals as witnesses, he swore on his soul that he would set out for the Holy Land on August 15, 1227, and that he would take with him one thousand knights who would be maintained out of his own pocket for a period of two years or pay a penalty of fifty marks for each knight falling short of that number. Frederick swore further to provide transportation for another two thousand knights, each with three horses and retainers. Beyond that he was to put one hundred galleys and fifty transports at the disposal of the departing army. Then, adding to his burden, Frederick agreed to deposit one hundred thousand ounces of gold into a fund administered by Hermann von Salza, to be paid in five installments. When and if Frederick arrived in Outremer, the money would be refunded; otherwise it would be forfeited and used to finance another papal-inspired crusade. And he agreed to an excommunication if his oaths were not fulfilled.

Frederick had gained another two years to finish the subjugation of his island kingdom. And while he had agreed to bear the brunt of the costly crusade, he had established that he was to be the commander of the coming adventure. The pope and his Curia were out of the picture. Perhaps with centralized financial and tactical control there would be better chances of success. Both Frederick and Honorius came away satisfied that each had gotten the better part of the deal. Frederick was sure that he could abide by his oaths and eventually lead a successful crusade, thus winding up more secure on his Jerusalem throne; if he did not live up to his promises, then the pope could rest comfortably that the last word would be his with his power to excommunicate—and he would be much the richer for his efforts.

It was probably this year that there entered Frederick's circle

> the wondrous Michael Scott;
> A wizard of such dreadful fame
> That when, in Salamanca's cave,
> Him listed his magic wand to wave,
> The bells would ring in Notre Dame![8]

True to his own bent, and always determined to unmask the dishonest, the false, the traders in hope, Frederick was attracted to Michael Scott despite more than a hint of phoniness and charlatanism in the latter. Outwardly Michael, about fifty, seemed to be an ideal member of Frederick's entourage. He was a man of prodigious learning. He wrote treatises on natural philosophy and even a commentary on Aristotle, which he introduced at Oxford University. Yet he was given to recondite studies in astrology, palmistry, physiognomy, and alchemy. On this basis alone legend would place him as a cousin to the devil. As a matter of fact, it was believed after he died that his book of magic, which survived, could not be opened without inviting the wrath of evil fiends. As a man willing to stretch truth to the breaking point so long as it gratified his penchant for mixing with people who mattered, Michael enjoyed the advantages of court life. Never above dealing in augurs and casting horoscopes, it may well have been Michael who offered the prediction that Frederick would die near an iron door in a castle whose name was derived from the word *flower*, a prophecy that Frederick took seriously and remembered for the rest of his life.

Michael Scott has remained in the public consciousness through legend both in Italy and Scotland, where it may be possible to trace him to the Scott family of Balwearie in Fifeshire. Dante, with typical

Dante-esque flair, placed him in the eighth circle of hell with the fortunetellers and diviners, all of them with their heads in reverse so they are forced to walk backwards, tears streaming down their backs. Frederick saw the phony side of Michael and, from time to time, had doubts concerning his intellectual honesty.

According to one highly suspect tale, Michael and Frederick became obsessed with the idea of the actual distance separating the earth from the heavens. From a church roof Michael supposedly measured the distance, which he presented to his employer. Frederick, wanting to test Michael's veracity, and knowing the means by which he had achieved his estimate, caused the roof to be lowered a few feet; he then asked the astrologer to repeat his calculations. When Michael presented his new answer, he remarked that either the heavens had risen or that the earth had mysteriously sunk. Frederick embraced him and owned up to his prankish test.

High jinks aside, Frederick saw this trickster as the man who had translated al-Bitriji's Astronomy, Aristotle's Zoology, and Averroes's commentaries on Aristotle's writings, works that had enormous impact on the thinking of the Middle Ages. Accordingly, Frederick called on Michael to give thought to some bothersome ideas regarding life, the afterlife, science, and the natural order. Probably with Michael Scott's approval Frederick himself indulged in a "scientific experiment" that became legendary. Eager to learn whether our languages stem from a mother tongue to which we might revert unless taught otherwise, Frederick ordered that a group of children be raised by attendants who were admonished to speak not a word to them, in any language, under any circumstance. According to the story the experiment was terminated when all the children died "for lack of love." In an experiment concerning human digestion, he is said to have issued a command that two prisoners be fed a healthy meal. The one prisoner was instructed to exert himself with several hours of exercise, while the other was allowed to sleep off his feast. The two men were then killed and their stomachs cut open to see which had better digested his food. The prisoner who had slept won the official, if unrealized, nod of approval. If all of this seems rudimentary, it must be remembered that Frederick was a man of his time. No question was too insignificant or too complicated. Do we have limbs because we need them to perform specific functions; or do our limbs function as they do because we have them? Why does a rod appear broken when plunged into water? If the sea is the source of all worldly water, why is it salty and other ponds and lakes sweet? How does the earth exist in space? Why does a star appear larger in its ascendency than at its zenith? Michael Scott was the recipient of an endless stream of questions that Frederick regarded as pertinent to his understanding of the afterlife. Can love or hate be strong enough to bring a dead person back to life? Apparently the medieval concept of the satisfaction of merely basking in the Creative Light and the endless adoration of the Supreme Being did not much appeal to Frederick. What do the souls in heaven for an eternity do with their time? How many heavens and hells are there, and who inhabits them? In which heaven does God reside? Do souls recognize one another in the afterworld? One story has it that Frederick, in an effort to prove or disprove the mortality of the soul, had a man imprisoned in an airtight vat and left to die, supposedly demonstrating that, since the soul could not issue forth from the container, it died with the body. Philosophic discussions and treatises occupied much courtly time and thought. With the rich mixture of religions, cultures, and races in Frederick's circle this must have made for interesting argument. Like an early-day Leonardo da Vinci, Frederick was anticipating the Renaissance. He was a man seeking answers.

Besides arguing with his intimates and quizzing Michael Scott, Frederick experimented with bird and animal breeding. He established certain seasons based on breeding habits when hunting was forbidden, surely the first recorded example of closed hunting seasons, and certainly pleasing to any early-day environmentalist. His palace at Foggia became the center for the care and breeding of a wide variety of waterfowl. There was plenty of water at his castle there, and ditches were dug to create a network of waterways to attract herons and cranes, among other water birds. (These canals still show up in certain types of aerial photography.) In addition, he kept herds of water buffalo, sheep, and cows scattered through the realm. He raised bees, pigeons, peacocks, goats, and pigs. He bred horses, seeking to improve bloodlines by importing Barbary mares. Frederick was especially fond of horses. His own black stallion was named Dragon, and his master of horses, Giordano Ruffo, wrote *De medicina equorum,* which was used as a veterinarian guide for centuries. Along with animal husbandry Frederick encouraged the cultivation of sugar cane, hemp, cotton, wheat, millet, olives, and grapes.

Above all his pleasures and interests, Frederick was carried away by his love of falconry, which he studied earnestly, and of which the most significant product was his book, *The Art of Falconry,* where he argues for the nobility of falconry over other types of hunting. In a display of acute and systematic reasoning, he divides birds into groups based on their habitats, and then further on their raptorial or nonraptorial propensities. He wrote of the habits, reasons, and seasons of migration, of the birds' halting places, their mates, coitus, nesting habits, of their egg incubation, their care of chicks and their organs, even including the contours of their feathers. Several sections of his book are devoted to hunting with different kinds of falcons. As a result of the completeness of his book, Frederick has often been singled out as the first naturalist and the father of the science of ornithology.[9] And here, ultimately, in a profound and meaningful understanding of nature, is where the two titans of their age—Frederick Hohenstaufen and Francis Bernardone—meet, each with his own interpretation of the miracle of life, the one with doubts and curiosity, the other with total acceptance and faith.

While Frederick was indulging his quest for knowledge, marrying, perhaps neglecting his wife, and certainly alienating his father-in-law, Francis Bernardone was covering Umbria and the Marches on one last preaching cycle. In time it became apparent that he could not go through with it. The agonies of the stigmata were draining his health. His sight continued to worsen, and the winter became so severe that he was forced to give up. He was taken to San Damiano, to be nursed there by the tender and loving Clare. Of course, the Poor Clares were distressed. Francis was their holy hero, their spiritual father, their guide to heaven, the sun in their cloistered lives. Their sadness at seeing him in such straits was impossible to hide. To cheer them he became a troubadour again, writing a hymn exalting the poor life that they had chosen as their way to salvation, and at the same time lamenting the labors ahead of them, a subject with which he was familiar.

Francis was nearly blind now, and the least amount of light was torture to his eyes. Yet it was here at San Damiano, the scene of his first enlightenment, that he composed his famous hymn to light, his "Canticle to Brother Sun," to the great life-giver, to God, the magnificent Father of things animate and inanimate. He sang his wonder-filled thanks for the gifts of life and death, for his "sisters" the birds and his "brothers" the animals, for plants, water, sky, air, fire—all things sharing a common Father, and hence, in his mind, quite literally his siblings. His hymn to nature is from the heart, an insistence on the presence of God as he saw it, in every aspect of life, eternal and all-encompassing, as monumentally significant as the tiniest grain of sand. In every way Francis's "Canticle to Brother Sun," one of the first vernacular religious poems in the Italian language, is a laud for the meticulously ordered gift of nature, and for the gifts that nature, in its turn, dispenses. It is a divinely simple idea, all the more striking in that the year of its creation was also the probable year of the birth of perhaps the most sophisticated intellectual of the medieval Church, Thomas Aquinas. Few Western men have been able to comprehend the Oriental concept of man's place in the natural-universal scheme of things as did the stigmatized, blind, ailing bridegroom of poverty from Assisi. There is something biblical about Francis's seeing the world as a well-ordered praise to God expressed in the simplest of poetic lines and feelings. The "Canticle to Brother Sun" is a praise of nature sung by a poet who could no longer see it.

Highest, all-knowing imperial Lord,
We praise, glorify, and honor You.
On You every blessing.
Through You all things exist.
No one is worthy to take Your name.

While Francis was reveling in the inspiration of his great hymn to creation, Bishop Guido of Assisi and the podestà, Oportulo di Bernardo, were feuding in a venomous quarrel that soon had the religious and civic communities at odds. Oportulo was prominent in Assisi, a leader of authority and spirit, a landowner and family man, law abiding and capable of intimidating fury. He had been excommunicated by the bishop for acting contrary to a papal directive. Francis revered Bishop Guido as a man who had always been understanding of his eccentricities and had helped to nurture his order into being, while Oportulo had long been a devoted supporter of Francis and had rejoiced when his own daughter, Agnese, had entered Clare's convent at San Damiano. Francis was saddened to think of his two friends wasting so much energy in recriminations and mutual hatred, feeling that those who hate are as much to be pitied as those who suffer physical infirmities and pain. Worn out by suffering, Francis could still act the peacemaker. He was weary of the feud that had dragged on month after dreary month. Francis begged the podestà to bring his followers to the courtyard of the bishop's palace where he was being cared for. He wanted the antagonists to hear his song.

Before the two adversaries and their followers, Brother Pacifico—the troubadour brother—intoned the "Canticle to Brother Sun," alternating with the assembled friars, who repeated each verse according to a melody that Francis had taught them. Suddenly the podestà arose, his hands clasped and tears in his eyes. It was a universal prayer he was hearing, an apotheosis of nature, a glorification of all that we had lost in

Eden, the sun and stars, the wind, fire and water. The song pierced the richly woven pallium of the bishop, appealing to his heart, to the source of his forgiveness. The men bowed their heads in humility in the face of the blind poet's message of divine, creative love that penetrated every chink of the rude courtyard walls. It was after the praise by "our sister mother Earth" that Francis introduced a new verse for the occasion, a gentle call for peace:

Praise be My Lord
By those who suffer loss and pain,
Who bear the burden of infirmity
And are happy to bear Your yoke in peace.
They shall from You, My Lord, receive the heavenly crown.

With this pointed reminder, Podestà Oportulo fell on his knees before the bishop to beg his pardon for what suddenly seemed an inconsequential, finicky disagreement. The haughty bishop, a little bent with age, embraced Oportulo and likewise begged forgiveness.

It was decided then that Francis should journey to Rieti to consult a doctor who was expert in diagnosing eye diseases. With eyes bandaged so he would not have to bear the agony of light, he was led on horseback to the Guelf commune and residence of medieval popes. Even before the Romans Rieti had been a Sabine capital, but by the time of Francis's visit, most traces of that ancient people had vanished, though there were, and are still, some impressive expanses of ancient walls. There was a twelfth-century cathedral there, which has been supplanted by a fourteenth-century building. Laid out on a Latin-cross plan, the church displays a Romanesque facade and a medieval campanile whose bells echo sonorously through the overcrowded, well-kept streets and through the clear air toward Mount Terminillo nearby. A ground floor seven bays long and two wide, canopied by an arresting procession of Gothic arches, serves as a foundation for a ponderous bishop's palace dating from just after Francis's time. A theatrical-looking staircase leads out of a courtyard to the first floor above ground level, while a high arch connects the palace with buildings across the Via Cintia. Rieti is a quiet city, a place for restful cogitation, wine in sunlit sidewalk cafes, and the local *fregnacce!*—pasta flats with a sauce of tomato, oil, garlic, and parsley. Rustic. Delicious!

By this time it was September; the grapes were in full fruit and hay was being mowed. Pope Honorius, absent from Rome because of another of the interminable uprisings against papal leadership, was at Rieti with Cardinal Ugolino of Ostia and the usual religious entourage. The rest that Francis needed was not forthcoming as everyone wanted to visit this holy man who, they all knew, was well into the last stage of his life. He was moved on another six miles to the monastery of Fonte Colombo, in a wild, rocky setting, surrounded by ilex trees and, because of the quiet and *il torrente* that runs from mountain crevices, a stopping-off place for migrating doves, which gives the place its name (dove: *colomba*). Lovely Fonte Colombo is Francis's kind of country, all rustling leaves and twittering and cooing birds, flowers, and no man-made clatter. A narrow, twisting road leads upward into the mountains, into thick woods where stepped paths twist and contort into the melancholy quiet.

The Chapel of the Madonna (also called "of the Magdalene") is small. Tranquil. A fresco of Santa Chiara occupies the left wall of the tiny interior, facing a less ingratiating Magdalene on the right. Small modern stained glass windows bathe birds of various kinds in shafts of light. One feels Francis lurking here, perhaps even more so than at the Carceri outside of Assisi. The Sacro Speco at a lower level on the mountainside invites us to look down to it, but, alas, passage is barred. These are the places where Francis prayed, especially in the Chapel of the Madonna. But it was in the Sacro Speco that he suffered the ultimate agony and horrifying medical indignity.

According to Thomas of Celano, who supposedly was there, a doctor was summoned to determine what, if any, treatment could be administered. He brought along a cauterizing iron, which he placed in a fire until it was red hot. Francis turned to the fire and said, "My brother fire . . . the Most High created you strong, beautiful, and useful. Be kind to me in this hour, be courteous. . . . I beseech the great Lord who made you that he temper your heat now so that I may bear it when you burn me gently."[10]

By the time it was over, the side of Francis's face had been laid open and horribly burned. It was decided to move him back to Rieti, to the bishop's palace, while the wound healed. Another doctor visited him there and declared that the cauterization had been useless and dangerous. He recommended a perforation of both ears with a red-hot iron. One of the most moving legends concerning Francis's ordeal says that God sent musicians playing a zither and a harp to comfort him, to ease the pain, to distract his mind from earthly evils. The music was at the same time joyous and soothing—the music of angels.

1226

For all the excruciating pain of the treatments that Francis had undergone, they proved ineffective. In a search for further help, he was moved in April to the Alberino friary near Siena. It was here that he

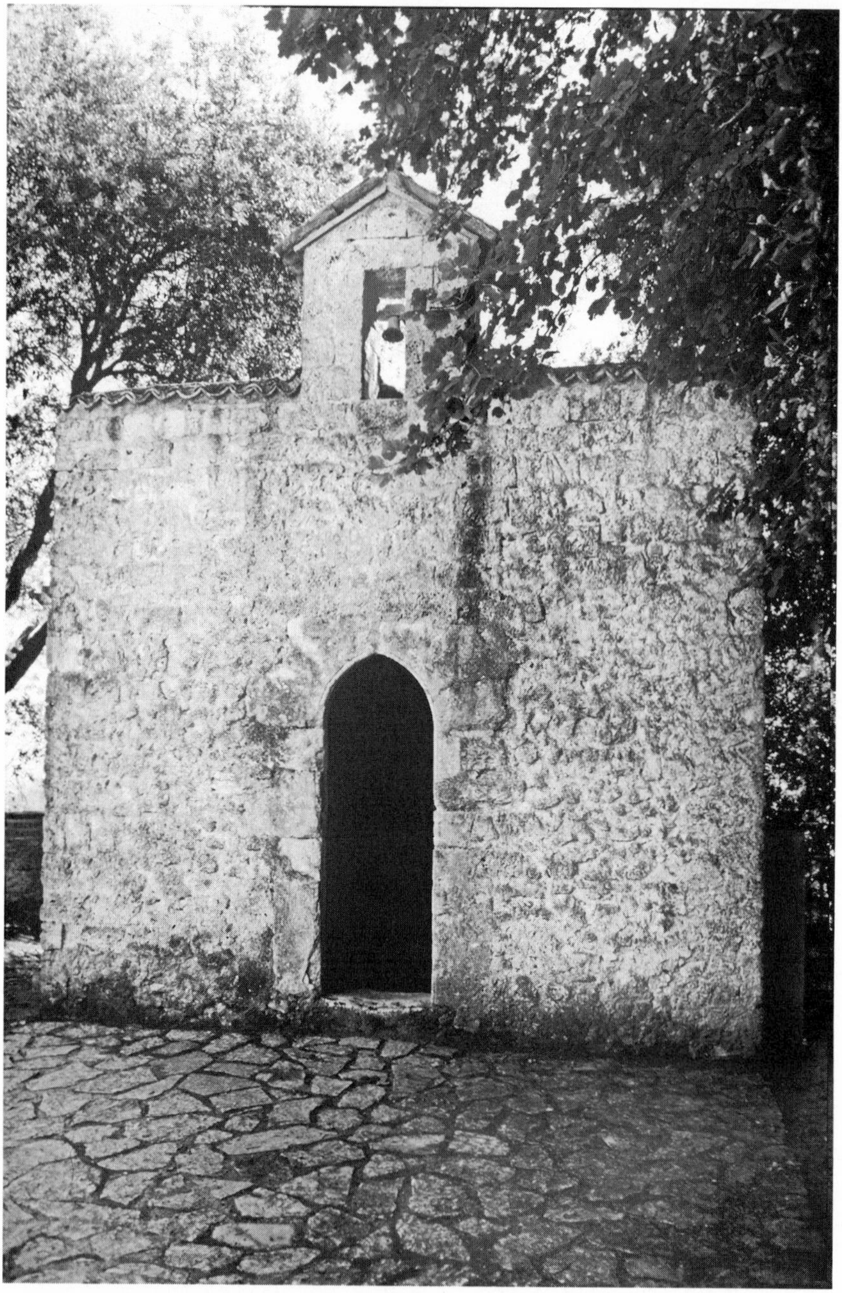

Chapel of the Madonna, Fonte Colombo, Italy

reaffirmed his love for his brothers, gasped out to Brother Benedetto of Pirano, who had to bend close to hear his words. It was more: it was a spoken testament of his belief in the rightness of his life of poverty and in the correctness of the linkage between his order and the Church. Within a few days Francis's health had improved sufficiently to gratify his pleas to be taken back to Assisi.

After a stop near Cortona because of his delicate condition, the sad procession made its way slowly back to the Porziuncola. Then—and one wonders at this constant moving him about—he was taken to Bagnara, a small recently completed friary high on the slopes of Mount Pennino, east of Nocera Umbra, where it was thought that the salubrious air might better his condition. (Thus far the author has been unable to locate the friary or its ruins and was told by a curtly hostile native that "Francis was never here!") As his end approached scenes of the most misguided, self-interested religiosity ensued, certainly bizarre by twenty-first-century standards but perhaps understandable in the context of medieval devotion. Francis was jealously guarded so that no city, in revenge against Assisi or in fanatical devotion to the sainted man, would try to make off with his body once his life was concluded. Tactlessly, it would seem, a delegation of knights from Assisi was sent to Bagnara to convince Francis himself that he must not allow anyone to claim the glory of ownership of his body. Francis was in agreement, expressing a desire to return to the source of his order—to the Porziuncola.

The melancholy procession was stopped by weather in Assisi. Francis was sheltered in the bishop's palace. A doctor, Bongiovanni, an old friend, came to see him, and spoke encouraging words. But Francis was not to be fooled, and he begged the doctor to tell him the truth. He was not afraid to die. He was told that he would die by the end of the month, or in early October. Francis clasped his hands in rapture. "Welcome, Sister Death," he said. Once again he became the troubadour. He ordered brothers Leo and Angelo to sing for him his "Canticle to Brother Sun." When they reached the final doxology, he stopped them, to murmur a new penultimate stanza:

Praised be My Lord
By Sister Death,
Whom no one can escape;
Oh, Woe to them who die in mortal sin;
And happy they who know Thy blessed will,
And so avoid a dreaded second death.

It was not in Francis's character to die in a palace. Legend has it that he was carried out of his natal city through the Moiano Gate and down into the plain. Back at the Porziuncola he set to his last work—the dictation of his final testament. In it he spoke of his loves and his griefs, his experiences in trying to draw together his order, his First Rule, his dreams and anxieties; and he ended with the admonishment that his testament was not to be argued about, or even interpreted. His words had been simply stated; they were to be understood in the same spirit.

Bedridden, blind, in agonizing pain, and sinking fast, Francis still had thoughts for those whom he had known in life: for his brothers in the order, for Clare and her sisters at San Damiano to whom he sent a message of comfort, and for the noble-born Jacopa dei Settesoli—his "Brother Jacopa"—who arrived at the Porziuncola almost miraculously as Francis was dictating a last message to her.

Late Saturday afternoon on October 3, at the time of a flamboyantly setting sun, with only two of his brothers present, Francis began to intone his last prayer, Psalm 142, the prayer of David in exile and hiding in the cave of Adullam. "I cried unto the Lord with my voice; with my voice unto the Lord did I make my supplication." And his brothers responded, "I poured out my complaint before him; I shewed before him my trouble." It was the cry of a spirit overwhelmed by the anticipated step before it, of a man who had no doubt, who knew he was returning to his point of origin. When his monks had wept out the last phrases—"Bring my soul out of prison, that I may praise thy name: the righteous shall compass me about; for thou shalt deal bountifully with me"—Francis was dead.

Then was born the final glorious legend. With a crescendo of joyous sound, a torrent of music, soft at first, and finally magnificently loud as the source of nature's orchestra came closer, descending with an almost liquid rush, a flock of skylarks fluttered down on the roof of Francis's cell. In the semidark of the late sunset, the airborne choir heralded Francis's transition from here to the hereafter, from body to spirit, from the earthly to the ethereal. No man has enjoyed a finer, more tumultuous fanfare from dark to light, from pain to comfort, from oppression to liberation, from turbulence to peace. To the believer no explanation is needed; for the nonbeliever it suffices to say that he had returned from the wars of life, that he had remained loyal to his convictions, indeed, had affirmed them. Scarred and burned by men's futile attempts to cure his physical ailments, wracked by the exquisite agonies of the passion of his miraculous stigmata, he had found his way to his final kingdom, unscathed, uncomplaining, joyful in the wealth of his poverty, and welcomed by the sweet song of his winged sisters. Many a saint may have asked for more, but surely none has received it. When his brothers laid his naked body on Mother Earth as he had requested, they sensed that his life—his corporal life—in a kind of biological absorption, a symbolic osmosis, was draining back into the great Mother of his sustenance. With the fluttering rise of the skylarks, a symphony of movement and music, Francis's spirit was carried aloft into the night to become one with the stars, to become a galaxy—or better, to become his Brother Sun. His brothers wept for their loss, but as much in joy for his final passage.

CHAPTER TEN

> Just judge of the avenging-punishment,
> work the gift of the remission (of sins)
> before the Day of the Reckoning.
> ***Dies Irae*, verse 11**

1226

While Francis was dying in Siena, Frederick was traversing the countryside north of Rome on his way to a meeting of German and Italian princes and churchmen scheduled for Easter Sunday in the city of Cremona, a place of heady memories dating back to 1212. Cremona was one of the few cities in Lombardy that he knew would pay him the respect that was his due. On passing through the Church-owned duchy of Spoleto without papal consent—a brusque act, maybe one of defiance—Frederick had demanded an armed guard drawn from the men of the region to escort him through their territory, thus protecting him from their own brothers. A paradoxical situation, but an emperor could not be too careful in volatile northern Italy! This mid-Italian area had long been under papal-imperial dispute, the emperors taking the stand that the lands were held by the popes only at imperial sufferance, with the popes maintaining that they were owned by the Church in perpetuity. Frederick's demand for an armed guard amounted to an unvarnished assertion of sovereign rights. As recently as six years before he had tacitly agreed that the lands were held by the Church, though in his mind he entertained the idea that they were revocable at the imperial will. Honorius was aware that in combination the Church-owned lands in the west, the duchy of Spoleto in the center, and the March of Ancona in the east effectively created a barrier across central Italy from the Tyrrhenian to the Adriatic Seas, between Frederick's northern empire and his southern kingdom. Should Frederick create as powerful a political machine in the north as he had in the south, it would be tempting for him to absorb that divisive wall of papal territory into his secular state. The affront of marching through Spoleto, and demanding protective troops on top of it, indicated how sorely he pined for the duchy. Papal outrage at Frederick's disrespect for protocol would be an understatement. Honorius fired off a letter:

> Be content with your own boundaries and seek not to encroach on the Patrimony of St. Peter. You have begun to harass the Church, no longer by deputy, but in person. The higher you rise, the more awful will be your fall. Remember the fate of Nebuchadnezzar and Pharaoh; aye, and of your own grandfather. He burnt the Porch of St. Peter's and worried the Church; he was punished like the Israelites of old, who were not allowed to enter the Promised Land; he was drowned before he arrived in Palestine. . . . The vengeance of God fell on his sons Henry and Philip. Why do you boast yourself in wickedness? We love you more than other crowned heads; we are therefore bound to rebuke you, when you go astray. Take care that God does not root you out of the land of the living; we must excommunicate you, if you persist in your wickedness.[1]

Frederick responded in kind, calling up every complaint he had against Honorius, his predecessor, and their policies, which brought down more rebuke from the papal heights. But Frederick had lost the fight even before it started. On the verge of moving into troubled Lombardy, he could not risk an outright break with the pope, and both parties knew it. Already many of the Lombard cities, led as usual by Milan but including Padua, Vicenza, and Treviso, had agreed to a twenty-five-year defensive league unmistakably aimed at the emperor—a reestablishment of the old Lombard League that had been directed against his grandfather. Word of Frederick's authoritarian laws in southern Italy were circulating throughout northern Italy, leaving the cities fearing a loss of freedom, especially their freedom to declare war against one another. The pope had to support outwardly any action that Frederick might take to get his stalled crusade on the road, the avowed purpose of the Cremona diet. But this spreading Lombard antagonism could not have been displeasing to him. Anything was acceptable that tended to thwart imperial power, except insofar as that power was used to benefit the Church.

The pope did nothing when the Lombards—along with Verona, now a member of the hostile coalition—blocked the passage of young King Henry and his German cavalry at Trento as they made their way along the narrow defile of the Adige River on their way to Cremona, causing Frederick, in helpless rage, to cancel his planned diet. With the whole adventure a washout, Frederick could take no view other than that the league was little more than a rebel state within his empire while the Curia, seeing it as a barrier against imperial encirclement, rejoiced. After a six-week delay at Trento, King Henry and his train returned to Germany, an unfortunate happening since Henry could have used some good fatherly advice at this time. It had been almost six years since Frederick had seen his son, years during which the young king had benefited from the late Engelbert of Cologne's sage confidence and courageous guidance. Now Duke Louis of Bavaria filled that vacated position, with results as yet undetermined.

While Henry turned his back to Italy, Frederick was fretting in Ravenna, haranguing away against a Church hierarchy that would tolerate the cities of the league when most of them were known to be hotbeds of heresy. This was no idle rhetoric on Frederick's part. Honorius himself had once decried against Milan as soaked in heretical poison. Believing in a balance of power between the religious and secular administrations, Frederick stood against heresy as actively as—sometimes more actively than—the popes. Besides, a weakened Church tended to negate, in his eyes, his own imperial clout. To save face, Honorius finally placed the league cities under papal ban. It was an idle gesture, and no one was fooled. Nevertheless, Frederick responded appropriately, exercising the temporal ban, outlawing the citizens of the condemned cities, and closing their schools. Before the year was out, fearing lest the anticipated crusade be aborted, the pope interceded between the emperor and the Lombard rebels, bringing peace by agreeing to lift the papal ban—provided that Frederick would lift the imperial ban. Getting the league members to swear not to seek revenge against Cremona and the other Ghibelline cities was a further string attached. More, they agreed to furnish four hundred knights for the coming crusade.

With typical Hohenstaufen persistence, Frederick was determined to go through with his sworn excursion to Outremer; but he was just as determined to endure no more hassling from the pope. After the Cremona diet fiasco he saw himself a victim of betrayal. He could best gain his ultimate objectives by playing the role of a wronged son of the Church who had come north with only one idea in mind: to assemble forces for the pope's crusade. Papal perfidy must have been obvious to the world. Honorius's arm-in-arm march with the heretical rebels was there for all to see. He was proving himself a traitor to Church and empire alike. Playing the wounded party, Frederick could afford to bide his time, firm in the conviction that this "incestuous" alliance of Church and heretics impaired the divinely willed constitution of a world united in the Church and the empire. Even more important to Frederick were the prestige of his empire and the honor of his person. He had been needled in a vital spot. Honorius, by his noncondemning attitudes and his positively saccharine affectations in settling the dispute, had all but condoned rebel treacheries. Only for the moment could Frederick afford to accept the put-down with outward good grace.

Ravenna, the city in which Frederick cooled his heels for several months, had been a pre-Roman city built on islands and piling in the Po delta. Time silted up the swampy areas between the small islands and the mainland, so that now it is situated several miles from the Adriatic. Greek geographer Strabo mentions that the city was founded by settlers from Thessaly, who abandoned it to the Umbrians. It was not taken by the Romans until around 191 BC. Augustus built the port of Classis three miles away as a base for the Roman navy, where it was reported that 250 ships could ride anchor simultaneously. Ravenna was a dismal station, fly- and mosquito-ridden, with recurrent malaria always a problem. The fifth-century onslaught of Alaric's hordes caused the Roman power center to be moved there. But that did not halt the decline. While the Eastern Roman Empire, centered at Constantinople, was flourishing, the western half fell more and more victim to its own internal decay, as well as to the continuing ravaging tribes from the northern woods. Under Odoacer, the first Germanic warrior-king of Italy, Ravenna stood for almost three years against the siege of Theodoric the Ostrogoth until Odoacer, agreeing to a joint rule with Theodoric, surrendered in March 493—and was murdered at a banquet by the conqueror's own hand.

Nine years after the death of Theodoric in 526, Byzantine emperor Justinian the Great sent his renowned general, Belisarius, to destroy the Gothic monarchy in Italy. Once achieved, Byzantine hegemony lasted for another ninety years, only to fall first to the Lombards, and eventually to the Franks under Pippin. Son Charlemagne himself was not above judicious vandalism, carrying off a bronze statue and columns from Theodoric's palace for use in his own imperial residence in Aachen. By the thirteenth century Ravenna was a Guelf-leaning independent republic, to be incorporated eventually into the papal see, where it remained until Garibaldi's unification of Italy in 1861.

Although Ravenna was a thriving, bug-ridden city in its Roman heyday, there is not a lot left to prove it. The monuments that tourists flock to date from after the fifth century. Frederick spent several months there, passing the time as was his wont by hunting, physical exercise, and long intellectual arguments with his confidants. Feeding his interests, he must have taken in numerous monuments, many of them built by his forerunners, including the quietly dignified, massive tomb of Theodoric. More than anything else, though, Ravenna claims rights to the most glorious conglomeration of the art of mosaic, a shimmering and sparkling world of sumptuous color as boundless as the elements, a most important broadside of Byzantine-inspired works the likes of which are not to be found in any other Western city, with the possible exception of Palermo. Frederick must have felt that he had come home to his own mosaic-enriched beginnings.

Ravenna's most noteworthy treasure is the mausoleum of the most interesting woman of the fifth-century Christian world, Empress Galla Placidia. Born to the purple (the daughter of Emperor Theodosius I) she married the king of the Visigoths and later became empress as consort of Constantius III. A small structure in cross form, the mausoleum is encrusted with marble and mosaics in rainbows of brilliant hues and shimmering golds, all backed by a star- and rosetta-studded blue. Saint Lawrence is represented looking angry, if not downright petulant, with the grill and fire of his martyrdom. An adolescent, graceful, and beardless Christ sits comfortably under a vault in a rocky, semi-arid landscape, dressed in a gold-and-blue-striped tunic, acting the gentle shepherd to his flock of long-tailed sheep. Floral patterns, geometric arrangements interspersed with figures, an especially charming little bath with two white doves, and a stag drinking from the Fountain of Life—"As the hart panteth after the water brooks," sings Psalm 42:1, "so panteth my soul after thee, O God." Endless riches make up the decorative scheme. Geometric patterns reminiscent of the Greek meander and, achieving a three-dimensional effect, enliven the interior with scintillating colors. One can feel an enormous affinity with the mosaics of this building, so simple from the outside that it gives no clue of the dazzling interior, mainly because of its small scale. The viewer is close to these tesserae of brilliant color, so close that one never mistakes the representations for painting, as can be the case in more distant situations.

With Theodoric and his Ostrogoth horde plunging into Italy, the controversial doctrine of Arianism made its entry into the normally orthodox land. The followers of the imported heretical teaching, which contradicted accepted Church dogma on the nature of the Trinity, built their own religious monuments in Ravenna. Theodoric himself caused Sant'Apollinare Nuovo to be erected as the palatine church and the cathedral of the Arian bishops, its name commemorating the legendary first bishop of Ravenna. It is widely admired for its interior triple register of mosaics. The upper band displays twenty-six graphic scenes—as graphic as mosaics can be, at any rate—from the life of Christ, the oldest extant mosaic cycle of the New Testament, including several scenes from the Passion—but none of the crucifixion. Immediately below is a band representing prophets and saints, while below that is the tour de force of the sumptuously decorative scheme, created after the church was given over to more orthodox (as opposed to Arian) worship in 560: the two processions of the saints and martyrs. Superb procession friezes were known from remote antiquity: the Parthenon Panathaea, Egyptian tomb decoration, the Babylonian, Assyrian, and Persian palace reliefs. But nowhere can we find processions of more austere tranquility or richer pattern, of more elevating stylization.

On the left side of the nave, over the columns separating that center aisle from the side aisle, is a procession of twenty-two holy virgins, all moving from the western end of the church—from the abstract Port of Classis—to follow the three Magi who offer their gifts to Mary and her son at the eastern end. The right side is reserved for representations

Sant'Apollinare Nuovo, Ravenna, Italy

of male martyrs moving toward the east from Theodoric's palace, to gather before Christ the Judge in company with an attendant angelic court. There is a regularity about both the placement and the attitudes of the figures, setting up a slow rhythm as precise as the columns below, the hesitant beat of a dignified, reverent procession. The figures carry crowns of their martyrdom and are typal rather than individual. Two small breaks: Saint Martin affects the same color as the Christ, and only Saint Lawrence among the white-clad males is swathed in gold. They appear to float incorporeally against a background of palm trees as evenly spaced as they are themselves. Their large, staring eyes are rapt in a beholding beyond our view, seeming outside of humanity, literally in a saintly, eternal order. The processions are so fixed that they enter the world of iconography: figured beyond what is perceived, they attempt to embody what is felt—what is known. Christian or not, no one who views these solemn, austere processions the length of the nave of Sant'Apollinare Nuovo, and who moves with them in their regular, measured rhythm, can fail to appreciate that they have experienced an event from another plane, another order, another reality. Francis of Assisi would have understood it perfectly.

But good things are yet to come: Christ the Friend, not long past youth, enthroned, backed by jewels and cushions. He is accompanied by four angels, large-winged, their faces a little more severe than the God they serve, their attitudes more rigid. Christ's hand is raised in blessing, a gentle gesture that hovers over a left hand holding a kind of scepter. The judge is smiling at us; none of that Eastern Pantocrator severity, the awesome judgmental forbiddance! Here we have an abiding friend, a judge willing to overlook human frailty as perhaps a trivial relapse from the ideal. His stare is steady; he sees right through us. He knows. Sublime in his majesty, he is not to be taken lightly.

Of special interest to Emperor-King Frederick must have been the Church of San Vitale, the model for Charlemagne's imperial chapel at Aachen, one of Frederick's most impressive stages. It is a dazzling church dedicated to a saint about whom little is known, though it is suspected that he and his wife, Valeria, were martyred during the un-Stoical persecution of Christians by devoted Stoic Marcus Aurelius. Occupying the site of a former fifth-century structure, San Vitale stands as one of the most stunning buildings in a city that has more than its share. Columns, capitals with their intricate impost blocks, and carved doorjambs were fashioned in the Byzantine quarries of Marmora and shipped to Ravenna. Clearly of Eastern inspiration, octagonal in plan, the great central space is surrounded by an ambulatory. Eight stout columns rise to a dome decorated, alas, by end-of-the-eighteenth-century frescoes, a discordant note in the overwhelming cacophony of vibrant colors and patterns, veined marbles, and glowing, thinly cut alabaster windows. The choir opens on a breathtaking crescendo of brilliant mosaic shimmer. The surface of the choir, from top to bottom, is covered with mosaics, allowing our eyes an ecstasy of free and unhampered movement over surfaces and ridges, planes and curves. The soaring arch that separates this presbytery from the main body of the church is decorated by glowing representations of Christ, the twelve apostles, and saints Gervase and Protase, called the first martyrs of the city of Milan, and presumed by some to be the sons of Vitale. In the vault of the chancel, the predominant colors are light yellow, gold, and blue, all arranged in swirling floral patterns that serve as background for four angels who, with arms aloft, support a central ring of fruits and flowers encasing a gleaming white Lamb of God.

Beneath the triforium galleries of the chancel are mosaics so decorative as to almost cause one to lose sight of their biblical significance. In cascades of richest greens and blues, augmented by warm reds, yellows and oranges, and sparkling golds, we find two stories from the life of Abraham, while across the chapel, incorporated into one scene, are the sacrifices of Abel and Melchisedek. There are representations of Jeremiah, Moses receiving the ten commandments, the chiefs of the twelve tribes of Israel, Aaron, Isaiah, Moses again—this time with the burning bush and his flock—the four evangelists with their symbols awaiting the divine messages in picturesque landscapes and surrounded by animals and birds.

In the apsidal half-dome Christ the Redeemer is enthroned on a globe of intense blue mosaic against a gold ground, radiating an aura of the divine as befits the universal setting. The youthful, beardless Christ, with ever-so-winsome a smile, is handing the crown of martyrdom to San Vitale, who is approaching timidly, being ushered into the divine presence by an angel, much harder, less benevolent in appearance than the Master. On Christ's left an equally austere angel is introducing Bishop Ecclesius, under whom the building of the church was realized and who is carrying a model of the church even as it exists today. The five pose in a landscape with a low horizon, as flower-strewn as an English country garden, and neatly arranged with geometrically stylized rocks and streams. As in other mosaics of this early period, the figures are conceived as pure rhythm, as flat arrangements of line and pattern, with no effort to model or to create an illusion of space.

San Vitale, Ravenna, Italy

ECLESIVS EPIS

Appropriate are representations of the Byzantine Emperor Justinian and his Empress Theodora, located slightly below and to either side of the court of the Redeemer. In blazing colors, worldly in pomp and circumstance, bejeweled and lively in vestments of ornate patterns and jazzy combinations of textures, the Byzantine court displays the power and wealth, not to mention the ritualistic solemnity of the most ceremony-minded court of its day. These mosaics were rendered after the takeover of Ravenna by the Eastern emperor, hence the prominence of the imperial personages, and especially of Archbishop Maximian, who consecrated the church in 547 and whose exquisite, if uncomfortable-looking, carved throne can be seen in the Archiepiscopal Palace Museum. What movement there is in these glorious mosaics is slow. The figures are rigid, with the trains of attendants as majestic as the rulers they accompany. But tiny informal gestures relieve the ceremonial stiffness: Theodora's attendant pushing back a drapery; one of Justinian's bodyguards looking straight at us wears a fleeting, almost self-conscious smile. Theodora's strands of jewels cascade from her headdress in rigidly vertical lines, like the burial adornment of Frederick's Empress Constance. Justinian's simpler pendants seem to swing as though set in motion by his slow gait. The women's robes are a miracle of variegated patterns and complex colors, with the lower edge of the empress's cloak showing a woven representation of the Magi offering their gifts; Justinian's men—but for Maximian, who is in gold, and the guards who wear more richly convoluted colors—are in dignified, austere white. The empress and her party are clearly standing in a festooned corridor complete with a spraying fountain. The bright purples and whites, the blues, reds and greens, and especially the golds, take on a prismatic sparkle that, working with the flat, stylized rendering of the garments, seems, as always in these mosaics, to place the figures on another plane of reality. The jewels, the beards, the attitudes speak of the world we know; the formality of the positions, the processional rigidity, the ritualistic placement of one character's foot overlaying another according to precedence, the slow movement speak of a world unknown by the rank and file. Here the corridors of power have been superseded by temples of ceremony, the world of orthodox religion, by the ritual cadences of the remaining half of the ancient Roman Empire. It was a colorful world, made geometric and formal beyond anything the Western Caesars ever knew. Such was the best of Ravenna in their time, perhaps the best in Frederick's time too. It was the last fling of a powerful empire on the edge of a centuries-long decline. By Frederick's century Ravenna was sleeping the sleep of age, long past her great moment as the center of Western culture. She had only her memories. But what memories they were!—perhaps enlivened, certainly romanticized by the poetic melodies of Dante, a political exile from Florence, who died there in 1321.

Frederick was ready to move south. With the Cremona diet in tatters, Lombardy in greater confusion than ever following the league's success at facing up to him, and his route home risky, it was time to go. Loyal Pisa sent him a group of armed stalwarts who escorted him to their city inland from the mouth of the Arno and the two islands of Caprara and Gorgona that float offshore. At Pisa he made the acquaintance of the most noteworthy mathematician of the age, the man who was responsible for introducing Arabic numerals and the zero into Europe: Leonardo Fibonacci (Leonardo da Pisa). Unlike Michael Scott, Fibonacci was a scientist's scientist, always legitimately above board, though in fairness to the former it must be remembered that astrological writings and predictions were the more or less honorable means by which many medieval scholars earned their livings. Fibonacci had already written his *Practica Geometriae* by 1220, and even earlier his *Liber Abaci.* Frederick was familiar with both of them. The mathematician solved difficult problems that Frederick presented to him and that had been suggested by his court philosopher, Giovanni da Palermo. Frederick, in turn, received and solved problems given to him by Fibonacci. Because of this contact Fibonacci long maintained an association with members of the imperial court. He would shortly write his *Liber Quadratorum,* a treatise on square numbers, which he would dedicate to Frederick. Worshipping at the altar of mathematics and natural science, dialectic and philosophy, both Occidental and Oriental, Frederick was in his element in Pisa. Renowned for the versatility of his interests and drawing the most brilliant men of his day to his court, he set a pattern to be emulated by princes of the coming Renaissance and caused a veritable avalanche of thinkers to enlist for positions as his civil servants. Frederick could gain some satisfaction even though his Cremona Diet had failed. There was Pisa itself to be enjoyed.

The Piazza dei Miracoli, the grassy piazza that fronts on and surrounds the cathedral, is a museum of Romanesque architecture at its most opulent. Pisan Romanesque is a style that influenced building as far away as Apulia, Sardinia, and Corsica, which were once her possessions. Few piazzas in the world command the adoration and tourist interest of this great green square, adorned—as though the cathedral were not enough!—by the tourists' favorite campanile, the leaning tower. With its list increasing yearly, it has been estimated that, unless something is done to arrest its movement, the tower will fall sometime during the present century. It started to lean during its building stage, probably because its foundations are only ten feet deep and of the same diameter (fifty-two feet) as the structure itself. Six open arcades of the round tower repeat the loggias of the western facade of the cathedral, while elongated blind arches delineate the ground story. An eighth story is smaller than the others and contains the bells. It was from the top of this remarkable tower that Galileo, between 1589 and 1591, proved that bodies of different weights fall with the same velocity. But the tower was standing ignored, leaning and unfinished, when Frederick saw it.

Frederick must have visited the greatest symbol of Pisan pride: the cathedral. The valor and nobility of purpose when, conjointly with Genoa, Pisa routed the Muslims from her area of the Mediterranean in the latter part of the eleventh century are on display here. As magnificent as a reliquary, its most interesting details are the south transept bronze doors by Bonannus Pisano, doors that should have been striking to Frederick in their similarity to the same artist's work at Monreale in Sicily. Here in Pisa Cathedral, in the most economical terms of design and in low relief, Bonannus tells the story of Christ from the Annunciation to the Ascension. Sparing the kinds of superfluous detail that themselves became points of departure in the later Renaissance, he tells his stories as succinctly as is possible in the metallic arts.

In a fanfare of bronze, three figures on horseback climb a slow arc representing a hill, while in the background is the explanatory, raised word *MAGIS*. Under the curve of the hill, in a kind of cave effect, are the small figures of Adam and Eve in the Garden of Eden, reminding us that the coming of Jesus was necessitated by their fall into original sin. The baptism of Christ is graphically presented, almost comically in that the River Jordan, in which Jesus is standing neck deep, looks more like a cord of wood stacked up around Him. Herod, wearing a crown too large for his head, supervises the Massacre of the Holy Innocents, pathetic little skinny bodies flung to the ground like a pile of toothpicks while the killer raises a sword to do his dirty work and a helpless mother looks on. It may be shallow relief with only the barest suggestions of place, but it is none the less horrifying for that. The mother's gesture of incapacity is understated in remarkable contrast to both Herod's disinterested, uninvolved command and the executioner's brutal move. And there are the pathetic babies!

Joseph hurries Mary and the Babe off to Egypt, carrying his effects on a stick—for all the world like a modern hobo. Because of the limited space of individual panels, the Last Supper has become a more selective dinner than one expects, with only seven guests. John, in the medieval

Massacre of the Holy Innocents, Pisa Cathedral, Italy

way, is asleep. All in all, there are twenty-four panels on the doors, twenty of them describing events from the New Testament.

By November Frederick was back in Sicily, the land of his perpetual longing. Having collected his wife Yolanda at Salerno, he was finally where he belonged, amid the sounds of foreign tongues, foreign and yet familiar, relishing the salubrious climate, relaxing in the embraces of his forebears' pleasure domes: La Zisa, La Favara, La Cuba. There, adjoining the cathedral where his grandfather, father, mother, and wife Constance were interred, was the anachronistic Loggia dell'Incoronata, the scene of his presentation to his subjects on Whit Sunday 1198, the day of his coronation. The neighborhood churches called Martorana and San Cataldo touched nerves of exquisite piety in Frederick, piety for the sterling deeds of his ancestors. But no place could arrest his attention as completely as the mosaic-encrusted Cappella Palatina, the royal chapel built by Roger II, small as such temples go, but with its two thrones clear in their implied insistence that the Church is only half of God's domain. In the name of the pope, the archbishop of Palermo could lord over Church affairs all he wanted from his dais but leave the secular world to Roger and his descendants on theirs. Frederick would occupy his throne on his own dais, facing the archbishop, his hand on his sword. The archbishop should have no truck with the sword, was Frederick's implied statement: let him wield his crucifix. And with his loyal friend Berard as current archbishop of Palermo, there was no confusion on that. Frederick still had it in mind to get on with his plans for crusade. Even his reticence to find fault with an unhelpful pope would seem to indicate that he still had it in mind not to make waves but to get on with his preparations. He had motives beyond papal satisfaction, however; personally taking possession of Jerusalem in the name of Yolanda and adding that sacred city to his list of holdings was too tempting to forgo.

1227

At San Germano two years earlier Frederick had agreed that he would leave on crusade in August 1227, under pain of excommunication should he renege. But Honorius did not live to see the ships sail. He died on March 18, 1227, and was buried in the basilica of Santa Maria Maggiore in Rome, probably not much lamented on either side of the papal-imperial struggle that seemed to be increasingly dividing Italy. To Frederick he had been a carping nuisance, not devoid of hypocritical viciousness; to the Curia he was too lenient, too easy on shrewd, tough-thinking Frederick, lacking in the strong qualities of his political-minded predecessor, Innocent III. In retrospect the papacy was beginning a gradual internal decay, a steady weakening that was to accelerate with the next pontiff and finally reach the nadir of self-interest and profligacy during the Renaissance. It is often said that Honorius was a mild man, quick to recognize threats to the papacy, honorable, a primate of exemplary patience. He was also conniving and quite capable of double-dealing. It was he who, in 1225, issued instructions to launch the final terrible "crusade" against the Albigensians of

Languedoc, which led ultimately to their cruel extermination in 1244 at Montségur in the mountains of southern France. Not only did he not succeed in checking the growth of imperial power, but he did a creditable share of creating such enmity between his office and Frederick's that any kind of team play was foredoomed to failure.

Worse yet, the man who succeeded Honorius would prove more intransigent and dogmatic, more resolute in his determination to tame the imperial lion, and uncompromising beyond Frederick's wildest imaginings. He would show himself a man determined to set against the emperor one of the most righteous moral forces of the century—the two booming mendicant orders, the Franciscans and Dominicans. If Francis was looking down from his heavenly throne, it must have devastated him to see his brothers aimed point-blank at the troublesome emperor and those fickle, spiteful Romans. Francis, who had held that the Church should be rebuilt spiritually—not secularly—had intended his magic to work benignly, persuasively. Instead, in the hands of ambitious churchmen, his brothers moved more and more outside the cloisters that were once so sacred until they did their own hefty share to bring down the imperial house.

The new pope, who took the name Gregory IX, was none other than Ugolino dei Conti, cardinal-bishop of Ostia, friend and mentor of Francis Bernardone and cousin to Innocent III, under whose influence he had matured. Gregory IX is described as a vigorous churchman, of noble form and countenance, endowed with an almost youthful ambition, retentive memory, and penetrating mind. Law was his forte, along with persuasive eloquence. Despite his worldliness he was still unpretentious enough, as we have seen, to go on record befriending, protecting, and encouraging Francis Bernardone in his pursuit of the simpler way of the mendicant. He would in the future even write hymns to this saint. The following year he would lay the foundation stone for the preposterously inappropriate and pretentious church in Assisi and at the same time canonize his friend. But Ugolino/Gregory was a complex personality, a man of fiery temper and inextinguishable passion. He could be at the same time a fervent ascetic in love with Franciscan ideals and an implacable opponent of the secular genius whom he saw as his greatest enemy. Face-to-face with this two-sided adversary, Frederick would need skill, daring, and a willingness to fight for his tightly controlled imperial domain. Beyond that he would do well to cater to a similarly thinking loyal court.

Following his election and enthronement, the new Pope Gregory IX toured on horseback around the walls of Rome, accepting the plaudits of the temporarily good-humored citizens. Hymns were sung as he rode by; clouds of incense rendered the air less fetid. Tapestries and streamers cascaded from balconies, while garlands festooned the public buildings bordering the pontifical route. Fanfares announced his coming as Rome was trumpeted into delirium. City officials in their embroidered silken robes, bishops and clergy, Greeks, Jews, members of the Curia, and simple tourists all heralded the coming of the new Vicar of Christ, the latest of a twelve-hundred-year line of successors to Saint Peter. On foot, one to either side, the senator and the prefect of the city led the papal mount to its destination at the Lateran Palace. Then Rome let loose its usual brawling celebration, the streets echoing with racy songs and ribald jests far into the night. By the time quiet had descended on the tired city, which sank slowly into its thick, springtime darkness as discarded torches burned themselves out in the streets, it was a foregone conclusion that change was in the air—one hoped for the better.

As expected, the spirit of the papacy underwent a vast change with the coming of Gregory. Stern, unbending, abrasive, he would follow his predecessors in giving Frederick no respite from crusade. It will be remembered that it was this pope, as cardinal-bishop of Ostia, who had handed Frederick the crusaders' cross at his imperial coronation in 1220 and who had heard the new emperor swear on the spot to set out for Outremer the following year. If Frederick had been expediently catering to Church desires to secure his imperial diadem, Pope Gregory IX, for his part, would have none of it. He was still master of his faculties and not so exhausted by years (though he was in fact eighty) as Honorius had been. He knew his Frederick—had known him since he was a child in Sicily. He saw the overwhelming Hohenstaufen ambition and stared it down, rather than shrinking before it as had Honorius on occasion. The first thing that Gregory did was to lay his cards on the table with a letter. And for once Frederick got good papal advice. "We are willing to grant you every indulgence that we can," Gregory wrote, "but take heed that you do not place yourself in a situation whence we may not be able to extricate you, even with the best will."[2] Then, heeding the words of chronicler Salimbene, who had remarked that the Lombards were "slippery as eels," Gregory followed up with a letter to them, ordering them to ready their responsibilities for the crusade.

The pope was ready to touch yet another sore spot, and Frederick should hear this warning, too. Word of his licentiousness had been spread mainly by uninformed common gossip through the courts of Europe and the East. The pope, in another letter, indicated to him his plan of attack, a plan that would prove eminently irksome to Frederick and satisfactory to Gregory in years to come. "God has bestowed on you the gift of knowledge and of perfect imagination, and all Christendom follows you. Take heed that you do not place your intellect, which you have in common with angels, below your senses, which you have in common with brutes and plants. Your intellect is weakened, if you are the slave of your senses."[3]

Outremer and crusade were to become well-gnawed bones of contention between Gregory and Frederick, who would have done better to look farther east, past the Caspian Sea and Khwarizm, past exotic Samarkand, Kiev, Moscow, and the Ural Mountains. Momentous events were taking place in the scattered camps of the Mongol hordes. For Jenghis Khan was dead, and the rule was about to slip into the hands of others who would eventually realize the old Mongolian dream—the invasion of Europe.

Frederick heard neither the rumblings in the East nor the pope's timely warnings. He was preoccupied with the kind of political game he enjoyed most. It seems that just the year before Sultan al-Kamil of Egypt had sent a mission to the Sicilian court. Able to converse in Arabic with the embassy, Frederick immediately struck up a remarkable and lasting friendship with its head, the Emir Fakhr ad-Din as-Shaikh, an intelligent man, cultivated in the arts of warfare, politics, and falconry, the very things that would attract Frederick. The two men hit it off so well that their friendship had a profound and positive effect on the coming crusade.

Fakhr ad-Din approached Frederick with offers of friendship from his master, who in the strangely circuitous manner of statesmen, had need of Frederick's help. Al-Kamil was caught in an endemic tangle of familial infighting. When the great Saladin had died in 1193, his empire, after the usual convolutions, was portioned out among al-Kamil and his two brothers, al-Ashraf, sultan of Babylon, and al-Mu'azzam, sultan of Damascus. Al-Kamil, the most imaginative of the three and the shrewdest, had his problems. Having entertained designs in company with his one brother against the other, he now saw his fraternal conspirator caught in a pincers movement between the object of their conspiracy, al-Mu'azzam, and a new ally, Jelal-ad-Din, shah of the Khwarizmian Empire, an empire reaching its zenith partly through having recently driven off a Mongol invasion. Jelal-ad-Din's rule extended now from Azerbaijan to the Indus River. If he and al-Mu'azzam were successful in their offensive war, then al-Kamil could foresee a future when he would be fending off the victorious allies. He would send his most brilliant representative, an expert in dialectic, a philosopher, a knowledgeable judge of horseflesh, and a subtle bargainer to boot—all characteristics held in high esteem by the brilliant emperor—to the court at Sicily. Enjoying the new game, Frederick, now a past master at biding his time, decided to do just that. Who could tell? An offer better than just friendship might be forthcoming. But the sultan of Egypt could be just as enigmatic as the emperor. As far as he was concerned, he could play the waiting game, too. The rules indicated that the next move was Frederick's.

During the year 1227 the trusted Archbishop Berard of Palermo was delegated to Cairo with Frederick's greetings, bearing gifts of gems and textiles, falcons, and most stunning of all, the emperor's own charger, complete with golden saddle. Al-Kamil made it clear that he would welcome Frederick and his army in the East, making no secret of the fact that, since Jerusalem was in the hands of his belligerent brother, al-Mu'azzam, and since that city would no doubt be the object of the crusaders' push, he (al-Kamil) would thus be relieved of the fraternal threat. Having in mind things going his way, he would be amenable to turning Jerusalem over to the Christians. Berard then moved on to consult al-Mu'azzam, and was left with the unmistakable impression that the latter would not budge an inch. By January 1228 Berard was back in Frederick's company in Apulia, bringing with him presents from al-Kamil, including the famous elephant.

While Berard was sounding out the situation in Outremer, Frederick busied himself with preparations for the pending adventure. To the surprise of all, the anticipated crusade suddenly became vogue, and the gathering of knights and "pilgrims" from all over Europe exceeded predictions. Hermann von Salza returned from Germany, where he had used Frederick's seed money to advantage, followed by a swarm of Germans who had been promised everything from good wages and positions of rank to eternal salvation. At Aachen, where he had gone to attend the coronation of King Henry's wife, Margaret of Austria, Hermann collared Landgrave Louis IV ("the Pious") of Thuringia and Henry of Limburg. Promises of monetary reward worked the usual miracles and fired both with new religious zeal. They were quickly followed by other worthies to the point that Hermann began to feel misgivings about the adequacy of Frederick's shipbuilding program.

An advance party—English and French under the leadership of the bishops of Exeter and Winchester—had already departed while troops continued to gather at Brindisi, the appointed jumping-off place. Italy's roads were clogged with jostling faithful, their horses and retainers bearing heavy battlefield impedimenta. Good to their words, Louis of

Thuringia and Henry of Limburg arrived, Louis at the head of a complete crusading army. North Europeans, having sailed the long way around Spain, now rode anchor in Brindisi's harbor. The pope, too, had finally gotten behind the effort and done his share of recruiting. In time there was no space for bedding down in the city of Brindisi, necessitating that large masses of the crusaders pitch camp outside the walls. Food began to run short, and as the summer heat increased, water came into demand. An epidemic of malaria broke out in the congested, unsanitary camps, causing a reactionary lack of enthusiasm for crusade and a breaking of ranks to return home. It was said that tens of thousands of pilgrims, with reason, abandoned the "holy war." But Frederick went on with his preparations, readying a special ship to carry himself and Landgrave Louis of Thuringia. Finally several thousand crusaders set sail on September 8 from Brindisi's shell-shaped harbor to a blaring fanfare and rousing cheers of "Godspeed!" But even then the venture was not free of difficulty.

They were hardly out of sight of land before both Frederick and Louis of Thuringia became bedridden. They had come down with malaria before departure, and the prognosis had been that the less putrid sea air would induce a cure. Their boat returned to Otranto just in time for Louis to receive the last sacraments before he died, leaving a mourning widow to an unhappy fate and to eventual canonization. Having already expended so much money and energy on the crusade, Frederick was determined to set sail once again. But within two days he was back in Otranto, this time on the insistence of his doctor, and with the concurrence of Hermann von Salza, and even of the new patriarch of Jerusalem, Gerold of Lausanne. He must put off another departure until he was hale, he was told. Hermann and Gerold were dispatched eastward, following in the wake of Henry of Limburg, who had sailed in August with a large contingent, and who was now declared the temporary commander of the combined forces.

Desertions became the order of the day when word got around that Frederick was not among the crusaders arriving in the Holy Land. Those who had already debarked there were dismayed, apparently thinking that either Frederick's ailment would prove fatal or that it was just another of his ploys to avoid taking the final step to the East. They forgot that he had more reasons than they for being there. He had spent more time and money than anyone, including the pope, on this "pilgrimage." He had it in mind to swing by Cyprus to assert his claims on that island, which of late had drifted away as an imperial fief. And beyond anything else, he wanted to lay claim, through his wife, to Jerusalem, even empty as that title may have been. Men tended to overlook the fact that he had been advised to return to shore not only by his associates, but also by the patriarch of Jerusalem, who had a lot to gain or lose himself. They also did not know that Frederick, as soon as his last troops had departed, headed for the baths at Pozzuoli, on a bay just west of Naples, to effect a cure. He was that sick.

In ancient days Pozzuoli (Puteoli) was a health resort of renown, faddishly popular among the Romans. Much of the ancient city is gone now, having fallen into the sea because of seismic activity. In 61 AD saints Paul and Luke, aboard an Alexandrian wheat ship called "Castor and Pollux," put into the thriving spa. The mole on which they disembarked is now under water, though supposedly still identifiable by bronze rings embedded in the concrete. By Frederick's time a cathedral had been built there, and the baths—still in operation—were being extolled by Peter of Eboli, whose treatise was illustrated by graphics depicting the various cures available. After Frederick's visit the spa came back into vogue, and Frederick himself thought enough of the curative treatments to build a hospital there for the poor. It may have been while he was at Pozzuoli—or shortly thereafter—that Frederick put one of his well-known propositions to Michael Scott, wanting to know why both salt and bitter waters flow forth from the earth and why some spa water is hot and some cold.

While Frederick was being restored to health at Pozzuoli, an embassy was dispatched to Anagni to explain his illness to Pope Gregory IX. They returned with word that the pope refused even to see them. Another mission, this one beefed up by the presence of Henry of Malta, the archbishop of Bari and Reggio di Calabria, and the duke of Spoleto, met with a similar reception, being interviewed only by the Curia. But the biggest shock of all was yet to come.

Toward the end of September, Gregory pronounced Frederick an excommunicate. The pope, strictly speaking, was within his rights: the emperor had agreed, after all, to that procedure at San Germano. But to Frederick and his supporters it seemed outrageously unreasonable to pronounce such a sentence without even having heard the case. To make matters worse, the pope reiterated the sentence at a meeting of Italian prelates held in November. Even before that conclave it was clear, when the original encyclical of astonishing violence went out from Anagni in October, that the pope was out to destroy Frederick. Using veiled truths and outright lies in an unprecedented manner, Gregory lashed out at the emperor by reviving quarrels and disagreements that had occurred between Frederick and the papacy since the days of Innocent III. In tear-jerking terms Gregory painted a totally false picture of the Church's role in the raising of its former ward:

> The Holy Apostolic See reckoned . . . on a nurseling whom she had brought up with the tenderest care; the Church had taken up the Emperor Frederick, as it were, from his mother's womb, fed him at her breasts, borne him on her shoulders; she had often rescued him from those who sought his life; instructed him with care and pain to manhood; invested him with the royal dignity; and to crown all these blessings, bestowed on him the title of Emperor, hoping to find in him a protecting support, a staff for her old age.[4]

Feeding the lie, Gregory blamed the loss of Damietta on Frederick, when in fact it was the papal legate, the proud and inept Cardinal Pelagius, who had been responsible. Gregory laid at Frederick's door the charge that he had not lived up to his agreement of gold payments, furnishing crusaders, and supplying transportation to Outremer—all of them false. Gregory went so far as to insinuate that the port of Brindisi had been chosen for the embarkation because it was a disease-ridden, unhealthy port, and that Frederick had deliberately undercut the venture by depriving the crusaders massed there of proper food. Cozying up to the Lombards again for the struggle that he was instigating, Gregory made no mention of their duplicity in not sending the paltry four hundred troops that they had promised as their penalty for having wrecked the diet at Cremona. He wrote to Stephen Langton, archbishop of Canterbury, that Frederick had cancelled his part of the crusade on a pretense of illness.

The only charge that Frederick would own up to was that he had not sailed off to Outremer. Any further explanations fell on deaf ears, unfortunately, for Gregory was fanning the fire of papal universal authority that was going to flare up with unprecedented fury around the person of Pope Boniface VIII at the turn of the century. Gregory's position was clear. He did not care, apparently, for the crusade one way or the other, successful or unsuccessful. His lying intransigence seems motivated solely by the idea of defeating his imperial adversary. Paradoxical in his determination, he was out to wreck the crusade and thus discredit Frederick before the world court of judgment. To combat Frederick's laying the foundation of his Siculo-German empire, Gregory believed that he had to go for broke. Obviously getting Sicily out of imperial hands would be the most efficient way of accomplishing the breakup of such a concentration of power. Vaguely concealed beneath his carping about Frederick's administration of the government of Sicily was the unmistakable suggestion that the ban of excommunication would be lifted when Frederick agreed to abandon all sovereign claims to his island. Wise as Gregory may have been in some ways, he gave no indication of it in his underestimation of his opponent.

To Frederick and many of his contemporaries it seemed that the pope's lust for temporal power was insatiable, that he was biting off more than he could chew. Frederick struck at papal intransigence and pride in letters that he sent off to the rulers of Europe, letters in which Pier delle Vigne's hand can be detected and that made clear the imperial hurt and astonishment as well as the determination to carry on with the crusade. Gregory now found himself in the awkwardly contradictory position of forbidding a crusade on the grounds that an excommunicate could not lead such an endeavor. Frederick fired off a volley of letters that strangely echoes those sent in his name to the European courts when he was living in fear of losing his kingdom to Markward of Anweiler back at the turn of the century. Only this time the Church was the villain instead of ambitious German and Norman nobles. And be assured that the brothers of the late Friar Francis were doing their share of "binding, loosing, punishing," of not sowing "the seed of the Word," but subduing men and wringing from them more money. Part of the world saw Frederick as having been shaped by God's hand; the Franciscans could see him only as the angel of doom. And only God, through the Church, could slay such an angel. While the brothers sincerely awaited reform in the Church, they had, apparently, lost sight of Francis's vision of spiritual as opposed to temporal reform. Still, it was axiomatic that the Church was the best anchor they had to hang on to.

1228

Even with Easter, the season of confession and forgiveness, Gregory IX refused to give Frederick a clue to the penance he must endure in order to have the ban of excommunication lifted. And all the while he contradicted his former stand by refusing to sanction—indeed, by forbidding—Frederick's participation in the crusade, part of which had long since debarked in Outremer and was already showing signs of degenerating into an exercise in expensive futility if the emperor himself did not arrive forthwith. In the meantime Frederick was building a support system, notably the Frangipani family in Rome, due to his generous shipments of wheat to that famine-stricken city during the past year. (Surely the pope could not turn his eyes from that gesture!) The Frangipani responded by exciting the populace to the point that during the Holy Thursday Mass (March 23), when Gregory again thundered forth his excommunication of Frederick along with his now-habitual denunciations, the congregation was stirred to resentful violence. They squealed catcalls and barked like dogs at the elevation of the Host. Then on Easter Monday they drove the pontiff from Saint Peter's Basilica, literally pursuing him through the streets, so terrifying him that he sought refuge in Perugia.

During this Easter season Frederick received word that the situation in Outremer was complicated by the unanticipated death of al-Mu'azzam, sultan of Damascus, which left his young son, an-Nasir Dawid, in his stead, and freed al-Kamil of the need for Frederick's help, now that he no longer feared an alliance between al-Mu'azzam and the Khwarizmians. Al-Kamil was so relieved, in fact, that he launched an immediate attack against his twelve-year-old nephew by which, with little difficulty, he took Jerusalem and Nablus. It was not long before al-Kamil and his brother joined hands again and agreed to a division of their nephew's lands. For all his former overtures of friendship and suggestions that he would turn Jerusalem over to Frederick, al-Kamil was now clearly in possession of the sacred city and was not about to give it up. All this despite the fact that he had only recently dispatched Fakhr ad-Din back to Frederick's court thoroughly coached in sweet words and promises. The two men renewed and enhanced their friendship, with Frederick going so far as to knight the Muslim and to give him permission to bear the Hohenstaufen coat-of-arms. Frederick realized the precariousness of the Christians' situation in the Holy Land and of his own claims to the throne of Jerusalem. Accelerating his preparations for departure, papal prohibitions or not, he sent off an advance party of five hundred troops, lest anyone entertain the notion that he was losing interest in that far-off land. With the Muslim instability in Outremer, Jerusalem had never seemed riper for conquest.

Still the pope remained adamant in his determination to prevent Frederick's departure. He was already threatening to release Frederick's subjects from their oaths of allegiance to him should he depart in defiance of papal orders, all of which had little or no effect. Having regained his health at Pozzuoli, Frederick was on the move with his old vigor. He visited Sessa Aurunca and Gaeta, where he garrisoned a new castle. When he held his Easter court at Barletta, the attending crowd was so enormous that the ceremonies had to take place out-of-doors. There his will was read, indicating his wish that his son, Henry VII of Germany, was to succeed him should he not return from Outremer. In the event that Henry died without issue, he was to be succeeded by Conrad, Frederick's son who was at this point just a few days old. The aftermath of the Barletta Diet was marred, and Frederick's position further complicated, when sixteen-year-old Yolanda, queen of Jerusalem and empress of the Holy Roman Empire, died on May 1, never having risen from the bed on which she gave birth to Conrad.

Poor Yolanda! Of Frederick's three wives (maybe four) she was the most victimized and the most pathetic. She had had little pleasure in life. Informed rumor had it that her stepmother had tried to poison her. Her father had abandoned her to political expediency. Her husband, for all his lusty ways, was showing signs of aging—heavy around the middle, flushed, and balding. He had ignored her, perhaps even deserting her for another on their wedding night. Under Frederick's tyranny she had lived in lonesome luxury in the Palermo harem, pining for her Eastern friends and relatives, slowly awakening to her resentment of the chattel role of the female—even a queen and empress—in male-dominated, treacherously violent thirteenth-century society. Now Frederick was in no better position concerning Jerusalem than had been John de Brienne a few years back—no longer a consort, but simply the guardian of the reigning monarch, Conrad. Frederick could make any claim he cared to, but the fact remained that his son's subjects in Outremer might take it into their heads to deny him his claim. Frederick knew that; and he knew they would be exercising rights to which they were entitled. Well, he would take care of that at the proper time.

Contrary to papal expectations, and showing how inaccurately Gregory had sized up his opponent, Frederick sailed from Brindisi on June 28, accompanied by the ever-faithful Archbishop Berard of Palermo, by Admiral Henry of Malta, by his chamberlain, Richard, who had been in the emperor's company since 1215 and had his complete confidence, and by Archbishop Jacob of Capua, another trusted churchman. There were some German attendants, and his Saracen teacher of Arab dialectic, Ibn-el-Gwasi.

Hearing of the embarkation Gregory was outraged that Frederick would sail secretly and, even worse, without confessing his sins and receiving absolution. The devil must have had a hand in it. But Frederick was making no secret of his departure or destination. He had left Rainald of Urslingen, duke of Spoleto, in charge of his realm. He had probably seen neither his new son nor the tomb of his wife in the Norman cathedral at Andria, shared today by another—the third—of his wives, and marked by the unremarkable legend:

Here lie the mortal remains of
Yolanda de Brienne
1228
and Isabella of England
1241
the august consorts of Frederick II, king of
Puglia and Sicily

Frederick knew the risks he was taking. Lombardy, under papal encouragement—no, meddling and conspiratorial understandings—was already temporarily lost to him. Tuscany was perhaps a little more secure due to endemic intercity distrust and rivalry that made it difficult to achieve any kind of unity, even against the emperor. Frederick knew that the moment he was out of Italy the pope would be sowing discord, releasing his subjects from allegiance, trying to dethrone him. He knew, furthermore, that Gregory would stir the always-ready-to-boil political stews in Germany. The truth was that Gregory had left Frederick no choice but departure. He had refused to lift the excommunication, while at the same time neglecting to state what penance would alleviate the ban. He had hinted that the only peace move he would accept would be complete forfeiture of the kingdom of Sicily. This was clearly out of the question! If Frederick had not sailed it would have been clear to the world that the pope had won the contest of stubborn wills. The only other thing that was just as clear was that Frederick had better be successful in the Holy Land. If he was going to triumph over the pope in this colossal face-off that was more important in his mind than triumphing over the Muslims, he had better come back with Jerusalem in his hands. Who could have predicted that he would do exactly that—and without so much as unsheathing a sword?

Chapter Eleven

I groan, as the accused:
my face grows red from (my) fault:
spare (this) supplicant, O God.
***Dies Irae,* verse 12**

1228

If Pope Gregory IX intended to sow ruin in Frederick's empire, this was the time to do it. Imperial disregard for papal authority and dignity could not go unpunished. Further stoking the pontifical fury was the acknowledged fact that among Frederick's entourage was a contingent of Saracen pages and court personnel, besides an army of Muslims from Lucera. Had Christendom ever imagined a force of "pilgrims" composed of infidel enemies who, making matters even worse, actually practiced their abominable religion with full approbation of the emperor himself? What kind of crusading army was that? In Gregory's mind Frederick preferred the followers of Mohammed to those of Christ, and he would make that allegation later. It would never occur to such a pigheaded pope (and he was not the kind of man to ask questions) that Frederick's use of Saracen troops was part of his calculated design in what he saw as his coming war of diplomacy with al-Kamil of Egypt. Far ahead of his contemporaries in imagination, intelligence, and daring, Frederick was risking everything on his perception of the Oriental mind, and on his own powers of negotiation. It was not a diplomatic solution that Gregory wanted. He quite literally demanded spilt Saracen blood. That was the sensible way of winning a crusade. Frederick must be gotten rid of, punished for his liberal thinking.

To this end Gregory set to work undermining imperial authority in Germany, a project singularly without success. He located a Guelf, a nephew of Frederick's old enemy Otto IV, and offered him the imperial diadem, as though he had the right to make such a suggestion. He was rebuffed by the assertion that the young man had no desire to die in the manner of his uncle, broken and deserted by his supporters after the Battle of Bouvines. Next, the German secular princes, as well as those of the Church, refused to heed various papal admonitions, either out of altruistic loyalty or in thanks for past favors—and hopes for future ones. Gregory's fury rose with the frustration of being unable to turn the world back to Innocent III's time of Romanish supremacy. Oh, for the days when the imperial crown could be granted to any number of willing papal puppets! Circumstance was forcing Gregory to watch the emperor go his own way, hopping from Italy to Corfu, from the Greek islands to the mainland, from Crete to Rhodes to Asia Minor. Frederick finally arrived at Limassol on the island of Cyprus on July 21, twenty-four days after leaving his kingdom. Thus began the saga of an excommunicated emperor wearing the crusaders' cross being shadowed by papal censure all the way to the Holy Land and beyond.

Under the late Amalric of Lusignan, king of Cyprus, the island had been counted as a fief of the Holy Roman Empire, thanks to Amalric himself, who had requested that he be permitted to do homage to Emperor Henry VI. But in the chaotic years following the latter's death, the kingdom had drifted free. With Frederick's idea of restoring the empire at least to the power it had known under his father, it stood to reason that he would lay over on the island until he had brought it back into the fold one way or another, by reason or by force. The ruler of Cyprus was eleven-year-old Henry I—son of King Hugh I and Alice of Jerusalem—whose mother was serving as nominal regent. Not having a mind for political infighting she had, some years ago, turned over the practical government to her uncle, Philip of Ibelin. The relations between Alice and her uncle were stormy, so it is rather surprising that on his death she agreed to the appointment of his elder brother, John, to the position.

John of Ibelin was a force to be reckoned with. He was the nearest male relative of both Henry of Cyprus and of Yolanda, Queen of Jerusalem, of whose death only a few east of the Mediterranean had heard. Enormously wealthy, a man of integrity and considerable respect, John was also learned, a linguist and a born diplomat. He practically owned the city of Beirut, and his wife, Melisande, was the heiress of Arsuf. None of this was enough to intimidate the emperor. On arriving at Limassol, Frederick summoned John, his sons, and the young king to court. Warned of Frederick's strength of will, John could hardly refuse the command. He was received with ostentatious honor and many gifts, including a ceremonial robe of crimson that Frederick insisted he wear in place of his robes of mourning for his brother, the better to indicate the joy he was supposed to feel at meeting the emperor. During the banquet in the Cypriots' honor, some of Frederick's men crept into the hall and stood with drawn swords behind each of the guests. Then Frederick stated his case: John of Ibelin must forfeit his fief of Beirut and all the revenues that had come to Cyprus since the death of King Hugh I. Ibelin eloquently and courageously refused both demands, and Frederick, because of his lack of ready manpower, was unable to do much more than demand hostages, including John's two sons and King Henry himself, and insist that John should accompany him to the Holy Land. After considerable disagreement and threatening behavior on both sides, it was finally agreed that the Cypriots should swear fealty to Frederick, that the hostages would be released, that both sides should swear to preserve the peace, and that John would come to Palestine as a crusader as well as to plead his case before the high court there. The boy-king would join Frederick's company. Aside from not having adequate forces to call Ibelin's bluff, Frederick's hand had been considerably weakened when word leaked out that his empress was dead and that he was no longer the king of Jerusalem, but only regent in the name of his son Conrad.

It is hard, but not impossible, to understand why Frederick took such a tough line with John of Ibelin, achieving at best a hollow victory. True, he needed a show of some kind of strength. First of all, he wanted to restore Cyprus to the imperial orbit. Beyond that, and more importantly, he saw himself as the long-anticipated liberator of the Holy Land, as the man who would release that territory from the clutches of the Saracens and return it to the Christians, a feat that the bickering and jealously self-interested Frankish barons had been unable to achieve even to their own advantage. But for all his reasoning he had succeeded mainly in alienating one of the most powerful and highly thought-of men of the eastern Mediterranean and in alerting the barons of Outremer to what they interpreted as his innate treachery. Frederick sailed for Acre on September 3 with the boy-king Henry, Ibelin, and the leading barons of the island in tow.

Forty-six years before Frederick's arrival at Acre, the ancient city had been visited by a Muslim from Spain who was touring the Mediterranean: Ibn Jubayr. His descriptions of this part of the world have been cherished as some of the most vivid accounts of eastern Mediterranean life of the Middle Ages. Acre, according to Ibn Jubayr, was not the most salubrious of places for a quiet weekend.

> It is the focus of ships and caravans, and the meeting-place of Muslim and Christian merchants from all regions. Its roads and streets are choked by the press of men, so that it is hard to put foot to ground. Unbelief and unpiousness there burn fiercely, and pigs [Christians] and crosses abound. It stinks and is filthy, being full of refuse and excrement.[1]

Frederick ran into unexpected trouble in Acre. Initially he was welcomed with strange music, with flowers and lush carpets strewn in his path. He was the triumphant overlord, the man of the century; he would settle once and for always the ownership of the hallowed territory. Hermann von Salza, the duke of Limburg, and Patriarch Gerold of Jerusalem were all on hand to welcome him. It made no matter that word had preceded him that Pope Gregory IX had excommunicated him a second time for setting out on crusade without papal sanction. The general feeling was euphoric; now that the emperor was there and proving his good intentions, the pope would relent and lift the ban so that the crusaders could get on with their business of killing infidels. Frederick's forces who had not already returned home in frustration at his temporary sick call gave him an ovation, in joint harmony with religious and governmental dignitaries kneeling before him to swear allegiance. He was not looked on with the same awe by the Muslims, however, who, seeing his clean-shaven face, regarded him as only half a man, hardly the kind of figure to inspire terror. And one Easterner described him as having an untrustworthy squint, though most commentators remark on his intimidating, steady gaze.

On the advice of Gerold, patriarch of Jerusalem, and the bishops of Outremer, Frederick sent Henry of Malta and the archbishop of Bari as delegates to the pope to inform him that he had arrived in the Holy Land and that he intended to fulfill his vow not to rest until the sacred shrines were in Christian hands. In the meantime, with his loyal adherents at his side, including Hermann von Salza and Berard of Palermo, Frederick settled down to await word from Rome and to start his diplomatic campaign vis-à-vis al-Kamil. Disquieting word had reached him already that his regent in Italy, Rainald, duke of Spoleto, responding to the papal negation of all oaths of allegiance sworn to Frederick by his magnates, and in a misguided effort to protect Frederick's interests, had invaded the Church's March of Ancona—and failed. Now the pope was gathering troops to invade southern Italy. Frederick saw that he had needs be quick in his diplomacy.

To Sultan al-Kamil, who had at one time all but invited the imperial presence to the East, Frederick had become an encumbrance. Having gained possession of Jerusalem without Frederick's help, al-Kamil envisioned himself as sole possessor of Palestine. By the time of Frederick's arrival, he and his brother al-Ashraf had their nephew, an-Nasir Dawid, holed up in Damascus and were laying siege. With Frederick in Acre, al-Kamil could not concentrate his attention or forces on Damascus. Besides, what would happen if Frederick decided to complicate matters by taking the side of the nephew? When Frederick sent ambassadors with gifts to al-Kamil, the sultan recognized the gesture by dispatching return gifts—fabrics, gems, Mehari camels, mules, bears, and monkeys. He sent as well his negotiator and Frederick's friend, Fakhr ad-Din, with instructions to open a dialogue and to keep it going as least until either Damascus fell or Frederick returned home. Beyond that the situation called for superabundant politeness and utter silence concerning the matter at hand. To add to Frederick's irritation, his straightforward appeal sent by delegates to the pope turned out to be a dismal failure. To prove how much of a bungle it was, Gregory dispatched two Franciscans to the Holy Land to inform the crusaders that they owed no allegiance to Frederick. Here again were the followers of the blessed Francis—a man dead not two years—being used to increase the secular power of an ambitious pope, the very thing against which Francis was adamantly opposed. How many times did the Church need to be reminded that Francis was inspired to rebuild spiritual leadership within the Church, for therein lay the strength and integrity of Christ's message to the world? Gerold of Jerusalem and the military orders were warned to give Frederick no help, indeed not even to associate with him. Another papal delegation tried to persuade Genoa—without success—to withdraw its supply support. Thus were hints of Christian duplicity carried into the Holy Land by the unlikeliest messengers. Only Berard of Palermo, Hermann von Salza and his Teutonic Knights, and a mere remnant of Frederick's original forces remained loyal.

His arrival ovation notwithstanding, Frederick was suddenly looked upon as a pariah, an enemy of the Church, a foreigner who had it in mind to practice his special brand of despotism over a resisting covey of Frankish barons. Papal interference split his forces down the middle: the English and the French, the Templars, and the Knights of Saint John on the one side watched with growing hostility and suspicion those faithful to the emperor—the Teutonic Knights, the Pisans, the Genoese, Sicilians, and Germans. Tensions were exacerbated by word from home that the pope had released all of Frederick's subjects from their allegiance to him. The nadir was reached when Gregory made letter contact with al-Kamil, begging him under no condition to agree to any kind of peace with Frederick. This from the successor of a line of popes who had, as he had himself, harangued all of Europe to mass their fortunes and forces to move against the sin-ridden infidels!

Understanding Western treachery perhaps better than the Westerners did themselves, al-Kamil did not lose his cool. He maintained a steady negotiating posture with Frederick, replying to the emperor's opening gambit with the response that he could never concede Jerusalem without losing face completely among his Saracen followers. Nephew an-Nasir Dawid, he argued, was proving a protracted irritant by stubbornly defending Damascus, proving to be not at all the push-over he was once thought to be. It looked as though the siege would go on for longer than had been anticipated. With that negative start to their negotiations, al-Kamil progressed to a more accommodating attitude. After several months of alternating bluff and admiration, Frederick decided to try to panic al-Kamil into agreement. He gathered together all the troops who could be talked into following an excommunicate emperor—probably fewer than eight hundred knights and ten thousand foot soldiers—and marched them south from Acre in Galilee, past Caesarea to Jaffa.

Aside from mention on a pylon at Karnak, the Bible is replete with references to Jaffa. The Lebanese wood for the building of Solomon's great temple in Jerusalem was landed there. Jonah sailed from Jaffa on the ill-fated boat from which he was hurled into the jaws of the whale. Saint Peter rested there for many days, exhausted after the eventful trip during which he raised Tabitha from the dead; there also, according to Acts 10:12, he had his extravagant vision of "four-footed beasts of the earth, and wild beasts, and creeping things, and fowls in the air." Held by Romans and Byzantines, Jaffa had been squabbled over for generations by the Arabs and the Christian crusaders, the latter having already captured it once in 1126, only to lose it to Saladin in 1187. During the third crusade Richard Lionheart recaptured it, but it was lost again almost immediately when Napoleon claimed possession in 1799. Today, enhanced by the cheek-by-jowl city of Tel-Aviv, a newcomer to history, Jaffa has reentered the mainstream of eastern Mediterranean life. Even though Frederick set to work diligently refortifying Jaffa, al-Kamil showed no sign of panic. He called Frederick's bluff by brusquely terminating negotiations until Frederick agreed to pay compensation for the Muslim villages he had pillaged along his route south.

1229

True or false, it is an oft-heard lament that historical circumstances prevented King Richard I of England and the great Saladin from being friends. They admired one another's talents and abilities from a distance; personal acquaintance might have made them affectionate friends. The same can be said for Saladin's son, al-Kamil, and Frederick Hohenstaufen. Without ever having met they maintained an honorable loyalty to one another. The abilities, tastes, and habits of sultan and emperor were so similar that it is quite sad to realize that they never had a face-to-face meeting. The story is told that on one instance when Frederick decided he wanted to visit certain sacred shrines pertinent to the life of Christ, the traitorous Templars, in league with Patriarch Gerold, sent word of the pending excursion to al-Kamil with the suggestion that it would be a convenient time to capture him. Al-Kamil forwarded the letter to Frederick, expressing his disgust over such rascality. As far as Frederick was concerned that was the end of any possible accommodation he might make with the military order. If some of his own countrymen could not appreciate Frederick's talents and ideals, al-Kamil was just the man to understand his universal character. As Frederick had founded Naples University, al-Kamil had founded a school in Cairo, and had spent enormous amounts of money privately to further education in his realm. Like his Western counterpart he wrote poetry and was noted for his politeness and gentleness of manner (though perhaps on this last he and Frederick would have parted company), as well as for his judgmental meticulousness. He liked nothing better than philosophical disputations with fifty or so scholars reclining on divans around his throne. Even his fears that he would lose face if he lightly gave Jerusalem to the Christians was echoed in Frederick's agonized claim that he would not have been such a hard bargainer had he not been afraid of losing prestige among the Franks. Determined and astute as al-Kamil was, Frederick finally won out—at least in his own eyes.

As far as the pope and the Curia were concerned, Frederick was simply proving himself more and more a child of the devil by negotiating with a Muslim. Gregory had received a sanctimonious letter from turncoat Patriarch Gerold of Jerusalem, reporting shamefully that the sultan further corrupted the already corrupt Frederick by sending him a bevy of singing girls and jugglers, people of ill repute, it was implied, who should not even be mentioned in the same breath with Christians. Frederick was accused piously of presenting Christian dancing women for the entertainment of Saracens with whom he was feasting. Freidank, a crusader and poet who generally took Frederick's side, lamented that negotiations were secret and that the two rulers acted like two misers who were arguing over three gold pieces to be equally divided. To ecclesiastical homebodies it was offensive that any part of the Holy Land be won without shedding the blood of the unbelievers. They held that there was something insidious in the secrecy of the negotiators, never mentioning, of course, that such formalities were made necessary by papal interference.

As for Gerold and Gregory, they would have done well to read some of the Muslim writings with which Frederick was familiar. It is a safe bet that Frederick knew the teachings of Ibn 'Arabi, the Spanish-born mystic now living in Damascus, who could have given them both a lesson in the essence of Christianity:

> My heart is capable of every form:
> A cloister for the monk, a fane for idols,
> A pasture for gazelles, the pilgrim's Ka'ba,
> The tables of the Torah, the Koran.
> Love is the creed I hold: wherever turn
> His camels, Love is still my creed and faith.[2]

When agreements were finally reached and the results made public, it was obvious that al-Kamil had given more than he had gained, that he had gone over as far as could have been expected to the Christian side of the bargaining table. His high esteem for Frederick was largely responsible for this effort, but so was his innate integrity, which was beyond even that of his father, Saladin, an infidel so highly regarded by Dante that he placed him in an Elysian situation, in the great Citadel of Human Reason. What is also obvious is that Fakhr ad-Din, in his friendship for Frederick as well as in his loyalty to his master, guided the two through the intricacies of the negotiations to eventual compromise.

Al-Kamil had to defend himself even against his own imams, who maintained that he had squandered away hard-gained territory and that he had sacrificed strategic safety. His nephew ordered public mourning for what he saw as a day of infamy. According to the new agreement Jerusalem was to be turned over to the Christians, except for the enclosure of the Temple of Solomon with its Dome of the Rock. The Templars—the Knights of the Temple of Solomon—were indignant that they were thus denied a return to their point of origin. But there was no way that Frederick could have accomplished what he did and still have wrested from al-Kamil that ground from which Mohammed took off on his flight to heaven. One mitigating condition allowed that, though the keys to the precinct would remain in Saracen hands, Christians would be permitted entry for prayer. In token of this freedom, a quid pro quo was established wherein the Saracens would be allowed to make pilgrimages to Bethlehem, now in Christian hands.

West of Jerusalem Frederick was awarded a corridor of land to the coast, as well as possession of Nazareth and some coastal cities such as Sidon, Jaffa, Caesarea, and Acre. A ten-year truce was established during which time Frederick would give no aid to either Christians or Saracens who might attempt to break the peace and would hold in check any who entertained ideas of attacking al-Kamil. He would further see to it that the kingdom of Jerusalem remained unfortified, although on the fulfillment of this last point there seems to be disagreement, depending on whether one reads Christian or Muslim sources.

When the terms of the truce were announced Frederick's German troops burst into ecstatic cheers. They saw that, by working together, the emperor and the sultan had brought a long-sought-after peace to the Holy Land. Yet beyond the rejoicing Germans there were few who celebrated. The Frankish Christians who had settled in Outremer admitted that Frederick had accomplished what no crusader had been able to do since the day that Saladin had conquered the sacred city of Jerusalem. Yet they lamented with some justification that strategically their position in the Holy Land remained shaky. Then—and Francis must have groaned on his heavenly throne!—there were those who complained that what land was won should have been taken by the sword, that infidels should have shed blood and died in the name of Christ. They were angry that the Muslims were allowed to maintain their own sacred shrines. The Templars protested that they were not given outright possession of the Temple of Solomon. And the Hospitallers, with no special ax to grind, simply refused to have anything to do with an emperor who, it seemed, deserved his sentence of excommunication. As philosophical non sequiturs certain chroniclers then and later leveled the old charges of Frederick's predilection for concubines—worse, *Saracen* concubines!—his epicurean appetites, his alleged avarice, and his infringements on the jurisdiction of the clergy.

The pope's wrath was the most noteworthy of all, though it sometimes verged on mere petulance. He allowed the rumor to be spread without contradiction through southern Italy that Frederick had died in Outremer, though he must have been too well informed to give that rumor credence. He denounced Frederick's treaty with al-Kamil in a letter to the archbishop of Milan, declaring that the emperor was anti-

Church, a foe of chastity, and condemned to hell. He was a disgrace to the memory of all martyrs who had died to save the Holy Land. His was a papal debauch of outrage that a treaty could be made with the Saracens against whom a righteous Christian abhorrence should be maintained. In an exemplary display of the very hubris of which he accused Frederick, Gregory saw that the emperor's diplomatic triumph could be interpreted by some as God's negative judgment on himself. He even attempted to minimize Frederick's achievement by pronouncing that God had not deigned to confer greater glory on the Christians. He heaped injury on insult by sending Frederick's ex-father-in-law, John of Brienne, into Apulia at the head of a papal army, causing Frederick to rail against Christian morality, displays of irritation which were as embarrassing to the Muslims as to the Europeans. Clearly Frederick's views of Christian motives and virtues were not adulatory.

The story is told that on a tour of the Dome of the Rock in Jerusalem, Frederick read an inscription placed there by Saladin: "Saladin cleansed this temple of the polytheists." Feigning ignorance, Frederick inquired who "the polytheists" might be. On the explanation that it was the Christians with their deification of the Trinity who were meant, he pursued his trend of thought further: Why the gratings over the windows? To keep out the birds. "Yet Allah has brought the swine among you," Frederick returned, using the most contemptuous Muslim term for the Christians that he could muster. This scorn was not especially pleasing to the Arabs, who regarded with suspicion a man who could mock his own religion and people. Neither were they pleased by his insistence that the muezzins continue their five calls to prayer, a daily ritual that al-Kamil had forbidden out of respect for him. "It is not right for you to do this for my sake," he admonished. "I would not have you do so in my country."

To an extent Muslim criticism of Frederick was a misreading. It was not only his contempt for his fellow Christians that goaded him into such behavior. From his childhood he had been a genuine admirer of things Eastern. Under the guidance of his tutor William Franciscus, he saw the Arabs as preservers of ancient learning, as well as valuable contributors to the fields of medicine, mathematics, and the sciences. He revered Arab thought and philosophy, their art of argument, indeed their whole culture. As far as he was concerned, the intellectual West had run its course and was trapped in an ecclesiastical mire. Only from the East did he receive the cognitive stimulation he craved.

For nearly a year while he was in the Holy Land, Frederick studied Arab architecture, including the much-venerated Dome of the Rock,

Dome of the Rock, Jerusalem. Photo credit: John S. Scott, Manhattan Beach, CA

the earliest great Islamic building still in existence in the twenty-first century, and stunning as viewed from Gethsemane with old Jerusalem in the background. Not typical of Islamic architecture, reflecting a pronounced Syrio-Byzantine influence, the sixty-foot-diameter dome, completed in 691 on Temple Mount, the site of Solomon's Old Testament temple, rests on a circle of columns, which in turn are surrounded by two concentric octagons. Inside it is a miracle of seventh- to eleventh-century mosaics and marble paneling, while the outside is covered with glazed tile of a style derived from ancient Middle Eastern civilizations and dating from the reign of Ottoman Sultan Suleiman (sixteenth century).

The Dome of the Rock is an icon to the three important religions of the area: the Jews and Christians hold it sacred because on the rock covered by the temple Abraham prepared the sacrifice of his son, Isaac; Islamic tradition holds that it was from this rock that Mohammed ascended into heaven. In both cases the Dome covers the site of monumental happenings in the history of man's faith. Some art historians hold that Frederick was inspired by the shape of the Dome of the Rock's octagon in his own design of the stunning Castel del Monte in Apulia, but that may be stretching it a bit.

What is not a stretch is that he did learn from the Muslims the use of hoods on hunting falcons, which must have been as interesting and pleasing to him as things of a more monumental nature. And it was apparently at this time that he adopted the Arab convention of a traveling harem. Though the harem was obviously not new to him, we do not read of his ladies being carted about in their palanquins and looked after by eunuch slaves until after his return from the East. Then, too, it was a good time for Frederick to brush up on his Eastern languages.

Frederick made his triumphal entry into Jerusalem on Saturday, March 17, despite threats of papal interdict on the whole city. There can be no stranger scene in history than that of the excommunicated emperor of the Holy Roman Empire, resplendent in imperial ostentation, leading his pilgrim army with ceremonial pomp into the Holy City in the name of all Christians, to the distant thunder of pontifical interdiction. On the next day, the fourth Sunday before Easter, Frederick went to the Church of the Holy Sepulcher, the original of which had been built by Constantine the Great over what was believed to be the tomb of Christ. Constantine instructed his architects to surpass in beauty all other buildings in Jerusalem with his church, whose destiny was to be vandalized by various peoples and finally demolished altogether by the mad caliph, al-Nakim, in 1009. Attended by Hermann von Salza and two churchmen, Berard of Palermo and Giacomo, archbishop of Capua, Frederick entered by an unimposing doorway into the transept of the irregular-shaped church with its bulbous dome projecting heavenward. On his left was (and still is) a domical building dating from 1099, almost certainly on the site of Constantine's fourth century shrine. To Frederick's right were the more conventional choir and apse structure built by the crusaders. Various religious groups hold rights to the collection of buildings that cluster about the church, and all have rights in the great rotunda and the tomb chapel itself, which has through the ages led to raging disputes—all in the name of gentle Jesus.

Unintimidated by papal anger, the Teutonic Knights accompanied Frederick, as did his loyal soldiers. Frederick had planned his act carefully. In a final gesture aimed defiantly at the heart of papal power, he raised the crown of Jerusalem from the altar and placed it on his own head, proclaiming without a trace of modesty that God, in an abundance of grace, exalted him above all princes. His following speech, translated into German and Latin by Hermann von Salza, was one of the few instances when Frederick softened his attitude of imperial detachment, so much that he even tried to explain away the myriad papal double-dealings, saying that had the pope known of his true intentions, he may have been more lenient in his judgment. Then he went further. Referring to Luke 1:68–69, Frederick proclaimed that the God of Israel "hath visited and redeemed his people, and hath raised up a horn of salvation for us in the house of his servant David." Other emperors may have claimed to be successors to King David. But Frederick was insisting that he was taking possession of his deserved inheritance, that he, like a true heir of David, was the king of Jerusalem. He saw himself as God's arbiter on earth, in secular matters what the pope was in spiritual matters. If not the equal of Jesus, he could at least be spoken of in the same breath. Later he would go even further, elucidating a claimed kinship with Jesus: "It fills us with joy that our Saviour Jesus of Nazareth also sprang from David's royal stock."[3]

If Frederick thought that his arrogant self-coronation coupled with his soothing words directed at papal treachery would melt the pope's hauteur, he was in for a shock. The next day the archbishop of Caesarea—in an attitude of embarrassment, to be sure—arrived under orders from Patriarch Gerold to place Jerusalem under interdict. The pilgrims who had left their homes and families and had suffered long deprivation for the privilege of worshipping at the sacred shrines were outraged. Frederick, in a tantrum of justified rage, instructed his followers to quit the city and to meet him at Acre. But even with his abandonment of Jerusalem, the hounding did not cease. Probably at papal instigation the Templars tried to ambush him for capture or assassination as he was headed for Jaffa. Nor was Frederick's anger assuaged by word from Italy that, at the head of papal armies, former father-in-law John of Brienne in company with Cardinal Pelagius—the same self-aggrandizing churchman whose ineptitude had doomed crusading efforts at Damietta—had succeeded in separating imperial forces, isolating one contingent in the Abruzzi and the other at Capua, and had already taken key cities in Apulia. It was time for Frederick to go home.

The invasion of the kingdom of Sicily was ill-inspired. It gave Frederick yet more ammunition to fire point-blank at the pope, and it gave poet Freidank the opportunity of pouring forth near-heretical venom in a thinly veiled call for revolt against the successor of Saint Peter: "Obedience is good as long as the Master worketh righteousness. If the Master seek to compel the servant to do what is wrong before God, then the servant must quit his master and follow him who doeth right."[4] Freidank's views did not go unnoticed, and eventually a portion of Europe's population saw Gregory himself as a heretic, if not verging on being the anti-Christ. For the moment, however, papal scheming was paying off. When Frederick left his Acre palace in the half-light of morning to board ship for departure, he was pelted with garbage.

After a short stop at Cyprus where he deposited King Henry I—no doubt glad to be back home after his trip to the Holy Land—and confirmed the ministers whom he had previously appointed, Frederick turned his ships toward Italy. At least he could hold the satisfying thought that, if he had not been cheered by his fellow Christians, he had been personally admired by those Saracens who knew him. And it would be a long time before they would forget him.

Frederick sailed against the warning of Thomas of Acerra to take precautions for his own safety and honor, since John of Brienne had garrisoned numerous ports with armed men and spies in order to capture him. Outstripping his own convoy, and making a record-breaking voyage—delay could mean the loss of both kingdom and empire—Frederick landed at Brindisi on June 10. And that was the end of the sixth crusade, which owed what success there was to Frederick's diplomatic skills and tenacity, and which owed its failures to human treachery, religious prejudice, and the hypocrisy of ecclesiastical personages from the highest office to some of the lowliest monks doing not at all the kind of work that Francis Bernardone had envisioned for his brothers minor.

As far as the rank and file of Christendom was concerned, Frederick had opened Jerusalem and other principal shrines of devotion in opposition to papal anathema. Just as important, he had arranged for routes of safe passage within the Holy Land itself. If the Templars were incensed that they had not gained possession and unlimited access to their cherished Temple of Solomon, then that was simply one of the transfers of ownership that was beyond Frederick's capabilities to arrange. In the meantime, Frederick could live with the accepted European view that he was the liberator of the land of Jesus. It was no matter to him or to popular opinion whether the hierarchy of the Church or the quasi-religious orders approved. Word filtered back to the West of the Templars' attempt to undercut Frederick's every move, how they had tried to capture, even assassinate him, how the pope had gone so far as to try to connive with al-Kamil to turn Frederick's triumphs into defeat. And men recited the poems of the popular Freidank, who cried in the name of the crusaders against the ban that had denied them access to Christendom's most sacred places:

O what in the world can a Kaiser do,
Since Christians and heathen, clergy too,
Are striving against him with might and main?
'Tis enough to craze e'en Solomon's brain! . . .[5]

As for the treacherous Templars, burned out in scandals of appalling squalor before the Middle Ages were over, they vanished in an orgy of heresy trials and witch hunts. The Hospitallers became heroes of history at Rhodes and Malta. The Teutonic Order laid the foundations of the kingdom of Prussia.

The pope, despite his wheeling and dealing, had already canonized Saint Francis (July 29, 1228). It is pleasant to think that Clare and her poor ladies had been present, enjoying an infrequent outing from the confines of the cloister. It is just as beguiling to see, in the mind's eye, "Brother Jacopa" arrive at the ceremony from wherever it was she lived in Assisi after Francis's death. Her home there, like Clare's San Damiano, had become a meeting place for disciples and a clearinghouse for donations to be passed on to the brethren. In any event, she had vowed she would not return to Rome again, but would remain in Assisi, walking the streets that Francis had walked, and continuing the work that he had undertaken. So it was until she died in 1274, "full of years," honoring her dear friend in death as she had in life. She was buried in the church of her spiritual mentor. Gregory had previously sent out an appeal for funds to build in Francis's name the huge basilica that dominates Assisi, and he had already laid the cornerstone for that memorial, which in its pretentious grandeur is such a far cry from anything admired by Francis. Gregory also issued a directive that Thomas of Celano, friar and friend of Francis, was to write a biography of the new saint. In fact Thomas wrote two of them, which are our main sources of knowledge concerning the life and legends of that gentle man.

All of this seemed to have little effect on Gregory's political thinking. With demonstrable ambivalence he called ever more stridently for war against Frederick Hohenstaufen, calls that went largely unheeded. On top of his other perfidies, had he not, until the very time that Frederick had arrived back in his realm, given credence to rumors of his enemy's death? Now here was the emperor in Barletta, standing before his subjects, who at first refused to believe that he was indeed Frederick. Once the fact was accepted that he had returned from Outremer hale and hearty, great rejoicing and rollicking around his banner took place. His army swelled with volunteers. A band of Teutonic Knights, returning from the Holy Land and forced to land at Brindisi because of inclement weather, joined him. It was noted with merriment that Frederick's troops advanced against the pope's while still displaying the red crosses of the crusaders. His followers—Sicilians, Germans, his loyal Saracens—banded together against the "soldiers of the keys," as the papal army was called. Rumors of papal deceit, which Frederick did nothing to contradict, swelled his base of support even further. John Vatatzes, schismatic Byzantine emperor of Nicaea in Bithynia, sent large sums of money, maybe angling for an advantageous marriage to one of Frederick's daughters, which he later achieved. Without hesitation Frederick set out to take back his kingdom, heading for Caiazzo, about eleven miles northeast of Capua, which was under papal siege.

The inhabitants of southern Italy were astonished. Here, after the rumor mills had ground out false tales of his death, his inability to maintain his kingdom, his gross cruelty, his downright fiendishness that would reduce Sicily to ashes, his thirst for blood that would never be slaked—here was Frederick riding the crest of a wave of popularity not too dissimilar to that which he had experienced in Germany in 1212, his banner flying, his soldiers loyal to a man. Cardinals, princes, nobles, the "soldiers of the keys," all seemed more than willing to scurry out of their dominions without even waiting to be attacked. It was an absolute rout of the papal armies. Even crusty old John of Brienne, again humiliated by his former son-in-law, scampered across the Volturno River into Church territory, whence he moved on with profound disillusionment to safety in his native Champagne. Cardinal Pelagius saved face—sort of—when he took himself to Monte Cassino, where he seized the abbey's treasury in order to pay his troops. When the mountain height proved too formidable for taking, Frederick allowed the cardinal an exit with full military honors, more by far than what he deserved. The town of Sora, so picturesquely situated on the Liri River, had to be taken by force. As a result it paid the ultimate price. Likened in Frederick's mind to ancient Carthage, its inhabitants were put to the sword, and the city was razed. On the other hand, the abbey at Cava, just north and inland from Salerno, was taken under special imperial protection because of proven loyalty. By the end of October, the last papal soldier was out of the southern kingdom; and so ended the rout of the "soldiers of the keys." Europe looked on admiringly. Frederick's main acts of vindictiveness were directed against Sora. There were the Templars and the Hospitallers, whose properties he confiscated. And there were some few instances of flogging and hanging turncoat soldiers and leaders whom he found in captured castles. But by and large the people of the kingdom of Sicily learned a practical lesson of the beneficences of Frederick's rule. They would never again welcome a papal army of deliverance.

1230

Had Frederick been so inclined, this would have been the ideal time to pursue the "soldiers of the keys" into papal territory; right up to the walls of Rome would not have been out of the question. That way he would have made it easy to take both the duchy of Spoleto and the March of Ancona, territories that he had long coveted. But he was more interested in making peace with Gregory: this indicates how strong a power the papacy was, how the office itself, regardless of individuals, still seemed to exist above and beyond wars, secular passions, and human treacheries. Frederick saw the man Gregory for what he was; but he also saw him as the Vicar of Christ. So it was that the ever-diplomatic Hermann von Salza, aided by several cardinals who were aware of the shortcomings of Gregory's policies, as well as many German princes and Pier delle Vigne in a minor role, arranged for a meeting of the two sovereigns to make their peace. It is incredible that Frederick, in every other way the victor over papal intrigue, came out on the short end of negotiations. He agreed to, and signed, a number of concessions at San Germano in July, giving up much that he had adamantly hung on to over the years, and all for the lifting of the ban of excommunication.

The most astonishing part of Frederick's acquiescence concerned the jurisdiction over, the taxation of, and the election of the clergy and Church hierarchy in his realm. From now on most of the clergy were no longer liable according to secular law and were no longer subject to taxation. Almost as astounding was Frederick's renunciation of the right of approval of episcopal elections, the very thorny right to which his Norman forerunners had clung so tenaciously. The Templars and the Hospitallers were to be recompensed for the lands that Frederick had confiscated, as were numerous faithless barons. It was at least humiliating to Frederick, who must have seen acceptance of these conditions as infringements on his sovereignty. It might even seem that he was being faithless to his own ideals. But he wanted absolution. He knew there was no way he could rule his realm, much less his empire, if he continued much longer as an excommunicate.

As time would prove, Frederick was acting the typical thirteenth-century ruler. Gregory had in no way given up his ideas of ruining him.

Frederick knew that. But he still had it in mind to establish his imperium in emulation of the ancient Roman Empire. For the moment he could afford to bide his time. He had his realm to restore to working order, and he had the very difficult problem of opposition-minded Lombardy. As long as the Lombards saw themselves as citizens of independent city-states, there was no way that Frederick's high-flown ideal of empire could be achieved. Furthermore, he had not given up his notion that he was God's secular regent on earth, as he had made unmistakably clear in his self-coronation speech in Jerusalem. From the time of his astonishing survival in the streets of Palermo, through his miraculous evasion of his enemies and his spectacular arrival in the transalpine city of Constance, his gathering of German forces and his defeat of Otto IV, his coronation as emperor and his successful crusade—in all of these happenings, he detected the guiding hand of God. He saw himself sitting on a God-ordained throne, as much the vicar of God as was the pope. He was the man who was ultimately responsible for the peace on earth that had been heralded over the manger in Bethlehem. And he would establish the peace as had the ancient Caesars. Feeling able to give a little, to bow down in deference to his nemesis in order to achieve his dreamed-of future goals, Frederick was driven toward rapprochement with the Holy See. Astonishing as it might have been to Christendom, an emperor who had recently been personally defamed by Gregory IX as having eaten and drunk with Saracens, who had been branded a blasphemer and Saracen sympathizer, suddenly became "the beloved son of the Church." On August 28, at Ceprano—today a dull, characterless town for the most part, whose saving grace is that it is not far from Naples—Frederick was finally absolved in the presence of a large official audience both ecclesiastical and secular.

Not everyone, however, was so sanguine in accepting this new brotherhood of rulers. Some viewed the suddenly quiet relationship of pope and emperor with contempt, seeing it as a disgrace to the Church. Troubadours sang with hostile joy of the demise of the Church. But criticism aside, pope and emperor, not to mention the ever-hostile Lombards, needed time. Frederick would never give up his vision of a papal-imperial alliance against the antagonistic forces of the world—especially the Lombards—as a product of God's ultimate plan. Throughout his life he would hold that the harmony of the empire was based on the coexistence of the two powers in perfect balance. The Holy Father had other ideas of manipulation and dominance, but he had been bested in his recent conspiracies against the crusading emperor; better to wait for a while. For a time—almost ten years, in fact—the dominant figures of Europe managed to bury their bones of contention and to smooth over the grave. But the truce was without substance. And the longer they waited, the more devastating the final political avalanche.

After Ceprano Frederick and Hermann von Salza journeyed to Anagni to dine with the pope. By August of the following year, Gregory formally recognized Frederick as king of Jerusalem. He could afford to by then, not having John of Brienne around to contest the claim, that opportunist having married one of his daughters to the child-emperor of Constantinople, giving him a new power base to occupy his energies. Gregory ratified the treaty made by Frederick and al-Kamil. He ordered that peace in the Holy Land was to be preserved at all cost. The only crusade led by an excommunicate had been acknowledged a success! Hallelujah!

But Frederick still had his work to do, not the least being to fight dishonesty and insurrection from within his own family. The world at large may have prayed for peace, and the Europeans may have been clamoring for harmony between Church and state. And God Himself, as Frederick proclaimed, may have established the former "boy of Apulia" as his secular vice-regent. But a resentful, power-jealous son, one who had already been designated to succeed to the imperial purple, had ways of thwarting even God's will. Henry, king of Germany, twenty years of age, was in no way going to make life easier for his father, who had enough to do managing a career vis-à-vis a pope who wanted to destroy him and princes who were just as jealous as he of their personal powers. And Henry should have been aware that disobedience was no way to win Frederick's love and respect.

For all his distractions Frederick was probably not immediately aware that one of his most admiring supporters—albeit one who tended to go a bit with the wind—a believer in German unity and a singer in praise of pure love, Walther von der Vogelweide, had died. Walther had spent the last six years on his small fief near Würzburg in Franconia. Once Frederick had been acclaimed king of Germany, Walther had remained reasonably loyal to the Hohenstaufen cause. He had supported Frederick's crusade and yet, paradoxically, could write in an almost Franciscan manner of toleration and brotherhood among men.

The most beautiful of Walther's lyrics ("Unter den Linden") is a virtual hymn to nature. It is said that when he died he left instructions that birds were to be fed on his grave every day. He was buried in a small garden—the Lusamgärtlein—in a twelfth-century cloister adjacent to the Neumünster in Würzburg. The cloister is gone now but for one gallery. A modern monument to Walther stands in the quiet shadows, adorned, when the author was last there, by a simple kitchen jar acting the vase for an exquisite yellow rose. More formally, Walther is honored by a statue in front of the *Residenz*, designed principally by Balthasar Neumann for the prince-bishops of Würzburg. There, as part of an attractive fountain complex, in company with painter Mathias Grünewald and sculptor Tilman Riemenschneider, Walther stands looking like a latter-day Saint Paul.

Now was the time of Francis Bernardone's two great humiliations—the one to his earthly remains, the other, and ultimate humiliation, to his creed. Tradition tells us that when Francis lay dying, he begged to be buried in the "Collis Infernus," a kind of Golgotha of Assisi where criminals were executed and sometimes buried. One of his closest friars, Brother Elias, was present at his deathbed. He must have heard that whispered request, assuming it is more than legend. But Elias would have none of the master's strange desire to lie among the unwanted, the criminals, the unholy sinners. Immediately he started wheels turning to build a mausoleum, complete with song-resounding vaults, frescoes, gold, marble, and alabaster. As we have already seen, the pope himself issued an appeal for funds, which started raining on Assisi from every corner of Christendom. One Simon Puzarelli donated a hill outside the walls of Assisi for a mausoleum-church. By this year the crypt was completed, though it would be another twenty-three years before the church would be officially consecrated.

Perhaps as exaggeratedly as the event itself, it is claimed that two thousand friars, bishops, and prelates converged on Assisi from all over Europe on May 25 to march from the Church of San Giorgio (Francis's parish church in which he had been temporarily interred, the site of which is now occupied by the Church of Santa Chiara) to the new crypt, his final resting place. One way or another the attendant religious and lay audience was not allowed to view the actual place of interment, a secret so closely guarded that it took until 1818 to find it. It is visible today above the crypt altar, encased in a massive pier of stone that has been partially cut away to allow a view of the casket. The crypt itself is not elaborate, but the two churches above it are. One can only wonder what mild expletive Francis might have uttered had he seen what his followers were up to in his name. And the man most responsible for the egregious denigration of Francis's ideal was one who should have known better—Brother Elias.

Hardly had Francis been laid to his final rest when an idea occurred to the intellectually slippery Gregory IX, made manifest in his bull, *Quo Elongati*. The final debasement! Gregory IX, previously Ugolino dei Conti, trusted friend and mentor of the saint he claimed to honor, protector of the order, decreed that Francis's testament had no binding power over members of the order because it had been written without consultation of the order's ministers. Furthermore, Francis's concept of poverty, as stated in his Rule of 1223, was reinterpreted in a manner that, by various quirky rationales, allowed members to use wealth, if not actually to own it. Thus was Francis divorced from his Lady Poverty through no fault of his own or of his bride, but through a third party—Madam Practicality. It had been a long and circuitous route from Francis's Bethlehem at San Damiano, with its talking crucifix, through the childhood of the Rivo Torto to the Gethsemane of the Porziuncola, to Rome, Damietta, and to his great moment—La Verna. Then the *Quo Elongati!* But Francis has had his resurrection. The fact remains that there are today over 50,000 avowed followers of his Rule. In addition there are others of myriad religious persuasions from all parts of the world who cherish him. *Il poverello* is beloved today as is perhaps no other saint in Christendom.

Chapter Twelve

Thou who forgave Mary [the sinful woman],
and favorably heard the (good) thief,
hast also given me hope.
***Dies Irae*, verse 13**

1231

A successful ruler needs a base to which he is emotionally, spiritually, and intellectually attached, a place whose inhabitants share his ideals and emotions, a place with which he identifies and which is identified through him. Frederick's abilities, if they were to be made to work successfully and not be frittered away in glib and dilettantish exercises, needed to find a receptive and adoring audience, an audience willing to adhere to his laws—as he himself was willing. Sicily, accustomed since ancient days to alternating tyrannical cruelties and benevolences, was as ready now to bend her back to autocratic admonitions and laws as she had been in the days of the coming of Frederick's Hauteville ancestors. It is reasonable to assume that Frederick was not blind to the idea that Sicily was "the mother of tyrants," as stated by Paulus Orosius as early as the fifth century, but that mainland Italy was "the clue to everything."[1] So it was here rather than in Germany, where Frederick had not been for eleven years, that he would establish his imperium, rigid and unchallengeable, the kernel of a vast empire, a model to those states and wide lands beyond papal holdings. Symbolically, perhaps, Frederick issued his new edicts from Melfi, that first bleak headquarters of his freebooting Norman forebears.

There is no more unlikely place than Melfi for the issuance of a code of laws meant to shake the world into the establishment of universal peace. In sight of the extinct volcano of Mount Vulture, Melfi occupies its own hilly pinnacle, quiet, primitive, unheralded by agents and unknown by tourists. Most guidebooks totally ignore this out-of-the-way town that was in medieval days a power center for the ambitious and successful. Made the capital of Apulia by the Normans, it figured largely in the machinations of popes, dukes, barons, and kings. The castle there was erected by Robert Guiscard. Along with Lagopesole, it became one of Frederick's favorite haunts in southern Italy.

Forests abound around Melfi as when they were explored by the emperor-huntsman and, farther back on the calendar, by the young Horace, who was native to the area. There is an intense blueness about the sky of lower Italy, a crystalline brilliance that seems as limitless as the matching sea. But Melfi is given to fogs too—heavy, chill, and opaque—penetrating every corner and to the marrow of every bone. Melfi is not far from Eboli, a town so poverty-ridden, underdeveloped, and drowning in hopelessness that it would prompt Carlo Levy to write his memoir "Christ Stopped at Eboli." Like so many inhabitants of this part of the Italian boot, the people of Melfi (and Eboli as well) are kind, curious about strangers, and given to quick smiles. If they were of more or less the same bent in Frederick's even harsher century, it is no wonder that he singled Melfi out as one of his favorite haunts and the headquarters for issuing his new code of laws.

Spooky underground churches replete with fresco remains, such as Santa Margherita, do little to assuage Melfi's general drabness, though the stout, eleventh-century campanile of the cathedral helps. It maintains its noble original form, except for its crowning octagonal upper story and pinnacle, while the rest of the church has been remodeled extensively through the centuries. Of special interest to Norman lovers are twin pompous griffins—emblems of the Norman masters—high on the tower in contrasting colored lava stone, themselves minor masterpieces of geometric decoration. A block or so away can one not smile at the sight of as handsome a Norman church doorway as one is apt to find anyplace, zigzag patterns and all, right next to the local *cinema?* With the propensity of the Italians to move through history so unconcernedly, it is a wonder the theater is not housed in the old Norman church! The Porta Venosina piercing the city's old protective wall is mossy and handsomely thirteenth century, though the towers and walls on each side of it are of a later period.

It was in August 1231 that Frederick published from Melfi his long-anticipated constitutions, his *Liber Augustalis,* first of all a rehash of existing but largely ignored Norman laws. With those laws as his ground, Frederick combined his own legislation from years back (as from Capua) with some new, all of which would be expanded still further in the future. His edict was the first great medieval codification of constitutional law whose influence on later European monarchs cannot be disregarded. The constitutions, which became binding on September 1, were compiled for use in Sicily, which included, of course, southern Italy. There was no way they could have been made applicable to the very different German thinking. But they were designed for the states of the future. Frederick was nothing if not the embodiment of divine law, which was to bring the ultimate peace on earth. In his dream his law would someday be the law of the world, including, as his father had dreamed, the Byzantine Empire. Unshakable in his belief in Rome, emperor and empire—with its "honor and rights," a phrase he repeated countless times verbally and in writing—he envisioned Constantinople as someday returning to her Roman mother. The title of his new table of laws made clear Frederick's position as emperor and his relationship to the ancient Caesars, an idea further generated by his imitation of the language of the enlightened code of law of Justinian the Great. But his *Liber Augustalis* was more than an imitation; it was an attempt to follow directly in the footsteps of Emperor Justinian the Great, sixth-century head of the Eastern Roman Empire. Furthermore, in the title he called on the sacred name of Augustus. So Frederick tied himself to memories of two ancient rulers, both of them admired for their civilizing contributions to the betterment of the human predicament. He went so far as to ape the Eastern bezant with his "Augustales," a stable gold coinage, in turn copied in the 1252 Florentine florin. He was doing everything in his power to reestablish the age of Augustus, which—a fact not lost on his contemporaries—was also the period of the son of God. Throughout the new edict it is clear that Frederick's intent was the prevention, rather than the punishment of crime. Going beyond his Norman predecessors, he welded feudal and Roman traditions to affect every aspect of life in the realm. Here is our first accurate impression of Frederick as the earliest of the princes of the coming Renaissance. He was creating history. Frederick utilized a team of jurists for the codification of his *Liber Augustalis*. Pier delle Vigne, with his cultivated facility for the written word, daily became more indispensable and a closer friend of his imperial master, as did Archbishop Giacomo of Capua. But the directing force behind the project was Frederick himself, peering over the shoulders of his thinkers and scribes, correcting, arguing, and cajoling them into realizing his dreams in law.

As we would expect, Pope Gregory took a dim view of the whole enterprise and renounced the 217 laws as denying the fundamental assumptions of Christianity, that is, salvation. Gregory, of course, saw himself as the legitimate heir to the Caesars—and his power, unlike

Frederick's, carried into the infinite afterlife. With his earthbound, very finite pretensions, Frederick would not hear of that. As God's regent he saw his laws as instrumental in the eradication of feudal violence and oppression, including Church oppression. He envisioned equal rights, justice for all—and equal responsibility. He aimed at the toleration of different, sometimes hostile religions. So here was each man stepping over onto the jealously protected turf of the other.

From the twenty-first century viewpoint, the most arresting single facet of Frederick's complicated new legal system was his assertion that all men were equal under the law, an astonishing enlightenment considering the nature of his times. In Frederick's eyes everyone, from emperor to lowest peasant, was entitled to justice, which was, in effect, dispensed from the imperial throne, albeit through justiciars who acted as governors of various provinces. Perhaps analogous to his concept of equality under law was Frederick's recognition of the common people—the Third Estate (the other two being clergy and nobles)—who may even have been summoned to the magnificent court at Melfi that celebrated the establishment of the new constitutions. Within two years Frederick would decree that representatives of the Third Estate meet twice a year to enact business appropriate to their social standing, though it must be admitted that in all probability his decree was prompted by social unrest, indeed, the uprisings that would occur in Sicily in 1233.

Again considering the times, Frederick's provisions for the women of the realm were truly enlightened, laying down for later ages a model that has not been faithfully copied. Rape was declared a capital offense, and pimping was punishable by relegation to slavery. To raise a daughter to the profession of prostitution—except in the direst financial hardship—could draw the severest penalties. Today we find nothing astounding about such laws. But such was not the case in Frederick's century when, in Cologne for example, a man could not be punished for rape if the woman had been alone on the street at night when she was accosted. In addition to the above, a woman was allowed, under Frederick's edict, to inherit property. Children could not be brought to trial, nor could "maniacs." Kidnappers were properly punished, as were those who neglected to give aid to victims of shipwreck. Frederick ridiculed the very idea of trial by ordeal and legally abolished the concept, as well as the use of love potions.

Beyond all of this the constitutions of Melfi laid down the working order of the civil service, tax collection, legal counseling, the control of weights and measures, the sale of unhygienic foods, the butchering of animals, and usury (forbidden to all but Jews). The jobs of justiciars and chamberlains, the admiral of the navy and marshal of the army, the secret police, and the heads of state financial organizations, and those in charge of import and export, were all clearly delineated. The land was divided into nine provinces, so cleverly drawn that they remained largely as Frederick deemed until Garibaldi's unification of Italy in the nineteenth century. Various state monopolies were affirmed: iron, salt, silk, hemp, and dyeing materials, with salt remaining to this day on the list of government monopolies along with the modern additions of tobacco and matches.

Frederick was in a comfortable position. He had established a peculiar sort of peace with the Church that would hold yet for a few years. He was idolized by a large part of Europe for having concluded a successful crusade with practically no cost in human life, and—to top it off—contrary to the pope's and the Curia's wishes. Now he had produced his inspired *Liber Augustalis,* recognized at once as enormous progress in the art of jurisprudence as well as an important civilizing document. Some might see the new laws only as rehashes of previous laws. But that is a false view. The new code was more than a listing of laws. It was a brilliantly reasoned structure whose building blocks were imaginative and innovative legal concepts held together by anciently ordained, tested, and proven mortar. Now Frederick could afford to lie back a bit, to indulge his Oriental love of luxury and study, and to gratify his well-known libidinous propensities that would bear fruit the following year.

Even at his age—he was a few years short of forty—Frederick kept himself in fair shape. Slowly inclining toward stoutness, he was still agile. He ate only one meal a day (in the evening) and could remain in the saddle for twenty-four hours at a stretch. He bathed daily, a habit he probably picked up in the East and which prompted unveiled criticisms from a mendicant monk who complained that he bathed even on Church festival days. Hunting was still his favorite recreational activity, which probably accounts for his physical adroitness and would in time lead to his creation of the aforementioned book on falconry, one of the more remarkable books of the Middle Ages. His auburn-blond hair was growing a little thinner now, but there continued to be something youthful about him, an agelessness, perhaps due to his habit of remaining clean-shaven. He could be winningly charming. He could also be a good friend, a quality not to be taken too lightly; friendships were important to him and not to be thoughtlessly betrayed, as Pier delle Vigne would learn. His gaze was still as direct as it had been in his youth—and just as deadly, evincing not a trace of inner feeling. He had not forgotten, and never would forget, his early humbler days; he touted himself now as "the man of Apulia."

Having run the gamut of political intrigue, dissemblance, and outright dishonesty, Frederick was in a position to lecture his sons on the duties and desirable qualities of a good ruler. Some revealing didactic letters exist that show Frederick as his sons' best educator. It is not enough, he points out, to be highborn, for kings and great men of the world need noble character and zeal for their jobs. If the common man perceives a ruler as great it is because the ruler has vision, is virtuous, wise, and honorable. Death, he reminds his sons, is the great equalizer, taking the powerful as well as the weak. The enlightened king is not afraid to act the pupil, but at the same time he must not be too humble, especially in his interchange with commoners, lest he harm the royal dignity. There were a few distracting claims on Frederick's attention in the next years—the calmest and most creative of his life—and the few were worthy of his notice. But for the most part he was in a comfortable place, able to enjoy extended periods of comparative relaxation to pursue the intellectual and cultural subjects so dear to his heart, before the forces of life would unite in a drowning swell of opposition too strong even for him.

Poetry was one of Frederick's first loves, as we have seen, and during his rule court poetry was set out in the vernacular Sicilian rather than in Latin, an example followed by the great Dante (using Tuscan Italian, of course), himself an ardent admirer of the emperor, whom he called "the father of Italian poetry." There was a flowering of poetic inspiration in Frederick's court, produced, according to Dante, by the questioning liberalism of the court itself, and which found its most natural expression in the local language. By using the vernacular instead of Latin, and then refining it with touches of Provençal and Tuscan, Frederick raised poetry to the rank of a court language. As in contemporary Provence, love poetry became the rage, along with expressions of the despairs of unrequited love. Frederick indulged himself in this medium, and his anguish could be as adolescently heartbreaking as that of the most ardent teenage swain, indicating that he was capable of genuine sentiment, perhaps not for a prolonged period, but at least for a time:

> For sure she did hurt and offend me
> since the moment she set me afire; that I know well;
> in fact her beautiful face has cut my heart to pieces.[2]

Members of the Sicilian court indulged themselves in poems of flowery language. Birds, weather, flowers, sunrises, and dusks were all material for the poet and not, incidentally, incompatible with the vision of Saint Francis. Under Frederick's guidance and the example of such as Giacomo da Lentino, often regarded as the inventor of the sonnet form, men like Rinaldo d'Aquino and his two brothers (relatives of Thomas Aquinas), Percival Doria, Arrigo Testa, Giacomino Pugliese, Pier delle Vigne, Jacopo Mostacci, and Frederick's eldest illegitimate son, Enzo, even crusty old John of Brienne, are known to have dabbled in the new poetry. Together they pointed the way to Dante, who with a monumental flourish opened the gate to the Renaissance. The Scuola Siciliana became the first school of poetry that can be called "Italian."

Now was Frederick approaching the height of his power. His ambitions fostered in him dreams—dreams of the impossible, it turned out—that would have carried his power and civilizing influence even further. But such was not to be. The pope recognized accurately that imperial ambitions of uniting Germany and Italy were a threat to his own territorial aims, that a large part of Church territory would be lost to the secular empire. Certainly the Lombards, with their long-established detestation of outside authority, could be counted on to oppose Frederick by any means they could contrive. The German princes, while basically in Frederick's camp, could not countenance his establishment of an Italian city—Rome—as the capital of his empire. They would certainly stand against that concept, gifts, benefits, and outright bribes notwithstanding. And there was yet another culprit to frustrate imperial ambitions, worse than the others because he was closer to Frederick's heart: his first-born son, King Henry VII of Germany.

The apparent father-son calm was misleading. Trouble was brewing, and not even beneath the surface. It was out in the open enough for anyone to see who cared to. It had been eleven years since Frederick had laid eyes on his son, now in his early twenties and well past the age that Frederick had been when he had affirmed his own right to rule and had seen his position vis-à-vis the pope as undignified. Since Frederick had not so much as set foot on German soil in those eleven years, it was with some justification that young Henry felt more knowledgeable about that northern part of the empire than his father. Had he been cleverer and wiser this could have worked in Henry's favor. But as things stood he was a match for his father in neither wisdom nor strength—nor even ruthlessness. And he was certainly not as capable of averting his eyes from voluptuous pleasures, seeing them as a way of life in themselves rather than as mere divertissements after the facts of life's business. While Frederick had been haggling with Pope Gregory IX at San Germano and Ceprano, Henry had been tilting at windmills in the person of the bishop of Liège, a joust pointless and futile, but nonetheless serious, losing for Henry several royal privileges, and for Frederick enormous amounts of imperial prestige.

When the German princes returned from Italy in 1231 after having helped arrange the Peace of Ceprano, they found Henry standing face-to-face against the bishop of Liège, taking the side of the citizens in a largely unimportant contest between them and the churchman. The princes saw Henry's stance as a betrayal of their interests and compelled him to hold a diet at Worms, where they formed a block of opposition. They forced Henry to relinquish his rights to coin money, to build fortifications on princely lands, to exact tolls and taxes, and more to the point, to give the princes added autonomy in their own domains, an autonomy now almost on a par with that of the ecclesiastical princes. It is true that Frederick himself had relinquished rights and granted favors, but he had done so only when he was sure of a tit-for-tat return, and for the most part, with ecclesiastical princes whose positions, being non-hereditary, were never so much a threat to imperial pretensions as were the secular. But Henry, by picking up the cause of the townspeople, by his hostility to the bishop and then to the princes, had gained nothing and lost much. Now more than ever, with his taming at Worms, the secular princes were petty sovereigns, flaunting their power, more capable of acting on their own, and consequently, more liable to turn their backs on the emperor when the chips were down. Such conditions could create dire results for Frederick's ultimate political goals, which were further threatened by the fact that randy Henry was clamoring to divorce his queen, Margaret of Austria, in favor of a new flame, Agnes of Bohemia. (Trouble was averted when Agnes took to a convent.) It would be to Frederick's advantage to have a meeting with his son—and soon. But even speed would not remedy the situation. Thus began a development that would climax in denigrating the emperor and bringing down the pope, and with him the last-act curtain of the Middle Ages.

The principal force working against Frederick and his dreams was the instinctive and implacable hatred of the Lombards to any person or government who they even suspected would deprive them of their jealously guarded forms of municipal self-government. Then, with the powerful body of the medieval Church behind him, there was always the pope, a man with courage hardly befitting a ninety-year-old and with that tenacious fear of a united empire. The current imperial-papal friendship was simply a gloss disguising the real intentions of both parties, but a believable-enough disguise to alert the Lombards to a power play in the making. And when Frederick issued a summons to the German princes and son Henry, as well as to ambassadors from the north Italian cities to attend a diet at Ravenna to commence on All Saints' Day (November 1), the Lombards acted in unison by resurrecting the Lombard League. The Alpine passes were blocked to German traffic, despite promises from the pope that he would use his good offices to assure the success of Frederick's meeting.

Taking the pope at his word, and wanting to appear intent on peace, Frederick arrived at Ravenna with a small party, including Berard of Palermo, as always, and Count Thomas of Aquino the Elder, of Lombard descent. A few loyal northern adherents were there—the lords of Parma, Pavia, and Cremona, for example. Word was not long in reaching the court that the German princes could not get through the Alpine barrier. Frederick bided his time. But the thought "So much for papal influence over the Lombards!" must have struck him. He postponed the diet until Christmas, filling in his time in this museum city of emperors and Gothic kings with the intellectual and collecting activities that were so dear to his heart. He set to work excavating the tomb of Galla Placidia that had become buried under litter and rubble and selected numerous works of sculpture, which he sent south for the adornment of his castles. By Christmas some of the German princes had, by hook or by crook, managed to cross the Alpine passes and made it to Ravenna. But Frederick was not prepared to let the disruptive cities off free. They had hit Frederick where it hurt the most. They had offended his office, which he considered the absolute source of civil law throughout the realm. Son Henry was noticeable for his absence. As far as Frederick was concerned, others had made it through by the Friuli route. Why not his son? The ban of the empire was laid on all those who had failed to make it to Ravenna.

1232

The Ravenna diet was mostly unsatisfactory except for Frederick's meeting old friends; and there were the pleasures afforded the natives, what with music, acrobats, performers of all sorts, and the chance to see the fabled imperial collection of lions, panthers, and the assortment of other exotic beasts and birds that the emperor clearly enjoyed having about him, especially the greatest curiosity of all, the elephant. All of this only added to the glamour of this Hohenstaufen, heaven-sent if ever an emperor was. A gloomy, frustrated Frederick left Ravenna in March prepared for two-fold action: in an effort to assure future freedom of movement over the Friuli-Austria passes, a visit to Venice was in order, however unenthusiastically the Most Serene Republic might react to the imperial guest; and, come what may, King Henry would get himself to Aquileia to kneel before the imperial presence during the coming Easter season. That was a demand, an undisguised summons.

As for Venice, there was no choice but to grant Frederick's request to enter the city to pay his respects at the shrine of the holy evangelist Saint Mark, though it takes some imagining to convince oneself that such a reason was important to him. He was welcomed by Doge Giacomo Tiepolo to the shimmering city, by this time on the verge of replacing Palermo as the most opulent and wealthy in Europe. Tiepolo's guarded hospitality was studied; the wealthy republic must not cozy up too much with the emperor for fear of endangering its coveted role as banker to the Lombard League. But the doge's not-too-effusive cordiality won spin-off dividends anyway in the confirmation of certain trading privileges in Frederick's southern kingdom. With an intellectual atmosphere similar to Palermo, the place of Frederick's education and very soul, Venice was the most exotic city he had ever seen. With its lagoons and canals, its gilt, bronze, and mosaics, it was a city of endless reflections and visual excitement. Frederick was just one more of the horde of celebrated personages who had visited, and would continue to visit, the sparkling city floating on her island-dotted lagoon. Gondolas were already in existence in Frederick's century (they are mentioned in chronicles as early as 1094), and it was a good thing, for few cities offer such rewarding sightseeing from slow-moving vehicles as did—does—Venice. Garden walls, trees weeping gently into the canals, curved bridges, the arches, towers and domes—all need slow, gliding, quiet passage to a proper love affair. And the gondoliers' hallooing warnings as they negotiate dangerous blind corners, while fracturing the silence, serve to emphasize by contrast the tranquility. If Frederick did not get a gondola ride, he missed one of the most intoxicating treats of his or our time.

The Piazza San Marco had been paved over by this time. The Doge's Palace was there, but not nearly as exotic in aspect as we know it—a lacey, overly intricate container for a pampered, overly vested lifetime autocrat chosen from the powerful rich. The Piazzetta had already been cleared and two columns erected there—one topped by the lion symbol of Saint Mark, the other by Saint Theodore and his dragon—by a young engineer named Nicolò Staratonio, creating an area between them which became the designated spot for public executions. It is nice that the Venetians hang on to the memory of Saint Theodore, the medieval symbol of the virtuous, stalwart hero of the Church, willing to fight evil in every form—hence his dragon-crocodile. (The French manage to get this hero idea across better than anyone in their concept of Theodore as seen on the south porch of Chartres Cathedral.) Before stealing the body of Saint Mark from its tomb in Alexandria and bringing it to Venice, the Venetians claimed Theodore as their patron. Once Saint Mark was elected, Saint Theodore was forgotten—but not completely. There he is, still posturing atop his column.

Venice was probably mobbed with tourists; it always has been, even in off-season months. Machiavelli said as much, elaborating further that the crowds are the source of the healthful atmosphere. Surely a modern environmentalist will have something to say about that! The normal thirteenth-century crowds of Venice would be swelled by the addition of Frederick's train of princes and nobles, his harem and menagerie, plus representatives from uneasy Lombard cities who came to spy, or just to watch out of plain curiosity. Ceremonies as seen in paintings by the Bellini family must have taken place before the reflections of the dome-undulating cathedral, not a cathedral then but the doge's chapel, a monument in a city of monuments, fabulously opulent and cheap looking, scruffy and glorious, an edifice at which "it is better not to look too closely, or the whole will begin to seem tawdry, a hodge-podge, as so many critics have said. The whole is not beautiful, and yet again it is."[3]

The present San Marco is what we have, and it is hard to imagine other than as it is. It is not inappropriate, therefore, to conjure up the processions filing through the crowded piazza, the music, the banners, the costumes of the nobility, the ecclesiastical vestments, those four tense horses watching from above, magnificent in their patinaed bronze, prancing, eyes panicky, nostrils flared—all of these features combine to create the kind of spectacle so cherished in the collective heart and mind of Venice, and that would be so lovingly, serenely painted in the fifteenth and sixteenth centuries by *la famiglia Bellini.* Frederick could afford to look up at those magnificent steeds—the real ones, of course, not the excellent copies we see today—and take some pride in the conduct of his recent crusade to Outremer, seeing that the life-size horses had been purloined from Constantinople in the wake of its frenzied rape by the armies of the fourth crusade.

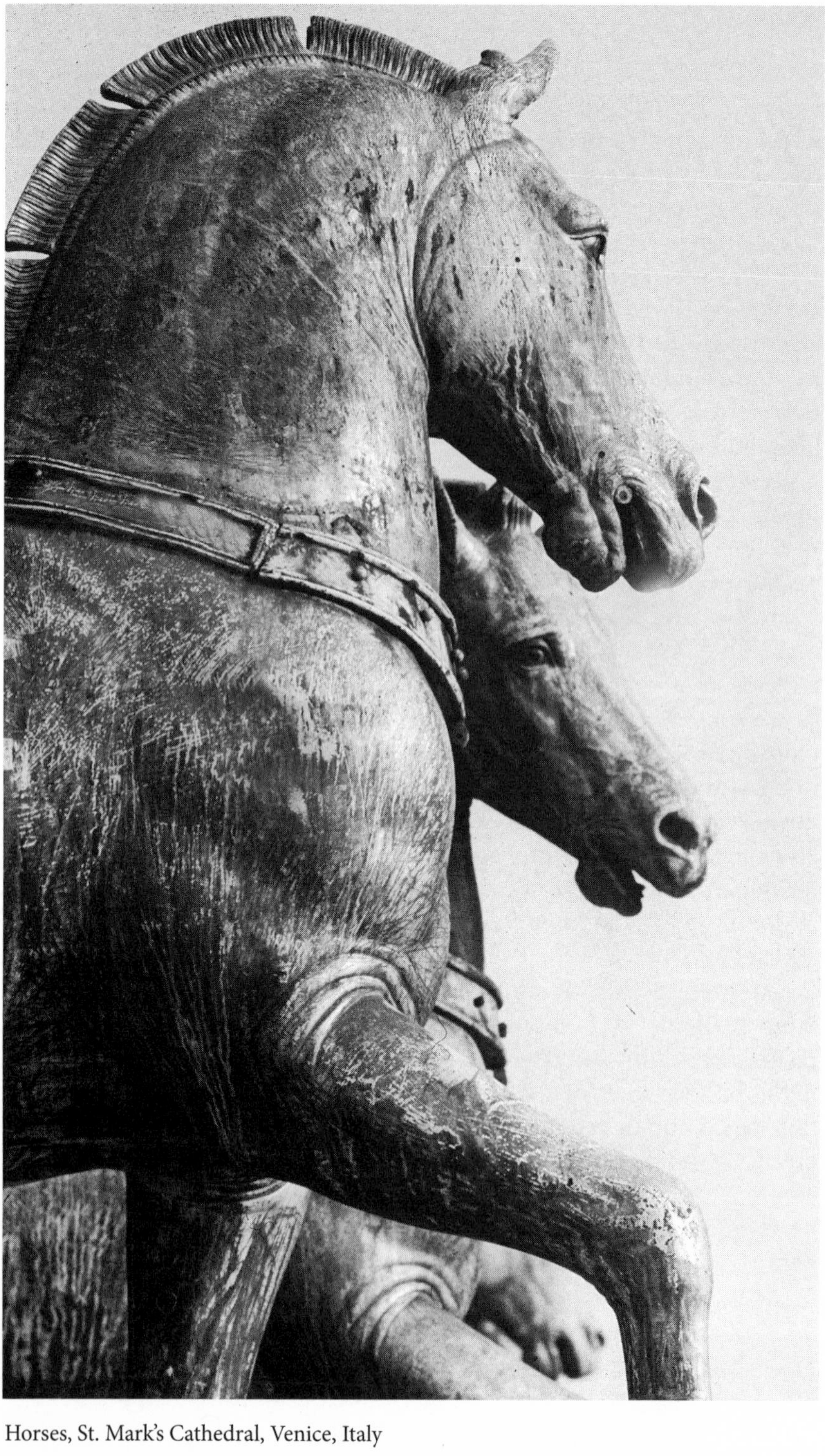

Horses, St. Mark's Cathedral, Venice, Italy

Platforms had been constructed in front of San Marco, on which perch Doge Giacomo Tiepolo and Frederick were enthroned, backed by the shimmering glory that elicited poetic rhapsodies from the naturally rhapsodic John Ruskin in *The Stones of Venice.* One wonders whether Frederick was aware that it was in the central doorway of Saint Mark's that Frederick Barbarossa had abased himself before Pope Alexander III in 1177, thereby ending one of the most destructive Church schisms in history. Today only a small porphyry plaque set in the pavement marks the spot of Barbarossa's humiliation.

The exuberant splendor of the outside of San Marco is but a preparation for the glories to be enjoyed within: arches, domes, stained glass; acres of mosaic; marbles, alabaster, precious jewels; paintings, sculpture, and columns of Byzantine inspiration. To the unprepared tourist entering San Marco can be an aesthetic knockout blow, an intoxication of textures and patterns, a visual hammering of more colors, brilliances and murky shadows than one is able to bear. The atrium, domed, dark, and mysterious, is itself a somber, dramatic, and sometimes humorous museum of Genesis. A beardless Christ stands before the obedient animals of his creation like a trainer demanding their attention; they face him, awaiting his command, tranquil with one another in the peaceable kingdom. Adam and Eve in the right-hand cupola clutch bundles of outsized leaves to hide their shame, Romanesque in their squatness rather than elegantly Byzantine. Abraham moves stiffly through the mosaics, as do Joseph and his brothers. A rickety tower of Babel rises futilely, its structural weakness mocking man's brazen pretensions. Noah heads for the ark, leading a colorful parade of domestic birds, while, inside, the ark is congested with men and beasts. The less-fortunate victims of the Deluge are shown in graphic horror worthy of a Hollywood filmmaker. When the waters recede, Noah releases his dove from a window of the packing-crate-like ark, while off to the right a carrion-feeder pecks at a drowned carcass. And Saint Mark sails toward his shipwreck off Venice, braving the Adriatic in a white-sailed dinghy, as imperturbable as an Eastern potentate, while his crew pulls at the sheeting in the face of rhythmical, regularly spaced waves.

The interior of San Marco gives literal meaning to the words "more so," carrying what we saw and enjoyed in the atrium to a climax so elaborate, so defiantly opulent and overdone as to make one feel that one had swallowed a fur. Heavy chandeliers swing from remote, shadowed domes ninety feet above. Mosaics glisten mysteriously in rainbow hues against gold backgrounds. A handsome icon-laden screen (iconostasis) separates the altar from its stadium-size nave. Pulpits and paintings, flickering votive lights and banks of candles, faint reminiscences of long-spent incense, and floor patterns like sumptuous echoes of Oriental rugs—all conspire to create a world as intoxicating as the smell of jasmine, as visually unexpected as a dream. God is here again and again watching, as it were, the Passion and Resurrection of his Son, the adoration of his immaculate consort, and the ministrations of his angels. Pictorializations from the New and Old Testaments give added meaning to the Word, and fanciful flowers, beasts, and birds augment it all in a kind of visual music. Nothing can equal the inside of San Marco, and that is not even to mention the treasury, a large part of it made up of booty from that shameful Christian-against-Christian outrage, the 1204 sack of Constantinople.

The most significant of all the precious items in San Marco is undoubtedly the Pala d'Oro, a coruscating reredos (altar screen) emblazoned with eighty enamels, gold and jewels and semi-precious stones to the tune of roughly 1300 pearls, 400 garnets, 90 amethysts and 300 emeralds. It is impossible to date precisely. While the Pala d'Oro would give pause to the most heavily jewel-encrusted dowager, it is the quickest road to humility. The central Christ figure, enameled, with gold hands and down-turned mouth and holding a bejeweled Book of Life, is an awesome presence, his eyes evasive but nonetheless severe. His halo is heavy with pearls and precious stones, and he is surrounded by jewels, not because they are symbolically or dogmatically meaningful, but because they are gorgeous. If all this sounds pretentiously glitzy, it is not. Man, with his limited comprehension of divine majesty, has no alternative but to turn to earthly wealth, to precious stones and metals. And on occasion how magnificently he makes that turn!

The two choir lofts, one under each of the domes at the ends of the two transepts, are distinctive features of the interior arrangement of San Marco, devices to be exploited by imaginative composer Giovanni Gabrieli who, in the sixteenth and seventeenth centuries, was choirmaster and musical director of the church. He wrote music making capital of these two balconies facing one another across the nave. By utilizing two choirs, two orchestras, two brass choirs—almost always two—Gabrieli caused them to sing toward one another, sometimes in unison, sometimes in oppositional dialogue, answering, even echoing one another, to overwhelm the congregation with trumpeting music and heavenly chorales. Even today, to generations accustomed to stereophonic sound, Gabrieli's music seems at one with the elaborate ornateness of San Marco. No instrumental praise to God and his heavenly court is more jubilant, no master chorale more richly textured or more apt.

Guidebooks do not do justice to Venice; there are, and always were, simply too many things to see there, the very face of the city itself being first on the list. The animated, colorful Grand Canal is a logical focal point, with its Ponte di Rialto, its lace-like Ca'd'Oro, numerous Renaissance palaces, the Accademia, and at the mouth of the canal, Longhena's Santa Maria della Salute. There is the majestically picturesque San Giorgio Maggiore, for the most part by Palladio, perched improbably on its little island on the toe end of the Giudecca. Who can forget the Bridge of Sighs—principal subject matter of so many bad paintings? It arches the narrow canal between the Doge's Palace and the prison, as depressing a monument to man's inhumanity to man as this author has had the misfortune to see. There are the quays, the churches, the markets, and one of the most beautiful outside staircases in the world (and that includes Francois I's famous decorated spiral stairs at the Château de Blois)—the spiral stairway of the Palazzo Contarini. And what about the grumbling vaporetti (water buses) always jammed to their gunwales, and the gondolas, the shops, and the restaurants? And not to worry about the wine; it is almost all excellent and all of it, of course, from the mainland. As part of all this, one must not forget Harry's Bar.

Venetian painting during its Renaissance heyday was famous for color and poetic light. How could the artists ignore all that shimmer and sparkle? Venice glories in endless works by Titian (he lived to be ninety-nine—and even then it took the plague to carry him off!), Veronese, the Bellinis, the mystical and sublime Giorgione, Carpaccio, Tintoretto, Tiepolo, Guardi, and Canaletto. As a final luxury no one who goes to Venice should miss a visit to the home of the late Peggy Guggenheim, a moneyed American with an impeccable taste for contemporary art that many another moneyed American should envy.

If Frederick responded at all like the majority of tourists through the ages, his stay in Venice was pleasant, relaxing, and too short. True, the Venetians maintained a steadily guarded mien, not wanting to do anything that would jeopardize their position in relation to the Lombard League. As far as Venice was concerned, Frederick was already powerful enough. The Most Serene Republic wanted elbow room to be free to join his enemies if it so desired. Even Frederick's commissioning of a new gold crown from a Venetian craftsman caused no end of agonizing until it was made manifestly clear that the transaction was a private matter, undertaken without official instigation or profit. But that was window trimming. We can be sure the Venetians made their profit. That was the way they were. Salimbene opined that they were greedy and stubborn.

> They would gladly subdue the whole world to themselves if they could; and they treat boorishly the merchants who go to them, both by selling dear, and by taking tolls in divers places in their district from the same persons at the same time. And if any merchant carries his goods thither for sale he may not bring them back with him: nay, but he must needs sell them there. . . . [4]

Frederick left rich offerings at the shrine of Venice's patron saint, and in return he received a splinter of the True Cross, which, with typical disregard, he passed on to Hermann von Salza. By the end of March he was in Aquileia, awaiting the arrival of his son who, according to imperial instructions, was to be housed in a separate city entirely—Cividale del Friuli. It was as though he did not want Henry near him. Perhaps separate cities would best dispatch that message to his indiscreet son.

It is only a short distance from Venice to Aquileia, a principal city of the ancient Roman Empire, named, according to legend, when an eagle (*aquila*) hovered overhead while the perimeter of the town was being furrowed with a plow. Though much cut down in size today, Aquileia will be remembered as a thriving Roman city of between three hundred thousand and five hundred thousand inhabitants to which Saint Mark was traveling when he was shipwrecked on an island in the lagoon that would one day give rise to the city of Venice. (It was after that shipwreck, when Mark was stepping ashore all dripping and breathless, that an angel is alleged to have appeared to him with the message, "Peace be to thee, Mark, my Evangelist," the motto that the Venetians adopted as their own, and that is emblazoned on countless representations of the Lion of Saint Mark that one sees around the world. During the Middle Ages Aquileia was the seat of the patriarchate, which had become increasingly powerful since its foundation in the seventh century. It will be remembered that one of its patriarchs had drawn down the tight-lipped ire of Pope Urban III for having performed the wedding ceremony of Frederick's mother and father, as well as crowning them with the iron cross of Lombardy. By Frederick's day ancient Aquileia had all but vanished, thanks to the depredations of Attila, that most unattractive of all Huns.

The refreshingly simple cathedral, the sole remains of Aquileia's medieval magnificence, which Frederick must have visited for the Easter services in 1232, had been built in the eleventh century by one Patriarch Poppo to replace a fourth-century basilica destroyed by Attila. The only reminder of that earlier building is a fine expanse of inlaid floor illustrating edifying stories for the early Christians, such as the eternal

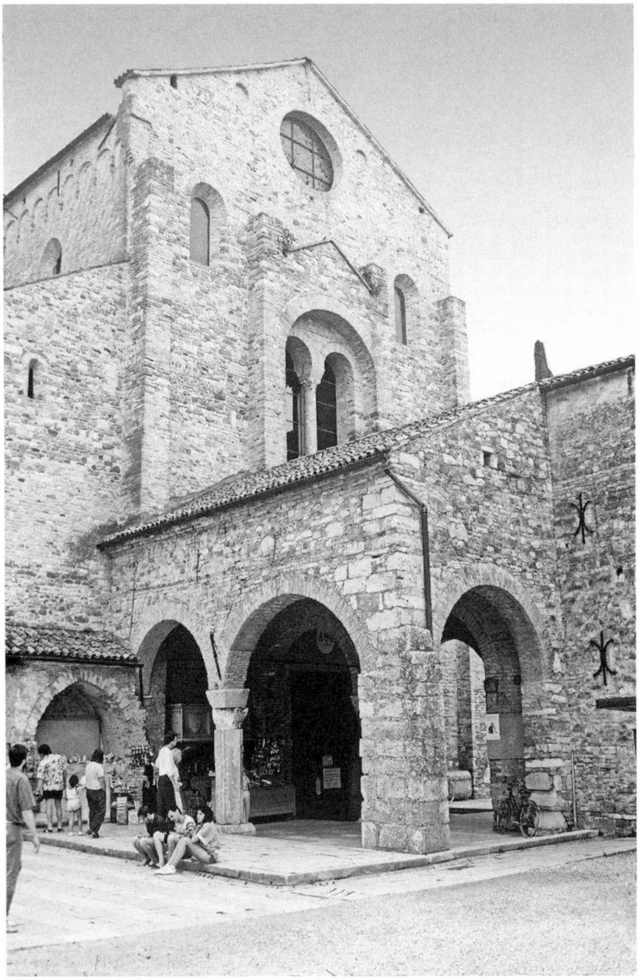

Acquileia Cathedral, Italy

struggles between the Church and wayward heretics (symbolized by a graphic contest between a cock and a tortoise), the Good Shepherd, and a mysterious rendition of Jonah fishing among a motley group of ugly little goblins. Archbishop Poppo's eleventh-century building is also laid out on a basilica plan, basically Romanesque in style, with a raised choir. Its capitals are especially striking, though the arches between them are Gothic and, together with the carinate (keel-shaped) ceiling, are products of the reconstruction following an earthquake in 1348. There are frescoes from the twelfth century, and those in the crypt feature the lives of Christ, Mary, and saints Mark (for obvious

Loculus, Acquileia Cathedral, Italy

reasons) and Ermagora (for obscure reasons). A fascinating touch is the crypt Crucifixion: while Christ's mother helps with the deposition of her Son's body, another of the Marys puts her hand over the eyes of one presumed to be the Magdalene to prevent her from seeing the gruesome sight. How like the twelfth century! An age as familiar with daily horror as any before or after could still view their adored religious personages as people who, like everyone else, lived lives of joy, love, hate, death, despair—and horror. In the church may be seen representations of the imperial family of Conrad II (c. 990–1039), the founder of the Salian dynasty.

There is a small structure inside Aquileia cathedral, a round stone building known as a "loculus," symbolic of the Holy Sepulcher in Jerusalem and used for the enactment of Easter ceremonies until 1595. Interesting but unattractive, it stands in the left aisle, the top of its circular wall acting as a base for a ring of stubby columns that support the conical roof. The use of circular structures to suggest the Holy Sepulcher was widespread during the Middle Ages. The Temple and Saint John's Priory Church, both in London, as well as several others, such as the chapel at Ludlow Castle, were meant to symbolize by imitation the sepulcher, for the devout the next best thing to making a pilgrimage with hordes of greedy, graffiti-scratching pilgrims, who could go most modern tourists one better by sometimes carrying hammers and chisels in their luggage. The loculus must have been used as an ersatz Holy Sepulcher when Frederick attended Mass in the cathedral on Easter morning. (Incidentally, anyone who goes as far as Aquileia should drive a few kilometers farther to see the tiny sixth-century cathedral in the colorful resort town of Grado.)

Smoldering away in Cividale del Friuli, King Henry VII did not have nearly as cosmopolitan a city to enjoy during his Easter stay in Italy, and the cathedral at which he no doubt heard Mass is no longer in existence. He might have seen the Oratory of the Convent of Santa Maria in Valle (il "Tempietto"), which stems from the eighth century—though Henry does not strike one as the kind who would enjoy that type of thing. Its resounding fame rests in six stucco relief figures high on the western wall, three to either side of an empty floral-ornamented niche, the ensemble a precious example of Lombard decorative art. The six figures stand in attitudes of absolute motionlessness reminiscent of Ravenna's Sant'Apollinare Nuovo, though the hands of the two center figures want to convey a certain stilted animation. Their robes are carved in long lines depicting decorative folds and in two instances a kind of embroidered surface ornamentation. Utterly classic in their timelessness, they reflect a rich appreciation of the Eastern arts, especially of Byzantium. With feet planted firmly on a supporting ledge, they express an eternity in a weightiness almost too heavy for the faded eighth-century frescoes and the elaborately fruit-rimmed arch below. They are expressive of the last period of Lombard prosperity and might.

Cividale's cathedral treasury contains the marble Ratchis altar, set up by a king of remarkable taste whose name has been attached to the title of the altar itself. Between 744 and 749 the king commissioned one of the finest examples of Lombard figurative art in the Friuli area. A tender, shallow-cut relief depicts the visit of Mary to her cousin Elizabeth, the two figures impossible to differentiate but for the cross engraved on the forehead of the one presumed to be Mary. The interlocked, comically dwarfish bodies, with their staring eyes, turned-down mouths, and clumsy companionship enact, nevertheless, eloquent gestures expressing deep emotional feeling. Another panel on the Ratchis altar depicts Christ in Majesty, enclosed in a palm-bordered mandorla supported by

Tempietto, Cividale del Friuli, Italy

Ratchis Altar, Cividale del Friuli, Italy

four highly stylized angels with enormous hands. A variety of rosette and cross decorations are scattered throughout the spaces of the composition along with, at the top, just over the head of the central figure, the approving hand of God the Father. It is a thoroughly delightful composition, with the four supporting angels anchored to the side borders as though they are standing horizontally rather than vertically. Of course, anything is fair in abstract art. And in the heavenly sphere as well.

Anxiously biding his time in Cividale, and not as intelligent a man as one might hope for in a king, Henry was not prepared for the stringent set of demands that were dictated to him from Aquileia; and he had to agree to full compliance before being admitted into the imperial presence. The humiliation of it all stunned him. He was an easygoing man who sang during morning ablutions, according to people who knew him. But this new development changed his easy manner and no doubt took the wind out of his song. In the evening he wept, it was said. A committee of archbishops, the dukes of Saxony, Meran, and Carinthia, and the patriarch of Aquileia took oaths to protect imperial interests and, in the event that the young king did not live up to his agreements, to declare war against him—and this with Henry's signed concurrence. It was to be nothing more than a period of probation. Even more denigrating, Henry was obliged to write a letter to Pope Gregory stating categorically that he would accept his own excommunication if he did not in every way obey his father. This had to be the ultimate put-down of a young man who, like Frederick himself at an even earlier age, wanted only to be independent enough to realize the role he felt he was born to play. He was on the downward path; uninventive and unimaginative as he was, there was no way that he would be able to divert his own plunge to ruin.

When Henry was finally confronted in person, it was not in the spirit of a warm father-son relationship, but rather of an offended, stern, demanding autocrat glaring down from his exalted heights on a wastrel vassal who seemed to be frittering away his and his lord's future. Frederick was angry, angry that his one legitimate son old enough to be involved in dynastic business was bungling the job so badly. Illegitimate Enzo, roughly the same age as Henry, had long ago proven his worth, being an active contributing member of the imperial court, entrusted with any number of important tasks devoted to the familial interests. And there were others of the younger generation of court families and hangers-on who were striving to get ahead, who were shouldering myriad responsibilities in the imperial interest. It was an open-and-shut case to all. Frederick lashed out at Henry of necessity. The young man's foolish policies would have broken the imperium in Germany by pitting the princes against their powerful overlord. As it stood, Frederick had to confirm the ill-conceived concessions that Henry had made to the secular princes after his confrontation with the bishop of Liège. That was enough! Having received lavish gifts from his father—Frederick's misguided way of buying loyalty—Henry and the princes returned to Germany, but only after giving pleasing assurances that they would start immediate preparations to join their overlord next spring in a war aimed at resolving the Lombard question. After his son, the Lombards were next on Frederick's hit list.

It was while Frederick was roving about the Friuli area, setting things to rights, establishing taxes (always taxes!), entertaining and getting to know his deputies better, that he befriended the brothers Ezzelino and Alberigo da Romano, both on the upswing, especially Ezzelino, a terrifying man, a tyrant in every sense. There was nothing restrained about Ezzelino da Romano's lust for naked power. Born the same year as Frederick, he eventually became the most hated and feared man in northeast Italy, though his reputation may largely be a figment of his enemies' imagination. He operated a reign of terror, sometimes even shortchanging the emperor himself. The claim has been made—surely an exaggeration!—that he maintained his power by sacrificing as many as fifty thousand men to his assassins and torturers. The fact that Ezzelino held women in contempt did not prevent Frederick from giving him one of his own daughters, Selvaggia, in marriage, though he had been married several times before. Cruel, proud, and not in the habit of bowing down to others, the Romano brothers were loyal to Frederick—most of the time—largely through self-interest. They would be handy men to have around during Frederick's future reign of fire. To start things rolling they attacked and took the city of Verona, thus assuring an open Brenner Pass to and from Germany.

Frederick needed supporters like the Romano brothers. And there were many just as vice-ridden and cruel, the lot of them no better than criminals, with nothing to recommend them to Frederick but their lack of conscience and their fearless contempt for every moral precept, which implied a willingness to do the imperial dirty work. Despite these associates Frederick nurtured his altruistic dream of a united empire. To realize this daunting ambition he needed loyal followers in both Germany and Italy. But it was not his idea to turn Germany into another Sicily. He did not entertain replacing the hereditary German princes with lay civil servants, jurists, and barons. It did not follow that what worked well for Italy and Sicily would prove satisfactory north of the Alps, where emperors before him had been frustrated by hereditary princes jealously guarding their governing prerogatives. It was not that he needed their wealth, though any emperor worth his salt could always use more money. They had little compared to the brimming coffers of Sicily. He was willing to buy their loyalty, especially since it would mean their helping to bring Lombardy to heel. Constantly aiming at greater independence, the princes saw their own loyalty as a trump card, an opening barter in the game of coaxing increasing benefits from the emperor. And Frederick was willing to play their game if, eventually, Lombardy could be shoehorned into his Italo-Sicilian scheme and the pope made to stick to his business of administering to the spiritual needs of his flock. An untroubled, loyal Germany would help him realize both of these ambitions, as well as his dream of a united empire.

When Frederick confirmed Henry's ill-conceived concessions to the German princes, he agreed to abandon his rights of building fortifications on their territories, as well as his rights of coining money and collecting tolls and taxes. With his abandonment of these jurisdictions, the princes became rulers of very nearly autocratic domains. Obviously the new conditions were bound to work against Frederick's plan of welding Germany into a single state and then attaching it to Italy since princes powerful in their own rights could hardly be expected to show overt interest in the fate of the empire. But for a time they were willing to cooperate and, in the imperial interest as well as their own, to maintain the peace. Frederick might be emperor-king in southern Italy, and he might be recognized as emperor in Germany; but more to the point, in Germany he was first among his peers. Well and good! But the outcome of this new princely independence—and the arrogance that of necessity went with it—could only be disastrous.

About this time Frederick's favorite son, Manfredi, was born to Bianca Lancia of a noble, but impoverished Piedmontese family. Bianca's brother (or uncle, we are not sure which) had long been in Frederick's service as administrator and friend. It will be remembered that Frederick met Manfred Lancia in 1212 when the king-emperor to be was on his way to Germany. Close in age, the two youths had been attracted to one another, and a lasting friendship developed. Manfred Lancia's name pops up on occasion in documents between the years 1218 and 1232 when, it seems, his family migrated to Frederick's court. Thereafter Manfred was much in the thick of things. It must have been through him that Frederick first beheld Bianca, who became his mistress and, in later years, his morganatic wife. We know nothing of the appearance of Bianca or even, for sure, whether she was married to Frederick, though most historians point to a number of conditions to indicate that she was.

Frederick and Bianca's son, Manfredi, was born at Venosa, the abbey and town intended as the mausoleum of Frederick's Hauteville ancestors; Robert Guiscard and several of his brothers were buried there. It is in a beautiful and wild area of southern Italy of which Frederick and the ancient poet, Horace, were especially fond. This was a place of Frederick's personal history; it was fitting that his new son, albeit illegitimate, was born there. As he had seen to Enzo, so would Frederick see to it that both Manfredi and Yolanda's son Conrad would receive proper court training and education in the subjects that the age thought important: the origin and potential perfection of the soul; the nature of the body; the things of the world and the universe; ideas of eternity. And he would insist on his own enthusiasms: literature, science and mathematics, theology and philosophy.

Before dismissing his German princes from Aquileia to their homeland laden with costly gifts, and himself heading for his beloved southern Italy, Frederick had several singular showy triumphs: he had drawn the Burgundian kingdom closer to his sphere so that it would soon for the first time make a not small contribution in his battle against the Lombard League; he had concluded peace talks with King Louis IX (Saint Louis) of France; and he had accepted from the sultan of Damascus a gorgeous, bejeweled, golden planetarium, which was shaped like a tent in which the heavenly bodies moved by means of a concealed mechanism. In return Frederick had delighted the sultan by making gifts of a white peacock and a polar bear, the second causing a sensation in Syria. Frederick's princes had the novel experience of attending a lavish bash that he hosted in honor of the Arab feast of the Hegira, which was, as far as Europe was concerned, a celebration unique to his court. Journeying to Apulia, then, he captured and imprisoned a number of Dalmatian pirates. On the surface things boded well for Frederick, his kingdom, and his empire—if only Henry could be counted on to behave himself, which was doubtful. Then there was always that pope and his Curia!

Chapter Thirteen

My prayers are not worthy,
but do Thou, Good (God), deal kindly
lest I burn in perennial fire.
***Dies Irae*, verse 14**

1232

Everyone—especially the two principals— knew that there was not room enough on the European stage for two actors of such consummate power, contempt, and dedication as Frederick Hohenstaufen and Pope Gregory IX. Nonagenarian Gregory was certainly not going to allow Frederick to usurp Church lands and papal temporal powers, which is exactly what would happen should a docile Lombardy be absorbed into the imperial realm. Frederick had already claimed Lombardy as his; but claiming was one thing, actually wielding his scepter quite another. He still envisioned the Holy Roman Empire as embracing the Church—but only as half of the whole, with the pope confining himself to his churches, convents, monasteries, and ecclesiastical palaces, where he could administer with a free hand for the betterment of men's souls. According to Frederick, secular power struggles, wars, taxes, and earthly justice were better left to lay authorities and their appointees. Each for his own reason, both pope and emperor were convinced that the present mirage of peace was beneficial. Each needed the other. Gregory needed Frederick's sword to protect the Papal States against the secular claims of every pope's habitual enemy, the voraciously land-hungry Roman populace; and Frederick anticipated that to tame the Lombard lion the pope's good graces were necessary. Both of them knew it was a fragile, temporary respite, that flashpoint had to be reached. And when it came, it would result in the termination of the golden day of imperial might and papal sovereignty, in short, the world as both of them knew it. For the moment both emperor and pope could give aid and comfort to the other, and both could benefit and rejoice in the other's discomfort.

Maintaining the centuries-long status quo, Gregory was locked in battle with antagonistic Rome. The citizens, always hankering for their rights, craved territorial expansion into Church lands. The pope, finally, had been forced yet another time to abandon the Eternal City and to cry to Frederick for help. But the emperor was himself locked in an insurrection in Sicily, where citizens were protesting their loss of civil liberties as dictated by his *Liber Augustalis.* Frederick sent his regrets that he could not personally lead his troops in defense of papal interests; but he could, and did, call on his Burgundian, Provençal, and German knights to move, which, even though it would take them a long time to get organized, was a gesture to make him look good in the eyes of Christendom. At least the pope had no grounds for complaint. Gregory reciprocated with a gesture about as meaningless; he assured Frederick that he would do everything in his power to back him vis-à-vis son Henry, though he personally would have liked nothing better than to see the two of them at loggerheads and the northern unity crumbling. To put a gloss on the situation, Gregory offered once again to act as mediator between Frederick and the hostile Lombards, to which—and one wonders why, considering the distinct lack of success of Gregory's last similar offer—Frederick responded by sending an embassy of his grand justiciar, Henry of Morra, along with Pier delle Vigne to the papal court. As before, little came of it.

In Outremer the situation was dark and disintegrating at an alarming clip, not because of Christian-Muslim enmity, but rather because of Christians lashing out at Christians. John of Ibelin, Frederick's appointed administrator of Cyprus, still smarting over his emperor's highhandedness four years before, had revolted against the imperial marshal of Palestine, Richard Filangieri. To show his good faith to Frederick, Gregory summarily deposed Patriarch Gerold of Jerusalem for having aided John. Then Hermann von Salza was sent to Outremer to staunch the wound, but the situation continued to deteriorate. Within the year Cyprus was lost as an imperial fief.

Frederick and Gregory could console themselves that, though each had given support to the other, neither had put the brakes on the other's decline. The Romans were happy that their ally, Frederick, had managed to wriggle out of a personal attack on them and their city in the name of the Holy Father; the pope was content that he had been able to give appearances of supporting imperial ambitions; and Frederick was comfortable in the knowledge that in the future he would be able to point out that he had ordered imperial troops to the papal defense, more impressive since it was the first time the Burgundians had been called up by the emperor. With an outward picture of harmony between emperor and pope—even the Romans were enjoying an atypical tranquility—the tendency was to forget Lombardy, the third corner of the troublesome triangle and the crux of the papal-imperial antagonism. But Frederick hadn't forgotten.

Now was the time to get the Lombards into line if it was to be done at all. Frederick begged the pope to call them to account for their past disloyalties and to be as severe on them as he himself had always been with heretics. Of course Frederick's definition of "heretics" included both those who were rebels against the empire as well as those disloyal to the Church. Gregory's definition concerned only the Church. Frederick might see the Lombard rebels as heretics, but Gregory regarded them warmly as blocks to imperial machinations to unite northern Europe and southern Italy. It was a no-win situation for the cities of northern Italy. If a town stood by Frederick, as Verona was forced to do at the behest of Ezzelino da Romano, it fell under papal interdict. If a city proclaimed its allegiance to papal wishes, it would be heretical in Frederick's cynical eyes. So any city that failed to accommodate itself either to the papal or the imperial will was branded heretic. And in both cases the city's action was regarded as rebellion against the divine will. It was abundantly clear that nothing but the direst situation could ever bring the two parties to mutual accommodation on this sorest of all problems. The Lombard League might be a blessing to Gregory IX, but it was only a nest of heretics within his state according to Frederick. He demanded unconditional obedience from these rebels; Gregory needed to do everything in his power to thwart such submission.

With all Frederick's talk and concern about heretics, one cannot help but wonder whether he understood that in his transalpine imperium a genuine inquisition was starting to roll, and with the admitted sanction of Pope Gregory. Conrad of Marburg, the most zealous of all inquisitors in Germany, was running amok in the name of the Church. He was a man totally vicious and absolutely indiscriminate in his acceptance of accusatory evidence. Without even questioning the accused, he would demand complete confession. If the frightened "heretic" protested his innocence, he was carted off to the stake, assured by the slim comfort that if he really was innocent, he would wear a martyr's crown in heaven. It is not surprising to learn that Conrad and one of his colleagues were murdered in 1233.

Considering the widespread unrest, it is easy to understand, even sympathize with, Frederick's preoccupation with building fortresses, ever enlarging and modifying existing ones, and his apparent disinterest in any other kind of architecture but for the occasional pleasure dome. Despite a lust for building he founded no abbeys, no convents, and only one cathedral—and that in connection with a whole town that he established. One of his Sicilian officials, Thomas of Gaeta, a trusted man who had been part of numerous missions to the papal court, had harped on Frederick for years to play the role of disseminator of the faith by building abbeys and churches; better churches and cloisters than fortresses, hunting lodges, and castles, he claimed to deaf imperial ears. But this year Thomas's message apparently sank in, the result being the cathedral at Altamura, the single religious edifice for which Frederick could claim credit.

Although sections of very ancient walls have been found, little else remains of an Altamura before Frederick's time. The old city had been destroyed in the ninth century by Saracen marauders and the population killed, scattered, or taken into slavery. It was on the site of the derelict ruins, about twenty-eight miles southwest of Bari and sixteen hundred feet above sea level, that Frederick decided to build his city and his cathedral. The protective walls of Frederick's Altamura rest on foundations of megalithic walls of a city of unknown name and probably encompassed the smallest possible perimeter. Built principally for protection, the city was limited by the very valid consideration of money but commonly evaluated by one's ability to get into it, rather than out.

One approaches cathedrals of Apulia humbly, through narrow, twisting streets of quarters that seem as old as time. The Porta di Bari is the best way into Altamura for it opens directly into the old quarter, whose streets lead to the cathedral. This is Frederick country, the Altamura of backstreets easy to get lost in. Sunlight is strong, stabbing through shadows correspondingly heavy, concealing, secretive. Always there are the *biricchini*—children of the streets—who regard the tourists as prey to be exploited as sources of never-ending cash or as funds of knowledge about unheard-of and exotic places. If they are sometimes indescribably dirty, they still boast the widest grins of the Mediterranean. And if they are bothersome, then that is just part of the game. Italian towns are noisy with shouts, cries, laughter, murmurs, groans. Then there is the wonderful quiet of evening or early morning. Outside stairs, balconies, arches, tunnels add to the thrills of discovery, pleasures only somewhat mitigated by the occasional native whose hostile stare sends the chilly message that you are invading private turf. There are little carvings all over town on doors, lintels, and walls, the kinds of things you see so often in Bari—angels' faces, flowers, small animals, stars. There may be a dearth of places to eat, but there is probably still a good hotel with a restaurant serving good pasta and dispensing loads of good cheer.

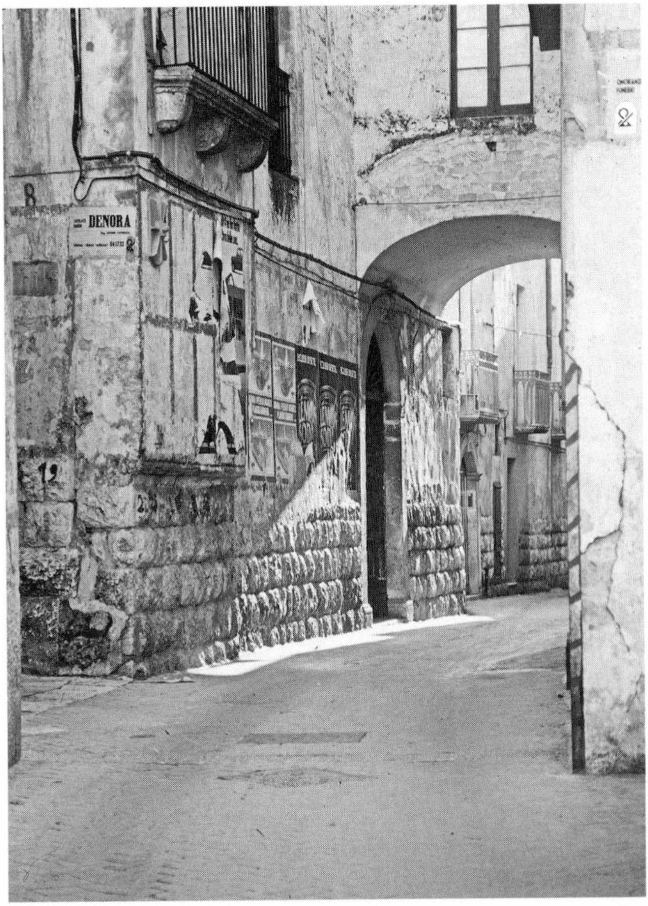

Street, Altamura, Italy

The church that one finally stumbles upon in Altamura is an anomaly, obviously Romanesque at first glance, but with two towers topped by baroque "cushion domes" and peaked by not very attractive spires. Changes have been wrought on Frederick's church, the most extensive rebuilding having taken place after an earthquake in the fourteenth century. There were sixteenth-century modifications, and then those strange domes and pinnacles of the seventeenth. The central porch of the west end, facing on the Via Federico II di Svevia, is the finest part of the church, with its twin pairs of columns resting on the backs of twin lions, a usual Italian device. The main portal is arched by scenes from the life of Christ, starting above the Virgin of the Annunciation on the right and ending over the angel of the Annunciation on the left. Mary is smiling wistfully, shyly in Gabriel's commanding presence and sits with her arms modestly folded over her breast. A graphic Last Supper acts as a lintel over the door, with John kissing Jesus and with all manner of food on a table tilted so that we can see what is being served. The inside is a horror of pink and beige marble and baroque ornamentation that tells us nothing about Frederick or his century. But there are few greater pleasures than to sit on the steps of the cathedral porch at Altamura and, well, just watch and hear the world go by.

1233

Almost without warning it looked as though luck had turned in Gregory IX's direction with a spontaneous arising in northern and central Italy that has been likened to a natural upheaval. It seemed that the entire peninsula was going to embrace the Church as the only way to earthly and heavenly salvation. The "Great Alleluia" was a sudden eruption, an explosion, the result of years of subsurface festering, that received some impetus from Frederick himself when his self-coronation claims in Jerusalem that he had come as God's chosen, as the salvation of the secular world, were circulated through Europe. The revivalist momentum was achieved also through the predictions and proclamations of Abbot Joachim of Flora, he who had envisioned such a dire future for the infant Frederick. His early-century apocalyptic warnings of the destruction of the world and the Last Judgment were awesome and fearful grist for the mill of human superstitious imaginations, sufficient to hold any man in thrall—at least through another century until Dante's *Divine Comedy*. The more fearful portions of Old Testament Jeremiah, Daniel, and Isaiah were reinterpreted along with the apocryphal visions of Saint John's Revelation. All was lost unless pathetic, groveling humankind performed proper penance to guarantee a blissful afterlife. This fear- and guilt-laden doctrine became the key to earthly life and, by extension, the starting point of the Dominican inquisitorial persecutions in northern Italy, encouraged with zest by Gregory, who thus branded himself as "the pope of the inquisition."[1] So Pope Gregory, an accomplished canon lawyer and brilliant promulgator of Church rights, could credit himself with that travesty of Christianity.

With all their power and the fear engendered by habitual heresy hunting, the Dominicans found their position in the world of the cloister untenable, especially when they saw the success of the Franciscans. Apparently disregarding the sympathetic friendship of Francis and Dominic, the Dominicans could not but envy their competitors for souls, especially since Francis had been canonized five years ago. And to make matters worse, Anthony of Padua, another Franciscan, had already been beatified, a giant step on his way to sainthood. Any self-respecting Dominican would hope and pray for at least equal status for his order's founding father. The bishop of Modena, a close friend of the Dominican preachers, as much as admonished them to get moving; since the Franciscans had a saint, they too should have one. With the bishop's call to establish a proper saint, with Frederick's coronation claim of fulfillment, with Francis Bernardone's message of holy penance and peace, and with Joachim of Flora's message of inevitable doom echoing down the years, the time was ripe for the Great Alleluia. It was also time for the bandwagon to gather its musicians.

Among the most flamboyant was Benedict of Parma, "Brother of the Horn," a vagabond strongly resembling John the Baptist in appearance. He went about the countryside trumpeting the faithful to church. There were others, Franciscans and Dominicans alike, who could outshine even the melodramatic Benedict. Giacomo of Reggio, who held a meeting between Calerno and Sant'Ilario, both immediately northwest of Reggio Emilia on the road to Parma, drew a mighty multitude from the surrounding land. There was Brother Leo of Milan, a famous preacher and a persecutor and confuter of heretics. There was Brother Gerard of Modena, who had been a friend of Francis. Giovanni da Vicenza, preaching in Bologna, was supposedly heard telepathically by Brother Gerard, who was standing in the Piazza Comunale in Parma. According to Matthew Paris, a Franciscan friar, Giovanni da Vicenza, could command eagles to stop in mid-flight and could walk across rivers without wetting his feet. And another, Guido Bonatti, self-proclaimed philosopher of Forlì, an astrologer alleged to be the wisest man in Italy, complained that he was never able to locate a single one of the eighteen men said to have been brought back from the dead by Giovanni. Dante relegates Guido to hell near Michael Scott, with the magicians and soothsayers and assorted mountebanks. For a while Giovanni da Vicenza met with incredible success, on one occasion on a plain near Verona, supposedly attracting over four hundred thousand faithful (surely exaggerated!) to hear him and to receive his blessing. Friar Giovanni and his sympathizing Franciscans were such a travesty on the thought and holy work of Francis Bernardone that one wonders how the order managed to survive the internal rot. Even such a brute as Ezzelino da Romano could not stand against Giovanni's appeal and was rumored to have agreed to his own demotion with tears in his eyes, misconstrued by the onlookers to have been tears of altruistic emotion.

Verona was for a time out of Frederick's sphere of influence, and the Brenner Pass to his northern empire was closed to him. Even so, the two principals, Francis and Frederick, would not have been hard put to admit that their aims had much in common: the restoration of the Church to the role of nonmoneyed shepherd of souls. Unaccustomed to secular power, Friar Giovanni abused his ducal privileges to such a degree that he was finally cast into prison, to emerge discredited, mad, and alone in his obscure world. One of the few cogent things that Brother Giovanni did was to support the movement to canonize Dominic Guzman, which event took place in 1234, the year after the Great Alleluia had died. It was that short lived.

No one gained from the Alleluia hysteria but Gregory IX, and only temporarily at that. Certainly Frederick, ruthlessly stamping out the Sicilian rebellion against his *Liber Augustalis,* did not. The only positive thing he could say about the revivalist movement was that it bypassed his Sicilian kingdom, allowing him a brief respite from imperial concerns to care for royal business in the southern realm and leaving his northern subjects to their business of fasting, flagellation, guilt enjoyment, and penance. To Frederick's detriment peace became so strong a watchword during the year 1233 that the on-again off-again Romans convinced themselves that they should accommodate their spiritual leader and invited him back to the Eternal City. Pope Gregory leaped at the chance, realizing that for the present there was no need for further overtures to his nemesis in Sicily.

The papal-imperial balance of power was restored when the Great Alleluia ground to an abrupt halt. Four days after an enormous conclave presided over by John of Vicenza, still riding high, outright warfare among the cities of Lombardy and the Treviso March restored the violent status quo. So much for the "peace" of the Great Alleluia. Before long endemic disorder was restored, as John of Vicenza languished in prison, the Romans reverted to their papal antagonisms, and the pope and Frederick could get back to their charade.

Through the rise and collapse of the Great Alleluia, the emperor, true to his bent, was more concerned with the Sicilian rebellion, seeing it as a sacrilegious assault on his divine office. For all his idealism there was a depth of cruelty in Frederick's heart for any form of insubordination. In this instance he showed himself merciless and treacherous, going so far as to renege on a promise of safe conduct to a crowd of trusting citizens who had taken refuge in a church. Invoking the anti-heresy laws of his own Constitutions of Melfi, he burned the rebels at the stake, except for the ringleaders who somehow wriggled free, escaping to Malta where they were later rounded up and hanged. The story of this treachery is one of the major blights on the reputation of the man who, for the most part, seems fair, sometimes forgiving. Other citizens suffered horrors of equal magnitude. The inhabitants of Centorbi, Traina, Capizzi, and Monte Albona saw their cities leveled, while they were resettled in the new city of Augusta, nineteen miles north of Syracuse.

Augusta Castle is centered by a courtyard, and the enjoyment of its bulky mass and strength is impossible to the casual viewer and left to the inmates of the prison who are currently housed therein. The strategic importance of the island, connected to the mainland by a bridge, was recognized by later Aragonese rulers, who fortified it still further. And it was from Augusta that the fleet of the Holy League sailed forth to defeat the Turks in the Battle of Lepanto in 1571, the battle that broke their hold on the western Mediterranean. The town has been badly treated by time, an earthquake in 1693, and allied bombing during World War II.

Few men in history have been such avid castle builders as Frederick Hohenstaufen—whether for protection (and it must be remembered that castles, even though people lived in them, were fundamentally of a defensive nature) or merely to impress rebellious subjects is immaterial. It must have galled his subjects to see money that had been extracted from them in the form of taxes used on projects that were obviously designed to keep them in line. In any case defensive construction was enough in evidence during Frederick's reign to prompt Thomas of Gaeta to again lecture his master that it would be better for him to look after the poor and to raise more buildings that would be pleasing to God, as did his Norman forerunners, even in the midst of wars.

Despite Thomas of Gaeta's exhortations, castle life was not all it is cracked up to be, and certainly not a bit the life that romantic novelists, movie makers, and poets make it. Castles, especially in northern Europe, were cold and drafty. Cisterns and water pipes suggest that the ultimate luxury of bathrooms may have had a place there. A castle worthy of the name might have had its own well, lead piping, bathtub, and latrine. The upper class was not indifferent to cleanliness. It is true that comfort was sacrificed for security, and to be "alone" was beyond even wishful thinking, what with armed guards clanking about, pages, priests, officials demanding attention, servants, dogs, children, and just hangers-on bustling in and out. Life in Frederick's castles may have been stimulating to the men whom he drew around his person. But think of the life of his womenfolk!—his queens and daughters, hoping for the attention they seldom received, pining for his favors and love, administering the household. And that was it. In a world where books and nighttime entertainment were rarities, where men preferred male company except in the bedroom—or, in Frederick's case, in the harem—any visitor to the castle, especially itinerant actors and musicians, troubadours, poets, acrobats, even favor seekers and just plain vagabonds—the latter sometimes with fascinating tales to tell of exotic places—would be welcomed and treated royally.

It was the woman's place to oversee the kitchen, where food was plentiful, if somewhat on the plain side until after the crusades when divers condiments and spices were introduced into Europe from the East. Some foreign foods had been imported at even earlier dates. Originating in Asia, for example, the artichoke may have been introduced into Sicily by the Saracens during the first millennium. Modern Sicilians still prepare artichokes—unlike the typically large American variety, these are small globes that are deliciously tender and eaten choke and all—the way the ancients probably prepared them. After pounding the vegetable lightly, head down, on a hard surface to spread the petals a bit, olive oil heavily laced with garlic and pepper is drizzled over it. The whole is placed directly on a wood fire and cooked and turned until heated through. The eater may reek of garlic, but at least a delicacy of indescribable *buon gusto* has been enjoyed—no, experienced. Food during the Middle Ages was cooked over charcoal or open flames and was, for the most part, healthful, consisting of the usual vegetables and meats, produced or hunted locally, but not totally without risk. Berthold of Ratisbon, who in 1233 was about thirteen and moving toward a life as a popular preaching Franciscan, singled out food providers at least three times as among the most accomplished swindlers of the age. A sterling example of sharpers, he proclaimed,

> are such as sell meat and drink, which no man can disregard. . . . If thou offerest measly or rotten flesh that thou hast kept so long until it be corrupt, then art thou guilty perchance of one man's life, perchance of ten. Or if thou offerest flesh that was unwholesome before the slaughter, or unripe of age, which thou knowest well and yet givest it for sale, so that folk eat it . . . thou art guilty of the blood of these folk. . . . So also do certain others betray folk with corrupt wine or mouldy beer . . . or mix water with the wine.[2]

For lack of something better to do as well as to keep warm, castle dwellers went to bed sometimes at sundown, sleeping nude and between furs. Beds were often high enough off the floor to need steps, this to protect against drafts. The odor of the stable was everywhere, mingled with the acrid smell of tanning leather and sweat. The castle that Frederick built at Augusta, and that gave rise to the new city around it, is situated on an island vaguely resembling the old quarter island of Ortygia at Syracuse and is probably the site of Xiphonia, a center for the production of a fragrant honey extolled by ancient poets. Augusta Castle was the largest of Frederick's Sicilian buildings and indicates even today that comfort was at least a consideration in its design. Only now and then was there a garden within the castle precinct, for enjoyment as well as for producing table fare.

Frederick must have realized that he was scratching a sore wound in quelling Sicilian unrest. If the northerners on the mainland objected to autocratic put-down, then certainly the southerners could be counted on to do the same in spades. No country has been so grossly mistreated as Sicily, an object for conquest since remotely ancient days, a land to be bled, a highway for predatory armies. The Phoenicians, those traders par excellence of the ancient world, set up commercial outposts there. Sometime-altruistic Greeks and always-ambitious Carthaginians had colonized the island long before the Romans. They had fought over it, governed and misgoverned it. Tyrants had ravaged it. The Romans themselves regarded their poor southern peninsula and island as undesirable, a backwoods, less than provincial—as do many moderns. After the Romans, barbarians from the north, Vandals and Goths, plundered its treasures. Popes, emperors, and kings coveted it. Pirates always infested the place. And it has been thus down through the ages, even to our own, making Giuseppe Lampedusa's novel, *The Leopard,* not unrealistic, but in fact one of the most accurate and classic assessments of Sicily's unhappy predicament. Harsh measures aside, Frederick's heart was always in his southern kingdom, and he was sincere in his desire to better the lot of his people, as were his Norman ancestors. But Frederick and his forebears were the exceptions.

Frederick looked on Sicilian peasants with a special toleration. Had they not proven themselves when he, as a child, wandered the tangled Palermitan streets? He realized now that his methods of putting down insurrection were not productive of a successful and prosperous rule and could almost certainly frustrate what he saw as his divine mission in life—the establishment of universal law. The ideal handling of the problem would be to stave off rebellion in the first place. By the end of this year, he was publishing edicts to prevent the recurrence of uprisings, one of the most curious being a prohibition on Sicilians marrying foreigners, curious in that his well-known liberality would seem to contradict the inherent prejudice of such a law. This particular law was promulgated in December, during his court in Syracuse, that boomtown set up by the ancient Greeks on the easily defensible Ortygia Island. Partly because of its advantageous situation Syracuse developed into the most intellectually, culturally, and financially active city of pre-Roman Sicily. As all cities must, Syracuse experienced doldrums after her moment of greatness, but by Frederick's day she was once more "in the chips" and enjoying a lively trade with North Africa and the eastern Mediterranean.

We have no way of knowing where Frederick bedded down when he held court in Syracuse since his Castello Maniace, which was then being built, could not be occupied until after 1239. Its commonly used name would seem to commemorate the eleventh-century Byzantine general, George Maniakes, who built a fortification there, a position shrewdly chosen for its defensive advantage on the extreme end of a spit of land jutting southward from the old-city island of Ortygia. Rectangular, with cylindrical towers on the four corners, Frederick's castle is of smooth stone blocks. The towers, convincingly strong and dissuasive of any form of rebellion, smack of Hohenstaufen energy and determination to bring about an envisioned better world. As in most of Frederick's Sicilian buildings, there is evidence of the coming French Gothic style. The main gate is outlined by a pointed arch, flanked by columns of red Brescia marble bearing carved lions. Stone corbels project from the wall to either side of the Gothic opening; at one time they acted as perches for two stunning Hellenistic bronze rams, one of which is on display in the National Archeological Museum in Palermo, magnificent in its virtuoso textural representations of flesh, horns, fur, and hooves. A masterpiece of realism it is, with its head turned, one leg delicately crooked, and its mouth open. One can almost hear a soprano bleat—a complaint or greeting, whatever was intended.

Inside, the Castello Maniace offers little to the seeker of Sicilian imperial lore. Yet the amenities that Frederick insisted upon are recognizable. The fireplace is there, flanked by brackets that at one time perhaps held treasures of classical antiquity, articles that Frederick—pre-Renaissance man that he was—always insisted on gathering. There are handsomely carved pilasters, with capitals in the forms of flowers and ferns. The rooms in the four towers have vaulted ceilings with lion-head corbels and, in one case, a crowned head that may well be a likeness of Frederick himself. So judiciously placed on its narrow land base, the castle commands superb views of the Mediterranean from windows in three directions, a plus in those days of dank and gloomy interiors.

Any openings, regardless of how narrow, that allowed warmth and the brilliant Sicilian sunshine to penetrate nooks and corners, which were dark even in the most clement of seasons, and that afforded glimpses of the bluest of azure-blue seas, would have been welcome architectural features. Permission is needed to enter the castle—though some of us have simply walked in, no questions asked.

Christianity came early to Syracuse, and its first bishop, said to have been a certain Saint Marziano, is remembered there by a crypt in his name. Four Norman columns remain in the crypt, replacements for fourth-century supports that were mutilated during the Islamic occupation. The capitals bear lively post-Norman carvings of the symbols of the evangelists, along with inscriptions from their gospels. Heavy, round arches create a somber atmosphere, a ponderousness that seems almost natural in its cave-like solidity. Their capitals give a welcome moment of refinement, an instant of relief from the brutish, yet lovingly carved stonework—almost a bit of frivolity. Evidence of religious belief, such as the crypt of Saint Marziano, is the best ancient man has to show us. It was his way of offering homage—a loving dirge in stone. Saint Paul is said to have preached in the crypt, which seems doubtful, and local belief holds that Saint Marziano was flogged at one of the columns in the northeast section of the crypt. On the same property are the Catacombs of San Giovanni (fourth century), second only to those in Rome. While the slowly self-extinguishing Great Alleluia preoccupied the north, Frederick moved about his island domain, certainly stopping at Catania for a look at its castle, which he was modifying, and which had once been occupied by Tancred of Lecce, the last, ill-fated Norman king. If any city has undergone a historical trial by fire, it is this baroque-enriched metropolis. In the shadow of lava-spewing Mount Etna, it has time and again been threatened, several times partially invaded, and twice ravaged to the last house by liquid fire.

Always it is the conical mountain that is the dominant presence, the endless views of which at the end of almost every street remind one that Etna is the compelling force and that Catania is in its direct line of fire, an open city as it were. Etna's presence is not a total negative. There are blessings that accrue from every devastating eruption, after the earth has cooled to allow once again its luxurious growth. Catania's oranges are sweeter than any in Sicily, and her grapes hang in pendulous clusters. Flowers abound as on no other mountain slope in Sicily. It seems incredible that the sides of Etna can restore themselves after repeated scorchings both natural and man induced. Roughly half a century before Frederick's coming Catania had been wiped out by earthquakes. It was devastated again in 1197 by Frederick's father when he claimed his imperial rights and again by allied bombers during World War II. Frederick's redoing of the old Norman castle at Catania was more than a remodeling: it was rebuilt as the grim Castello Ursino, square, solid, forbidding, defensively arrogant against squalid Catanian parking congestion, but housing the comfortable municipal museum surrounding a gracious central courtyard.

Of all the cities of Sicily, with the understandable exception of Palermo, Frederick's favorite was Enna, seeming to lie beyond time, and even sound, straddling a rough, sloping hinterland mountain almost three thousand feet high. It is gray—not dark or light gray, just gray—and more silent than most Siculo-Italian towns. The natives are more inward, more to themselves, content to be let alone and semi-isolated in their "navel of Sicily." Even their clothes are somber-hued and more often than not covered by black capes. Enna's children do not seem to laugh as readily as other children do, and the parents, while not hostile—indeed, they can be friendly and considerate—do not smile as openly as Mediterranean people generally seem to do. And if one wants to see a ritual straight out of the Middle Ages, then a visit to Enna on Good Friday is recommended; that is the day when the upward-sloping Via Roma becomes a modern Via Dolorosa, the way to Calvary, with children and black-robed, white-hooded adults, some carrying crosses, some flowers or candles, others censers, wending slowly toward the cathedral in the ultimate Lenten procession. It is a demonstration of belief, of guilt, grief, and expectation for the final glory of the Resurrection. If Enna was anything like this in the thirteenth century, one can understand why it was the favorite Sicilian city of two Frederick IIs—Hohenstaufen and Aragon.

Frederick built an enormous, twenty-towered castle on the highest point of Enna's mountain, overlooking magnificent fertile valleys and even Lake Pergusa, scene of the abduction of Persephone of Grecian myth. It could have caused only wise rethinking on the part of anyone lusting after a particle or two of Frederick's realm, manned as it was by a garrison from Lombardia Minor (southern Italy, hence its name *Castello di Lombardia*), a bunch tough enough to give pause to any would-be enemy. Only six of its towers remain, the most spectacular being the Torre Pisano, but even alone it is enough to allow a strong impression of defensive muscularity though the whole castle was touted as an imperial summer pleasure dome, or at least as luxurious as medieval stone castles would allow. At the end of the thirteenth

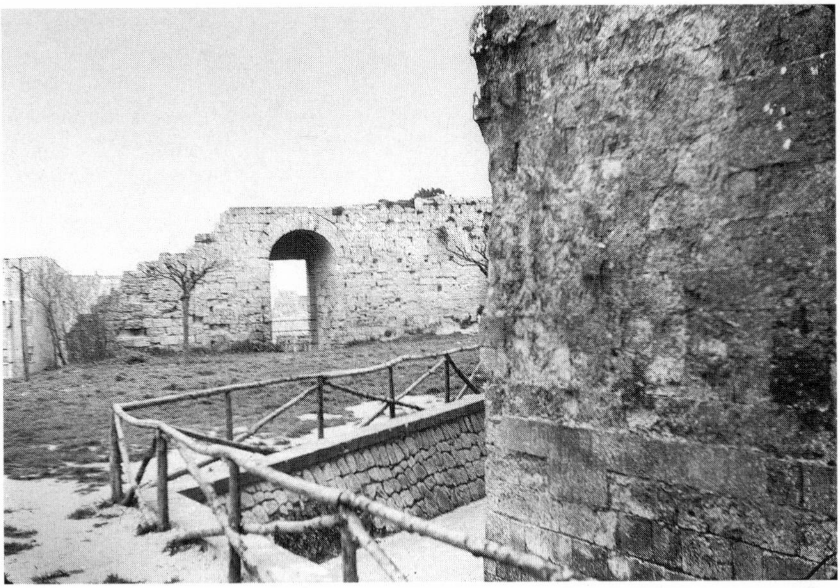

Castello Lombardia, Enna, Sicily

century, after the collapse of the Hohenstaufen dynasty, Frederick II of Aragon claimed Enna as his preferred city, and remodeled the imperial castle into a more salubriously palatial environment, which is, for the most part, what we have in today's remains—not much of Frederick, but historically invigorating.

More indicative of Frederick's full-blooded tastes, the Torre di Federico II is an octagonal tower that vaguely echoes his startling masterpiece, his Castel del Monte in Apulia. The Torre di Federico II, at the opposite end of town from the Castello di Lombardia, was three stories high but is now only two, with the single chamber on each floor linked by a spiral staircase incorporated into the thickness of the outer wall. At one time there was a curtain wall surrounding this vertical keep and enclosing additional buildings for court functions and functionaries. The fortifying wall is mostly gone now, which allows the tower a friendlier attitude, an atmosphere more in keeping with its original purpose as a place of retreat from the cares of governance and from Sicily's intense heat. The mellow ambiance is not lost on Enna's romantically inclined swains and their ladies, who seem to have a predilection for the area. It is a pleasure to imagine Frederick and his court enjoying some of those good barbecued artichokes in such euphoric surroundings.

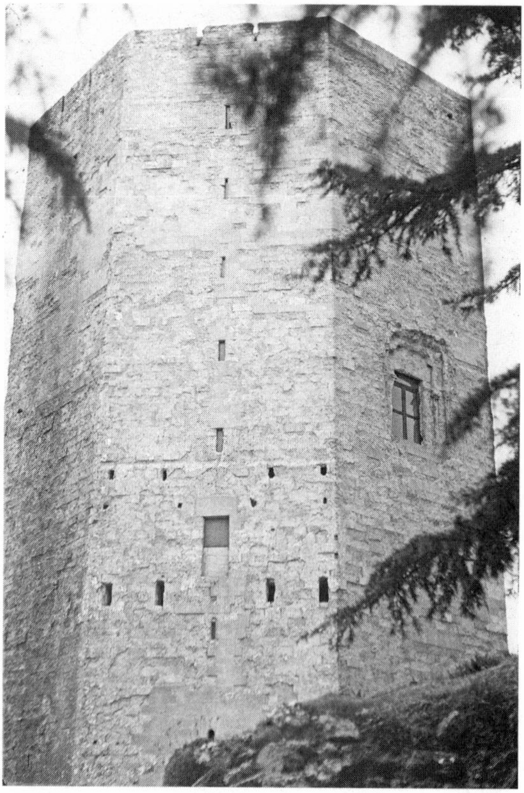

Torre di Federico II, Enna, Sicily

The tower refuge at Enna was another one of Frederick's "places of solace," built after the custom of his Norman predecessors, but instead of being located in one area, as at Palermo, they were scattered across the realm, especially in the eastern part of the island, close enough to one another to allow for convenient stopovers for an emperor and a court ever on the move. Permanent staffs were maintained in all the "places of solace," both in Sicily and on the mainland, which would indicate that they were kept in working order and ready for even unannounced occupancy. Men like Hermann von Salza, Archbishop Bertold of Palermo, and Pier delle Vigne were in the saddle daily going about imperial business. Surely these various castles, shelters, and pleasure houses were open to these confidants of the emperor when they arrived tired, hot, and dirty after a day on the road. Travel was no easier on Frederick, even in robust health as he was, for the roads were atrocious, ankle-deep in mud or clouded by dust. Adroitly spaced castles allowed journeys broken by periods of relaxation, ease, good food, and drink.

1234

It had been a time out of human memory since Europe had experienced such cold. Even the waters of the Venetian lagoon were frozen over. Roman mobs, hungry and desperate to feed their families, attacked the homes of rich cardinals, the Lateran Palace, and other Church properties. In the face of the despairing unrest, the pope was forced to flee yet again, this time to Rieti, whence he sent out appeals for help to the rulers of Europe. The situation in Rome became worse than even Gregory could anticipate when one Luca Savelli, nephew of the late Pope Honorius III, was elected the new senator, immediately gaining popular acclaim by declaring Church lands in Campania and Tuscany as public property whose towns should pay homage to the Roman people. Savelli went still further, pressing for the rights of the Romans to raise taxes, to issue their own coinage, to declare an end to clerical immunities, and for the exemption of all Romans from excommunication. The pope responded by wielding his ultimate, if now dulled weapon; he excommunicated the Romans to a man.

Basking in more clement southern Italy, Frederick recognized an opportunity when he saw it. Rumors had filtered down from Germany concerning the ill behavior of his son: that the young king was increasingly playing up to imperial enemies. Henry's fall seemed imminent, necessitating a measure of papal goodwill in the near future. Taking his six-year-old son Conrad to be offered as hostage, a token demonstration that Gregory, in his holiness, could not accept of course, Frederick joined the pope at Rieti, where he heroically proclaimed himself the papal protector. By being the only one of Europe's rulers who rose to the pope's defense, Frederick became once again master of the game. Gregory was not happy with that development, but if he wanted his Roman throne, palace, and churches back again, he had no choice but to accept what aid he could get, and from whomever. It was obvious to him that he was going to get no help from anyone but his friendly Hohenstaufen antagonist. Waxing into his role of golden knight of Mother Church, Frederick took the city of Viterbo, from which vantage point he could harass the Romans in their fortress at Rispampano near Tuscania. But his heart was not there. He would have preferred to be in southern Italy, hunting with his falcons. Besides that, he loathed fighting the Romans, who he felt were essentially sympathetic to his cause. He knew trouble was coming from the north, and he wanted relaxation before the storm. He left his troops to carry out the skirmishes from Viterbo and moved to Campania. It was not long before he received the welcome word that the Romans had been coaxed to the peace table.

In the spring of the year, Frederick stopped off at Capua with his son Conrad. He wanted to personally oversee a giant clearance project that had been undertaken in the northern part of the city, his preparations for an architectural wonder that would, in effect, serve as the first light for the dawn of the Renaissance one hundred years later. It was a bridge-gateway spanning the Volturno River and serving as a glorious centerpiece for a fortification system he envisioned. Clearly Frederick had it in mind to recreate the glowing art of the ancient Caesars, that art so spectacular in scale and rich decoration as to evoke the admiration of the world. The Capua bridge was the finest civil monument to Frederick's reign in southern Italy, serving as symbol and well as protection, hinting as it does at the superiority of the secular state over the Church.

Frederick saw his gate as two massive polygonal bases supporting round towers that sentineled both sides of the roadway leading to the bridge into the city. In his day Capua was a prosperous city, not at all the run-down, deprived community we know today, so the stout towers, ornamented with sculpture and holding between them a monumental arch, stood in keeping with a wealthy atmosphere already in evidence. As though the enormous size of the gateway were not enough, Frederick saw to it that sculpture was used profusely throughout: it was from this gate that the already mentioned portrait bust of Pier delle Vigne in the museum at Capua was rescued, a work that, in its adherence to the classical ideal so admired by Frederick, was long thought to have been lifted by the emperor from an ancient monument rather than being a thirteenth-century precursor of the Renaissance. (A statue of Frederick, which must have served as a focal point, is in the museum too, but thoroughly trashed by man and time.)

As a measure of Frederick's architectural sensitivity, it pays to examine the transitional device he utilized between the intrinsically incompatible polygons and the round towers, graceful marble connecting bands of shallow, inverted arches clinging to the curved surfaces and growing with absolute logic out of the bases. It was the perfect solution to a difficult problem, and one that was copied (and can still be seen) in the pigeon houses growing like giant mushrooms out of the top of the fourteenth-century castle at Benevento.

Alas, like so many of civilization's greatest works, the Capua gate surrendered to "progress," being laid low in 1557 by an age that regarded the canon as more important than visual inspiration. It is said that the Capuans wept when the connecting triumphal arch crashed to the ground and the towers were lopped off at their bases. Only a few rough sketches remain for us in the Imperial Archives in Vienna, those and the bases. And that is the extent of it.

Probably at the suggestion of Pope Gregory IX, Frederick had already dispatched Pier delle Vigne to London to sound out the possibilities of a marriage alliance between the emperor and Isabella, sister of England's King Henry III. Presiding over an ever-dwindling continental realm, Henry III could use a politically advantageous marriage in his Plantagenet house. The time was approaching when England's last line of defense would be the channel. Frederick, too, was in need of an advantageous marriage: an additional legitimate heir or two would be useful. Ominous news from Germany indicated that son Henry was living up to expectations. Move after inept move that the young man made was leading him ever closer to the chasm of obscurity, if not prison. That is not to say that he was totally without merit. His former mentor, Engelbert of Cologne, had imbued in him a certain altruism, which he displayed in his stand against the fanatical Conrad of Marburg when he nipped in the bud that nightmare-haunted man's projected crusade against heresy. And Henry absolutely turned his back on Gregory IX's plea for him to make himself more attractive to God by exterminating heretics. So one wonders how he could possibly have made the ultimate mistake that was to seal his fate. Beyond Henry, next son Conrad, nominal king of Jerusalem, was Frederick's only legitimate male heir. It behooved Henry to safeguard the interests of the house of Hohenstaufen, which he clearly did not intend to do.

Frederick had calculated his ride to Gregory's rescue with the reasonable expectation of a quid pro quo gesture from the Holy Father. The time was nigh to call on Gregory to accept his role in the coming events. Then, at just the time that Frederick was consulting Gregory in Rieti, word reached him that King Henry had made a supremely insulting move against the German ecclesiastical princes. With his usual outlandish propensity for doing the wrong thing, he had freed the inhabitants of the Rhineland cities from their allegiance to their bishops. In the resulting unrest Henry's brother-in-law, the duke of Austria, attacked the territory of the duke of Bavaria, a staunch supporter of the emperor. Frederick was livid, but he had to admit that the timing was perfect. According to their 1232 Aquileian agreement Gregory had no choice but to lower the boom of excommunication on the wayward, treasonous son. It was not long before Frederick was made further aware of just how treasonous his son could be. It surpassed his wildest dreams.

During the autumn of 1234, representatives of King Henry, Anselm of Justingen and Walter of Tannenburg, had negotiated a secret agreement with Milan, the most treacherously dissatisfied of Frederick's enemies, the worst of all possible choices. The hush-hush alliance was to be opened for renewal every ten years; regardless of how the conspiring parties might try to soft-pedal it, this was clearly a long-term project. It is hard to pinpoint why or how Henry deluded himself into such a compromising move unless he saw it as a sure way of unseating his father or at least of preventing him from using the Alpine passes on a trip to Germany that was obviously in the offing. Frederick had too many loyal adherents in Germany for Henry to get away with it. A few bishops were loyal to Henry—those of Augsburg, Worms, and Würzburg, for example—along with the abbot of Fulda and a handful of secular nobles. Beyond that there was no one of consequence in his camp. As far as Frederick was concerned, he could take only one stand: this was naked insurrection. Yet further outrage was flung in his face.

Rubbing salt into the wound of filial disloyalty, Milan offered Henry the iron crown of Lombardy, that coveted emblem denied to Frederick all these years since he had returned from Germany as new king and expectant emperor. There was no way that Henry's deposition could have been more assuredly guaranteed.

For a good part of this period of adamant foolishness, Henry was ensconced in the Rhine city of Boppard, the Roman Bodobriga, founded as an outpost station by Drusus around 20 BC. Situated on the left bank of a sweeping, dramatic curve of the Rhine River, Boppard became a royal residence of the Merovingian dynasty and then a free imperial city. The medieval castle squats in ruined splendor near some ancient Roman walls. Below the castle, the Church of Saint Severus was built to house relics of that saint, which were brought to Boppard from Trier in the tenth century. It is a singular building for, aside from being elaborately and tastefully decorated inside, it has two spires, which are located between the nave and the choir so that they take on the external appearance of transepts. An excellent Romanesque portal emphasizes the western end, and inside is a most charming smiling Madonna, brightly colored and happy, her back to a crucifix of expressive tragedy hanging in the soaring triumphal arch. Both are of the thirteenth century. The Church of Saint Severus was in use when Henry was holding court in Boppard (it had been dedicated in 1225), though not in the state that we know it. A Benedictine nunnery—the Marienberg—is nearby and played a minor but sad role in a legend local to Boppard.

Across the Rhine from the medieval city are two castles, the Sterrenberg and the Liebenstein, double ruins called collectively *Die feindlichen Brüder* ("the Hostile Brothers"). So close together and with a wall between, theirs is a strange tale. It seems that dour and staid Count Johann of Sterrenberg had two sons: Heinrich, fair-haired, openhearted, and quiet; and the younger Conrad, dark, passionate, and impetuous. Both men, coming out of their teens, fell in love with a distant cousin, Angela, who had been orphaned as a baby and had lived from that time at Sterrenberg. Dreaming golden dreams of heroic glory, the sons chafed to be off on crusade, but their father, advancing in years, demanded that one stay home to tend the property should anything happen to him. The aggressive Conrad was finally dispatched to Outremer, but not until he announced his betrothal to Angela. (In some versions of the legend she is called Hildegarde, which, considering the venue, does seem more reasonable.) Conrad was absent for a longer time than was anticipated, and Angela, tired of waiting, made a play for Heinrich, who, in his loyalty to his brother, rebuffed her advances. When Conrad finally returned as the hero he had dreamed of being, Angela, by this time totally smitten, confessed her love for the more reticent brother. Conrad, in a fit of jealous fury, attacked the loyal Heinrich and was himself wounded. Feeding his outrage further, he vowed never to see or speak to either of them again. Conrad left Sterrenberg and constructed a twin fortress on the same hill, a scarped rock known ironically as Liebenstein—"the Stone of Love." Every year Conrad heightened and thickened the wall between the castles. Heartbroken, Angela entered the nunnery of Marienberg. Nothing could get either of the brothers from his castle, and no communication existed between them. No woman was allowed within either castle. Each brother died in his eighties without ever seeing the other again. The value of the two castles today lies in the spectacular views that they command of sweeping curves of the Rhine and the beginning of the Rhine Gorge as it extends south toward the legendary Loreley where, legend tells us, an enchantress bewitched boatmen with sweet songs and lured them to their deaths.

Even disloyalty could have its advantages. With Henry so proficiently painting himself out of the picture, his father had the ideal justification and opportunity for seeing to it that a more trustworthy supporter was placed in the risky, sensitive spot of successor. Pope Gregory reaped no advantage, however. The moment he consented to Henry's excommunication, Gregory placed himself in a position of extreme embarrassment at the short end of the deal. Having accomplished the act, which must have been distasteful to him, Gregory found himself face-to-face with a solid body of obsequiously friendly Lombards who were now allied with the traitorous, excommunicated, disloyal son of Frederick. It would need every bit of curial ingenuity to extricate the Holy Father from his quandary for which even the most intricate Byzantine reasoning would have been hard put to find an answer. With his back squarely against the wall, Gregory did the only thing he could. He had to support Frederick in whatever action the aggrieved father took against his son, in a sense taking the stand that it was a Hohenstaufen problem that must be worked out within the family. At the same time he would ignore as much as possible the treacherous behavior of his Milanese allies. For Frederick's part, he would head for Germany.

1235

Frederick decided to reenact the role he had played as "the boy of Apulia" in 1212. With only a small company of armed troops for support and with seven-year-old Conrad in tow, he would in every way dazzle his northern subjects. He traveled with a pomposity befitting his majesty, his wagons loaded with gold and silver, gems and costly linens. His collection of exotic animals was the highlight of his magnificence, and his Saracen and Ethiopian guards were the height of curiosity. His wealth was in anticipation of the usual imperial handouts and was made possible by his new hearth tax called *la collecta,* but designated in cruder terms by his complaining Sicilian subjects. In addition there was his harem, complete with its host of husky Saracen guards, the total company of which was persuasive of the superior nature of the emperor, as far as the German on the street was concerned. Not known for his modesty, Frederick was aware that his most salient characteristics were the magic of his personality, his wealth, and the glamour of his lifestyle. In April his German princes met him en masse at Aquileia, where he arrived by boat from Rimini. With his train steadily growing in size, Frederick rode on through Friuli and the Austrian province of Styria and into Germany. There was one small unpleasantry at the border of Styria. Duke Frederick II of Austria, brother-in-law to fading King Henry and the last of the notorious but able Babenberg family, demanded two thousand marks from the emperor to help him in his current war against Hungary and Bohemia. Frederick Babenberg was called "the Quarrelsome," and quarrelsome he was. He had never made a pretense of getting along with the Hohenstaufens, or anyone else for that matter. Frederick, of course, refused the extortionate demands. He had his own financial drain.

"The *Man* from Apulia" wanted to give the impression of coming again in peace, God's chosen peacemaker, fate itself. Once in Germany the magic of his name attracted droves of the faithful and borderline-faithful to his banner. By the time he arrived at Ratisbon (modern Regensberg) on the right bank of the Danube and the residence of the early dukes of Bavaria since the sixth century, Henry's ill-fated insurrection (if that is what it can be called) had dematerialized. It may have been at Ratisbon that the duke of Bavaria, a man of unwavering fidelity to Frederick's cause, received his reward when his daughter, Margaret, was betrothed to Prince Conrad, both of the youngsters being all of seven years old.

When Frederick came to Ratisbon he was returning to his imperial roots, the city having been a favorite of Charlemagne, and a preferred residence of several subsequent Carolingian emperors. It was also one of the richest towns of the region. Ratisbon had served as the place for the establishment of the Wittelsbach family as dukes of Bavaria by Frederick Barbarossa in 1180, a position that the family relished until the revolution of 1918. It was outside the walls of Ratisbon in 1809 that the world almost rid itself of one of its notorious bloodletters, Napoleon, who was wounded there, a singular occurrence. Occupied since the Celts first settled a site that they called Ratabona, it had prospered throughout antiquity and up to the advent of the Wittelsbachs. During Frederick's century Ratisbon enjoyed the happiest time of its history.

The oldest medieval monument in Ratisbon is a three-aisled basilica that was constructed over the tomb of Saint Emmeram, a seventh-century bishop of Poitiers who had come to Bavaria, perhaps on the invitation of Duke Theodo I, and at the hands of whose men-at-arms he died a martyr. To this basilica of Saint Emmeram, splendid cloisters were added a short time before Frederick's visit and are today much as they were then. One of Saint Emmeram's most noteworthy inmates was, in 1235, preparing to enter that monastery: Berthold of Ratisbon, a most rigidly moral preacher in an age of rigid morality, who seemed to have had it in for women with his lashing out at their dress "with all the crimple-crispings here and the christy-crossings there, and the gold thread here and there . . . nought but a bit of cloth after all!"[3]

Saint Emmeram's is one of the few German churches that boast a detached bell tower in the Italian manner. It is fronted by an extremely fine Romanesque porch protecting excellent sculpture figures of Emmeram, Jesus, and Saint Denis, which are some of the earliest medieval works in Germany and reflect influences from the hieratic art of the East. Saint Emmeram stands in impressive dignity, an almost-divine aloofness. The enthroned Christ figure above the door is like something from an illuminated manuscript, while at his feet is a medallion showing Abbot Reginwart who lived in the eleventh century. The figures all show remnants of the original coloring, which augments their subtle echoing of medieval manuscripts. The simple Romanesque marvels inside have been desecrated, alas, by lavish rococo additions by the sixteenth- and seventeenth-century partner-brothers, Egid Quirin and Cosmas Damian Asam, all curves, curls, and golden shells that tell us nothing of the more primitive but aesthetically more honest Middle Ages—and certainly add not a whit of charm.

Saint Wolfgang (c. 930–994) is buried there in a properly somber crypt decorated with shallow reliefs on the capitals of the columns, a stone throne, unoccupied of course and certainly not designed for comfort, but primitively monarchical, worthy of a ruler, or perhaps a saint. The curved, rigidly vertical back enforces, even in the mind, an attitude of majesty, of arrogant condescension. Neither Wolfgang nor

Throne, crypt of St. Wolfgang, Ratisbon (Regensburg), Germany

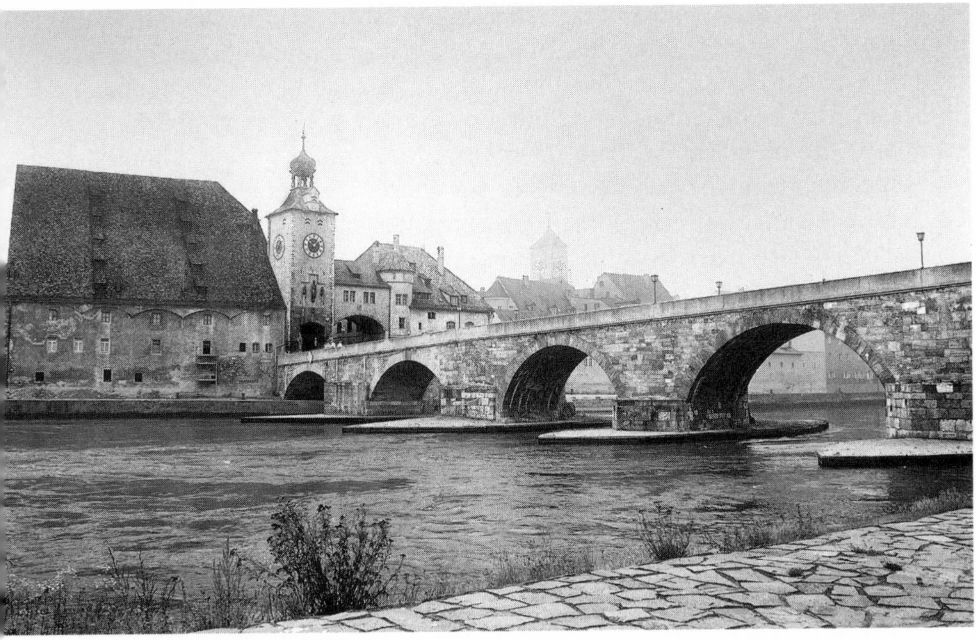

Steinerne Brücke, Ratisbon (Regensburg), Germany

Emmeram would claim the chair on those grounds, especially the latter whose leg bones lie in a silver reliquary beneath an altar—all that remains of the itinerant missionary saint.

Frederick never saw the cathedral at Ratisbon, since it was not begun until the year of his death. But he must have been familiar with the Chapel of All Saints, standing in what is now the cathedral cloister, its origin going back to the eighth century and with twelfth-century frescoes, preserved to this day in near perfect condition. The lively subjects of the frescoes are the Christ in Glory in the central dome, surrounded by the chosen people of the Great Tribulation as envisioned by John (Revelation 7:4–8), the number 144,000 in his account exceeding by far those shown in the small chapel!

Ratisbon is a delight to explore on foot. Highly recommended is a walk along the left bank of the Danube and then back toward the old city across the sixteen-arched stone bridge, the Steinerne Brücke—in its day considered an engineering miracle, as well it should have been. Dating from 1135–46, it is an excellent vantage point from which to view the towered medieval houses, reminiscent of those in Bologna and San Gimignano, built by the rich merchants of the city. The dedicated bridge-walker will be interested in the Historische Wurstküche to the left of the old salt warehouse, just off the end of the Steinerne Brücke as you face the city. There is no better wurst than the marvelous sausages served at this, one of the oldest eating establishments in Germany, which the Regensburgers will tell you was established to feed the men who worked on the twelfth-century bridge. There is a mellow feeling of camaraderie as one shares a long table with others, never strangers for more than a few minutes. How pleasant to imagine a convivial Frederick at one of those tables on the quay by a sluggishly moving Danube! And the beer! The word "unbelievable" does not do it justice. It must be stated in German: *unglaublich*. There! That says it. To the uninitiated, the *Weissbier* might be interesting. It is a local beer that tends to be cloudy and sweeter tasting than more familiar brews.

A good hike beyond the old city district, the twelfth-century Church of Saint Jakob, called the *Schottenkirche* after the Irish (Scotti) Benedictines who founded the monastery to which it was attached, is one of the few Bavarian Romanesque buildings that remains complete to this century. The north doorway is rich with an enormous expanse of Romanesque carvings that take up a good third of the exterior length of the nave. While the themes of the carvings remain a bit obscure, certain elements can be identified with no trouble: Christ and his apostles are high up on the wall, with the Virgin and unidentified emperors to left and right. There are dragons and composite figures and pictures of the underworld that just might ring a bell in the twentieth-century mind. Inside, a magnificent wooden rood at the choir entrance dates from about 1200, and a late twelfth-century crucifix speaks well of the taste of the burgers who donated these objects.

Frederick in Ratisbon, the pope in Rome, and assorted rulers of Europe, Constantinople and Outremer, none of them had their ears cocked to the rumbling of heavy cart wheels, the clashing of armor, the pounding of cavalry horses' hooves on the hard desert clay of the Far East. They had heard rumors that the Mongol hordes were approaching, but they paid no attention. Frederick had more pressing concerns: the pope, Lombardy, the always-intractable German princes, his son. He may not have been in a hurry to confront Henry. It was clear that the young man was dangling already from the imperial hook. Let him squirm for a while. He was trying desperately to hold a few fellow travelers and his castles, especially Trifels, where were housed the crown jewels. Finally at the behest of sage Hermann von Salza, it became apparent even to this slow-witted young king that there was no way but unconditional surrender to his father, a fearsome thought to anyone, but surely more awesome to the son.

Chapter Fourteen

Among the sheep offer (me) a place
and from the goats sequester me,
placing (me) at (Thy) right hand.
***Dies Irae,* verse 15**

1235

Crowning a sharp ridge overlooking the Neckar River, the Hohenstaufen palace at Bad Wimpfen is impressive even in its ruins. An interesting detail toward greater livability unfolds in an arcade of small columns set in a massively solid stone wall through which light was coaxed into its now fragmented great ceremonial hall. Shining new when Frederick billeted there, it stands as one of the best examples of Hohenstaufen castle building in Germany. It is obvious that under the Hohenstaufens creature comforts were more and more the architectural focal points, something more than protection: home as opposed to mere shelter; palace as opposed to castle. Stylistically there is little unusual about the palace other than its gentle nudging of the longed-for concept of comfort. Essentially, it remains a bulwark of a building, a reminder that the dynasty of Holy Roman emperors was, in the end, German, regardless of the southern graces they may have adopted. Not long after Frederick's death the structure was sold off piece by piece, hence its derelict state, its materials going to buildings by the local merchants, lords, and rich townsmen. The "Blue Tower" (the highest building in town) and the "Red Tower" offer the sightseer ample evidence of the heavy-shouldered set of Hohenstaufen architecture, aside from affording magnificent views of the winding Neckar River.

With narrow, hilly streets lined by half-timbered houses, and terminated by old city gates, Bad Wimpfen gives a more-than-vague notion of medieval atmosphere, even down to the jarring rumble of iron-shod wooden cartwheels over cobbled streets. The internal combustion engine and the piercing squeal of horns may interrupt a medieval reverie,

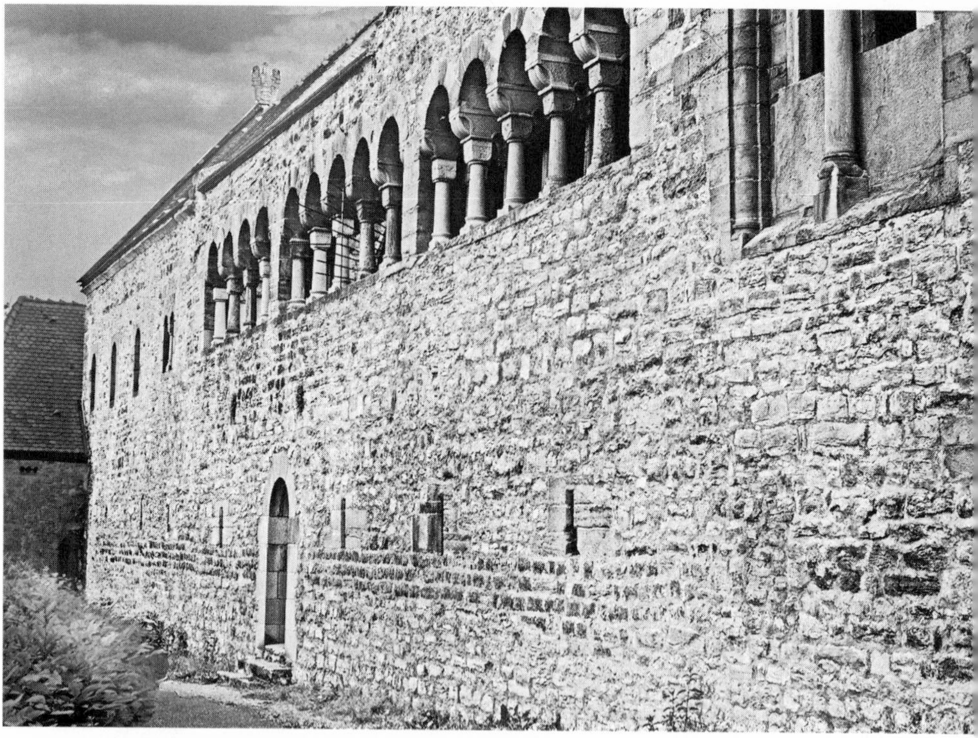

Hohenstaufen Castle, Bad Wimpfen, Germany

but only occasionally. For the most part it is human noise—laughter, footsteps, window-to-window gossip—that soothes the tired tourist enjoying a glass in a sidewalk *Weinstube* or, better yet, *Kaffee und Torten* in a *Konditorei* (bakery). The Romanesque Collegiate Church in the lower city with its rugged, heavy facade reinforces the overall impression. Though the rest of the church, which is dedicated to Saint Peter, is Gothic, the west facade achieves grandeur and a monumentality not easily forgotten. It was built, it would seem, by stonemasons well versed in the architecture of the city of Paris.

Father and son, the Hohenstaufens finally met at Worms, but only after Henry was soundly rebuffed by his father at Wimpfen. He was not even allowed into the imperial presence. He was taken a veritable prisoner and forced to accompany Frederick's colorful retinue down the rhapsody-inducing Neckar River, with its occasional "moment of absolute bliss, a moment of magical perfection . . . spread over the azure and gold sky, in the clear gray clouds on high, over the elms and weeping willows bent over the still water, over the expanse of ancient houses of various hues, their windowpanes lit up by the last rays of the sun. The houses . . . almost unreal, pierced with windows . . . like eyes, intricately arranged, violet-colored, shadowy, made of silver, copper, and dancing smoke, thronged with the infinite silence of the dead."[1] It's a safe bet that Henry had no eye or ear for such heady pleasures as the procession wound past Heidelberg to the Rhine and thence to Worms, where he was immediately clapped into prison. Bishop Landulf, who had ill-advisedly supported Henry's ambitions, was ordered out of Frederick's sight when he attempted to partake of the official greeting at the door of Worms Cathedral—a building rich in legendary-historical lore.

Henry was brought before Frederick's throne in early July. Uncharacteristically diffident, he entered the room, which was packed with resplendently garbed courtiers gathered to watch the showdown. Henry threw himself at his father's feet, as though this display of filial shame and repentance would result in a less severe display of justice. How little Henry understood his father's frame of mind when he thought mere show would assuage the imperial fury! The traitorous son lay on the floor for what must have seemed an eternity. No one moved or gave the command to arise. Finally, at the behest of a few of the princes, Frederick signaled that Henry should regain his feet. Looking dazed and confused, Henry apparently did not have the mental wherewithal to comprehend what was happening to him. He begged his father's forgiveness and renounced his claim to the German kingdom and to his worldly wealth. Without further ado, and to his bewilderment, he was dispatched to prison in Heidelberg, where he languished until finally being escorted to Rocca San Felice in Apulia, cleverly chosen for its location at the center of a security triangle formed by Melfi, Benevento, and Salerno. Further humiliation was inflicted when a man whom Henry regarded as an enemy, the duke of Bavaria, was appointed his jailer. Henry had saved his own life by begging forgiveness and renouncing his rights, but he had forfeited his freedom and any further familial contact. He was isolated from Frederick's presence for the rest of his life, an empty life that dragged on for another seven years. Anselm of Justingen, one of the partners in revolt and the arranger of the treaty with Milan, fared better. He fled to the court of the quarrelsome Duke Frederick II of Austria, where he was warmly welcomed and achieved a safe refuge. It was a bitter sorrow for Frederick, this disloyalty on the part of his eldest son, upon whom he had set such high hopes. But the safety of the empire and his own honor were at stake.

No doubt it was from the north door of Worms Cathedral, the ceremonial entrance in close proximity to both the imperial and the bishop's palaces, that Frederick banished Bishop Landulf from his presence. One likes to think that he may have glanced upward above the doorway to a bent-column framed space where had been placed the "Golden Bull" of 1184, Frederick Barbarossa's solemn proclamation of imperial freedom to the city, some of which is still readable. Below, in the tympanum, are parts of the emperor's salutation in which he frees Worms from hereditary tribute and predicts for the city a well-earned liberty.

The anonymous poet of the Nibelungenlied uses this doorway as the setting for his version of the confrontation of the two queens, Brunhild and Kriemhild, each basing her claim on the mistaken notion that her husband is superior to the other's, when in fact the husbands are, in the way of recondite medieval storytelling, equals. Brunhild, married to Kriemhild's brother, has a crush on Kriemhild's husband, Siegfried. The disagreement becomes so venomous as to be the turning point in the tale, resulting in the death of Siegfried. With him went an untold number of worthy knights and the kingdom of Burgundy. (According to Wagner's version Siegfried's death leads ultimately to the destruction of Valhalla.) Legendary swain Siegfried wooed Kriemhild in the rose garden, which is still pointed out to gullible tourists on the opposite side of the Rhine, and which gave its name to *Der Rosengarten*, a thirteenth-century poetic saga.

We can identify the point where the imperial palace adjoined the cathedral. A small doorway at ground level was the private entrance for the emperor and, higher up, another door (walled in now) once led from the empress's quarters to her private prayer area on a cathedral balcony. One version of the tale would have us believe it was at this doorway that occurred one of the more grisly scenes of the legendary revenge of one queen on another, Brunhild on Kriemhild.

> [T]he corpse of Siegfried of Niebelungland [was] carried in secret to Kriemhild's apartment and set down on the threshold, so that she should find him there before daybreak when she went out to matins, an office she never overslept. . . . From the moment she learned of Siegfried's death she was the sworn enemy of her own happiness. . . . And the laments of his friends mounted to such a pitch that the palace and the hall and indeed the whole city of Worms echoed mightily with their weeping.[2]

Worms Cathedral had its genesis in the sixth and seventh centuries, when the Merovingian kings built a church and a palace on the Rhine River where once a Roman temple and several administrative buildings

Cathedral, Worms, Germany

had stood high enough to escape flooding. Barring that of Trier, this Merovingian cathedral may have been the earliest in Germany. Some of the remains of the first church lie beneath the floor of the present structure, which was consecrated in 1018 and was certainly completed by 1228. The imperial palace occupied by Frederick has long since vanished, as have most of the historic buildings, including the Bischofshof, the place of the 1521 Diet of Worms, which listened to and then condemned Martin Luther, touching off the Reformation. Cathedral buildings—the palace Church of Saint Stephen, the administrative buildings of the convent, the ten-sided baptistery on the southeast side—are gone now, victims of the devastations of the French under Mélac in 1689, the allied raid of February 21, 1944, and—in the case of the cloister—because it had simply outlived its purpose. It was torn down to make better use of the stone.

Built of red sandstone, the cathedral presents an imposing four-square mien, with a block-like eastern end (though, surprisingly, it is semi-circular inside) and a glorious western end representing the zenith of German Romanesque architecture. With its rose windows and perfectly placed arcades of columns, its round towers to either side visually defining the space north and south, with its choir and apsidal polygons in as well-balanced a relationship of ascending forms as one is likely to find, it gives the impression of overpowering grandeur, of dignity and richness beyond compare. The western end is truer to Frederick's Romanesque age than is the eastern, which suffers the indignity of baroque intrusions by eighteenth-century master Balthasar Neumann. An endless array of pillars, statues, and decorations, including a choir stall partially blocking the view of a brilliant twelfth-century fresco of Saint Christopher, is not likely to induce spiritual profundity. The interior western end, with its four windows brilliantly exploiting the afternoon sunshine and underscored by blind arcades made even handsomer by the expertly utilized zigzag patterns of their ribbing, may be the highest expression of the late Romanesque period in Germany. The western choir originally commemorated the victory of Christianity, led by Emperor Otto I, over Magyar (Hungarian) tribes on Saint Lawrence's Day in 955 in the Lechfeld near Augsburg. There are few places in Germany—indeed, in Europe—where one is so overwhelmed by perfection of form, space, and light as in this sanctuary. Its impeccable proportion ranks with Norman interiors in Italy and England, with Hagia Sophia in Istanbul, and with Spain's Court of the Lions.

Frederick never knew the cathedral's south portal as it was built around 1300, but he would have approved it as an architectural balance to the emperor's portal on the north side. The usual way of entry into the church, it is adorned, on the inside, by a twelfth-century sculpture of Christ enthroned, with Mary to his right and Saint Peter on his left. Originally an exterior decoration on this same portal, the sculpture was relocated inside in 1300. In a swirling cascade of rhythmic line drapery, Christ raises a (now missing) right hand in blessing, while his left holds the book with the usual proclamation, "I am the Way, the Truth and the Life." His face is without emotion, his eyes wide in the Romanesque manner. Mary and Peter, while as stylized in body as the Christ, still seem more expressive of life, of flesh and blood. Christ is on a different level, unapproachable. He is not the stern Judge of Byzantium. Yet there is a hint of innate inflexibility in his personality, inviting us to follow his lead but unsympathetic to our refusal. Mary and Peter are more coaxing; Christ makes an offer of salvation. That is as far as he goes.

In a small, dark, and uninviting chapel by the south door we find another relief—charming and of the same period. Daniel, lounging comfortably in the lions' den, is in the act of lecturing to the beasts; and they seem more receptive than anyone has reason to expect. With faces more human than leonine, they mouth him in a friendly fashion, one licking his knee, another his hand. Overhead an angel carries the prophet Habakkuk bearing a bowl of broth for the condemned man, who, we are inclined to hope, will share it with the affectionate beasts.

As though his cathedral were not sufficient claim to fame, Bishop Burchard constructed three imposing monasteries in a kind of protective ring around the central church: in the north was the monastery of Saint Martin, one-time home to the jolly, disrespectful Archpoet; in the south Saint Andrew; and in the east Saint Paul. These three collegiate churches are still a very visible part of Worms. Saint Andrew's is a municipal museum. Saint Paul's still has its cloister and outer monastic buildings, along with a choir of the early thirteenth century. Saint Martin's displays an interior similar to the cathedral and a majestic doorway flanked by eight columns. An eleventh-century synagogue, the oldest in Germany, is in Worms and of topical interest in light of an event that will tax Frederick's ingenuity in the following year. Near the synagogue is a small section of the medieval city hall. For the epicurean inclined, the north suburb Church of Our Lady (*Liebfrauenkirche*), situated in extensive vineyards, has given its name to the popular *Liebfraumilch,* the genuine article of those particular vines being sold under the name of *Liebfrauenstift.*

Worms, specifically its cathedral, was the setting on July 15, 1235, for one of the most stunning pageants of the century, the wedding of Frederick Hohenstaufen and Princess Isabella, daughter of King John of England. Negotiations and preparations for the marriage had been progressing for almost a year. Pier delle Vigne had made two trips to England to ascertain that the union was agreeable to both emperor and king. The princess's feelings on the matter were apparently not investigated. With the successful conclusion of the consultations, Pier moved into the position of one of Frederick's top diplomats. The princess brought a dowry of such proportions as to makeeven an imperial eye bat—thirty thousand marks sterling, far beyond that brought by Henry II's daughter, Princess Joan, when she was shipped off to Sicily to marry Frederick's cousin, the Norman King William II. Isabella was, from all accounts, stunning as only a twenty-one-year-old can be, bowling over almost everyone who laid eyes on her. When she raised her veil before the curious townswomen of Cologne, she is said to have created a sensation. Her crown was of the finest gold, studded with jewels, and decorated with images representing the four "Martyr Kings" of England. Chests of jewels and necklaces, silks and cushions for the marriage bed—she did not know what was in store for her in this wise!—completed her dowry. Even her cooking pots were silver! Heavy taxation of the English may have defrayed the cost of all this puffery but probably had little to do with steadying the shaken imagination of the more practical German housewife. It is not difficult to imagine what deposed Henry thought when word of the festivities reached him in his Heidelberg prison, especially remembering that not too long ago Isabella had been under consideration as his spouse.

Having sailed from Sandwich on England's east coast, Isabella had landed at Antwerp, whence she had progressed in sumptuous procession to Cologne. For six weeks she remained there, enjoying elaborate festivities and historic rituals of flowers and music. At last word reached her at her quarters in the house of the provost of Saint Gereon that the emperor was prepared to receive her at Worms. A sizeable army was sent to escort her thence, as well as to protect her from possible abduction by allies of Louis IX of France. That king was uneasy at the prospects of this coming together of England and Germany, necessitating papal attempts at placation, as well as Frederick's personal assurances of his own good intentions, and a reminder that he had enjoyed good relations with the last two kings of France. On the negative side, there was carping over Isabella's lineage. She was a mere princess, and some members of the German court felt that any new empress should bring at least a kingdom as her dowry. This was debated on the typically specious grounds that she was a descendant of King Alfred and could thus trace her lineage to Adam!

The July 15 wedding ceremony was a pageant of incomparable splendor, what with four kings in attendance, along with eleven dukes, counts and prelates, knights and countless self-serving charmers. Though the marriage was not consummated until the following day, court astrologers having advised Frederick to delay action until a more propitious time, the celebration proceeded afoot on the completion of the nuptials, with jousting, acrobats, music, and singing by German, French, and Italian poets. Food and wine was served in prodigious amounts, especially the latter, for the Germans were noted even as early as the Middle Ages for having a tendency to get in their cups. More than that, Worms was close enough to France to take advantage of the fine vineyards there.

None of the celebration in her honor was witnessed by the new empress. Once she had served her purpose in the marriage bed, she was whisked off to the care of Saracen eunuch guards, and that only after Frederick had assured her that she was with son. Official word was dispatched to the English king apprising him of the imperial opinion. Having satisfied himself of his own potency, Frederick dismissed Isabella's train of attendants, which included an old crusading companion, the bishop of Exeter, and assorted English envoys, sending them back to England laden with gifts including three leopards, destined, as symbols of the English royal arms, to become early members of the Tower of London menagerie. Isabella was allowed to keep only two of her ladies-in-waiting. Like her predecessor Yolanda, she would be considered little more than a bearer of Frederick's legitimate successors, a curious stance for a man so given to adulating memories of his own mother, frequently speaking of her as "divine" and in other exalted terms never employed by previous or subsequent German rulers. There was simply no room in Frederick's life for women as co-rulers, helpmates, or even as mothers. His first queen, Constance, was the exception. As for the others, isolated in the harem, they were almost unknown even to their own children. And neither they nor Frederick's mistresses, worn out as child bearers and satisfiers of an extremely active libido, lived for long, with the exception of his beloved Bianca Lancia, who may even have been his wife, and who was probably very much in his mind and eye at the time of his marriage to Isabella. It would seem that Frederick had a halfhearted working relationship with Isabella, but it was never manifest in public. Henry III of England voiced his irritation that his sister was never seen wearing her crown. Aside from being gorgeous, Isabella was civilized and witty, and this must have been pleasant to her husband. He supplied her with a constant flow of the latest toys, musical instruments, and games, some of which were seen and remarked upon by her brother, Richard of Cornwall, himself to be elected king of the Romans in 1257.

Smugly satisfied that there was another legitimate male heir on the way, Frederick moved on in mid-August to a dazzling diet at Mainz, which lasted three months and was terminated in November at Augsburg. A German code of laws was initiated, which, like Frederick's Melfi Constitutions, contained both ancient and contemporary laws amalgamated into a new order and exceeding anything that had been done before. Furthermore, Frederick saw to it that his new laws were published in the German language, the first time that the northern vernacular was utilized in this manner, indicating the emperor's recognition that German was civilized on a par with Latin. Overshadowing all of the above, son Henry's treacheries were given paramount consideration, resulting in a most important decree:

> Whatever son shall drive his father out of his castles or other property, or shall burn it or plunder it, or shall conspire with his father's foes, or plot against his father's honour or seek his father's destruction . . . that son shall forfeit property and fief and personal possessions and all inheritance from father and mother, and neither judge nor father shall be able to reinstate him, for ever.[3]

So was Henry legally negated.

There was a further accomplishment during the Mainz diet. Officially ending the ancient feud, Otto of Lüneberg, the Guelf nephew of the late Emperor Otto IV, paid homage for his possessions and swore allegiance to Frederick. As a mark of favor Frederick created a dukedom and bestowed it upon Otto as a hereditary imperial fief. To celebrate the happy termination of the traditional contention, a High Mass was sung later in Augsburg Cathedral, and an elaborate feast followed (for twelve thousand knights, it was claimed—surely an exaggeration). It was the beginning of the end of the aristocratic imperium, which would increasingly bend before bourgeois pressure, the very force to which Frederick was so implacably opposed. But for the moment Frederick took justifiable pride in his accomplishments at the Mainz-Augsburg diet, the last exhibition of the Holy Roman Empire in full glory.

Only one note at Augsburg was destined to sour the sweet taste of success: on summoning the troublesome Duke Frederick II of Austria, "the Quarrelsome," to defend himself for sheltering Anselm of Justingen, the emperor was snubbed by his failure to appear. Frederick then terminated the diet and moved on to his favorite of all German imperial homes, Hagenau, where he enjoyed a peaceful Christmas, despite a second no-show on the part of the ill-tempered duke of Austria. With that, Frederick declared his foe an outlaw and his duchy forfeit, appointing several of his loyalists to open a war that, in time, he himself would have to terminate.

1236

Frederick's relaxation at Hagenau and his enjoyment of Barbarossa's extensive library there was interrupted early in the new year by an incident that demanded his attention, ingenuity, and wisdom. An uprising and massacre of Jews in the city of Fulda focused his attention on an accusation that they had, in the course of a spring ritual, sacrificed a Christian boy. Knowing the Jewish religion, Frederick disposed of the allegations and then, to reinforce his judgment, requested the other Christian rulers of Europe to inquire of knowledgeable Jews in their realms as to the nature of Jewish rites. The results, of course, were a total vindication of his stand. Having enacted the part of a medieval Solomon, Frederick decided on a spring progress of the western sector of his imperium.

A stop at Strasbourg, an imperial city since the time of his uncle, Philip of Swabia, gave him the chance to see the marvelously inventive Pillar of Angels, which was newly completed and already positioned in its designated home, the still unfinished cathedral. Most medieval churches utilized a rendition of the Last Judgment, almost invariably on the inner or outer wall of the western facade. At Strasbourg a columnar form was chosen for a striking rendition of final doom, centrally located in the south transept, just inside the portal. A Last Judgment suggested through the use of individual, almost isolated figures, was ingenious and without precedent. The column cluster is in eight parts, four attached columns and four detached. Starting about ten feet above floor level, four bases adorned with the symbols of the evangelists act as footings for the figures of the evangelists themselves. Marvelously eloquent they are, each with his own special dignity and personality: John radiating elegant grace; Mark gathering his robes in his hand as though not to soil them; Luke all fire and brimstone; Matthew looking every inch a Roman patrician.

Above the evangelists are four angels of the Last Judgment, each holding a trumpet to herald the end of the world. With deliciously curvaceous figures, their robes cling like the "wet drapery" of Hellenistic sculpture. They stare down at us. But they are not forbidding; rather they seem sweet-faced, gentle, half-smiling as though encouraging us—or at least expressing their sympathy for our plight. They lean to the task of holding their instruments with a kind of balletic grace, anticipating the effect of their awful message. Ensconced above these pleasant harbingers of doom is the ultimate Judge, sadly looking out into space, and accompanied by three angels of Christ's passion, one holding the cross and three nails, another the crown of thorns, and the third empty-handed now in the absence of the lance that he at one time bore. They avoid our stares, looking with their Master into middle distance as though envisioning the prophesied blessing and damnation. All of the angels have simple, gracefully formed, solid-looking wings of stone that make no effort to imitate the fragile delicacy of feathers. The

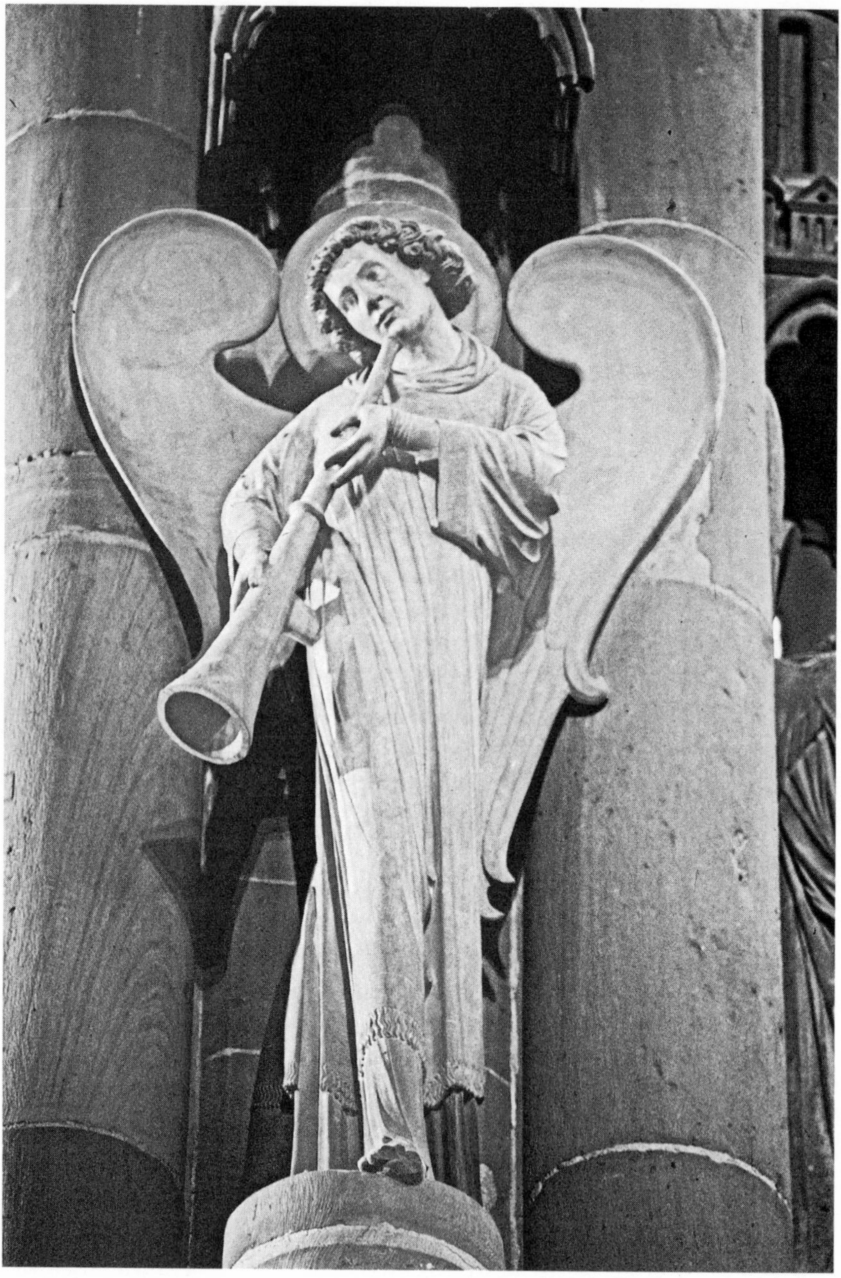

Pillar of Angels, Cathedral, Strasbourg, Alsace, France

whole ensemble is backed by the soaring interior of one of France's finest Gothic churches. Two brilliant rose windows throw down torrents of light of divers colors that all but convince the susceptible that the millennium is indeed imminent.

If one is disturbed by thoughts of ultimate destruction (though the Pillar of Angels is not grim in the manner of most renditions of the subject), then a glance to a side wall allows a change of pace, but not mood: a towering, ornate astronomical clock dating from 1550 and displaying, among other wonders, a perpetual calendar—perpetual until Doomsday, that is. But even the clock is not going to let the squeamish viewer off the hook. In an open oriel is a skeletal figure of Death holding a scythe and a bone, acting the marshall over a passing review at quarter-hour intervals: a child, a man, a mature soldier, and finally an old man bent with years. So each hour is brought to a close with a solemn reminder of the passage of life, dreary perhaps, but a profoundly felt, ever-present awareness of the frailty of earthly existence. If all this is too much, there are always smiling faces scattered throughout the cathedral—note especially the relaxed figure studying the Pillar of Angels from a balcony in the south transept. The very optimism of Gothic, so exemplified here at Strasbourg, soaring to the heavens as though the stone itself were levitated, rising in vertical dignity, arching in slow curves the firmament it encloses, is enough to lighten the spirits of even the dourest tourist suffering a surfeit of Madonnas and cathedrals—and Last Judgments and astronomical clocks.

There is an endless array of things to see at Strasbourg, a favorite city of generations of tourists, the author included. An ample portion of the most interesting sights are located in the nucleus center of Strasbourg's vibrant life, in the cathedral square, with its street mimes, musicians, and numerous outdoor cafes. Everywhere one looks there is a delight to the eye: carved posts, half-timbered houses, balconies and shaded courts, gilt figures, church spires, waterfalls at some of the canal locks, confection shops (of course)—and those eloquently graceful angels on that pillar!

From Strasbourg Frederick headed for Colmar with—one presumes, though the records make no mention of it—a layover at Sélestat, a city under imperial protection. A lovely, quiet little town, Sélestat has no traffic to speak of and is the ideal place to enjoy lunch or just a cup of coffee on a Sunday morning. Deeply resonant church bells call the faithful from their homes and from the surrounding countryside, with only the occasional feeble tinkle of a bicycle echoing through the streets. Frederick devised ingenious and questionable schemes for raising always-much-needed funds. With the lavishness of his expenditures he was in perpetual search of new sources of income. His exchequer was low, and at Colmar he came upon a tempting opportunity. A lord by the name of Wölfelin, whose wisdom was in higher repute than it deserved, had surrounded Colmar with sturdy defensive walls. He is generally given credit for endowing this exemplary act, though some accounts of the story maintain that he raised his money by a grievous extortion that he levied upon his serfs and tenants. In addition to the city walls, he frittered away fortunes to build castles dotting the Alsatian area, the very worst things he could have done in the eyes of any prince, king, or emperor. Worried lest Wölfelin entertain delusions of power, Frederick had him and his sons thrown into dungeons until they coughed up sixteen thousand marks from their ill-gotten hoard. He might have been able to wrest even more had Wölfelin not requested leave to visit his wife, who unconjugally smothered him during the night so that he might not confess to his remaining treasures.

Colmar is one of the most enchanting towns of Alsace, the major part of it dating from after Frederick's time, though it is none the less charming for that. The Church of Saint Martin is of his century and was surely in the planning stage when he was there. Parts of it are obviously inspired by Reims Cathedral, and it has a rich facade with tympanums of the Adoration of the Magi and the Last Judgment. Among its treasures is the *Madonna of the Roses*, a miracle of detailed realism by Martin Schongauer, who was born in Colmar about 1450. But Colmar's tour de force is the ten-painting Isenheim Altarpiece by a German contemporary of Michelangelo, Matthias Grünewald. In the Unterlinden Museum, the centerpiece Crucifixion is awesome in its horror, its blunt realism, and in its shattering distortion, which, in theory at least, could serve as a starting point for the twentieth-century German Expressionists. And the nightmare painting of the *Temptations of Saint Anthony* could be considered in a like manner related to the modern surrealists. Few painters have so successfully painted from the back recesses of their minds. Grünewald's *Temptations* is formidable enough to make Gustave Flaubert's written account of the same legend seem merely a romantic joke. Paul Hindemith's musical version of the painting in his *Mathis der Mahler* is more to the point, with its broken rhythms and jarring dissonances, its deep cry from the wilderness of a man's mind.

It is a point worth remembering that Frédéric Auguste Bartholdi, the designer of the Statue of Liberty, was born in Colmar in 1834. The studio where he worked still stands and serves as a museum. There is no statue in the world more widely recognized than Bartholdi's Bedloe's Island torchbearer, and yet it is probably a safe bet that not one

American in a hundred knows the name of the artist responsible for it.

By April of 1236, Frederick was in the city of Speyer, parading triumphantly down the impressive avenue built for imperial ostentation a century before and leading from a city gate straight to the cathedral. He could look fondly and with an arrogant smile at this largest of European Romanesque churches, seeing it as a monument to imperial power. The Salian emperor, Conrad II, the builder of the cathedral, was buried there in a magnificent crypt, as was his son, Henry III. Frederick surely related to the bulky structure since his Uncle Philip of Swabia was interred there in 1208 in a tomb still to be seen.

Time has not dealt fairly with Speyer Cathedral; wars, fires, and the depredations of man have wreaked their toll. It is still a majestic building, as much for its size as for anything. Among the interesting devices employed by the medieval craftsmen are inventive little carvings on the main portal depicting monkey-like figures, winged dragons, and strange, long-eared squirrels. These are all part of the architectural scheme of the portal and must have added no end of delight to the drab lives of the medieval churchgoers. Speyer Cathedral was familiar to Saint Bernard of Clairvaux, that persuasive hawker for a more activist Church. It was here in 1146 that he collared Conrad III of Hohenstaufen, king of Germany, successfully browbeating him into playing a part in the second crusade. At first Conrad refused. But later Bernard, speaking as though he himself were divine, reminded the king in no uncertain terms of his heaven-sent benefits. Conrad was not Frederick, not the kind to stand against such forcefully persuasive argument; he relented and agreed to go along with the disastrous expedition, at the same time giving Frederick Barbarossa his initial spotlight exposure on the world stage.

Rulers need public exposure, and this was no less certain during the Middle Ages than it is today. Having made his progress through Alsace, Frederick journeyed to Marburg on the Lahn River for a May 1 celebration of the reentombment of his sainted kinswoman by marriage, Elizabeth of Hungary, who had been canonized just the year before. (Her husband, Louis, was Frederick's second cousin and, it will be remembered, died at Brindisi in 1227 on the eve of Frederick's crusade.) Frederick laid the cornerstone for the church that was being built in her name by the Order of the Teutonic Knights, and which would be consecrated in 1283. But even in this early stage of construction, it had already become a popular shrine for this sweet, self-effacing widow of Landgrave Louis IV, "the Pious," from whom the city had received its municipal charter.

Francis Bernardone would have loved Elizabeth. Though not a member of his order, she was Franciscan to her fingertips. Had she followed the life dictated by birth, she would have been a queen instead of a woman of penance and asceticism. Customarily depicted in rich robes and carrying in her gathered skirt a profusion of roses, Elizabeth holds behind her back a loaf of bread to be given to the poor, a reference to a legend concerning Elizabeth and her husband. Cornering his wife one day as she was leaving the Wartburg carrying in her apron a load of bread for the poor, Louis demanded to see what she was hiding. With no choice left to her, Elizabeth threw open her apron to display a profusion of fresh roses. The miracle is supposedly what converted him to his piety—and one would think so!

Society was not ready for Elizabeth; even her mother-in-law mocked her religious attitudes as the behavior of a "tired old mule." Unlike the queen she was born to be (her father was King Andrew II of Hungary), she wore rough clothes of scratchy, untreated wools and flatly refused to wear a crown of gold since Christ had been crowned with thorns. Following the death of her husband in Brindisi, Elizabeth and her children were driven from her palace by Louis's family, while her brother-in-law, the despicable Henry Raspe IV, declared himself regent in place of what to him was an obviously demented woman who was squandering the family wealth by her unbounded charity. On their return from crusade, her husband's Teutonic Knights reestablished her in her rightful place. Henry Raspe was forced to relinquish many of the perquisites that he had assumed, and Elizabeth's son, Hermann, was set up in Wartburg Castle as the lawful heir to the landgraviate of Thuringia. Elizabeth, however, determined to live on in Marburg, keeping up her life of pious seclusion and charity, befriending the friendless, establishing a hospital, and administering to the poverty-stricken sick. She died in 1231, exhausted by the severity of the life she had chosen under the guidance of the sadistic, heretic-haunted Conrad of Marburg, and was canonized by Pope Gregory IX a mere four years later.

The Church of Saint Elizabeth at Marburg (begun in 1235) is French in feeling and apparently used as its models the cathedrals at Amiens and Reims. It boasts some rich ornamental stained glass of the thirteenth century, fortunate in a country where much of the historical glass has been lost. The doors display intricate ironwork that may be the best of thirteenth-century Germany. At the entrance to the chancel, a rood screen backs an altar over which hangs a 1931 monumentally moving crucifix by Ernst Barlach.

Reliquary of St. Elizabeth, Marburg, Germany

During the ceremonial disinterment of the remains of Elizabeth, it is said that a sacred oil was seen to flow there from, quickly collected and distributed to churches and monasteries throughout the land by the Teutonic Knights who were eager to create a cult around her memory. As part of the service Frederick placed a crown on her head, the very emblem she so abhorred in life. Eventually her relics were deposited in a splendid reliquary of gilded silver and copper created by a Rhenish master between 1236 and 1250, showing scenes from her life, and ornamented by figures of her fellow saints, all of them lively and abstract enough to set any determined agnostic to dreaming of a world beyond the merely mundane. This richly textured shrine can be viewed in the old sacristy off the north side of the chancel. It no longer contains the sacred relics, however. During the Reformation austerity, Count Philip of Hesse determined to end pilgrimages as religious exercises and had the relics removed and reinterred in an unidentifiable grave.

On the site of Elizabeth's original grave, there is a thirteenth-century altar showing pathetic lunatics, beggars, and cripples with crutches and walking stools—the people to whom she so dutifully ministered—praying to her as she lies in her casket. Always it is the downtrodden and underprivileged who play the large part in the stories and legends of this kindly woman. A second altar to Saint Elizabeth has Gothic frescoes, one of them portraying Frederick II himself attending the opening of her tomb. He is standing in a group of four celebrants, crowned, red-robed, looking properly worshipful, and carrying the cross-topped orb of his office.

Dominating the city of Marburg is the great castle. The two most interesting rooms were built at roughly the same period as the Church of Saint Elizabeth: the small chapel and the Rittersaal (the hall of knights). The latter is a two-aisled, ten-vaulted grand room, considered to be the most spacious nonsacred room in German Gothic architecture. Here was held the dramatic Colloquy of Marburg of 1529, at which Martin Luther and reformer Huldrych Zwingli of Zurich met to discuss problems concerning their differing views of the doctrine of transubstantiation, on which no agreement was reached.

Ceremonial duties in Marburg accomplished, Frederick determined that his problems with the Lombards had gone on long enough. Pope Gregory IX needed no miraculous revelation to tell him that his main allies against imperial encroachments were in grave danger. To try to forestall a war that suddenly seemed imminent, or maybe avoid it completely, Gregory relied on a favorite old papal device: he called for an immediate crusade, a totally transparent summons since the treaty that Frederick had worked out with Sultan al-Kamil of Egypt still had another four years to go. Frederick and his German princes, who were as keen as he to see the traitorous Lombards punished for their befriending of ex-king Henry, would not hear of another crusade. Making clear that his target was Italy, Frederick threw down the gauntlet to both pope and Lombards when he tore up the papal demand for crusade and ranted that to sail against the infidels while "heresies" continued to proliferate would be tantamount to administering medicine without extracting the offending weapon. It would cost enormous sums of money to outfit an eastbound fleet and army, he claimed. His war against the Lombards was, in Frederick's mind at least, Holy War enough—and probably in Gregory's as well, if the truth be known.

Recently in the Lombard city of Mantua, a mob of Patarene heretics had crucified the bishop over the cathedral altar. After consultation Frederick agreed to allow the pope some time to arbitrate, but, knowing his singular lack of success at that sort of thing, he did not maintain an easy optimism. In fact, he allowed the pope only until Christmas to work out what settlement he could. Interpreting as weakness the emperor's apparent desire to maintain a cordial relationship, Gregory insisted that Frederick agree beforehand to accept without condition any plan that he might be able to come up with. Frederick treated the absurd demand with the contempt it deserved. But still hoping that something might come of all the talk to avert war, he sent trusted Hermann von Salza to Rome, where he joined Pier delle Vigne, who was already dickering there as Frederick's envoy. A meeting was scheduled, but when the Lombards did not show up, Hermann, in a bit of a huff, headed back to Germany, refusing to return even when word reached him en route that the Lombards had subsequently arrived.

Frederick came out ahead in this nip-and-tuck game-playing, since he could with justification claim that the Lombards were shrewdly pitting the emperor and the pope against one another, knowing that they would always enjoy papal support because the pope needed them more than they needed him. No one was so foolish as to think that the Lombards relished the company of the papal Curia. It was simply that the Church was a useful ally in their determined battle against being swallowed up by imperial greed, with the concomitant loss of precious freedom to pursue their own obstinately ambitious ways.

Almost to a man the German princes were behind Frederick. They were anxious to get on with the fray, remaining undaunted by Gregory's flimsy arguments that the bone of contention with the emperor was an alleged mismanagement of his southern Italian kingdom. When that argument failed, the pope went on with endless demands that a new crusade be launched. Later, when it seemed that the emperor might gain from a crusade, Gregory would be the first and most vociferous to oppose it. In the course of the increasingly acrimonious debate, Gregory went so far as to invoke a most exaggerated interpretation of the spurious Donation of Constantine, in which that emperor was supposed to have conferred sovereignty on the pope over the entire Western Roman Empire. Furthermore, Gregory argued, Pope Leo III's crowning of Charlemagne as Holy Roman Emperor on Christmas morning 800 AD in no way implied surrender of papal jurisdiction over the ancient realm. Frederick was unfazed. No doubt he was consulting his scholars and astrologers, among them a newcomer from Antioch, Master Theodore, who had probably been sent to the imperial court by al-Kamil. Master Theodore rose to instant prominence and, among other duties, was put in charge of Frederick's continuing correspondence with Arab leaders.

There was a time when Gregory, in a humbler position in Church hierarchy, had seemed in sympathy with the Franciscan way, which, properly promoted, could have remade the face of Europe through a better understanding of the balance of power and of Europe's relationship with the Near East. The Church to the Church, Francis said. The state to the state. In a sense this was a revitalization of the "render unto Caesar what is Caesar's" motif. But no one seemed to hear, especially not the emperor and the pope. Even the Franciscan order itself was divided along similar lines.

Everyone was choosing sides: pope against emperor; the Lombard League, with Milan as the driving force, against the loyalist cities led by Cremona; Azzo d'Este, formerly in the imperial camp but now a papist, against Ezzelino da Romano, tyrant of Verona. The cities of northern Italy seethed convulsively as the facedown of the Middle Ages came closer to realization. Frederick's representatives were dispatched across the realm, arguing, cajoling, persuading, speaking in the most idealistic terms of their master and the benefits of his rule. Pier delle Vigne was in Piacenza addressing the citizens concerning Frederick's planned visit for purposes of holding a diet there, a meeting that never materialized as it turned out. Pier cleverly chose as his focal point Isaiah 9:2: "The people that walked in darkness have seen a great light: they that dwell in the land of the shadow of death, upon them hath the light shined." Here again Frederick was being equated with the Messiah, albeit this time by one of his adherents. Piacenza remained largely skeptical and soon embraced the standard of the Lombard League, of which she had been one of the originators. In a quid pro quo Bergamo deserted the league.

The loss of Piacenza was severe. Located at the end of the Via Emilia on the right bank of the River Po, it was throughout the Middle Ages one of the principal trade centers of Lombardy. Along with Verona and Pavia, it served as a clearinghouse for barges fighting the torrents of the Po laden with commercial wealth from Venice and other Adriatic centers, to be distributed to southern Italy or sent northward over the Alps to Germany and the Baltic.

Christianity came early to Piacenza. The fourth-century cathedral of Sant'Antonio had fallen into ruins by the ninth century and was largely rebuilt in the eleventh, to be redone yet again in the thirteenth. Most accounts list 1122–1233 as the building dates. It was in the Cathedral of Sant'Antonio that deputies of the Lombard League had ratified the 1183 Peace of Constance with Frederick's grandfather, Barbarossa. High on the left tower of the western front hangs the *gabbia*—a metal cage in which naked criminals were displayed to public scorn. Despite that melancholy relic, the outdoor trattoria-pizzeria facing the cathedral is a pleasant place to enjoy good food and wine while watching piazza romances, parents doting over gurgling babies, or misbehaving little boys looking for trouble, all to the tune of deeply resonant cathedral bells.

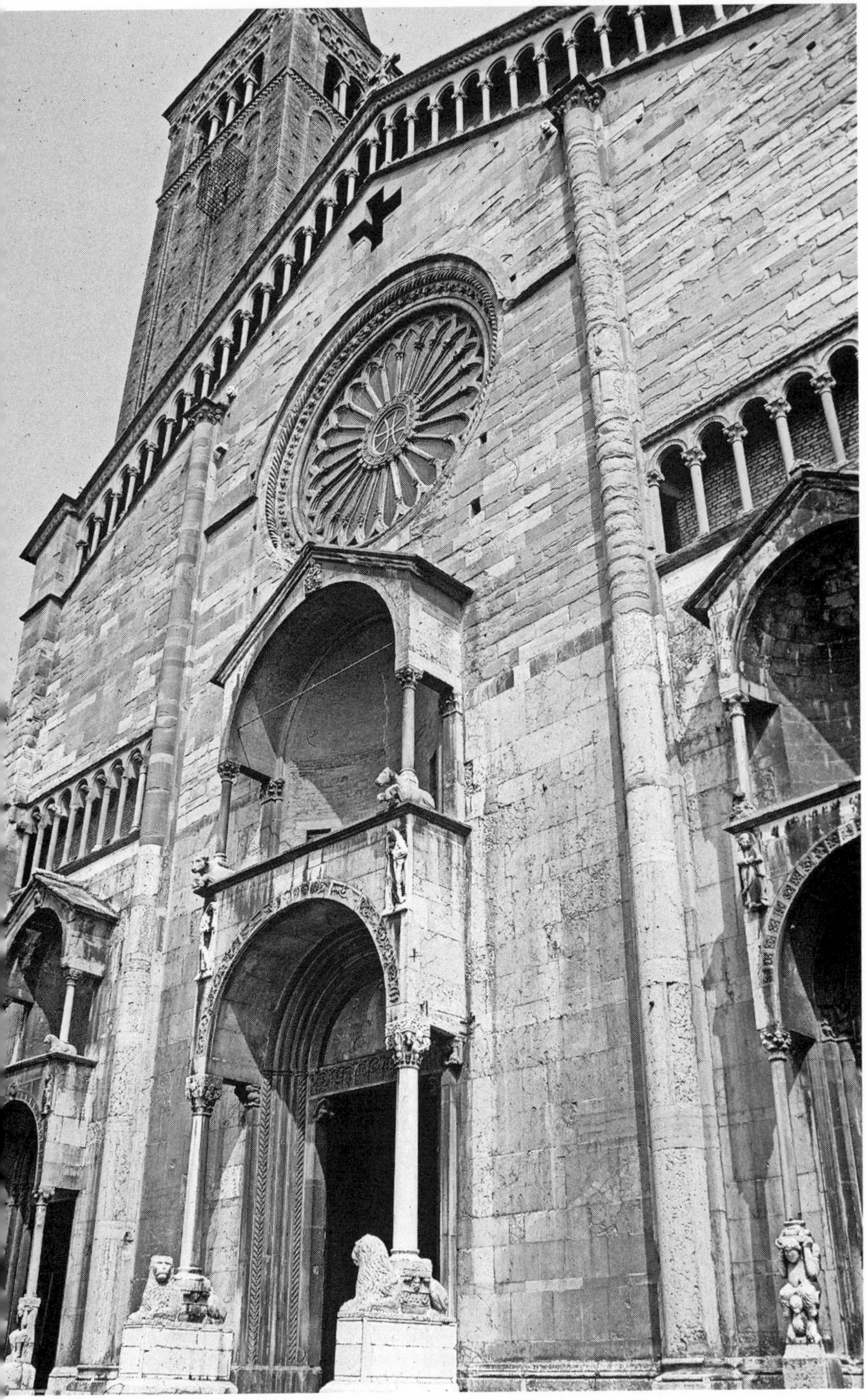

Cathedral of St. Anthony, Piacenza, Italy

The sprawling building is in the Lombard Romanesque style, with a nave and two side aisles, and transepts that do not project beyond the exterior aisle walls. Rows of massive columns dividing the cathedral nave from its aisles are carved with reliefs representing the donor guilds of craftsmen, singularly appropriate for a city as industry-oriented as Piacenza. They are in the charming, clumsy style of one Nicolaus, who dominated the Emilian sculptural scene in the first half of the twelfth century. Originally the nave was covered by an exposed beam roof, which was replaced by vaulting in Frederick's century, a practice of such frequency as to be astonishing when one considered the wars, sieges, upheavals, and destruction of the times. A graphic figure of John the Baptist on the porch of the north portal is by the much-acclaimed Nicolaus or his workshop (or both), as is the right portal of the front. With his expertise in flowery calligraphy, and between harangues in Piacenza, Pier delle Vigne must have been intrigued by the mosaics in the crypt and transepts of the Church of San Savino, which are important examples of the decorative arts of the time. The aisle of San Savino houses a veritable zoo of monstrous animals, bulls, horses, lions, and foxes that rear and glower, prance and cavort into interlacements of astonishing inventiveness and entertaining fantasies.

Despite the endemic mayhem of the age, there was a ferment of building activity in northern Italy, and some of the finest secular architecture of Europe was done during Frederick's tenure. Piacenza's aristocratic Palazzo del Comune is among the most beautiful in Italy, with its pointed arch arcade at ground level and its curiously dissimilar round arches above, piercing a heavy brick facade. Between two arches on the second level is a curiously small Romanesque Madonna regally surveying the spacious piazza. The whole ensemble is topped by a procession of fan-shaped Ghibelline merlons seeming to indicate that the city was loyal to Frederick's cause, which it never was.

Emperor and pope were aware that the final stage of the battle for empire had been joined. It would take yet a while for things to reach a roiling boil, but it was inevitable that both the empire and the Church would be severely damaged, if not brought down. Gebhard of Arnstein, a Thuringian nobleman always loyal to Frederick, a personal friend and imperial legate in Tuscany, had already arrived at Verona with five hundred mercenary knights and one hundred mercenary archers. He had come to reinforce Ezzelino da Romano, who was having difficulty holding off assaults by turncoat Azzo d'Este, a man suffering terminal jealousy of Ezzelino's growing power and of the reliance placed on him by the emperor. After a period of fifth-column undermining of Azzo's position in Vicenza, Ezzelino notified the emperor that the time was propitious for an attack. The Lombard League troops allied with Azzo fled in the face of the coming assault.

Vicenza, "city of one hundred towers," was burned on November 1, a merited fate according to the chronicler Richard of San Germano. The city was all but destroyed in one of the most horrifying rampages of the century—extraordinary, considering that it was, in reality, a mere skirmish before the main joining. Even the city walls were demolished. It was probably only moderately comforting that Frederick dealt leniently with Vicenza's inhabitants, restoring to them their ruined property and appointing over them an imperial podestà. Other cities—Ferrara, Padua, and Treviso—promptly fell into the imperial palm. Still in Vicenza, Frederick received word concerning that quarrelsome Babenberger, Duke Frederick of Austria. After being declared an outlaw he had been cornered by imperial forces in his own stronghold at Wiener Neustadt and the adjacent family-owned castles of Starhemberg and Seebenstein. Defying his captors, he broke free and was now dominating the area south of the Danube and the border of Styria. Greater insult, he had routed Frederick's forces.

South of Wiener Neustadt, Seebenstein can be reached only by a strenuous climb of about twenty minutes, but it is ultimately rewarding for its two gateways, its bridge, and tower, not to mention its inviting, grassy picnic spot. To the north, Starhemberg—also a tiring climb on foot—is more complete, with a large section of curtain wall remaining (though a length of it has fallen down the steep hill), a kitchen with a huge chimney, and a chapel in a twelfth-century tower. Both of these places are wild and off the beaten track, which adds to the evocative moods and imagined sounds of other ages. The more interesting of the two is Starhemberg, but determination is needed to breach the occasional bramble patches that guard the stronghold.

With still-smoking Vicenza back in the imperial hands and the inhabitants preoccupied with rebuilding their homes, Frederick determined that the time was right to put the contentious Duke Frederick of Babenberg out of action for all time and to take Austria as though it were in fact his Hohenstaufen patrimony. Like the Lombards, in Frederick's eyes the duke was no better than a renegade "heretic," an outlaw with the single saving grace that he was a patron of Neidhart von Reuenthal, a kind of Pieter Breughel of poetry. Peace in Europe could be more successfully achieved without his troublesome presence for, childless as he was, if he could be made to forfeit his claims on Austria and Styria, Frederick Hohenstaufen could then arm them

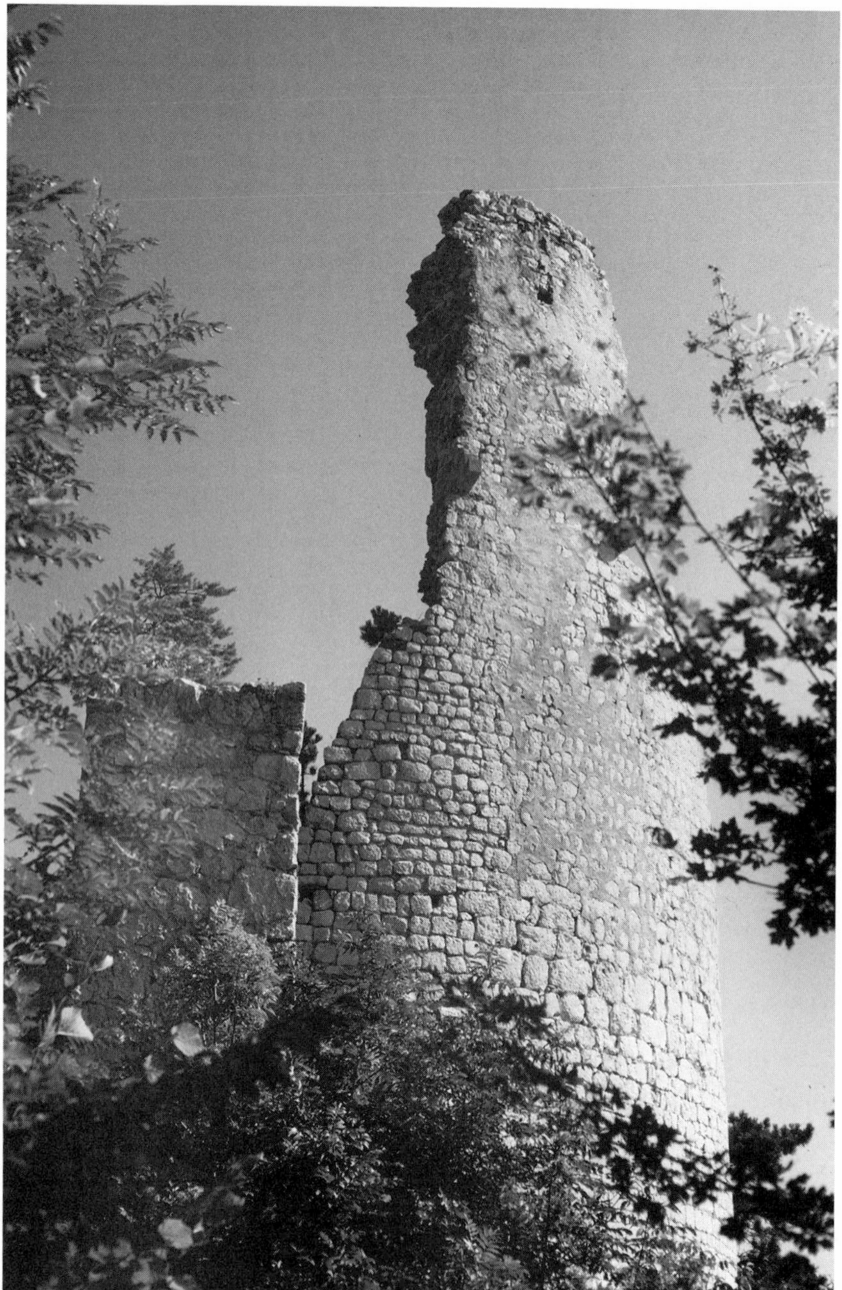

Starhemberg Castle, Austria

as key positions in his imperium. Most of Austria had already fallen before the German armies in the name of the emperor, but Babenberg was still in a position of advantage and able to stir up his contentious brew. Frederick did not want to divide his armies between Italy and Austria; and with the approaching winter making his showdown with the Lombards a little less urgent, he opted for crossing the Carnic Alps into Austria for a final object lesson to the wayward duke.

1237

Even distracted as he was about the questionable loyalties of the Babenberg duke of Austria, who was again barricaded in Wiener Neustadt, Frederick was increasingly intent on resolving the question of his own succession. Empress Isabella, despite her husband's bragging confidence on the consummation of their marriage, had finally, after two years, given birth to a daughter, Margaret—not the offspring Frederick had so categorically anticipated. Perhaps the thorny problem of succession should be tackled while he was still riding high on his triumph over Vicenza and cowing Frederick Babenberg.

With the new year Frederick moved on to Vienna. During a splendid end-of-January court he brought the question into the open. It says much about the power he was now wielding that he was able with a minimum of effort to convince the body of his court to approve the election of nine-year-old Conrad, king of Jerusalem, as his heir—and this without requesting papal approval! Sumptuous feasting and celebrations were held to conclude the diet that made the young Conrad the new king of Germany and, by implication, the future emperor. Thus was designated before the fact that the emperorship was now conceived as a hereditary office, an ambition entertained, but never realized, by every previous Hohenstaufen. Then, in a powerfully magnanimous gesture, and while the Babenberg duke grumbled and cursed in his Wiener Neustadt hideout, Frederick declared the city of Vienna an imperial city, and Austria and Styria were proclaimed imperial fiefs. Next, in a proclamation contradictory for a man as enlightened as Frederick, he bowed to widespread prejudice by barring Jews from public office, lest they "abuse" the Christians.

Despite the haughty confidence of Frederick II's proclamations, which implied deposition of the Babenberger duke, they did not long prevail. Frederick the Quarrelsome emerged from his Wiener Neustadt lair immediately after the emperor left the area, carrying on his troublesome sniping at imperial forces until he eventually won back virtually all he had lost. The emperor himself made light of his own succession by refraining from crowning Conrad, probably afraid of a repeat performance of the unwise King Henry. He appointed the archbishop of Mainz and Henry Raspe, unprincipled brother-in-law of Saint Elizabeth, to rule Germany temporarily as imperial representatives. Frederick then headed for Speyer, where he held a second diet to make the gesture of allowing the princes of Germany not present at Vienna the privilege of ratifying Conrad's election. His main preoccupation, however, was to prepare for his coming collision with the Lombards, the long-anticipated, go-for-broke struggle that everyone dreaded, particularly Pope Gregory IX and his Curia.

Chapter Fifteen

After the accursed have been silenced,
given up to the bitter flames,
call me with the blest.
***Dies Irae*, verse 16**

1237

The Venetians were feeling threatened. Watching the hostile and always brutal Ezzelino da Romano tyrannize over the March of Treviso, and expecting to see Frederick swooping in any day from the north to make a clean conquest of Lombardy, did nothing for the serenity of the Most Serene Republic. Worried over the outside chance that Frederick and the Lombards might reach some sort of accord, if only a temporary one, the clever Venetians scotched that by getting an anti-imperialist mayor installed in recently defected Piacenza. It was the way of the times. Piacenza, too hopelessly divided by internal contention to reach any kind of meeting of minds on the selection of a native-born podestà, elected to go for a foreigner. Padua and Treviso already had Venetian mayors. Why not a Venetian for Piacenza? Venice was only too willing to supply one, though she had not yet, and never would, tolerate a foreign podestà on her own canal. But certainly one elsewhere—say, Piacenza—would have a strengthening effect on the Lombard League. The new podestà promptly persuaded Piacenza to agree never to accept a podestà harboring imperial interests. This was all well and good until it became obvious that Frederick did not have Venice in mind as his Italian linchpin.

A line drawn on a map from Parma to Cremona to Verona—reinforced by Ferrara and the soon-to-be-won Mantua—assumes the shape of an arrow aimed right at the heart of Milan. Holding that threat in abeyance, Frederick opted to go first after the city of Brescia, which, barring one of the principal northern routes to Milan between lakes Iseo and Garda, could serve as a tactical convenience. He had his German army with him, along with seven to ten thousand Saracen archers from Lucera, a contingent of Apulian knights, plus levies from Bergamo and other Ghibelline towns of Northern Italy. Brescia, backed by its Milanese allies, had the advantage of falling back into the city they were defending. Some estimates place the total numbers at twenty thousand for Frederick and just under that number for the Lombards.

Increasingly panic-stricken, Pope Gregory IX tried again to open negotiations with the emperor. But the die had been cast, especially now with Milan frantically preparing for the worst. Frederick made the first move by taking a few scattered towns that might prove nettlesome during the showdown. When he had the choice he invariably chose open field warfare, eschewing the sieges that were the usual medieval military maneuver. Sieges were drawn-out affairs and too often led to little more than bitter frustration. But the Milanesi were cagey. Even when Frederick drew them away from his first important target, Brescia, he could not coax them into open combat. In a state of near despair as November cold and rain closed in and the fighting season was well-nigh at an end, Frederick realized he must somehow trick the enemy into out-and-out battle. If he could convince them that he was leaving the field in disappointment and disgust to head for winter bivouac, perhaps he could catch them with their guard down. Nearby Cremona would be the logical sham headquarters.

At this point the right decision could put Frederick on the peak of the figurative mountain he had been climbing since he had passed secretly through this territory some twenty-five years before, a hunted youth on his way to Germany to claim his place in history. The wrong move could plunge him into the yawning abyss below, a trap already littered with the pathetic remains of countless ambitious men through time who had reached beyond their capabilities. He made the right move: he broke camp at Pontevico and with the usual pandemonium crossed the Oglio River and marched south toward Cremona. While he and contingents of cavalry and Saracen archers turned aside, eventually to lie in wet ambush near Soncino, he dispatched a small remainder of his troops on to Cremona, a convincing dodge to calm Lombard fears. The enemy was convinced all right. With Pietro Tiepolo, podestà of Milan and son of the doge of Venice, as their leader, they set out northward for Palazzolo sull'Oglio, thinking that Frederick had disengaged them. Then they turned west for Milan, their homes, wives, children, parents, and sweethearts. When word reached Frederick via his spies that the enemy was headed homeward, he moved northward again, intercepting them on November 27 almost in the shadow of the castle of the town of Cortenuova.

Before the imperial troops burst from the wood in which they had concealed themselves, one of Frederick's knights created the proper confusion by suddenly appearing before the homeward-bound Lombards to announce that his master was poised for the kill. Then, to brassy calls of trumpets and yells of the attackers, an instant tornado of destruction was unleashed. Frederick's Saracen archers suffered heavy losses trying to take Milan's *carroccio* (chariot), but his mounted knights saved the day by galloping to the rescue. A dreadful slaughter followed, with the Milanesi, to their everlasting pride, defending their cumbersome, wheeled rallying shrine. The imperial troops were merciless, heeding neither pleas for life nor promises of reward. Imitating their emperor and leaders and fed up with Lombard troublemaking, they took to the job at hand with relish, no less delirious than the imperial butchers themselves, as Pier delle Vigne described the scene. The victims, hopelessly outclassed and by comparison ridiculously undertrained, could only pray for mercy from their attackers first and then from God, before spilling their blood into the soft mud of the battlefield. Nightfall prevented Frederick from taking the town of Cortenuova, but it was no loss. And when morning dawned it was discovered that the Milanesi had skulked away in the darkness, abandoning their dead and dying friends, their castle, arms, baggage and—what was more humiliating—a large part of their battered, mud-mired *carroccio*. Even the small bit of it that they managed to cart away was later left by the wayside as the fugitives struggled over the rain-flooded roads.

Northern Italy trembled. Never would Frederick's power go beyond that which at this moment he embraced. His troops cheered the victory while mopping up a gang of prisoners, including Pietro Tiepolo. With casual optimism Frederick failed to dispatch troops after the fleeing enemy. And that was mistake number one. A formidable percentage of those fugitives reached Milan and lived to fight another day. For the moment Frederick wanted only to savor the sweet nectar of success: lawgiver, diplomat, crusader, general, leader of the intelligentsia, poet, patron of the arts—the man of his century. His trumpeted second victorious entry into elaborately festooned Cremona was the show of a conquering Caesar. His famous elephant pulled what was left of the *carroccio* of Cremona's bullying enemy, its standard dragging ignominiously on the ground, the yellow imperial banners flying triumphantly overhead, and Podestà Pietro Tiepolo bound to the lowered mast, his wrists chained together. Fair weather or foul, celebration was in the air with the realization that no longer did Cremona need to fear her neighboring foe, now cut down to humiliating size by the most powerful

Hohenstaufen of them all, the temporal law-and-order dictator who would, it was foreseen, eventually relegate the resolutely antagonistic spiritual leader of Christendom to his Roman palaces and churches.

Writing to his brother-in-law, Richard of Cornwall, Frederick estimated ten thousand of the enemy slain or taken prisoner, but this is surely victorious hyperbole, in keeping with which he forwarded Milan's *carroccio* as a gift to the city of Rome, in whose name his victory was ostensibly won. Pope Gregory could have been only appalled when he saw the symbolic victory chariot of his beaten allies hauled through the crowded streets of Rome, dragged now by mules instead of noble white oxen. His horror grew when he heard Frederick's message to the Romans that left no doubt in anyone's mind that he intended on making their city his capital. And where would that leave the pope? Clearly there was no room in that city for two such ambitious men. Better that the pope go back into his churches, leaving Frederick free to wander the corridors of power. To assure his motives and his success, Frederick presented the most intoxicating delight of all to the Roman ear and the most distressing to the pope's: "Soldiers of Rome! Soldiers of the Emperor"—the new battle cry that he had originated for his legions. Where did that leave Gregory, who firmly believed that the emperor was merely the sword arm of the Church?

Frederick's efforts to negate the power of the pope and the Curia led to the criticism that he was a bad Catholic, devoid of any feeling of loyalty to God. However, he always claimed to see, and acknowledged with thanks, the guiding hand of God behind his successes. As statesmen and politicians before and since, he would maintain as dogma that his was a divinely ordained career. More than ever he saw himself as a prime instrument of God's order, one who alone had been singled out by that awesome power to be caretaker of his mundane dominions. With Rome as his capital and with all Italy in the palm of his hand—and no pope to worry about in a temporal sense—the Roman Empire of ancient days would again be an actuality. He was not the Antichrist. In some respects he may have been a better Catholic than the pope and the members of the Curia. His desire was to negate the Church politically, so that it could fulfill more completely the intentions of the founding apostles. It could be said that in this Frederick was thinking like a Franciscan. Like Francis, Frederick had in mind a Church with ideals that had brought it into existence in the first place. So the balance of power: with Francis the objective had been life-long, life-fulfilling; with Fredrick it was short-lived, to the detriment of succeeding Hohenstaufens.

1238

Now was Frederick exalted above all men. In May 1236 he had written an angry letter to Pope Gregory IX, stating, among other items of contention, that Italy was his rightful inheritance. This blatant claim had stunned Gregory. Now his assertion that his victory over Gregory's allies was a triumph of God over the devil (the implication of a horned pope was clear) must have taken the old man's breath away. Frederick wrote to the citizens of Rome that his first thoughts were always for them and for their city and the reestablishment of it as the capital of civilization. Using the most flattering language always, he inspired nostalgia for the classical empire, while promising to aim at the restoration of the nobility of the ancient city and its customs.

It was easy for Frederick to flatter, and his promises were justified. Apparently nothing could stop him now. Had he not just proven that he was obviously the chosen of God? Even his enemies must appreciate now that he had not been too far afield in 1229 at the altar of the Holy Sepulcher when he claimed that the Almighty had raised him beyond mere royalty and that he was of the house of David. A fuming pope, an abysmally depressed and frightened Milan, and a gaggle of nervously vacillating northern Italian cities (Lodi flopped over to Frederick's side almost at the instant of the Lombard defeat) further added to his glory. He was in charge of the present, of every physical aspect of men's lives. According to some he was even in charge of the pope, though that assessment was not quite accurate. He was prepared to acknowledge the pontiff's sovereignty over the souls of his subjects, both before and after death. But that was as much as he would admit.

In December, following Cortenuova, Milan approached the archenemy with more than ordinary peace proposals. With only three league cities left to her defense—Brescia, Alessandria, and Piacenza—she could hardly do otherwise. A Franciscan acted as spokesman for a group of nobles and citizens of Milan, approaching Frederick in Lodi, where he was spending the winter months preparing his spring offensive against his blustering enemy. Frederick received the embassy from a seated position. Even then he appeared sufficiently menacing, bulky as he was, muscular, and hinting of a terrible energy. That reptilian-eyed stare alone was enough to intimidate the already anguished and edgy delegates. At first he played the part of the benevolent ruler, speaking of his desire to rule as any king should.

First Milan offered to accept Frederick as sovereign. Once that was made clear, they announced that they were prepared to supply him with ten thousand soldiers annually for use in the Holy Land during the crusade, which was increasingly being talked up since the ten-year truce with the Muslims was due to expire next year. Adding to the probability of a new crusade, news had recently reached Frederick that his friendly adversary, Sultan al-Kamil, had died. Al-Kamil was profoundly mourned by the emperor, who complained a few years later when Outremer was obviously slipping out of Christian hands, that things would have been different if al-Kamil were still alive. In addition to their bargaining, the Milanesi offered to pay a large indemnity for damages they had perpetrated in defense of their independence. Frederick was not to be mollified. Encouraged by success, and egged on by loyal Ghibelline cities, he demanded unconditional surrender. And therein he made his second mistake, perhaps the biggest of his career. The Milanesi were earnestly seeking peace. But they had their pride. And fears. They remembered Barbarossa's cruel destruction of their homes and churches. Knowing themselves to be especially hated by Frederick, they could not count on the clemency he had in the past displayed to other league cities. In short, having learned by experience, they could not now surrender unconditionally. Better to die fighting, they told the emperor point blank, than by starvation, treachery, or the stake.

Some in Frederick's inner circle tried to dissuade him from what seemed to be turning into a vengeful retribution. Why another war with the Lombards, even his daughter Violante asked, since he already had everything in his kingdom that he could want? Frederick is said to have acknowledged that she was correct, but at the same time, he claimed, he could not turn back at this point without dishonor. Again his unfailing insistence that the honor of the empire and his office remained paramount propelled the great drama of Frederick's life and the ultimate unrealizability of his dream.

Such was his conception of empire. It had been with him since the days of his lonely childhood when, fearful of the likes of Markward of Anweiler, and cared for by the generous people of Palermo, he had held to himself his rigid belief that he was destined to control Rome and the Occidental kingdoms. The idea was not new in his time. The Archpoet had sung the same in Barbarossa's day. But this time it looked as though such was about to come to pass. Perhaps Frederick was on the verge of reestablishing a second age of Caesar Augustus. The people were hopeful; the pope was dismayed. Frederick's poets hymned him by comparing him to the first Caesar. He was, they claimed, the embodiment of the prophesies of Merlin and the ancient sibyls. Pier delle Vigne, by this time so close to the emperor, was like another Virgil to his Augustus. And, having received with jubilation Milan's *carroccio,* the Romans were willing, indeed eager, to accept their role as subjects at whose pleasure this modern Caesar reigned. It would seem that the new Caesar could not miss. A son had been born to him in the weeks after Cortenuova, named Henry, as though trying to make amends for the errors of his father. Understandably, no one—no one—could anticipate that his comparatively benevolent reign was shortly to metamorphose into a reign of fire.

Had he been able to maintain an appropriate-sized standing army, Frederick might have been able to stand against the dominant force of thirteenth-century Italian politics—communal pride. But northern Italy, with no passion to permit anything even remotely resembling a national pride, was, in a sense, a conglomeration of guerrilla factions intent on striking the minute the would-be conqueror's back was turned, all of them defending their own independence and proving, because of their deeply ingrained unwillingness to unite, the more formidable collective foe. At the peak of this pyramid of distrust, there was always the pope and his thoroughly suspicious Curia, ever churning the currents of unrest, poisoning the atmosphere with visions of temporal supremacy. Yet even some of Frederick's apologists maintain there is argument in favor of the papal view. Perhaps the pope was not as unwise as it first seemed by using the Franciscan order to further his cause. The Church to the Church. The state to the state. Had Frederick succeeded in realizing his dream, the Church would have been reduced to a mere zero, with a leader forever mouthing off about imperial hubris, but unable to correct the sinner. The two forces must inevitably clash, both of them at once irresistible and unstoppable. And in their initial hysteria the citizens of Milan became suspicious, seeing the pope as party to Frederick's evil. Rabble roamed the streets, looting churches, destroying property and religious works, and hanging crucifixes upside down. Later, when Frederick's demands became known, they took hold of themselves, the better to reach a genuine consensus. Then they hardened their resolve, becoming as adamant in their refusal as the emperor was in his insistence on unconditional surrender.

Strategically Lodi was a perfect place for Frederick to winter, being on the right bank of the River Adda just before it flows into the Po, and centrally situated in a rough parallelogram formed by his four most dangerous opponents—Milan, Brescia, Piacenza, and Alessandria. Barbarossa had founded New Lodi in the middle of the twelfth century after the original city had been laid low by Milan. Not much of history is left at Barbarossa's Lodi, however, though there are some Renaissance points of interest. The most intriguing medieval remains of New

Lodi are small traces of city walls, with a round, heavy-topped tower, brutish and overgrown with wild shrubbery, and the Cathedral of San Bassiano. On the doorjambs of the cathedral entrance, one to either side, stand Adam and Eve in their repentant grief, angular in their remorse. Eve, on the left, looks at us in quiet pain, her right hand over her abdomen as though to hide both her shame and the life within. Her eyes are large, staring, disbelieving. On the right a forlorn Adam tries desperately to clothe his body with a knee-length robe. He evades our eyes and crosses his left leg over the right to deny the very essence of his masculinity. Terribly moving they are in their tragedy, their inability to live up to God's command, and in their essential humanness.

On the high altar of the crypt of the cathedral is a brutal carving, a head of Saint Bassiano himself done in dark red Veronese marble. His face is craggy; his mouth turned down in a rigidly determined expression. It is hard to like this man, to think of him as being saintly. And yet there is a quality in his ugly arrogance that smacks of uncertainty and self-consciousness. A strangely unhappy face!

Lodi Vecchio (Old Lodi) is a few miles east of the Colle Eghezzone, the slow-rising hill on which Barbarossa's Lodi stands. It had been established by the Boii, a Celtic tribe, only to be taken over by the Romans, whose walls, forum, and street outlines can still be vaguely traced. The early basilica of San Bassiano stands in isolated grandeur, so old that it had already been rebuilt by the tenth century—and would be again after Frederick's time. The inside is colorful, with animated human figures and animals in still-brilliant hues of terra cotta, green, blue, and black. Winged animals and beasts of burden decorate the ceiling in a galaxy of stars and a mixed company of saints and angels. Unpainted carvings on the columns both contrast with and enrich the paintings, with the semi-humorous relief animals doing all the things that animals do.

Frederick's winter was not spent lolling about Lodi waiting for fighting weather to return. He toured northern Italy, accepting the homage of city after frightened city until the Lombard League was effectively dismantled, at least for a time. In keeping with imperial designs and in place of a former Milanese, Florence, not a member of the league, dutifully appointed a new podestà. Frederick went beyond his immediate sphere by appealing to the principal rulers of Europe for support to enable him to take on the insurgent Lombard cities, with the result that his armies were swelled by forces and supplies from well beyond his territory—from England, Spain and France, Hungary, from Oriental sultans, and even from Byzantine Emperor John Vatatzes, still maintaining a fugitive government at Nicaea, and still kissing up to the emperor. It was the time of Frederick's greatest strength as these troops joined his regulars, along with contingents from Burgundy, Sicily, Florence, Rome, and the Romagna. A well-equipped army from Germany under the nominal command of the boy Conrad traversed the Alps to join Frederick at Verona, to which he had moved for the Easter season.

Ezzelino da Romano advised that Brescia be the first target of Frederick's spring offensive, arguing reasonably that that enemy stronghold should be eliminated as a potential irritant on the imperial right flank once the climactic siege of Milan got underway. A siege camp was set up in the narrow strip of land between Brescia and the Mella River, which flows southward there, eventually emptying into the Oglio and thence into the Po. War machines were drawn up: battering rams, trebuchets, ballistae, portable towers, mangonels, all the most advanced and formidable attack mechanisms known to the age. All were readied for the onslaught.

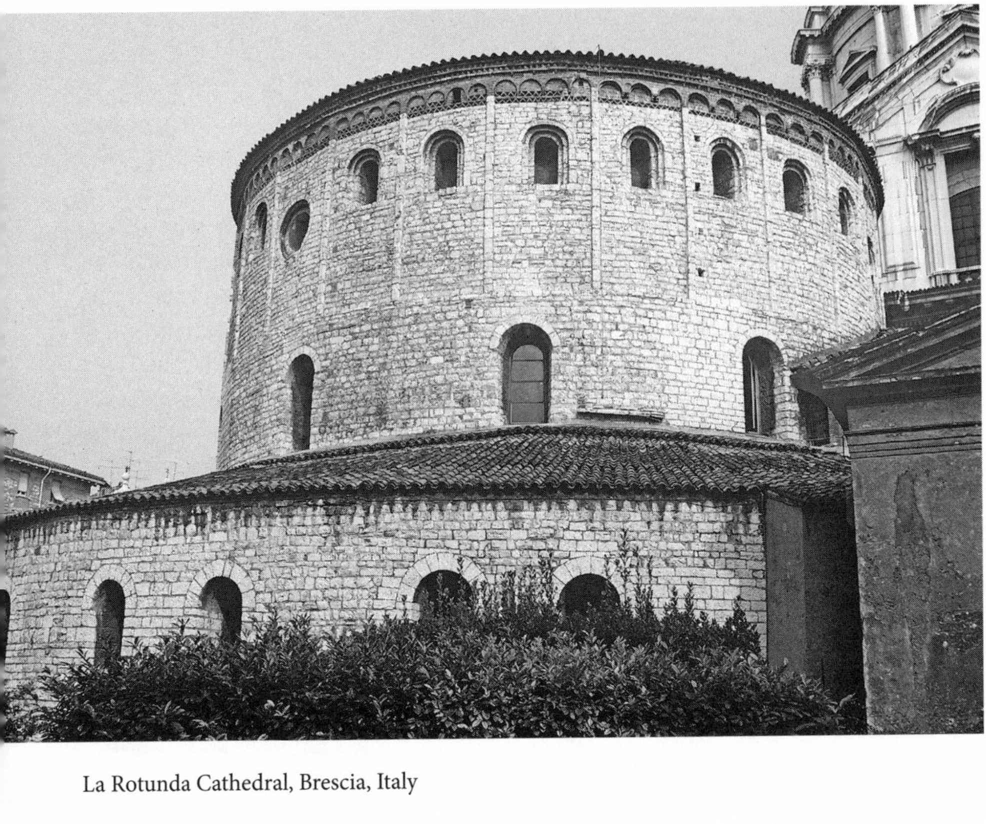

La Rotunda Cathedral, Brescia, Italy

Frederick was defied by a city surrounded by daunting walls. It entered history as Roman Brixia, and some few broken remains of that civilization were, and still are, in evidence. Behind Brescia's walls terror reigned, but not defeatism. The citizens feared Frederick's determination to force Lombardy into his empire. They were familiar with the sometimes-exaggerated tales of his heartless vengeance and with his prideful defense of the honor of his role as God's secular representative, as he interpreted that vague office. They were also aware of his overriding resolve that the "rights" of his empire would not be dishonored. Meetings were called in La Rotunda (the old cathedral) to pray at the crypt of San Filastrio. As its name indicates, the church is round with its high central portion domed and supported by a ring of columns. It had been built on the site of the Church of Santa Maria Maggiore of the sixth and seventh centuries, of which some pavement mosaics still remain. La Rotunda, dimly lit because of small windows, offers a refreshing respite in its cool interior, as well as an escape from the ubiquitous Italian din. One interested in Aldous Huxley's thingness of things—the experience of the materials from which they are made—might consider La Rotunda's stoneness of stone, hard, durable, as unyielding as the stalwart citizens who prayed in it and then turned to face the enemy. The problem—and this holds for more than a few of Brescia's places of interest—is finding the building open. It is, however, worth the trouble, not only for the admirable curve of its ambulatory, but to see the gorgeous twelfth-century Cross of the Field. Of beaten gold and enamel "gems," it displays graphically, if not realistically, the dead Christ on the cross, with Mary and John mourning from the ends of the two arms. It is shallow relief, but nonetheless moving, for the central figure is terrible in its awkward, twisted lifelessness. It is as severe a reflection of the age that produced it as is the stone building that shelters it. Nearby a communal palace of the twelfth century is dominated by an even older People's Tower, a soaring lookout that was used to keep an eye on the activities of Frederick's besieging army.

There is the stunning Cross of Desiderius in Brescia, made for that last Lombard king who died circa 786 and who ought to be acclaimed an art patron on the basis of this single object. Fixed on a wooden core covered by a sheet of metal alloy, it shows the figure of an enthroned Christ at the central crossing, giving his blessing and surrounded by the four evangelists. It is claimed that there are encompassed within the work 212 stones, cameos, and gems of colored glass. Frederick would have been riveted by a study of this cross made for a king who was roundly defeated by Charlemagne, the first of the line of emperors for which office Frederick was currently fighting. The eighth-century convent of San Salvatore looms nearby, rigidly rectangular and frescoed. If one craves the out-of-doors to breathe in Brescia's bracing air, there are no fewer than seventy-two fountains to enjoy within the city perimeters. For the stout of heart perhaps a stiff grappa is in order, an Alpine spirit distilled from the pips, stalks, and skins of the grapes after smooth wine has been extracted. Guaranteed to lacerate the palate!

Frederick's attack on Brescia had barely started when, to his extreme irritation, his great siege engineer, a Spaniard by the name of Calamandrinus, was captured. Calamandrinus knew how to respond to Brescian wooings when, on top of bribe money he was offered a house and a comely wife, unmistakably a better life than bivouacking with Frederick from campsite to campsite. The engineer responded by designing defensive machinery for his new patrons, mechanisms able, in turn, to destroy the imperial constructions which he had himself previously designed. On July 11 the siege began. And that was Frederick's third big mistake. It was to prove the disastrous turning point in his life. Years later he would still be fighting for the subjugation of Lombardy, a battle he could never win and one that would become increasingly demeaning and frustrating.

The Brescians were too terrified to surrender. Frederick, his anger growing daily, could not understand how a small city could stand against the might of his battle-toughened forces in combination with those that had been sent to him by sympathetic rulers. But the defenders' fears only fed their determination to hold out. In his growing frustration Frederick resorted to elaborate cruelty, a demonstration of that streak of heartlessness that showed itself occasionally in him and his family. He bound Lombard prisoners (some of them captured at Cortenuova) to his siege engines and temporary wooden fortresses, thinking to protect those instruments of war from the defenders' ballistae. Rather than allowing that to deter them, the Brescians followed his example and hung imperialist prisoners by their arms along the walls of their city in line with Frederick's battering rams and then continued to fire upon the enemy. They were not content to hide behind their walls waiting for the all-out attack. At night they made risky sorties against the imperialists, often inflicting telling damage, and on one noteworthy raid in October they almost succeeded in making it to Frederick's headquarters tent.

Plague broke out among Frederick's war horses and beasts of burden. Unusually severe deluges of rain harassed the attackers until, finally weakened by the wet and by the devastating night attacks, morale broke. Frederick decided to negotiate. But his peace emissary, Bernardo

Orlando di Rossi of Parma, also betrayed him, for unknown reasons convincing the Brescians to keep up their determined resistance; Frederick would quit, he assured them. Frederick did that. He burned his siege engines and retired to friendly Cremona. (Brescia was not so lucky in 1512, when even her courageous obstinacy could not save the city from being sacked by the French under Gaston de Foix, in an ordeal from which she has never recovered.) Frederick dismissed his Ghibelline troops to their native cities and sent a large part of his German contingent back across the Alps. All in all he had to admit to a fiasco, to being betrayed by di Rossi and to being defeated by a city whose taking was intended to be only the first step in a systematic program that was to make all Italy his. But the greatest damage of all—the negation of the idea of his invincibility—had been done. Enemy cities, and more than a few friendly ones, suddenly saw the feasibility of reassessing their positions and strengths. The spell had been broken, never to be recast. Old Pope Gregory IX (he was almost one hundred years old now) mustered the energy to leap into the fray by declaring open sympathy for the Lombard cause. Rumors were circulated that Frederick was a denier of the fundamental Christian doctrine of transubstantiation, that he wanted to establish a new religion with himself on the papal throne. His moral life was called into question in lurid gossip concerning his alleged habitual indulgence in every known heinous vice, instigated and spread further by Nicholas of Carbio, a papal confidant and one of the most accomplished character assassins of the century.

On a more practical level, Pope Gregory had engineered an alliance of Genoa and Venice, marked by their openly declared enmity for the emperor—not too difficult a feat, considering that Genoa was still smarting from having her Sicilian merchant bases taken from her, and Venice was in a tantrum over Frederick's treatment of their doge's son (the captured podestà of Milan), who had been relegated to an Apulian prison. Among the welter of conditions of the alliance were two of special significance: any civil power that contradicted the spiritual authority of the pope was to be considered a common enemy; no rapprochement would be made with Frederick without Gregory's express approval. Yet it was a fact that during the siege of Brescia, even while the salacious rumors were being circulated and the alliance confirmed, Gregory had made several hypocritical moves indicating that he wanted to maintain a papal-imperial dialogue. He had sent Frederick's old acquaintance and head of the Franciscan order, Brother Elias, to speak for the Curia. Equally hypocritical, Frederick had responded by dispatching ambassadors to Rome, though he had continued to stir anti-papal feelings even within the Curia. All that was past now. To act as new papal legate to Lombardy, Gregory sent a genuine Frederick hater and master of intrigue, Gregory of Montelongo, to wreak what damage he could. It was not long before he had reunited the Lombards in their league and fired up their common imperial antipathy. Next, in a missive sent out by the pope, Frederick was fingered as the anti-Christ predicted in the Second Letter of Saint John, as the instigator of the quarrel with the Lombards (a purposeful distortion of the facts of the conspiracy of King Henry of Germany), as a persecutor of monks in his southern kingdom, the wreaker of evil against the Templars and the Knights of Saint John, the suppressor of churches and monasteries, a discourager of potential converts to Christianity, a friend of Saracens, and the evader of a new crusade to boot. Clearly Gregory entertained no desire for peace with Frederick, and vice versa. The pope would not desist. And Frederick was not up to further papal browbeating.

Contemptuous of papal ambitions and hostilities, Frederick busied himself arranging the marriage of his natural son Enzo with the newly- and twice-widowed Adelasia, an heiress who claimed a sizeable portion of the island of Sardinia. Flying in the face of ancient papal assertions of ownership based on the ill-reputed Donation of Constantine, Frederick was implying that eventually the whole island would be absorbed into the empire. No one took papal claims to Sardinia very seriously and had not since the days of Frederick Barbarossa, and even earlier. As a result of jockeying about for ownership between Genoa and Pisa, Adelasia had come into possession of two of the four provinces of the island. With Cagliari, which she already owned through one of her previous marriages, she was a desirable widow indeed. Frederick moved almost before Adelasia could don her weeds and won the grieving widow over to looking with favor on the handsome young Enzo, who had been knighted in October and stood contrary to the papal pleasure, which had anticipated a husband more faithful to the Holy See than an illegitimate son of an "infidel emperor." In spite of threats of excommunication, Adelasia made her choice, and it was not in the best interests of the Curia. With the marriage accomplished, Enzo was declared king of Sardinia by his father and dispatched to his new realm. Frederick then took his court to Padua for the winter. It did not take long for a white-hot letter of protest from the pope to reach him.

Enzo was the most attractive of Frederick's children, and all of them were good looking enough. Well built, blond, and blue-eyed, he had been born to a German woman with whom Frederick had had a liaison during his first trip north of the Alps. Enzo grew to be an ostentatiously daring young man, with a quick smile, a light heart, and a joy in living. Always first into battle, he had an energy to match his father's. He was personable and liked by all who knew him—even imperial antagonists. In his later years, all of which were spent in captivity, he remained the toast of his captors. He was not as naturally intelligent or as well read as his father, but historians never tire of pointing out that he was an accomplished poet, mentally active, consistently good-natured, and as far as his contemporaries were concerned, almost beyond reproach—no small triumph for a public figure of any period. And if we can believe in the sincerity of his poetry, he seemed to have a rather heroic and romantic view of honor, public life, and life in general.

> I judge wise and knowing
> who does his work with reason,
> and who knows how to adapt to the moment
> and to live in peace with people,
> so that no one can find any reason
> to blame him for what he does.[1]

1239

When Frederick settled for the winter at Padua, he chose for his headquarters the monastery of Santa Giustina, a saint about whom we know little other than that she was "the glory of Padua." The uninteresting facade of Santa Giustina that faces on the spacious, oval sculpture park, the Prato della Valle, was rebuilt in the eighth and ninth centuries and then again in the Renaissance. Padua had been a thriving commercial and cultural center centuries before Frederick's time. And his contemporary, austere and outspoken Saint Anthony of Padua, in no way lessened those aspects of this lively, arcaded community in which Frederick himself had established the university in 1222.

Saint Anthony was a mighty force in Padua—so much that even today one forgets that he was in truth Portuguese. Having traded the Augustinian for the Franciscan habit in 1220, Anthony had tried to emulate those five Brothers Minor who had been martyred in Morocco. His health would not permit him to remain there, and he was sent back to Italy, where he rose, in time, to being the best known of the Franciscan preachers. He may have met his beloved Francis Bernardone in Assisi. If so, he was certainly inspired by his mentor. It was said that no church was of a size to hold the vast numbers of people who gathered to hear him speak. Ceremonies had to be held out-of-doors, on hillsides, in meadows. Anthony was a magnet, drawing crowds for miles around, for people, once they heard him, could not get their fill of hearing more. There was nothing trivial or self-effacing about his sermons; indeed, he became famous for his outspoken attacks on the corruption of the courts, the debilitating effects of luxurious living, and that fair target for every preacher of the period, heretical beliefs. He seemed to be afraid of no one, going so far as to denounce Archbishop Simon de Sully, who had invited him to preach in Bourges.

The popular Anthony—he went Saint Francis one better by preaching to the fish, no less!—was the first great theologian of the order, though he was destined to die at a young age. His sermon to the creatures of the water was poeticized in 1808 by Achim von Arnim and Clemens Brentano in their *Des Knaben Wunderhorn*, and then brought into the sphere of music by Gustav Mahler in his song cycle of the same name. (Mahler later reused the musical idea in the scherzo of his Second Symphony.) According to the poets, though the sermon pleased the fish, none of them was better off for having heard it.

Anthony died on June 13, 1231, in Padua, worn out by religious activities and as ready to go as had been his mentor. It is said that, like Francis, he died with a song on his lips. He was canonized within a year and was named a doctor of the church by Pope Pius XII in 1946. The building of the vast basilica of Saint Anthony, which dominates the city of Padua like a heap of enormous bulbs, was already eight years along when Frederick was there. Eventually it evolved into the gargantuan structure we know today, in the form of a Latin cross, roofed by seven cupolas, and the embodiment of an unattractive fusion of Romanesque forms with elements of the Gothic and Byzantine.

In the center of Padua, the Palazzo della Ragione was already looming over the colorful, verdurous Piazza delle Frutte and Piazza delle Erbe by the time the imperial court wintered there. It was not as high then as it is now since the top floor with loggias was added in 1306. The grand salon in this huge building was originally decorated with frescoes by the incomparable Giotto, but these were replaced after a fire by Giovanni Miretto, a Paduan, who utilized astronomical and astrological motifs for his paintings. The subject matter of Miretto's frescoes, though dating from a time after Frederick, illustrates the power of the intellectual flood that was emanating from his court. With the coming of Michael Scott to the imperial court, and for years after his death, astronomical and astrological ideas increasingly penetrated into the visual arts. Previous to the advent of Scott, the sun and moon, and perhaps a few stars, were the only heavenly spheres used as aesthetic devices, and then solely as symbols of Christian beliefs. Now, pointing the way to the Renaissance, the stars and planets, the birth signs, months, seasons and years, and men's activities as they might be influenced by the aforementioned, all became legitimate and inspiring subject matter in the arts.

By far the finest sight in Padua is the small Scrovegni Chapel, built on the ruins of a Roman arena and so called the "Arena Chapel." It was built by the son of one Reginaldo Scrovegni, a notorious usurer of Padua, as a kind of bail payment to get his father out of hell after Dante had placed him there in circle seven. Regardless of what we may think of young Scrovegni's line of thought, at least we can give him credit for hiring the foremost painter of his day to decorate the interior of his chapel: Giotto. Giotto di Bondone started painting the Scrovegni Chapel around 1303. Too bad! Frederick would have marveled. There are a few other buildings in Padua with which Frederick could have been familiar—the Church of the Hermits and the Church of Santa Maria del Carmine, for example—but they have been so brutalized by man and time, rebuilt sometimes again and again, as to be almost unrecognizable as of his age. But the Scrovegni! Sheer perfection, an unalloyed message, an infinitely complicated, eloquently simple message arching the firmament from the thirteenth to our twenty-first century. How beautiful is Giotto's telling of the meeting of Mary and Elizabeth, the tender breath, the shared feminine secret! How compelling the barely three-dimensional movements of Christ through a world that Francis would have found as compatible as his beloved Assisi! Here, indeed, is the beginning of the Italian Renaissance, the investigation and representation of the world as we see it and want to know it.

The spring of the new year introduced two fateful incidents into the long and stormy relationship of Church and state, incidents calculated to foster the cataclysm. On Palm Sunday Frederick's close friend and associate, the grand master of the Knights of the Teutonic Order, Hermann von Salza died at Salerno. Bitterly disappointed, he had shared Frederick's dream of emperor and pope ruling jointly a world in which material and spiritual concerns and objectives were clearly delineated, where neither power made obeisance to the other, but rather maintained a clearly marked-out position of mutual respect, understanding, and if possible, affection. Hermann had two lives—representative of the emperor and trusted noncurial confidant of the pope, a model of honor and loyalty in a century when neither seemed important. He was so unimpeachable in virtue that he could, with impunity, rebuke both the Lateran and his imperial benefactor. Pope and emperor saw Hermann as a man who could bend ears with straight messages from both camps. In line with his own dream of a kind of early-day United Nations, a Europe united in peace, Hermann never knew real tranquility. Ever on the move from southern Italy to Rome, from Sicily to Germany, then back to Rome, or perhaps to the Holy Land or England, he always carried in his heart the best interests of all concerned.

It was good that Hermann von Salza died not knowing of the final shattering of his vision, the ultimate collapse of what structure there was of unity between emperor and pope that he had labored so industriously to build, the rupture itself brought about by the second fateful event of the spring: Frederick's second excommunication. Now there was no hope for an amicable relationship with the papacy, nor would there be for the ten years or so remaining of Frederick's life. On Easter Sunday priests intoned the dreaded words from the pulpits of Christendom after the pope had publicly read the decree on Holy Thursday. There were many trumped-up reasons for the ban: Frederick's alleged mistreatment of the Sicilian Church; his failure to return lands that had been taken from the Hospitallers and Templars; his stirring up of dissatisfaction and revolt in Rome. Gregory never mentioned the Lombard question—the largest single point of difference. Another item, the most curious of the lot, especially in that it so intricately involved the Lombards, cites Frederick's failure to further a new crusade now that his ten-year truce with the Muslims had expired. It was perfectly obvious to any observer except Gregory (and probably to him, too, if the truth were known), that as long as the Lombard question remained unresolved, there was no way that Frederick could have torn himself from his realm to sail off to some Eastern shore. Then, too, despite his talk, Gregory was not all that interested in a new crusade. A loss of the Holy Land might be agreeable as long as Frederick was brought down with it. To that end, in the same month of Frederick's excommunication, men assembling in Lyons for the new crusade that the pope had been harping about, received without warning a message from Gregory forbidding the adventure until the following year. He ordered the would-be crusaders to return to their homes. "Soldiers of God," who had outfitted themselves for the "holy war" by selling their property and mortgaging their homes, found themselves suddenly betrayed. Their fury was so burning that they almost took out their revenge, which should have been directed at Gregory, on his messenger.

Throughout the heat of the papal-imperial imbroglios, despite his clear dislike of Gregory, his own vociferous accusations and determined defenses of the rights and honors of his empire, Frederick left the door open for accommodation. Realizing the impracticality of contacting Gregory, he took to writing letters to the Curia maintaining that he sought above all a harmonious working arrangement with the Church. He distinguished between the Curia and the man, insisting that the body of the College of Cardinals was surely superior to one pope. A working plan for Christendom was introduced into Frederick's arguments in which a general council composed of German princes and the ruling figures of Europe would work hand in glove with the pope and the Curia, a plan that years later would achieve a good deal of support. Always in his communications the learned, suave, and colorful style of Pier delle Vigne is discernible, so it was inevitable that the rumor mill cranked out stories that Frederick planned to start a new church with Pier as its high priest. Nothing, of course, could have been further from the truth. He was quite simply ahead of his time to the point where there was no way his contemporaries could understand either his innovations or his motives. Propaganda and showmanship aside, Frederick still had little to show for his all-out efforts, political or religious. The communal spirit of independence was just too strong for him; and papal haranguing was a sinister and distracting irritant. Such was the persistent weakness of his position.

Faced with the realization of his excommunication, and foreseeing the effect it would have on his imperium, Frederick was stunned, unable to understand why the pope had acted so precipitously. The loyal Pier delle Vigne addressed the imperial court and leading Paduans on Frederick's virtues. He complained that Frederick was being vilified for being the finest, most idealistic emperor to rule the Holy Roman Empire since Charlemagne. And he laid responsibility squarely at the feet of the Curia. The hurt of the undeserved punishment was his key phrase—an idea cribbed from Ovid's *Heroides*.

Deserved or undeserved, Frederick was not one to bear punishment patiently. He did more than complain. He railed against the bishop of Rome in letters to kings and princes everywhere, starting an avalanche of name-calling that helped the reputation of neither of the antagonists. He spoke of Gregory as a roaring lion, a polluted priest, a defiler of God's Church obviously not worthy of being the spiritual guide he was set up to be. The pope was a mad prophet sitting in his court and issuing dispensations for gold, and then greedily counting the profits. Gregory responded in kind. Frederick was an apocalyptic composite beast from the sea whose mouth was good only for blaspheming, an emperor admired and supported by infidels, a reincarnation of Simon Magus, a destroyer of the Church, a man who claimed that the world had been victimized by three deceivers—Moses, Mohammed, and Jesus, the latter whose mother he derided as a virgin. He was a scorpion, a wolf in sheep's clothing, a man without modesty and intoxicated by his own power. Gregory even went back to Frederick's aborted crusade of 1227, suggesting that the emperor had poisoned his noble companion, Louis of Thuringia, in Brindisi. In return, then, the pope was a second Balaam. He was compared again and again to the anti-Christ and to the rider of the red horse of the Revelation, the rider who could abolish peace from the earth. The pope was a dragon, an angel of hell, the sun attempting to obscure the moon, when in reality both lights were divinely created to illuminate the world. Clearly, there was no way these two powers could ever cooperate again. Any restraint Frederick had shown in the past was cast to the winds, for he knew that, as far as Gregory was concerned, no action was the sign of a weak ruler incapable of looking after his own interests. Frederick saw himself now as free to act in any way his conscience dictated to preserve his position and his empire.

As he had foreseen, rebel cities were encouraged, indeed instructed by the excommunication, resulting in breaks and attempted breaks from his hegemony. He was on the move for the rest of the year, back and forth across northern Italy, snuffing first this flame, then that, never attempting hands-down victories but merely trying to extinguish the conflagrations. City after city caused alarm. Friends proved themselves false, men such as Alberigo da Romano, who, unlike his brother Ezzelino (of whose brutal power he was intensely jealous), proved one of the most treacherous of allies. In company with one-time friend Azzo d'Este, who had only recently resworn fidelity to the emperor, Alberigo defected by taking possession of the city of Treviso in May, driving out the imperial podestà. Frederick had already given his daughter Selvaggia in marriage to Ezzelino as one way of calming things but more than a family connection was needed to bring tranquility. Ravenna was induced to revolt by Cardinal Sinisbaldo Fiesco, cardinal-priest of San Lorenzo in Lucina, soon to become Pope Innocent IV. In the meantime, Frederick-hater Gregory of Montelongo brought Milan and Piacenza into an alliance like that between Venice and Genoa, in which both parties agreed not to make peace with the emperor without the consent of the pope, whoever that might be (since Gregory was evidently nearing his end). Formally England maintained a pro-Frederick stance. In spite of the fact that weak Henry III was the emperor's brother-in-law, he maintained a hands-off attitude, taking neither one side nor the other. King Louis of France confirmed his usual loyal and friendly stand for Frederick.

In Germany, thanks to Conrad of Thuringia, who took the place of Hermann von Salza as grand master of the Teutonic Knights, things were kept on an even keel against the blasts of the papal delegate, Albert of Bohemia. Almost to a man the German princes refused to buy papal rhetoric and invective. When Gregory tried again to instigate the election of a new emperor, they refused to allow him any part in the election process, pointedly reminding him that it was his task to perform coronation rites on the man chosen by the elector-princes themselves.

Frederick continued his steady round of letters to important kings and princes. He maintained that all princes should see themselves threatened by papal invective and duplicity, that the pope's attempt to bring down the most noble emperor was merely the beginning of an effort by the Church fathers to seize all temporal power for themselves. Frederick realized that his southern kingdom was especially vulnerable to Church depredations. As a seal against any temptation to spoliation, those purveyors of papal propaganda, the Franciscan friars from Lombardy, were driven unceremoniously from the realm. But there was dissension even in those ranks. Brother Elias, never rigorously loyal to the principles of Francis Bernardone, but nevertheless a friend and follower of the saint and now minister general of the order—even he was won over to Frederick's side, a situation not difficult to understand when one considers how far removed from the pope Francis probably would have been had he lived to see the carryings-on of his former mentor. No lover of poverty and obedience, Elias *was* a lover of the Church. Like Francis, he saw the Franciscan order as a prime instrument in the establishment of the glory of that Church, and therefore of God. Now he watched as his order was debased by being turned into a mere propaganda tool of the pope. In the face of the severe criticism of his contemporaries, Elias maintained the position of counselor to Frederick, at times going so far, it was reported, as to absolve receivers of the papal anathema.

Reasoning that the government should be in the sure hands of the man who had the most to lose, Frederick took over direct control of the administration of his realm, even though the governing body he had appointed when he went to Germany—Archbishop Berard of Palermo, Count Thomas Aquino, and Enrico da Morra, among others—had functioned excellently in his name. Despite the distractions of northern Italy, Frederick still managed to revitalize the government of his southern realm, to reorganize its armed forces, and to exact new taxes (not popular!)—all processes carried off efficiently by an absentee ruler, which speaks well for the machinery of the administration that he had organized. In July Frederick awarded his son Enzo the title of vicar for the whole of Italy in a letter by which he gave him unlimited "imperium" in his pursuit of peace. Now, as his intention indicated, southern Italy was to be joined to northern, and both of them to Germany to establish his one vast empire—his promise to the late Pope Innocent III to avoid linking them notwithstanding. This intent may have long been clear to many of his contemporaries, but now for the first time it was out in the open. Enzo was a brilliant strategist and had little trouble taking over the March of Ancona, Jesi, Macerata, and the duchy of Spoleto. Darkening the picture, though, the city of Spoleto remained a papal enclave along with Terni, Perugia, and Assisi.

By September Milan was once again the target of Frederick's siege engines. Advantageously protected by walls of daunting proportions and able to utilize and change the courses of surrounding irrigation streams, the outnumbered Milanesi could bide their time, ignoring Frederick's efforts to entice them into a showdown battle in the open. Finally in October Frederick withdrew his forces. After taking, for a short time, a strategic bridge across the Po near Piacenza, he visited several cities and wound up the year in Pisa where, in absolute defiance of papal orders, he attended Mass and even preached from the pulpit a sermon on the subject of peace. Depending on how one looked at it, it was an inspired gesture and one that touched off a new direction in his propaganda. From this time on his letters and proclamations assume a messianic ring, a holier-than-thou posture, a counter to Gregory's "anti-Christ" attitudes that were a direct extension of Frederick's quasi-divine, self-appointed stand at the Holy Sepulcher in 1229. A new height of messianic utterance was reached in a letter that he wrote to Jesi, the city of his birth, a communication of biblical tone and reckless audacity, considered in context of the time. "The instincts of nature compel us to turn to thee, O Jesi," he wrote, "the place of our illustrious birth, where our Divine Mother brought us into the world, where our radiant cradle stood. . . . Thou, O Bethlehem, city of the March, are not least among the cities of our race; for out of thee the leader is come!"[2]

CHAPTER SIXTEEN

Kneeling and bowed down I pray,
My heart contrite as ashes:
Do Thou [, my End,] care for my end.
***Dies Irae*, verse 17**

1240

An aggressive, systematic confrontation with the Church was the only way that Frederick could hope to save his imperium. By February of the new year, he was moving through the papal patrimony unopposed. A host of cities, including Foligno and Viterbo, the latter traditionally loyal to the Church, submitted to his authority. Before long he was at the gates of Rome itself, causing the desertion of several cardinals from the papal camp and alarm in the Lateran inner sanctum. Aged Pope Gregory was reported as being in a state of acute despair. The Roman citizens were cheered by the imperial presence at their walls and gave every indication of pleasure at the prospect of the pending downfall of the intransigent pontiff. Then the pope, inventive to the end, pulled one of the tricks of his trade that by its very improbability seemed to be magic. Distressed by the desertion of that faction of cardinals, and seeing ultimate defeat hammering on the gates of the Eternal City, he went to the hostile people in the streets. On February 22, without advance notice, he appeared in procession, surrounded by hymn-singing loyalists, all of them turned out in their finest showy vestments, and bearing censers, relics of the True Cross, and the heads of saints Peter and Paul. The Romans, Ghibelline sympathizers that they were, jeered this transparent appeal to religious sentiment until old Gregory turned to face them. With a dignity that only he among men could muster, he excited their sense of duty in the face of an emperor out to wreck Mother Church. One man he may be, he affirmed, but he was not willing to bow down to another man's threats. He uncovered the sacred relics, admonishing his audience, now frozen in silence, to look on the relics for which their city was venerated. With a gesture dramatic in the extreme, he removed his own tiara and placed it on the relics, calling on the saints to protect their city since no longer were its citizens willing. It was a show of incomparable imagination, determination, and appeal. The crowd was speechless, incapable of any response but the sign of the cross.

Shaking his head in disbelief at the quixotic nature of the most notoriously fickle people of the century, the emperor was stopped dead at the gates of the Holy City. A doddering pope had upstaged a vigorous, determined emperor half his age by appealing to ancient religious sentiment. Frederick may have been the herald of the coming Renaissance, but the country of its approaching birth was not yet ready for him. He had no choice. By the end of March, he was back in his southern kingdom, wounded but wiser, more determined than ever to get to the task of uniting the south to the imperial north and to Germany. He had already started by appointing son Enzo as vicar for the whole of Italy. His eyes always steady on the future, Frederick initiated a massive reorganization of the kingdom and its administration. By May he was chafing to spring again into military action, with the declared objective of annexing papal territories—the duchy of Spoleto, the March of Ancona, indeed the whole of the patrimony of Saint Peter—thereby divesting the pope of all temporal power and relegating him solely to spiritual governance. Not to be ignored was his intention of intimidating Gregory into lifting his order of excommunication.

Conrad of Thuringia, neatly filling the office of grand master of the Teutonic Order once enjoyed by Hermann von Salza, was serving as delegate of the German princes and doing his best to snuff a fuse that seemed to be sputtering to an early explosion. He arrived in Rome, where he negotiated with several cardinals rather than the Holy Father, whom he saw as too intransigent to allow for meaningful discussion. The slight stung Gregory where it hurt. He stiffened his attitudes further, becoming more resistant than ever when Cardinal Giovanni Colonna quarreled with him and told him that he would no longer recognize him as pope. The few cardinals working to reconcile the papal-imperial differences would meet with no success in the face of Gregory's implacable suspicion of the equally disbelieving Frederick. Some showpiece negotiations collapsed in July, mainly because of papal insistence that the Lombards be included as active participants in whatever bargaining sessions were forthcoming. Then, in a desperate effort to bring Frederick to heel, Gregory abridged his rights and called a general council to meet in Rome during the Easter season of the following year. Knowing that Gregory would assume the responsibility of excluding anyone even remotely considered an imperial sympathizer, Frederick resisted, reasonably asserting that a general council by its very name should be composed of members chosen by both sides in any dispute. He had no bones to pick against holding a council. He had several times promulgated the idea himself. But this was clearly so rigged a scheme that he could in no way endorse it. He forbade his subjects from making the trip to Rome and warned others that they would incur great risk if they chose to go.

By this time Frederick had suffered several reverses in the Romagna, causing him to focus on Bologna and Ravenna. Ravenna fell easily after a siege of less than a week. Bologna, however, proved a more complicated story. He could not afford to attack the university city without first taking nearby Faenza, a free agent ideally situated to act as a gadfly. Blockade failed to bring Faenza to her knees. With winter coming on, and remembering the Brescia debacle, Frederick proceeded to erect a complete wooden town surrounding the beleaguered city, taxing his own treasury until it verged on financial disaster. He was forced to issue leather money stamped with the imperial eagle, which was later redeemed at promised value. But this was only after he had rifled the churches of Sicily of their treasures, a signal to Venice to get into the act, which she did by burning two Apulian towns and capturing an imperial galley near Brindisi. Now Venice, too, must be made to pay. The Nicaean emperor, John Vatatzes, was requested to plunder any Venetian possession within his sphere of activity. Imperial galleys set forth from Ancona against the Venetians. So desperate was Frederick for a victory that he dragged Milan's former podestà, Pietro Tiepolo of Venice, from his Apulian dungeon and hanged him in full view of Venetian galleys harassing Brindisi harbor.

1241

Faenza fell in April after eight months' siege, and then only after famine within the city so weakened the citizens as to distract them from imperial troops tunneling beneath their walls. Ever the showman, Frederick entered Faenza in triumph, bragging of his own "inexhaustible clemency" and "overflowing gentleness." Thus, like a judgmental god, he forgave the terrified and sick citizens their transgressions.

No one goes to Faenza today to find Frederick's world. Of its earlier history Faenza has little to show, so rebuilt and remodeled are its monuments. The traveler goes there, however, to study ceramics, for Faenza has been famous for that craft since the twelfth century.

She later enhanced her fortunes by importing new techniques from the Near East via Spain. The invention of tin enamel allowed Faenza, Orvieto, and Siena, as well as Paterna in Spain, to develop the attractive decorated pottery known as faïence, also called majolica, a word thought to be derived from the island of Majorca. Such is Faenza's historic claim to fame.

Frederick's threats against delegates traveling to Gregory's general council were so pointed that word went out from the Lateran to proceed as much as possible by sea. Genoa and Venice were friendly, amenable to transporting Church dignitaries at exorbitant rates and in absolute secrecy. Prospective council members arrived in Genoa secretly, but aware that Frederick had friends there: the Dorias, the Spinolas, and his recently appointed Admiral Ansaldus de Mar. A contingent of the church fathers got cold feet at the last moment, but the rest of the delegates boarded ships to run the Sicilian-Pisan imperial gauntlet. Courageous men! Aboard twenty-seven galleys and thirty-three transports, they set sail, daunted by the prospects but determined. They had reasons for their nervousness. They were nailed by Frederick's fleet between Italy and Corsica, specifically between the islands of Montecristo and Giglio. Three Genoese ships got free; the rest were captured but for three galleys that were sunk with all hands. Four thousand prisoners were taken, including more than one hundred prelates and two cardinals. At first both the prisoners and their wardens were welcomed by Enzo at Pisa, but his hospitality was cut short by his father's order to hustle the churchmen off to prison. Depositing the inferior clerical prisoners in Pisan dungeons, Enzo imprisoned the bigwigs in the imperial castle at San Miniato, west of Florence almost on the road to Pisa, whence they were shipped off to captivity in Apulia.

San Miniato was the residence of imperial governors of Tuscany. Frederick must have been thrilled by the sight of its castle stronghold built by his grandfather, Frederick Barbarossa. From its battlements there are panoramic views of Tuscany and the Arno Valley. San Miniato is one of the most charming hilltop towns in Tuscany, its battlements and high retaining walls, its stepped streets and comparative quiet allowing an escape into a centuries-old milieu. When the sunflowers (the Italians have such a lovely word, *girasole,* turn-with-the-sun) are blooming on the lower hill and in the surrounding valley, one seems to bask in a perpetual medieval sunshine. Countess Matilda of Tuscany (1046–1115), staunchly anti-imperialist to the end, inherited this wealthiest state in Italy at the age of nine. It was her donation of land to the Holy See that made up the large part of the patrimony of Saint Peter.

The imprisoned churchmen appealed to Pope Gregory's decency to make peace with Frederick and thus alleviate their misery. Several of them had already died in their Apulian confines, victims of the primitive conditions under which they were forced to exist. Contrary to his self-promotional pronouncements, there was an innate Satanic ruthlessness in Frederick's vindictiveness, people said, a dark side that smacked of being devil-inspired, all of which did nothing to mend the widening cracks in his trumped-up claims of kinship with the Divine. In victory he was looked upon with awe, albeit inspired in good part by fear. Riding a wave of public esteem that was at once fearful and admiring, Frederick determined to settle matters once and for all by capturing the city of Rome, and with it the pope. Then, from the very center of Christendom, he would be able to dictate the terms of the agreement he wanted, as well as relegate the pontiff to his appropriately religious throne. But he vowed he would never give up trying to reason with Gregory, a task that he himself viewed as hopeless.

To no avail it was called to papal attention that Frederick had sounded an alarm—anemic at best—by publishing concern about the advancing tides of Mongol invaders. This should have been not only the emperor's concern, but the pope's—all Europe's—because the avalanche was seen as becoming a threat to all of Christendom. Too many German princes, even some traditionally loyal to the Ghibelline standard, saw the wave of Tartars as emblematic of four major civilizations on a collision course: Christian, Asian, Jewish, Muslim, each with its own religion and claims to hegemony that allowed little room for the others. Frederick's refusal to turn from papal name-calling and cat-and-mouse dodging over the map of Europe, while his German princes fretted for an imperial leader to guide them against the new enemy from the East, would do Frederick's cause no good in this last decade of his life. The pope, too, remained adamant, unfazed by a popular view that with Frederick's sea victory God had pointedly indicated whose side he was on, a belief encouraged by Frederick, who crowed that the judgment of God from on high was proof enough of the righteousness of his cause. God had declared in his favor! Songs and poems were composed and sung in his honor, and at least one priest—a Dominican—preached that Frederick's victory was indeed an act of God and clearly illustrated the divine prejudice. The public view was not unmitigated admiration, however.

Shortly after his naval coup Frederick utilized the services of his brother-in-law, Richard, earl of Cornwall, as ambassador to Gregory. Richard came to Italy from Outremer full of dire reports on the horrendous conditions in that far-off land. The East was going to be lost to the Muslims, he predicted. Faced by this man who came in peace with firsthand experience in affairs of the East, stiff-necked Gregory, who saw him only as a relative of the despised emperor, would have nothing to do with him. Frederick, on the other hand, gave Richard the red-carpet treatment, ordering diversions, bloodlettings, baths, and medical therapies to offset the rigors he had suffered in Palestine. Imperial courier or not, what Richard really wanted was to see his sister, Empress Isabella. He was entertained in her apartments, where he found her surrounded by every sort of luxury, by toys, musical instruments, servants, and guards. Jugglers were brought in for his amusement, as were two dancing girls who especially turned his eye as they performed atop enormous glass globes.

Without warning, but not unexpectedly, a mirage of the end of Frederick's troubles was delivered by messenger. The ninety-four-year-old fighter for Church supremacy, Gregory IX, had breathed his last; his death commenced a two-year vacancy of the papal office, one of the

Right doorjamb, Basilian Monastery, Grottaferrata, Italy

most agonizing periods in Church history. Frederick received the news at his headquarters at Grottaferrata in the Alban Hills, nine miles south of Rome, a choice location on the site of an ancient Roman villa, and embracing a view of the Roman Campagna against which he was currently mapping a campaign.

Grottaferrata was already famous in Frederick's time for its Basilian monastery founded in 1002 by Saint Nilus, who did not live to see its completion. A sixteenth-century addition of ramparts and moats by Pope Julius II does nothing to harm the medieval aspect of Nilus's abbey, including the star of the show, an excellent Byzantine-style doorway ornamented as it is by cats' heads, dogs, lantern-jawed men, flowers, grapes, and arabesques inlaid here and there with tiny bits of ceramic color. Arching the marble lintel, a stiffly Byzantine Christ, Mary, and saints John and Bartholomew crown an eleventh-century wooden door. An even older marble baptismal font graces the atrium. Inside a veritable carpet of boldly designed Cosmati stone adds cheer and elegance, while the Chapel of Saint Nilus is decorated with frescoes by Domenichino (seventeenth century). The abbot's palace exhibits an eleventh- or twelfth-century pallium with needlework biblical scenes. As for the rest, it is an unhealthy mixture of Italian baroque, and Byzantine styles, including some unattractive icons, an exception being the two-panel, graceful Annunciation on the doors of the iconostasis. The effect is to leave one in a quandary—admiring and yet dissatisfied.

Pope Gregory IX had lived almost a century, a century when men who appeared hardier by far had succumbed to all manner of epidemics and plagues. His death could have demeaned the emperor: with no pope the conquest of Rome might have had little meaning, at best a Pyrrhic victory, an empty histrionic gesture to invite ridicule. Frederick's alternative was a verbal blast that the earth had finally seen the end of its leading preventer of peace, a panderer of evil, a disturber of the human condition, and the cause of much suffering and bloodletting.

Hate breeds hate—and feeds ambition. Neither of these powerful rulers was stronger than when his hatred for the other was at its height, the governing passion, the motivation for action. Of the two, though, Gregory was the more enigmatic. For all his sincere admiration for his dead friend from Assisi, there was little of Francis's spirit in Gregory's political vision. One wonders sometimes what he could have seen in Francis Bernardone. Gregory was a wrathful and savage man. He saw himself as the stalwart avenger, fighting the monster from the infernal deep. Frederick must have rejoiced at the demise of the man who had stood in the way of his forward-thinking dream of world unity. He had been more successful than his apostolic adversary. By his vision and energy the secular empire had been raised as a political institution. The world itself became a kind of forum with Frederick as its center. Some Arab observers saw him as the greatest Western prince since Alexander the Great. Other rulers circled like satellites around his sun, a sun that should have been incapable of involving itself in affairs less than imperial. Each lesser planet in its own orbit reflected the ultimate sun, Frederick believed, and so carried the center body to a greatness impossible to achieve alone. Though it seemed for a while that such a galaxy was on the verge of reality, it was not to be, either during Frederick's lifetime or after.

Gregory, by carrying the warped vision of Innocent III beyond even what that political genius had envisioned, had debased the Church to a scandalously dishonest, greedy, and conniving institution. Most rulers recognized that they were challenged by Church-instigated problems. Frederick might rail at them to protect their divinely appointed systems against the Church's encroachments, but he would not be successful. His sun would burn out. It was incomprehensible to Frederick that his fellow rulers did not champion him as they could have. Had not God singled him out for the imperial diadem? He must have sensed that in truth the kings did not trust him. Without exception he had the power to destroy them should they stand in his way. Yet they knew that had the Church triumphed over Frederick, the most powerful of the lot, then their days surely would be numbered.

The popes and the Curias had reason for their fears of the Hohenstaufen line. Frederick's implied assertions of divinity were enough to give pause to anyone who claimed to be God's representative on earth. Members of the Curia believed avidly that the pope was the vicar of Christ, and they his working forum, though one wonders how they could have maintained this elevated view, seeing the moral decay of the Church during these hectic years. Perhaps it is more easily understood considering Frederick's implacability, his daunting insistence on the sacredness of his imperium—his arrogance. After all, there were some members of the Curia—Cardinal Giovanni da Colonna, for example—who were exemplary in behavior and viewpoint. All that aside, any man or group who impinged on the Church's claims of Divine appointment could not be tolerated. Divine right of kings was bad enough; but to claim, or even hint at, kinship with the Divine was unconscionable.

Seeing his world threatened by an ambitious pope, Frederick unjustly generalized that the priests were as bad as their superiors since, having taken their vows, they owed allegiance to no one beyond the institution of the Church. They tended toward oppression through greed, he cried, while fattening themselves on alms cajoled from the common man, who could ill afford the giving. In Frederick's eyes nothing would do but that the state be emancipated from the Church. Frederick had known no father. He may have been sincere in his frequently made assertion that he wanted to look to the pontiff as a father. And the psychological implications of that idea are fraught with significance. At the very least it had to be jolting to him to see the spiritual father wallowing in treacherous scheming for his debasement. In the end both powerful adversaries—empire and Church—would come crashing down in the wreckage of the Middle Ages.

The struggle had already set Frederick on the road to ruin. The crusade had taught him that he dare not leave his realm as long as Gregory was alive, during which time a foe potentially a thousand times more dangerous than the pope or the Muslims was hammering on the gates of the empire. Europe was immobilized by the portent of Mongolians marching westward. They had already ravaged Russia and destroyed Kiev. Even when they swarmed across the Polish and Hungarian frontiers, Frederick dared not leave his kingdom open to Gregory's depredations. He should have been leading Europe's mightiest against the hordes from the East. Instead, he was besieging the hardly important town of Faenza and speaking hollow phrases about his "inexhaustible clemency" and "overflowing gentleness." He was tracking down Christian churchmen at sea and finally stomping around outside the walls of Rome while Gregory was dying inside. With a letter-writing campaign voicing his opinion that now God, in his infinite wisdom, would see to it that a more fair-minded man would sit on the throne of Saint Peter, he marched off to his southern realm where, for the next twenty-two months, he remained.

An expedition to sally forth and meet the terrible Mongol invasion, which was recognized now as a threat to Germany itself, had been called in the name of thirteen-year-old King Conrad. Yet the best Frederick could do in his post-Gregory ennui was to send some fatherly instructions on the conduct of the anticipated confrontation and perhaps a small detachment of horsemen to stem the limitless tide of Mongols in the Danube area. There are reports that brave Enzo, emulating his father's former youthful dash, led a few thousand cavalrymen to join his half brother Conrad in Hungary, but they are not totally supportable. Germany was saved through no effort of the emperor. The Polish cavalry entered Latin Christian history by doing its part to save the north, while the excommunicated emperor involved himself in what seemed to many of his princes to be situations of miniscule importance. In any event he was not at hand to lead forces of his own in defense of his, Italy's, and Germany's interests.

Even disagreeable Duke Frederick II of Austria ostensibly went to the aid of King Bela of Hungary, but his motives were purely selfish. He would have liked nothing better than to see Bela go down in defeat before Mongol raiders so that he himself could annex Hungarian lands west of the Danube. He sowed discord wherever he went, eventually taking over several areas from Bela after capturing that king, who was the only man actively holding his own against the Eastern terror. Duplicitous from head to toe, Duke Frederick went his quarrelsome way, never moving eastward against the Mongols, but inviting other nations to send their finest to Europe's defense, allowing them to use Austria as their road to the front. When King Bela sent urgent pleas for help to Frederick, the pope, and Louis IX of France, he was rebuffed from all quarters. Frederick claimed he had to march on Rome and bring the pope to heel; then he would be in a position to offer help. The pope claimed that he could do nothing as long as he had the worry of Frederick on his mind. The slender, angel-faced Louis, with his usual grace, simply wrung his hands and said to his mother, Blanche of Castile, that should they not be stopped, then the Mongols would send them to the eternal reward of the righteous in heaven. And all the time Frederick the Quarrelsome was sowing his usual discord. By the time old Gregory died in Rome there had been a several-month lull in the fighting on the eastern front, creating a false sense of security among Europeans. Anxieties faded, and troops turned homeward. But irreparable damage had been done, and Frederick's reputation would never regain its luster. Then the Danube froze over.

Under the leadership of Batu, grandson of Jenghis Khan, the Mongols had crossed the frozen river and sacked the richest city in Hungary—Gran, now Esztergom—almost on the sweeping curve where the Danube turns south after flowing eastward from Vienna. Downstream, Pest was used as a jumping-off point for another pack from the east side of the Danube to attack Buda on the west bank. The Mongols were on the march to Austria, and scouts actually reached the outskirts of Vienna. Wiener Neustadt was attacked. At the same time a small reconnaissance force reached the very edge of panic-stricken Udine, only sixty miles from Venice, and was advancing ever closer to the Dalmatian Coast. Then it started moving in the direction of Dubrovnik. To any reasonable observer only a combined European army, probably under Frederick Hohenstaufen, might have saved the day. Even then, they would have been the underdogs standing against the best army in the world.

Weighed down by cumbersome armor and comparatively slow-moving, on elaborately decked-out mounts, they would have found it nearly impossible to outmaneuver the lightly encumbered enemy who, "sullen, fatalistic, phlegmatic and callous . . . could suffer without complaint and kill without pity."[1] At this point Europe could have used an Alexander Nevsky, prince of Novgorod, who was successfully holding off lesser invaders—the Swedes—in the north. But no savior was evident.

As is the case more often than not, it was familial ambition that frustrated Mongol determination. Some said it was an act of God. In any case it was not any action by Frederick. Ogedei, the great khan, the supreme leader of the Mongol swarm, died of excessive drink, a broken, dissipated man, encouraged in his vice by a wife who wanted her son to succeed to the leadership. So ended the threat of a Mongol invasion, as the hordes, bound by tradition, did an about-face and marched eastward to faraway Karakorum to pay their respects and to elect a new great khan. Eastern Europe had been ravaged; the land had been wasted, the population depleted. Only Batu and his troops remained behind at his lavish camp at Sarai ("Golden Camp") near the River Volga north of the Caspian Sea. Batu would don the trappings of the great khan himself. Under his ambitious design, Sarai became a new capital rivaling even Karakorum and from it later rode forth the Golden Horde. But the Mongols had missed their opportunity; Europe would not again be laid out so vulnerably before them. Eventually they passed into history, literature, and legend, to be absorbed, in a sense, by the very cultures that they had conquered.

Rome was without its leading citizen. The ten cardinals who were at liberty (out of twelve, since two had been captured in Frederick's sea coup) were reluctant to meet for any election of a new pope until Frederick helped their situation by releasing his prisoners, which he flatly refused to do. Matteo Rosso Orsini, dictatorial senator of Rome, (helped to power by Gregory, incidentally) tired of the delays. Determined to operate under a pope of the same mold as Gregory IX, he virtually imprisoned the available cardinals in the ancient and derelict Septizonium, abandoned now since "Brother Jacopa" dei Settesoli had moved to Assisi to live out her life in the clear Umbrian air of Saint Francis. Then, acting with the senator's approval, the appointed guards so flagrantly abused and deprived the old men, inundating them with urine and excrement and feeding them inadequately, that Cardinal Robert of Somercote, an Englishman, died shortly afterwards. Pope-elect Celestine IV succumbed within seventeen or eighteen days following his election. He died before he was even consecrated and after only one official act—an unsuccessful attempt to excommunicate high-handed Matteo Orsini. Matteo, not pleased with the prospects of another enforced election, had imperialist Giovanni da Colonna clapped into prison, feeding the flames of a family feud that would last for generations and, on more than a few occasions, reduce Rome to a battlefield. Three Guelf-leaning cardinals stayed in Rome, while the remaining four fled to Anagni, whence they refused every entreaty to return for a new election, at least until Frederick would release the two cardinals he still held. But Frederick was obstinate, which paid off eventually when he won over to his side one of the two—Otto of Saint Nicholas. Perhaps now, he reasoned, he stood a bare chance of getting a supreme pontiff with whom he could work.

Death visited the house of Hohenstaufen when at the end of the year, on December 1, Frederick's English empress, Isabella, died while giving birth to a daughter. Only two of the four children she bore survived her, one of them being the now three-year-old Henry. Isabella was only twenty-seven, the second of Frederick's wives to die in childbirth, and there is no reason to believe that he mourned any more for her than he had for the others. She was buried in the dark, heavy-arched Norman cathedral at Andria where her predecessor, Yolanda, also lay.

1242

Within three months of the death of the empress, the House of Hohenstaufen was visited again by the ghostly presence. Young Henry VII, imprisoned since the year of Frederick's marriage to Isabella, died—it would seem by his own hand—on February 12. He had been relocated from San Felice to Nicastro with the intent of keeping him in southern Italy and out of the mainstream of the more troublesome political affairs. It was in the course of yet another move that he intentionally rode his horse either off a bridge or over the side of a cliff into an abyss below. There is some evidence that Frederick may have summoned him to his court for forgiveness and that the unknowing Henry, deep in the depression that must have enveloped him, believed he was on his way to execution. The mystery will never be solved. But what is known is that in this case Frederick grieved deeply, weighing his torment as a father against the sentence that he as emperor-judge had been forced to administer. And his load was not lightened by the funeral obsequies in which he was likened to the biblical Abraham who was, similarly, called upon to sacrifice his own first-born. Frederick wrote a sad letter on the death of Henry. Significantly, he relates himself to both David (an ancestor of Jesus, remember) weeping over Absalom, his first son, and to Julius Caesar mourning over his son-in-law, Pompey. If he could not weep for his wives, Frederick could experience genuine grief for a disloyal son: "The feelings of the father overpower those of the Judge, and we are forced to bewail the death of our eldest son. . . . We confess that though we could not be bent by our son when alive, we mourn him when dead."[2]

1243

On June 25 the Church was given a new leader, but only after Frederick had reluctantly complied with the wishes of the Curia and released his cardinal prisoners, on the condition that character-assassin Gregory of Montelongo, still an agent for the Curia and still actively sowing seeds of subversion in northern Italy, be recalled—an agreement that the new pope refused to honor. Twenty months after the death of short-lived Pope Celestine IV, the understaffed College of Cardinals elected courteous and cultivated Sinibaldo Fieschi of Genoa, who chose the name of Innocent IV, which in itself was enough to send shivers of anticipation through Frederick's stocky frame. Frederick expressed satisfaction with the election of a pope whose family, the counts of Lavagna, had imperialist connections. Indeed, they had received their title from Frederick himself. Yet shrewd Innocent IV would prove the most disconcerting threat of all Frederick's papal adversaries. From now on the immense and formidable power of the Church over the destinies of men was in the hands of a master manipulator and an expert lawyer. Religious feeling was not a part of the man's character. Mystical depth played a secondary role in the face of worldly interests. Manipulation of moral purpose was the end-all of the papal raison d'être. With God on his side, Innocent IV was in every way but warfare superior to his imperial adversary. Within a few days Innocent made known his policy, causing Frederick to observe ruefully, "No pope can be a Ghibelline." It became abundantly clear that the papal-imperial struggle was not merely a battle between two very pigheaded men; it was a fight to the death between the priestly and the secular ruling castes and could at times become astonishingly petty.

Publicly Frederick had rejoiced in the establishment of the new papacy. He sent legates to the Lateran with congratulations and assurances of peaceful intentions and obedience—save where the rights and the honor of the empire were concerned. The pope responded by sending a return embassy to the imperial court with a message of similar intentions of peace, providing only on the release of the rest of the prisoners taken at Giglio and the righting of the wrongs performed by Frederick against papal interests, especially his invasion of the Papal States. For his part, said Innocent, he was willing to make amends for any wrongs committed by the Church—"which is inconceivable." Frederick hedged; and immediately the quarrel gained momentum. He could never, of course, admit to his own excommunication. The Lombards could never be a part of his negotiations with the pope, he said, a condition that Innocent clearly had in mind, for he knew that once Frederick had his vengeful way in Lombardy, the security of the Papal States would be jeopardized. In addition, Frederick brazenly tried to bargain his way into possession of the Papal States, arguing that he was willing to recognize them as papal fiefs. This was precisely what Innocent and a whole series of popes before him feared the most, an undivided union of northern and southern Italy in the control of a single man, be it Frederick, his forerunners, or his heirs. Furthermore, with Innocent's encouragement, the papal legate, Gregory of Montelongo, went on determinedly undermining the imperial position in Lombardy. Then, if more proof of the impossibility of reconciliation were necessary, there arose further evil in the person of one Cardinal Ranieri to seal once and for all the fate of the impossible dream.

Never again would Frederick be pitted against so odious an adversary as Cardinal Ranieri, a man with a taste for every kind of deceit, vilification, cunning, and foul play, as long as he furthered the influence and power of the Church hierarchy. His loathing for the emperor was so overblown as to soar into the realm of the demented. He was of the school of political churchmen who equated spiritual and secular power and who made ethical conduct and morality subject to material and political interests. Ranieri was a native of Viterbo—which had been taken by Frederick in 1240, remember—and was consistently in opposition to any kind of peace overtures between Church and empire. Now this year he saw his opportunity to scuttle what meager progress had been made. Evidence indicates that Innocent himself backed Ranieri's seizure of the imperial stronghold at Viterbo, his guarantee of safe conduct for its guards, and their consequent massacre. At any rate, Frederick believed that Innocent was party to the affront and betrayal and so accused him. By September Frederick was back at the walls of Viterbo, fighting to regain his stronghold in a siege that resulted in his overwhelming defeat.

With the emperor distracted, Innocent gave Gregory of Montelongo and Bernardo Orlando di Rossi the nod to rekindle rebel antagonisms in Lombardy by assuming jurisdiction of Parma. He annulled Enzo's marriage to Adalasia and consequently any claims that young man might have on Sardinia. His back to the wall, Frederick negotiated through Cardinal Otto of Saint Nicholas, one of only two papal representatives whom he could trust, the other being Giovanni da Colonna. Even by a stretch of imperial imagination, the peace could not have been more humiliating. If adhered to, it would simply have dismembered the empire and negated the ideals for which Frederick had all of his life been fighting. Cardinal Otto, who had become convinced of the legitimacy of Frederick's views while he was in captivity after Giglio, was scandalized by Ranieri's malevolent massacre of the imperial loyalists as they marched out of the Viterbo fortress. How could success ever be expected, Frederick asked Otto, if all shame be set aside, if good faith be despised, if conscience be beyond reason and without conviction, if no trust could be put in the honor of spiritual fathers? What would hold men together? What could be expected to bring about a reconciliation in this very serious quarrel if the promises of the holy legate, no, of a cardinal, could be so easily negated? While Otto of Saint Nicholas was not suspect in Frederick's view, the emperor was never again free of suspicion of churchmen. He vowed vengeance against Viterbo even, he swore, at the cost of losing his chances at Paradise. But worse was yet to come.

1244

It would have been irrational for Frederick to assert that, following the betrayal and slaughter of his troops at Viterbo, any accommodation between emperor and pope could be possible. Yet on Holy Thursday Frederick's spirits were buoyed when a provisional peace settlement between the two was spelled out before Innocent IV and a vast crowd in the piazza in front of the Lateran. One of Frederick's representatives was the extremely intelligent imperial court judge Thaddeus of Sessa. Thaddeus was a weighty man, if we can go by the prominent-featured portrait bust of him in the Museo Provinciale Campano in Capua, mellow, and probably soft spoken, which admittedly is reading quite a bit into a marble portrait seven centuries old. What we know for sure, however, is that he was wise, and a loyal and cherished intimate of the emperor. Speaking for the emperor, Thaddeus, Pier delle Vigne, and Count Raymond of Toulouse swore to Hohenstaufen peaceful intentions in a ceremony witnessed by cardinals, the Roman senator, and crowds of citizens. Emperor Baldwin of Constantinople was there in

Thaddeus of Sessa, Museo Provinciale Campano, Capua, Italy

Rome to beg for a handout, money being as hard to come by in the East as in the West. Without lifting the ban of excommunication, the pope went so far as to call Frederick "a devoted son of the Church" and "a believing prince." There was no treaty, only a preliminary to a treaty. Yet Frederick was sufficiently optimistic to write to son Conrad in Germany advising him to broadcast the glad tidings throughout his realm. Enter the Lombards, whom this pope, like the last, insisted be part of the peace process.

On arriving in Rome to ratify the treaty, the Lombard delegation immediately turned thumbs down. They refused to accept any part of it. Their predicament vis-à-vis the emperor came first, they claimed, even before papal problems. After all, they did not hesitate to point out, their years of mistreatment were the reason for Frederick's excommunication to begin with. What everyone knew had finally been said. Like his predecessor, Innocent bent over backward to mollify the Lombards, transparently agreeing to changes that he knew would be unpalatable to Frederick, among them that Church lands must be returned and the

Giglio prisoners freed before the lifting of the ban of excommunication. There was no way that Frederick could do this; and he knew the pope knew it. Should Innocent suddenly get it into his wily head to demand new concessions, then Frederick's leverage would be lost. But he still had a trump card to play. To Innocent's horror the imperial-sympathizing Frangipani family offered to cede to Frederick certain of their fortifications within the city of Rome, some of which had been constructed in the ruins of the Colosseum. Frederick played his card wisely. He asked for a face-to-face meeting with the pope, which was agreed to. But Innocent had an ace up his sleeve, too. He appointed twelve additional members to the College of Cardinals, which in itself made Frederick raise his guard. But not far enough. Frederick moved his court to Terni, near Narni, the agreed-upon site for the meeting. As though playing a gigantic game of chess and in answer to Frederick's move, Innocent responded with one of his own to Civita Castellana, there ostensibly to await the laying of the final plans. Then Innocent overtrumped.

On June 27 he moved to Sutri whence, in the dark hours of the morning, in disguise, and in the company of four cardinals and a handful of servants, he deserted his court and bolted for Civitavecchia. By arrangement, a Genoese fleet awaited there to carry him off to Genoa where, on July 7, he landed to the joyous, welcoming psalm, "Blessed be he that cometh in the name of the Lord." Genoa may have been delirious in her reception, but the papal presence could wear thin after a while. At the same time the rest of Europe cast a wary eye on the prospect of having a voluntarily exiled Innocent IV as a guest on their sovereign soil for an indeterminate time, for that was clearly what he had in mind. This is not to mention the nerve-shattering prospect of antagonizing the fuming, outsmarted Hohenstaufen emperor. As a last resort Innocent, ailing and not really fit for travel, was carried in a litter across Piedmont and over the Alps to Lyon, arriving with an ostentatious papal flourish. He had his full court reassembled by December 1, and there he would remain for the next six years in a preview run of the "Babylonian captivity" at Avignon. Now generally viewed as a frightened fugitive from imperial tyranny, the pope was out of the empire and beyond Frederick's reach, in a city ruled by an archbishop-prince and a commune. Innocent was free to take what vindictive action he wanted. He was free to call the Gregory-instigated general council, which, under his domineering control, could be counted on to go through the motions of deposing the emperor. The only hope for Frederick to avoid this prospect—though he always maintained correctly that neither the pope nor the Curia, singly or together, had the authority for imperial deposition—was to make peace with the intractable pontiff. While his henchmen were sowing discord elsewhere, Innocent set the wheels in motion to gather the council, scheduled to meet in June 1245. Adding to his frustration, Frederick was now distracted by an uprising in Parma where Innocent's Fieschi family was prominent and he himself especially well represented by his handsome brother-in-law, Bernardo Orlando di Rossi, Frederick's turncoat emissary during the siege of Brescia. Frederick sent troops to Parma and arranged the election of a new podestà, one of his Sicilian courtiers, Teobaldo di Francesco, later to turn traitor also.

When Innocent IV came to Lyon, he established residence in a city founded by Lucius Munatius Plancus, whose tomb the eighteen-year-old Frederick might have seen at Gaeta. Roman statesman Agrippa made Lyon the starting point for the four great roads that were to traverse Gaul. Augustus favored the city, and Claudius was born there. Some remains of early Christianity are found at Lyon, along with traces of Roman baths, a forum, and certain religious structures and altars. The transepts and choir of the Cathedral of Saint-Jean had long been finished by Innocent's time, though the west portal with its three sculptured doorways would be left for the next century, and even then were badly damaged by Calvinist troops in 1562. Next to the cathedral on the south side, the Choristers' House is adorned with Romanesque blind arcades and sculptural patterns and is the finest medieval building in Lyon. More than adequately the two together serve as a centerpiece for the Saint-Jean quarter, the medieval area of Lyon that hugs the right bank of the Saône.

The heavy, solidly Romanesque Church of Saint-Martin d'Ainay, with its reused ancient columns and its twelfth-century mosaic floors, had been rebuilt almost a hundred years before Innocent's stay. The decorative capitals and bas-reliefs are especially entertaining in their Romanesque simplicity and naive clumsiness: birds and fish, lions and fantastic animals, plant patterns, scenes from the Old and New Testaments enliven the perceptions of the twenty-first century as they did those of the Middle Ages. Adam and Eve are there, and their humble shame before God is, in its primitive, honest storytelling, undeniably moving. The Great Creator stands in the presence of Cain and Abel, a picture of unconcerned aloofness, while to the right Saint Michael fights off the creatures of hell. Dark and cool inside, Saint-Martin d'Ainay is topped by a hefty central tower, especially handsome from the outside, block-like and solid, but refined by four open arches on the upper level of each side.

1245

Frederick was not prone to kowtow to anyone, much less a tricky pope. He had one more point to make, a point so strong that with a more reasonable pope on the throne it probably would have made a difference. In August 1244 Jerusalem had fallen to the Khwarizmian Turks, which horde then joined forces with the Egyptians to administer a devastating defeat to the Christians at Gaza, certainly negating whatever political progress Frederick and his emissaries had gained in

St. Martin d'Arnay, Lyon, France

years past. It was the beginning of the end of the Western presence in the Holy Land. King Louis IX of France, the most virtuous of the monarchs of his time, had already announced his coming crusade, a grateful quid pro quo for a miraculous recovery from a malarial infection of December last year. Should Frederick and Louis be able to join hands on this venture, it would bode well for its success, a prognosis more reasonably optimistic than for any of the other ill-timed, ineptly managed excursions. Frederick, confronting the symbolic humiliation of a ritual deposition, and on the encouragement of the patriarch of Antioch, who as much as anything else was afraid for the safety of the East in the path of the again-raging Mongols, tendered his offer to lead a crusade to embattled Outremer. He went beyond reasonable expectations by suggesting that he would not return to Europe without papal consent for a period of three years. Then he went beyond even that by claiming that he would leave, with no strings attached, the resolution of the Lombard question solely up to the pope. On the surface it was a clear signal to Innocent that he had won the game, though he must have wondered why Frederick chose this particular time to marry his illegitimate daughter, Constance, off to the Nicaean emperor, John Vatatzes, especially considering that the bride had not yet reached the age of puberty and that Vatatzes himself was older than Frederick. It proved a good political union, which is what it was intended to be, with Vatatzes supplying Frederick with men and arms for the rest of his troubled years.

Frederick must have known that Innocent IV was so bent on his destruction that he would not accept his proposals regardless of how appealing they were, in which case he could proclaim to the world his own virtue. Then again, Frederick's craving for peace—he was almost fifty-one years old now—may have persuaded him to this capitulation. Historians argue, too, that he wanted to go east, to leave Europe in favor of King Conrad, hoping his son would not incur the same debilitating struggles that he had faced throughout his life. Certainly it is easy to understand that Frederick, even energetic and robust as he was, was tired of the constant battle, the perpetual circle of intrigue and betrayal that seemed to lead nowhere and might now be pointing to the destruction of the empire. He might pine for the more laid-back lifestyle of the East, for the scientific and philosophical discussions for which he had developed such a taste when he was on crusade, for the arts with their spiritual and mystical slant. Whatever Frederick's reasons for his willingness to go east, the despicable Cardinal Ranieri, having heard rumors that Innocent was inclined to accept Frederick's submission, determined to block his adversary once again.

Journeying northward to a springtime imperial diet that he had called at Verona, Frederick paused at Viterbo to administer a token vengeance on the traitorous city. Like a man deranged, Ranieri so exaggerated his report to the Curia concerning the minor damage done to the Marches of the Papal States that Frederick was again branded the anticipated anti-Christ. The trumped-up horrors Frederick was accused of included the indirect murders of Gregory IX and his own son Henry

VII and the murder by poisoning of his three empresses. The latter accusations are more credible since Frederick had already contracted to marry Gertrude, niece of Duke Frederick II of Austria (the contract was speedily voided when the frightened bride-to-be refused). Ranieri crowed that Frederick was in revolt against heaven, that he was a man worse than Herod in that Herod slew only Jesus, while Frederick would destroy God. Once again he was a denier of the Faith, the despoiler and corrupter of the world, a poisonous serpent, a would-be dethroner of popes. Ranieri's was an attack of duplicity and vicious lying unmatched in the history of propaganda. By his diatribes he saw to it that the dim light of papal-imperial accommodation was snuffed out.

In Verona preparing for the diet he had summoned, Frederick was at first unaware of Ranieri's attacks. He was enjoying the company of seventeen-year-old Conrad, neither of them aware that this was the last companionable meeting they would know. Conrad cut a fine figure of a youth fast growing into stalwart manhood. From the look of him, he would in time be a worthy defender of the empire. After Frederick's experiences with the contrary and hostile Henry, Conrad was soothing comfort. The surroundings were pleasant. Not yet the city of rebellious subjects familiar to Romeo and Juliet, Verona was orderly and calm as she basked in the light of the imperial presence.

Strategically protected by two sharp loops in the swift-flowing Adige River, Verona had been a thriving city of the Roman Empire, of which ample remains testify, including an enormous amphitheater, a theater, two arches of the Ponte de Pietra, and some walls and gates of the third century. The Piazza delle Erbe, now the main produce market, is on the site of the ancient forum and, together with the Piazza dei Signori, with its statue of Dante and its twelfth-century town hall, is surrounded by excellent medieval buildings. Theodoric the Great, king of the Ostrogoths, was familiar with Verona, and so was Odoacer, the first of the barbarian rulers of Italy. Both Lombards and Franks resided in this celebrated ancient city.

Verona is rich in buildings that date from early Christian days, the most spectacular being the Basilica of San Zeno, named for the first bishop and patron saint of the city, who died in 371. In every way a superlative example of Romanesque architecture, it was erected in the fifth century but did not achieve its present form until the twelfth, when the crypt (with its charming sculptural burlesque of the fable of Reynard the Fox in which, as always, the beast's cunning wins out) was opened by raising the floor of the choir higher than the nave. This arrangement, though not unique, theatrically dramatized the altar end of the church. There are medieval frescoes inside and an altarpiece by Andrea Mantegna showing an enthroned Madonna in company with angels and saints. The choir screen supports statues of Christ and the apostles, which show vague traces of northern European Gothic influences, while still remaining essentially Romanesque.

The basilica's greatest treat, however, is the west doorway, flanked by ferocious lions astride which every child wants to be photographed, and with bands of twelfth-century sculpture on either side by Guillelmus and Nikolaus, the latter of whom did work on the cathedrals here and in Ferrara and Piacenza. Stylized scenes from the Testaments are shown, so magnificently stylized as to make us feel that we really are witnessing miraculous events, as well as stories concerning Veronese history in ornamental relief. The two huge bronze doors, made up of reliefs bolted to a wooden core, are of at least partly German workmanship and inspiration and show stories from the life of San Zeno and from the Bible.

At first glance the bronze slabs seem flat and primitive, with little detail. Only on closer scrutiny does one become aware of the overriding vigor and subtle élan, the charm, of the forty-eight shallow reliefs. With what remarkable energy and economy does the unknown artist fill the square panel allotted to the expulsion of Adam and Eve from the Garden of Eden, not tropically lush and verdant but skimpily planted with exotic, two-dimensional flora—decorative, yes, but right to the point! How graphic is the story of Herod's lust, John the Baptist's decollation, and Salome's dance, she looking like some exotic slug without a bone in her body! God in Glory is stunted, the head being too large in the Romanesque manner, but faith and the desire to glorify are never in doubt. With what natural ease the artist breaks through a decorative molding to make room for a mourning Mary at the deposition from the Cross and with what expertise he abstractly arranges the soldiers in the flagellation, all of them wearing strange, conical hats like something out of *The Mikado*. San Zeno is there in the sacred company, as are Balaam astride his donkey, and Jesse reclining on a couch, acting the root to the tree of the generations of Jesus. There are masks of monsters and saints, ugly and serene, grotesque and lovely, works harkening back to Augsburg but in some ways more satisfying. While Augsburg echoes Teutonic thunder, San Zeno's doors in their naiveté, their graceful embellishments and ornamental excesses, betray the innate, fun-loving tastes of the people for whom they were created. The reliefs are a far cry from Ghiberti's coming realistic excesses at Florence. And they are the better for it.

Expulsion from Eden, San Zeno, Verona, Italy

While Frederick basked in the pleasure of his son's company at Verona, the adulations of his loyal German princes, and the considerable money consignments from his new son-in-law, John Vatatzes, Innocent IV went on manufacturing evidence and mustering energy for his presentation at the Lyon general council. As Frederick later pointed out, the council was in no sense of the word "general" since many members were absent when the conclave finally gathered—in fact, less than one-third the number of churchmen present at Innocent III's celebrated Lateran Council of 1216, and a paltry number compared to the five hundred who would attend Gregory X's 1274 meeting in this same city. Innocent IV quickly disposed of some Church business that he considered inconsequential—but not without moments of discomfort, as when Hugh de Digne, Franciscan friend of Salimbene, sounding like a second Saint Paul, hurled abusive criticism at the gathering.

Sitting in the lofty choir of Lyon cathedral, flooded in the brilliant colors of the thirteenth-century stained glass, Innocent IV intoned the usual tiresome complaints against the emperor, all of them eloquently refuted by Thaddeus of Sessa. The emperor was, according to Innocent, guilty of heresy and sacrilege, the latter for having taken prisoner the prelates caught by his navy at Griglio. He had been a part of the marriage arrangements of his daughter with schismatic emperor John Vatatzes. He had employed Saracens to kill Christians; indeed, was he not a friend to Saracen rulers? In the eyes of the church Frederick had sinned by negotiating with infidels. Furthermore, conveniently overlooking Altamura, he built no churches in the name of the Lord and made no contributions to charity. He had hired assassins—an interesting accusation in light of Innocent's actions in the near future. It is difficult to see this pope as interested in anything beyond the destruction of Frederick Hohenstaufen politically and, as time would tell, physically.

Thaddeus of Sessa defended his master, but his arguments were rudely brushed aside. Envoys from France and England were given no chance to question papal logic, and the patriarch of Aquileia was threatened with the loss of his office if he spoke. By July 17 Innocent had wrung from the council a decree of deposition of an emperor painted as wallowing in sin. Enthroned in this glorious house of God, surrounded by a shimmering prism of windows in a forest of soaring columns, and as though it were within his jurisdiction to unseat an emperor, Innocent intoned his words of deposition:

> We . . . after careful deliberation with the Holy Council, by virtue of the power bequeathed by Christ to us in the person of St. Peter, hereby declare [Frederick], who has proved himself unworthy of the Crown, to be bound by his sins and cast off by the Lord, and we hereby strip him of all his honours, and we release his subjects from their oath of allegiance to him as Emperor and King; and we decree excommunication against any who shall hereafter abet or counsel him. The Electors of the Empire are free to choose a successor in his room; as to the Kingdom of Sicily, we will make such provision for it as may seem expedient to us.[3]

In counterpoint to the culminating Te Deum, Thaddeus of Sessa lamented that now the heretics could rejoice and the Mongols arise and make merry. Innocent responded that he had done his duty; now God could do what he would with the East. Thaddeus's last point, while well taken, was not entirely fair.

Shortly after arriving in Lyon, Innocent had sent two embassies to Mongolia to visit the court of the great khan. Unfortunately, Innocent dispatched a letter with a friar, Johannes de Plano Carpini, a Franciscan and former friend of Francis Bernardone, in which he demanded with an arrogance and lack of understanding that bordered on stupidity that the great khan accept Christianity. After traveling for fifteen months, enduring atrocious hardships, resting over in the ruined city of Kiev, and visiting Batu at his Golden Camp, Johannes finally reached the new great khan, Kuyuk, son of the late Ogedei, near Karakorum. By the time he made it back to the pope at Lyon in 1247, he was an exhausted, sick courier, bearing only the kind of insulting letter that Innocent deserved, a counterdemand that the pope recognize Kuyuk's suzerainty and, in company with all the princes of the West, do homage to him. Johannes de Plano Carpini did leave his mark, though. He has gone down in history as the first explorer of Mongolia and, what is more, wrote about it in what could be the most arresting terms of any Western Christian writer of the Middle Ages.

When word of Innocent's deposition reached Frederick in Torino, the emperor's fury knew no bounds. Although he expected the worst, nothing had prepared him for the presumption of a pope who would aspire to deprive him of his empire and kingdoms and even foreclose the futures of his heirs. Donning one of his crowns, he bellowed that he had not, and would not, give up his crowns without shedding blood. No longer would he serve as anvil to Innocent's hammer, he swore. From now on he, Frederick, would be the hammer!

The battle had been joined again. Once more Frederick's famous circular letters began to make the rounds of the courts of Europe, warning that others' turns would follow should Innocent IV be allowed free rein for his special kind of energetic vindictiveness. The rulers must resist in Frederick's name—or feed the notion that it was indeed a papal right to depose princes. He lashed out at Innocent's avarice and shameless nepotism, his hypocritical cries of poverty. Now was the decay of the papacy running rampant; now was the man of God destroying with his un-Christian pride, his egotism and self-interested bids for power, the spiritual ties that had held the medieval world to the Church, the very foundation of the European social structure.

King Louis IX of France took time off from preparing his crusade and, with Queen Mother Blanche, tried to reason with Innocent late in the year at Cluny. But in a conference that is said to have extended over seven days, he met with no success with the obdurate pope, even though he argued that the success of his coming crusade depended on the good offices of Frederick Hohenstaufen, his political knowledge, his Eastern connections, and his assistance in supplying troops, money, and provisions. By the end of the conference, it had become clear to Louis and to most observers that the pope was interested only in putting an end to papal-imperial negotiations. Frederick and his house were to be brought down as far as the pope was concerned, and that was the end of the matter. It is a singular fact of the tragic impasse that now it behooved a secular prince to try to unite Europe to fight its religious battles, while the vicar of Christ foundered about in the most dismal political swamp, which with his half-crazed struggles for both survival and vengeance, became more and more like a quicksand from which he would never extricate himself.

1246

The year 1246 brought imperial fortunes to a low beneath anything Frederick could have envisioned in the heady days of his Cortenuova triumph. In March his son-in-law, Count Richard of Caserta (he was married to Frederick's natural daughter, Violante), arrived at Grosseto, where Frederick had retired to indulge in some good hawking there in the pine woods. Very much to the pope's knowledge—probably even by his instigation—an outrageous plot had been hatched to murder the emperor, his son Enzo, and Ezzelino da Romano. Richard arrived just in time, as it turned out, for the assassinations were scheduled to be perpetrated during a banquet to be held the following day and were to be augmented by revolts throughout the Italian peninsula.

Not unaware of impending disaster, Frederick had been uneasy for several weeks. Had not natural phenomena indicated a coming event of catastrophic proportions? Seas had been running unseasonably high; electric storms were occurring without warning; strange portents seemed to be spreading to the heavens where stars, even the sun and the moon, were suddenly given to unpredictable behavior. But worst of all to Frederick was his perusal of the list of conspirators—most of them considered good, trusted, and dear friends. Especially troublesome was the listing of three of the ringleaders: Jacopo da Morra, son of his faithful and justicial friend, Enrico; Teobaldo di Francesco, a steady member of the Sicilian court, commander of ill-destined Capaccio, and just this past year entrusted with the job of podestà of Parma; and Pandolfo di Fasanella, who for years had quietly fulfilled the difficult post as Frederick's vicar-general of Tuscany. If Frederick needed proof of the allegations, Jacopo da Morra's and Pandolfo's precipitate flight from Grosseto provided it, just as Pandolfo's refuge in Rome indicated who had been the guiding light behind the scheme.

On the surface of it, hate-monger Bernardo Orlando di Rossi of Parma had been the main instigator, but apparently he had acted at the behest of his brother-in-law, the pope. Good-looking Bernardo could be very convincing, especially when he was dealing in duplicity. Teobaldo di Francesco had found it impossible to stand against his blandishments, especially against promises by Bernardo that he would be given the realm of Sicily as his reward. Even some of Frederick's administrative trustees in Sicily, men who had been imperial confidants for years, were mixed up in the plot and were being counted on to spread insurrection when word got out that Frederick was dead. One, Roger de Amicis, must have been especially revered by the emperor as he, along with Jacopo da Morra, was one of the first writers of poetry in the Italian vernacular, in itself enough to endear him in the emperor's heart. All of this had a profoundly devastating effect on Frederick. But the nadir had not yet been plumbed.

Misinformation surfaced that Frederick was dead. Cardinal Ranieri, in a paroxysm of heroic optimism, ran up the banners and invaded imperial territory—and ended up scuttling back from whence he had come. After twenty years of relative calm, uprising surfaced throughout the southern realm, where even smatterings of Frederick's trusted Saracen battalions arose in rebellion. Leaving Enzo and the formidable Ezzelino da Romano in charge of northern territories, Frederick headed south to tackle the situation, which he found not too difficult thanks to the precipitate action of son-in-law Richard of Caserta. He was granted a bonanza of evidence implicating Innocent IV when he intercepted a letter from the pontiff, encouraging the rebels in their last two stubbornly resisting strongholds. Scala, north of Salerno, and Capaccio, in sight of ancient Paestum, were the last enclaves of insurrectionists, with Scala being taken even before Frederick's arrival by another of his sons-in-law, Thomas Aquino. The revolt in the south never achieved the popular support that the northerners had hoped for, despite the widely disseminated claims that Frederick was dead. Thanks to the command of Teobaldo di Francesco, Capaccio held out far into the hot, dry summer months. With the final collapse of their defenses, the rebel garrison trooped out through the fortress gateway—which is still standing, though nothing remains within, and the area has been turned over to agriculture. They marched into a fate worse than the mere death they had recently faced. They were blinded, then had their noses and one hand and one foot cut off before they were condemned to be burned, hanged, drowned, or dragged behind horses until dead. In a refinement of symbolic torture, some of them were sewn into leather bags with poisonous snakes and thrown into the sea. Teobaldo and his closest associates were kept barely alive, to be paraded about the realm and exhibited as living evidence of the inadvisability of revolt, and were finally burned to death. The rebels' women consorts disappeared into the prisons of Palermo. For the first time in recorded history, a pope had been part and parcel of a plot to murder an emperor. And he had failed.

In the months following the conspiracy, word was leaked that Parma was ripe for insurrection. Enzo and Manfred Lancia set on the city of Parma, where they captured some key participants, mostly followers of Bernardo Orlando di Rossi. But some seventy of them, including Bernardo, eluded capture and fled to Piacenza and Reggio, from where they contacted Gregory of Montelongo for further scheming. Frederick continued to fan the flames of recrimination, and thereby use adversity to strengthen his position, by letting the world know of the pope's orchestration of both the attempt on his life and the uprisings. It was too good an opportunity not to be utilized. But he would go even further, becoming ever more tyrannical and vengeful, in the process unleashing an avalanche of hate and violence—a veritable rain of fire.

Not satisfied with polluting the political waters of Italy, Innocent IV got to work on Germany, starting with the religious hierarchy itself through threats and excommunications, silencing or getting rid of archbishops who were not properly sympathetic with papal reasoning. Digging until he found a nucleus of discontent that he could exploit among the Rhine bishops, Innocent went so far as to have Landgrave Henry Raspe of Thuringia elected "king" of Germany. This was the same Henry who had so cruelly expelled his sister-in-law, Saint Elizabeth, from her lands on the death of her pious husband in 1227 and who had been appointed regent of the kingdom by Frederick himself only a few years before. He was supported by ecclesiastical princes only—there were no secular princes attending the "election" and not many ecclesiastical ones, for that matter. Most of the lay princes maintained their fidelity to the emperor.

In a world of unlikable men—even his name strikes an unpleasant chord—Henry Raspe stands as a sterling example of one of the worst. As though his treatment of his sister-in-law, Elizabeth, were not enough to guarantee him a place of honor in the annals of despicable behavior, Henry had wavered for and against Frederick time after time, most noticeably in 1241, when under Gregory IX there had been some talk of setting up an anti-king. Now, on May 22, he finally made his treachery irretrievable when he consented to wear the false crown (he was never either crowned or anointed) in opposition to Conrad's legitimate reign. About the only decent thing that Henry Raspe could have done at this point would be to die, which he did the following year, to Innocent's chagrin. The election of Henry was not generally recognized in Europe, but that in no way mitigates the treachery and high-handed presumption of both the pretender to the German throne and Innocent IV.

Expert in the questionable legalities of European politics as he was, Innocent was capable of moving further into the nadir of diplomatic presumption. He wrote to the sultan of Egypt, encouraging that honorable Muslim to break a treaty with Frederick. This was a major duplicity on Innocent's part, considering his horror expressed at the Council of Lyon on the subject of diplomatic relations with Muslim leaders. The sultan replied as Frederick would have expected, calling Innocent's motives into question so unmistakably as to shame forever the Holy Father, including the supremely acrimonious reference to papal ambassadors who "have spoken of Christ, whom we know how to glorify better than you do."[4] He gave instruction to his ambassador to the imperial court to pass on the word of Innocent's duplicity to Frederick. Surrendering to total anger and hatred, if not revulsion, Frederick published his "Reform Manifesto," denouncing the clergy as slaves who were increasing their personal wealth at the expense of demeaning their piety. He harkened back to the old days when priests and pontiffs led apostolic lives "emulating their Master's humility," and when princes obeyed them because of their persuasive holiness. He postulated rhetorical questions concerning the rights of churchmen to bear arms, to fight, and to kill with lethal weapons, rather than to wield the weapons of heaven. He criticized the mobs who could venerate such obscene caricatures of the Church's founding fathers and namesake.

Frederick was thinking like Francis Bernardone, who would have returned the Church to the humble beginnings that Frederick was alluding to, who would have had the Church reembrace her forgotten spouse, Lady Poverty. It would be idle to pretend that Frederick stood alone against the mighty Church, that he was for the most part misunderstood by a complacently obedient Christian congregation. There were members of the mendicant orders who still saw their calling in the light of idealism and self-abnegation. They no more took to doing the papal dirty work than Francis would have. Especially in Germany the mendicants were standing in accusatory opposition to the regular clergy. Many among the followers of saints Francis and Dominic saw the anti-Christ in the bosom of the Church—not, as the vicar of Christ so loudly proclaimed, at the head of the empire. A document surfaced, penned by a mendicant brother, Arnold by name, entitled "Innocent IV, Anti-Christ." The same brother also claimed to have endured a vision from Christ during which the pope and his followers showed themselves the true enemies of the Father, the destroyers of the gospels. Prayers were asked for the success of Frederick and his sons against the machinations of the pope. One wonders what Francis would have thought of those of his followers who seemed more than eager to give aid and comfort to the series of such pontiffs. Would he, as Franciscan legend tells us, have been enthusiastic in his yearly rescue of his friars from purgatory on the anniversary of his death?

Within the Curia itself there were those who saw the evil of Europe not in the person of the excommunicated, ineffectively deposed emperor, but in the person of the deposer, "the Servant of the Servants of God." Much of the Church hierarchy of France was in open revolt against Innocent's blatant nepotism, his selling of indulgences, and his frank profiteering by absolving "crusaders" from their vows to take up arms in a "crusade" against Frederick. It became vogue to declare for the "crusade" in order to gain promised indulgences and then buy a way out with cash on the line. To the swell of anti-papal propaganda, Frederick kept adding his own outraged letters and manifestos. He and his day mark the stirrings of the breakdown of papal sanctity that was to climax in the equally turbulent days of Martin Luther three centuries later. The fatal wound in Church-empire harmony continued to fester and widen. No political unguent or theological poultice was going to cure this ever-more-debilitating pain. And once Frederick made up his mind to strike iron with iron, he must stand accused as much as his papal adversary for contributing to the common misery and historical shame. Their animosity was in perfect balance; neither hated more—or less—than the other. Like grudge fighters or gladiators, the two champions faced one another, squaring off for a fight that neither could win.

Chapter Seventeen

That sorrowful day,
on which will arise from the burning coals
Man accused to be judged:
therefore, O God, do Thou spare him.
***Dies Irae*, verse 18**

1247

Frederick could not allow Henry Raspe's usurpation to go unchallenged. A false friend he was, and that was itself sufficient to fire the imperial wrath. But a false king was carrying betrayal beyond the realm of law. It was a frustration of God's plan for the orderly governance of the empire, and eventually of the world. Given that no abridgment of the dignity and honor of the empire, the southern realm, or the emperor's sacred trust was to be tolerated, Raspe's treason was out of the range of anything so insignificant. It was a naked bid for power, and Frederick decided to go to Germany for a showdown. And while he was about it, he would swing by Lyon for a confrontation with the conniving author of the usurpation. He had barely mounted his horse and turned his eyes toward Burgundy when word reached him that Henry Raspe was conveniently dead, which left Conrad, for the moment at least, unopposed as legitimate king. Raspe's demise mercifully brought the male line of his family to an end, and his lands were returned to the Hohenstaufen sphere, to be headed by Albert of Meissen, who was betrothed to Frederick's daughter Margarete. It would be six months before the German ecclesiastical princes would elect another ghost-king, this time nineteen-year-old William of Holland, who would be no more effective than was Henry Raspe.

Frederick did not abandon his idea of a march on Lyon. He had already set the wheels in motion by betrothing his natural son Manfred, now about fifteen years old and growing into an uncommonly handsome man, to Beatrice of Savoia, thereby guaranteeing year-round open mountain passes into Burgundy. Though Manfred had been born out of wedlock, Frederick always thought of him as a legitimate son. He honored him as such and in addition maintained with the young man an affectionate relationship. Though he loved his other children, especially Enzo, Manfred was his favorite. It was to him that Frederick dedicated his book on falconry, and it was Manfred who lovingly created a second edition of that lost work after his father died. Frederick maintained an equally tender relationship with Manfred's mother, Bianca Lancia, and there is evidence (but nothing definitive) that he may have married her. We know that he lavished properties on her, including Monte Sant'Angelo, which was traditionally a part of the dowers of the queens of Sicily. Her brother, also a Manfred, was sometimes referred to in official documents as "our beloved relation."

Setting the stage for a final showdown between Church and state, Frederick solidified his positions politically and through family ties. In addition to forming a new link with the house of Savoia through Manfred, he married off his natural daughter Catherine to the Marquis del Carretto, whose lands bordered Genoa, and then married Enzo to a relative of Ezzelino da Romano. Both acts were calculated to strengthen his grip on northern Italy. Considering that another of the emperor's natural sons, Frederick of Antioch (whose name suggests Asian origins on his mother's side) held Florence within the imperial sphere, and that Viterbo had recently returned to the fold and was nominally ruled by the nine-year-old Henry, son of Isabella, things were, all in all, looking good. In April he appointed his most loyal friend and fellow-poet, Pier delle Vigne, as chancellor of Sicily and protonotary of the imperial court. Pier was now second only to the emperor, the most trusted of his advisors, the ranking diplomat and fiscal expert of the Sicilian court. It would seem that Frederick was very much in control of things.

By this time the pope was feeling himself a virtual prisoner in Lyon. While Innocent was dangerous at any time, a penned-up Innocent was worse. No secular ruler could be found who was willing to harbor him, and after running out on Frederick the way he had, he could not safely make a return trip to Rome. As always with stirrers of political waters, when dangers arise of drowning in waves of their own making, they cry that they are being victimized. So it was with Innocent, who complained that the emperor was marching on him in vengeance, a claim that was true only in that Frederick aimed to humiliate his antagonist once he was able to confront him with his deceits.

King Louis IX of France, siding with anyone who stood against the blatant corruption of the mid-thirteenth-century Church, knew the emperor intended no physical harm. What would be gained by making a martyr of the pope? It was an extremely delicate situation for fair-thinking Louis. Preparing for crusade as he was, Louis needed to maintain cordial relations with Frederick, whose son, Conrad of Germany, was also the legitimate king of Jerusalem. His permission was a prerequisite for entry into that territory. (The fact that Jerusalem was currently in Muslimhands affected no one's thinking.) If Louis habitually maintained a neutral, sometimes conciliatory posture concerning Frederick's continuing contest with the popes, Frederick was not always as level in his dealings with the king of France, whose envoys kept the emperor informed about the French preparations for crusade, which, after studying, he passed on to the sultan of Egypt. As it turned out, Louis had to do nothing. Papal agents and relatives were at work again in Italy.

Frederick was in Torino, ready to set out for Lyon. After waving his troops off, he learned by messenger that a core of papal Guelfs, motivated by former friend Bernardo Orlando di Rossi, had hatched an elaborate, half-baked plot and were fortifying the imperial city of Parma. Enzo, in charge of northern Italy, could do nothing about it. He was away, besieging the Brescian castle at Quinzano d'Oglio. On a day when a prominent Ghibelline wedding party was in progress, Bernardo gave the signal, and his cohorts together with the seventy Parmesan exiles who had eluded Enzo the year before staged an attack to capture the city. More than a little in their cups, the Ghibelline celebrants were lured from the nuptial feasting by what must have been a less-than-portentous attack. The imperial podestà fell, and the rest of the defenders, in general not behaving in an exemplary manner, were either killed or captured. Then Enzo made a mistake. Instead of hurrying back to the beleaguered city before defenses could be contrived by the small band of attackers and the swelling band of turncoat natives, he went on a scouting operation to gather reinforcements, finally setting up his camp a few miles from Parma's walls. Relief was pouring into Parma from Mantua, Piacenza, Milan, from Ferrara and Reggio. Genoa sent bowmen, as did Innocent's kinsman, the count of Lavagna. The defenders worked night and day raising palisades and digging trenches, hammering out weapons and stockpiling supplies. Parmesan spirits were high, inspired by the presence of Bernardo Orlando di Rossi, the magnificently built, handsome traitor whom the emperor would gladly have hung by his thumbs. But the great hope of the Guelfs was Gregory of Montelongo, a master of intrigue. A sensualist, gouty, he had several times been approached by Frederick, who had promised to make him the most important man of his court, next to himself, of course, if he would but leave the service of the Church. The time it took Enzo to canvass Cremona, Bergamo, and Pavia (the levy from Pavia was commanded by Hugo Boterius, son of one of Innocent's sisters, who would remain rigidly loyal to Frederick) gave the rebels the time they needed to organize their defenses, making it impossible for Enzo to attack without his father's help. Parma was shaping up as the stage upon which the fate of the empire would be played out.

Turning his attention from Lyon, Frederick summoned his troops back from their trek across the Alps. It was not long before he was alongside his son, where with tough Ezzelino da Romano they hemmed the rebels into Parma by completely surrounding it. Outwardly Frederick made light of the insurrection; but he fooled no one. Parma was strategically important as it commanded the main route to southern Italy. Should Parma break free of Hohenstaufen control, who could foretell the damage to the empire and the extent of the domino effect, especially in commune-minded Lombardy? Already the revolt had triggered unrest and uneasiness enough, scattered brush fires that Frederick's sons and lieutenants were instructed to water down while he besieged the more important Parma. He did not allow himself to be distracted by the defection of Florence, a Ghibelline city that he scrupulously avoided because of an astrologer's prophecy that he would die *sub flora*—in a place whose name derived from the word *flower*. By the good graces of the podestà, Frederick of Antioch, the Guelfs had for years been tolerated in Florence. When they followed Parma's example, Frederick of Antioch repaired to Prato, some eight miles to the northwest, where there was a newly finished castle refuge.

It was probably at the time of Frederick's stay in Pisa in 1226 that he initiated the building of two castles in Tuscany, one at San Miniato and the Castello dell'Imperatore in Prato. The latter was built on the perimeter of the old city walls, and though it is square rather than octagonal, it still calls to mind Frederick's greatest existing building, his yet-to-come Castel del Monte in Apulia. In its echoing of his southern architecture, it is of a kind rarely seen in Tuscany. Squarely atop its earthy knoll and constructed of smoothly cut stone blocks, it utilizes four burly corner towers, with pentagonal towers in the center of each of the four sides. There is a no-nonsense aura about this defense bulwark, its thickset presence an implied dare to assault, despite its disarmingly inviting, recessed entrance. With high walls topped by Ghibelline crenellations, the gray stone emphasizes its enormous bulk, its cold disdain for the daily activities and peaceful traffic that swirl around it, even reduced as it is to acting the centerpiece of a small park or an open-air theater for

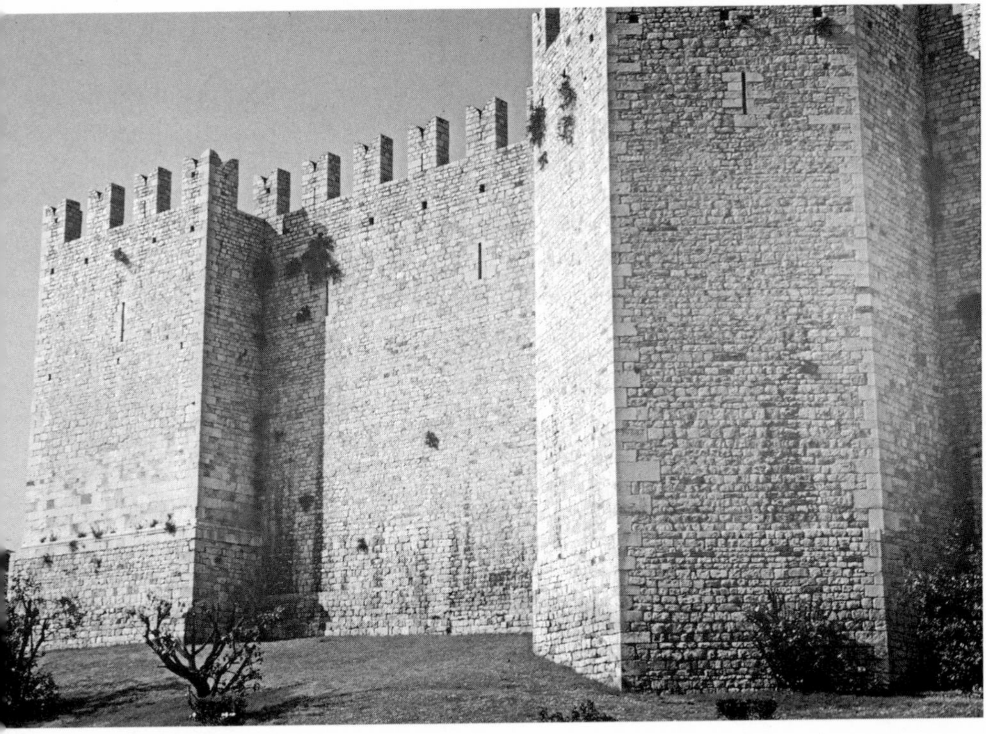

Castello dell'Imperatore, Prato, Italy

rock concerts, ear-splitting amplification and all. Forced to play second fiddle to Florence, Prato would never come close to that great city's wealth and cultural glory. Yet Frederick thought of it and its Castello dell'Imperatore as a pivotal point in his vast defense system. And it does have its treasures—the belt of the Virgin, for example, by tradition given to the apostle Thomas during a miraculous vision and brought to Prato by a knight returning from the Holy Land in 1130. How it came into his possession is not a part of our story.

While Frederick of Antioch was gathering forces in Prato, preparations for his return to Florence proceeded apace, largely under the direction of the determined leader and imperial sympathizer Farinata degli Uberti. From his high Uberti family towers, Farinata took the offensive against the Guelfs, enabling Frederick of Antioch to take back the city and drive the anti-imperial enemy to locales more compatible with their troublemaking while he and Farinata razed their family towers. Farinata is interesting in his own right. A giant of a man, he some years later earned the citizens' everlasting gratitude by successfully arguing against his own Ghibellines, who would demolish the city of Florence in an act of pitiless vengeance. On the other hand, his memory was not quite so sacred to Dante, a Florentine and a Guelf, who placed him in the sixth circle of hell. Farinata was posthumously declared a heretic in 1283. According to the poet he can foretell the future with precision but has no knowledge of the present or the past, thus by Divine justice voiding the intellect of the heretic after the Judgment when there is no future.

Pockets of insurrection were being retaken by Frederick II's men-at-arms in scattered areas of Italy, while the defenders of Parma settled down for a long siege, hoping against hope that one Cardinal Ottaviano Ubaldini, an opportunist of little ability in anything but vacillation between Guelfs and Ghibellines and a hedonistic enjoyment of life, wealth, and sexual delights, would manage to get through to them with desperately needed supplies. A prince of the Church who lived in a luxury rivaling the much-criticized emperor's, he played politics simply for the love of the game, loyal to no side but his own. One of Ubaldini's troubles was that he had no overriding passion, apparently not even for the religion he claimed to espouse. The story is told that once when he had lost a large sum because of the Ghibellines, he blasphemed, "If there be such a thing as a soul, I have lost mine to the Ghibellines!" The first phrase was sufficient to condemn him to Dante's hell along with other heretics like Frederick and Farinata. Not surprisingly, even when a way was finally opened for him to deliver his supplies to starving Parma, Ottaviano reneged by disbanding his army, thereby betraying those who were so doggedly, if rashly, depending on him. The cardinal's inability or cowardice notwithstanding, Gregory of Montelongo and his cohorts managed to bolster the spirits of the suffering citizenry, who, since they were defending their homes and families, were more interested in survival than Frederick's paid mercenaries were in assault.

Remembering his successful siege of Faenza, Frederick undertook to build a fortified wooden city in the shadows of the walls of Parma, bragging that one day soon he would replace Parma with this new city, relocating the citizens and sowing salt over the leveled remains of the old. So would he terminate once and for all the life of time-honored, ancient Parma. It is said that his siege city had clearly demarcated streets, a canal for water, a palace for Frederick and his harem, a marketplace, and a church. In an ebullient mood, and with tragically misplaced optimism, he named his wooden city "Vittoria."

Winter cold descended on the Italian peninsula. Frederick and his troops (many with their families) lived in relative comfort, while the suffering of the Parmesans was increased to the limits of endurance. To boost morale Gregory of Montelongo resorted to counterfeiting messages from without, assuring that help was on the way. Never one to let a sleeping dog lie, Frederick fueled the general misery and fright by seeking revenge on all who had anything to do with the defection and defense of the city. Captured prisoners were executed in cold blood every morning in clear view of the walls of Parma. In his fury, and apparently in a fear that verged on paranoia, Frederick became ever more ruthless. With or without cause, he began to harbor a dread of being poisoned. Denunciations became the name of the game. He listened more and more to accusations and talebearing. Proscriptions and banishments from his court followed. Torture and hangings were the rule. Bishop Marcellino of Arezzo, a turncoat vassal, was executed after having been dragged behind a horse. Seeing its broad streets and sun-saturated squares, one can be excused for not realizing the endless series of Ghibelline atrocities, the horror and misery of imperial revenge on a hapless citizenry.

The monk Salimbene, a native of Parma whose supposed house of birth is pointed out just to the right of the cathedral baptistery, reports that the Parmesan women got wind of Frederick's determination to wipe out their city and replace it with his new Vittoria. They assembled in the cathedral to pray to the Virgin, who is venerated there with special fervor. Indeed, the cathedral is dedicated to the Assumption of Mary. Salimbene reports that, "[the] better to gain her ear, they made a model of the city in solid silver, which I have seen, and which was offered as a gift to the Blessed Virgin."[1] Mary in her turn, according to Salimbene, prayed to her Son, who responded as Solomon had prefigured him in I Kings 2:20 when he faced his mother, Bathsheba: "And the king said unto her, Ask on, my mother: for I will not say thee nay." And with that he promised to deliver the city of Parma.

Few places in Italy are more pleasurable than the Piazza del Duomo, an austere square emanating charm and warmth, dominated by the Lombard-Romanesque cathedral with its delightful open loggias and two-tiered, lion-supported porch, the great bulk crowned by a ponderous octagonal dome. The inside of the dome is entirely covered by a flamboyant fresco depicting the Assumption of the Virgin by Correggio (died 1534), a work of jarring complexity in these austere Romanesque surroundings. Also inside are the episcopal throne and a splendid *Deposition from the Cross*, both by Benedetto Antelami, the latter signed and dated 1178. It is the earliest of his known works, especially interesting in that it manifests, even at his early age of about twenty-eight, most of the characteristics that we think of as his style. The stiff iconography in no way interferes with his attempt at realism beyond the realm of human experience, even while it tells of human tragedy and shortcomings. With what wondrous, sweet gentleness Christ reaches down even in death—softly, oh, so softly!—to give a comforting stroke to the side of Mary's face!

The north portal of the baptistery, that portal facing the cathedral and called the Portal of the Virgin, is surmounted by Antelami's lantern-jawed Mary enthroned, holding a stern-faced Child who looks the image of his mother. Rather than tender, the overall feeling in her steady (Hohenstaufen?) stare is one of majesty, a precedence over humanity, perhaps even a monumentality in the stoniness of her rough-hewn features. Prestigious, yes, but she does take some getting used to.

Madonna by Benedetto Antelami, Baptistry, Parma, Italy

1248

Early this year, on February 18, Frederick undertook a falconry expedition as a means of relaxation away from his siege city of Vittoria. A feint was made by the Parmesan garrison when a detachment sallied forth from Parma and lured Vittoria's commander, Manfredo Lancia, into pursuit. With Vittoria undefended, the body of Parmesan troops, along with an avalanche of half-starved but audacious citizens, descended on the few remaining soldiers and torched the entire wooden city. The most tragic loss to Parmesan desperation was the loyal and brilliant Thaddeus of Sessa. That noble man, so gentle and kind-looking in his Capuan portrait, was captured and displayed to the joyous citizenry, following which he had his hands amputated and was cast into prison where he died. Prisoners, including the imperial harem and their eunuch guards, were carried away by the victorious citizens along with enormous stocks of food, herds of cattle, horses and mules, gold, silver, and precious stones, and—more the humiliation—the cherished *carroccio* of imperial Cremona. Even the imperial crown, "which was of great weight and value, for it was all of gold, inlaid with precious stones, with many images of goldsmith's work standing out, and much graven work," was carried triumphantly into Parma by "a little man of mean stature"[2] named Cortopasso ("Short-step") and deposited in the sacristy of the cathedral. The imperial scepter was lost. Frederick's gold seal vanished, either stolen and hidden or destroyed in the conflagration. On top of everything else, in addition to the confiscation of his library with its scientific books and its maps, Frederick's decorated manuscript on falconry, said to be embellished with designs in gold and silver and with a likeness of the emperor himself, disappeared. It was this book that Frederick had dedicated to Manfred and which Manfred worked so hard to duplicate after the death of his father.

Frederick hurried back to the flaming Vittoria. There was nothing he could do but beat a retreat, to mourn profoundly the fate of his respected friend and defender at Lyon, Thaddeus of Sessa, and to heap coals on his already scalding hatred of the pope. He and his court left the smoldering ruins and repaired first to Borgo San Donnino, some fourteen miles northwest of Parma on the Emilian Way and now known as Fidenza.

Three days later Frederick was back at the walls of Parma, apparently undecided whether or not to renew the siege. Enzo, eager to atone for his gaffe, was for it, as was Ezzelino da Romano. But Frederick decided against it and turned instead to strengthening his hold on the Cisa Pass near Pontremoli, southwest of Parma, essential to communications with his southern realm. It was there in that gorgeous Apennine pass, very green, with deep ravines and soaring tree-covered peaks, that his troops captured the odious Bernardo Orlando di Rossi, who for some reason had abandoned his native Parma. He was without further ado chopped to pieces.

The loss of Parma was Frederick's most serious setback ever. Legends of his invulnerability, already shaken by his backing down at Brescia and his reticence about facing the Mongol hordes, were now irrevocably shattered. The effects were far-reaching and seemed to indicate an imminent victory for the Church, whose pontiff knew no depth too low to acquire money for financing his scheme to eliminate the Hohenstaufen breed. Aside from filling his coffers by allowing sworn "crusaders" against Frederick to buy their way out of their oaths, he handed out Church property to the faithful hierarchy, who were interested only in acquiring those benefices for their monetary value. This practice made the recipients look more kindly on the papal cause and become more willing to cough up the funds that Innocent cried for. He encouraged the sale of indulgences, and he practiced blatant usury. Breaking the Hohenstaufen grip was more important than any law or concept, religious or temporal, and Innocent never pretended otherwise. At least in that way the man was not a hypocrite.

In a chain reaction touched off by the defeat at Parma, the Romagna was lost, as was the March of Ancona and certain smaller cities around Spoleto. Even worse, there was little Frederick could do about it, a state of affairs that tended to feed his growing paranoia. With the loss of the imperial treasury at Vittoria, cash again became his overriding concern, though son-in-law John Vatatzes did his best by sending him sizeable sums. Frederick leveled new taxes over the entire realm, but those schemes took time to activate and even more time for the money to start flowing in. He borrowed funds at exorbitant rates of interest. For the most part he maintained a positive manner, but those who knew him saw that he was increasingly short-tempered and nervous. Since the Mongol threat the strains of a regime in disarray had been showing. Frederick could no longer count on German loyalty since the papal agents north of the Alps, while not meeting with spectacular success, were still getting through to a number of the ecclesiastical princes. The troublesome archbishop of Cologne, Conrad of Hochstaden, who just this year had laid the foundation stone for his cathedral, created unrest along the Rhine when he and the archbishop of Mainz invaded Hohenstaufen territory. On this crumbling foundation Innocent IV could establish a structure of disenchantment and insurrection without the calming presence of

Louis IX of France around to dissuade him. Headed for Cyprus and the fulfillment of his crusading pledge, that determined monarch had sailed off from Aigues-Mortes on August 25. On board with him as he left the harbor of the ancient walled city in the marshes of Provence was his brother Charles, Count of Anjou, who by 1266 would be ensconced on the Hohenstaufen throne of Sicily.

While things in Germany were admittedly dicey, they were not hopeless. Through his marriage to Elizabeth, daughter of the duke of Bavaria, King Conrad managed to secure his hold on that region. In another three years Elizabeth would present Conrad with a baby boy, Conradino (little Conrad), who would, in a tragically youthful burst of energy so reminiscent of the teenage Frederick, fire the imagination of the world in an ill-fated effort to gain his imperial destiny. To King Conrad's holdings was added a large part of the duchy of Austria, in turmoil since the recent unlamented death without heir of the frosty, abrasive Duke Frederick, the last of the Babenbergs. Still it would seem that the German princes, while not in open revolt, were anticipating the possible collapse of the imperium and were acting accordingly. Out of self-interest in an every-man-for-himself environment, some loyal German knights came south to take a stand by the side of their emperor. At this point Frederick must have regretted his disinterest in Germany when the Mongols were looming on the horizon! Perhaps—only perhaps—his German vassals would have felt a greater tug of loyalty to him in his current tribulations. But he was far from helpless. To consolidate his position he opened negotiations for a possible marriage to the daughter of Duke Albert of Saxony, polishing his image by journeying to Piedmont and taking over the city of Vercelli, a thriving community today with no lack of Italian gregarious humor and willingness to offer unasked-for advice to passing strangers.

At Vercelli a progressive-thinking Frederick must have come to know the church and abbey of Sant'Andrea. Architect Benedetto Antelami's deliberate blend of old Romanesque with the new French Gothic style might have brought a wry smile to the emperor's face. When last seen by the author the northern tower, tall, thin, at odds with the grumpy weight and solidity of the western facade it adorns, offered a humorous touch by rooting in the roof tiles a bush the size of a tree, not unlike a plume on a warrior's pointed helmet.

The interior is more obviously Gothic, more of a piece, with attention given to the effects of light to accent and exalt the linear verticality. The light is striking in its quality—not dark and dim as in so many churches. And how cool is the interior on a hot July afternoon! How much a part of God's refreshing world it must have seemed to the medieval believer entering from the stifling, dusty streets! The patterns of bricks, manufactured in a variety of shapes—all sorts of curves and points and arabesques—filling their own special places and edged with blue patterns of plants and stars, add a colorful jauntiness to this earthbound speck of Paradise.

The tranquil cloister is perfectly proportioned and shaded, making it an ideal place for a young laborer to take a smoking break from polishing the sanctuary's fine wooden choir stalls. How evocative it is of the silence of the cloistered world—and how at odds with the thunder of Frederick's planet beyond the columns, the arches, the light and shadows!

1249

Feeling every inch the controller of human destiny and emerging victor over evil, Innocent continued to broadcast to all who would listen that he could be counted upon never to make peace with Frederick or any of his offspring. Beyond that, talk of peace without the inclusion of the Lombards was out of the question. As early as autumn 1248 Innocent had published his objectives concerning a projected takeover of the kingdom of Sicily. Finally he started moving. He was undisguisedly blunt when in April 1249 he appointed Cardinal Peter Capoccio for the job, replacing master hater Cardinal Ranieri, who retired to Rome, where he died late the following year. Peter Capoccio came from a noted Roman family. He had done Innocent's dirty work in the past, having been a prominent member of the mission to Germany that brought about the election of William of Holland. He was regarded as a true papal loyalist and as such was to be given full rein in Sicily to bring about the fall of the Hohenstaufens. Innocent was blatantly after the ultimate trophy: the uncontested secular rule of Europe and the implied subjugation of all princes to his will.

Frederick was stunned. He was holding his own—barely. But he was in for an even greater jolt, one that no doubt did much to increase his already obsessive suspicion, if not outright distrust, of everyone around him. Still reeling from the loss of his trusted confidant and companion Thaddeus of Sessa at Parma, he now confronted the bitterest disillusionment: Pier delle Vigne was accused of treason. Precisely what the allegations were remains a mystery. What is known is that Pier, "who held both keys to Frederick's heart, / locking, unlocking with so deft a touch / that scarce another soul had any part / in his most secret

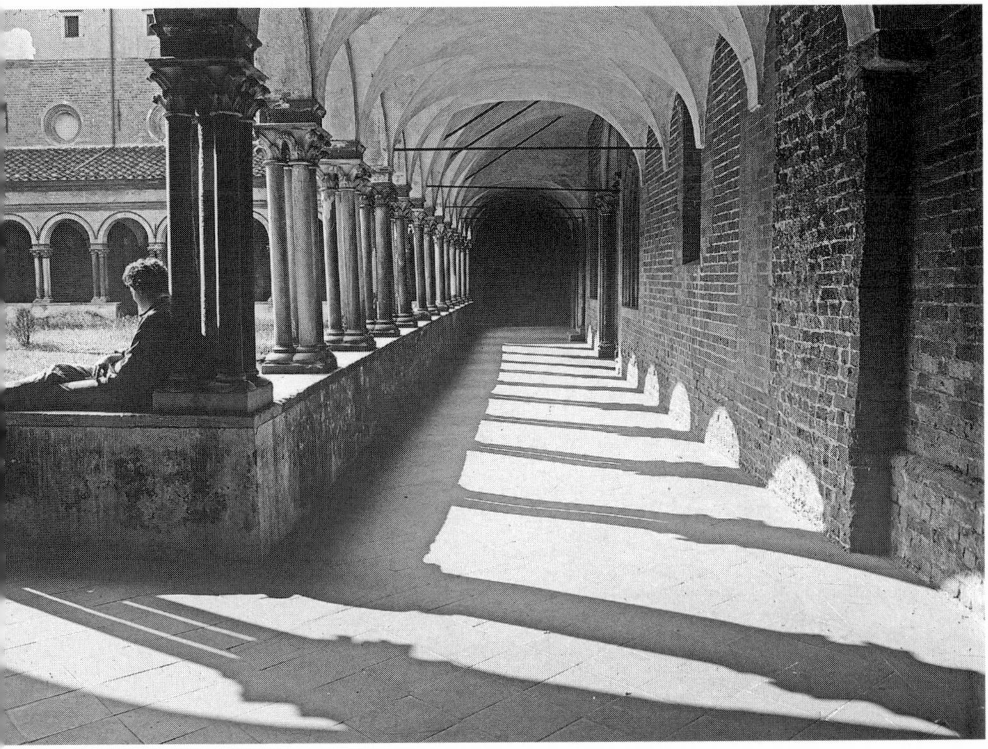

Cathedral cloister, Vercelli, Italy

thoughts,"[3] was with Frederick when they arrived in Cremona in January, after having been to Piedmont to attend the politically beneficial marriage of Manfred to Beatrice of Savoia. A month later Pier was in disgrace and in prison—first there, then later at Borgo San Donnino. Without doubt Pier was the object of intense jealousy among the courtiers, who saw him enjoying too much the perquisites that they might enjoy themselves had he not been in such an exalted position. Beyond the treason charges, it may have been bandied about that he had been party to that historically verified plot to poison the emperor, a rumor not to be accepted as a likelihood. Certainly there was ample opportunity for Pier to embezzle on a sumptuous scale, and for him to break the laws (if he did) was infinitely worse than a criminal act on the part of a lesser courtier. There was always the chance that Frederick's suspicions were piqued beyond the point of endurance. His correspondence reveals his belief that Pier was guilty of corruption, embezzlement, or the misuse of funds entrusted to him.

Opinion at the time was so divided that there never has been a clear verdict of history, and judicious minds then and after have always hesitated to find fault with delle Vigne's behavior. Dante, from the distance of the next century, seems convinced of Pier's innocence when he meets him in the Wood of the Suicides in the seventh circle of hell, rather than among the traitors in the ninth, and hears him explain:

> That harlot, Envy, who on Caesar's face
> keeps fixed forever her adulterous stare,
> the common plague and vice of court and palace,
>
> * * *
>
> inflamed all minds against me. These inflamed
> so inflamed him that all my happy honors
> were changed to mourning. Then, unjustly blamed,
>
> * * *
>
> my soul, in scorn, and thinking to be free
> of scorn in death, made me at last, though just,
> unjust to myself. By the new roots of this tree
>
> * * *
>
> I swear to you that never in word or spirit
> did I break faith to my lord and emperor
> who was so worthy of honor in his merit.[4]

Pier's guilt for whatever he was charged with was affirmed at his trial. The evidence of the verdict and Frederick's personal belief aside, it is difficult to imagine the cultured, hardworking Pier giving in to temptations from enemies of the empire. As punishment for his "crime," he was blinded and imprisoned at San Miniato (or Pisa) where he killed himself, some claimed by bashing his head against the wall or column to which he had been chained.

One wonders what Frederick may have thought when, amid all his troubles, word reached him that, in far-off Egypt, Damietta had fallen to Frankish troops under the leadership of King Louis IX. Louis may have learned some lessons from the fifth crusade and its stalemated failure at the walls of Damietta, but he learned nothing from Frederick's sixth crusade, won by the arts of negotiation. Despite his slender, rather anemic build, and despite his appearance of saintliness to some, Louis projected the very image of the active, sword-wielding crusader, saying on one occasion that the only way to deal with a nonbeliever was to plunge a sword into his nonbelieving body as far as it would go. It was the friend of Frederick, Fakhr ad-Din, whom Louis faced in battle, the one he could have faced across the negotiating table had he a mind for it. But King Louis, apparently believing his own words, refused outright to talk to a Muslim. Even when Sultan Ayub of Egypt, the tubercular son of al-Kamil, offered to buy back Damietta and cede Jerusalem to the Franks, Louis rejected the offer. Like so many before him, he held to the tenet that a crusade, by its very nature, should be won by spilling Muslim blood. His crusade was doomed.

One would think that the year 1249 had already brought the nadir. But more was yet to come. It was a disillusioned emperor who headed south from Pisa after the trial and suicide of Pier delle Vigne and after receiving word that the structure of détente that he had built in Outremer had come to nothing. While resting over in Naples, Frederick received the sad word that his natural son, Richard of Teate, was dead. Other than some scattered battle accounts and affirmations that he served his father well as vicar-general of the Romagna and Spoleto, we know little of Richard. We do not even know Frederick's feelings for him other than that they must have been to a certain extent warm since he had been invested with a good deal of authority. Politically the death of Richard was a loss to Frederick, but nothing compared to the ultimate disaster.

The most loyal, the bravest, most handsome and aggressive of Frederick's sons, the vice-regent of all Italy, Enzo, answered an appeal from Modena to help them fight off an attack by Bologna. He had been left to administer in the north while a depressed Frederick took himself to southern Italy and Sicily, the land he most loved. Gathering his bodyguard and some knights from Cremona, Enzo set off in a protective frenzy from Modena. On May 26 at Fossalta, on the edge of Modena's territory, Enzo became embroiled in a small, intrinsically unimportant skirmish with the enemy. His horse was shot from under him, and he was captured with a body of his knights and foot soldiers. The Bolognesi were ecstatic as they led the prize of the century back to the palace of the podestà, where he would remain a prisoner for twenty-three years until he died March 14, 1272. For all Enzo's fortitude and misfortune, Modena by the end of the year had capitulated to its Bolognese enemy.

The "Palazzo del Re Enzo" was new at the time of the internment of its illustrious prisoner, having been finished in 1246. It has since been restored, but it is still the kind of building to conjure poetic thoughts of a heroic age and of the plight of the brilliant, loyal young man, cultured and refined, who could bewitch his captors into admiration and undisguised pleasure in his company while they yet confined him to the day of his death. Enzo was never mistreated. He was allowed all the visitors he craved in his natural gregariousness; even the city's Ghibelline adherents were allowed access to him. Among them he cultivated especially Pietro Asinelli of the family who built the taller of Bologna's two outlandishly leaning towers. In his comfortable but confining prison Enzo could only long for freedom in the sunny hills of Tuscany and the plains of Apulia, crying his anguish in a poem that may well have been written during his incarceration:

> Go my little song,
> and greet my Lord;
> and tell him all the anguish I suffer.
> He who holds me in his power
> holds me so tight
> that I won't be able to live.
> Greet Tuscany for me,
> that queen of all
> where every courtesy reigns;
> and go to the Puglian plain,
> the great Capitanata
> there where my heart is night and day.[5]

Frederick would be hard put to replace Enzo. His world was crumbling. He was out of sync with his times. He tried every kind of negotiation for his son's release, but the captors vowed they would never let him go, scoffing with thinly disguised mock humility that sometimes even a not-so-great dog can hang on to a wild boar—*a cane non magno saepe tenetur aper.* To an extent Enzo's void was filled by Uberto Pallavicini, a man as ruthlessly efficient as Ezzelino da Romano. Of medium stature and alarmingly strong, Uberto cut a grotesque figure with his shock of black hair and one empty eye socket; it was noised about that a cock had picked out his eye when he was an infant. He shared Frederick and Ezzelino's disdain for the sanctity of the papal person. The Church carried no religious significance for him: he considered it nothing more than a base for just one more ambitious politician fighting for material gain. Like Ezzelino he would eschew the comforts of the sacraments on his deathbed.

Even with Umberto Pallavicini as an ally, Frederick's life had reached its lowest point due to the loss of Enzo. He needed his son to help him fight his battles and to administer the realm. The strain was showing in Frederick's eyes and in his actions. For a time his health failed, and he fell victim to a severe skin disease. But by the end of the year, he had recovered somewhat, and even grieving as he was for Enzo, he returned to the task of empire building with his usual bounce. He began to talk again of putting the Lombards down once and for all. Having long entertained thoughts of visiting Conrad in Germany, Frederick took increasing interest in the idea as the negotiations progressed for a possible marriage with the daughter of Duke Albert of Saxony.

1250

With the end of Christmas celebrations and the coming of the new year, Frederick's fortunes picked up. His son-in-law, Emperor John Vatatzes, continued to send him material and human reinforcements for the coming battles he was mapping. Piece by piece, city by city, northern Italy was pulled back into the Ghibelline mold. Piacenza turned Ghibelline and was ruled jointly by Uberto Pallavicini and his partner in viciousness, Ezzelino da Romano, enough to cause any would-be troublemaker's flesh to crawl. It was not long before Parma along with its *carroccio* was back in the fold. Other cities as well were won back by Frederick's lieutenants: Assisi, Senigallia, Pesaro. Cardinal Peter Capoccio was trounced resoundingly and with an enormous loss of men before he could even cross into the southern realm on his assigned papal takeover mission. With Conrad keeping things in line in Germany, even the treacherous Rhine bishops had been forced to seek a truce.

Sobering word reached Frederick that his old friend and conversationalist Fakhr ad-Din had been killed on February 8, hacked down in battle by a company of Templars. He had been serving as general of the Egyptian troops defending Mansourah against attacks by King Louis's crusaders in the swampy Nile delta. Louis had unwisely chosen that way to Cairo, and though the crusaders were victorious for the moment, they were not to win the war. With an open-ended stalemate at Mansourah, Louis at long last tried to negotiate with the infidels in April, offering to exchange Damietta for Jerusalem, the offer he had disdainfully turned down once before. Now it was too late. Within a few days he and his entire army were prisoners of the Egyptians. An enormous ransom was eventually raised for the liberation of Louis, including the surrender of the city of Damietta, but it would be yet another four years before he would set foot in his realm again.

Louis's plight was depressing news. Though he himself had not always proven scrupulously loyal to Louis, Frederick remembered that that king had generally been sympathetic to the imperial predicament in the face of a hostile Church. Yet the emperor could gain from Louis's failed crusade. Innocent was being roundly cursed as the man who, because he had made it unfeasible for Frederick to join the crusade, had guaranteed its failure. Furthermore, he had diverted too many knights away from Louis's "holy war" in order to wage his own unholy crusade against the emperor. Innocent could not have been comforted by these widely voiced opinions, nor could Frederick's renewed status in Italy and Germany have bolstered his morale. As a matter of fact, at this point Innocent was so uneasy and faced such a bleak outlook—Louis had gone so far as to send word to him from the Holy Land to patch up his quarrels with Frederick or be prepared to leave Lyon—that he begged King Henry III of England for asylum in his French holding of Bordeaux. Henry refused, on the sobering grounds that Innocent was too profoundly despised ever to find a friendly home in that territory. Equally discommoding, Innocent was almost broke. In spite of his active traffic in indulgences, simony, and nepotism, his coffers were all but empty. Knowing that Frederick was anticipating a trip to Germany, Innocent envisioned him sweeping by Lyon for a face-off confrontation, the last thing that a nearly penniless pontiff on a shaky throne wanted. The general view had it that the emperor's star was again ascendant and that heaven was once again on his side. Bleak was not the word for Innocent's plight. Black would be better.

Lagopesole in the mountains south of Melfi was one of Frederick's favorite "places of solace." After spending the summer there, resting in anticipation of the more strenuous life of northern Italy and Germany, he moved to Foggia. He was in the country he loved above all others except Sicily, the land that prompted the boast when he was at the pinnacle of his power that, dazzling as was the title of emperor, he still did not consider it demeaning to be known as "the man of Apulia." His residence in Foggia was the largest and most sumptuous of all his mainland palaces. Accounts from the time describe a place of spacious halls, gardens, fountains, and courtyards. It is said that its magnificence was such that Frederick gave instructions that his prisoners from Cortenuova were to be guided through the marble halls of the residence so that they could be properly impressed with his grandeur and brilliance. So much more the tragedy that nothing remains of it but a hard-to-find single vestige—a doorway with an arch supported by carved eagles. Maimed, scarred, and battered as they are, we can yet divine the pride and majesty of their positions as they scrutinize the passersby. An inscription records that the palace was built according to Frederick's instructions by one Bartholomew and that the royal city became famous through its glory. In the vicinity of Foggia, Frederick ordered other palaces and lodges to be built, along with fish ponds and aviaries, stables and kennels. The waterways that Frederick caused to be dug around these sites, aside from aiding the cultivation of vineyards, attracted all manner of waterfowl, which served as game for his falcons. Most of the sites have been reduced to earth mounds surrounding the former lodges, and many of them are in desolate places. Quantities of pottery have been found on these now agricultural locations, some of it unique to Frederick's world.

An ebullient Frederick had come to the hunting land of his choice, but he was observed by his followers to be a sick man. Not one to give in easily to ailments of the body, he insisted on setting out for Lucera, the sprawling castle compound—a veritable city—manned by his favorite Saracen guards. On the way he even digressed for a brief hunting expedition. Bravado aside, however, he could not continue. He was finally carried in a litter to another of his "places of solace," the castle of Fiorentino, with a severe case of dysentery.

Frederick sensed that this sickness was to be his last. His chief justiciars were summoned at his request. Most prominent at his bedside was his eighteen-year-old son, Manfred, of all his children the most like him. There was also present the most loyal archbishop Berard of Palermo, friend through the years and the counselor who had accompanied the "boy of Apulia" when he was only eighteen and starting out in quest of his crown and destiny. Count Robert of Caserta arrived, along with the Sicilian physician, Giovanni da Procida, who in 1282 would play a half-legendary role in the great break for freedom known as the "Sicilian Vespers." Frederick dictated his will in the presence of these and other chief officers of the state. To King Conrad went the empire and the kingdom; Henry, son of Isabella, was willed the kingdom of Arles or Jerusalem, the choice being left to Conrad; Manfred was appointed vicar-general of the Italian-Sicilian state and was given the principality of Taranto; his grandson Frederick—son of the first guileful Henry—was given the duchy of Austria. They all had their work cut out for them. Perhaps to cleanse his own mind and soul, Frederick stipulated that to the Church was to be returned all rightful possessions—provided that the honor of neither the emperor nor the empire was sullied.

Having made known his will, Frederick seemed to regain a rallying strength. When he asked where he was, he was told that he lay in the castle of Fiorentino. He thought then of his lifelong avoidance of the city of Florence and the disturbing prophecy that he would die in a place whose name was derived from the word *flower*. Had avoiding Florence been in vain? He asked to be told more precisely where he lay and was told that his bed was against a walled-up opening that had formerly led to the castle tower, and that concealed behind the masonry was the original old iron door. He knew then that the prophecy of his soothsayer was being realized in its totality: "You will die by an iron door in a place whose name is derived from the word *flower*." The prophecy had run its course. And with it so had his life. He did not want to die. But he faced the inevitability of the divine will.

As late as December 12 it seemed that stubborn Frederick might yet conquer fate. He spoke of getting up from his bed perhaps the next day and of again enjoying the hunt. He ate some pears cooked with sugar, prescribed by a Salerno medical book as being a cure for internal disorders. But by December 13 he was clearly dying. He had himself robed in a Cistercian white habit and received absolution from his beloved Berard of Palermo. And with that he died. It was the feast day of Sicilian Santa Lucia, whose name derives from *lux*—light.

Frederick had requested that he be buried in Palermo, simply and without fanfare by the side of his father, Henry VI, in company with his courageous, embittered mother, Constance, and his first wife, the other Constance in his life. Despite his instructions, however, a solemn and elaborate procession wended through the realm, down the boot of Italy, past Canosa di Puglia, where was buried a cousin twice removed, a man equally heroic in his way, and similarly defeated by the forces of life: Bohemund, Prince of Antioch, giant-sized son of Robert Guiscard, the deceased emperor's great-uncle. Frederick was accompanied by his openly mourning Saracen guards and a cortege of officials, whose armor was draped in black. A ceremonial stop was made at Bitonto, where he lay in state before the most dramatic of backgrounds, the cathedral, a home for a veritable zoo of sculptured animals and imaginary beasts cavorting with abandon around doors and windows at both the western entrance and the eastern apsidal facades. This sublime temple remains a monument to the piety and taste of Frederick's eleventh-century Norman forebears. The cathedral houses an elegantly carved marble pulpit with strange figures believed by some to represent Frederick and Isabella of England and two of his sons. And Frederick would have been comforted by the awareness that he lay almost in sight of the most

Cathedral, Bitonto, Italy

palatial of his hunting palaces, the Castel del Monte, one of the singular architectural triumphs of the entire medieval period.

No single structure built to Frederick Hohenstaufen's specifications is more imposing than this massive castle taunting the heavens in solitary splendor on a rise overlooking the vast Murge—the Apulian foothills and plain. While it may have served partially as a defense outpost, it was clearly intended more for imperial delight and comfort, as the finely carved capitals, the severely handsome entryway flanked by lions, the interior latrines watered by lead pipes from a roof cistern, and the delicately modeled window frames all attest. Of all Frederick's castles, that of the mount is the most logical. Built on an octagonal plan of rough-cut, yellowish-gray limestone, it is brought into stunning

Castel del Monte, Italy

harmony by eight octagonal towers protruding from the wall junctures, an Eastern device that Frederick may have picked up in Outremer, perhaps directly from the Mosque of Omar in Jerusalem, which he admired. It has also been suggested that Frederick may have wished to vaunt the imperial glory by creating an enormous functioning monument suggesting the eight-sided crown of the Holy Roman Empire. And, indeed, it is golden, especially late in the afternoon, when the unequivocal Apulian sun engenders dense shadows, dramatizing and articulating the great mass of this imperial diadem. The octagonal central body of Castel del Monte, all planes and angles, seems to flow into the towers, which themselves enforce the coherent unity by their repetition of the basic form. A concave, octagonal courtyard wraps around the majestic, convex exterior, multifaceted, its walls without start or finish, infinitely enclosing a very finite space. All doors come in, it seems; none go out. The building is an exercise in geometry.

The eight trapezoidal rooms of the ground floor are repeated almost exactly on the floor above. They are made gracious by marble paneling, brick and stone patterns, mosaic floors, vaulted ceilings and rose-colored columns veined with blue and lavender and topped by Gothic capitals. Three of the upper-floor rooms appear to have been designed for the emperor's personal use. One of them has a triple Gothic window, the largest in the castle, which commands a breathtaking view of the city of Andria, the birthplace of Conrad, and the burial place of Conrad's mother, Yolanda, and Isabella of England. The presence of a private bathroom suggests Frederick's pagan preference for bodily cleanliness. Other rooms were surely equipped with large fireplaces and art works both ancient and modern, as well as books and manuscripts on the sciences and expanses of heavy drapery to deaden the sound and cut drafts. Peculiar to the Castel del Monte is the strange architectural device of controlling traffic flow by connecting the rooms. Frederick's natural, if sometimes latent distrust of those around him may be the explanation. The one entrance from the outside world can be easily surveyed from imperial quarters above. The solid perimeter walls are pierced by typically medieval light slits, shielding the inside from the devastating brilliance of the southern sun, while still allowing ample interior light in the manner of the more gracious Renaissance.

Few castles in any country conjure feelings of such majesty, such luxury in the Eastern manner, and such dramatic strength, all emphasized by the barrenness of the surrounding olive tree–dappled hillside. There is a kind of movement in the design, a feeling of revolving form in the exact repetition of the protruding towers, giving the building an aura of power, a design logic without beginning or end, an immortality. Castel del Monte is, in a sense, the emperor himself, indomitable, arrogant, proud, a model of logical organization and of luxurious ostentation. There is poetry in its rhythms and exacting repeats. Here in this favorite Murge of Frederick's realm, shaped like his imperial crown, enthroned on a dais of arid earth (in his day covered by forest) that he envisioned, as though seeing through the eyes of Saint Francis, as God's triumphant mundane creation, rises the supreme monument of the most enlightened, the most visionary of medieval rulers, a despot to be sure, at once the climax of his own age and the prophet of the next, the acting medium between the Middle Ages and the Renaissance. It is an arresting thought that the gorgeous Castel del Monte is only a short hop from Frederick's Norman ancestors' first mountain lair, Melfi.

The Castel del Monte and its environs seem a wondrous place of joy and rest, neither dark nor glaringly bright—a kind of quiet gray between two extremes. Francis would have loved it. Through the still,

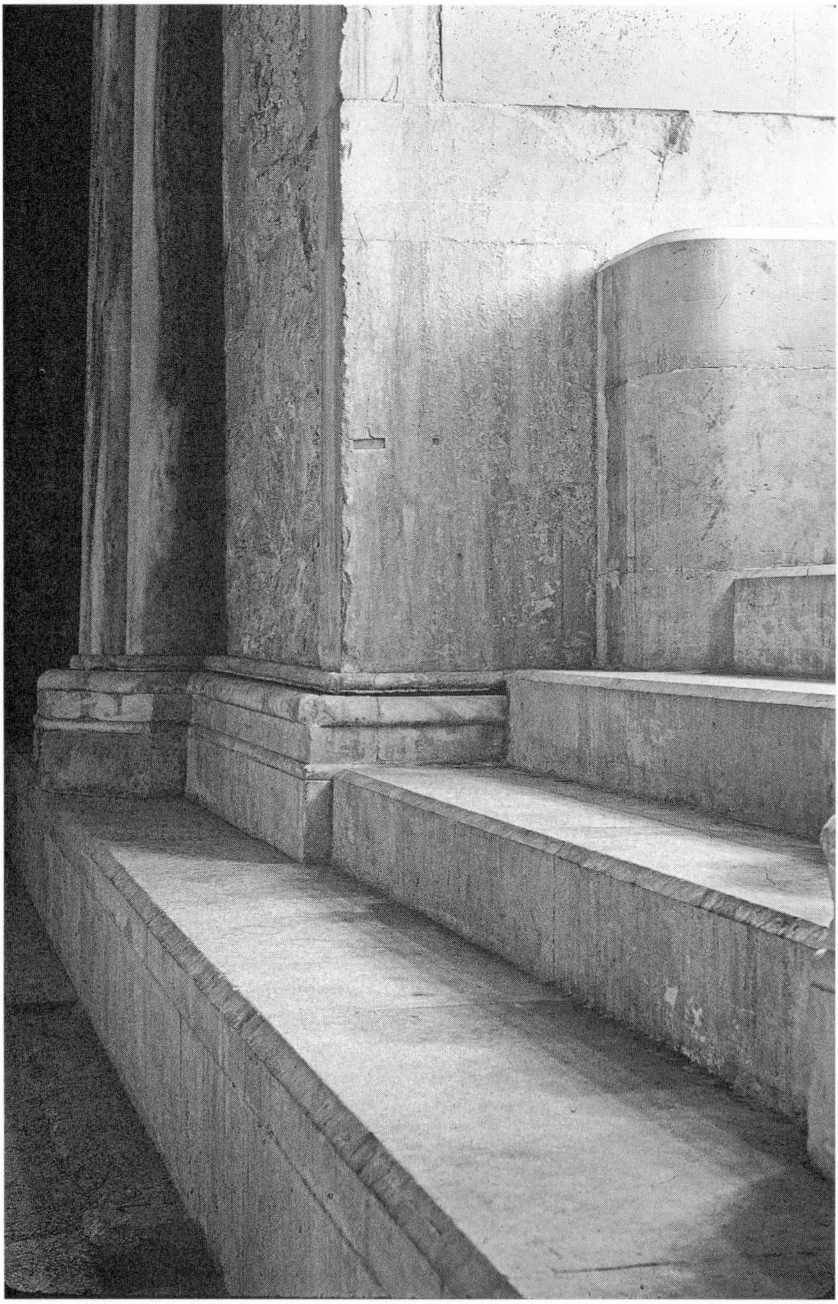

Window seat, Castel del Monte, Italy

dry silence of the Apulian summer, one can hear sparrows nesting in the crevices of these ancient walls and watch the slow-circling hawks hovering above. From this Atlantean structure that seems to shoulder the cobalt sky, from windows with their handsome marble seats and steps that turn each opening into a proscenium, Francis and Frederick together would have taken in sweeping views of the realm, the empire, and the world under Brother Sun. They also would have witnessed the end of the Hohenstaufen line, the destruction of the Holy Roman Empire and its laws that Frederick had envisioned, along with God's world of love as Francis had dreamed.

To the mournful blare of trumpets, the flutter of imperial banners, the muffled clangor of veil-draped armor, and the resonant tattoo of drums, Frederick's body was borne to Gioia del Colle, where he lay in state in his castle, which looms formidably above its surrounding town and houses a reconstructed medieval kitchen, heavy with stone arches and a cavernous walk-in fireplace. The procession moved on to Taranto, whence the trip to Messina was accomplished by boat. The sad cortege made its way to Patti, where the evil Markward of Anweiler had died in agony forty-two years before, and then on to glorious Cefalù Cathedral, the supreme creation of Frederick's maternal grandfather, King Roger II, the first of the royal line. Faithful subjects stood in silence to watch as "the wonder of the world" was carried past—the man "at whose feet lay the universe and on whom God smiled," as Manfred put it to Enzo when he wrote, informing him of their father's death. Along the northern coast road of Sicily, Frederick was carried to Palermo, not the city of his birth, but the source of his education and inspiration.

Frederick was interred in garments of fine Arabian silk, richly embroidered with Kufic characters in gold thread. He wore a crusader's cross on his left shoulder and a red mantle embroidered with imperial eagles and clasped by a brooch of emeralds and amethysts. His spurs were attached to his boots, which were embroidered with small deer. His sword was interred with him, as was his orb, and on the middle finger of his right hand he wore a gold ring with a large emerald. On his head was placed a richly jeweled crown. Frederick was laid in a porphyry tomb made to receive his maternal grandfather but which had, for abstruse reasons, remained unused in the cathedral at Cefalù until sixty years after the great king's death, when it was transferred to Palermo in anticipation of Frederick's final sleep. The body of the tomb is supported by porphyry lions, a pair sitting back-to-back at each end, while the gabled lid is embellished with the symbols of the four evangelists and the figure of Frederick.

Frederick—God's regent, the anti-Christ, favored of God and hated by his vicars on earth, the devil's confidant, "wonder of the world," the sun of Italy, the glory of Germany, friend of Muslims, linguist, poet, mathematician, judge, king, emperor—had returned to the city that had raised him from beggary, educated him, inspired and determined him to seek the fulfillment of his destiny as he saw it. At last, rest.

Frederick's tomb, Cathedral, Palermo, Sicily

EPILOGUE

Faithful Lord Jesus,
grant them rest.
Amen.
***Dies Irae*, verse 19**

Young Henry, Isabella of England's son, died at fifteen, less than three years after Frederick. And that year (1253) marked the dedication of the enormous Church of Saint Francis in Assisi, the final affront to the groom of Lady Poverty. If the elaborate crypt of the retiring little saint were not negation enough, there rose above it two churches, one above the other—"like a Babylonian tower," scoffed Goethe[1]—each one to become a veritable museum of artists over a period of several centuries. While one admires the frescoes by the likes of Simone Martini, Cimabue, the Lorenzetti brothers, and the sublime Giotto, one can't help hearing what a far cry they are from Francis's basic principles. In the upper church Giotto covered the walls with frescoes of the life of Francis, done with a tenderness and sweetness unknown in the arts until the coming of this artist and his model.

One wonders what the spiritual lover of Francis, gentle Chiara Favarone, thought on seeing the basilica rising each day higher and higher from its steep hillside. But she was busy with her own priorities, composing an austere rule for her Poor Clares. Pope Innocent IV finally gave in to her on August 9, 1253, and confirmed her set of regulations. Two days later she joined Francis in death.

King Conrad, Frederick's heir, could not face the prospect of endless struggle in Germany. A year after his father's death, having narrowly escaped an attempt on his life by the abbot of Saint Emmeram at Ratisbon, where he had been spending Christmas, he left Germany to Innocent's man, usurper William of Holland, and came to Italy to stake out his claim there. But he died of a fever in 1254 at age twenty-six. That same year Innocent IV, broken by sickness, disillusionment, and the exertions of his approximately forty-seven years, died in Naples.

During the battle of Benevento in 1266, Manfred, Conrad's half-brother, was killed defending Hohenstaufen claims to Sicily against the onslaught of Charles of Anjou, brought into Italy by French pope Clement IV. Charles claimed the realm, but too zealously, as it turned out. There was yet one remaining free representative of the Hohenstaufen dynasty in the legitimate male line: Conrad's son—Conradino, the Italians call him—little Conrad.

Conradino was fifteen years old when he left Swabia to come to Italy to claim his inheritance, very much as his grandfather had before him, but going in the opposite direction. He was greeted as a hero in a Rome laid with rugs and festooned with silks and banners. Arches were erected from the bridge of Sant'Angelo to the Capitoline Hill. Conradino was acclaimed legitimate king. He was cheered and hymned as a fresh-faced young man chosen by God to give new life to Frederick's vision and a renewed sense of destiny to the fickle populace. He was with his Ghibelline family. Four weeks later Conradino was in the clutches of Charles of Anjou, having been betrayed after the battle of Tagliacozzo (1268). With him were a few loyal friends who were executed. (One was imprisoned for thirty-two years in the Castel del Monte—strange that that glorious house should serve such a purpose!)

With Charles of Anjou watching from a prominent place in the Piazza del Mercato in Naples, earning for himself an indelible reputation for calloused heartlessness, Conradino was beheaded, a fate without precedent for a king taken in war. As his head fell from the block, an eagle—the Hohenstaufen symbol—swooped out of an azure sky and dipped its right wing into the pooling blood. Then, carrying the precious relic of the last free representative of the great line, it vanished into the heavens. At least, that is what people say.

Charles of Anjou was unopposed as Charles I of Naples and Sicily. Brave Enzo would try to save the situation with an attempted escape from his Bolognese palace, but he was caught in the act and returned to his luxurious confinement, where he died in 1272. Charles I's day came with the Sicilian Vespers in 1282, which put Peter III of Aragon on the southern throne.

The piazza of Conradino's murder is now a dismal place: noisy, exhaust-belching automobiles and trucks; lines of tattered awning-covered stalls of produce, cheap toys, and shoddy household appointments; heaps of empty plastic containers; city dirt and dust; shrill crowds; and the ubiquitous, painful decibles of recorded rock and heavy metal. But Conradino found his quiet rest in the Church of Santa Maria del Carmine at the edge of the piazza. Inside there is a statue in his memory. He is tall, a straight-backed young man, with a deep chest and a hand on his sword—Frederick's grandson to his finger tips! But he was not given a chance. And Frederick would have wept for him.

Conradino, Santa Maria del Carmine, Naples, Italy

Endnotes

Prologue

1. Kington, *History of Frederick the Second,* 1: 30–31.

Chapter One

1. Dante Alighieri, *Paradiso,* Canto III: 114–16.
2. Scherer, *History of German Literature,* 1: 193.
3. Pacaut, *Frederick Barbarossa,* 98.
4. Thomas of Celano, *St. Francis of Assisi,* 6–7.
5. Fortini, *Francis of Assisi,* 37.

Chapter Two

1. Kington, *History of Frederick the Second,* 1: 89.
2. Norwich, *Kingdom in the Sun*, 362.

Chapter Three

1. Newman, *Stories of the Great Operas*, 4.
2. Heer, *Medieval World*, 194–95.
3. Thomas of Celano, *St. Francis of Assisi*, 40.
4. Kantorowicz, *Frederick the Second*, 54.

Chapter Four

1. Barzini, *Italians*, xi.
2. Morton, *Traveller in Italy*, 158.
3. Freeman, *Herbs for the Mediaeval Household*, 11.
4. Ibid., 6.
5. Aston, *Peirol*, 139.

Chapter Five

1. Thomas of Celano, *St. Francis of Assisi*, 20.
2. Runciman, *History of the Crusades*, 3: 140.

3. Demus, *Encyclopedia of World Art*, 10: 639.
4. Kantorowicz, *Frederick the Second*, 160.
5. Binns, *Innocent III*, 70.
6. Temko, *Notre Dame of Paris*, 212.

Chapter Six

1. Bury and others, *Cambridge Medieval History*, 6: 711.
2. Fortini, *Francis of Assisi*, 380.
3. Bishop, *Saint Francis of Assisi*, 127.
4. Masson, *Frederick II*, 64.
5. Kantorowicz, *Frederick the Second*, 104.

Chapter Seven

1. Goethe, *Italian Journey*, 20.
2. Coulson, ed. *The Saints*, 147.
3. Norwich, *Kingdom in the Sun*, 389.
4. Milman, *History of Latin Christianity*, 4: 289.
5. Kington, *History of Frederick the Second*, 1: 201.
6. Concerning this oddity of only a single senator, Georgina Masson explains it as well as anyone: "When the Senate was revived in 1144 there were fifty-six senators. This continued almost without intermission until 1204, when it became the custom to elect annually only one, or at most two, senators, who were assisted by counsellors. This practice continued with one intermission until 1358, after which the Senator was appointed by the Pope." Masson, *Frederick II*, 359.

Chapter Eight

1. Machiavelli, *The Prince*, 122.
2. Van Cleve, *Emperor Frederick II*, 140.
3. Kantorowicz, *Frederick the Second*, 121.
4. Aston, *Peirol*, 162–63.
5. Ibid., 163.
6. Leo of Assisi, *Mirror of Perfection*, 381.
7. Englebert, *Saint Francis of Assisi*, 278–79.
8. Van Cleve, *Emperor Frederick II*, 154 (quoting Jamal-ed-Din).

Chapter Nine

1. Dante Alighieri, *Paradiso*, Canto XI: 94–96.
2. Kantorowicz, *Frederick the Second*, 293.
3. Bonaventure, *Life of Saint Francis*, 506.
4. *Little Flowers of Saint Francis*, trans. T. Okey, 113–114.
5. Ibid., 115.
6. Francis's stigmatization was the first recorded and has remained the most celebrated. However, there have been over three hundred reported cases of a similar

phenomenon since then, three of them in the twentieth century: Gemma Calgani of Lucca (died 1903), Theresa Neumann of Konnersreuth, Germany (died September 18, 1968), and Padre Pio (died September 22, 1969), who lived the last years of his life at San Giovanni Rotondo on the Gargano peninsula, where he caused an up-to-date hospital to be built to care for the poor of southern Italy.

7. Translation by Carmen Mion. For the original, see *Speculum: A Journal of Mediaeval Studies* 1: 93–94.

8. Scott, *Lay of the Last Minstrel*, XII:138–42.

9. For Frederick's *The Art of Falconry (De Arte Venandi cum Avibus)*, see the excellent edition translated and edited by Wood and Fyfe.

10. Thomas of Celano, *St. Francis of Assisi*, 271.

Chapter Ten

1. Kington, *History of Frederick the Second*, 1: 260.
2. Ibid., 284.
3. Ibid., 285.
4. Milman, *History of Latin Christianity*, 4: 325.

Chapter Eleven

1. Ibn Jubayr, *Travels of Ibn Jubayr*, 318.
2. Nicholson, *Literary History of the Arabs*, 402.
3. Kantorowicz, *Frederick the Second*, 201.
4. Ibid., 198.
5. Kington, *History of Frederick the Second*, 1: 334.

Chapter Twelve

1. Goethe, *Italian Journey*, 240.
2. Translation by Carmen Mion. The complete original poem can be found in *Speculum: A Journal of Mediaeval Studies* 1: 89–90.
3. McCarthy, *Venice Observed*, 50.
4. Coulton, *From St. Francis to Dante*, 195.

Chapter Thirteen

1. John, ed., *The Popes*, 228.
2. Berthold of Ratisbon, in Coulton, *Life in the Middle Ages*, 3: 59–60.
3. Ibid., 65.

Chapter Fourteen

1. Levi, *Linden Trees*, 97.
2. *Nibelungenlied*, 133–135.
3. Kantorowicz, *Frederick the Second*, 410.

Chapter Fifteen

1. Translation by Carmen Mion. The original can be found in *Speculum: A Journal of Mediaeval Studies* 1: 404.
2. Masson, *Frederick II*, 303.

Chapter Sixteen

1. Chambers, *Devil's Horsemen*, 53.
2. Kington, *History of Frederick the Second,* 1: 534.
3. Ibid., 2: 368.
4. Masson, *Frederick II*, 338.

Chapter Seventeen

1. Coulton, *From St. Francis to Dante*, 119.
2. Ibid., 120.
3. Dante Alighieri, *Inferno*, Canto XIII: 58–61.
4. Ibid., Canto XIII: 64–75.
5. Translation by Carmen Mion. The original can be found in *Speculum: A Journal of Mediaeval Studies* 1: 400.

Epilogue

1. Goethe, *Italian Journey*, 107.

Bibliography

For the reader who is not already satiated, the reader who is simply curious enough to investigate the subject or tangential subjects further, even the one who wants easy-to-read references, the following bibliography makes no pretense to being definitive. It consists of books that have been utilized in the text, either as simple references or as footnotes. Additional sources have been included that the author feels may be of interest, together with some that from his own point of view were found to be especially interesting, helpful, or amusing. The emphasis, but not the insistence, is on books in the English language.

Abulafia, David. *Frederick II: A Medieval Emperor*. London: Allen Lane the Penguin Press, 1988.

Agnello, G. *L'Architettura Sveva in Sicilia.* Rome, 1935.

Allshorn, Lionel. *Stupor Mundi.* London: M. Secker, 1912.

Almedingen, E. M. *St. Francis of Assisi.* New York: Knopf, 1967.

Ambrosini, Maria, and Louisa Boggeri. *The Secret Archives of the Vatican.* With Mary Wollis. Boston: Little, Brown, 1969.

Andrewes, Patience. *Frederick II of Hohenstaufen.* London: Oxford University Press, 1970.

Ariès, Philippe, and Georges Duby, eds. *A History of Private Lives: Revelations of the Medieval World.* Translated by Arthur Goldhammer. Cambridge: Belknap Press of Harvard University, 1988.

Armstrong, Edward A. *Saint Francis: Nature Mystic.* Berkeley: University of California Press, 1973.

Ashdown, Charles Henry. *European Arms and Armour.* New York: Brussel and Brussel, 1967.

Aston, S. C. *Peirol: Troubadour of Auvergne.* Cambridge: Cambridge University Press, 1953.

Banister-Fletcher, Sir. *A History of Architecture on the Comparative Method.* 14th ed. New York: Charles Scribner's Sons, 1948.

Barber, Richard. *The Penguin Guide to Medieval Europe.* Harmondsworth, UK: Penguin Books, 1984.

Barraclough, Geoffrey. *The Crucible of Europe: The Ninth and Tenth Centuries in European History.* Berkeley: University of California Press, 1976.

———, trans. and intro. *Mediaeval Germany, 911–1250* [essays by German historians]. Oxford: Basil Blackwell, 1938.

———. *The Medieval Papacy.* London: Thames and Hudson, 1968.

Barzini, Luigi. *The Italians.* New York: Atheneum, 1965.

Batterberry, Michael. *Art of the Middle Ages.* New York: McGraw-Hill, 1974.

Bäuml, Franz H. *Medieval Civilization in Germany, 800–1273.* New York: Frederick A. Praeger, 1969.
Beckwith, John. *Early Medieval Art.* New York: Frederick A. Praeger, 1964.
Benvenisti, Meron. *The Crusaders in the Holy Land.* Translated by Pamela Fitton. Jerusalem: Israel Universities Press, 1970.
Binns, L. Elliott. *Innocent III.* n.p.: Archon Books, 1968.
Bishop, Morris G. *The Middle Ages.* New York: Mariner Books, 1970.
———. *Saint Francis of Assisi.* Boston: Little, Brown, 1974.
Boase, T. S. R. *Kingdoms and Strongholds of the Crusaders.* New York: Bobbs-Merrill, 1971.
———. *St. Francis of Assisi.* London: Thames and Hudson, 1968.
Bonaventure. *The Life of St. Francis.* Translated by E. Gurney Salter. With *The Little Flowers of St. Francis* and *The Mirror of Perfection* by Leo of Assisi. New York: Everyman's Library, 1951.
Boni, Ada. *Italian Regional Cooking.* New York: Bonanza Books, 1969.
Bradford, Ernle. *The Shield and the Sword: The Knights of Malta.* London: Fontana/Collins, 1972.
———. *The Sword and the Scimitar: The Saga of the Crusades.* New York: Gollancz, 2004.
Bridge, Antony. *The Crusades.* London: Granada Publishing, 1985.
Briffault, Robert S. *The Troubadours.* Bloomington: Indiana University Press, 1965.
Brion, Marcel. *Frederick II de Hohenstaufen* [in French]. Paris: Librairie Jules Tallandier, 1978.
Brockway, Wallace, and Herbert Weinstock. *Men of Music,* rev. ed. New York: Simon and Schuster 1950.
Brooke, Christopher Nugent Lawrence. *Europe in the Central Middle Ages, 962–1154.* Harlow: Longman, 2000.
———. *Medieval Church and Society.* New York: New York University Press, 1972.
———. *Monasteries of the World.* New York: Crescent Books, 1982.
———. *The Twelfth Century Renaissance.* New York: Harcourt, Brace and World, 1969.
Brooke, Rosalind, and Christopher Brooke. *Popular Religion in the Middle Ages.* London: Thames and Hudson, 1984.
Brown, Raphael, trans. *The Little Flowers of St. Francis.* New York: Image Books (Doubleday), 1958.
Bryce, James. *The Holy Roman Empire.* New York: AMS Press, 1978.
Burman, Edward. *The Templars: Knights of God.* Wellingborough: Thornson Publishing, 1986.
Bury, J. B., et al. *The Cambridge Medieval History,* vol. 6. New York: Macmillan, 1929.
Busch, Harald, and Bernd Lohse, eds. *Gothic Europe.* Translated by P. Gorge. New York: Macmillan, 1959.
Cairns, Trevor. *The Middle Ages* (Cambridge Introduction to the History of Mankind, Book 4). Cambridge: Cambridge University Press, 1972.
Carretto, Carlo. *I, Francis.* Translated by Robert R. Barr. New York: Orbis Books, 1980.
Cassady, Richard F. *The Norman Achievement.* London: Sidgwick and Jackson, 1986.
Chambers, James. *The Devil's Horsemen: The Mongol Invasion of Europe.* New York: Atheneum, 1979.
Cheetham, Nicolas. *Keepers of the Keys.* New York: Charles Scribner's Sons, 1982.
Cheney, Christopher Robert. *Medieval Texts and Studies.* Oxford: Oxford University Press, 1973.

Chesterton, Gilbert K. *St. Francis of Assisi.* Garden City, NY: Doubleday, 1924.
Cohn, W. *Hermann von Salza.* Breslau: M. and H. Marcus, 1930.
Comyn, Sir Robert Buckley. *The History of the Western Empire: From Its Restoration by Charlemagne to the Accession of Charles V.* London: W. H. Allen, 1841.
Contamine, Philippe. *War in the Middle Ages.* Translated by Michael Jones. Oxford: Basil Blackwell, 1984.
Coulson, John, ed. *The Saints: A Concise Biographical Dictionary.* New York: Hawthorne Books, 1958.
Coulton, George Gordon. *From St. Francis to Dante.* London: David Nutt, 1906.
———. *Life in the Middle Ages,* 4 vols. in 1. New York: Macmillan, 1930.
———. *Medieval Panorama.* London: Collins, 1961.
———. *The Medieval Scene.* Cambrdige: Cambridge University Press, 1930.
———. *Medieval Studies.* 2 vols. Boston: Beacon Press, 1959.
———. *Medieval Village, Manor and Monastery.* New York: Harper Torchbooks, 1960.
Crichton. G. H. *Romanesque Sculpture in Italy.* London: Routledge and Paul, 1954.
Cronin, Vincent. *The Golden Honeycomb.* London: Granada, 1980.
Cunningham, Lawrence, ed. *Brother Francis.* New York: Harper and Row, 1972.
———. *Saint Francis of Assisi.* San Francisco: Harper and Row, 1981.
Curtis, Edmund. *Roger of Sicily and the Normans in Lower Italy, 1016–1154.* New York: G. P. Putnam's Sons, 1912.
Dahmus, Joseph H. *Dictionary of Medieval Civilization.* New York: Macmillan, 1984.
———. *Seven Medieval Kings.* Garden City, NY: Doubleday, 1967.
Dante Alighieri. *The Inferno.* Translated by John Ciardi. New York: New American Library, 1954.
———.*The Paradiso.* Translated by John Ciardi. New York: New American Library, 1961.
Davis, Henry William Carless. *Medieval Europe.* London: Oxford University Press, 1960.
Decker, Hans. *Romanesque Art in Italy.* Translated by James Cleugh. New York: Harry N. Abrams, 1959.
Demus, Otto. *Byzantine Art and the West.* New York: New York University Press, 1970.
———. *Byzantine Mosaic Decoration.* New Rochelle, NY: Caratzas Brothers, 1976.
———. *Encyclopedia of World Art.* New York: McGraw-Hill, 1965.
———. *The Mosaics of Norman Sicily.* New York: Philosophical Library, 1950.
———. *The Mosaics of San Marco in Venice.* 4 vols. Chicago: University of Chicago Press, 1984.
De Sanctis, Francesco. *History of Italian Literature.* Translated by Joan Redfern. 2 vols. New York, 1968.
Detwiler, Donald S. *Germany: A Short History.* Carbondale: Southern Illinois University Press, 1976.
De Wald, Ernest T. *Italian Painting, 1200–1600.* New York: Holt, Rinehart and Winston, 1961.
Downs, Norton, ed. *Basic Documents in Medieval History.* Princeton, NJ: D. Van Nostrand, 1959.
———. *Medieval Pageant.* Princeton, NJ: D. Van Nostrand, 1964.
Dronke, Peter. *The Medieval Lyric.* London: Hutchinson, 1968.
Dunlop, Sir John Kinnenmont. *A Short History of Germany.* London: O. Wolff, 1965.
Durant, Will. *The Age of Faith.* New York: Simon and Schuster, 1950.
Einstein, David G. *Emperor Frederick II.* New York: Philosophical Library, 1949.

Englebert, Omer. *Saint Francis of Assisi.* Translated by Eve Marie Cooper. Chicago: Franciscan Herald Express, 1965.

Erbstösser, Martin. *The Crusades.* Translated by C. S. V. Salt. New York, Universe Books, 1979.

———. *Heretics in the Middle Ages.* Translated by Janet Fraser, Leipzig: Edition Leipzig, 1984.

Eschenbach, Wolfram von. *Parzival.* Translated by A. T. Hatto. New York: Penguin, 1980.

Esser, Kajetan. *Rule and Testament of St. Francis.* Chicago: Franciscan Herald Press, 1977.

Ferguson, George. *Signs and Symbols in Christian Art.* New York: Oxford University Press, 1954.

Finley, Moses I. *A History of Sicily.* With Denis Mack Smith and Christopher Duggan. New York: Viking Penguin, 1987.

Finucane, Ronald C. *Soldiers of the Faith.* New York: St. Martin's Press, 1983.

Fisher, Herbert. *The Medieval Empire.* 2 vols. London: Macmillan, 1898.

Flores, Angel, ed. *An Anthology of Medieval Lyrics.* New York: Modern Library, 1962.

Fortini, Arnaldo. *Francis of Assisi.* Translated by Helen Moak. New York: Crossroad Publishing, 1981.

Frazer, Sir James George. *The Golden Bough.* New York: Macmillan, 1951.

Frederick II Hohenstaufen. *The Art of Falconry, Being the De Arte Venandi cum Avibus of Frederick II of Hohenstaufen.* Translated and edited by Casey A. Wood and F. Majorie Fyfe. Stanford: Stanford University Press, 1943.

Freeman, Margaret B. *Herbs for the Mediaeval Household for Cooking, Healing and Divers Uses.* New York: Metropolitan Museum of Art, 1943.

Friederich, Werner Paul. *History of German Literature.* With Oscar Seidlin and Philip A. Shelley. New York: Barnes and Noble, 1962.

Fuhrmann, Horst. *Germany in the High Middle Ages, c. 1050–1200.* Translated by Timothy Reuter. London: Cambridge University Press, 1986.

Gabrieli, Francesco, trans. *Arab Historians of the Crusades.* London: Routledge and Kegan Paul, 1969.

Gasnick, Roy M., comp. and ed. *The Francis Book.* New York: Macmillan, 1980.

Germany: A Phaidon Cultural Guide. Englewood Cliffs, NJ: Prentice-Hall, 1985.

Gibbon, Edward. *The Decline and Fall of the Roman Empire,* New York: Modern Library, 2003.

Gies, Frances, and Joseph Gies. *Life in a Medieval City.* New York: Crowell, 1969.

———. *Life in a Medieval Village.* New York: Harper Collins, 1991.

Gillingham, John. *Richard the Lionheart.* New York: Times Books, 1978.

Goethe, Johann Wolfgang von. *Italian Journey, 1786–1788.* Translated by W. H. Auden and Elizabeth Mayer. New York: Schocken Books, 1968.

Goldin, Frederick. *German and Italian Lyrics of the Middle Ages.* Garden City, NY: Anchor Press, 1973.

———. *Lyrics of the Troubadours and Trouveres.* Garden City, NY: Anchor Press, 1973.

Gottfried von Strassburg. *Tristan.* Translated by W. H. Auden and Elizabeth Mayer. Harmondsworth, UK: Penguin Books, 1960.

Green, Julien. *God's Fool.* Translated by Peter Heinegg. San Francisco: Harper and Row, 1985.

Gregorovius, Ferdinando. *History of the City of Rome in the Middle Ages.* Translated by A. Hamilton. London: G. Bell and Sons, 1902.

Grousset, René. *The Epic of the Crusades.* Translated by A. Hamilton. New York: Orion Press, 1970.

Gunn, Peter. *A Concise History of Italy.* New York: Viking Press, 1972.

Hampe, Karl. *Germany under the Salian and Hohenstaufen Emperors.* Translated and with an introduction by Ralph Bennett. Totowa, NJ: Rowman and Littlefield, 1973.

Harvey, John. *Mediaeval Craftsmen.* New York: Drake Publishers, 1975.

Heer, Friedrich. *The Holy Roman Empire.* Translated by Janet Sondheimer. New York: Frederick A. Praeger, 1968.

———. *The Medieval World.* Translated by Janet Sondheimer. New York: New American Library, 1961.

Herlihy, David, ed. *Medieval Culture and Society.* New York: Harper and Row, 1968.

———. *Medieval Households.* Cambridge: Harvard University Press, 1985.

Hermann, Placid, trans. *XIIIth Century Chronicles.* Chicago: Franciscan Herald Press, 1961.

Holl, Adolf. *The Last Christian.* Translated by Peter Heinegg. New York: Doubleday, 1980.

Hollister, Charles Warren. *Medieval Europe: A Short History.* New York: John Wiley and Sons, 1964.

Hoyt, Robert S. *Europe in the Middle Ages.* New York: Harcourt, Brace, 1957.

Hubert, Jean. *The Carolingian Renaissance.* With Jean Porcher and W. F. Volbach. Translated by James Emmons, Stuart Gilbert, and Robert Allen. New York: George Braziller, 1970.

Ibn Jubayr [Abu 'l-Husayn Muhammad ibn Ahmed ibn Jubayr]. *The Travels of Ibn Jubayr.* Translated by Ronald J. C. Broadhurst. London: Jonathan Cape, 1952.

John, Eric, ed. *The Popes.* London: Burn and Gates, 1964.

Joinville, Jean de, and Geoffrey de Villehardouin. *Chronicles of the Crusades.* Translated and with an introduction by M. R. B. Shaw. New York: Dorset Press, 1985.

Jörgensen, Johannes. *St. Francis of Assisi.* New York: Image Books (Doubleday), 1955.

Kantorowicz, Ernst H. *Frederick the Second, 1194–1250.* Translated by E. O. Lorimer. New York: Frederick Ungar, 1957.

———. *The King's Two Bodies.* Princeton, NJ: Princeton University Press, 1957.

Kauffmann, C. M. *The Baths of Pozzuoli.* Oxford: Bruno Cassirer, 1959.

Keen, Maurice. *The Pelican History of Medieval Europe.* Harmondsworth, UK: Penguin Books, 1969.

Kessel, Dimitri. *Splendors of Christendom.* Commentary by Henri Peyre. Lausanne: Edita Lausanne, 1964.

Kidson, Peter. *The Medieval World.* New York: McGraw-Hill, 1967.

Kieckhefer, Richard. *Repression of Heresy in Medieval Germany.* Liverpool, UK: Liverpool University Press, 1979.

Kington, Thomas Lawrence (later Oliphant). *History of Frederick the Second, Emperor of the Romans.* 2 vols. Cambridge: Macmillan, 1862.

Kininmonth, Christopher. *Sicily.* London: Jonathan Cape, 1965.

Koch, Hannesjoachim Wilhelm. *Medieval Warfare.* New York: Prentice-Hall, 1978.

Kossak, Zofia. *Blessed Are the Meek.* New York: Roy Publisher, 1944.

Lamb, Harold. *Charlemagne.* New York: Bantam Books, 1958.

Lampedusa, Giuseppe di. *The Leopard.* Translated by Archibald Colquhoun. New York: Pantheon Books, 1960.

Landay, Jerry M. *Dome of the Rock.* With the editors of Newsweek Book Division.

Wonders of Man Series. New York: Newsweek, 1972.
Lawrence, Clifford Hugh. *Medieval Monasticism.* London: Longman, 1984.
Lawrence, David Herbert. *Movements in European History.* Oxford: Oxford University Press, 1981.
Leach, Maria, ed., and Jerome Fried, assoc. ed. *Dictionary of Folklore, Mythology and Legend.* 2 vols. New York: Funk and Wagnalls, 1950.
Leithe-Jasper, Manfred, and Rudolf Distelberger. *Vienna, the Kunsthistorische Museum.* Translated by Elsie Callander and Ilse Seldon. London: Philip Wilson Publishers, 1982.
Leo of Assisi. *The Mirror of Perfection.* Translated by Robert Steele. New York: E. P. Dutton, 1951.
Levi, Carlo. *Christ Stopped at Eboli.* Translated by Frances Frenaye. New York: Farrar, Straus, 1947.
———. *The Linden Trees.* Translated by Joseph M. Bernstein. New York: Alfred A. Knopf, 1962.
The Little Flowers of St. Francis. Read by Cyril Cusack, Caedmon Records, TC 1112, 1959.
The Little Flowers of St. Francis. Translated by John Steven McGroarty. Westwood, NJ: Westwood Hills Press, 1932.
The Little Flowers of St. Francis. Translated by T. Okey. With *The Mirror of Perfection* by Leo of Assisi and *The Life of St. Francis* by St. Bonaventure. New York: Everyman's Library, 1963.
Luchaire, A. *Innocent III.* 6 vols. [in French]. Paris, 1905–08.
Lyon, Bryce D., ed. *The High Middle Ages, 1000–1300.* New York: Free Press, 1964.
Machiavelli, Niccolò. *History of Florence and of the Affairs of Italy.* New York: Harper and Brothers, 1960.
———. *The Prince.* Translated by Luigi Ricci. Revised by E. R. P. Vincent. New York: New American Library, 1957.
MacKenzie, Donald A. *German Myths and Legends.* New York: Avenel Books, 1985.
Mack Smith, Denis. *A History of Sicily.* 2 vols. London: Chatto and Windus, 1968.
Maehl, William Harvey. *Germany in Western Civilization.* University: University of Alabama Press, 1979.
Mahler, Gustav. *Des Knaben Wunderhorn.* Philips Recording 9500 316.
Mâle, Émile. *Religious Art from the Twelfth to the Eighteenth Century.* New York: Noonday Press, 1949.
Mango, Cyril. *Byzantium, the Empire of New Rome.* New York: Charles Scribner's Sons, 1980.
Marcuzzi, Luigi. *Aquileia.* Sacile, Italy: Edizione Zanette, 1985.
Masson, Georgina. *The Companion Guide to Rome.* New York: Harper and Row, 1965.
———. *Frederick II of Hohenstaufen: A Life.* New York: Octagon Books, 1973.
Matthew, Donald. *Atlas of Medieval Europe.* New York: Facts on File, 1983.
McCarthy, Mary. *Venice Observed.* Paris: G. and R. Bernier, 1956.
Mills, Dorothy. *The Middle Ages.* New York: G. P. Putnam's Sons, 1935.
Milman, Henry Hart. *History of Latin Christianity,* vol. 4. London: John Murray, 1855.
Miskimin, Harry A. *The Medieval City.* Edited by David Herlihy and A. L. Udovitch. New Haven, CT: University Press, 1977.
Momigliano, E. *Federico II di Sveva.* Milan, 1948.
Montaigne, Michel Eyquem de. *Travel Journal.* Translated and with an introduction by Donald M. Frame. Foreword by Guy Davenport. San Francisco: North Point Press, 1983.

Morton, Henry Canova Vollam. *A Traveller in Italy.* New York: Dodd, Mead, 1964.
———. *A Traveller in Rome.* New York: Methuen, 1957.
———. *A Traveller in Southern Italy.* New York: Methuen, 1969.
Mose, Paul. *The Saint and the Sultan.* New York: Random House, 2009.
Mundy, John H. *Europe in the High Middle Ages, 1150–1309.* Edited by Denys Hay. London: Longman, 1973.
Munz, Peter. *Frederick Barbarossa.* Ithaca, NY: Cornell University Press, 1969.
Murphy, Thomas Patrick, ed. *The Holy War.* Columbus: Ohio State University Press, 1976.
Music of the Crusades. Argo Records, ZRG 673.
Music of the 12th and 13th Centuries. Vol. 1 of Anthology of Middle Age and Renaissance Music. EMS Recordings 201, 1951.
Musolino, Giovanni. *The Basilica of St. Mark in Venice:* Translated by John Guthrie. Venice: Ferdinando Ongania, 1955.
Newman, Ernest. *Stories of the Great Operas.* Philadelphia: Blakiston Co., 1930.
Nicholson, Reynold A. *A Literary History of the Arabs.* Cambridge: Cambridge University Press, 1930.
The Nibelungenlied, prose version. Translated by Arthur T. Hatto. Baltimore: Penguin Books, 1965.
Norman, Alexander Vesey Bethune. *Arms and Armor.* New York: G. P. Putnam's Sons, 1964.
———. *Warrior to Soldier, 449–1660.* With Don Pottinger. London: Widenfeld, Nicholson, 1966.
Norwich, John Julius, ed. *Great Architecture of the World.* New York: Random House, 1975.
———. *The Italians.* New York: Harry N. Abrams, 1983.
———. *The Kingdom in the Sun.* New York: Harper and Row, 1970.
———. *Venice, The Rise to Empire* [companion volume, *Venice, The Greatness and the Fall*]. London: Allen Lane, 1977.
Oke, Richard. *The Boy from Apulia.* London: Arthur Barker, 1936.
Oman, C. W. C. *The Art of War in the Middle Ages.* Ithaca, NY: Cornell University Press, 1984.
Otto of Freising. *The Deeds of Frederick Barbarossa.* Translated and annotated by Charles Christopher Mierow and Richard Emery. New York: Columbia University Press, 1953.
Pacaut, Marcel. *Frederick Barbarossa.* Translated by A. J. Pomerans. New York: Charles Scribner's Sons, 1970.
Partner, Peter. *The Murdered Magicians: The Templars and Their Myth.* New York: Barnes and Noble Books, 1993.
Pereira, Anthony. *Discovering Sicily.* London: B. P. Batsford, 1972.
———. *Naples, Pompeii and Southern Italy.* London: B. P. Batsford, 1977.
Pernoud, Régine. *The Crusaders.* Translated by Enid Grant. Philadelphia: Dufour Editions, 1964.
Pevsner, Nikolaus. *An Outline of European Architecture.* Baltimore: Penguin Books, 1960.
Pfistermeister, Ursula. *Nuremberg.* Nuremberg: Hans Carl, 1975.
Pilkington, Roger. *Small Boat on the Moselle.* London: St. Martin's Press, 1968.
Pirenne, Henri. *A History of Europe.* Translated by Bernard Maill. London: George Allen and Unwin, 1961.

Pirie-Gordon, C. H. C. *Innocent the Great: An Essay on His Times.* London: Longmans, Green, 1907.

Platt, Colin. *The Atlas of Medieval Man.* New York: St. Martin's Press, 1980.

Poole, Reginald Lane. *Illustrations of the History of Medieval Thought and Learning.* New York: Dover, 1920.

———. *Lectures on the History of the Papal Chancery.* Cambridge: Cambridge University Press, 1915.

Powell, James M., ed. *Innocent III: Vicar of Christ or Lord of the World.* Boston: D. C. Heath, 1963.

Prescott, Orville. *Lords of Italy.* New York: Harper and Row, 1972.

Previté-Orton, C. W. *The Methuen History of Medieval and Modern Europe, 1198–1378,* vol. 3. London: Cambridge University Press, 1951.

———. *Outlines of Medieval History.* Cambridge: Cambridge University Press, 1929.

———. *The Shorter Cambridge Medieval History.* Cambridge: Cambridge University Press, 1952.

Price, Lorna. *The Plan of St. Gall in Brief.* Berkeley: University of California Press, 1982.

Raymond, Ernest. *In the Steps of St. Francis.* New York: H. C. Kinsey, 1939.

Richey, Margaret Fitzgerald. *Studies of Wolfram von Eschenbach.* Edinburgh: Oliver and Boyd, 1957.

Rörig, Fritz. *The Medieval Town.* Berkeley: University of California Press, 1969.

Ross, James Bruce, and Mary Martin McLaughlin, eds. *The Portable Medieval Reader.* New York: Viking Press, 1949.

Rossi, Ferdinando. *Mosaics.* Translated by David Ross. New York: Praeger, 1970.

Runciman, Steven. *A History of the Crusades.* 3 vols. Harmondsworth, UK: Penguin, 1981.

Saalman, Howard. *Medieval Cities.* New York: Braziller, 1968.

Schearer, C. *The Renaissance of Architecture in Southern Italy: A Study of Frederick II of Hohenstaufen and the Capua Triumphator Archway Towers.* Cambridge: Heffer and Sons, 1935.

Scherer, Wilhelm. *A History of German Literature.* Vol. 1. Translated by Frederick Cornwallis Conybeare. New York: Charles Scribner's Sons, 1888.

Schwartz, H. M. *Sicily.* New York: Studio Publications, 1956.

Scott, Martin. *Medieval Europe.* New York: Dorset Press, 1986.

Scott, Sir Walter. *The Lay of the Last Minstrel.* Edited and with notes by William J. Rolfe. Boston: University Press, 1896.

Shearer, Cresswell. *The Renaissance of Architecture in Southern Italy.* Cambridge: W. Hefner and Sons, 1935.

Shepard, William P., and Frank M. Chambers. *The Poems of Aimeric de Péguilhan.* Evanston, IL: Northwestern University Press, 1950.

Sherley-Price, Leo, trans. *Saint Francis of Assisi: His Life and Writings as Recorded by His Contemporaries.* New York: Harper and Brothers, 1959.

Sherrill, Charles Hitchcock. *Mosaics in Italy, Palestine, Syria, Turkey and Greece.* London: John Lane, 1933.

Slaughter, Gertrude. *The Amazing Frederick.* With drawings by Robert Hill Taylor. New York: Macmillan, 1937.

Smail, R. C. *The Crusaders in Syria and the Holy Land.* Vol. 82 of Ancient Peoples and Places Series. New York: Praeger, 1973.

Smith, Charles Edward. *Innocent III: Church Defender.* Baton Rouge: Louisiana State University Press, 1951.

Smith, John Holland. *Francis of Assisi.* New York: Charles Scribner and Sons, 1972.

Southern, Richard William, ed. *Essays in Medieval History.* London: St. Martin's Press, 1968.

———. *The Making of the Middle Ages.* London: Hutchinson, 1953.

———. *Western Society and the Church in the Middle Ages.* Harmondsworth, UK: Penguin, 1970.

Speculum: A Journal of Mediaeval Studies, vol. 1. Cambridge: The Medieval Academy of America, 1926. For poems ascribed to Frederik II and "Red Fredericus" by Herman H. Thornton, page 87 and following.

The Splendors of Italy. New York: G. P. Putnam and Sons, 1964.

Steinbicker, Earl. *Day Trips in Germany.* New York: Hastings House, 1984.

Stephenson, Carl. *Mediaeval History: Europe from the Second to the Sixteenth Century.* Edited and revised by Bryce Lyon. New York: Harper and Row, 1935.

Stubbs, William D. D. *Germany in the Early Middle Ages, 476–1250.* London: Longmans, Greene, 1908.

Sumption, Jonathan. *Pilgrimage: An Image of Mediaeval Religion.* Totawa, NJ: Rowman and Littlefield, 1975.

Temko, Allan. *Notre Dame of Paris.* New York: Viking Press, 1955.

Thomas of Celano. *St. Francis of Assisi: The First and Second Life of St. Francis.* Translated by Placid Hermann. Chicago: Franciscan Herald Press, 1962.

Thompson, James Westfall. *Economic and Social History of the Middle Ages.* 2 vols. New York: Frederick Ungar Publishing Co., 1966.

———. *Feudal Germany.* Chicago: University of Chicago Press, 1928.

Tierney, Brian. *The Crisis of Church and State, 1050–1300.* Princeton, NJ: Prentice Hall, 1964.

Tillmann, Helene. *Pope Innocent III.* Translated by Walter Sax. Amsterdam: North-Holland Publishing, 1980.

Toesca, Pietro, and Ferdinando Ferlati. *Mosaics of St. Mark's.* Translated by Joyce Templeton and Gustina Scaglia. New York: New York Graphic Society, 1958.

Toynbee, Arnold J. *A Study of History.* New York: Oxford University Press, 1947.

Untermeyer, Louis. *Blue Rhine Black Forest.* New York: Harcourt, Brace, 1930.

Van Cleve, Thomas Curtis. *The Emperor Frederick II of Hohenstaufen: Immutator Mundi.* Oxford: Clarendon Press, 1972.

Vasari, Giorgio. *The Lives of the Artists.* Abridged and edited by Betty Burroughs. New York: Simon and Schuster, 1946.

Vernadsky, F. *The Mongols and Russia.* New Haven, CT: Yale University Press, 1953.

Volborth, Carl-Alexander von. *Heraldry—Customs, Rules and Styles.* Poole, UK: Blandford Press, 1981.

Voltaire. *Annals of the Empire.* Translated by William F. Fleming. Paris: E. R. DuMont, 1901.

Von Wahlstatt, Kurt Blücher. *Know Your Germans.* London: Chapman Hall, 1951.

Voragine, Jacobus de. *The Golden Legend.* Translated by Granger Ryan and Helmut Ripperger. New York: Arno Press, 1969.

Waddell, Helen. *Medieval Latin Lyrics,* 5th ed. London: Constable, 1966.

———. *The Wandering Scholars.* Garden City, NY: Doubleday, 1955.

Wagner, Richard. *Die Meistersinger.* Translated by H. Corder and F. Corder. Hollywood: Huber Publications, n.d.

Waley, D. *The Papal State in the Thirteenth Century.* London: Macmillan, 1961.

Walther von der Vogelweide. *Songs and Sayings of Walther von der Vogelweide.* Translated by Frank Betts. n.p., n.d.

Watkins, Paul. *See Sicily.* London: Format Books, 1974.
Whicher, George F. *The Goliard Poets.* Cambridge, MA: University Press, 1949.
Wiegler, Paul. *The Infidel Emperor.* New York: E. P. Dutton, 1930.
Wilkinson, Frederick. *Arms and Armor.* New York: Grossett and Dunlap, 1971.
Willemsen, Carl A., and Dagmar Odenthal. *Apulia: Imperial Splendor in Southern Italy.* Translated by Daphne Woodward. New York: Frederick A. Praeger, 1959.
Winston, Richard, and Clara Winston. *Notre-Dame de Paris.* With the editors of Newsweek Book Division. New York: Newsweek, 1971.
Wolfe, Ivor de. *The Italian Townscape.* New York: George Braziller, 1966.
Wolfram von Eschenbach. *Parzival.* Translated and with an introduction by Helen M. Mustard and Charles E. Passage. New York: Vintage Books (Random House), 1961.
Zarnecki, George. *Art of the Medieval World.* New York: Harry N. Abrams, 1975.
Zeffirelli, Franco. *Brother Sun, Sister Moon* [motion picture]. 1973.

INDEX

Page numbers in italics refer to illustrations.